Enterprise Architecture for Integration

Rapid Delivery Methods and Technologies

DISCLAIMER OF WARRANTY

For a listing of recent titles in the *Artech House Titles in Computing,* turn to the back of this book.

Enterprise Architecture for Integration

Rapid Delivery Methods and Technologies

Clive Finkelstein

Software to accompany this book is available for download at:

http://www.artechhouse.com/static/downloads/finkelstein_713.zip

ARTECH HOUSE
BOSTON | LONDON
artechhouse.com

Library of Congress Cataloging-in-Publication Data
Finkelstein, Clive.
Enterprise architecture for integration: rapid delivery methods and technologies/Clive Finkelstein.
p. cm.
Includes bibliographical references and index.
ISBN 1-58053-713-8 (alk. paper)
1. System design. 2. Computer architecture. 3. Computer software—Development. I. Title. II. Series.

QA76.9.S88F527 2006
005.1'2—dc22 2005058857

British Library Cataloguing in Publication Data
Finkelstein, Clive
Enterprise architecture for integration: rapid delivery methods and technologies.
1. Enterprise application integration (Computer systems) 2. Software architecture
I. Title
005.2'76

ISBN-10: 1-58053-713-8

Cover design by Igor Valdman

International Standard Book Number: 1-58053-713-8
Library of Congress Catalog Card Number: 2005058857

10 9 8 7 6 5 4 3 2 1

To my wife, Jill—my friend, my companion,
and the love of my life

To our daughter Kristi, our son-in-law Bill,
and our two beautiful granddaughters, Megan and Apryl

Contents

CHAPTER 15

Foreword

I cannot sufficiently impress you with the significance of Clive Finkelstein's book *Enterprise Architecture for Integration: Rapid Delivery Methods and Technologies.* Those of us who are alive and in the workforce in 2006 are the transition generation, in transit from the Industrial Age to the Information Age, much like those of several centuries ago as the world changed from the Agricultural Age to the Industrial Age. Hopefully, many of us will be survivors in the massive, global revolution that is currently being waged: the Information Revolution. I always have said that the best place to be in a revolution is on the winning side. Clive Finkelstein is providing a strategy that will position an enterprise to be on the winning side.

The academics make the case that it takes a lifetime to make the transition from one global environment to another. The scientific measurement for one lifetime is a 40-year life cycle and there is some evidence that we began the transition somewhere between 20 and 25 years ago. That would suggest that we may have only 20 or 25 years to go before we will know who has successfully made the transition and who has been left behind.

Although we have not yet seen the Information Age and no one knows positively all of its characteristics, much has been speculated and written about. Likely, the most widely read and credible series of books were those authored by Alvin Toffler (*Future Shock,* Random House, 1970; *The Third Wave,* William Morrow, 1980; and *Powershift,* Bantam Books, 1990). Thanks to him and others, not to mention our own personal experience, our understanding of some of the characteristics of the Information Age is taking shape.

First, major changes clearly are taking place. Business is no longer going to be as simple as "get yourself a good product or service and then go find a bunch of people to sell it to." The Information Age business is "get yourself a good *customer* and then *you* go find the *range of products and services* required to keep that customer a good customer." The Information Age business is far more complex than Industrial Age businesses. The day you have to treat each customer as an individual and customize (integrate) the enterprise response to the customer requirement, you are signing up for orders-of-magnitude increases in complexity. From the perspective of the enterprise, it is no longer a case of "the market is integrated." Now it is, from the perspective of the customer, "the enterprise is integrated." Those who have to deal with the process of integration—customer or enterprise—have to accommodate the complexity. The concept of "stovepipes" is anathema to the Information Age enterprise. The enterprise is going to have to be integrated. How do you suppose the enterprise is going to get integrated? By accident? By writing some more code? By wishful thinking? I submit, the people who are building the enterprise systems … automated *and* manual … are going to have to produce enterprise-wide, integrated implementations if there is going to be any enterprise-wide integration. Complexity is escalating dramatically. No longer is it adequate just to get the manual and automated systems to work.

A second characteristic of the Information Age that is becoming abundantly evident is the dramatic escalation of the rate of change. We are all running out of time. I'm running out of time. You are probably running out of time. IS is running out of time. The enterprise is running out of time. From a consumer (customer) perspective, we all need "custom products, mass-produced in quantities of one for immediate delivery" because we do not know the nature of the product we want to take delivery on until we want to take delivery. From the supplier (enterprise) perspective, you cannot wait until you get the order to engineer and manufacture your response (think about homeland security!). You cannot anticipate and manufacture and have in storage every finished good the consumer is ever going to want to take delivery on. You are likely going to have to engineer parts (not finished goods), prefabricate them and have them in inventory before you ever receive an order—and the parts are going to have to be cleverly engineered such that they can be assembled into more than one finished good It is totally unreasonable to think that you can engineer parts that can be assembled into automobiles, supercomputers, locomotives, and peanut butter sandwiches. You cannot expect to engineer parts that can be assembled into anything. No—there indeed are limits. The limits are whatever the scope of the *enterprise* is. The engineering will have to be done "enterprise-wide." The manufacturing name for this concept is *mass customization.*

The same conceptual approach will be required for the enterprise as for any product if the enterprise "owners" (management) are unable to define the nature of the enterprise implementation they need until the moment they need it. Also, regardless of whichever implementation they want, they will want it integrated, enterprise-wide. This will be particularly critical for service-based enterprises because the enterprise services are simply the enterprise as viewed from the perspective of the customer.

In any case, some principal characteristics of the Information Age are extreme complexity and extreme rates of change. The question for the enterprise is "How do you intend to deal with orders-of-magnitude increases in complexity and orders-of-magnitude increases in the rate of change?" Do you think this is not happening? The question is not "Is this going to happen?" The only question is "What are you going to do about it?"

Seven thousand years of known history of humankind would suggest that the only known strategy for complexity and change is *architecture.* If it (whatever it is) gets so complex that you can't remember all of the details all at one time, you have to write it down ... describe it ... architecture. If you cannot describe it, you cannot create it. After you get it (whatever it is) created and you want to change it, how do you change it? You start with what you wrote down ... architecture. The key to complexity and change is *architecture.*

I submit that if you do not have an enterprise architecture strategy, you do not have a strategy for addressing orders-of-magnitude increases in complexity and orders-of-magnitude increases in the rate of change and, therefore, you are likely to have a very difficult time maintaining your viability in an Information Age environment.

Clive's book is not about the Zachman framework. In fact, Clive refers to other books about the Zachman framework, including a book that I have authored. Clive's book is a methodology book. He provides a summary overview of the framework graphic because he maps his methodology against the framework. The framework provides a context within which the logic of a methodology can be expressed in an understandable manner. Furthermore, the framework provides a structured definition of enterprise architecture that Clive exploits, whereas historically enterprise architecture is an issue that most methodologies have tended to ignore.

Engineering for flexibility is a function of separating independent variables. Therefore, when I say "parts," I mean independent variables. In framework terms, this means "primitive" models. "Primitive" does not mean granular. It means a single abstraction from a single perspective, independent variables, a single cell of the framework. But this is a framework issue and not appropriate for this foreword or this book. I happened to put enterprise names on one of the graphic representations of the framework because I was interested in engineering and manufacturing enterprises.

Because I originally articulated the framework, the methods and tools vendors have wanted me to "endorse" their specific method or tool as the "exclusive" tool for "implementing" my framework. I have deliberately kept the framework quite independent of all tools and methodologies for several reasons. First, I do not believe there is one way to "do" enterprise architecture as prescribed by the Zachman framework. I believe there are *N* different ways to realize enterprise architecture as expressed by my framework, some likely better than others. Second, I do not have a warm feeling that many of the methods and tools vendors that have been operating in the Industrial Age have any idea about the implications of enterprise architecture in general and the Zachman framework specifically. Third, associating the framework schema with a particular method or tool would not make any sense at all, any more than associating the periodic table, a two-dimensional classification system for (primitive) chemical elements, with Dow Chemical or Glaxo Smith-Kline or whomever. The schema is universal and quite independent of and certainly not owned by the process owner, that is, the tool or methodology provider.

In the Industrial Age, the enterprise value proposition for computers was "better, faster, cheaper." Computers were better than people because people make mistakes and computers do it the same way every time. Machines are faster than people and machines are cheaper than labor. If "better, faster, cheaper" is the enterprise value proposition, it will drive you to a very short-term approach for implementation because the very moment you discover something repetitive going on in the enterprise that is not automated, it is actually costing you quality, time, and money (better, faster, cheaper). There is an incredible incentive to get the systems implemented as soon as possible. Anything that inhibits implementation is "analysis/paralysis." This value proposition has spawned a whole genre of rapid application development—style methods and tools.

In contrast, if accommodating extreme complexity and high rates of change are the enterprise value proposition, then the engineering design objectives are integration, flexibility, alignment, interoperability, reduced time-to-market, security, and so forth—*not* simply implementation. The Information Age value lies in creating an inventory of knowledge about the enterprise, knowledge assets, enterprise architecture knowledge assets, primitive models. These primitive models must have been engineered for integration, flexibility, alignment, and so forth. Before there is an order for any implementation, such as that from the inventory of primitive models, virtually any manifestation of the enterprise can be assembled to order by the click of a mouse. Now we are talking rapid application development ... however, somebody has to get the primitive models engineered and into inventory before the order is received.

This is all physics. Nothing is happening by accident. If you want integration and reusability, then you are going to have to build enterprise-wide primitive models. If you want alignment, then you are going to have to define what you are aligning to, that is, the higher row models. If you want flexibility, then you are going to have to build primitive models and keep them separated until you want to implement them. If you want to accommodate change, then you are going to have to build primitive models and retain them to serve as a baseline for managing change. If you want to reduce the time it takes to implement systems, then you are going to have the primitive models in inventory before you get an order for implementation. If you want quality, then you are going to have to make the primitive models explicit and make them explicit at excruciating levels of detail. And so on. Let me give you some friendly advice: There is no such thing as a free lunch ... and there are no "silver bullets" (I think that was the name of an article by Fred Brooks years ago).

If all you want is implementation as soon as possible, then "you start writing the code and I'll go find out what the users have in mind" (the caption on an old cartoon) later.

Although I have known Clive Finkelstein for more than 25 years, and although we were coming from entirely different perspectives—he from a methodology perspective and I from an architecture perspective—we were both arriving at the same conclusions. The end object is *not* simply to get the systems to run and, therefore, it is *not* adequate simply to write code. Engineering work, *enterprise* engineering work has to be done because the enterprise problem in the Information Age is integration, flexibility, reusability, quality, security, reduced time to market, and so forth. Yes, you have to get to implementation as soon as possible, but if you are not assembling the implementations from the primitive models that are already in inventory, that is, enterprise architecture, before you get the order, all you are going to end up with is more code, that is, more legacy. And, it makes no difference what technologies you are using or how many lines of code you can write per day, you are just building more legacy that is *not* integrated, *not* flexible, *not* reusable, *not* secure, *not* aligned, *not* quality, and *not* very rapid either!

Clive's methodology is one of the few methodologies that I know of in 2006 that actually addresses some of the enterprise engineering design objectives that go far beyond just getting the code to run. I hope you can see why I said at the outset that I could not sufficiently impress you with the significance of this book.

A lot of work needs to be done and we are running out of time. At the point in time at which the enterprise is critically dependent on accommodating extreme complexity and extreme rates of change, it is going to be too late to start working on enterprise architecture because enterprise architecture is not simply one more implementation project. Enterprise architecture is a different way of life. At least some enterprise architecture work is going to have to be in place before the enterprise becomes critically dependent on it. I recently asked someone in one of my seminars how long they thought they had before they had to have some major pieces of this in place ... 20 years? ... 10 years? ... 5 years? Their response was "We needed this 2 years ago!" It will not be long before we will know which enterprises have gotten some of this work done ... and which haven't!

I hope you enjoy Clive's book as much as I have.

John A. Zachman
President, Zachman International
Glendale, California
March 2006

Preface

The most critical issue facing government, defense, and commercial enterprises today is the rapid pace of change in almost every industry. With the rate of technological change increasing, together with today's budget and competitive pressures, enterprises must be able to change rapidly ... often just to survive—let alone to succeed.

The need to transform from today's inflexible business environment to an agile enterprise that can change direction rapidly has never been greater. Yet the structures, processes, and systems that we have today are inflexible: They are incapable of rapid change. And more computer hardware, or software, or packages, or staff, or outsourcing is not the solution. They are part of the problem.

The solution requires methods and technologies for rapid business change—with systems that also change in lock-step. This is *not* a computer problem. It is a business problem, one that needs strategic direction from senior management and strategic planners, with these directions then translated into rapid action by business experts working with IT experts.

What are needed are methods that enable senior managers—together with their planners, business managers, business experts, and IT staff—to work together to achieve business change, with each group contributing its specific expertise. The methods to achieve this are being successfully applied by many enterprises today. But these methods need new thinking. The tried and true ways no longer work. We need new ways to make the required business change transformations.

Our current systems development methods have served us well for developing operational information systems in the period of managed change that we had up until the 1990s. But now the pace of change is much faster than we ever anticipated when those systems were first built.

Historically, these systems have been difficult to change. The systems and databases that we built in the early years of the Information Age to enable our organizations to be more responsive to change are now monolithic and resistant to change. Today, they inhibit the ability of our organizations to change rapidly in order to compete ... sometimes even to survive. We are chained to inflexible systems that no longer respond to the rapid change environment of today—let alone the even greater change environment that we will find ourselves in tomorrow.

We need to build more flexible systems for the future that can change easily, rapidly, and often. To achieve this, the systems development methods that we use should take a different focus for the future. They must be able to identify potential future changes early. We must also build systems and databases differently, so that they can be changed rapidly to support vital business changes. These changes must be capable of being made within weeks, even days—not in years as is the case today. This book addresses enterprise integration using enterprise architecture methods and technologies. Enterprise architecture achieves *business integration.* It requires a focus on the future: through methods for strategic business planning, for creating a balanced scorecard, and for governance. These strategic planning methods are covered in Part I.

Business integration is also achieved by enterprise architecture methods that address the integration of data, processes, locations, people, events, and motivation for an enterprise. Enterprise architecture (EA) methods are briefly introduced in Chapter 1; they are covered in detail in Part II of the book, with methods to identify priority systems for rapid delivery into production in 3-month increments.

Enterprise integration also includes *technology integration*—using the technologies of extensible markup language (XML), enterprise application integration (EAI), enterprise portals, Web services, and service-oriented architecture (SOA) with business process management (BPM) languages that are automatically generated from process or workflow diagrams. These technologies can be used to deliver priority systems rapidly into production in 3-month increments and are covered in Part III of the book.

We are at a dramatic and historical point of convergence: in business and in technology. The Internet and associated technologies today enable all of the customers, suppliers, and business partners of an enterprise to work together at electronic speeds. These technologies are transforming organizations. Processes that took days or weeks to complete previously by using mail, fax, and courier communications now take hours, minutes, and sometimes even seconds. This is the direct consequence of technology.

But technology alone is not the answer. To achieve any degree of success in enterprise integration, technology integration must be used within a coherent, integrated enterprise, through business integration. Most enterprises still have a long way to go to realize business integration.

To appreciate what still has to be achieved, we need to review what I call the *process engineering bible*. I describe it in this way because it has had a dramatic effect on the way in which organizations function. To consider its impact, we need to review its message. But first:

- What is its title?
- Who was the author?
- When was it published?

Perhaps we can identify the book by first considering its author:

- Was it Michael Hammer or James Champy of *Reengineering the Corporation* [1] fame? No, it was neither of them.
- Was it Ken Orr [2], Ed Yourdon [3], or Tom de Marco [4] of *Software Engineering* fame? No, it was not them either.
- Well, was it Peter Drucker of *Management* [5] and *Strategic Planning* [6] fame? No, not him.
- Was it W. Edwards Deming of quality control fame? No, not him either.
- Was it Alfred Sloan or Henry Ford? No, the book I am referring to was published long before all of these eminent people.

So which book am I talking about? As soon as I give you the author and its title—with its publication date—its significance will become apparent. The reference is as follows:

- Adam Smith, *Wealth of Nations* (1776) [7]

This was one of the most influential books at the start of the Industrial Age. It described the evolution from the Agricultural Age to the Industrial Age. It was the foundation for most industrial enterprises in the late 18th century and into the 19th century.

To understand the importance of Smith's *Wealth of Nations,* we will review part of his first chapter. Box P.1 provides an extract from Chapter 1 of *Book One.* Its language is unusual today. I have included part of the initial paragraphs; to help readability I have added comments in parentheses to indicate the terminology that we use today to describe the same concepts.

The principles that Adam Smith advocated broke complex processes into simpler process steps. He showed by using technologies available in his day that an illiterate workforce could be trained to carry out each step repetitively. In this way they were able to achieve much higher levels of productivity that if one worker carried out each step in turn. Smith showed that component steps could also be combined in different ways for new, improved processes. These are the same concepts that we still use today for *reusability,* using *object-oriented methods.*

Box P.1: Extract from Adam Smith's "Wealth of Nations"

EXTRACT FROM BOOK ONE: *"Of the Causes of Improvement in the Productive Powers of Labour, and of the Order According to which its Produce is Naturally Distributed Among the Different Ranks of the People."*

CHAPTER 1: *"Of the Division of Labour"*

"... To take an example, therefore, from a very trifling manufacture; but one in which the division of labour has been very often taken notice of, the trade of the pin-maker ... a workman ... could scarce ... make one pin in a day, and certainly could not make twenty. [In today's terminology he is referring to *serial operation.*]

But in the way in which this business is now carried on, not only the whole work is a peculiar trade, but it is divided into a number of branches of which the greater part are likewise peculiar trades. [In today's terminology this refers to *object-oriented methods.*]

One man draws out the wire, another straights it, a third cuts it, a fourth points it, a fifth grinds it at the top for receiving the head; to make the head requires two or three distinct operations [object-oriented encapsulation]; *to put it on is a peculiar business, to whiten the pins is another; it is even a trade by itself to put them into the paper; and the important business of making a pin is ... divided into about eighteen distinct operations ....* [object-oriented methods]

I have seen a small manufactory of this kind where ten men only were employed ... they could, when they exerted themselves, make among them about twelve pounds of pins in a day ... upwards of forty-eight thousand pins in a day. Each person, therefore ... might be considered as making four thousand eight hundred pins in a day. [object-oriented reusability]

But if they had all wrought separately and independently... they certainly could not each of them have made twenty, perhaps not one pin in a day [serial operation] ... ; *that is, certainly, not ... the four thousand eight hundredth part of what they are at present capable of performing, in consequence of a proper division and combination of their different operations."* [object-oriented reusability]

P.1 Evolution from the Industrial Age to the Information Age

Adam Smith's breakthrough was the foundation for late eighteenth-century–early nineteenth-century industrial enterprises. With the focus mainly on manufacturing physical items, this period also saw the same concepts applied to knowledge-based processes for bank loans and for insurance policy applications. Instead of manufacturing steps, a loan application or a policy application approval process was broken down into discrete steps to be carried out by different people, each skilled in assessing an aspect of the relevant application. Each process step was carried out in a defined sequence: One step was completed before the next step in the sequence was started. The result was the definition of *serial processes.*

As the application form was routed to each person in the approval process, details of the relevant applicant and the current status of the process were recorded in handwritten ledgers; these were called the applicant ledger or the customer ledger. Each person involved in carrying out a process step kept an individual record of every applicant or customer that worker had processed, and the stage the applicant had reached in the approval process.

The twentieth century saw an improvement in these process steps with the introduction by Henry Ford of the *assembly line* method of automobile manufacture. The vehicle being built physically moved along each section of the assembly line, where different components were added in each step of the assembly process.

This period also saw the introduction of *parallel processes,* in which two or more processes could be carried out concurrently, with each process step executed independently of other process steps. An example is the parallel construction of the body of the automobile, while its engine is constructed at the same time. Each parallel process path is thus independent of the other parallel paths, until they need to converge. Only when the automobile has to be driven off the assembly line does the engine have to be fitted into the car.

By the middle of the twentieth century, the industrial enterprise had evolved into a complex series of manual processes. The pace of progress had seen most enterprises evolve to use increasingly complex business processes, with rapidly growing transaction volumes to be manually processed. And what was the result? These enterprises found *they were operating in a continual state of manual chaos!*

Then the computer came on the scene in the second half of the twentieth century. From the late 1950s—through the 1960s, 1970s, and up to today—we have seen manual processes being automated by computer. What was the result? The processes were automated, but we took the existing manual processes and then automated them essentially *as is,* without much change. That is, the automated processes were being executed as the manual processes used to be, but faster and more accurately. *In so doing, we moved from manual chaos ... to automated chaos!*

Enterprises tried to hide this automated chaos. Through to the mid-1990s, most enterprises could confine their automated chaos to the back office. They presented a calm, in-control, front-office appearance to the outside world. They tried to emulate the graceful swan, gliding silently across the glass-like surface of a lake with no apparent effort. The furious paddling activity—trying to move ahead—was hidden beneath the surface.

But with rapid acceptance of the Internet in the second half of the 1990s, the chaos moved from the back office onto the front doorstep of enterprises: through their Web sites. *Customers could visit these enterprises with the click of a mouse. But they could just as quickly leave with the click of a mouse if they did not find what they needed!*

The reason they left is not because of what the automated processes could do; rather, they left because the processes did not provide what the customers needed. This was often due to redundant processes and redundant data, which, by definition, are nonintegrated. Another term for nonintegration is *disintegration.* That is, by automation most enterprises had evolved from nonintegrated manual processes to *disintegrated automated processes.*

The problem, however, is much worse than this! Most automated processes today assume that the technologies of the past still apply. The manual processes that they automated required paper-based forms that were mailed, or later faxed. So their automated counterparts are based on forms that are also printed to be mailed or faxed. On receipt at their destination, the data in these forms are manually reentered into relevant systems—with manual work, with extra staffing to do that reentry, with delays, with errors, and with associated costs.

In Part III of this book, we will see how technologies can be used to convert printed forms automatically into electronic forms using the extensible markup language. These XML forms can be transmitted electronically to receiving applications within an enterprise or between enterprises. This is called *enterprise application integration.* It replaces mail transmission and manual reentry based on paper-based systems that were designed for completion over weeks or days. Instead, paper forms are replaced by electronic forms and systems that intercommunicate within minutes or seconds—anywhere in the world.

The problem is that automated systems that assume intercommunication with printed forms and manual reentry over weeks and days do not work well when asked to intercommunicate with electronic forms that bypass the need for manual reentry—and that are completed in minutes or seconds. What is the basic reason for this dichotomy?

Today we have twenty-first-century enterprises that utilize twenty-first-century technologies, yet most enterprises today still use eighteenth-century disintegrated business processes!

The business processes—originally designed based on principles set by Adam Smith in 1776—have not evolved to take advantage of the technologies we have available today. This is a business problem; not a technology problem. It requires business decisions. It requires business expertise. These are the basic ingredients for business integration.

Part II of this book shows how business integration for business transformation is realized by enterprise architecture. But the real architects of an enterprise are not found in its IT department. This leads us to two important principles:

1. Enterprise architects are the senior managers who set the directions for the future, based on processes designed for that future and its technologies. But the future cannot continue to be based on eighteenth-century business processes that no longer respond to the rapid-change environment of today ... and even greater change tomorrow.

2. The future will be based on business transformation through processes that use the technologies of today and tomorrow to complete in minutes and seconds what before took days and weeks ... with strategic directions set by senior management, and with business experts and IT experts working together in a design partnership.

Enterprise architecture methods of enterprise engineering enable business experts and information technology (IT) experts together to identify reusable business activities, reusable business processes, and integrated databases for business integration. These take advantage of the latest technologies for technology integration—with integrated twenty-first-century enterprises that have been transformed through the use of reusable twenty-first-century processes.

P.2 Reading Strategies for the Book

This book has been designed so that each chapter stands alone and covers all of the concepts of each relevant method or technology. It has been written as a how-to text that serves the needs of a diverse audience: senior executives (CEOs, COOs, CFOs), business managers and business experts, senior IT executives (CIOs, CTOs, IT managers), project managers, business analysts and systems analysts, technical IT staff, and enterprise architects. I will address each of these roles and interests, highlighting the parts of the book that will be of greatest interest to you.

P.2.1 For All Readers

The book starts with an overview of enterprise architecture and enterprise engineering. Chapter 1 is required reading for all readers; it is a nontechnical, introductory chapter. It covers business and IT concepts of enterprise architecture and enterprise engineering from a management and an IT perspective. It establishes the fundamental principles on which the book is based. It should be read by all readers.

P.2.2 Business and IT Executives and Methodology Readers

Part I, Enterprise Architecture for Managers, is for business managers and business experts, as well as the IT staffs who will work with them on enterprise architecture projects. The chapters in this part introduce balanced scorecard and strategy maps, strategy analysis, and governance analysis. A brief overview of each chapter is provided here, with a more detailed overview given at the start of Part I:

Chapter 2 discusses the concepts of balanced scorecard and strategy maps, which can be used as a catalyst for business transformation. These are catalysts for Part II; using enterprise architecture methods to ensure that systems and databases provide required balanced scorecard support.

Chapter 3 describes the strategy analysis management methodology, which is used to identify requirements and set directions for the future. This rapid-delivery method for business planning and balanced scorecard is used by senior managers and their business experts to define business transformation directions for the future enterprise. It is introduced with many examples, together with a business planning questionnaire template (in Word) on the accompanying CD-ROM.

Chapter 4 introduces governance analysis. Many countries have enacted legislation for corporate governance. For example, the United States' Sarbanes-Oxley Act of 2002 requires internal control reporting for senior management to ensure that financial reporting and other governance controls are in place. Enterprise architecture enables governance analysis frameworks to be dynamically defined for each enterprise for internal control reporting purposes.

Part II, Enterprise Architecture Methods, covers several business-driven methods used for enterprise architecture. Each chapter fully describes relevant methodology concepts, with examples and case study exercises to test your understanding together with sample solutions. These chapters are discussed briefly next, with more detail about each chapter given at the start of Part II.

Chapter 5 discusses enterprise architecture as used by the U.S. federal government as the federal enterprise architecture framework (FEAF) and by the Department of Defense (DoD) as the DoD architecture frameworks (C4ISR and DoDAF). The chapter shows how the latest enterprise architecture methods enable dramatic savings to be achieved, delivering key business processes and systems into production in 3-month increments.

Chapter 6 describes business-driven data mapping. This data modeling methodology is used by business experts and IT experts working together in a design partnership. It uses business examples to show how integrated data are defined, with case study exercise problems and sample solutions on the accompanying CD-ROM.

Chapter 7 discusses strategic modeling for rapid delivery of enterprise architecture. This is a key methodology chapter. It shows how project plans can be derived from data maps, either manually or automatically. These plans enable high-priority business subprojects to be identified for delivery in 3-month increments. Many business examples are used, together with case study exercise problems and sample solutions on the accompanying CD-ROM.

Chapter 8 covers strategic alignment, activity and workflow modeling, and business rules. It shows how matrices are used to achieve alignment and define the governance analysis framework discussed in Chapter 4. Workflow models and business rules are used in Part III for automatic generation of executable code.

Chapter 9 describes the use of business normalization to determine future business directions. This enables business knowledge to be used to identify future data needs for business transformation. It includes business examples, together with case study exercise problems and sample solutions on the accompanying CD-ROM.

Chapter 10 completes Part II. It discusses menu design and screen design, briefly also covering physical database design and transaction performance analysis. It discusses process modeling, which is used to define reusable business processes.

P.2.3 IT Technical Staff and Technology Readers

Part III, Enterprise Architecture Technologies, covers the technologies and vendor products that are used to deliver priority databases, activities, and processes (as defined in Part II) into production. Each chapter provides a stand-alone description of the relevant technology, with representative vendor products that use the technology and the strategies adopted by these vendors. Product descriptions are included on the accompanying CD-ROM.

Chapter 11 covers enterprise application integration concepts. It introduces the basic concepts of XML and EAI that are used throughout Part III. The CD-ROM discusses a number of software products that are offered by EAI vendors.

Chapter 12 introduces the concepts and technologies that are used by enterprise portals. It describes their use for rapid delivery of priority information and content resources in enterprise integration projects. Several vendors and their products are discussed on the CD-ROM.

Chapter 13 describes Web services for real-time integration. Concepts and technologies are introduced in this chapter, along with the evolution of Web services. Many Web services vendors and their software products are discussed on the CD-ROM.

Chapter 14 introduces the concepts of service-oriented architecture and business process management languages. Four BPM languages and the business process modeling notation (BPMN) are described. These offer the potential to transform systems development in twenty-first-century enterprises, with XML-based BPM languages automatically generated as executable code directly from workflow models or process models. The strategies used by SOA and BPM vendors are discussed, with a number of products from these vendors on the CD-ROM.

Chapter 15 brings together the methodology and technology parts of the book. On the CD-ROM modeling tools are discussed from several vendors, along with their products. These tools capture the semantic meaning from business models in Parts I and II, for business integration with the technologies in Part III. The chapter summarizes the methodology and technology principles from the book, concluding with the directions that methods and technologies are expected to take for the future.

P.2.4 Enterprise Architecture Readers

Enterprise architecture readers will want to read the entire book to understand the business methodologies in Part I and Part II, and the rapid-delivery technologies in Part III. With this audience in mind, the book has been structured to lead you progressively through each method and technology.

The end result of this emphasis on enterprise architecture is the rapid delivery of priority activities, processes, databases, and systems into production in 3-month increments. For this reason, I suggest you read the book from cover to cover.

P.3 Accompanying CD-ROM

A CD-ROM is provided with this book containing additional book material as well as student editions of several modeling tools.

P.3.1 Book Materials on CD-ROM

The CD-ROM includes additional book materials, such as questionnaire templates, case study problems and sample solutions, and product descriptions. The following Part II and Part III files are provided in the Book Materials folder on the CD-ROM as listed in Tables P.1 and P.2.

P.3.2 Format Conventions for the Book

The book is structured for ease of use both as a textbook for universities as well as for business and technical readers. Part II includes questionnaires and problem exercises—together with sample solutions—so you can assess your understanding of the concepts that are covered. These questionnaires, problems, and solutions are included as Word or PDF files on the accompanying CD-ROM (see Table P.1). See

Table P.1 Additional Files for Part II in Book Materials Folder on the CD-ROM

Part II File Name	*CD-ROM File Contents*
"Chap-03-Questionnaire.doc"	Chapter 3: Business Planning Questionnaire Template (in Word)
"Chap-06-Problems.pdf"	Chapter 6: Data Mapping Problems (in PDF)
"Chap-06-Solutions.pdf"	Chapter 6: Data Mapping Sample Solutions (in PDF)
"Chap-07-Questionnaire.doc"	Chapter 7: Strategic Modeling Questionnaire Template (in Word)
"Chap-07-Problems.pdf"	Chapter 7: Strategic Modeling Problems (in PDF)
"Chap-07-Solutions.pdf"	Chapter 7: Strategic Modeling Sample Solutions (in PDF)
"Chap-08-Problems.pdf"	Chapter 8: Strategic Alignment Problems (in PDF)
"Chap-08-Solutions.pdf"	Chapter 8: Strategic Alignment Sample Solutions (in PDF)
"Chap-09-Problems.pdf"	Chapter 9: Business Normalization Problems (in PDF)
"Chap-09-Solutions.pdf"	Chapter 9: Business Normalization Sample Solutions (in PDF)

Table P.2 Additional Files for Part III in Book Materials Folder on the CD-ROM

Part III File Name	*CD-ROM File Contents*
"Chap-11-Products.pdf"	Chapter 11: Enterprise Application Integration Product Descriptions (in PDF)
"Chap-12-Products.pdf"	Chapter 12: Enterprise Portal Product Descriptions (in PDF)
"Chap-13-Products.pdf"	Chapter 13: Web Services Product Descriptions (in PDF)
"Chap-14-Products.pdf"	Chapter 14: Service-Oriented Architecture Product Descriptions (in PDF)
"Chap-15-Products.pdf"	Chapter 15: Modeling Tools Product Descriptions (in PDF)

Activation of Ful Capactiy Projects in the Product Descriptions file "Chap-15-Products.pfd" on the accompanying CD-ROM.

Each chapter in Part II includes endnotes that also indicate the name and location of the relevant file. Figures or reports in each Problem file are prefixed with "P" (such as Figure P6.1 or Report P7.1), while figures in each Solution file are prefixed with "S" (such as Figure S6.1). All endnotes for files on the CD-ROM are shown as numbered superscripts and appear at the end of the file.

Part III includes product descriptions for many vendors that offer products based on the technologies discussed in each technology chapter, so you can understand how the various technologies are used. These product descriptions are included as PDF files on the accompanying CD-ROM (see Table P.2).

Each chapter in Part III includes endnotes indicating the name and URL for further details of relevant vendors or products. Figures in each Products PDF file are prefixed with "P" (such as Figure P13.1). All endnotes for files on the CD-ROM are shown as numbered superscripts and appear at the end of the file.

P.3.3 Modeling Tools on CD-ROM

The CD-ROM also includes free, single-user student editions of several modeling tools from Visible Systems Corporation [8]. This includes the following products:

- *Visible Advantage Enterprise Architecture Edition* is a modeling tool offering powerful enterprise architecture planning and analysis support, with project examples from the book. It supports strategic planning, with integrated logical and physical data modeling, activity modeling, and process modeling. Based on a concurrent relational repository for single-user or multiuser environments, it also supports model analysis validation and automatic derivation of project plans from data models using entity dependency analysis (see Chapter 7) for full-scale enterprise architecture planning and analysis.
- *Visible Analyst Enterprise Framework Edition for Zachman Framework* is a modeling tool that is used for enterprise architecture design and development. Models can be exported and imported between Visible Advantage and Visible Analyst, which offers support also for software engineering and UML. It includes structured analysis and design modeling capabilities, object-oriented modeling, and database modeling support for forward engineering and reverse engineering. It includes model validation and uses an integrated repository for single-user or multiuser environments. The Zachman framework is used as a front-end interface for better management of repository objects.
- *Visible Developer* is a code generation tool for enterprise architecture deployment, with automatic code generation of Visual Basic, ASP, Visual Basic .Net, ASP .Net, and C# .Net of customizable, executable, and layered applications. It can seamlessly and automatically connect generated applications to multiple legacy databases. This deploys a common and consistent multitiered application framework. It generates 80% to 90% of code based on database code patterns, while managing application-specific code without change when regeneration is required.

- *Visible Polaris,* for issues management, task management, and project management of the software development life cycle (SDLC), is used for enterprise architecture change management. It includes task and workflow management, automated defect tracking, consolidated project information in the form of bug tracking, defect tracking, issue tracking, problem tracking, and automated ticketing. Easy to learn and use, it is configurable to enterprise architecture processes and integrates with all EA activities (planning, analysis, design, development, and deployment).

Refer to Chapter 15 for further descriptions of each of these products. Review also on the CD-ROM several tutorials and manuals that are provided with the included products.

P.4 University and Corporate Use of the Book and CD-ROM

The book and the student edition modeling tools on the CD-ROM have been designed to be used by universities and other educational institutions for undergraduate and postgraduate courses. These can be used by large commercial, government, and defense organizations also for internal training of business and IT staff. The educational materials provided include a comprehensive reference text and student edition software tools for strategic planning, data modeling, activity modeling, process modeling, and object-oriented modeling in UML; for automatic code generation in VB, ASP, VB .Net, ASP .Net, and C# .Net; and for change management.

P.4.1 Structured Chapters for Rapid Delivery

Each chapter in the book has been designed to stand alone, if required. It covers a specific methodology or technology for rapid delivery of enterprise architecture. The book, however, is actually intended be used in its entirety: All methods and technologies in the chapters are presented in the recommended sequence for rapid delivery of enterprise architecture.

Each chapter covers introductory concepts, with increasing detail as the student works through each topic. For the methodology chapters in Parts I and II, problems and sample solutions on the CD-ROM enable each student's understanding to be tested. For the technology chapters in Part III, product examples and vendor strategies are discussed. Each chapter summary covers the key principles that have been learned. Product descriptions are included on the CD-ROM.

P.4.2 Using the CD-ROM for Full-Capacity Case Study Projects

The modeling tools, code generation, and change management tools supplied on the CD-ROM enable more extensive undergraduate projects to be set, based on the student edition versions that are provided. Each of these limited-capacity student edition products can also be converted to the full-capacity product for use in one full-capacity project using each tool—at no further charge. This makes the tools on the CD-ROM invaluable for student development of larger projects for postgraduate and doctoral theses.

P.4.3 Licensed Use of Course Presentation Materials

The concepts in the book are based on a series of public and in-house courses presented by the author worldwide [9]. These courses are delivered by PowerPoint with full instructor notes, and also include many video clips by John Zachman and Clive Finkelstein.

These presentation materials are designed to be used as the basis for easy introduction of enterprise architecture methods and technologies to your educational curriculum. Each course contains sections that correspond to specific chapters of the book. They provide more detail than can be included in the book. While new developments will be published as separate editions of the book every 2 to 3 years, each course is continually maintained with the latest, up-to-date methodology and technology developments.

These PowerPoint materials, with full instructor notes and video clips, can be licensed for use within universities or other educational institutions as part of their curriculum or for internal use by commercial corporations, government, or defense departments. Annual maintenance support entitles you to maintenance releases of the latest developments incorporated in each course. To help introduce these courses into an organization, Teach-the-Teacher (TTT) courses for lecturers and instructors will be presented on site by Clive Finkelstein. Options for certification are also available, if required [10].

P.5 Copyright and Trademark Acknowledgments

All product names and all registered and other trademarks that appear in this book are, and remain, the property of their respective owners. They have been included for reference purposes only. Any further information about any product or service referenced in this book should be obtained from the relevant product or trademark owner, based on the links supplied in the references section at the end of each chapter, or other links that are obtained through appropriate Internet searches.

P.6 Other Acknowledgments

I would like to acknowledge the input and suggestions provided by the following people:

- John Zachman, president of Zachman International, and Stan Locke, managing director of Zachman Framework Associates. Many thanks for their extensive support and suggestions in relation to Chapters 1 and 5, and elsewhere.
- Thanks go to Joe Butchko (U.S. Air Force, Retired) for his assistance in Chapter 5 on the use of enterprise architecture at the air mobility command of the U.S. Air Force.

- Thanks go to Bob Weisman, enterprise architecture practice manager of CGI in Ottawa, Canada, for his input in Chapter 5 on FEAF in federal government, as well as the use of enterprise architecture, C4ISR and DoDAF in the defense forces of the United States, Canada, the United Kingdom, and NATO. Thanks also go to Bob for his technical review of the entire book.
- Thanks to Doug Erickson for his input in Chapter 5 on his project experience at the Ohio Bureau of Workers' Compensation.
- Thanks also go to Mike Tiemann for his assistance with the enterprise architecture planning (EAP) approach used by Steven Spewak, referenced in Chapter 5.
- Many thanks also go to Ram Kumar in Sydney for his review of Chapters 13 and 14 and his suggestions for improvement based on his role as an OASIS working group chairman.
- I would like to thank George Atallah, IBM federal systems in Washington, D.C., for his input and redbook references on virtualization and on-demand directions in Chapter 15.
- Many thanks also go to George Cagliuso, chairman, and Mike Cesino, president, of Visible Systems Corporation for supplying the accompanying CD-ROM containing versions of their products: Visible Advantage, Visible Analyst, Visible Developer, and Visible Polaris.

Endnotes

[1] Hammer, M., and J. Champy, *Reengineering the Corporation,* London: Nicholas Brealey Publishing, 1993.

[2] Orr, K., *Structured Systems Development,* New York: Yourdon Press, 1977.

[3] Yourdon, E., and L. Constantine, *Structured Design: Fundamentals of a Discipline of Computer Program Systems Design,* Englewood Cliffs, NJ: Prentice-Hall, 1978.

[4] De Marco, T., *Software Systems Development,* New York: Yourdon Press, 1982.

[5] Drucker, P., *Management: Tasks, Responsibilities, Practices,* New York: Harper & Row, 1974.

[6] Drucker, P., *Management Challenges for the 21st Century,* New York: HarperCollins, 1999.

[7] Smith, A., *An Inquiry into the Nature and Causes of the Wealth of Nations,* 1776. Often called just *Wealth of Nations.*

[8] Further information on software products is provided in Chapter 15 on the CD-ROM and is also is available at http://www.visible.com.

[9] Course outlines of some public and in-house courses that are presented by Clive Finkelstein worldwide are available at http://www.ies.aust.com. Course outlines accessible from the *Courses* link of any page present concepts suitable at the information systems and business school undergraduate level. Project descriptions accessible from the Projects link of any page also cover concepts suitable for postgraduate and doctoral levels.

[10] Further information on licensing of course presentation materials, on Teach-the-Teachers training, and on certification options are available at http://www.ies.aust.com. Click on the *Courses, Certification,* and *Projects* links from any page. Please use the e-mail facility provided by the *Contact Us* link from any page to e-mail your interests and discuss your needs.

CHAPTER 1

Enterprise Architecture and Enterprise Engineering

In the preface we discussed the evolution of enterprises: from the Agricultural Age to the Industrial Age and then to the Information Age. We saw that we evolved from manual chaos using manual processes to automated chaos using automated processes. The manual processes were essentially automated *as is,* without effective redesign of those processes to take real advantage of the new technologies that were employed. The result today is that we have twenty-first-century enterprises with systems that use twenty-first-century technologies, *yet most enterprises today still use processes that were originally designed in the eighteenth century!*

The enterprise architecture methods of enterprise engineering as described in this book enable business experts and IT experts together to identify reusable business activities, reusable business processes, and integrated databases for *business integration.* These take advantage of the latest technologies for *technology integration.* The result is the evolution to integrated twenty-first-century enterprises that have been transformed through the introduction of reusable twenty-first-century processes!

Chapter 1 addresses the role of enterprise architecture for enterprise integration. To understand this, we will first discuss the evolution of enterprise architecture.

1.1 The Evolution of Enterprise Architecture

Enterprise architecture was developed by John Zachman while with IBM in the 1980s, after observing the building and airplane construction industries and the IT industry. He saw similarities between the construction of buildings, airplanes, and the information systems used by an enterprise.

These industries manage the design, construction, and maintenance of complex products by considering the needs of different people. Figure 1.1 illustrates the *owner* in the building industry, who uses *architect's drawings* to decide that the building addresses specific requirements. For airplane manufacture, the *owner* uses the high-level work breakdown structure of the plane to determine requirements. For information systems, the *owner* uses a *model of the business* to determine the enterprise needs.

The *designer*, however, needs a different set of diagrams: *architect's plans* for the building, sets of *engineering design* diagrams for the plane, or *information system models* for the enterprise.

DIFFERENT PERSPECTIVES

Buildings	Airplanes	Enterprise
	OWNER	
Architect's Drawings	Work Breakdown Structure	Model of Business
	DESIGNER	
Architect's Plans	Engineering Design	Model of Info System
	BUILDER	
Contractor's Plans	Manufacturing Engineering Design	Technology Model

Figure 1.1 The owner, designer, and builder are interested in different diagrams or representations from their perspectives in the design and construction of buildings, airplanes, and enterprise systems.

The *builder* relies on still different types of diagrams: *contractor's plans* for construction of the building, a *manufacturing engineering design* for plane construction, or *technology models* for information systems.

In addition, there are a number of different questions—called *primitives* or *interrogatives* or *abstractions*—that also need to be considered. These are illustrated in Figure 1.2.

What is needed is important to know. This is represented in Figure 1.2 by *material*, such as *bills of materials* for buildings and planes, and *data models* for information systems. *How* these are used is indicated by *functions*, such as *functional specifications* for buildings and planes, and *functional models* for information systems. *Where* is also important, as indicated by *location*—in *drawings* for building and plane construction and in *network models* for information systems.

DIFFERENT ABSTRACTIONS

WHAT	HOW	WHERE
Material	Function	Location
Bill of Materials	Functional Specifications	Drawings
Data Models	Functional Models	Network Models

Figure 1.2 Different questions (or abstractions) also need to be considered in the design and construction of buildings, airplanes, and enterprise systems.

Bringing these concepts together, the result is a matrix of five rows and three columns. These represent the perspectives of the *planner,* the *owner,* the *designer,* the *builder,* and the *subcontractor,* who are all interested in what, how, and where.

The last row addresses the *functioning enterprise.* The sixth row is not normally counted in the five main rows of the Zachman framework. Further, different documentation, models, or representations may also be utilized in each cell of the Zachman framework as shown by Figure 1.3. For example, reading down column 1—What (*Data*)—of this figure we see that:

- The cell formed by intersection of the *objectives/scope* row (of interest to the *planner*) and the data column shows that a "list of things" is relevant to this cell.
- The cell intersected by the *owner* row and *data* column is the "enterprise model"—also called the *strategic model.* We will discuss the role of strategic models in more detail in Part II of this book. For example, in Chapter 7 we will see that the strategic model enables enterprise-wide data integration to be realized.
- The cell for the *designer* row and the *data* column shows that "logical data model" documentation applies to this cell. This expands the strategic model to integrated logical data models with data attribute detail.
- The *builder* row and *data* column cell contains the "physical data model" for subsequent data implementation in target databases.

	What Data	**How** Function	**Where** Location
PLANNER **Objectives/Scope**	**List of Things**	**List of Processes**	**List of Locations**
OWNER **Conceptual**	**Enterprise Model**	**Activity Model**	**Business Logistics**
DESIGNER **Logical**	**Logical Data Model**	**Process Model**	**Distrib. Architect.**
BUILDER **Physical**	**Physical Data Model**	**System Model**	**Technol. Architect.**
SUBCONTRACTOR **Out -of-Context**	**Data Definition**	**Program**	**Network Architect.**
FUNCTIONING ENTERPRISE	Data	Function	Network

Figure 1.3 Different model representations exist in each of 15 cells to address the perspective of each row and the focus of each column.

- The *subcontractor* row and *data* column cell contain "data definition" scripts for the physical installation of these databases.

Reading down column 2—How (*Function*)—and column 3—Where (*Location*), we also see that each row has various representations in the cells for these columns as well. Several types of models may also be relevant to each cell. These models should all be well defined, but this complete definition is difficult to achieve in most enterprises.

For all things that we consider in business or day-to-day life—whether for buildings, for planes, or for complex enterprise systems—there are in fact six independent variables. These are based on the six primitive interrogatives: *what, how, where, who, when,* and *why.*

There are a further three columns—Who, When, and Why—in the complete *Zachman framework for enterprise architecture*. These additional interrogatives are shown in Figure 1.4, which illustrates a complete Zachman framework. In most enterprises, we will see that the models represented in these additional 15 cells are rarely well defined. We will also see in Part II that column 6—Why (*Motivation*)—is a very important column: It typically defines the business needs of an enterprise for the future.

Figure 1.4 shows examples of typical model contents for each cell. For example, the How column (column 2) shows that an *Activity Model* is relevant to the Owner row (row 2). This is a key cell, because it enables the return on investment (ROI) of alternative activities to be assessed through activity-based costing (see Chapter 8).

	What Data	How Function	Where Location	Who People	When Time	Why Future
PLANNER Objectives/Scope	List of Things	List of Processes	List of Locations	Organization Structure	List of Events	List of Goals Objectives
OWNER Conceptual	Enterprise Model	Activity Model	Business Logistics	Work Flow	Master Schedule	Business Plan
DESIGNER Logical	Logical Data Model	Process Model	Distributed Architecture	Human Interface	Process Structure	Business Rules
BUILDER Physical	Physical Data Model	System Model	Technology Architecture	Presentation Interface	Control Structure	Rule Design
SUBCONTRACTOR Out-of-Context	Data Definition	Program	Network Architecture	Security Interface	Timing Definition	Rule Specifications
FUNCTIONING ENTERPRISE	Data	Function	Network	Organization	Schedule	Strategy

Figure 1.4 The complete Zachman framework for enterprise architecture is based on a further three columns, for a total of six columns and five rows—making up 30 cells. Each cell may contain various types of models, as illustrated in this figure.

As a further illustration, column 2, row 3—a cell of interest to the Designer—shows that a *Process Model* is relevant for this cell. We will discuss process models in Chapter 10.

In summary, the framework rows therefore indicate different views (or perspectives) of people in the enterprise, from the perspectives of the *planner, owner, designer, builder,* and *subcontractor.* (The last row, "the functioning enterprise," is not normally counted.) The framework columns also address different primitive questions (also called interrogatives or abstractions) of *What, How, Where, Who, When* and *Why.*

The book *Enterprise Architecture Using the Zachman Framework* [1] provides an excellent introduction. In fact, to gain an overall appreciation of the Zachman framework, this book should be read even before the landmark e-book by John Zachman himself, *The Zachman Framework for Enterprise Architecture: A Primer for Enterprise Engineering and Manufacturing* [2].

1.2 Using the Zachman Framework for Enterprise Architecture

The focus of enterprise architecture initially should be based on *rows 1 and 2*, from the perspectives of the *planner* and the *owner*. These perspectives typically focus on the motivation as indicated by column 6 (*Why*), which represents business plans for the enterprise. Clear strategic directions can then be provided to row 3 (for the *Designer*), row 4 (for the *Builder*) and row 5 (for implementation by the *Subcontractor*).

The complete Zachman framework for enterprise architecture is illustrated now in Figure 1.5, showing representative models for each of the 30 cells. This

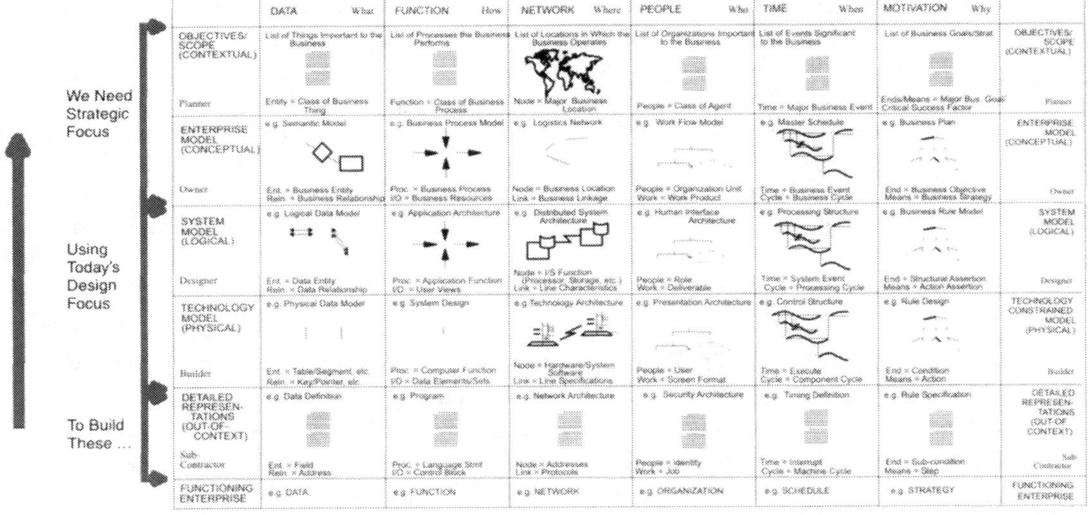

John A. Zachman, Zachman International

Figure 1.5 The Zachman framework for enterprise architecture illustrates how we have traditionally taken a bottom-up focus to the Designer's row 3; we have then built down again from row 3. We have not typically taken the perspectives of the Planner or the Owner rows into account. (Courtesy of John A. Zachman.)

framework is available on the CD-ROM as a large foldout page [3]. Print this page now; leave it for easy reference as you read further.

Traditionally, in building enterprise systems we have taken a bottom-up view. We have looked at the existing systems—whether manual or automated—represented by the bottom row of the framework. From this view, we have looked at ways in which current manual or automated systems have been implemented. We examined ways to improve these systems: either by automating manual systems or by using new technology to improve existing automated systems. We have taken a design focus from the perspective of row 3 (*designer*) and then moved back down again to rows 4 and 5 (*builder* and *subcontractor*), using different technologies to bring about the desired improvements. This approach, however, is quite technical. Traditionally, it has been difficult to include the perspectives of the *owner* (at row 2) or the *planner* (at row 1). Parts I and II cover methods that involve senior managers and business experts in enterprise architecture.

1.2.1 The Difference Between Primitives and Composites

John Zachman makes the case that by addressing the six primitives (the interrogatives or questions of *what, how, where, who, when,* and *why*) very complex *composites* (such as buildings, planes, or enterprise systems) can be developed. Answers to these questions, he states, can be used to capture knowledge that is needed to construct any complex (composite) object.

He notes that by taking a top-down approach, building construction and airplane design have developed interchangeable parts that can be reused. He gives the example of standard doors and windows in buildings. He points out that "the Boeing 737, 747, 757 and 767 airplanes were designed so they all use a standard undercarriage. But it is hard to achieve reusability if each component is built from scratch each time" [2].

He develops this reusability principle further by saying that [2]:

> The IT industry has tried to build reusable code or components by using object-oriented methods. But we have not been particularly successful to date. We do use O-O to build reusable components for screen design and other systems components. But we have not been very successful using O-O methods to identify many reusable activities and processes within an enterprise. Enterprise reusability is only achieved effectively by taking an enterprise-wide approach: not in detail across the enterprise, but broadly to encompass the whole enterprise.

This enterprise-wide view is illustrated in Figure 1.6 as horizontal "slices" in each cell. For example, a high-level view of the business plans for an enterprise is shown by the horizontal slice at the top of each cell for column 6 (Why) with row 1 (Planner), and column 6 (Why) with row 2 (Owner). We will see in Part I that strategic planning uses strategy analysis in Chapter 3 to identify these horizontal slices in column 6 as a high-level *list of goals/objectives* and high-level business plans. These comments introduce an initial three enterprise architecture principles—out of a total of six key principles:

	What Data	How Function	Where Location	Who People	When Time	Why Future
Horizontal Slice — PLANNER Objectives/Scope	List of Things	List of Processes	List of Locations	Org Structure	List of Events	List of Goals/Obj
OWNER Conceptual	Enterprise Model	Activity Model	Business Logistics	Work Flow	Master Schedule	Business Plan
DESIGNER Logical	Logical Data Model	Process Model	Distrib. Architect.	Human Interface	Process Structure	Business Rules
BUILDER Physical	Physical Data Model	System Model	Technol. Architect.	Presn Interface	Control Structure	Rule Design
SUBCONTRACTOR Out-of-Context	Data Definition	Program	Network Architect.	Security Interface	Timing Definition	Rule Specs
FUNCTIONING ENTERPRISE	Data	Function	Network	Organization	Schedule	Strategy

Figure 1.6 An enterprise-wide approach is shown as a horizontal band across the full width of each cell. A high-level view of the models within each cell is shown as a narrow "slice" for the enterprise-wide band at the top 10% of each cell.

- Column 6 (Why) for both the Planner and Owner rows are two important primitive cells, used as a starting point focus based on the business plans defined for the future.
- Each horizontal slice extends across the full width of its cell, to show that it is "enterprise-wide." Because this horizontal slice is "high level," it typically extends down to only approximately 10% of the depth of a cell.
- The full depth of a cell represents "an excruciating level of detail," to quote John Zachman [2].

Similarly, these high-level business plans are used to identify people in the *organization structure* (column 4—Who, row 1—Planner) who have business expertise in the areas addressed by those plans, together with knowledge of the high-level data that are required to implement the plans within the enterprise. This highlights the fourth principle:

- Column 4 (Who) for the planner row is another key primitive cell. It identifies business experts in the organization structure who know the data and the processes that are suggested by the business plans.
- Column 1 (What–*Data*) with row 1 (*Planner*) in Figure 1.6 shows a *List of Things* as a high-level horizontal slice in that cell. Column 1 (What–Data) with row 2 (*Owner*) further represents this data as an *Enterprise Model.* A high-level horizontal slice of an Enterprise Model—called a *Strategic Model*—applies to this cell. Chapter 7 describes how strategic modeling is used to develop a strategic model as horizontal slices for these two cells. The fifth principle is therefore:

- Column 1 (What) for the Planner and Owner rows are two important primitive cells. They define the strategic model as the integrated data resource (of the enterprise model) that is required by the business plans.

Furthermore, horizontal slices in column 2 (How–Function) for row 1 (*Planner*) and for row 2 (*Owner*) represent a high-level *List of Processes* and high-level *Activity Models*. Part II will show how a data model can be used to identify a list of processes in column 2, row 1 as a *List of Activities*. This list is then used to identify and define activity models in column 2, row 2. Chapters 7 and 8 discuss how reusable activities can be identified from data models, for further documentation as activity models for ROI analysis through activity-based costing. The sixth principle of enterprise architecture is therefore:

- Column 2 (How–*Function*) for the Planner and Owner rows are two important primitive cells. They identify reusable business activities from the strategic model (in an enterprise model) and from the business plans.

Other methods are discussed in Part II for these primitives: column 3 (Where–*Location*); column 4 (Who–*People*), and column 5 (When–*Time*) for each of rows 1 and 2 (Planner and Owner).

1.2.2 Identifying Reusable, Priority Areas for Early Delivery

The high-level focus of the horizontal "slice" at the top of each cell, shown by Figure 1.6, enables priority areas to be identified that need to be implemented first. These are shown as vertical "slivers" in Figure 1.7, extending for the full depth of the cell at an "excruciating level of detail" [2] for the subset of the cell represented by the sliver.

Horizontal Slice / Vertical Sliver

	What Data	How Function	Where Location	Who People	When Time	Why Future
PLANNER Objectives/Scope	List of Things	List of Processes	List of Locations	Org Structure	List of Events	List of Goals/Obj
OWNER Conceptual	Enterprise Model	Activity Model	Business Logistics	Work Flow	Master Schedule	Business Plan
DESIGNER Logical	Logical Data Model	Process Model	Distrib. Architect.	Human Interface	Process Structure	Business Rules
BUILDER Physical	Physical Data Model	System Model	Technol. Architect.	Presn Interface	Control Structure	Rule Design
SUBCONTRACTOR Out-of-Context	Data Definition	Program	Network Architect.	Security Interface	Timing Definition	Rule Specs
FUNCTIONING ENTERPRISE	Data	Function	Network	Organization	Schedule	Strategy

Figure 1.7 Priority areas for early delivery are identified as vertical "slivers" within each cell, which extend to the depth of the cell. Resources are allocated to these priority areas (slivers) so they can be defined, built, and delivered first.

From the planners' and owners' perspectives in rows 1 and 2 of Figure 1.7 we can see that vertical slivers in each cell enable greater detail to be defined in priority areas. These areas progress to detailed definition (represented by the full depth of the vertical sliver in each cell) for rapid implementation using appropriate tools and technologies. Thus, these areas can be delivered early, before other, less important areas that can wait until later. Part II discusses methods for rapid identification and definition of reusable activities and processes. Part III discusses technologies that are used to deliver these activities and processes rapidly into production as systems.

Rows 1 and 2—from the perspectives of the Planner and Owner—are critical for business transformation. These two rows are used to identify reusability opportunities within an enterprise.

Figure 1.8 highlights rows 1 and 2 (Planner and Owner) of the Zachman framework. A number of cells in these rows are vitally important. We have discussed that *Business Plans* in column 6 (Why) are the most important because such plans are used to set directions for the future. This is developed further in Chapters 3 and 7. We also discussed that column 4 (Who) identifies the *Organization Structure* in row 1. This enables business managers and business experts to identify relative priorities based on the business plans.

The business plans from column 6 are used to develop a high-level *strategic model* in column 1 (What). This is an important cell: It is vital in identifying the integrated high-level data that are needed to manage the progress of the enterprise toward the future. Activity models in column 2 (How) are also vital: These activity models are used to identify critical activities that should be carried out by the enterprise in the future.

John Zachman comments that "enterprise architecture is used for the management of enterprise change." In fact, "if enterprise architecture is not used," he says [2], "there are only three options for managing enterprise change: by trial and error; by reverse engineering; or by going out of business!"

Reusability Definition

	What Data	How Function	Where Location	Who People	When Time	Why Future
PLANNER Objectives/Scope	**List of Things**	**List of Processes**	**List of Locations**	**Org Structure**	**List of Events**	**List of Goals/ Obj**
OWNER Conceptual	**Enterprise Model**	**Activity Model**	**Business Logistics**	**Work Flow**	**Master Schedule**	**Business Plan**
			Reusability Definition			
DESIGNER Logical	Logical Data Model	Process Model	Distrib. Architect.	Human Interface	Process Structure	Business Rules
BUILDER Physical	Physical Data Model	System Model	Technol. Architect.	Presn Interface	Control Structure	Rule Design
SUBCONTRACTOR Out-of-Context	Data Definition	Program	Network Architect.	Security Interface	Timing Definition	Rule Specs
FUNCTIONING ENTERPRISE	Data	Function	Network	Organization	Schedule	Strategy

Figure 1.8 The Planner and Owner rows (rows 1 and 2) are used for Reusability Definition. The Owner row is most effective in its ability to identify enterprise-wide reusability opportunities.

1.3 Enterprise Engineering for Rapid Development

From this brief introduction to enterprise architecture, we will look at typical systems development problems. The typical approach that is used to design and build enterprise systems with traditional systems development methods is summarized here:

- Systems requirements have typically been defined by IT staff, by interviewing users to determine their operational business needs.
- The designs that are established are then based on technology, with application design, database design, and object design reflecting that technology.
- These designs are then implemented to meet desired business performance requirements.

This traditional approach to systems development has been *technology dependent* and has resulted in problems:

- The *business needs* have been difficult to determine. If these needs are not understood or expressed clearly, the designed systems may not address the real needs of the users and management.
- The systems that are developed are typically not aligned with corporate goals that set directions for the future. This is one of the main problems with systems development today.
- But the strategic directions are not clear; yet they must be understood if IT is to design flexible systems that support the strategic directions.

In fact, problems with traditional development methods are much greater than suggested by the preceding list. The business needs have traditionally been decided by reviewing the operational processes of the business. These processes were determined based on strategic plans typically defined many years ago, sometimes more than a decade ago.

Yet in the early 1990s we had no idea—not even in our wildest predictions of the future—that we would today be able to communicate instantly with customers, suppliers, and business partners anywhere in the world, through the Internet. The environment that we accept today as the norm was way beyond our most fanciful imagination.

The strategic plans defined in the 1990s did not anticipate that these organizations would today communicate with each other in seconds. They assumed communication would be as it had always been, by mail—or later by fax—with responses received days or weeks later. The most rapid response these business processes assumed was at best in hours. The business processes we still use today were never designed to respond in seconds.

This point is vitally important and should be emphasized:

> The traditional systems development approach—interviewing users based on existing business processes and then identifying their future needs—does not work well in periods of rapid change, such as today.

In fact, I will make this point stronger:

> If we base our needs for the future on operational processes that we still use today, we are implicitly assuming that the future will be similar to the past. This is very dangerous; few industries and enterprises can say today that their future will be like their past. Most know that the future will be quite different. The only certainty we have is that the processes we will need then are quite different from the processes we use today.

This brings me to emphasize a very important principle for change:

> We must design for tomorrow based not on operational processes still used today. We have to design for tomorrow by using new activities and processes tailored for the environment of the Internet—which represents our present and our future—so that enterprises can respond in seconds or minutes, not in days or weeks.

Enterprise engineering provides support for business transformation: a future where *the only thing that is constant ... is change itself*. Businesses must change, to compete with other organizations in their relevant markets. This is true for commercial organizations that compete with other organizations. It is true for government departments that compete with other departments for government funding. And it is also true for defense departments, which compete with hostile defense forces, and also with friendly defense forces for limited resources.

Competition today demands systems that can change easily, to support rapid business transformation. Many business changes may need significant change or redevelopment of systems. Yet most of those systems were not designed for change. Existing systems may need massive modification to support essential business changes. Often it is faster to throw the existing systems away and start over again, developing new systems from scratch. This can still be slow and very costly.

The advantages and benefits of technology were not clear in the early 1990s to many senior managers. It was sometimes difficult to get funding approval for new projects and funding for the resources that are vital for success. But the Internet and the Y2K problem in the late 1990s demonstrated to management the dramatic impact—both positive and negative—that technology can have on the enterprise.

We discussed earlier that we have taken a bottom-up view with traditional methods in building systems for the enterprise. We looked at the existing systems—whether manual or automated—as represented by the bottom row of the Zachman framework for enterprise architecture.

From a bottom-up view, we looked at ways in which current manual or automated systems have been implemented. We then examined ways to improve these systems: either by automating the manual systems, or by using technology to improve existing automated systems.

As discussed with Figure 1.5, we have taken a design focus from the perspective of row 3 (Designer) using traditional methods, and then moved down again to rows 4 and 5 (for Builder and Subcontractor), using technologies to bring about the desired improvements. We saw that this approach is quite technical. Traditionally, it has been difficult to include the perspectives of the Owner (at row 2) or the Planner (at row 1).

How can we address these problems and involve the Planner and the Owner in setting transformation directions for the future? We will now consider solutions to these problems arising from the traditional approach to systems development:

- The systems that are to be developed for the future must support the corporate goals. This is the most common systems development problem today.
- We must therefore determine the goals for the future. But goals are expressed in business terms, not systems terms. What should we implement?
- We earlier discussed that IT departments must be aware of strategic directions so they can design for the future. In the 1990s this was difficult because most IT departments did not participate in strategic planning. However, this is changing; many CIOs now come from the business side rather than from IT.
- Yet we have seen that IT must build systems based on strategic plans if those systems are to be aligned with corporate goals. They must be based on activities and processes designed for the future, not the past.
- If this is done, technology can then offer competitive advantage: It can be used to help achieve the strategic plans and corporate goals, with new activities and processes that respond in seconds or minutes—not in days or weeks.

Today, enterprise engineering resolves these problems with systems development. It enables business experts and IT experts to work together in a design partnership using modeling tools (previously called CASE tools for computer-aided software engineering). Enterprise engineering utilizes modeling tools and methods for business transformation by business experts and IT experts to do the following:

- Build systems for the future that can support the corporate goals.
- Identify goals for the future in business terms, so that IT can determine what to implement in systems terms.
- Provide strategic business planning methods so that the IT department can participate in strategic planning with management.
- Enable IT to build systems based on the strategic plans so that those systems are aligned with corporate goals.
- Technology can then offer competitive advantage—used to help achieve the strategic plans and corporate goals.

We will now examine the business-driven enterprise engineering methodologies in more detail. These methods support all phases of the systems development life cycle (SDLC). Figure 1.9 illustrates that phases above the line are technology-independent methods and focus on the business. They apply to rows 1–3 (Planner, Owner, and Designer) of the Zachman framework. These methods are strategic business planning, data modeling, and function modeling:

- The strategic directions set by management provide input to strategy analysis, discussed in Chapter 3 for column 6 of the Zachman framework.

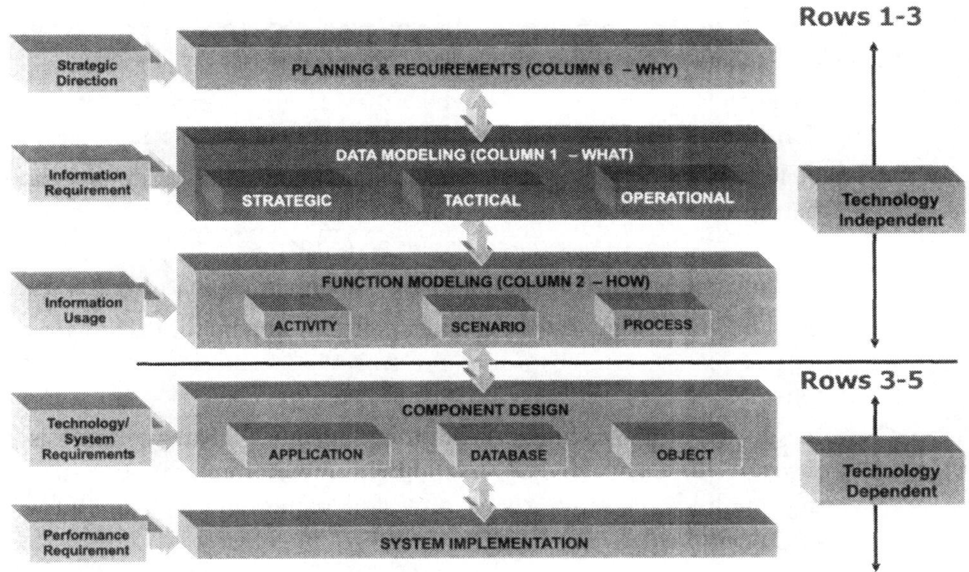

Figure 1.9 Enterprise engineering supports all rows of the Zachman framework, with rapid implementation of priority enterprise architecture areas.

- These plans indicate the information requirements of management that are input to data modeling in column 1. Strategic, tactical, and operational data modeling are covered in Chapters 6, 7, and 9.
- Plans and data models define information usage as input to function modeling, for activity modeling, scenario modeling, and process modeling in column 2. These are covered in Chapters 8 and 10.

These phases of Figure 1.9 define technology-independent business requirements and address enterprise architecture rows 1–3 (for the Planner, Owner, and Designer). Phases below the bold line in the figure are technology dependent. They address enterprise architecture rows 3–5 (for Designer, Builder, and Subcontractor). These methods address component design and systems implementation:

- Technology and systems requirements of the business provide input to systems design. Internet technologies and object-oriented methods in this phase are used for application design, database design, and object design of systems to be deployed on corporate intranets and/or the Internet.
- Identified performance requirements then provide the input required by the systems implementation phase.

The first enterprise engineering phase is strategic business planning. This identifies the planning and requirements needs of the enterprise for the future. Strategic plans are represented by column 6 (Why) in the Zachman framework. Strategic business planning uses the method of strategy analysis to determine the strategic plans for the future, as discussed in Chapter 3. Strategy analysis is used to accomplish the following:

- Identify goals from existing strategic plans, so that a clear understanding can be reached of the business needs of the enterprise.
- Help develop business goals (where they do not yet exist)—or refine any goals that already exist—to ensure that business results are clearly stated.
- Help develop project goals from business goals—or refine any project goals that already exist—to ensure that the business results and the project results can be clearly expressed and define what the project must achieve.
- Consider alternative technologies for implementation as discussed in Part III.
- Provide knowledge of strategic business planning methods and terminology to help IT experts and business experts provide technology input to the business plans.
- Guide an organization's technology agenda. Strategy analysis identifies priorities for early delivery. In conjunction with the other enterprise engineering methods, it supports a powerful rapid-delivery capability for large organizations.

After strategy analysis, strategic modeling methods use business plans to develop a strategic model. This is used to develop an enterprise architecture portfolio plan (EAPP) for project planning. We will learn in Chapter 7 how to develop project plans from data models. We will derive required project plans for enterprise architecture implementation. We then use technology for early delivery of priority systems.

Looking at the data modeling phase in more detail in Figure 1.9, Strategic business planning identifies the information requirements of management and provides input to this phase:

- Strategic business plans provide input to strategic modeling, to develop a strategic data model, called a *strategic model.* This is discussed in Chapter 7.
- Analysis of the strategic model produces an EAPP as mentioned earlier.
- The strategic model, the EAPP, and tactical business plans all provide input to tactical data modeling, to develop tactical data models.
- The EAPP, tactical models, and operational business plans also provide input to operational data modeling, to develop operational data models.
- Data modeling and business normalization methods—discussed in Chapters 6 and 9—are used to develop strategic data models, tactical data models and operational data models.

Data modeling is used to develop a strategic model from strategic plans for the rapid development of high-level business data models. These data models are used to develop project plans to deliver high-priority and high ROI systems early.

Data modeling also helps to identify various alternatives, leading to business benefits. This provides business justification for technology alternatives, funding approval for the technology, and resources for implementation.

The EAPP report is a deliverable from strategic modeling and strategic model analysis. We will see in Chapter 7 that this establishes clear project plans for priority projects. It leads to detailed development of approved projects. Tactical and operational data models then define databases in detail, ready for implementation.

Function modeling addresses column 2 (How) of the Zachman framework. It is based on the information usage of management, as determined by the strategic plans defined by strategy analysis (in column 6—Why). Information requirements of management (from data models in column 1—What) also provide input to function modeling, which includes the following:

- *Activity modeling*: This indicates *what* has to be done to provide the required information to management. Activity models address column 2 (How) in rows 1 and 2 (for Planner and Owner) and are discussed in Chapter 8.
- *Process modeling:* This indicates *how* processes are to be carried out, based on required activities. This addresses column 2 (How) in rows 2 and 3 (for Owner and Designer) and is described in Chapter 10.
- *Scenario modeling:* This indicates *who* is involved in activities and processes. It identifies people from the organization structure (in column 4—Who, row 1—Planner) based on strategic alignment matrices in Chapter 8.

Function modeling is used to model business activities as activity models (also using activity-based costing) and as process models that define business processes. It aligns activities and processes to strategic plans to support corporate goals, project goals, and system goals. It is used for development of approved projects, to define business objects for object-oriented development. Function modeling ensures that systems can change rapidly.

We earlier discussed the component design phase. We saw the typical approach that has been used to design and build enterprise systems previously with traditional systems development methods. However, by using the prior technology-independent phases of enterprise engineering, the business needs for the future are now clearly defined from strategic plans and business plans as a result of these methods:

- *Strategy analysis* to define strategic business plans for the future.
- *Data modeling* to develop strategic, tactical, and operational data models.
- *Function modeling,* using activity modeling, activity-based costing, process modeling, and scenario modeling.

The business priorities are now clearly defined from business needs and project plans in Parts I and II. Data models are now fully developed at strategic, tactical, and operational levels to address future needs. Activity models and process models are now fully developed, with business processes defined as business objects for future needs and environments. Technology is then used for rapid development as discussed in Part III. This use of enterprise engineering is summarized in Box 1.1.

1.4 Using Enterprise Architecture for Enterprise Integration

At the start of this chapter we discussed that enterprise integration depends on business integration and also technology integration. Business integration is achieved

Box 1.1: Enterprise Engineering for Enterprise Architecture

The use of enterprise engineering methods for enterprise architecture results in rapid definition of a strategic model for an enterprise—typically over 2 days—in a facilitated modeling session with business experts from relevant project areas of the enterprise. In Chapter 7 we discuss several strategic models developed in 2-day facilitated modeling sessions for a number of organizations.

From a strategic model defined in a 2-day facilitated modeling session, an enterprise architecture portfolio plan report is developed. The EAPP report identifies priority enterprise architecture areas for rapid delivery and implementation. For small and medium enterprises, the EAPP report is typically developed and documented in a total elapsed duration of 4 weeks, including the 2-day facilitated modeling session to develop the strategic model. For large enterprises, the development and documentation of the EAPP report typically takes 8–12 weeks because of the greater enterprise complexity.

The EAPP report is developed using entity dependency analysis methods covered in Chapter 7. These project plans are the basis for later development of tactical and operational data models (in column 1) and activity models and process models (in column 2) of the Zachman framework. This leads to rapid implementation of priority systems for the priority project areas.

With this analysis and the technologies covered in Part III, priority business activities and processes (as priority project areas) can typically be delivered into production in 3-month increments for small and medium enterprises. For large enterprises, these priority areas are delivered into production in 6-month increments due to greater enterprise inertia.

through the use of enterprise architecture and related enterprise engineering methods. Technology integration is achieved with the use of XML, EAI, enterprise portals, Web services, and SOA, as discussed in Part III. We will now discuss some of the implications of business integration.

1.4.1 The Importance of Metadata

Enterprise integration is critically dependent on a clear definition of the *metadata* used in an enterprise. When asked to define the meaning of metadata, most IT experts respond with a definition of "data about data" or "information about information." These definitions are meaningless to nontechnical business managers. They do not even begin to explain the meaning of metadata, let alone its vital importance for enterprise integration, business integration, and technology integration. Yet a clear definition of the metadata of an enterprise—referred to as *enterprise metadata*—is vital for success in each of these integration endeavors. A better definition of metadata is provided by the nontechnical analogy provided in Box 1.2.

As we discussed in relation to Adam Smith in the preface, enterprises have historically evolved with different terminology in various parts of the organization. The need for a common language for communication in an enterprise was not recognized. Consider the problems that arose as computers were introduced to automate processes and data. We discussed that this introduced problems of data redundancy, data maintenance redundancy, and process redundancy. To achieve business integration and technology integration for business transformation, common terminology must be used.

Data modeling is used to identify metadata and define what each term means. These definitions are captured by data modeling tools and stored in a repository. Agreed-on common terms, with other enterprise terminology, constitute the *enter-*

Box 1.2: A Nontechnical Introduction to Metadata

Consider how we communicate by phone. Because all countries are interconnected by the global phone network, we can dial any number at random and a phone will likely ring somewhere in the world. However, if the person who answers it speaks a different language, communication may not be possible. But by using an interpreter or a translation dictionary, we are able to communicate regardless of the spoken language.

Now consider that different "language" or terminology may be used in various parts of a business. We call this *jargon.* For example, finance people and engineering people may not understand each other because they use different terms to refer to their areas of knowledge.

Consider also that different terms can mean the same thing in various parts of the business, such as "customer," "client," and "debtor." These words are synonyms. They are used, respectively, by the sales department and order entry department, by the credit control department, and also by the finance department. Each synonym refers to a buyer of products or services from an enterprise. To communicate most effectively, a common term must be agreed on and its exact meaning defined and documented so that all parties know what that term means. A more appropriate definition of metadata follows:

> Metadata documents an organization's terminology and meanings. It documents the enterprise language typically as an enterprise glossary of terminology.

This glossary is the enterprise equivalent of a translation dictionary as discussed earlier.

prise glossary that we discussed in Box 1.2. The enterprise glossary is the language dictionary of a business, similar to the translation dictionaries used with different spoken languages.

We discussed that data modeling methods are used by enterprise engineering. These methods are described extensively in Part II. They define metadata. Their use is vital to achieve business integration. Their use is also vital to implement enterprise architecture for business transformation.

To illustrate the problems that arise from a lack of definition of enterprise metadata, we will consider a hypothetical enterprise in Box 1.3: XYZ Corporation. XYZ is a sales and distribution organization that purchases products and services

Box 1.3: XYZ Case Study Example

Both the sales department and the order entry department of XYZ accept orders from "customers." They keep details of customers in a database table called CUSTOMER.

The credit control department keeps similar details, but it uses different terminology. It refers to people who buy from XYZ on credit as "clients," not customers. Details are kept in a CLIENT table.

The accounts receivable section in the finance department uses different terminology also. It calls the people who pay for orders "debtors," with details kept in a DEBTOR table. Multiple copies of each organization's address are stored in these tables.

If an organization that deals with XYZ as a customer, client, or debtor is also a supplier of products, then the purchasing department uses different terminology yet again. Such organizations are "suppliers," with details kept in a SUPPLIER table. Payment by XYZ of the supplier's account balance is managed by accounts payable in the finance department, who call these suppliers "creditors," with details kept in a CREDITOR table.

If an organization—known to XYZ variously as a customer, client, debtor, supplier and creditor—later changes its address, all of these address copies must be updated and synchronized so that they contain the same changed address.

from its suppliers to sell to its customers. We will use this as a case study example throughout the book.

Redundant data present no problem if their values do not change. But if data values are volatile and hence can change—such as an address—then every redundant version of the address in each database table must be changed to contain the latest correct value.

We can see the problem that arises if different terminology is used throughout XYZ. Each of these terms represents the same organization: a "customer"—for sales and order entry; a "client"—for credit control; a "debtor" or "creditor"—for finance; a "supplier"—for purchasing. These synonyms all identify a buyer of products and services from XYZ, or a supplier to XYZ. To communicate effectively, a common term must be agreed on and its exact meaning defined and documented so that all involved understand what that term means.

The preceding example considers the various roles that an organization can take in dealing with XYZ. A common term should be used throughout XYZ Corporation. We will discuss this further in Chapters 6, 7 and 9 when we discuss data modeling methods to identify metadata.

1.5 Summary

The summary is as follows.

- We discussed the need to transform from today's inflexible business environment to an enterprise that can change direction rapidly. Methods and technologies are needed for rapid business change—with systems that change in lock-step.
- Business change depends on enterprise integration. This includes business integration using enterprise architecture methods to define integrated data and reusable business activities and processes. Enterprise architecture methods are covered in Part II of this book.
- Enterprise integration also includes technology integration, that is, the process of using technologies to deliver integrated data and reusable processes rapidly into production as shared databases and systems. Enterprise architecture technologies are covered in Part III of this book.
- The problem is that today we have twenty-first-century enterprises that use twenty-first-century technologies ... yet most enterprises today still use eighteenth-century disintegrated business processes!

The business processes—originally designed based on principles set by Adam Smith in 1776 as discussed in the preface—have not evolved to take advantage of the technologies we have today. We need integrated twenty-first-century enterprises together with transformed twenty-first-century processes!

- We discussed the problem of redundant data versions in most enterprises. When data values change, all redundant versions must be updated to synchronize with that change. With redundant data, we moved to data maintenance chaos!

- We saw that data modeling methods define metadata. Their use is vital for business integration. Their use is also vital to implement enterprise architecture.
- We discussed concepts of the Zachman framework for enterprise architecture. We discussed that the real architects of an enterprise are the senior business managers who set strategic directions for the future, based on business plans and strategies, and processes designed for that future and its technologies.
- We discussed enterprise reusability. We saw that the Planner and Owner rows of the Zachman framework are critical for reusability. These two rows enable reusability opportunities to be identified within an enterprise.
- We discussed the concepts of enterprise engineering, which is used to identify reusability opportunities based on business plans for rapid delivery of priority areas into production.

Summarizing enterprise engineering as used with the Zachman framework, the preferred way to implement for the needs of the future follows:

- We must design for tomorrow based on business plans for the future. We should use activities and processes tailored for the environment of the Internet—which represents our present and our future—so that enterprises can respond rapidly.
- Enterprise architecture should therefore first address rows 1 and 2, from the perspectives of the Planner and the Owner.
- Column 6 (Why) defines the business plans for the future. These plans are an important starting point.
- Column 4 (Who) is used to identify the business managers and business experts responsible for implementing the business plans.
- The business experts are used to identify the data needed for the future in column 1 (What). They also identify activities and processes in column 2 (How).
- Clear directions can then be provided to row 3 (for the Designer), row 4 (for the Builder), and row 5 (for implementation by the Subcontractor).
- The result is the development of flexible systems based on the needs of the future, to be implemented rapidly using Internet technologies and tools.

Endnotes

[1] O'Rourke, C., N. Fishman, and W. Selkow, *Enterprise Architecture Using the Zachman Framework,* Boston, MA: Course Technology, a division of Thomson Learning, 2003.

[2] Zachman, J., *The Zachman Framework for Enterprise Architecture: A Primer for Enterprise Engineering and Manufacturing,* Glendale, CA: Zachman International, 2003, http://www.zachmaninternational.com.

[3] The complete Zachman framework is available as a PDF file on the accompanying CD-ROM. Print this now, in color if possible, and use it for reference as you read though the book. This PDF file has been included with permission from Intervista Institute (http://www.intervista-institute.com).

PART I

Enterprise Architecture for Managers

Part I is directed to business managers and business experts, as well as IT staffs who will work with them on joint business-driven enterprise architecture projects. It covers strategic planning and governance methods. It shows how these methods are used with a balanced scorecard for strategy-focused organizations. The chapters in Part I form a catalyst for Part II, which uses enterprise architecture methods so that strategies for governance and for balanced scorecard measures can be implemented effectively throughout the enterprise.

Chapter 2: Balanced Scorecard and Strategy Maps. The balanced scorecard approach has been used successfully as a catalyst for business transformation. The directions established by balanced scorecards and strategy maps provide a catalyst for Part II, which uses enterprise architecture methods to ensure that systems and databases are developed to support balanced scorecard measures.

Chapter 3: Using Strategy Analysis to Define the Future. This chapter introduces the rapid-delivery, business-driven methodology of strategy analysis for business planning and balanced scorecards. It is used by senior managers and their business staffs to define business transformation directions for the future enterprise. Strategy analysis is introduced with examples, together with case study exercise problems and sample solutions.

Chapter 4: Governance Analysis Using Enterprise Architecture. Many countries have enacted legislation for corporate governance, such as the Sarbanes-Oxley Act of 2002 in the United States. This requires internal control reporting for senior management to ensure that financial reporting and other governance controls are in place. Enterprise architecture enables governance analysis frameworks to be dynamically defined in each enterprise for internal control reporting.

CHAPTER 2

Balanced Scorecard and Strategy Maps

Part I covers methods for enterprise architecture that provide information needed by senior and middle managers in the enterprise. Chapter 1 covered the basic concepts of enterprise architecture and enterprise engineering.

In this chapter we discuss balanced scorecard and strategy maps. We will see how these tools assist management by representing business plans visually. We will see the need for strategy analysis methods, which we cover in detail in Chapter 3. In Chapter 4 we will see how enterprise architecture can be used for governance analysis.

Each chapter's focus is shown in relation to the Zachman framework, which was introduced in Chapter 1. This is illustrated in Figure 2.1, with the specific cell of the framework highlighted. We will discuss methods for column 6 (Why), in particular, rows 1 and 2 for the Planners and Owners of the enterprise. (*Note:* As with the Framework PDF on the accompanying CD-ROM, column 3 of this screen shot should show Location, not Network.)

2.1 Introduction to Balanced Scorecard and Strategy Maps

Strategic business planning has been the emphasis of good management since the 1960s through the early books by Chandler [1], Ansoff [2], Andrews [3], Drucker [4], Porter [5, 6] and many others [7, 8]. However a problem with most strategic planning methods has been in translating the plans into action, as most memorably summarized by Ackoff [9]:

> Most corporate planning is like a ritual rain dance: it has no effect on the weather that follows, but makes those who engage in it feel that they are in control. Most discussions of the role of models in planning are directed at improving the dancing, not the weather.

The 1996 book *The Balanced Scorecard: Translating Strategy into Action,* by Robert S. Kaplan and David P. Norton [10], had a large impact on the discipline of strategic planning. This book was followed in 2001 by *The Strategy-Focused Organization: How Balanced Scorecard Companies Thrive in the New Business Environment* [11], which reported on the success of the early application of the balanced scorecard in many enterprises. Kaplan and Norton's 2004 book, *Strategy Maps: Converting Intangible Assets into Tangible Outcomes* [12], built on the experience of other successes in the implementation of balanced scorecard and strategy maps.

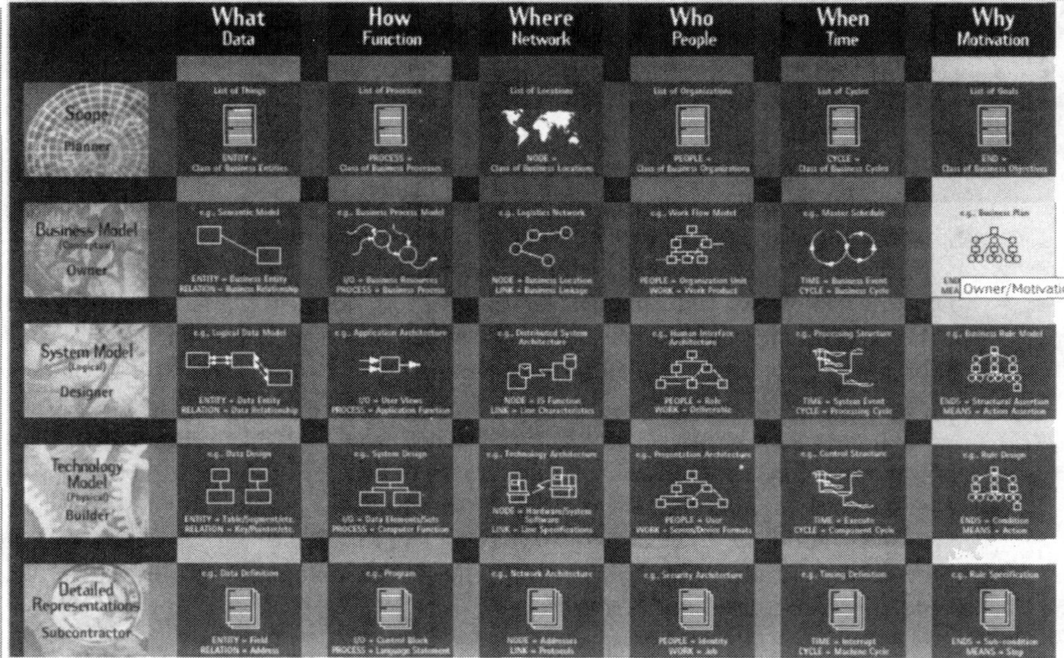

Figure 2.1 Strategy analysis addresses Zachman framework, column 6, rows 1 and 2.

In this chapter, we will draw on principles introduced in these three books. In so doing, we will see the advantages offered by balanced scorecard and by strategy maps. We will also see where additional methods can provide further support. To provide this support, we will cover the methods of strategy analysis in Chapter 3 and governance analysis in Chapter 4.

2.2 Basic Concepts of Balanced Scorecard

The 1996 book by Kaplan and Norton introduced the basic principles of balanced scorecard [10]. Their next book in 2001 reinforced the five principles of successful strategy-focused organizations [11] and are discussed next.

2.2.1 Translate the Strategy to Operational Terms

Balanced scorecard concepts were introduced in 1992. A balanced scorecard clearly shows the important aspects of each strategy in a consistent way. An example is discussed later in relation to Mobil Corporation, as illustrated in Figure 2.2.

In designing a scorecard, the first question is: What is the strategy? From this, it is illustrated in a strategy map; this clearly shows the dependent aspects in a strategy. Examples of Mobil's strategy map are shown as Figures 2.3 and 2.4. The development of this strategy map is discussed later in the chapter.

As described by Kaplan and Norton, "the measurement linkages of cause-and-effect relationships in strategy maps show how intangible assets are transformed into tangible (financial) outcomes." They state: "Intangible assets ...

	Strategic Themes	Strategic Objectives	Strategic Measures
Financial	Financial Growth	F1 Return on Capital Employed F2 Existing Asset Utilization F3 Profitability F4 Industry Cost Leader F5 Profitable Growth	• ROCE • Cash Flow • Net Margin Rank (Vs Competition) • Full Cost Peer Gallon Delivered (Vs Competition) • Volume Growth Rate Vs Industry • Premium Ratio • Non-gasoline Revenue and Margin
Customer	Delight the Customer Win-Win Dealer Relations	C1 Continually Delight the Target Customer C2 Build Win-Win Relations with Dealer	• Share of Segment in Selected Key Markets • Mystery Shopper Rating • Dealer Gross Profit Growth • Dealer Survey
Internal	Build the Franchise Safe and Reliable	I1 Innovative Products and Service I2 Best in Class Franchise Teams I3 Refinery Performance I4 Inventory Management I5 Industry Cost Leader I6 On Spec, on Time	• New Product ROI • New Product Acceptance Rate • Dealer Quality Score • Yield Gap • Unplanned Downtime • Inventory Levels • Run-out Rate • Activity Cost Vs Competition • Perfect Orders
Learning and Growth	Motivated and Prepared Workforce	L1 Climate for Action L2 Core Competencies and Skills L3 Access to Strategic Information	• Employee Survey • Personal Balanced Scorecard (%) • Strategic Competency Availability • Strategic Information Availability

Figure 2.2 Mobil's Balanced Scorecard (*From:* [11], Figure 2-5, p. 42. © 2001 Harvard Business School Press. Reprinted with permission.)

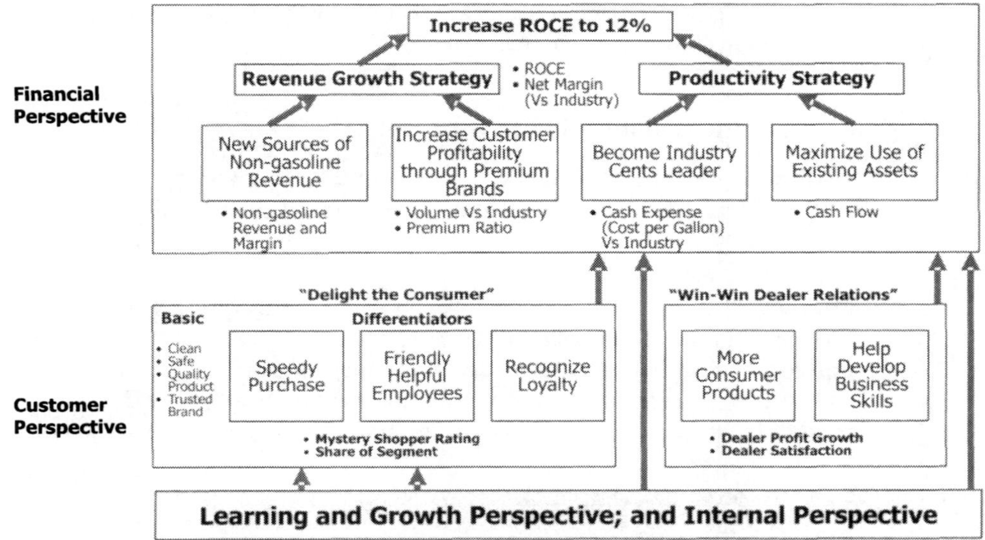

Figure 2.3 Mobil's strategy map, part 1, reading from the top down. (*After:* [11], Figure 2-6, p. 42.)

usually have little standalone value; their value arises from being embedded in coherent, linked strategies." They emphasize that [11]:

> The scorecard's use of quantitative, but non-financial, measures—such as cycle time, market share, innovation, satisfaction, and competencies—allows the value-creating process to be described and measured, rather than inferred.... The Strategy Map and its corresponding Balanced Scorecard measurement program

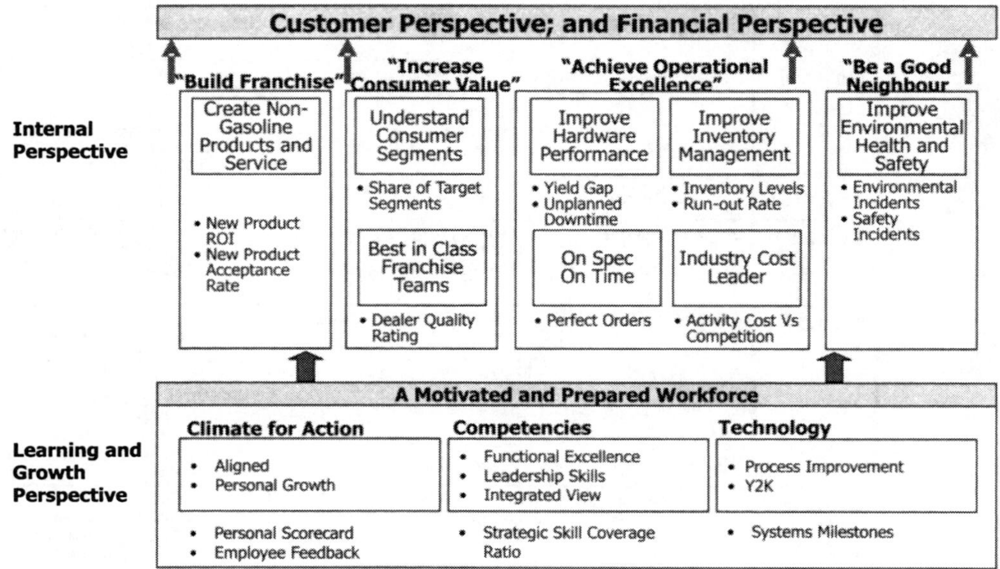

Figure 2.4 Mobil's strategy map, part 2, reading from the top down. (*After:* [11], Figure 2-6, p. 43.)

provide a tool to describe how shareholder value is created from intangible assets. Strategy maps and Balanced Scorecards constitute the measurement technology for managing in a knowledge-based economy.

2.2.2 Align the Organization to the Strategy

From the definition of balanced scorecards and strategy maps, Kaplan and Norton make the logical point that the organization should then be aligned to the strategy [11]:

> Organizations are traditionally designed around functional specialties such as finance, manufacturing, marketing, sales, engineering and purchasing. Each function has its own body of knowledge, language, and culture. Functional silos arise and become a major barrier to strategy implementation, as most organizations have great difficulty communicating and coordinating across these specialty functions.

They go on to say that [11]:

> Strategy-focused organizations, however, break this barrier. Executives replace formal reporting structures with strategic themes and priorities that enable a consistent message and consistent set of priorities to be used across diverse and dispersed organizational units.... Business units and shared service units become linked to the strategy through the common themes and objectives that permeate their scorecards.

2.2.3 Make Strategy Everyone's Everyday Job

The implementation of new strategies requires the cooperative efforts of all managers and their staffs in an organization. Kaplan and Norton ask the important question [11]: "How do you move strategy from the boardroom to the backroom and thus to the front lines of daily operations and customer service?"

Balanced scorecards and strategy maps clearly communicate the new strategy to the organization. But should this be done? The authors say: "... some managers are skeptical about communicating strategy to the entire organization, fearing that valuable information could be leaked to competitors." In discounting this fear, they quote Brian Baker from Mobil, talking about the Mobil strategy (discussed later) and communicating it to all employees [11]: "Knowing your strategy will do them little good unless they can execute it. On the other hand, we have no chance of executing our strategy unless our people know it. It's a chance we'll have to take."

Kaplan and Norton discuss organizations that were successful in implementing balanced scorecards and strategy maps. They found many of these organizations had cascaded high-level corporate and business unit scorecards to lower levels of the organization, through the definition of personal scorecards and personal objectives. They said that: "... instead of cascading objectives through the chain of command, as is normally done, the complete strategy was communicated in a top-down fashion."

But what is not clear from their books is how to implement the new strategy and how to determine the areas of implementation responsibility for each manager and staff member. They refer to the need for strategy analysis to achieve this implementation, but provide little guidance in how this is achieved.

Chapter 3 describes a very effective method for strategy analysis that is used to address this need. It enables the new strategy to be implemented at all management levels throughout an organization. The strategy is reflected in personal scorecards and personal objectives for each manager. Strategy analysis takes the broad strategic directions and the dependent measures as documented in balanced scorecards and strategy maps and translates these into supporting goals, objectives, strategies, and tactics at all levels of the organization. In Chapter 3 it achieves full management accountability for implementation, by building these statements into each manager's and staff member's job description.

2.2.4 Make Strategy a Continual Process

Quite independent of a balanced scorecard, government departments in many countries have linked strategy to the budget process. Each department is required to show how next year's budget is linked to the strategic plans for that same period. This has had great effect of improving the strategic planning process in these departments. In many countries, however, there has not been any review of the effectiveness of implementation of the previous year's budget against the relevant plans, before a new budget is approved for the next year's plans. There is no *effective accountability*.

Kaplan and Norton found that many companies that had achieved success with balanced scorecards had linked strategy to the budgeting process. A balanced scorecard "provided the yardstick for evaluating potential investments and initiatives.... Companies have discovered that they needed two kinds of budgets: a strategy budget and an operational budget" [11].

They found that these companies introduced management meetings for accountability to review strategy, where these meetings did not exist in the past.

Some introduced open reporting, making performance results available to everyone in the organization. "Building on the principle that 'strategy is everyone's job,' they empowered 'everyone' by giving each employee the knowledge needed to do his or her job." Kaplan and Norton noted that [11]:

> Finally a process for learning and adapting the strategy evolved.... The scorecard design process helped to make the cause-and-effect linkages in the strategic hypotheses explicit. As the scorecard was put into action and feedback systems began reporting progress, the organizations could test the strategies' hypotheses.... Instead of being an annual event, strategy became a continual process.

2.2.5 Mobilize Change Through Executive Leadership

From the organizations that were successful in implementing balanced scorecard and strategy maps, the authors found that "the single most important condition for success is the ownership and active involvement of the executive team.... A successful Balanced Scorecard program starts with the recognition that it is not a 'metrics' project; it's a change project." They found that:

> Initially the focus is on mobilization and creating momentum, to get the process launched. Once the organization is mobilized, the focus shifts to governance, with emphasis on fluid, team-based approaches to deal with the unstructured nature of the transition to a new performance model. Finally, and gradually over time, a new management system evolves—a strategic management system that institutionalizes the new cultural values and new structures into a new system for managing. The various phases can evolve over two to three years.... Once the change process is launched, executives establish a governance process to guide the transition.... The creation of strategy teams, town hall meetings, and open communications are all components of this transitional governance.

We will see a governance analysis method in Chapter 4 that assists with the balanced scorecard shift from mobilization to governance.

In addition to linking balanced scorecard to the formal planning and budgeting process, many of the successful organizations linked executive compensation to the scorecard:

> By linking traditional processes such as compensation and resource allocation to a Balanced Scorecard that described the strategy, they created a *strategic management system*. The scorecard described the strategy while the management system wired every part of the organization to the strategy scorecard.

The experience and the impressive results that were achieved by many successful organizations are described in *The Strategy-Focused Organization* [13].

2.3 Basic Concepts of Strategy Maps

The balanced scorecard was first introduced "to overcome the limitations of managing only with financial measures. Financial measures reported on outcomes and lagging indicators, but did not communicate the drivers of future performance." We will now look at the structure and content of strategy maps and see how they make strategies for value creation more explicit from four different perspectives:

1. *Financial:* The strategy for growth, profitability and risk viewed from the perspective of the shareholder.
2. *Customer:* The strategy for creating value and differentiation from the perspective of the customer.
3. *Internal Business Processes:* The strategic priorities for various business processes, which create customer and shareholder satisfaction.
4. *Learning and Growth:* The priorities to create a climate that supports organizational change, innovation and growth.

As discussed in Kaplan and Norton's 2004 book, *Strategy Maps* [12], the balanced scorecard provides a framework for describing strategies that create value. This framework is discussed next and is shown on the left of Figure 2.5 for private-sector organizations, which measure success in terms of financial value as a return to shareholders. The figure shows similar components for public-sector and nonprofit organizations on the right.

Financial performance provides the definition of a private-sector organization's success in the value that is returned to the shareholders, expressed on the left of Figure 2.5, by answering the question: If we succeed, how will we look to our shareholders? The strategy for these organizations is to create sustainable growth in shareholder value.

Private-Sector

The Strategy

Financial Perspective

"If we succeed, how will we look to our shareholders?"

Customer Perspective

"To achieve our vision, how must we look to our customers?"

Internal Perspective

"To satisfy our customers, which processes must we excel at?"

Learning and Growth Perspective

"To achieve our vision, how must our organization learn and improve?"

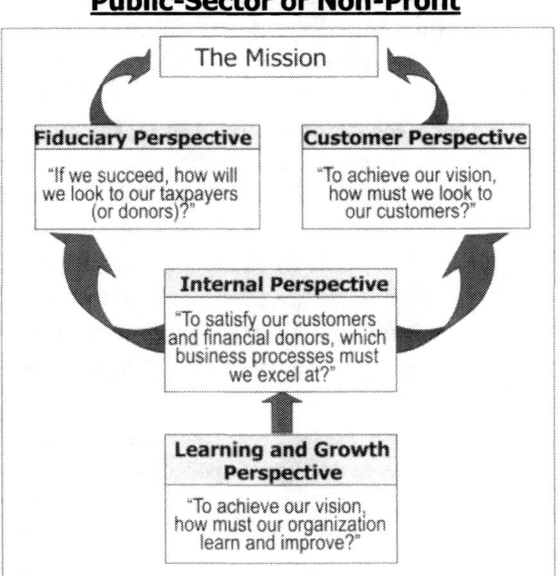

Figure 2.5 Strategy maps show the dependent components of a strategic plan. This shows a private-sector organization example on the left and a public-sector or nonprofit organization example on the right. (*From:* [12], Figure 1-2, p. 8. © 2004 Harvard Business School Press. Reprinted with permission.)

Value is achieved from targeted customers by measuring lagging indicators of customer success, such as satisfaction, retention, and growth. This answers the question: To achieve our vision, how must we look to our customers?

Internal processes create and deliver value to customers by answering the question: To satisfy our customers, which processes must we excel at? The performance of these processes is a leading indicator of subsequent improvements in customer and financial outcomes.

Learning and growth objectives describe how people, technology, and the organization all combine to support the strategy. They answer the question: To achieve our vision, how must our organization learn and improve?

On the right, Figure 2.5 shows that public-sector and nonprofit organizations measure success not in financial terms, but in terms of the value that is returned to taxpayers or donors from a fiduciary perspective or in terms of the value to customers from a customer perspective.

The ultimate definition of success for public and nonprofit organizations is performance in achieving their mission. They typically cover a wide focus in their mission and so must define their social impact differently from a result that reflects financial value as is true of private-sector organizations. An example of a public-sector mission for a government social security department is: "To achieve social security policies that meet the needs of the community and deliver entitlements and services with fairness, courtesy and efficiency."

The mission for public-sector and nonprofit organizations shown on the right of Figure 2.5 focuses on meeting the needs of the customers who benefit from the services that they deliver, by answering the question: To achieve our vision, how must we look to our customers?

The fiduciary perspective answers the additional question of: If we succeed, how will we look to our taxpayers (or donors)? It reflects the objectives of taxpayers or donors who provide the funding for the organization's continued operation.

The internal perspective addresses these two constituencies by answering the modified question: To satisfy our customers and financial donors, which business processes must we excel at? This must be done while the learning and growth perspective is the same as for private-sector organizations on the left of Figure 2.5.

An example of a strategy map that shows how an organization can create value is shown in Figure 2.6 for a private-sector organization.

The financial perspective in Figure 2.6 illustrates four strategies that all work together to create long-term shareholder value. We can see there are two productivity strategies: "improve cost structure" and "increase asset utilization." There are also two growth strategies: "expand revenue opportunities" and "enhance customer value."

These financial perspective strategies are addressed from the customer perspective in terms of the customer value proposition by product/service attributes of price, quality, availability, selection, and functionality. There are also relationship factors of service and partnership as well as image factors of brand.

We can also see from Figure 2.6 that internal processes support customer perspective attributes and factors through operations management processes of supply, production, distribution, and risk management; customer management processes of selection, acquisition, retention, and growth; innovation processes of opportunity

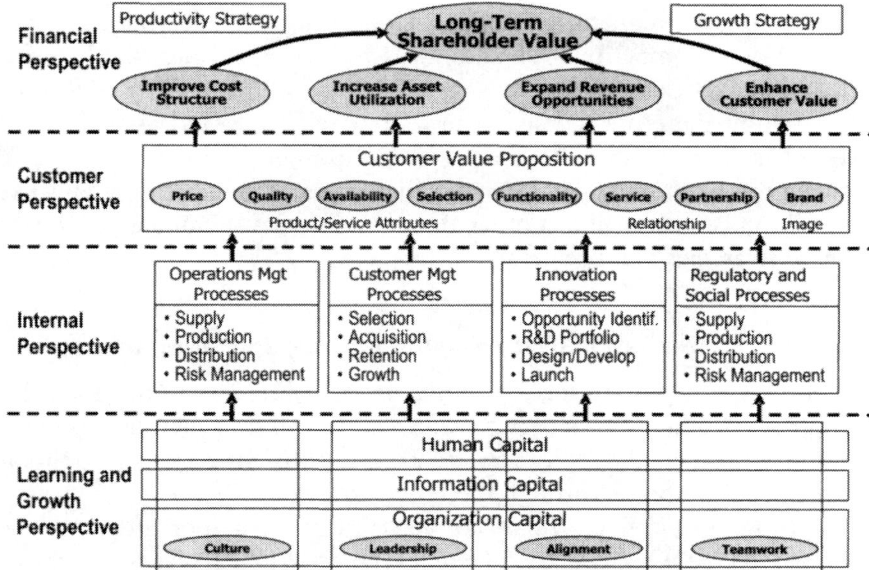

Figure 2.6 Strategy maps show value creation (*From:* [12], Figure 1-3, p. 11. © 2004 Harvard Business School Press. Reprinted with permission.)

identification, R&D portfolio, design and development, and launch; and finally regulatory and social processes of supply, production, distribution, and risk management.

The learning and growth perspective at the bottom of the figure shows human capital, information capital of databases and information systems, and the organization capital of culture, leadership, alignment, and teamwork. We can clearly read the strategy map in Figure 2.6 from the top down, or from the bottom up, and see all of the dependencies that contribute to the success of the strategy. For a real-life example, refer to Mobil's strategy map, illustrated earlier in Figures 2.3 and 2.4.

2.4 Examples of Balanced Scorecard and Strategy Maps

The effectiveness of a balanced scorecard and strategy maps is documented in Chapter 2 of *The Strategy-Focused Organization* by Kaplan and Norton [11]. Chapter 2 discusses the results that Mobil North America Marketing and Refining (Mobil) achieved in the mid-1990s. In the early 1990s, the company was inwardly focused, bureaucratic, and inefficient. By 1995 it had been transformed by its use of a balanced scorecard, with a turnaround in operating cash flow of $1 billion per year. In a few short years it had become the industry profit leader. We will discuss how this was achieved by Mobil in this section.

2.4.1 Differentiation of Mobil North America Marketing and Refining

Like other companies in its industry, Mobil had attempted to compete through a product leadership strategy that stressed brand image and product characteristics.

But with its competitors using a similar strategy, it was hard to differentiate any Mobil competitive advantages. Most competition was based on price and location.

Mobil therefore defined a new strategy that would appeal to customers who purchased more gasoline than average, purchased more premium than regular-blend products, were willing to pay higher prices for a better buying experience, and would purchase products other than gasoline at a retail gas station. Let's examine these strategies in more detail.

2.4.2 Differentiation of the Financial Perspective at Mobil

The new strategy addressed two areas of differentiation: (1) Reduce costs and improve productivity across its value chain, and (2) generate higher volume on premium-priced products and services. If successful, Mobil reasoned that its profit margins would improve through these two strategies.

Mobil's high-level financial objective was to increase its return on capital employed (ROCE) from its current level of 7% (which was below the cost of capital) to 12%, and to achieve this within 3 years. This is illustrated in Figure 2.7 from the financial perspective.

This financial objective was supported by a revenue growth strategy based on ROCE and on net margin when compared to its competitors in the industry. It defined two strategies to achieve this. The "new sources of nongasoline revenue" strategy added new revenue from other sales of automobile services and products such as car washes, lubricants, oil changes, minor repairs, and some replacement parts. This objective was measured by nongasoline revenues and margins. The second strategy was "increase customer profitability through premium brands." In addition to volume growth, Mobil wanted a higher proportion of sales in premium product grades that had a higher margin than regular grades. It set two measures for this growth strategy: volume growth versus industry growth rate, and percentage of volume in premium grades.

It also established a productivity strategy for cost reduction and asset productivity. Cost reduction focused on a strategy to "become industry cost leader" by measuring operating cash expenses versus the industry—using cents per gallon to normalize for volume. Its asset productivity strategy to "maximize use of existing assets" focused on being able to handle greater volumes from its growth strategy without expanding its asset base. It used cash flow, net of capital spending, as the

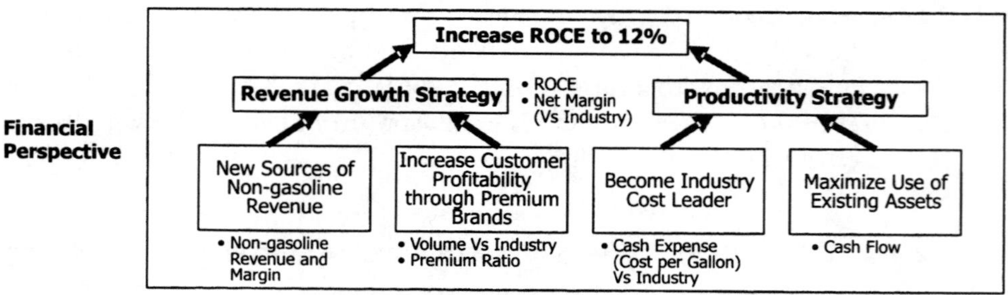

Figure 2.7 Mobil's strategy map—the differentiated financial perspective. (*From:* [11], Figure 2-1, p. 31. © 2001 Harvard Business School Press. Reprinted with permission.)

measure of the benefits from generating more cash (or throughput) from existing assets plus any benefits from inventory reductions.

Pursuing conflicting strategies of productivity and growth can often lead to strategic error if not managed well. The strategy map in Figure 2.7 allowed Mobil to balance conflicts and reduce the risk of applying these two conflicting strategies.

2.4.3 The New Customer Perspective at Mobil

With its revenue growth and productivity focus and the now-well-defined contributing strategies and their measures, Mobil needed to know how to generate the desired growth in volume, both in margins and in nongasoline revenues. The marketing department had identified five distinct consumer segments in the gasoline-buying public:

- *Road Warriors* were defined as higher income middle-aged men. They drive 25,000 to 50,000 miles per year, buy premium gasoline by credit card, purchase sandwiches and drinks from a convenience store, and sometimes wash their cars at the car wash. This group represents 16% of the market.
- *True Blues* are also 16% of the market. These are men and women with moderate or high incomes who are loyal to a brand and sometimes to a specific gas station. They typically buy premium gasoline and pay in cash.
- *Generation F3* represents 27% of the market. These are generally upwardly mobile men and women—half under 25 years old—who drive a lot and snack heavily from the convenience store.
- *Homebodies* are 21% of the market. These are usually housewives who shuttle their children during the day and use whatever gas station is based in town or along their route of travel.
- *Price Shoppers* represent 20% of the market. They are not loyal to any brand or gas station and rarely buy premium gasoline. They are often on tight budgets.

Mobil rationalized that it was too expensive to try to appeal to each of these segments, so it decided on a strategic choice to focus on the first three segments. Road Warriors, True Blues, and Generation F3 represented around 60% of the total market. It decided not to appeal to the other segments, the Homebodies and Price Shoppers who make up the remaining 40% of the market. Mobil reasoned that they would be less attracted by its premium-grade growth strategy.

Mobil then decided that it needed to determine how to attract, retain, and deepen its relationship with customers in the three targeted segments. Its research identified the attributes that represented a great buying experience for these customers:

- Immediate access to a gasoline pump—to avoid waiting for service;
- Self-payment mechanisms at the pump—to avoid waiting to pay;
- Covered areas at the pumps—to protect customers from rain and snow;
- 100% availability of product, especially premium grades—to avoid stock-outs;

- Clean restrooms in the gas station;
- Satisfactory exterior station appearance;
- Safe, well-lit stations;
- Convenience store, stocked with fresh, high-quality merchandise;
- Speedy purchase;
- Ample parking spaces near the convenience store;
- Friendly employees;
- Availability of minor car services.

To ensure that these qualities were available at each of its gas stations, it used "mystery shoppers" from an independent third party to visit each gas station unannounced. The job of the mystery shopper was to evaluate every station each month against 23 criteria, which included all of the criteria just listed.

The monthly mystery shopper rating was the measure that Mobil used to determine how well each station performed for its targeted customers. It reasoned that increases in the mystery shopper score would translate into increases in its market share of the three targeted segments.

However, Mobil did not sell directly to these customers, but only through the gas station owners who were often independent. These dealers were franchised to Mobil; they purchased gas and lubricant products from Mobil to sell to consumers in Mobil-branded gas stations. Previously they did not consider their retailers or distributors as strategic partners; in fact, many of these dealer relationships were quite adversarial.

To succeed with its strategy, Mobil realized that it had to stop treating these dealers as rivals. They adopted a new objective to increase the dealers' profitability from the targeted customer segments. Its target objective was to have its dealers become the most profitable franchise operators in the country so that Mobil could attract and retain the best people.

The dealers benefited from higher revenues from the targeted market segments in three ways: (1) The increased sales of premium grades increased the total revenue that was produced by each dealer; (2) by increasing market share in the three targeted segments, higher quantities of gasoline would be sold with a higher percentage for premium grades; and (3) the dealers would also have an additional revenue stream from the sale of nongasoline products and services—such as convenience store and car services—some revenue of which would also flow back to Mobil.

Mobil set an objective to create a win–win relationship with dealers and measured this objective by the gross profits that could be split between the dealers and Mobil. The result of the customer perspective of this strategy is illustrated in Figure 2.8.

2.4.4 The Internal Process Perspective at Mobil

To directly link to the customer objectives discussed in the preceding section, Mobil now needed to develop objectives and measures in its business processes. It identified two important internal processes:

Figure 2.8 Mobil's strategy map—the customer perspective. (*From:* [11], Figure 2-3, p. 36. © 2001 Harvard Business School Press. Reprinted with permission.)

1. Develop new products and services.
2. Generate dealer profits from nongasoline revenues.

The first objective addressed the development of new offerings at the gas station. The second objective supported the new win–win relationship with dealers and Mobil's own financial objectives. If dealers could increase revenues and profits from products other than gasoline, then dealers would rely less on profits from gas sales to meet their profit targets.

In addition to processes aimed at improvements in customer objectives, Mobil also included other objectives and measures in the internal business processes for its gasoline and lubricant refining and distribution operations. They defined measures for those operations that emphasized low cost, consistent quality, improved use of assets through reductions of plant and equipment downtime, and elimination of environmental, safety, and health-threatening incidents. Most of these related to the cost reduction and productivity themes of the financial perspective. Because Mobil was producing a commodity product, it did not expect to create a competitive advantage from these processes; merely to improve the efficiency and effectiveness of these refinery and distribution operations. Provided these processes operated well, the competitive advantage was expected to come from the improved customer experience and the resulting profits. These internal processes are illustrated in Figure 2.9.

2.4.5 The Learning and Growth Perspective at Mobil

From its earlier understanding of the financial, customer, and internal process perspectives, Mobil next had to define objectives for the foundation of its strategy: the skills and motivation of its employees and the role of information technology. They identified three strategic objectives for the learning and growth perspective:

1. Core competencies and skills;
2. Access to strategic information;
3. Organizational involvement.

The first objective addressed the level of skills and the competencies that were needed to execute the vision. The second objective focused on information systems that would provide the strategic information needed to execute the strategy. The third objective needed to promote an understanding of the organizational strategy

Figure 2.9 Mobil's strategy map—the internal process perspective. (*From:* [11], Figure 2-4, p. 39. © 2001 Harvard Business School Press. Reprinted with permission.)

and create an environment in which all employees were motivated and empowered to achieve the vision. The result of this perspective is illustrated in Figure 2.10.

The Mobil balanced scorecard is summarized in Figure 2.11. This has been adapted and summarized from Figure 2.5 in *The Strategy-Focused Organization* [12]. Refer to that figure for the complete balanced scorecard.

The strategy map for the balanced scorecard in Figure 2.11 has been summarized for Mobil in Figures 2.3 and 2.4, both of which have been adapted from Figure 2.6 of *The Strategy-Focused Organization* [11].

2.5 Steps to Develop Balanced Scorecards and Strategy Maps

I summarized one example of the successful use of a balanced scorecard and strategy maps by Mobil North America Marketing and Refining in the preceding discussion. Many other examples of implementation successes are documented in the books by Kaplan and Norton [14]. These include examples for private-sector organizations as well as public-sector and nonprofit organizations. Refer to their books for a complete discussion of the following steps, which were used successfully by Mobil in their scorecard-building process:

1. Assess the competitive environment.
2. Learn about customer preferences and segments.
3. Define a strategy to generate breakthrough financial performance.
4. Articulate the balance between growth and productivity.
5. Select the targeted customer segments.

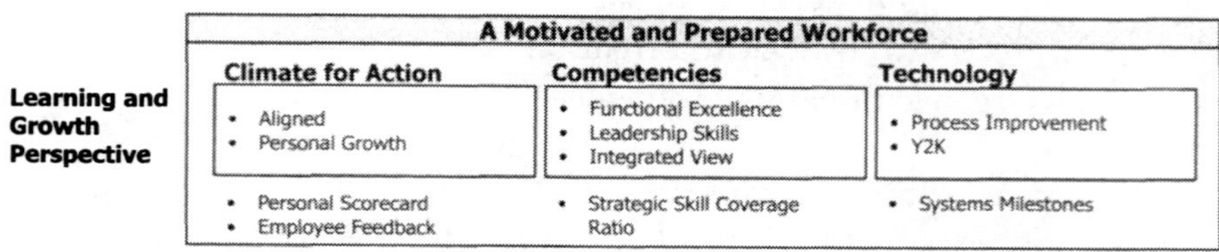

Figure 2.10 Mobil's strategy map—the learning and growth perspective. (*From:* [11], Figure 2-5, p. 41. © 2001 Harvard Business School Press. Reprinted with permission.)

	Strategic Themes	Strategic Objectives	Strategic Measures
Financial	Financial Growth	F1 Return on Capital Employed F2 Existing Asset Utilization F3 Profitability F4 Industry Cost Leader F5 Profitable Growth	▪ ROCE ▪ Cash Flow ▪ Net Margin Rank (Vs Competition) ▪ Full Cost Peer Gallon Delivered (Vs Competition) ▪ Volume Growth Rate Vs Industry ▪ Premium Ratio ▪ Non-gasoline Revenue and Margin
Customer	Delight the Customer Win-Win Dealer Relations	C1 Continually Delight the Target Customer C2 Build Win-Win Relations with Dealer	▪ Share of Segment in Selected Key Markets ▪ Mystery Shopper Rating ▪ Dealer Gross Profit Growth ▪ Dealer Survey
Internal	Build the Franchise Safe and Reliable	I1 Innovative Products and Service I2 Best in Class Franchise Teams I3 Refinery Performance I4 Inventory Management I5 Industry Cost Leader I6 On Spec, on Time	▪ New Product ROI ▪ New Product Acceptance Rate ▪ Dealer Quality Score ▪ Yield Gap ▪ Unplanned Downtime ▪ Inventory Levels ▪ Run-out Rate ▪ Activity Cost Vs Competition ▪ Perfect Orders
Learning and Growth	Motivated and Prepared Workforce	L1 Climate for Action L2 Core Competencies and Skills L3 Access to Strategic Information	▪ Employee Survey ▪ Personal Balanced Scorecard (%) ▪ Strategic Competency Availability ▪ Strategic Information Availability

Figure 2.11 Mobil's Balanced Scorecard (*From:* [11]. © 2001 Harvard Business School Press. Reprinted with permission.)

6. Determine the value proposition for the targeted customers.
7. Identify the critical internal business processes to deliver the value proposition to customers and for the financial and productivity objectives.
8. Develop the skills, competencies, motivation, databases, and technology required to excel at internal processes and customer value delivery.

2.5.1 Methods for Defining Strategies, Processes, and Systems

As discussed earlier, very little guidance was provided by Kaplan and Norton regarding the methods to be used to define the strategies needed to address the steps just listed. They defined *what* had to be done to develop strategies, but did not indicate *how* to do this. Many strategy methods that are used depend on the internal environment and culture of each individual organization. However, a wide body of knowledge exists about methods to define strategies that can be used as a starting point for this guidance.

The focus of this book is to document methods that provide greatest assistance. These are briefly summarized here and described in greater detail in later respective chapters.

Chapter 3: Using Strategy Analysis to Define the Future. This chapter describes the steps for definition of strategies that are documented using a balanced scorecard and strategy map principles as discussed in this chapter. It demonstrates an easy-to-use method for defining scorecard measures and also personal scorecards. It includes many examples, together with case study exercises and sample solutions. It uses a business planning questionnaire that provides input for the definition of appropriate strategies.

Chapter 4: Governance Analysis Using Enterprise Architecture. This discusses internal control reporting matrices that are used for corporate governance, based on matrices defined using methods in Chapter 8. Other matrices can be used that enable balanced scorecard and strategy map measures and objectives—identified in this chapter and defined in Chapter 3—to be implemented and tracked to measure the effectiveness of strategies for financial, customer, internal process and learning and growth perspectives.

Chapter 5: Methods for Building Enterprise Architecture. This chapter discusses the impact of the Clinger Cohen Act of 1996 in the United States, which mandates the use of enterprise architecture by government departments and by the DoD. In fact, DoD considers the lack of use of enterprise architecture for projects greater than $1 million a criminal offense! The chapter discusses several methodology alternatives for implementing enterprise architecture and their financial results. It then describes a sequence and methods for implementation in 3-month increments.

Chapter 6: Using Business-Driven Data Mapping for Integrated Data. This chapter describes methods for defining and designing integrated databases. These are used to provide the needed information system support, identified by the above strategies in terms of the learning and growth perspective.

Chapter 7: Strategic Modeling for Rapid Delivery of Enterprise Architecture. Priority business activities and processes and required database support determined in the internal process perspective and the learning and growth perspective are identified in Chapter 7 for rapid delivery into production. Typically, these activities and processes can be delivered in 3-month increments, using the technologies discussed in Part III.

Chapter 8: Strategic Alignment, Activity and Workflow Modeling, and Business Rules. Matrices identified in Chapter 4 are defined using methods in this chapter. Activity models and activity-based costing methods enable new activities to be designed as determined for the internal process perspective. Workflow models are also designed that can use business rules and the rapid-delivery technologies described in Part III.

Chapter 9: Using Business Normalization for Future Business Needs. In this chapter additional methods are described that are used in conjunction with Chapters 6, 7, and 8. These define business needs that must be addressed by strategies for financial, customer, internal process, and learning and growth perspectives that were determined in the balanced scorecard and strategy maps.

Chapter 10: Menu Design, Screen Design, Performance Analysis, and Process Modeling. Processes that were identified from business activities in Chapter 8 are further defined in this chapter, for later implementation using particular technologies described in Part III.

The methods described in the Chapters 3 through 10 provide assistance for the development and implementation of the strategies, activities, processes, and databases needed for implementation of balanced scorecard and strategy maps.

2.6 Summary

The following is a summary:

- Strategic planning has suffered from difficulties in communicating the content, context, and dependencies of defined goals, objectives, strategies, and processes of business plans.
- The development of a balanced scorecard and strategy map principles in the early 1990s by Kaplan and Norton provided a powerful, visual representation that communicated the key strategies and their dependencies that are essential for business success.
- We covered the basic concepts of strategy maps and the perspectives that they communicate: financial perspective, customer perspective, internal process perspective, and learning and growth perspective.
- We examined key differences between strategy maps for private-sector organizations and those for public-sector and nonprofit organizations.
- We reviewed the experience of Mobil North America Marketing and Refining in their use of balanced scorecard and strategy maps.
- We reviewed the steps that Mobil used to define and implement its balanced scorecard and strategy maps to achieve success as the industry profit leader in a few years, with a turnaround in operating cash flow of $1 billion per year.
- We concluded the chapter by discussing the methods that are needed to define and implement strategies identified by the balanced scorecard and strategy maps. These methods are described in later chapters of Parts I and II.

We will now move to the most important of these methods in the next chapter. Chapter 3 describes the steps and application of strategy analysis. This method is used to define and implement strategies for the future, with full accountability.

Endnotes

[1] Chandler, A. D., *Strategy and Structure: Chapters in the History of the American Industrial Enterprise,* Cambridge, MA: The MIT Press, 1962.

[2] Ansoff, H. I., *Corporate Strategy,* New York: McGraw-Hill, 1965.

[3] Andrews, K. R., *The Concept of Corporate Strategy,* Homewood, IL: Irwin, 1971.

[4] Drucker, P., *Management: Tasks, Responsibilities, Practices,* New York: Harper & Row, 1974.

[5] Porter, M., *Competitive Strategy: Techniques for Analyzing Industries and Competitors,* New York: The Free Press, 1980.

[6] Porter, M., *Competitive Advantage: Creating and Sustaining Superior Performance,* New York: The Free Press, 1985.

[7] Galbraith, J. R., and D. R. Nathanson, *Strategy Implementation: The Role of Structure and Process,* St. Paul, MN: West Publishing, 1978.

[8] Rowe, A. J., et al., *Strategic Management and Business Policy: A Methodological Approach,* 3rd ed., Reading, MA: Addison-Wesley, 1990.

[9] Ackoff, R. L., "On the Use of Models in Corporate Planning," *Strategic Management Journal,* Vol. 2, 1981, pp. 353–359.

[10] Kaplan, R. S., and D. P. Norton, *The Balanced Scorecard: Translating Strategy into Action,* Boston, MA: Harvard Business School Press, 1996.

[11] Kaplan, R. S., and D. P. Norton, *The Strategy-Focused Organization: How Balanced Scorecard Companies Thrive in the New Business Environment,* Boston, MA: Harvard Business School Press, 2001.

[12] Kaplan, R. S., and D. P. Norton, *Strategy Maps: Converting Intangible Assets into Tangible Outcomes,* Boston, MA: Harvard Business School Press, 2004.

[13] In *The Strategy-Focused Organization* [11], read the experience and results achieved by Mobil North America Marketing and Refining, CIGNA Property & Casualty Insurance, Brown & Root Energy Services' Rockwater Division, and Chemical (Chase) Retail Bank.

[14] Many of these examples are included in Kaplan and Norton's 2001 book, *The Strategy-Focused Organization* [11], based on 5 years of experience following the publication of their 1996 book. The 2004 book, *Strategy Maps* [12], includes additional experience.

CHAPTER 3

Using Strategy Analysis to Define the Future

In Chapter 2 we discussed balanced scorecard and strategy maps. Books by Kaplan and Norton [1–3] provide valuable insight into this visual approach to documenting strategic plans, but they offer little guidance on the development of strategic plans. Chapter 2 and this chapter include references to methods written by many others on this subject. However, what is missing from the methods is an approach for rapid refinement of existing strategic plans. That is the focus of this chapter on strategy analysis.

Chapter 3 describes the strategy analysis methodology. This applies to the Why column for the Planner and Owner rows (column 6, row 1, and column 6, row 2) [4] of the Zachman framework discussed in Chapter 1. Strategy analysis is used to define business plans for the future as shown in Figure 3.1. Our focus is to learn how to use business planning methods for the later rapid delivery of enterprise architecture in Part II. In Chapter 8 we will discuss the implementation of business plans as business rules, which apply to the Why column for the Designer, Builder, and Subcontractor rows [C6R3] through [C6R5].

Strategy analysis is used to refine existing plans, or build them if they do not yet exist. It is a method that can be used at corporate, business unit, and business function levels of an organization to define clear, concise strategic business plans, tactical business plans or operational business plans. Strategy analysis is used to:

- Define business goals, issues, and strategies.
- Address identified problems and opportunities.
- Establish strategy and technology requirements.
- Define functional responsibility and accountability.

3.1 Strategy Analysis in Business Planning

At the corporate level, strategic business plans provide guidance for the organization, which comprises many tactical business units and operational functional areas:

- Tactical business plans are used to manage each tactical business unit.
- Operational business plans are used to manage operational functional areas, which carry out many business functions.

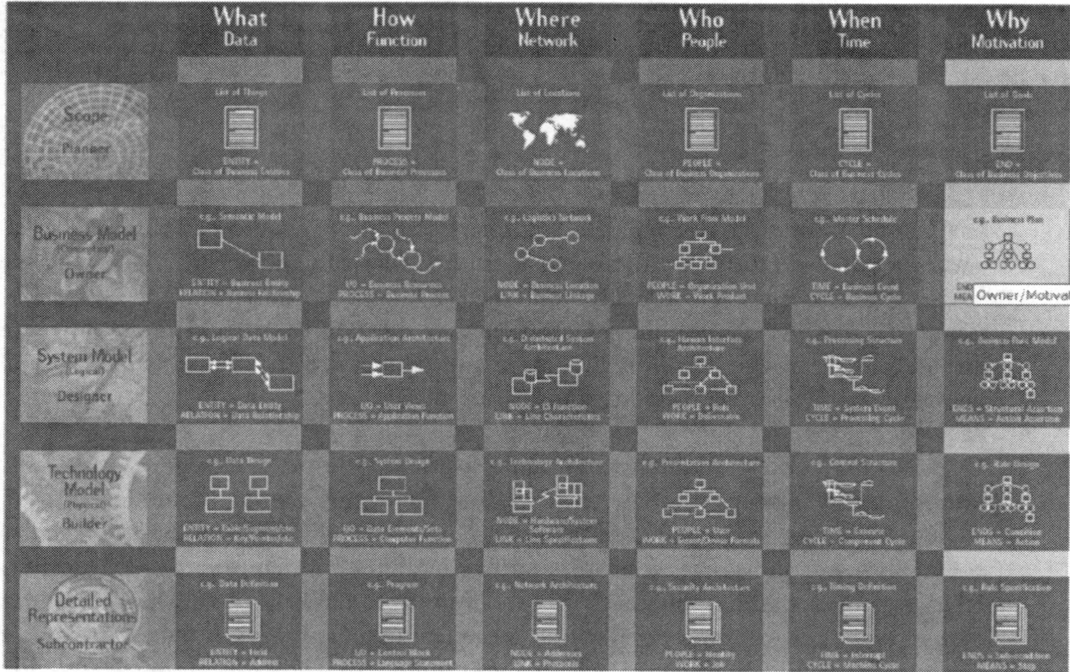

Figure 3.1 Strategy analysis addresses the Zachman framework Why column for the Planner [C6R1] and Owner rows [C6R2].

Strategy analysis can be used to define these plans so that the needs of managers at each level are clearly understood and expressed. Figure 3.2 shows the hierarchical nature of these business plans. Plans documented at one level provide input to define plans at the next lower level. At this level, problems or opportunities may be identified that need clarification or resolution from the higher level managers. We will call these *issues*. By examining these issues, we will see that strategy analysis helps us to identify strategies that address problems or opportunities. There may be many alternative strategies. The proposed strategies are presented along with the issues to manage-

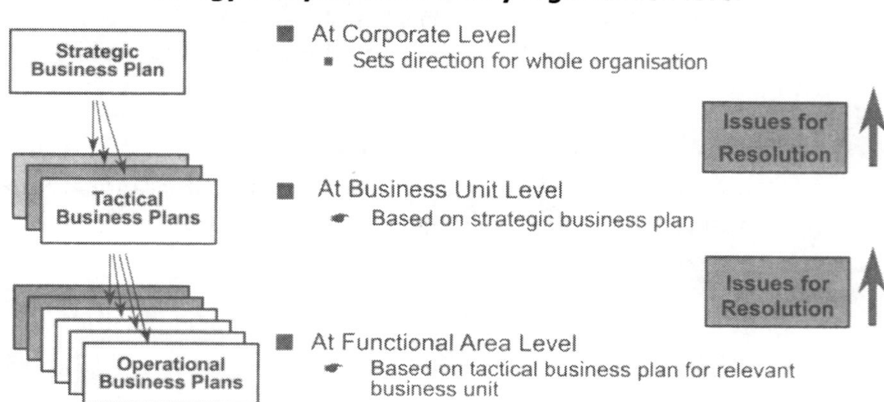

Figure 3.2 The hierarchical nature of business plans.

ment for their direction or resolution. For example, the resolution of an issue associated with a business function may require the introduction and use of new technologies. This feedback obtains management agreement for directions to be taken by the organization and the resources needed for implementation.

Managers who participate in strategy analysis are decision makers at all organizational levels, as well as staff who develop recommendations for them. It is their responsibility to ensure that business plans are well defined and clearly understood. By participating in strategy analysis, they use their organizational knowledge to develop business plans that incorporate that knowledge.

Strategy analysis can also be used to develop a formal business plan rapidly if no documented plan presently exists. It defines the vision, mission, core values, goals, objectives, strategies, and key performance indicators of the organization, and also defines business functions and business function accountabilities. It will establish directions and priorities for later development (see Chapter 7) of a strategic model. It can be easily applied at all business levels.

Later in this chapter we present an example of how strategy analysis can also be used to define the specifications for a sample project. For example:

- It identifies business and project goals, with business reasons for the project.
- It determines business functions to be supported after implementation.
- It identifies technology strategies, showing how technology can assist functions.
- It identifies business system requirements and obtains higher management agreement that those requirements are valid.

These specifications can all be expressed as project goals.

3.1.1 Using Strategy Analysis

We will use an example to illustrate the application of strategy analysis. This example will demonstrate the use of strategy analysis as a proactive planning method.

We will examine the strategic plan of a hypothetical company, XYZ Corporation. This is documented as a mission statement and associated critical success factors (CSFs) (Table 3.1). These typically are major factors that managers determine are important for the success of an organization. We will later use this strategic business plan to decide the directions that XYZ should take for the future and the goals and strategies that XYZ should establish to help it achieve that plan.

The mission statement in Table 3.1 indicates that XYZ can potentially operate in any industry or market that enables it to achieve a return on investment (ROI) of 20%. But a problem exists with the present CSFs: They are not clearly stated. Expressed in only one or two words, they are subject to misinterpretation. You can demonstrate this quickly to yourself by asking two or three people what "market analysis" means to them. You will find that each person has a slightly different idea of its meaning, and how XYZ can use market analysis in planning its future directions. The statements must be defined more explicitly. We will see how strategy analysis provides the required clarity of definition.

Table 3.1 Example Mission Statement and CSFs

XYZ Mission and Purpose	Develop, deliver, and support products and services that satisfy the needs of customers in markets where we can achieve a return on investment of at least 20% within 2 years of market entry.
XYZ Critical Success Factors	Market analysis Market share Innovation Customer satisfaction Product quality Product development Staff productivity Asset growth Profitability

3.1.2 The Quality of Planning Statements

To be effective, a strategic plan must be clear and unambiguous. We can test this as follows. Does the XYZ strategic plan in Table 3.1:

- Provide sufficient guidance for XYZ?
- State clearly what is to be done in XYZ?
- Constitute an effective strategic plan for XYZ?

Each of these questions, when applied to the earlier plan, leads to an answer of "no." The plan in its present form is confusing. Its quality is low. We will examine in more detail how planning statements are expressed so we understand them better, for their later use in strategy analysis.

A mission statement is also called a "mission and purpose." To provide clear guidance it should answer Drucker's questions [5]:

- What is our business?
- Who is the customer?
- Where is the customer located?
- What products or services does the customer want from us?
- What does the customer consider as value?
- What is the customer prepared to "pay"?
- What will the business be, in the future?
- What should the business be, in the future?
- What is the key strategic thrust?

The mission statement must clearly answer these questions. Most organizations focus on business processes—on "how" they operate, rather than "what" their reasons are for existence. Few ask themselves "What is our business?" Fewer still ask the related questions: "What will our business be if we make no changes?" and "What should our business be?" This latter question helps us decide on the changes that should be made, if we are to succeed in the future. It helps us determine the key strategic thrusts.

Many organizations focus on the products and services that they deliver to their customers, rather than first finding out the needs of those customers. By understanding those needs, a better appreciation of existing (or new) products and services that satisfy those needs can be gained. By knowing what customers consider as value, we can better decide whether price is important, or quality, or service. Some are internal customers who will "pay" not by price, but in other ways—such as by "political" or other support.

When these questions are used in conjunction with an enterprise architecture project, each manager becomes an internal customer. Their needs must be understood, so that information "products and services" can be designed and delivered to satisfy those needs. The answers to all of these questions must be known. From a clear expression of the mission, there may be many statements of goals that indicate what the organization must achieve to realize the mission (see Figure 3.3).

There may be many concerns or issues (perhaps expressed by CSFs) associated with these goals. These indicate problems that impede—or opportunities that enhance—the achievement of the goals. Understanding these will help us to define relevant strategies. These strategies specify what we must do to achieve the goals, and so realize the mission. A goal may have many strategies; these represent alternative strategies from which the best strategies to achieve goals must be selected. Strategies will later be implemented as business activities.

An understanding of the many concerns and issues associated with these strategies will help us also to decide relevant tactics. Tactics and tasks are defined that specify how we will carry out the strategies to achieve the goals. These tactics or tasks will later be implemented as business processes.

Strategy analysis comprises a series of steps that progressively develop these statements. In the following section we will see how clear, unambiguous tactical business planning statements are developed from the earlier XYZ mission and CSFs. Irrespective of the quality of the initial planning statements, those statements are catalysts for the definition of refined statements at the next planning level. We will later use these planning statements in Chapter 7. In that chapter we will develop a strategic model that will help us to identify the information needs of management.

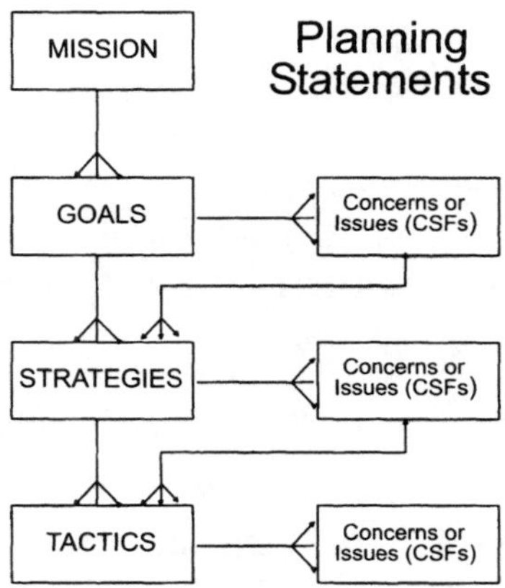

Figure 3.3 Relationship between planning statements.

3.2 The Steps of Strategy Analysis

Strategy analysis has nine steps, as discussed in the following subsections. We will carry out each of these steps using the XYZ example to understand their application to strategy analysis when used for business planning. These steps define the high-level horizontal slices of the Zachman framework as discussed in Chapter 1, addressing Why for the Planner [C6R1] and Owner rows [C6R2]:

- Step 1—Understand the mission and purpose.
- Step 2—Identify the major business areas.
- Step 3—Determine what has to be achieved.
- Step 4—Identify issues representing opportunities or problems.
- Step 5—Determine what will achieve or resolve the issues.
- Step 6—Define Key Performance Indicators (KPIs).
- Step 7—Identify the current functions that exist.
- Step 8—Allocate functional responsibility to implement strategies.
- Step 9—Define job responsibilities for each function.

3.2.1 Step 1—Understand the Mission and Purpose

To understand the mission and purpose, we must be aware of the environment in which the organization operates and how the environment will change in the future. Geography, industry, markets, legislation, the economy, and technology all affect the environment. They also affect the public- and private-sector organizations that operate in that environment as partners, customers, suppliers, and competitors. These all influence the mission statement. Drucker [5] comments that "[C]lear definition of mission and purpose makes possible clear and realistic business objectives. It is the foundation for priorities, strategies, plans and work assignments."

The vision statement for an enterprise defines where the organization is going and how it will get there. It is the organizing force behind every corporate decision. Core values are factors that are important drivers of decisions or activities. These can be incorporated in the mission statement. Two examples of typical mission statements are shown in Table 3.2.

Each statement in Table 3.2 can be tested by questions discussed earlier in Section 3.1.2 on the quality of planning statements. These mission statements are not perfect, but they certainly provide better guidance than the mission of XYZ in Table 3.1.

The objective of this step has been to understand the mission and purpose. An ideal mission should be timeless—it should identify directions now and into the future. It should clearly express:

- What the business is doing now;
- What is happening in the environment;
- What the business should be doing in the future;
- It should broadly indicate markets, customers, products, and services.

Table 3.2 Examples of Typical Mission Statements

A Corporate Mission for a Private Sector Company	We are the leading provider of electronic and fiber-optic connections and accessories. We bring the benefits of modern products and their technologies from the world's leading suppliers. We will create and satisfy the needs of professional users to achieve physical connections for communications or control purposes. We are skilled and dedicated people working in partnership with our customers to satisfy their needs and their expectations for our long-term mutual benefit. Our major focus is to provide exceptional service and value so that we will be their first choice. We will increase the value of our company, and improve the economic well-being and quality of life of our customers, suppliers, staff, and other stakeholders.
A Document Management Unit Mission for Local Government	To provide any individual or organization who is located predominantly within our local government area, or anywhere in the country or overseas, document-based information: about the activities for which our authority has responsibility, either as prescribed by legislation or on an elective basis, or that enhances decision making by elected members and/or our employees. Our primary focus is the efficient and effective provision of timely, accurate, and complete document-based information consistent with the recipient's security classification and the document-based information's release status.

Corporate and business unit mission statements, as we saw earlier, are expressed at a very high level. They can be difficult to use as catalysts for enterprise architecture. We will see that strategy analysis helps us to define business plans at the next lower level, which becomes an excellent catalyst for enterprise architecture.

3.2.2 Step 2—Identify the Major Business Areas

From the understanding of the mission gained from Step 1, we will now analyze its focus further to identify major business areas that should be involved. These are based on the organization structure, as indicated by the Who column for the Planner row [C4R1] of Figure 3.1. Business experts from these areas will be invited to participate in later strategy analysis steps.

We will use the earlier XYZ strategic planning statements in Table 3.1. We will start by examining the mission and purpose statement, looking for explicit and implicit nouns in the statement. There will typically be 6 to 10 major nouns. These nouns should enable us to determine what parts of the business are involved. For example:

> Develop, deliver, and support *products* and *services* which satisfy the *needs* of *customers* in *markets* where we can achieve a *return on investment* of at least 20% within two years of market entry.

The nouns in italics in the mission statement above suggest the major business areas in which XYZ Corporation is involved (see Table 3.3). Managers from each of the business areas listed in Table 3.3 are invited to participate in the remaining strategy analysis steps. They may attend alone—or they may prefer to bring along business experts from their areas to participate with them.

Table 3.3 XYZ Corporation's Major Business Areas

Noun	*Involved Business Area*
Product (or service)	Production/service delivery
Customer	Sales and distribution
Need	Product development, R&D
Market	Marketing
Investment (or performance)	Finance

3.2.3 Step 3—Determine What Has to Be Achieved

Step 3 focuses on identifying and refining goals. This depends on the policies set by management, which define "the rules of the game." *Policies are qualitative guidelines that define boundaries of responsibility in the organization;* they must be known if valid goals are to be defined based on those policies. They enlarge on the mission statement. They are the internal rules (as company policies) or external rules (as legislation, laws, and so forth) that the business follows to achieve its goals.

Goals are typically layered hierarchically and are made up of principal goals and contributing key performance indicators (KPIs) or CSFs. In most organizations there are three to, typically, six major goals whose achievement is critical to realize the mission. The number of goals that are identified decides the duration of strategy analysis. Six goals typically take 3 to 5 days for managers to discuss all relevant factors, as they complete the steps of strategy analysis. More goals than this will require greater time for discussion in planning sessions.

Goals and objectives are measurable targets. To be measured, they must of course be quantitative. They have three characteristics—measure, level, and time:

- The *measure* defines what performance indicator will be used for measurement.
- The *level* indicates what result value must be achieved.
- The *time* specifies when that result should be achieved.

If only two of the three characteristics are defined, goals and objectives are meaningless; all three must be known for quantitative targets.

Notice that measure, level, and time focus on *what* and *when*, not yet on *how*. Only when we know what result is to be achieved and the time frame, can we determine the most appropriate strategies or tactics—which indicate *how*.

Typically goals are long-term targets, whereas objectives are generally short term. Some industries reverse these. In one industry, long term may be 2 years; for another industry in a rapid-change environment, long term might only be 6 months. We will use the term *goals* in this chapter to refer to both goals and objectives. The rate of change in an industry or in the environment affects the focus of goals. Technology can also affect the rate of change. For example, due to rapid technological change one Internet year equates to more than 7 years of change in real time. This rate of change is expressed by the term *Internet time.*

We do not have clear statements of goals for XYZ. We only have poorly defined CSFs in Table 3.1. We will ask managers and business experts from XYZ—drawn from the business areas identified in Step 2 for the Who column in the Planner row

[C4R1]—to define relevant statements in a planning session. We will ask them to identify the goals that they believe will lead to realization of the mission.

In this book it is difficult to achieve the real-life interactivity of an actual planning session. Because of this, we will instead evaluate the wording of each goal defined by the managers and business experts, to assess whether their goals are clearly defined. The statements they developed for the asset growth, profitability, market share, and market analysis CSFs in Table 3.1 are documented next.

- *Asset growth:* "Monitor performance of all aspects of our business so that each activity has a favorable effect, directly or indirectly, on our mission ROI."
- *Profitability:* "Monitor financial performance of all activities to ensure that profit and cash flow projections are achieved according to, or ahead of, plan."
- *Market share:* "Achieve the targeted annual market share (expressed as ...) for the chosen market segments of XYZ."
- *Market analysis:* "Analyze existing and emerging markets on a regular basis, to assess market growth, potential market size, and potential market competition."

The first statement on asset growth is not quantitative. It does not include measure, level, and time and so is not expressed as a goal statement. Neither does it communicate qualitative guidelines or boundaries of responsibility; it is therefore not a policy. Instead it describes what to do and so is a potential strategy statement.

The same arguments can be made for the statements of profitability and market analysis. They are not quantitative and so are not goals. They do not provide qualitative guidelines and so are not policies. They also describe what to do and so are potential strategy statements.

The third statement on market share is almost a quantitative target. Market share is a measure, but the level and time have not yet been defined. The statement is almost complete; when level and time are defined it will potentially be a goal statement. We will refine this statement later in the chapter.

Only one out of the four earlier statements was found to be a potential goal. This is not unusual. Statements often specify what to do, rather than define what is to be achieved. Only when we understand what has to be achieved (goals) can we determine what we should do (strategies) and how we should implement them (tactics).

We could ask the managers and business experts to change the other three statements of strategy so that they are quantitative goals. They may define better statements next time. But we will defer this refinement until we have completed more of the steps of strategy analysis. We will find that these later steps give us a better appreciation of what is to be achieved, so that we can later come back to refine the preceding statements. We can still make good use of them in their present form for the next strategy analysis step.

3.2.4 Step 4—Identify Issues Representing Opportunities or Problems

When we know problems or threats that are barriers to, or that impede, the achievement of goals—or when we are aware of the opportunities or technologies that enhance or facilitate their achievement—we can then determine the most relevant strategies to follow for those goals. In the following discussion we will refer to these collectively as *issues*. Issues can be internal or external to the organization.

As well as defining issues in this step, we can also list the organization's strengths and weaknesses. With our understanding of opportunities and threats, we can analyze strengths, weaknesses, opportunities, and threats in a SWOT analysis, sometimes renamed using a more memorable acronym "WOTS up?" [6].

In this step we will examine the issues that the XYZ managers and their staff define for the statements in Step 3, focusing on asset growth, profitability and market share. We will sit in on their planning session and hear how they consider the potential barriers or problems that impede, and the opportunities or technologies that facilitate or enhance the statements—considering both internal and external factors. We will also hear how they identify strengths and weaknesses. The chief financial officer (CFO) describes the factors they identified. From this, we learn a little about XYZ Corporation:

> XYZ experienced major asset growth in the late 1990s, when our industry expanded rapidly due to the ready availability of funding. At that time we entered some markets that had only a short life. These markets are now in decline. Other markets were not researched well before entry, resulting in high market entry costs and low profitability. Much fixed interest debt was accepted, which must be serviced and is very costly today.

As spokesman, the CFO then moves on to the issues relating to profitability:

> In the first few months following my recent appointment as CFO, I found that I had inherited a sorry situation. We have been very profitable, but our products were of poor quality and we provided very poor service to our customers. We were a monopoly in our industry. We became arrogant because our customers had nowhere else to go. But because of poor quality products, high prices, and poor service, each year our annual report was a public relations nightmare.

The CFO told us how XYZ had resolved this problem. He spoke of previous decisions taken to reduce the source of the annual negative media exposure.

> We were so profitable we delayed financial reporting. We carried high interest costs and we had poor cash flow management—because this reduced the profits. In fact, we had no budget control. We spent money like water. That certainly had an impact on our bottom line.
>
> Profitability was achieved in spite of ourselves. Our monopoly position was a license to print money. Now our industry is deregulated. We have competitors who view our historical poor performance as a golden market opportunity. We are rapidly losing market share. We are now losing money when we can ill afford to.

Wow! He certainly pulled no punches! Interestingly, in planning sessions the identification of problems or threats leads to a flood of issues. Sometimes identifying opportunities is equally productive. We will not look yet at how we can address these issues. That will be done in the next strategy analysis step. Instead we list them as bullet points. Let us now hear from the marketing manager who picks up the same theme:

> In those days we had no market share information as we had 100% of the market. We were a monopoly with no competitors. Competitors were legally prevented from entering our industry by legislation that was enacted to protect us.
>
> We had all of the market and we were very profitable. We did not expand the market further. But our corporate image was very poor because of our lousy service and poor products.
>
> We had limited product ranges: our customers could only buy what we sold, not what they needed. Our pricing policy for products was also high and inflexible. If our customers did not like what we offered them, too bad!
>
> We were arrogant and we are now paying the cost. Our competitors designed products that corrected our product deficiencies. They sell those products way under our prices. We can't even match them because our costs are so high. They tailor their products to the customer's exact needs. How about that! And their service is outstanding. Whenever I have used their products I have been amazed that they can do so much at such a low price compared to us.

These comments are all summarized as bullet points in Table 3.4. The issues identified in their planning session, with bullet points of identified strengths and weaknesses, are included in the following comments.

By examining issues, strengths, weaknesses, opportunities, and threats in this step, we learned a lot about XYZ. Problems or threats are readily identified in a planning session that focuses on issues; most managers are well aware of them. Opportunities will also be well known. Potential technologies that can help are also identified by the IT staff who may also participate in these planning sessions.

The participants also know their strengths and weaknesses. Sometimes similar points appear in each. For example, staff are experienced (a strength), but they are arrogant (a weakness); they are cash rich (an opportunity), whereas competitors have an aggressive, competitive sales capability (a threat).

Strengths and weaknesses can be identified more formally than in Table 3.4 by using an internal appraisal approach [7]. Similarly, we can analyze our competitors by "wearing their hat." An internal appraisal can be carried out for each competitor in turn—particularly those that represent threats—so that we understand them better. This analysis uncovers weaknesses that we can attack, or identifies strengths of which we must be aware.

From an internal appraisal of competitors, areas of *comparative advantage* can be identified. These are areas where we are strong and our competitors are weak. We also know where our competitors are strong and where we are weak. An understanding of these respective comparative advantages allows us to identify vulnerabilities in our competitors that can be attacked.

When comparative advantages are used in this way, competitive advantage is gained. We should use our strengths to gain opportunities, while also attacking our competitors' weaknesses. We also should use our strengths to protect our weaknesses and avoid threats mounted against us. An understanding of comparative advantage and competitive advantage principles helps us to identify the information that management needs to enable them to make the best competitive decisions. Michael Porter provides additional detail on these subjects [8–10].

Competitive advantage applies to commercial organizations in the private sector. It also has relevance for public-sector, government organizations. Every organi-

Table 3.4 Assessment of Concerns and Issues

Asset Growth

"Monitor performance of all aspects of our business so that each activity has a favorable effect, directly or indirectly, on our mission ROI."

Issues:

Many investments in declining markets

High market entry cost into marginal markets

High debt levels for assets in sunset markets

Profitability

"Monitor financial performance of all activities to ensure that profit and cash flow projections are achieved according to, or ahead of, plan."

Issues:

Delayed financial reporting; poor financial control

High interest costs; poor cash flow management

Poor budget control

Market Share

"Achieve the targeted annual market share (expressed as ...) for the chosen market segments of XYZ."

Issues:

No market share information (unavailable or inaccurate)

Competitor activity (analysis not available)

Market definition (growth rates and size not known)

Corporate image (poor)

Product range definition (limited)

Pricing policy (high and inflexible)

Strengths

Large, cash-rich organization

Established market position

Experienced, capable staff

Weaknesses

Poor financial control and management

Arrogant, reactive corporate culture

Poor customer service and products

Limited experience in a competitive environment

Bureaucratic organization with long decision paths

Opportunities

Cash-rich organization

Established market infrastructure

Leader in new technologies

Threats

Competitors are nimble with short decision paths.

Competitors excel in market and product innovation.

Competitors have good research and development capability.

Competitors have aggressive, competitive sales capability.

zation competes with others. In the public sector, this competition is indirect. Government organizations all compete with others for resources: the funding and budgets needed to operate. One government department may gain funding at the expense of others. Competition therefore applies to all organizations: private sector, public sector, and defense.

It is not appropriate in this book to address these subjects in more detail. During strategy analysis, after identifying our own strengths and weaknesses we can informally "wear the hat" of our major competitors—especially those that threaten us—to identify their strengths and weaknesses. Formal internal appraisal and external appraisal techniques for comparative advantage and competitive advantage are discussed in [11].

3.2.5 Step 5—Determine What Will Achieve or Resolve the Issues

With this knowledge of issues (strengths, weaknesses, opportunities, and threats) we have an agenda. We know what has to be corrected or protected—this is reactive. We know where we should focus our strengths to achieve opportunities or take advantage of technologies—this is proactive. And our understanding of comparative advantage helps us to use our strengths as weapons for competitive advantage to resolve the issues, while being aware of our weaknesses. We will use this new understanding to identify relevant strategies in this step.

The tendency of most organizations is to address their problems to protect themselves against their threats and correct their weaknesses. This reactive approach places the organization at a disadvantage; at best it will equal its competitors, not better them.

Instead the emphasis should be to identify strategies that will realize the opportunities, using technologies and strengths as competitive weapons. This proactive approach will enable the organization to gain the initiative. It can diminish the impact of problems, threats, or weaknesses so that they are less important. It leads to aggressive strategies that focus on competitive advantage.

Aggressive strategies that use strengths or technologies to attack competitors where they are vulnerable can divert their attention. It takes the initiative to "do unto them before they do it unto us!"

We will now ask the XYZ managers to review each issue listed in Step 4. They should ask the following questions for each point discussed in that step:

- What should we do to take advantage of the opportunities?
- What technologies are available to assist us?
- What strengths can we use to help us?
- What has to be done to resolve the problems?
- What should we do to protect ourselves from the threats?
- What should we do to correct our weaknesses?

The focus of these questions is *what* should we do, not *how* do we do it. Only when we know what we should do can we select the best strategies. Only then can we decide how to carry them out. Only then can we define relevant tactics and processes to implement the strategies.

The relationship between these statements is shown in Figure 3.4. They focus on the concerns and issues that have to be faced in order to achieve goals and objectives within the boundaries defined by policies and the mission.

The XYZ managers identify many alternative strategies that they feel will address the issues and achieve the goals. They discuss each statement in turn, start-

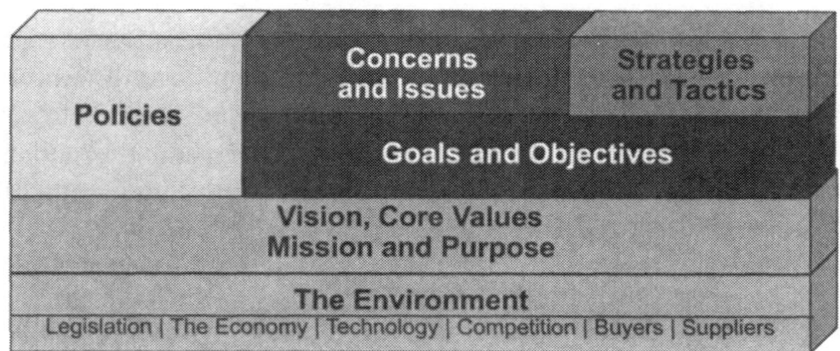

Figure 3.4 A stable strategic plan takes its foundation for the mission and vision from the environment. Strategies and tactics address issues, to achieve goals and objectives within the boundaries defined by policies.

ing with the issues listed in Table 3.4 under asset growth in Step 4. According to the CFO:

> The issues for asset growth suggested that we need to establish criteria for minimum return on investment of assets. Obviously, investments that do not meet the criteria should be sold. We also need strategies to assess the profitability of markets, and to exit unprofitable markets. Further, these strategies will allow us to assess new potential markets before entry.

Based on these comments, the XYZ managers defined the following strategies for asset disposal and market exit.

- *Asset Disposal Strategy:* Identify assets that cannot provide a return within 2 years consistent with the mission ROI, and dispose of them at the best possible price.
- *Market Exit Strategy:* Identify markets that are unprofitable and in decline, and exit those markets at the lowest possible cost.

The CFO then continued with the assessment of the profitability issues in Step 4:

> These issues suggest that we need strategies to improve our financial reporting and financial control. We also need strategies to improve our budgeting and cash flow management.

The XYZ managers defined profitability and budget control strategies for these issues.

- *Financial Reporting Strategy:* Implement flexible financial reporting systems that can be introduced at any organizational level and that can provide profit and loss statements for any defined reporting frequency, with associated balance sheet statements.
- *Budget Control Strategy:* Establish and maintain strong budgetary controls for all expenditures, linked directly to revenue achievement. All financial statements

must clearly show actual revenue and expenditure against budget, and indicate percentage change from the previous reporting level.

These strategies were easy to define, once the issues were understood and the managers knew what had to be done. The marketing manager then addressed the market share issues from Step 4:

> If we measure market share, we also must know market size and growth. A market share strategy is only effective if we can increase market share faster than the market growth. If not, we are losing market share. We also must know our competitors' shares, because their total share helps us assess ours. We must also define strategies that enable us to decide product ranges and pricing for different markets.

As we saw earlier, XYZ has historically operated as a monopoly. It had no competitors, so today it has no competitive analysis information. It suggests that strategies are needed to survey existing and potential markets to determine potential market size, growth rates, identification of competitors, and their market share. These surveys should also identify the needs of current and new customers in those markets.

Information from market surveys will permit analysis of existing and potential markets. Decisions can be made of products to satisfy those needs, product ranges, and pricing for each market. After discussion, the managers suggested the following strategies:

- *Market Survey Strategy:* Ensure regular surveys are undertaken to determine market size and our market share, and to understand the needs and the expectation characteristics of our chosen and potential market segments.
- *Product Range Strategy:* Establish and maintain a product range definition that recognizes the strength of our products and technology, and the capabilities for bundling products into innovative packages.
- *Product Pricing Strategy:* Establish and maintain a pricing policy that will sustain long-term achievement of market share targets by market segment, which is consistent with achieving profitability targets.

In deciding on these strategies, the managers relied on two strengths of XYZ: It still had a large (but shrinking) market share, and it was cash rich. They also knew their competitors were small and financially vulnerable. XYZ had no in-house expertise for market survey, market analysis, or competitive analysis. But it had deep pockets. It could buy expertise by outsourcing to outside market research consulting organizations.

So far in strategy analysis we have discussed three of the CSFs in Table 3.1 of the strategic plan—asset growth, profitability and market share. Discussion of the other CSFs will lead to an agreement on wording for statements, identification of issues, and definition of potential strategies. Steps 3, 4, and 5 are repeated, as shown in Figure 3.5, until all have been considered.

At this point, we have agreed (in Step 3) on the wording of statements that define the intent of the CSFs from Step 1. Other statements may have been added in

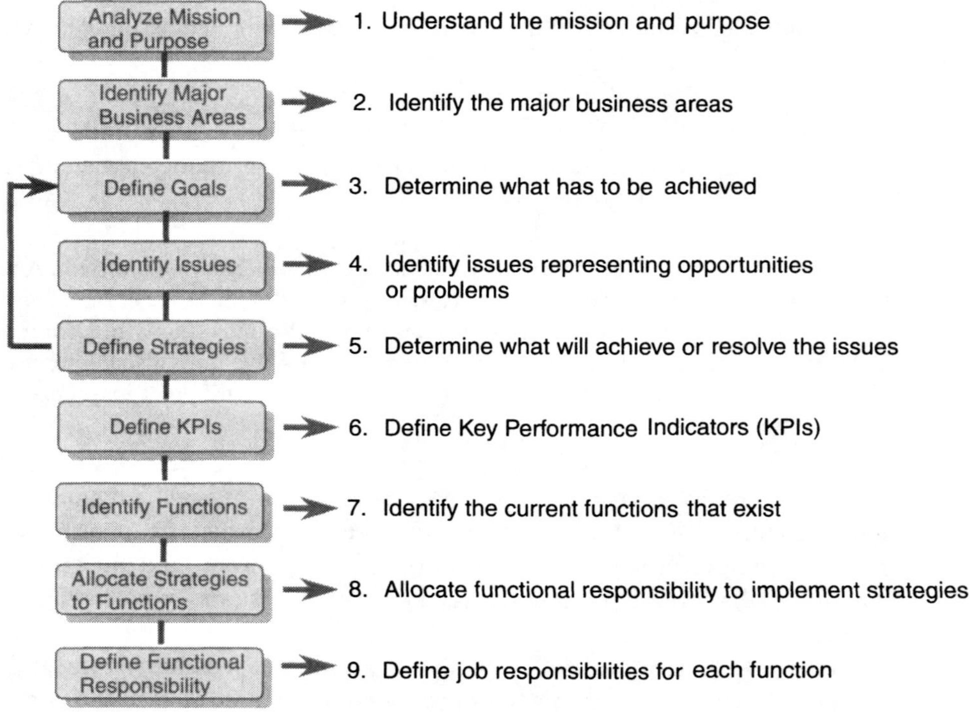

Figure 3.5 The steps of strategy analysis.

later planning sessions. We considered issues (Step 4) that indicate problems or threats, opportunities or technologies. We carried out an informal SWOT analysis by including strengths and weaknesses. We defined strategies (Step 5) to address these issues based on identified SWOTs. We repeated these three steps as shown in Figure 3.5 until all statements, issues, and strategies had been covered.

We are now ready to move to the next step. This identifies quantitative measures that will enable managers to assess the effectiveness of strategies, once implemented. This is where the earlier work starts to pay dividends. We will identify information that will later be delivered to the managers.

3.2.6 Step 6—Define Key Performance Indicators

We saw that performance measures are quantitative: They clearly express the measure, the result level to be achieved, and the time for that achievement. We defined goals and objectives as quantitative targets with long-term goals and short-term objectives. We refer to both, collectively, as goals. But targets change over time, typically in the level or the time for achievement. We will see how to express goals that accommodate change.

A goal or objective statement must define the performance measure clearly. But rather than change the wording of level or time for each change, we will instead cross-reference the statement to key performance indicators (KPIs). We will use KPIs to express the level and time. Changes in either or both of these only need to reference the relevant KPI. KPIs cannot only be used to define goal achievement, but also can monitor the effectiveness of strategies. For example, the product pricing strategy was defined earlier as "Establish and maintain a pricing policy that will sustain long-term achievement of market share targets by market segment, which is consistent with achieving profitability targets." We can set market share targets in particular market segments by reducing sales price. But customers must be aware of these prices. Market share depends not only on pricing, but also on advertising. Advertising costs money; a manager must decide what proportion of funding should be allocated to advertising.

We now come to the role of a manager. Is it to manage people? Yes, but it is more than that. Is it to manage funds, or equipment, or other resources? A manager certainly must manage these resources, but still has to do more. In fact, the management of resources is a manager's "tools of the trade." A manager's job is easy to define, but difficult to do: It depends on information feedback. The job of a manager can be defined as follows:

- To allocate resources optimally, to achieve defined objectives.

The managers refined the market share strategy (while observing the pricing strategy) as follows: "Achieve the targeted annual market share based on unit market share KPI for the chosen market segments of XYZ." The earlier market share strategy has been changed such that it now cross-references the unit market share KPI. This KPI is defined and defined qualitatively the unit market share KPI as follows:

- *Unit Market Share KPI:* The unit market share KPI monitors market growth in total units and unit sales growth targets by quarter. These targets are managed by varying total and proportional funding for advertising and product cost reduction technologies, to achieve decreases in sales price with consistent gross margins. The unit market share KPI defines each of these targets.

Finally, we will check the statements against the pricing strategy to satisfy ourselves that it has not been violated.

- *Pricing Strategy:* Establish and maintain a pricing policy that will sustain long-term achievement of market share targets by market segment, which is consistent with achieving profitability targets as follows (further definition is detailed).

We observed the pricing strategy, using technologies to bring about product or service cost reductions while maintaining consistent gross margins and hence profitability. We have refined the market share strategy and defined a new unit market share KPI. We are now ready to move on to the next strategy analysis step.

3.2.7 Step 7—Identify the Current Functions That Exist

The refined strategic plans for XYZ are now taking shape. But these plans are pointless unless their implementation is well managed. Specific managers must be given this responsibility. The final steps of strategy analysis focus on assigning implementation responsibility for these planning statements to relevant parts of the business.

We first must be aware of the current functions. These functions are typically intertwined with ownership (and empires). A *function* is defined as a group of related activities and can be executed across multiple business units. Some business activities can also be shared across several functions. We need to identify or define function responsibilities independently of how the organization is currently structured. The managers provide us with a list of the current functions of XYZ:

- Corporate;
- Finance;
- Forecasting;
- Marketing;
- Sales;
- Research and development;
- Production;
- Purchasing;
- Personnel.

For each strategy, we can identify the principal business activities. We may have to derive new functions and activities that are needed for some strategies in addition to the current functions in the preceding list. The next strategy analysis step helps us do this.

3.2.8 Step 8—Allocate Functional Responsibility to Implement Strategies

This step helps us to establish action plans for strategy implementation. It allocates responsibility for achieving goals and KPIs. A matrix is developed, with each strategy on a separate row and each function listed as a column heading in Figure 3.6. We will see in Chapter 4 that matrices help in identifying corporate governance responsibilities.

For each strategy in turn, the managers decide which function has primary responsibility for managing implementation of that strategy. A solid bullet in the cell for the relevant primary function column signifies this responsibility; there can only be one solid bullet in each row.

Other functions may also need to be involved; they have secondary responsibility for implementation. An open bullet in a cell indicates that a function has secondary responsibility. The primary function is responsible for coordinating each secondary function for implementation of the strategy. The result is the business function–strategy matrix illustrated in Figure 3.6. There are more strategies listed in that figure than we have discussed in this chapter.

Notice in Figure 3.6 that arrows highlight some columns. These indicate new functions that XYZ will need to support. For example, the managers defined *market data* and *market analysis* strategies to implement the market survey strategy. These are part of a market research function that XYZ does not currently have; therefore, a new column, Market Research, was added to the matrix for this function. This does not imply that XYZ has to establish a new market research department: It can outsource this to an external market research firm to carry out the function on its behalf. But XYZ may

LEGEND

● Primary resp.

○ Shared resp.

Strategy	Function													
	Corporate	Finance	Mkt Research	Forecasting	Marketing	Sales	R & D	Product Mgt	Production	Purchasing	Education	Personnel		
Asset Disposal	○	●												
Market Exit		○	○	○	●									
Financial Reporting		●		○	○	○								
Budget Control		●		○	○	○								
Market Data		○	●	○	○	○								
Market Analysis		○	●	○	○	○								
Market Needs Analysis		○	○	○	●									
Technology Monitoring			○	○	○	○	●							
R & D			○	○	○		●							
R & D Funding		●	○	○	○									
Customer Satisfaction Survey			○	○	○	●		○						
Sales, Support & Customer Training					○	○		○			●			
Quality Control								○	●	○	○			
Product Maintenance Improvement								○	●	○	○			
Product Review								●	○	○	○			
Product Release						●		○	○	○	○			
Career Planning	○	○	○	○	○	○	○	○	○	○	○	●		
Staff Incentives	○	○										●		

Figure 3.6 Business function–strategy matrix. Arrows identify new functions not currently supported by XYZ Corporation.

need to appoint a market research manager to liaise with this firm, and receive their market analysis results from the market data they obtain through market surveys.

A sales, support, and customer training strategy was also defined by the managers in Figure 3.6. The education function was given primary responsibility for implementing this strategy. Because XYZ does not currently have this function, it should appoint an education manager to select and liaise with external education firms to carry out this outsourced training on its behalf.

Finally, the product review strategy has been allocated to a product management function. Again, an arrow highlights this new function in Figure 3.6. We earlier discussed that XYZ had entered many markets at high cost, where those markets did not give a satisfactory return. This was found to be due to a lack of coordination between the functions of R&D, product development, production, sales, and marketing. The managers decided a new product management function should be established to coordinate other functions for new products and markets. Product management is responsible for product review, and for the product range and product pricing strategies discussed earlier.

The business function–strategy matrix in Figure 3.6 enables primary and secondary implementation responsibility to be allocated for each strategy. It leads to proactive management of strategy implementation. Each strategy is allocated to at least one function, with new functions identified and added as required.

3.2.9 Step 9—Define Job Role Responsibilities for Each Function

The business function–strategy matrix in Figure 3.6 also allows job role responsibilities for each function to be identified. This is used to document the responsibilities for each manager appointed to a job role to manage these functions.

For example, in Figure 3.7 an arrow highlights the Finance column. Reading down, we see solid bullets that identify each strategy where the chief financial officer (CFO) has primary job role responsibility, as manager of the finance department. We also see open bullets that identify strategies where finance and, hence, its CFO has secondary job role responsibility to participate with other functions.

We will now use Figure 3.7 to focus on asset disposal, financial reporting and budget control, which we defined earlier in Step 3 [12]. This will incorporate the strategies and their KPIs or objectives as action plans for the CFO job role description. The result for the CFO is documented in Table 3.5. We will see that this job role description also becomes the tactical business plan for the finance department. The strategies, with identified issues, strengths, and weaknesses from Step 4, and the KPIs or objectives defined in Step 5, can now be consolidated as a position statement for the job role of CFO.

As we discussed earlier, goals are long-term quantitative targets, whereas objectives are short-term targets. We can see from the job role description in Table 3.5 that the CFO has defined objectives for asset disposal, financial reporting, and budget control strategies, using the same names. These are definitely quantitative, because they define measure, level, and time quite clearly. For example, the asset disposal objective defines the measure as "following Board approval, dispose of

LEGEND
● Primary resp
○ Shared resp.

Strategy	Corporate	Finance	Mkt Research	Forecasting	Marketing	Sales	R & D	Product Mgt	Production	Purchasing	Education	Personnel
Asset Disposal	○	●										
Market Exit		○	○	○	●							
Financial Reporting		●		○	○	○						
Budget Control		●		○	○	○						
Market Data		○	●	○	○	○						
Market Analysis		○	●	○	○	○						
Market Needs Analysis		○	○	○	●							
Technology Monitoring			○	○	○	○	●					
R & D			○	○	○		●					
R & D Funding		●	○	○	○							
Customer Satisfaction Survey			○	○	○	●		○				
Sales, Support & Customer Training					○	○		○			●	
Quality Control								○	●	○	○	
Product Maintenance Improvement								○	●	○	○	
Product Review								●	○	○	○	
Product Release						●		○	○	○	○	
Career Planning	○	○	○	○	○	○	○	○	○	○	○	●
Staff Incentives	○	○										●

Figure 3.7 Job role responsibilities can be read down each function column.

Table 3.5 CFO Job Role Description and Tactical Business Plan for the Finance Department

Position:	Chief financial officer
Reports to:	President and CEO
Asset Growth	Monitor performance of all aspects of our business so that each activity has a favorable effect, directly or indirectly, on our mission ROI.
Issues	Many investments in declining markets High market entry cost into marginal markets High debt levels for assets in sunset markets
Asset Disposal Strategy	Identify assets that cannot provide a return within 2 years consistent with the mission ROI, and dispose of them at the best possible price.
Asset Disposal Objective	Following Board approval, dispose of all nonperforming assets within 12 months.
Profitability	Monitor financial performance of all activities to ensure that profit and cash flow projections are achieved according to, or ahead of, plan.
Issues	Delayed financial reporting High interest costs Poor cash flow management
Strengths	Profitable Cash rich
Weaknesses	Poor financial reporting Poor budget control
Financial Reporting Strategy	Implement flexible financial reporting systems able to be introduced at any organizational level, and which can provide profit and loss statements for any defined reporting frequency, with associated balance sheet statements.
Financial Reporting Objective	Implement financial reporting systems within 6 months that provide profit and loss, balance sheet, and cash flow reporting within 1 day of the close of any defined financial period.
Budget Control Strategy	Establish and maintain strong budgetary controls for all expenditures, linked directly to revenue achievement. All financial statements must clearly show actual revenue and expenditure against budget, and indicate percentage change from the previous reporting level.
Budget Control Objective	Implement budget control systems directly linked to financial reports according to the budget control strategy, within 6 months.

nonperforming assets"; the level is "all" (100%) and the time is "within 12 months." The financial reporting objective defines the measure as "implement financial reporting systems that provide profit and loss, balance sheet, and cash flow reporting"; the level is "within 1 day of the close of any defined financial period" and the time is "within 6 months."

By progressively applying the steps of strategy analysis we have developed a precise job role description for the CFO. But it is more than that. We see that this also becomes the tactical business plan for the finance department.

This represents the high-level horizontal slice of the Zachman framework for the Why column in the Planner [C6R1] and Owner rows [C6R2] as discussed in Chapter 1, for rapid delivery of priority enterprise architecture subprojects.

Strategy analysis can be applied at each lower management level to ensure that this tactical business plan is implemented correctly. The objectives defined at this level become "goals" for achievement at the next lower level. The finance managers and the staff who report to the CFO identify issues associated with the achievement of these objectives. They define "strategies" that address these issues. These in fact become tactics for implementing strategies defined by the CFO.

3.2.10 Benefits of Strategy Analysis

Strategy analysis is easy to learn and use, yet it is quite rigorous. It normally requires 3 to 5 days of planning sessions by managers in a business planning workshop [13] to develop tactical business plans in an organization. Strategy analysis delivers many benefits. It:

- Produces clear, performance-based statements of policies, goals, objectives, strategies, KPIs, and action plans (tactics).
- Implements business plans at all management levels.
- Produces a clear definition of quantitative goals and objectives.
- Defines KPIs for performance measurement of changing goals.
- Defines strategies to address opportunities and resolve issues.
- Defines objectives or KPIs so that strategies can be implemented correctly and in a timely fashion.
- Defines tactics for implementation of plans at lower levels.

We have discussed the use of strategy analysis to develop, or refine, business plans at all management levels of an organization. Strategy analysis can also be used to develop project specifications for enterprise architecture projects or for other projects of interest. In the next section we will review how strategy analysis is used for this purpose.

3.3 Strategy Analysis for Project Specifications

Strategy analysis is used to define specifications for projects where none presently exist, or to refine current specifications so that the business requirements and project focus are clearly expressed. Changes are made to the steps of strategy analysis for this project focus. These changes are listed here and discussed in the following paragraphs:

- Step 1—Examine business and project mission statements.
- Step 2—Identify project goals and performance criteria.
- Step 3—Define clear business and project goals.
- Step 4—Identify the business problems or opportunities.
- Step 5—Determine strategies to address problems or opportunities.
- Step 6—Define key performance indicators.
- Step 7—Determine which business functions are to be supported.
- Step 8—Identify managers and business experts from each function.
- Step 9—Schedule joint participation by business and IT experts.

3.3.1 Step 1—Examine Business and Project Mission Statements

This step identifies the business areas to be addressed by the project. These areas may be in specific business units or in certain functions of the organization. Typically, this step examines existing business and project mission statements to understand the business purpose of each area.

Where they are missing, a mission statement should be defined for each involved business area. Ideally, a manager or experienced staff member from each area should define these statements. They are intended for use by the project team to define project specifications, and so should also be reviewed (and corrected where necessary) by other managers of each business area.

Where statements do exist, this step clarifies those existing statements as required. It ensures that the purpose of each business area is clearly documented. From this greater business understanding, a project mission statement is then defined.

3.3.2 Step 2—Identify Project Goals and Performance Criteria

From the project mission, preliminary project goals are defined and performance criteria are established. For example, a project goal may be defined to design and build a data warehouse. A performance criterion may be to complete the warehouse by a certain date. But to build the data warehouse on time, without first ensuring its ability to deliver required information needed by management, is pointless. These preliminary project goals and performance criteria must be expanded into more detailed goals and criteria.

3.3.3 Step 3—Define Clear Business and Project Goals

Projects typically support business goals. For example, the achievement of a business goal may depend on the ready availability of accurate information for management. The strategy that management defined to achieve this goal was to implement a data warehouse to derive and deliver the required information. This was the main reason for initiating the project in Step 2.

For this example, project goals must be defined that clearly specify what information is needed to support the business goals. These business goals and the project goals must both be known if the project is to achieve those goals. They must fully define what results will achieve those goals.

3.3.4 Step 4—Identify the Business Problems or Opportunities

The business problems or opportunities are generally well known; in many cases they are the reasons for establishment of the project. But it is important here to apply the complete strategy analysis Step 4 as discussed earlier. This identifies all relevant business issues: problems, threats, and opportunities for the business areas. It identifies strengths and weaknesses. These all provide input to the next step, to decide specific strategies to be followed by the project.

3.3.5 Step 5—Determine Strategies to Address Problems or Opportunities

The understanding gained from Step 4 above enables specific features or characteristics of the project to be defined. These are strategies to address identified issues, using relevant technologies and drawing on specific strengths (or addressing weaknesses) as required.

From this examination, the best strategies are selected to achieve the project goals and business goals. These project strategies clearly define *what* the project has to do to achieve the project and business goals (but not yet how). It is typically only in the technical design of the project that the detailed tactics for implementation are defined, that determine *how* the strategies will be implemented.

3.3.6 Step 6—Define Key Performance Indicators

Now key performance indicators can be defined to ensure that the project strategies established in Step 5 are correctly implemented. These KPIs typically define measures that enable the functionality of implemented project strategies to be tested. They permit assessment of the ability to support achievement of related project or business goals.

3.3.7 Step 7—Determine Which Business Functions Are to Be Supported

From the preceding steps, a clear definition of business and project mission, as well as business and project goals, issues, strategies, and KPIs, will emerge. But during these steps, some changes may have occurred in the specification of the project that could affect other parts of the organization.

This step therefore provides an important cross-check. All areas and functions that are affected by the project are listed, so representatives from those areas can be identified in the next step.

3.3.8 Step 8—Identify Managers and Business Experts from Each Function

A project strategy–function matrix is developed in this step. This lists relevant business strategies and all project strategies each as a separate row, with all affected areas and functions as columns. Primary responsibility for each business or project strategy is shown as a solid bullet in the relevant column. An open bullet shows secondary responsibility of all other affected columns.

3.3.9 Step 9—Schedule Joint Participation by Business and IT Experts

The matrix developed in Step 8 allows primary and secondary responsibility areas or functions to be identified for each strategy row. It also allows all strategies for an area or function column to be readily identified by reading down that column. Managers, business experts, and IT experts with detailed knowledge of each relevant business or project strategy can now be easily identified. Their knowledge will be needed to develop a strategic model, as discussed in Chapter 7.

3.4 Preparation for Strategy Analysis

In this section we will discuss the preparatory steps for business planning. We will use a questionnaire [14] to obtain planning statements for later strategy analysis refinement.

3.4.1 Business Planning Questionnaire

A questionnaire is often helpful as a catalyst to obtain relevant planning statements from business managers who are responsible for implementing part of the business plan. A partial questionnaire, with some responses, is shown in Boxes 3.1 through 3.3.

Box 3.1: Organization's Mission and Purpose Statement

As you are aware, we are experiencing rapid changes in our environment, in our industry, and in our markets. You have been invited to participate in a Business Planning Workshop, which has been scheduled as advised separately by e-mail. This questionnaire provides input for that workshop. Please enter your responses after each question in the Microsoft Word document attached to the e-mail message.

All responses are totally anonymous, so please feel free to answer each question candidly and completely. We encourage frankness and forward-looking suggestions. Insert as much text as you need, to respond fully to each of the following questions.

Please complete and return the Word document, with your inserted questionnaire responses to us as an e-mail attachment, by the specified date in our e-mail message to you.

We need to assess the effectiveness of our enterprise mission and purpose to address the needs of the future. The following questions request your feedback.

1. Define the Mission and Purpose of our Organization

a) Our Current Mission and Purpose is expressed as follows:

"We supply products and services to address the needs of our customers, wherever they are located. On their behalf we will research and source the most appropriate products from the world's leading suppliers. We are skilled and dedicated people working with our customers to satisfy their needs and expectations for our long-term mutual benefit. We will provide exceptional service and value so that we will always be their first choice. We will increase the value of our Company, and improve the economic well-being and quality of life of our customers, suppliers, staff, and other stakeholders."

b) Please Comment on the Mission Statement. Please be candid—provide positive or negative comments and indicate any suggestions for improvement.

- *This mission is very flexible, but it does not define any boundaries for products or suppliers. Are we restricted in any way?*
- *The mission does not define which customer types are acceptable.*

c) What Should Our Mission and Purpose Be? Will the mission statement in a) above help guide our future? Suggest improvements or provide suggested rewording.

- *There are no pricing or profitability criteria to guide us in deciding which customers or products we can address.*
- *For governance and security reasons, the mission should provide criteria to determine any products and services or customers that are not acceptable to our future direction.*
- *There are no economic criteria defined that enable us to decide how much research is appropriate to address a customer's request.*

Box 3.2: Business Unit Mission and Purpose

2. Define Your Mission and Purpose: *This will help us ensure that all areas are working together to support our organization's direction for the future.*

a) What Is Your Mission Now? Please document the mission and purpose of your area, as you understand it.

- ***Project Management:*** *We will establish a project to manage the research and sourcing of each customer's product requirements, based on their identified needs and location. For each customer project, we will research and source the most appropriate products from the world's leading suppliers.*

b) What Will This Mission Be in the Future? Is this mission statement suitable also for the future?

- *As worded, there are no pricing or profitability criteria to guide us in deciding which customers or products we can address.*
- *Governance and security criteria should be defined to identify any projects that are not acceptable to our mission.*
- *There are no economic criteria defined that enable us to decide how much research is appropriate to address a customer's request.*

c) What Should This Mission Be in the Future? Please reword or refine your mission statement to address what you feel is needed for the future.

- ***Project Management:*** *We will establish a project to manage the research and sourcing of each customer's product requirements, based on their identified needs and location. For each customer project we will assess the customer based on profitability, product pricing, governance, and security criteria. Based on guidelines defined with the criteria, we will research and source the most appropriate products from the world's leading suppliers.*

Box 3.3: Policies, Objectives, or Strategies

3. Prioritize Policies, Objectives, or Strategies: We need to understand the policies, objectives, or strategies for your area of responsibility, and their relative priorities.

a) List and Prioritize the Relevant Policies, Objectives, or Strategies for Your Area: Please list all policies, objectives, or strategies first, then review them and indicate their relative priorities as follows: 1 = high priority; 2 = medium priority; 3 = low priority.

	POLICY, OBJECTIVE, OR STRATEGY	PRIORITY
1.	*Each project must have a project owner, responsible for allocating and managing the project budget.*	1
2.	*Each project must have a project manager, responsible for completing the project by the scheduled date, within budget.*	1
3.	*Projects are only authorized that can achieve project objectives by the scheduled completion date, within budget.*	2

The questionnaire is completed before a business planning workshop [15]. As preparation for the workshop, it enables managers to provide input based on their understanding of the planning statements for their areas of management responsibility. A questionnaire template is provided on the CD-ROM that accompanies this book, as discussed in Section 3.5.1. The completed questionnaire is used as a catalyst for strategy analysis as used in the workshop, based on the steps in this chapter.

Each manager completes the questionnaire personally—it is not done in a group or by committee. Individual input from each manager is required. To encourage all respondents to provide completely candid answers, the responses are kept completely anonymous.

On receipt back from all participants, the responses to each question are combined so there is no way the consolidated answers can be used to identify the original respondents. With such anonymity, all participants are encouraged to provide as much candid feedback as possible, both positive and negative.

Boxes 3.1 through 3.3 include the first three questions of the following list. These are shaded in the boxes—to distinguish them from responses, which are shown as *bulleted italics*:

1. Define your organization's mission and purpose.
2. Define your business unit's mission and purpose.
3. Prioritize policies, objectives, or strategies.
4. List existing and potential markets.
5. List existing and potential products and services.
6. List existing and potential channels.
7. List strengths, weaknesses, opportunities, and threats.

These questions and sample responses are discussed next. All questions are shown in the complete questionnaire template included on the CD-ROM, as discussed later.

3.4.2 Enterprise Mission and Purpose

The questionnaire starts by quoting the mission statement of the enterprise. Each person is asked to comment on the quoted mission. The respondent is asked to suggest how the mission statement could be improved, and to suggest how it should be expressed for the future [16]. Each question in Box 3.1 is shaded, with sample responses in *bulleted italics*:

- The mission of XYZ Corporation has been inserted in the questionnaire as Question 1a in Box 3.1. Please take a moment to review this statement.
- Question 1b asks for comments about the mission statement. These comments have been consolidated, anonymously under Question 1b in Box 3.1.
- Question 1c asks for comments on what the mission should be, for the future. Sample replies are consolidated under Question 1c in Box 3.1.

These initial questions establish a firm foundation for later questions. They encourage comments about the present mission and purpose statement for the enterprise, and then ask the participants to suggest what is needed for the future. It focuses their attention on broad enterprise directions, in preparation for more detailed questions later.

3.4.3 Business Unit Mission and Purpose

The next questions ask for the mission and purpose statement of each participant's area of responsibility. Regardless of whether each person has management responsibility to define or change this statement, all are encouraged to provide suggestions for change.

- Question 2a first asks the participant to quote the mission statement for his or her particular area. A sample mission statement for the Project Management Business Unit of XYZ is shown in Question 2a of Box 3.2 as *italics*.
- Question 2b asks each participant to comment on whether this mission is also suitable for the future. Sample responses for Question 2b of Box 3.2 are shown.
- Question 2c asks for suggested wording that would address the preceding comments for the future. The response to Question 2c in Box 3.2 provides a suggested reworded and refined mission statement.

3.4.4 Policies, Objectives, or Strategies

Box 3.3 shows sample responses for the third question, which asks for statements of the policies, objectives, or strategies that apply to each participant's area. Earlier, we were quite specific when we discussed these terms. However we do not want to be pedantic in the questionnaire; all we need is each participant's own words.

We will later use these statements as catalysts for strategy analysis. At that time we may reword the suggested statements. Notice that Question 3 in Box 3.3 does not clarify what the terms mean; it only invites input—shown as *numbered italics*.

Question 3a asks for the policies, objectives, or strategies to be listed. It asks for relative priorities that apply to each statement, where 1 = high priority; 2 = medium priority; 3 = low priority. Sample responses are shown in Box 3.3.

3.4.5 Processing of Questionnaire Responses

As the responses to the questionnaire are received, all participants' responses are consolidated under each question. This consolidated response is then reproduced for each attendee at the business planning workshop, over 5 days. It becomes a catalyst for discussion during the workshop. Each strategy analysis step is covered in turn, and then the workshop attendees immediately apply that step using their consolidated responses as a starting point for discussion and refinement.

3.4.6 Refined Policies, Objectives, or Strategies

Below we can see the partial result of later applying Step 4 of strategy analysis in this chapter to the policies, goals, or objectives statements that were provided as responses in Box 3.3. Compare the responses in Box 3.3 with those shown in Table 3.6 to see refinements that were made.

Table 3.6 Application of Step 4 of the Strategy Analysis Method to Further Refine Earlier Thinking

	Refined Policy, Objective, or Strategy	*Priority*
1	Projects are initiated by a project owner, who requires completion of the project to deliver defined business objectives within an agreed budget and time.	1
2	A project manager is allocated to a project by the project owner. The project manager has responsibility to manage the project to completion, to achieve defined project objectives by the planned time and within the allocated budget.	1
3	Projects are authorized by management based on planned capability to achieve project objectives within an agreed budget and time, for a defined return on investment (ROI).	2

3.4.7 Markets, Products and Services, Channels, and SWOTs

The remaining tasks not addressed by Boxes 3.1 through 3.3 are shown in the following list. They address current and potential markets; products and services; channels; and strengths, weaknesses, opportunities, and threats (SWOTs). These and subset questions are included in the questionnaire template as discussed next.

4. List existing and potential markets.
5. List existing and potential products and services.
6. List existing and potential channels.
7. List strengths, weaknesses, opportunities, and threats.

3.5 Questionnaire Templates for Enterprise Architecture

This section discusses a business planning questionnaire template that can be tailored to address your enterprise needs. It invites input prior to a business planning workshop that uses strategy analysis. A strategic modeling questionnaire template can also be tailored and used prior to a facilitated strategic modeling session.

3.5.1 Business Planning Questionnaire Template

A template is provided on the CD-ROM that accompanies this book to help you prepare a business planning questionnaire before a business planning workshop [17]. The business plan from that workshop becomes the high-level horizontal slices of the Why column for the Planner [C6R1] and Owner rows [C6R2] of the Zachman framework as discussed in Chapter 1. This becomes the starting point for enterprise architecture using the methods described in later chapters.

3.5.2 Strategic Modeling Questionnaire Template

An enterprise architecture project may not have any authority to change the strategic plans, or to define or refine lower level tactical or operational business plans. In this case a business planning workshop is not relevant. The enterprise architecture starting point is still the Zachman framework Why column for the Planner [C6R1] and Owner rows [C6R2]. A strategic modeling questionnaire is used instead as the input to a facilitated strategic modeling session [18]. To illustrate this, Boxes 3.1 through 3.3 will later be used as catalysts for strategic modeling in Chapter 7.

3.6 Summary

In this chapter we covered the business planning method of strategy analysis for rapid delivery of enterprise architecture, using the Zachman framework Why column for the Planner and Owner rows.

- We discussed strategy analysis, to define business plans if none presently exist or to refine existing plans. This method is easy to learn and can be used to define business plans for any management level or for any project.
- We discussed how a business planning questionnaire is used to obtain planning statements as input catalysts for a business planning workshop. We used sample responses to see how consolidated questionnaire responses are prepared.

We are now ready to move to Chapter 4, where we will cover methods that apply to the application of these business plans for governance analysis.

Endnotes

[1] Kaplan, R. S., and D. P. Norton, *The Balanced Scorecard: Translating Strategy into Action,* Boston, MA: Harvard Business School Press, 1996.

[2] Kaplan, R. S., and D. P. Norton, *The Strategy-Focused Organization: How Balanced Scorecard Companies Thrive in the New Business Environment,* Boston, MA: Harvard Business School Press, 2001.

[3] Kaplan, R. S., and D. P. Norton, *Strategy Maps: Converting Intangible Assets into Tangible Outcomes,* Boston, MA: Harvard Business School Press, 2004.

[4] I will abbreviate these Zachman framework column and row references from this point on as [C6R1] and [C6R2]. For easy reference, see the Zachman framework PDF on the accompanying CD-ROM.

[5] Drucker, P., *Management: Tasks, Responsibilities, Practices,* New York: Harper & Row, 1974.

[6] Rowe, A. J., et al., *Strategic Management and Business Policy: A Methodological Approach,* 3rd ed., Reading, MA: Addison-Wesley, 1990.

[7] A number of useful strategic planning techniques are described in Chapters 10–13 of Finkelstein, C., *An Introduction to Information Engineering,* Sydney, Australia: Addison-Wesley, 1989.

[8] Porter, M., *Competitive Strategy: Techniques for Analyzing Industries and Competitors,* New York: The Free Press, 1980.

[9] Porter, M., *Competitive Advantage: Creating and Sustaining Superior Performance,* New York: The Free Press, 1985.

[10] Montgomery, C., and M. Porter, (eds.), *Strategy: Seeking and Securing Competitive Advantage,* Boston, MA: Harvard Business Review Press, 1991.

[11] The concepts of internal and external appraisal are covered in Chapters 8–14 of Finkelstein, C., *Information Engineering: Strategic Systems Development,* Sydney, Australia: Addison-Wesley, 1992.

[12] We did not earlier discuss the R&D funding strategy in Figure 3.7, so I have not included it in the CFO job role description.

[13] The project description for the business planning project phase and a business planning workshop is available from the IES Web site at http://www.ies.aust.com. Click on the Projects link from any page.

[14] Earlier versions of this questionnaire appeared in books by Clive Finkelstein [7, 11], where it was called a management questionnaire.

[15] The business planning workshop is part of the business planning project phase [13].

[16] The intent is not to change the mission as such, but to focus on its directional role for the future.

[17] A questionnaire template is included as the Word file *Chap-03-Questionnaire.doc* in the *Book Materials* folder on the CD-ROM. This can be tailored to your organization for input to the business planning workshop. If you wish, this workshop can be personally presented on your premises by Clive Finkelstein. Visit the IES Web site at http://www.ies.aust.com and click on the Contact Us link.

[18] The same questions still apply as discussed for a business planning workshop. In this case it is called a *strategic modeling questionnaire.* A CD-ROM template for this questionnaire is discussed in Chapter 7.

CHAPTER 4

Governance Analysis Using Enterprise Architecture

In Chapter 3 we covered the strategy analysis methodology. We focused on the Why column for the Planner [C6R1] and Owner rows [C6R2] of the Zachman framework, used to define business plans for the future.

This chapter describes a practical approach using enterprise architecture for rapid compliance with business governance requirements, such as the United States' Sarbanes-Oxley Act of 2002. It shows how internal controls can be established by senior management using a governance analysis framework (GAF). This is used to document the relationships within an enterprise that support financial and other reporting requirements. It is based on a comprehensive organizing framework using the Zachman framework, as well as proven enterprise architecture methods and tools for the documentation and management of the GAF. It ensures that senior management is able to comply with the internal control reporting requirements of Section 404 of the Sarbanes-Oxley Act of 2002.

Like Chapter 3, our governance analysis focus in this chapter is also on the Why column for the Planner [C6R1] and Owner rows [C6R2]of the Zachman framework, as shown in Figure 4.1.

4.1 Responsibilities Imposed by Sarbanes-Oxley

The Sarbanes-Oxley Act of 2002 (also called *Sar-Ox* or *SOX*) assigns responsibility to senior management of public and nonpublic organizations in the United States [1]. It also is applied in various forms by other countries throughout the world. Of particular concern is Section 404 of the act, titled Management Assessment of Internal Controls [2]. Typical examples of the difficulties that face senior management to ensure they support SOX are issues related to internal control over financial reporting of public companies and issues related to judgments and estimates that may change over time. These are discussed in [3].

The required internal controls vary from enterprise to enterprise. They need to be tailored to the industry or industries in which the organization operates, and are typically unique for each enterprise—where internal controls are determined by its business activities and processes as well as its financial controls. They are closely related to the IT systems and databases that the enterprise uses for financial and other reporting.

For example, a simple test that can be applied in an organization is to ask staff why they carry out a specific business process, financial or otherwise. This is a ques-

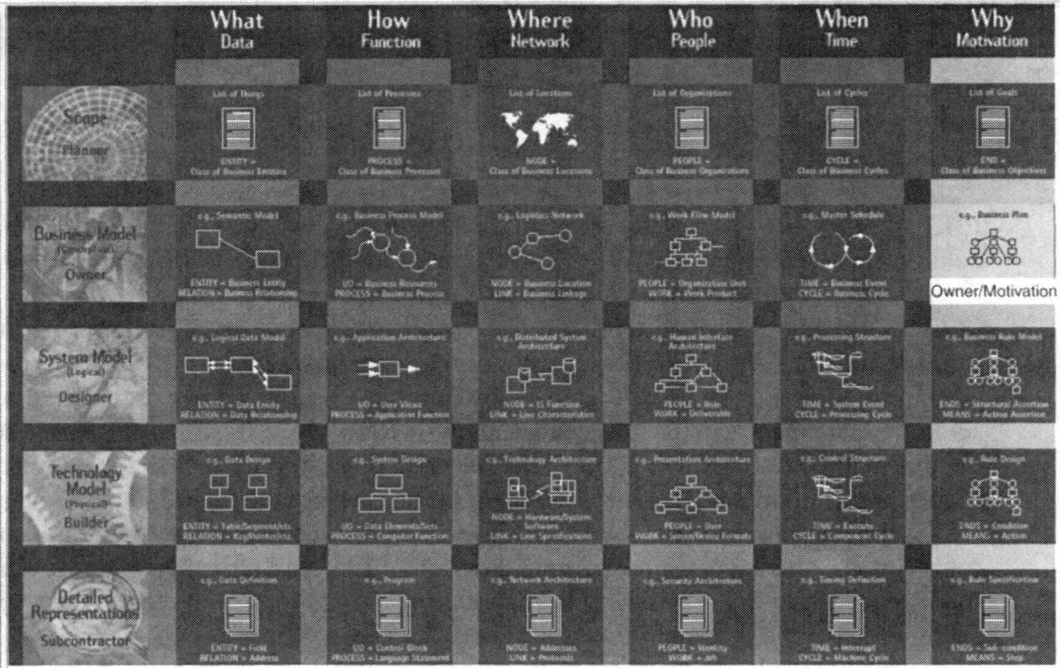

Figure 4.1 Governance analysis addresses the Why column for the Planner [C6R1] and Owner rows [C6R2] of the Zachman framework.

tion that may be asked by an auditor to see whether internal controls referenced by management do actually work. When a person is asked, "Why do you do that process in that way?" the response is often "Because we have always done it that way." This answer indicates that the reasons—even if they were once known—have become lost to history. It is a warning signal to the auditor and to management that the internal controls are not working in that particular case.

Another example of some of the questions that auditors must ensure are adequately addressed is shown in Figure 4.2, in relation to multiple-location testing considerations. These questions relate to business units and locations and are generally tested first by auditors. They should be easy for most enterprises to answer. Difficulty answering these simple questions may indicate more serious deficiencies in internal controls. This can lead the auditor to pose more difficult questions, where the detail of the answers is less important to the auditor than the demonstrated fact that senior management does have relevant answers available.

4.1.1 Typical Internal Control Questions

For complete satisfaction that internal controls have not only been implemented, but also work in practice throughout the enterprise, senior managers need to show that answers are available for management and audit questions to determine SOX compliance. These relate to key resources that are needed, such as data, business activities and processes, locations, people or business units, and events. The answers should relate back to strategic and tactical business plans that have been defined by management as follows:

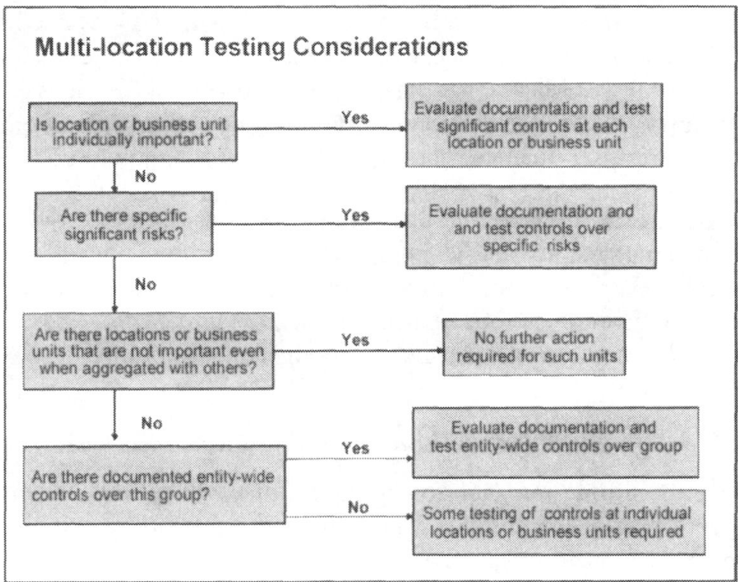

Figure 4.2 Multiple-location testing considerations for auditors in relation to internal control reporting for Sarbanes-Oxley. (*Source:* File *2003_0822_Sarbanes-Oxley_Omnibus_Final_rev.pdf* in *2003_0822_pcaob.zip* as discussed in [3].)

- *For data:* What do the data represent? How are the data processed? Where are they used? Who is responsible for the data? When are the data used? Why are the data needed? Do these data support the strategic and tactical business plans?
- *For processes:* How do we execute our processes? What data do they use? Where are they processed? Who is responsible for the processes? When are these processes used? Why are the processes needed? Do they support strategic and tactical business plans?
- *For locations:* What data does the location need? How are processes executed in the location? Who is responsible for the location? When is the location involved in key events? Why does the location exist for the enterprise? Do the business plans for each location support the strategic and tactical business plans?
- *For business units or people:* What data do the business units need? How are key processes executed in each business unit? Where is each business unit located? Who is responsible for the business unit? When is the business unit involved in key events? Why does each business unit exist? Do the business plans for each business unit support the strategic and tactical business plans?
- *For business events:* What data does each business event need? Which processes are initiated by each business event? Where do business events occur? Who is responsible for these business events? When do they occur? Why do they occur? Do the business events support the strategic and tactical business plans?

- *For business plans:* What data do the business plans need? How do processes support the business plans? Which locations do the business plans apply to? Who is responsible for these business plans? When does each event occur that supports the business plans? Why do the business plans exist? Do tactical and operational business plans support the strategic plans?

An auditor expects the answers to most of these questions to be available to senior managers, at least when applied at the strategic level—and for key financial aspects at the tactical level also. But the reality in most organizations is much different. Apart from questions relating to "where" and "who," the answers for many of the preceding questions are extremely difficult to obtain.

4.1.2 Managing Internal Controls Using Enterprise Architecture

These are simple internal control questions: what, how, where, who, when, and why. If controls are in place, these questions should be capable of being answered from the different perspectives of management and staff levels in an enterprise. The answers available to senior managers (as the planners and owners of the enterprise) are likely to be less detailed than those needed by middle managers, business experts, and IT staff (as the designers and builders of the enterprise).

These six questions are represented by the six columns of the Zachman framework for enterprise architecture. (See more detailed discussion in Chapters 1 and 5 and the Zachman framework PDF file in the *Book Materials* folder on the accompanying CD-ROM.) In Chapter 1 we saw that each framework cell should contain primitive models. Enterprise architecture has previously been considered to be an IT responsibility, but when used by managers, it enables precise *governance analysis*. For example, a matrix shows the relationships that exist between two columns. Each matrix can be used by managers to answer questions such as who and what; where and who; how and why; why and what and so on.

The designers, builders, and subcontractors (often outsourced) work with the business experts who understand the business processes of the enterprise. Based on this business knowledge, IT staff design and build systems and databases that support those processes. They provide the data, information, and processing needed for day-to-day operational functioning of the enterprise. They are represented by the bottom three rows of the Zachman framework in Figure 4.3.

	What	How	Where	Who	When	Why
PLANNER Objectives/Scope						
OWNER Conceptual						
DESIGNER Logical						
BUILDER Physical						
SUBCONTRACTOR Out-of-Context						
FUNCTIONING ENTERPRISE	Data	Function	Network	Organization	Schedule	Strategy

Figure 4.3 The Zachman framework for enterprise architecture is used to create a governance analysis framework as an internal control reporting approach to comply with Section 404 of the Sarbanes-Oxley Act of 2002.

In most enterprises, senior managers are not involved in enterprise architecture (EA), which has been considered by many to be a computer discipline. Although this is true in part, EA is also a business discipline. It enables business experts and IT staff, working together, to establish and define internal controls—as systems to support key business processes and databases that are needed for internal control reporting. However, when used by senior management, enterprise architecture also provides methods for business transformation as discussed later.

It is the responsibility of senior managers—as the planners and owners of business plans, data, processes, locations, business units, and events that are used to manage the enterprise—to define the objectives and scope of the internal controls. It is also their responsibility to provide the high-level perspective or view that is needed to manage these controls. These perspectives are defined in the first two Zachman framework rows in Figure 4.3. It is important to note that senior management involvement in enterprise architecture for SOX internal control reporting is missing in most enterprises today.

In the past, the absence of these controls has merely been embarrassing. With the legal implications of Sarbanes-Oxley noncompliance, however, an inability by senior managers—due to the complexity of most enterprises—to answer internal control reporting audit questions takes on a new personal meaning. What is needed is a governance analysis framework that is both easy to create and easy to use and that can be used to obtain answers for relevant internal control reporting questions.

4.2 Governance Analysis Framework (GAF) for Sarbanes-Oxley

The Zachman framework provides a way to cut through the complexity of today's enterprises and document the relationships that exist between each column for each row. These relationships are illustrated as matrices, shown in Figures 4.4 through 4.7 and discussed next. They address governance of the project management business unit of a typical enterprise. These matrices are based on a high-level strategic model of the enterprise, which was introduced in Chapter 1 and discussed further in Chapter 7. The definition of the matrices is described in detail in Chapter 8.

The right window of Figure 4.4 shows an organizational structure for project management in some organizations. Under the project management business unit are three business units: financial management, resource management, and schedule management. These business units represent model views of the enterprise.

The left window shows a typical governance analysis framework matrix. This relates business planning statements (goals, objectives, policies, KPIs, strategies, tactics, and so forth). The statements are shown as rows and address the question of *why*. These are the Project Management planning statements that we discussed in Box 3.3 in Chapter 3. Relevant business units (based on the model views in the right window) are shown as columns of the matrix; they address the question of *who*.

Reading across a row in Figure 4.4 shows ticked business units that are responsible for, or involved in, implementing the relevant planning statement for that row. For example, the P3 Project Authorization (Policy) row that is highlighted shows the business units that are involved: F1 Strategic Model, F2 Project Management, F3 Financial Management, and F4 Resource Management. This clearly answers the

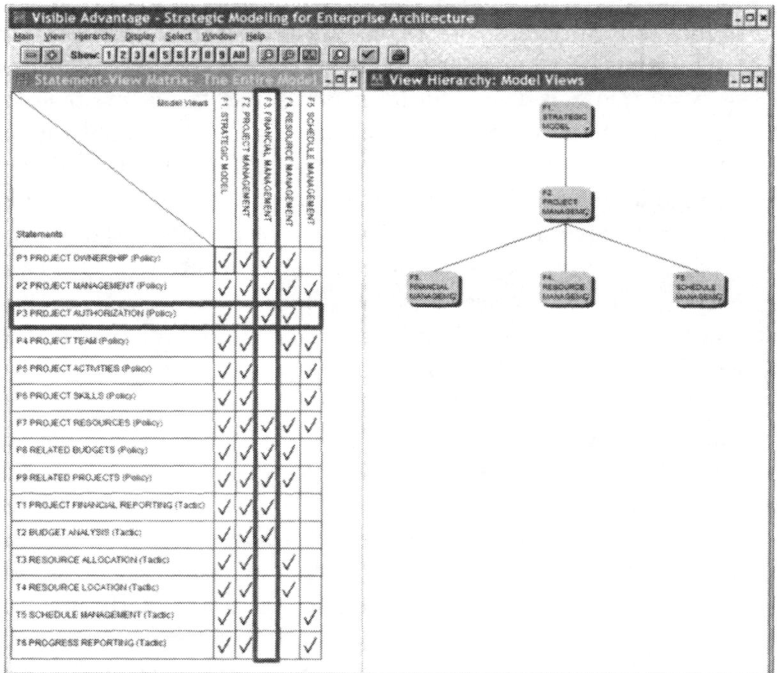

Figure 4.4 Typical GAF matrix that relates *why* (as rows for planning statements) and *who* (as columns for business units).

question of who is responsible for managing, or involved in implementing, this statement.

Reading down a column in Figure 4.4 indicates the subset of planning statements that the relevant business unit column is responsible for, or involved in implementing. For example, reading down the F3 Financial Management column, the ticked planning statement rows together represent the tactical business plan for financial management in the business unit. By referring to the detailed text in those planning statements, these rows clearly answer the financial management question of *why* for financial reporting.

Figure 4.5 shows a similar matrix that lists business activities for financial management as rows, with the relevant business planning statements shown as columns. This matrix is initially blank when it has just been created for the particular organization. It provides a governance analysis framework that is still to be completed by knowledgeable business experts. When completed as shown in the figure, it can be easily used to answer the questions of how and why.

Reading across a row in Figure 4.5 with an understanding of the relevant business activity for that row, the financial management business experts refer to the relevant planning statement text for each column. They tick those planning statement columns that require the relevant activity.

On completion of the matrix in this way, some internal controls for financial management have now been documented for later reference. For example, reading down a planning statement column in the matrix answers the question of how the planning statement is implemented or managed based on the activity rows that are

Activity-Statement Matrix 1. Initial Strategic Model

Activities: \ Statements	P1 PROJECT OWNERSHIP	P2 PROJECT MANAGEMENT	P3 PROJECT AUTHORIZATION
A1 Project Budget Management	✓	✓	✓
A2 Project Objective Management			✓

- Matrix relates Activities to Plans
- Indicates "Why" Activity exists
- Each Activity is shown as a Row
- Each Planning Statement is a Column
- Reading across a row shows Planning Statements for that Activity, or "Why"
- Reading down a column shows all Activities for that Statement

Figure 4.5 Typical GAF matrix that relates *how* (as rows for business activities) and *why* (as columns for planning statements).

ticked. Reading across an activity row answers the question of why the activity is carried out, for all of the planning statement columns that are checked.

Figure 4.6 provides a further internal control matrix. It relates business plans (shown as planning statement rows) with data (shown as data object columns). When this governance analysis framework matrix has been completed, it can be used to answer *what* and *why*.

For example, reading across a planning statement row in Figure 4.6—such as for the P2 Project Management (Policy) row—each data object column is ticked that provides data in support of the full text of that planning statement.

On completion of the matrix, by reading down a data column, each ticked row shows the planning statements that the data supports, hence answering the question of why the data are needed. Reading across a planning statement row indicates the data that are available to support that statement and associated management decision making. This answers the question of what; it shows the data that support the relevant statement.

A fourth GAF matrix is also very important. This is shown in Figure 4.7. It lists business activities as rows, with data objects as columns (named *Entities* in the figure). To complete this matrix, business experts who are knowledgeable in a listed business activity row will tick each data column that the activity requires. The resulting completed matrix in Figure 4.7 enables the questions of *what* and *how* to be answered. Reading down a data column, each activity row that has been ticked indicates how the data are used. Reading across an activity row, each column that

Statement-Data Matrix: 1. Initial Strategic Model

Statements \ Data Objects	BUDGET	OBJECTIVE	PERSON	PROJECT	PROJECT BUDGET	PROJECT MANAGER	PROJECT OBJECTIVE	PROJECT OWNER
P1 PROJECT OWNERSHIP (Policy)	✓			✓	✓			✓
P2 PROJECT MANAGEMENT (Policy)	✓	✓		✓	✓	✓	✓	✓
P3 PROJECT AUTHORIZATION (Policy)	✓			✓	✓	✓	✓	✓

- Matrix relates Business Plans to Data
- Indicates "What" is required by Plans
- Shows Planning Statements as Rows
- Shows Data as Columns
- Reading across a row shows Data that is required for that Statement
- Reading down a column gives Subset of Planning Statements for that Data

Figure 4.6 Typical GAF matrix that relates *why* (as rows for planning statements) and *what* (as columns for data objects).

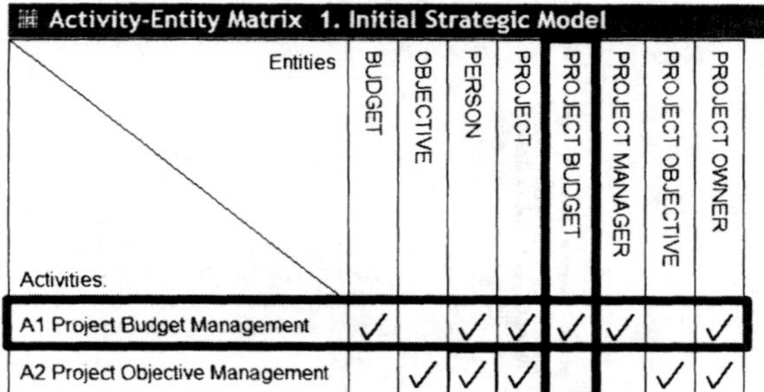

Activity-Entity Matrix 1. Initial Strategic Model

Activities \ Entities	BUDGET	OBJECTIVE	PERSON	PROJECT	PROJECT BUDGET	PROJECT MANAGER	PROJECT OBJECTIVE	PROJECT OWNER
A1 Project Budget Management	✓		✓	✓	✓	✓		✓
A2 Project Objective Management		✓	✓	✓			✓	✓

- Matrix relates Activities to Data
- Indicates "What" Data is required
- Each Activity is shown as a Row
- Each Data Entity is a Column
- Reading across a row shows Data required by that Activity, or "What"
- Reading down a column shows all Activities that use the Data Entity

Figure 4.7 Typical GAF matrix that relates *how* (as rows for business activities) and *what* (as columns for data).

has been ticked indicates what data are required. We will later see in Chapter 7 how we can derive the data needed by an activity.

Other matrices are also needed to be able to answer each of the internal control questions posed earlier. Relevant matrices are identified next, with reference (in parentheses) to earlier figures where appropriate:

- *Data matrices:* data to processes (see Figure 4.7); data to locations; data to people or business units; data to events; data to business plans (see Figure 4.6);
- *Process matrices*: processes to data (see Figure 4.7); processes to locations; processes to business units; processes to events; processes to business plans (see Figure 4.5);
- *Location matrices:* locations to data; locations to processes; locations to people or business units; locations to events; locations to business plans;
- *People or business unit matrices:* people or business units to data; people or business units to processes; people or business units to locations; people or business units to events; people or business units to business plans (see Figure 4.4);
- *Business event matrices:* business events to data; events to processes; events to locations; events to people or business units; business events to business plans;
- *Business plan matrices:* business plans to data (see Figure 4.6), business plans to processes (see Figure 4.5); business plans to locations; business plans to people or business units (see Figure 4.4); business plans to business events.

When senior managers use governance analysis framework matrices as described here, they are able to demonstrate that they have a powerful management tool for internal control reporting as required by the Sarbanes-Oxley Act of 2002.

The development of the matrices just summarized is discussed in Chapter 8. This development is discussed at an overview level in the next section.

4.2.1 Developing a Governance Analysis Framework

It is important to note that none of the matrices discussed in Figure 4.4 through 4.7 were manually defined. Manually determining the relevant row and column titles for each of these tailored matrices is extremely difficult; to keep them manually updated continually as the enterprise changes over time is even more difficult. Only if all matrices are kept up to date over time can they be relied on for effective internal control [4]. When other matrices that have also been listed above are considered, manual definition and maintenance of these matrices for internal control reporting purposes is no longer a practical or realistic option. Instead, the row and column titles for each matrix in these figures were automatically generated from strategic model by a modeling tool (discussed later), based on a rigorous governance analysis methodology. Each generated and tailored matrix provides a governance analysis framework to be completed by relevant business and IT experts.

When completed, these matrices provide a powerful internal control reporting capability. Furthermore, this automated support enables the matrices to be easily kept up to date over time as required by SOX. Any relevant changes are automatically applied to all other matrices that are also affected. The methodology, the steps, and the modeling tools used to achieve this automatic matrix creation and maintenance are discussed later in this chapter.

These matrices are generated from the business plans that are defined and agreed on by senior management for the enterprise. Such plans define the strategic directions that the senior management team establishes to manage the enterprise today, and provide direction as it moves into the future. These strategic plans provide a catalyst to develop a tailored strategic model for the enterprise.

A strategic model provides a "picture of the business," similar in concept to the layout of a city. A city map clearly shows the layout of streets ("where") and the access routes that define "how" to get there. It also indicates "what" is located in parts of the city. Given a reason ("why") to take a given route at a certain time ("when"), people ("who") can use the map to navigate through any city. The development of a strategic model is discussed in detail in Chapter 7.

What is missing in most enterprises is a similar map (or picture) of the business. A city map can be bought from news agents in that city, but no news agent sells strategic models for enterprises. In the absence of a strategic model for your enterprise, it is hard to answer the questions we discussed earlier. As a result, internal control reporting is quite difficult. A strategic model (developed and tailored to an enterprise) enables senior managers, as well as middle managers, expert business staff, and IT staff, to see the data, activities and processes, locations, business units or people, the business events, and the business plans that all need to be managed effectively for internal control reporting.

From the strategic model, the governance analysis framework matrices discussed earlier become dynamic. They are automatically generated. For example:

- The strategic data of vital importance for financial reporting and internal control reporting is defined as the strategic model is developed. These data are automatically used to create the data columns in Figures 4.6 and 4.7.
- The strategic model also enables key business activities and processes to be identified and named. These identified activities and processes are automatically used to create the activity rows shown in Figures 4.5 and 4.7.
- The planning statements from strategic plans that are used as the catalyst to develop the strategic model are automatically used to create the statement

rows shown in Figures 4.4 and 4.6 and statement columns shown in Figure 4.5.

- The named business units responsible for, or involved in, implementing the business plans are automatically used to create the business unit columns in Figure 4.4.
- Similarly, the strategic model is automatically used to create the relevant rows and columns of many other matrices as discussed earlier.

The role of the strategic model is vital for automatic creation of the governance analysis framework matrices discussed earlier, for internal control reporting. Methods and tools for developing and maintaining these internal controls are discussed next.

4.2.2 Methods and Tools for Governance Analysis

The development of a tailored strategic model for an enterprise is the vital first step toward establishing internal control reporting based on dynamic governance analysis framework matrices that can be automatically generated as discussed earlier. The method used to achieve this is called *strategic modeling.*

A typical strategic modeling project to define a tailored strategic model for an enterprise takes 25 days—typically spread over 3 months as illustrated later in Figure 4.8 and discussed in Chapter 7. This 25-day period does not result in completed GAF matrices, but it does automatically create each relevant blank dynamic matrix row and column name, tailored to the terminology enterprise.

The completion of a strategic modeling project in this time frame depends on corporate buy-in and support by senior management. It requires the senior management team and their direct reports to participate for 2 days in a facilitated session near the start of the 25-day period to help develop the tailored strategic model. Their active commitment is vital: It ensures that their key needs for internal control reporting are incorporated into the strategic model. For success, a senior manager who is prepared to act as the sponsor or "champion" of the strategic modeling project is

25-day Project for Enterprise Architecture Delivery in 3-month Increments

Governance Analysis Project Task	Days	Mth 1	Mth 2	Mth 3	...	Mth N
1. Establish Project Plan for Governance Analysis and Identify Senior Management Participants	2					
2. Distribute Business Planning Questionnaire and Consolidate All Responses under each Question	18					
3. Conduct Strategic Modeling Facilitated Session using Consolidated Responses in Plan as Catalyst	2					
4. Analyze, Identify and Document Potential Priorities within Strategic Model from Facilitated Session	12					
5. Derive Governance Analysis Framework (GAF) Matrices for Review and later Matrix Population	10					
6. Review Strategic Model Analysis and GAF Matrices to set Priorities for GAF Matrices and GAF Systems	1					
7. Commence Population of Priority GAF Matrices for Use in Governance Internal Control Reporting	N					
8. Commence 3-month Incremental Delivery Projects of Priority Systems to Support Senior Management	N					

25 Days

Figure 4.8 Project plan for governance analysis strategic modeling projects.

needed to convince other managers that they should actively and personally participate in the 2-day facilitated session.

Two days is a significant demand on their limited time availability, but it is essential. Although this facilitated session with management has been reduced in some cases to 1 day, the accuracy, usefulness, and maintainability of the resulting GAF matrices suffer if the senior management team is not actively involved. If their direct reports participate on the second day, it is critical that senior management spend at least a further half-day to review the additional detail provided when they were absent from the facilitated session.

Given this input from senior management team and their direct reports, a detailed analysis is carried out by the facilitator in the remainder of the 25-day period as shown in Figure 4.8. This strategic model analysis identifies key data, business activities, locations, business units, and business events for the business plans that were used as catalysts.

The result of this strategic model analysis is documented in an enterprise architecture portfolio plan (EAPP) report. This is the main deliverable from a strategic modeling project [5]. This report includes an executive summary and key recommendations, with a description of the methods used to maintain the delivered tailored GAF matrices over time. Appendices are also included that document all components of the defined strategic model for internal control reporting as follows:

- *Business plan:* Documents the strategic business planning statements that were used as the catalyst for the facilitated strategic modeling session. These address the *why* questions for SOX compliance.
- *Strategic model:* Documents the enterprise strategic model and high-level tactical models for key business units. These models are represented as data maps that show a "picture of the business."
- *Strategic data:* Documents the underlying data represented in the enterprise strategic model and high-level tactical models for key business units. This answers the *what* questions for SOX compliance.
- *Business activities:* Identifies key business activities that are reflected in the strategic model, as determined during and after the facilitated session. This answers the *how* questions for SOX compliance.
- *Business activity clusters:* Documents automatically derived project plans that identify the data required by each activity. This identifies activities that can be reused throughout the enterprise—with large potential cost savings from this reuse. This also answers the *how* questions for SOX compliance.
- *Business locations:* Lists key locations (where relevant) that were identified during and after the facilitated session. This answers *where* questions for SOX.
- *Business units:* Lists key business units identified during and after the facilitated session based on the high-level tactical models from the strategic model. This answers the *who* questions for SOX compliance.
- *Business events:* Lists key business events (where relevant) identified during and after the facilitated session. This answers the *when* questions for SOX compliance.

- *GAF matrices:* Documents blank governance analysis framework matrices from the data, activities, locations, business units, events, and business plans from the earlier appendices. This includes the four tailored matrices discussed in Figures 4.4 through 4.7 and other matrices as required.

The EAPP report and its contents (as described earlier) provide a high-level documented view of tailored internal control reporting from the perspective of senior management. These matrices then must be completed by relevant business experts as discussed earlier. The strategic GAF matrices are typically defined later as more detailed matrices by key business units.

Tactical modeling projects—each similar to the strategic modeling project—can in turn be undertaken in parallel for each of these business units. The planning and conduct of tactical modeling projects are described in Chapter 7. Tactical models are the "vertical slivers" we discussed in Chapter 1 (see Figure 1.7). Tactical modeling projects can typically be completed in 1 to 3 months, depending on business scope. The problems previously experienced with traditional methods (see Chapter 1) in moving from design models into implementation are addressed by the rapid delivery methods in Part II and technologies in Part III. Together, these enable tactical models to be delivered rapidly into production in 3- to 6-month increments.

Strategic modeling and tactical modeling projects have been completed for large and medium commercial enterprises throughout the world. Some of these projects are described in Chapter 7 [6]. Governance analysis frameworks for internal control reporting are also vitally important to large government departments and defense departments. Strategic modeling and tactical modeling projects for government and defense have been completed in the United States, Canada, Australia, and New Zealand. The success of each project was due largely to a sponsoring senior manager who acted as the "champion" for the project. The ability to develop the tailored definition of a strategic model, together with the appendices and matrices discussed earlier, depends on the methods that are used for strategic and tactical modeling projects as described in Part II.

Most important is the ability to develop a governance analysis framework that is tailored uniquely to an enterprise—and to complete this GAF in 25 days within an elapsed 3 months. Most modeling tools require much of the definition to be carried out manually over many months (sometimes even over years), but not in days. Their lack of automated tools for dynamic maintenance may further mean that this maintenance must also be done manually.

The strategic and tactical modeling projects discussed used two modeling tools to complete these projects rapidly. These are Visible Advantage and Visible Analyst, both available from Visible Systems Corporation [7]. Screenshots of Visible Advantage were shown earlier in Figures 4.4 through 4.7. Visible Analyst, with its full support of the Zachman framework for enterprise architecture as a clickable interface, is shown in Figure 4.1. Other modeling tools can also be used, such as Telelogic System Architect [8]. Tools are also available for automatic code generation and for problem tracking [9]. These modeling tools are all discussed in Chapter 15.

An important comment was included in the preceding discussion about the EAPP report. This was the reference to *strategic model analysis,* which was briefly mentioned in relation to business activity clusters. These clusters are automatically generated by Visible Advantage as project plans, which are used for rapid delivery of priority business processes into production in only 3 to 6 months. This capability for rapid delivery is vital in today's rapidly changing world. Priority business processes can be implemented in this rapid time frame that also use the latest technologies (see Part III) based on XML, Web services, service-oriented architecture, and business process management (BPM) languages. Furthermore, BPM languages can be automatically generated as executable code from process models, workflow models, or similar diagrams. This means that business processes can be rapidly delivered into production, and also can be easily and rapidly changed as the business changes.

An important point is the ability of the modeling tools used in Figures 4.4 through 4.7 to automatically identify reusable activities as part of their analysis of the strategic model. Business activity clusters are derived automatically by entity dependency analysis and clearly identify reusable activities as discussed in Chapter 7. These reusable activities are a catalyst for business transformation.

4.2.3 Business Transformation Using Enterprise Architecture

A rapid business transformation capability is vital for success in today's rapid business change environment. Even today, most organizations still use business activities and processes that were defined before the advent of the Internet. These older activities and processes do not enable the full benefits and cost savings of the Internet to be realized effectively. The reusable activities and processes identified in the EAPP report, when they are later implemented, often become catalysts for business transformation and can typically represent potential annual cost savings of hundreds of millions of dollars for large enterprises [10].

The EAPP reports produced from strategic modeling and tactical modeling projects use modeling tools to provide the documentation that is needed. This is an added by-product of the enterprise architecture methods used for governance analysis as discussed in this chapter. The methods and tools are similarly used to implement transformed business activities and processes for business transformation enablement. These are discussed in more detail in Part II.

4.3 Step-by-Step Approach for Governance Analysis

Finally, the methods discussed earlier in this chapter can be applied rapidly in a manageable step-by-step approach as listed next. These steps are illustrated in Figure 4.8, which is keyed to each step described next:

- Step 1—Establish plan for strategic modeling project.
- Step 2—Capture initial business planning input as catalyst.
- Step 3—Conduct strategic modeling facilitated session.
- Step 4—Carry out strategic model analysis.

- Step 5—Derive governance analysis framework documentation.
- Step 6—Review matrices and governance implementation plan.
- Step 7—Manage progressive completion of GAF matrices.
- Step 8—Manage implementation of governance analysis systems.

4.3.1 Step 1—Establish Plan for Strategic Modeling Project

A project plan is established to manage the tasks that will be carried out over the elapsed 3-month period of a strategic modeling project. This involves identifying senior managers and their direct reports who will participate in the 2-day facilitated session and the later review session after analysis of the strategic model. The facilitated session is scheduled to take place over 2 days at a convenient date for all managers, following Step 2.

4.3.2 Step 2—Capture Initial Business Planning Input as Catalyst

Strategic modeling uses the strategic business plans of the enterprise as a catalyst. These are expanded with input from all participating managers (who were identified in Step 1) using a business planning questionnaire tailored from the strategic plans. This questionnaire was discussed in Chapter 3 and is included as a template on the CD-ROM [11]. It requests anonymous responses for each question from each manager, 3 weeks prior to the 2-day session. All responses are returned to a central point a few days prior to the scheduled facilitated session, where all manager responses to each question are consolidated under that question—maintaining full anonymity to encourage uninhibited discussion during the facilitated session. The strategic plans and all consolidated questionnaire responses are entered into the modeling tool that is to be used in Step 4 for later strategic model analysis.

4.3.3 Step 3—Conduct Strategic Modeling Facilitated Session

The scheduled 2-day strategic modeling facilitated session is undertaken with all of the invited managers present, using the consolidated responses to the business planning questionnaire as a catalyst. From these, with further expansion of business strategies by the group of managers based on questions asked, the facilitator progressively develops a "picture of the business" on a whiteboard to represent the strategic model, as discussed in Chapter 7. This model is used by the facilitator and managers to identify, to name, and to prioritize key business activities and processes that exist within the strategic model. As required by the enterprise, key locations, organizational units, and business events may also be listed if they are not already documented elsewhere.

4.3.4 Step 4—Carry Out Strategic Model Analysis

On completion of the facilitated session, the facilitator enters the strategic model into a modeling tool [12]. This tool is uniquely able to analyze and automatically identify the data required by each key business activity or process prioritized by the managers during the session. Business and IT experts, working together under the guidance of the facilitator, develop textual definitions for identified data, activities, and processes represented in the model. These data and activity definitions are entered into the modeling tool, together with the lists of key locations, organizational units, and the business events that were obtained from available documentation or separately listed during the session in the absence of that documentation.

4.3.5 Step 5—Derive Governance Analysis Framework Documentation

Following analysis of the strategic model in Step 4, the agreed names from the facilitated session and associated definitions of data (what), activities and processes (how), locations (where), organizational units (who), business events (when), and business plans (why) are used to derive the key matrices identified by the enterprise as needed for subsequent GAF matrix completion in Step 7. Further analysis by the modeling tool also automatically derives the EAPP report, discussed in detail in Chapter 7. This EAPP report is used to determine the implementation plan for governance analysis.

4.3.6 Step 6—Review Matrices and Governance Implementation Plan

The managers who participated in the facilitated modeling session in Step 3 return for the 1-day review session scheduled at the end of 25 days, on completion of Steps 4 and 5. The governance analysis framework matrices that were derived are reviewed, along with the governance implementation plan determined from the EAPP report. Required changes or reprioritization of the associated GAF matrices are discussed and documented. These changes are made immediately on completion of the review session by the business and IT expert team, under the guidance of the facilitator.

4.3.7 Step 7—Manage Progressive Completion of GAF Matrices

The business and IT experts used to develop definitions in Step 4 and make changes in Step 6 are assigned to progressively complete each required governance analysis framework matrix. The matrices are reviewed and kept up to date by iterating through Steps 6 and 7. As the enterprise changes over time, these two steps are repeated periodically to ensure that all matrices reflect changes to the governance status of the enterprise, for up-to-date internal control reporting.

4.3.8 Step 8—Manage Implementation of Governance Analysis Systems

As governance analysis systems are identified to support key GAF matrices for further internal control reporting to senior management, the governance implementation plan reviewed in Step 6 is used for rapid delivery of these systems. These are managed as tactical modeling projects, as described earlier and using the same approach detailed in Steps 1 through 7 for strategic modeling projects. These systems are delivered into production in 3-month increments, using the technologies discussed in Part III.

4.4 Summary

The following is the summary:

- Internal controls will vary from enterprise to enterprise. They need to be tailored to the relevant industry or industries within which the organization operates; they are also typically unique for each enterprise.
- With the legal implications of Sarbanes-Oxley noncompliance, the inability to answer internal control reporting audit questions takes on a new personal meaning for senior managers. A governance analysis framework is needed that is both easy to create and easy to use and can be used to obtain answers for relevant internal control reporting questions.
- Senior management needs to show that answers are available that address typical internal control questions of what, how, where, who, when, and why. They are shown as columns of the Zachman framework for enterprise architecture.
- Enterprise architecture enables precise governance analysis by senior management. It also provides a very effective capability for business transformation enablement.
- An example was discussed of a governance analysis framework that uses matrices to create and maintain relationships between Zachman framework columns that enable each of these questions to be answered.
- A strategic model that is developed and tailored to an enterprise enables senior managers, middle managers, expert business staff, and IT staff to see the data, activities and processes, locations, business units and people, the business events, and the business plans that all need to be managed effectively for internal control reporting.
- From the strategic model, the governance analysis framework matrices are automatically generated. A strategic modeling project over a 25-day period identifies key data, business activities and processes, locations, business units, and business events for business plans. This is documented in an EAPP report, the main deliverable from the strategic modeling project.
- The EAPP reports produced from strategic modeling and tactical modeling projects provide the documentation and modeling tool capabilities that are needed for internal control reporting for Sarbanes-Oxley.
- As an added by-product of the governance analysis framework methods described in the chapter, similar methods and tools can also be used to implement transformed business activities and processes for business transformation enablement.

We are now ready to move to Part II, where we cover enterprise architecture methods.

Endnotes

[1] A summary of links about the Sarbanes-Oxley Act of 2002 is located at http://www.aicpa.org/sarbanes/index.asp. The full text of the act is available from these resource links as *Sarbanes-Oxley Act 072302.pdf*. A summary of key sections of the act is available at http://www.aicpa.org/info/sarbanes_oxley_summary.htm.

[2] Section 404 states that it is "the responsibility of management for establishing and maintaining an adequate internal control structure and procedures for financial reporting."

[3] The following two quotations are from *Key Issues Document–FINAL.pdf* in *2003_0822_pcaob.zip*, which can be downloaded from http://www.aicpa.org/sarbanes/index.asp.

"Management is required to document the system of internal control over financial reporting. As required by the Sarbanes-Oxley Act of 2002 (SOX), section 404 (Management Assessment of Internal Controls), management will be required to assess the effectiveness of these controls. The ASB [Auditing Standards Board] believes that the evidence management uses to support its assertion about the effectiveness of its internal control also should be documented. The ASB believes that a failure to document the system of controls or the evidence used in making the assessment should be considered a weakness in internal control...."

"Management must recognize that judgments and estimates are subject to second-guessing, and an assessment can change in a subsequent period if new information becomes available. As a result, the system of internal control over estimates is particularly sensitive because the auditor or a regulator might conclude that the internal control system was either not appropriate or not functioning because it allowed an inappropriate estimate to be booked in the first place. This will be true for any account or control where there is a greater degree of subjectivity."

[4] This maintenance over time is required to accommodate changes that occur in procedures and estimates, as specified by the SOX quotations in [3].

[5] The development of an EAPP report is described in Chapter 7.

[6] Clive Finkelstein has completed many strategic and tactical modeling projects in 20 to 25 days throughout the world. Many of these have provided rapid delivery of priority enterprise architecture areas into production in 3 to 6 months as described in Chapter 7.

[7] Further information on *Visible Advantage* and *Visible Analyst* can be obtained from Visible Systems Corporation in Lexington, Massachusetts, at http://www.visible.com. Both of these modeling tools are included on the accompanying CD-ROM.

[8] This modeling tool was previously known as *Popkin System Architect*. Popkin Software was purchased in 2005 by Telelogic. Further information is available at http://www.popkin.com.

[9] Visible provides an automatic code generation tool, *Visible Developer*, as well as a problem tracking and version control tool, *Visible Polaris,* which are also on the accompanying CD-ROM.

[10] A large government department was able to identify potential cost savings of this magnitude in the development and later maintenance of new systems for these reusable activities. They were able to eliminate much of the data redundancy in their databases.

[11] A questionnaire template is included as the Word file *Chap-03-Business Planning Questionnaire.doc* in the Book Materials folder on the accompanying CD-ROM. In Chapter 3, we saw that this is tailored to your organization for input to the business planning workshop. It also provides input for governance analysis in a strategic modeling facilitated session. See Chapter 7 for further discussion of the Strategic Modeling Questionnaire Template.

[12] Visible Advantage is typically used to carry out automatically this strategic model analysis, as discussed in Chapter 7. Further details are available at http://www.visible.com.

PART II

Enterprise Architecture Methods

Part II covers various methods for implementing enterprise architecture. The emphasis of these methods is to identify priority data, business activities, and business processes, and then deliver these priority areas in 3-month increments as production systems. Each chapter covers a specific methodology, with examples, case study exercises, and sample solutions on the accompanying CD-ROM so that readers can ensure they have a complete understanding of the relevant method.

Chapter 5: Methods for Building Enterprise Architecture. This overview chapter discusses the use of enterprise architecture for federal government and the Department of Defense (DoD) in the United States. It covers the federal enterprise architecture framework (FEAF) and the DoD architecture frameworks (C4ISR and DoDAF). It describes significant cost savings that have been achieved in past multiyear projects using enterprise architecture. The latest EA methods now enable these savings to be achieved in 3-month increments, delivering key business processes as production systems in that time frame. The steps that achieve this rapid EA delivery are covered in detail in the remaining methodology chapters of Part II.

Chapter 6: Using Business-Driven Data Mapping for Integrated Data. Data modeling has previously been used by IT data administrators in conjunction with interviewing business experts. This chapter describes a business-driven methodology for data mapping that is used by business experts and IT experts working together in a design partnership. It establishes the essential foundation for data integration, so that common data can be shared throughout an enterprise. The chapter uses many business examples, with case study exercise problems and sample solutions on the accompanying CD-ROM.

Chapter 7: Strategic Modeling for Rapid Delivery of Enterprise Architecture. This chapter describes entity dependency analysis, which is used to identify reusable business activities and business processes from data models. This is a key method that is used to derive project plans manually or automatically from data models. This method enables high priority business subprojects to be identified for delivery in 3-month increments. The method has been used during the last 20 years as an integral part of business-driven enterprise engineering, but has not previously been published or used in data modeling until now. It is a significant advance in the discipline of data modeling. The chapter shows how a strategic model is defined with senior managers in a facilitated modeling session. It discusses many business examples, with case study exercise problems and sample solutions included on the accompanying CD-ROM.

Chapter 8: Strategic Alignment, Activity and Workflow Modeling, and Business Rules. An important step in enterprise architecture is strategic alignment: so that data as well as processes, locations, people, events and business plans all support each other. This chapter shows how matrices are used to achieve this alignment; these define the governance analysis framework discussed in Chapter 4. The chapter covers activity modeling and activity-based costing to define and optimize transformed business processes. It shows how to derive workflow models from activity models. It describes how business rules can be identified for use in these workflow models. These workflow models can be used by the BPM languages discussed in Chapter 14 for automatic generation of executable XML-based code.

Chapter 9: Using Business Normalization for Future Business Needs. Traditional normalization—used widely in data modeling—is a technical discipline typically used to interview business users. This chapter describes the principles of business normalization: a business-driven method that is actively used by business experts and IT experts working together in a design partnership. It enables the knowledge of business experts to be used to define future data needs for business transformation, in a way that has not yet been effectively achieved by using traditional normalization. It includes many business examples, along with case study exercise problems and sample solutions on the accompanying CD-ROM.

Chapter 10: Menu Design, Screen Design, Performance Analysis, and Process Modeling. This chapter covers the principles used for designing menu structures and screen formats from a data model. It discusses physical database design and transaction performance analysis. It describes a technology-independent process modeling method, used to define reusable business processes that can be implemented in any programming language. This can be used with object-oriented methods and languages, as well as the new BPM languages as described in Chapter 14.

CHAPTER 5

Methods for Building Enterprise Architecture

In Part II we will cover methods for implementing enterprise architecture. In this chapter we review the federal enterprise architecture framework (FEAF) used by government departments in the United States and other countries. We also review evolution of the DoD architecture frameworks in the United States (C4ISR and DoDAF), which are also used by defense departments in other countries. We discuss the open group architecture framework (TOGAF), which is used by many commercial organizations and government agencies. We will discuss how enterprise engineering is used with these and other methods for rapid delivery of priority enterprise architecture areas into production in 3-month increments.

Enterprise architecture and enterprise engineering achieve business integration in the enterprise for more effective technology integration. But before examining enterprise architecture methods in this and the following chapters, we should briefly review the evolution of systems development methodologies.

5.1 Evolution of Systems Development Methodologies

Methodologies that have evolved since the beginning of the Information Age have helped us to examine current manual processes so we could automate them. From rudimentary methodologies in the 1960s, by the 1970s these had evolved into the *software engineering methods*. Michael Jackson [1], Ken Orr [2], Ed Yourdon [3], Tom De Marco [4], and others were key originators of the software engineering methodologies, which are also called structured methods.

5.1.1 Evolution of Software Engineering

The software engineering methods analyzed current manual processes, documenting them with data flow diagrams (DFDs) and functional decomposition diagrams (FDDs). The structure of modular programs to automate these processes was documented using structure charts (SCs). Programs were then written in various programming languages to execute the automated processes.

As discussed in the preface, in automating manual processes as is, we moved from manual chaos to automated chaos. Common manual processes, used in various parts of the enterprise, had often evolved in quite different ways. For example, a process to manually accept an order (an order entry process) may differ according to how the order was received: by mail, by phone, or from a salesperson. The process may also depend on the specific products or services ordered. The result is the evolution of different manual processes, all intended to achieve the same objective: accept an order for processing. When these processes were automated, we found we also had many automated order entry processes. We had lost sight of the principle of reusability, as discussed in Chapter 1.

This added to the automated chaos: When a change had to be made to a process, the same change had to be made to every version of that process throughout the enterprise. Every program that automated the different versions of the process had to be changed, often in slightly different ways. The result was also chaos—*program maintenance chaos!*

With software engineering, each DFD that was defined for a process identified the data that it needed as *data stores*. Each different version of the same process often resulted in redundant data store versions implemented for each automated process, moving us to *data maintenance chaos!*

Whenever a change had to be made to data values for maintenance purposes, such as by changing a customer's address, every version of that address had to be changed. This was redundant data maintenance processing. Redundant staffing was needed to do this redundant work. And because redundant data maintenance programs were developed independently, these data maintenance workers also had to be trained in the different operating procedures that were used for data entry by each data maintenance program. This resulted in redundant training.

These types of redundant costs are regularly incurred by every enterprise today: in redundant data maintenance costs for redundant data value changes, in redundant staffing, and in redundant training to carry out this work. These redundant costs have a negative effect on the bottom line—in reduced profits for commercial enterprises, and also reduced cost effectiveness for government or defense enterprises. These redundant costs can amount to hundreds of millions of dollars annually for large organizations.

5.1.2 Evolution of Information Engineering

In this same period—from the late 1960s through the early 1970s—Edgar Codd, a research fellow at IBM San Jose Labs, developed the relational model from mathematical set theory [5]. This was the foundation of the relational database technology that we still use today. The first relational database management systems (RDBMSs) were released by IBM Corporation (IBM DB2 RDBMS) and by Oracle Corporation (Oracle RDBMS) in the late 1970s and early 1980s.

From the mid-1970s, three approaches emerged, as discussed next, to apply concepts of the relational model to the methods that were used for database design. The first approach was from the United Kingdom and Europe [6, 7], the second approach was from the United States [8, 9], and the third approach was business driven and emerged independently in Australia [10]. Each addressed the development of data modeling methods, using normalization to eliminate redundant data versions.

The business-driven approach evolved into integrated methods for information, using a rigorous engineering discipline, called *information engineering* (IE). Originally developed by Clive Finkelstein [11], IE was popularized worldwide throughout the 1980s by James Martin. Further books showed the use of business-driven information engineering [12, 13]. This evolved into what is today called *enterprise engineering* (EE). Part II covers in detail the latest enterprise engineering methods as they are used for enterprise architecture.

5.1.3 Evolution of Object-Oriented Methods

In the late 1980s, the concepts of object-oriented (O-O) development and the unified modeling language (UML) were developed by Grady Booch [14, 15], James Rumbaugh [16], and Ivar Jacobson [17, 18]. Object-oriented methods based on UML were found to be very effective in developing reusable code. They use a number of diagrams to model various aspects for O-O development: class, state transition, use-case, collaboration, sequence, and activity diagrams.

Booch, Rumbaugh, and Jacobson established Rational Corporation to develop associated UML modeling tools. They popularized UML and Rational software tools, which were widely used in the late 1990s. When IBM purchased Rational Corporation in 2003, Rational became a subsidiary of IBM. The Rational software tools became IBM software tools [19] (see also Chapter 15).

5.2 Review of Enterprise Architecture

In Chapter 1 we discussed the basic concepts of enterprise architecture, with its origins in building and airplane design and construction. We were introduced to the Zachman framework for enterprise architecture, with its six columns—the interrogatives What, How, Where, Who, When, and Why. We saw five rows that represented the perspectives of Planner, Owner, Designer, Builder, and Subcontractor as illustrated in Figure 1.7 of Chapter 1. We discussed in Part I the challenge of gaining senior management support for enterprise architecture. The methods used for building enterprise architecture are described in Part II and are overviewed in this chapter.

5.2.1 Business Knowledge Is Needed for Enterprise Architecture

We saw in Chapter 1 that enterprise architecture should be applied in a top-down approach using business-driven methods. Business expertise is therefore critical. Enterprise architecture requires business specialist experts, including IT, to work together in the same project team in a *design partnership*. Business experts know the business; IT experts know the capability and limitations of computers. They each need to draw on their respective areas of expertise as each cell of the Zachman framework is defined in detail.

Enterprise architecture builds on this business knowledge and allows business specialist experts—with technical expertise from IT experts—to apply their respective knowledge to determine the most effective technology and process solutions for the business. Business and IT experts are both critical decision resources for your enterprise. This point is illustrated next by some nontechnical, business-oriented examples.

5.2.2 Technology Decisions Using Enterprise Architecture

IT today is regarded as an "overhead" commodity expense by many enterprises. Because of its potential long-term impact on an enterprise, IT decisions should be treated exactly like any other business investment decision. For example, the following criteria apply to every investment decision made by the business, whether for building a new plant, building a new manual system, or building a new automated system:

- What costs are involved in building the particular plant/system?
- What benefits will be delivered by the completed plant/system?
- How long will it take for the completed plant/system to realize these benefits?
- What is the expected ROI that will be delivered by the completed plant/system?
- Will the completed plant/system enhance (or inhibit) future *business flexibility?*

The most important criterion is the last bulleted point. Any plant or system that is built today must support and enhance the ability of the business to change rapidly—whenever required—in the future, *because the only thing that is stable today ... is CHANGE itself!!!*

Plants or systems that are built today must be capable of being changed easily, fast, and often! The emphasis of enterprise architecture in row 1 (Planner) and row 2 (Owner) leads to a corporate ability to change rapidly: through the use of common, shared data, and through common, reusable activities and processes. This is a key tenet of business transformation enablement.

5.2.3 Enterprise Architecture and the Pace of Change

We discussed in Chapter 1 that most technology decisions that are based on traditional systems development approaches do not enable the enterprise to change easily—if at all. They focus on automating current business processes. Yet business processes are typically the most volatile parts of enterprises.

To be able to be changed easily, rapidly, and often, systems must be built on the most stable part of the enterprise. Today, processes are extremely volatile, but data are much more stable. Consider the following examples:

- Accounting processes in the past involved pencil, paper, and double ledger accounts. Today most accounting processes are automated. Yet the data on which accounting is based have not changed to the same extent, *not for hundreds of years.*
- Banking in the nineteenth and early twentieth centuries involved passbooks with handwritten teller entries. Today most banking is automated via ATMs, phone banking, or Internet banking. The banking processes have completely changed. Yet the data held by each bank have not changed to the same extent, *not for hundreds of years.*

- Building processes have changed over the years with new building technologies and materials. Yet the data used for the design and construction of buildings have not changed to the same extent, *not for hundreds of years.*

Data do change, but they change much more slowly than processes. We discussed in Chapter 1 that current business processes in most enterprises are based on strategic plans set by management some 5 or 10 years ago. The systems for tomorrow must be based on strategic plans that are defined today, for that future tomorrow.

We also discussed that the processes of yesterday assumed that communication with customers or suppliers took days or weeks (via mail). With the processes of today and tomorrow this communication now takes minutes—often seconds. In fact the processes of yesterday (designed for communication over days and weeks) may not work well in the rapid response and rapid business change environment of today, let alone tomorrow.

The only thing we can be certain of is that today and tomorrow are quite different from yesterday. Business activities and processes will almost certainly change, often much faster than the existing systems in an enterprise can themselves be changed. This ability to change rapidly is a major focus of enterprise architecture for business transformation.

5.3 Government Methods for Building Enterprise Architecture

There has been much activity in defining approaches for building enterprise architecture. We will cover some of these approaches in this section. References are provided where additional information about each approach can be found.

We first discuss the federal enterprise architecture framework. This mandates—by law—that all U.S. federal government departments must use enterprise architecture. We next examine how enterprise architecture was introduced into the DoD, and how it has been adopted by defense departments in many other countries.

5.3.1 Federal Enterprise Architecture Framework

The U.S. federal government has mandated that enterprise architecture be used by all government departments and agencies, as detailed in the Clinger-Cohen Act of 1996. This is the basis for the federal enterprise architecture framework (FEAF), defined by the U.S. government CIO council. The FEAF is well documented and readily available from the Internet [20]. The FEAF approaches enterprise architecture from four levels:

- *Level I:* This is referred to as the view from 20,000 feet. When parachuting from a plane, the earth is very distant from this height. This is the highest FEAF level, introducing eight major federal enterprise architecture components: architecture drivers, strategic direction, current architecture, target architecture, transitional processes, architectural segments, architectural models, and standards.

- *Level II:* This represents the view from 10,000 feet. The earth is also indistinct from this height. Level II expands detail in the eight components that are needed for federal enterprise architecture. It shows greater detail of the business and design components of the federal enterprise architecture.
- *Level III:* This is the view from 5,000 feet. Some detail is apparent, but it is still blurry. The FEAF report states that [20]: "It shows three design architectures: data, applications, and technology."
- *Level IV:* This is the view from 1,000 to 500 feet. From this level the detail can be overwhelming as the earth rushes toward you. The FEAF report comments [20]: "It identifies the kinds of models that define the business architecture and the first three design architectures: data, applications, and technology. It defines enterprise architecture planning."

The first three levels provide high-level views of the enterprise architecture. It is only at Level III that a relationship to the Zachman framework is seen. The FEAF report clearly shows how the FEAF maps to the Zachman framework.

The federal enterprise architecture framework draws on the work by Dr. Steven Spewak called *Enterprise Architecture Planning* [21]. This work provides guidance on how to define the top two rows of the Zachman framework, for the Planner and Owner. The design of systems is defined in row 3 (Designer) of the Zachman framework. The FEAF makes the point that the EAP approach used by Spewak does *not* address design [20]. It is different from the EAPP discussed in Chapters 1, 4, and 7. Spewak's enterprise architecture planning is described in the FEAF report as follows [20]:

> EAP defines the blueprint for subsequent design and implementation and it places the planning/defining stages into a framework. It does not explain how to define the top two rows of the Zachman Framework in detail but for the sake of the planning exercise, abbreviates the analysis. The Zachman Framework provides the broad context for the description of the architecture layers, while EAP focuses on planning and managing the process of establishing the business alignment of the architectures.

EAP is planning that focuses on the development of matrices for comparing and analyzing data, applications, and technology. Most important, EAP produces an implementation plan. Within the Federal enterprise architecture, EAP will be completed segment enterprise by segment enterprise.

The approach used by Spewak is expanded in Figure 5.1. The following discussion from the FEAF report refers to the four EAP "layers" shown in Figure 5.1 [20].

- *Layer 1—Getting Started:* This layer leads to producing an EAP work plan and stresses the necessity of high-level management commitment to support and resource the subsequent six components (or steps) of the process. Planning initiation covers, in general, decisions on which methodology to use, who should be involved, what other support is required, and what toolset will be used.
- *Layer 2—Where We Are Today:* This layer provides a baseline for defining the architecture to be and the long-range migration plan. Business Modeling is a

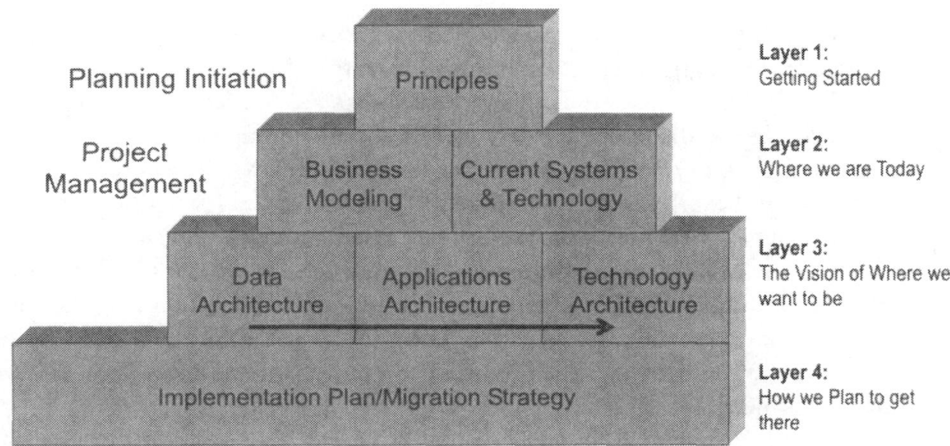

Figure 5.1 Layers of Spewak enterprise architecture planning. (*From:* [21]. © 1992 S. Spewak. Reprinted with permission.)

compilation of a knowledge base about the business functions and the information used in conducting and supporting the various business processes. Current Systems & Technology defines current application systems and supporting technology platforms.

- *Layer 3—The Vision of Where We Want to Be:* The arrows delineate the basic definition process flow: data architecture, applications architecture, and technology architecture. Data Architecture defines the major kinds of data needed to support the business. Applications Architecture defines the major kinds of applications needed to manage that data and support the business functions. Technology Architecture defines the technology platforms needed to support the applications that manage the data and support the business functions.
- *Layer 4—How We Plan to Get There:* Implementation Plan/Migration Strategy defines the sequence for implementing applications, and lays out a schedule for implementation, a cost/benefit analysis, and a clear path for migration.

Level IV of the FEAF redefines the Zachman framework based on the terminology used throughout Version 1.1 of the FEAF report. These terms are mapped to the first three columns of Zachman framework (What, How, and Where) as follows:

- Data Architecture is mapped to column 1 (What);
- Applications Architecture is mapped to column 2 (How);
- Technology Architecture is mapped to column 3 (Where).

However, the perspectives (rows) of the Zachman framework are not changed. They are used without modification with the Zachman terminology for Planner, Owner, Designer, Builder, and Subcontractor in the federal enterprise architecture framework.

The FEAF was initially developed based on the first three Zachman interrogatives, the What, How, and Where columns. The FEAF report therefore includes a complete definition of the content of the 15 cells of these first three columns of the

Zachman framework (see Figure 1.7). It includes a similar definition in an Appendix (added later) to document the content of the other 15 cells: Who, When, and Why.

The FEAF also uses the concept of "slivers" as vertical and horizontal portions of a cell. As we discussed earlier, we will be more precise in this chapter. We will refer to a *horizontal slice* as a high-level view within a cell, whereas a *vertical sliver* moves to an "excruciating level of detail" within the cell (to quote John Zachman).

The actual FEAF is composed of five basic models as shown in Figure 5.2. The use of these models and demonstrating compliance is crucial for Office of Management and Budget (OMB) approval for resources. The FEAF models, as well as useful information pertaining to the FEAF and how to use it, are available for download [22]. Figure 5.2 illustrates the hierarchical relationship between these five models, as discussed next.

The Performance Reference Model (PRM) is a framework for performance measurement that provides common application measures throughout the federal government. It allows agencies to better manage the business of government at a federal strategic level while providing a means for gauging progress toward the target FEA. Version 1.0 of the PRM was issued in September 2003 in two volumes: with the first one detailing the model; and the second one focusing on how to use it.

The Business Reference Model (BRM) in Figure 5.2 is a function-driven framework for describing the business operations of the federal government independent of agencies that perform them. At the time of this writing, the BRM was in its second revision and Version 2.1 (with the defense addendum) had been published.

The Service Component Reference Model (SRM) is business driven and is a functional framework that classifies service components and describes how they support business and/or performance objectives. The SRM, constructed hierarchically, is structured across horizontal service areas that provide a foundation for reuse of applications, application capabilities, components, and business services. Version 1.0 was completed in June 2003.

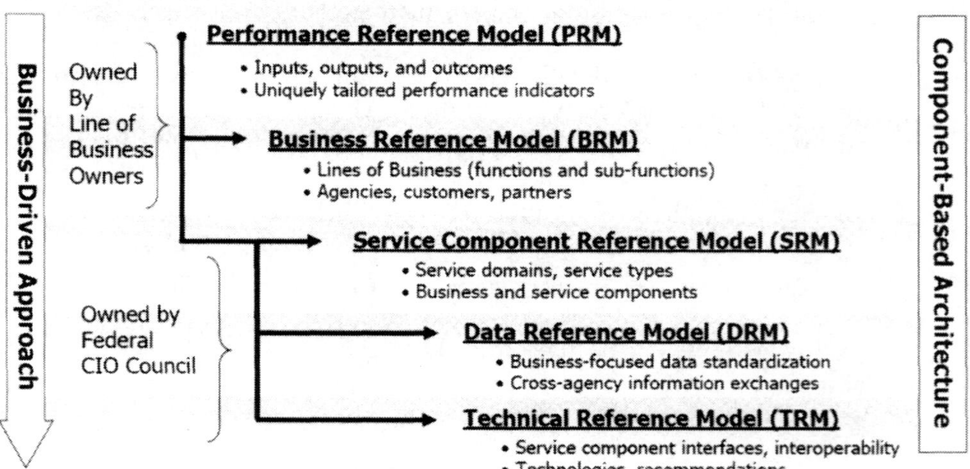

Figure 5.2 Five basic reference models of the FEAF and their relationship to each other. (*From:* [22]. © 2004 FEA Program Management Office. Reprinted with permission.)

The Technical Reference Model (TRM), for which Version 1.0 is now available, was created to:

- Provide a government-wide reference model that unifies agency TRMs and existing e-government guidance.
- Focus technology standards, specifications, and recommendations on those that embrace the Internet and related approaches.
- Create a foundation that focuses heavily on the secure delivery and construction of service components and their interfaces.
- Identify layers of a component-based architecture, the supporting technologies, and recommendations for each.

The Data Reference Model (DRM) was released October 20, 2004. It describes, at an aggregate level, the data and information that support program and business line operations. The first DRM volume states that it is "the starting point from which data architects should develop modeling standards and concepts." It is stated as the "foundation, which describes essential components for later DRM Volumes. These combined volumes support data classification—thus enabling horizontal and vertical information sharing."

The aim of the FEA reference models is to ensure that technology is business-driven and the emphasis is on standardizing the business functions (Zachman rows 1 and 2 in column 2) in the BRM. This function-driven approach was useful in that it enabled departments and agencies to rationalize their information technology infrastructures across the various lines of business, services, and/or programs.

As shown in Figure 5.3, these business functions were directly linked to one or more service components that enabled their execution. Subsequently, the components were then linked to the TRM that detailed the technologies to be employed to implement the components. The DRM enables both government developers and software vendors to have clear-cut guidelines for creation of a new generation of

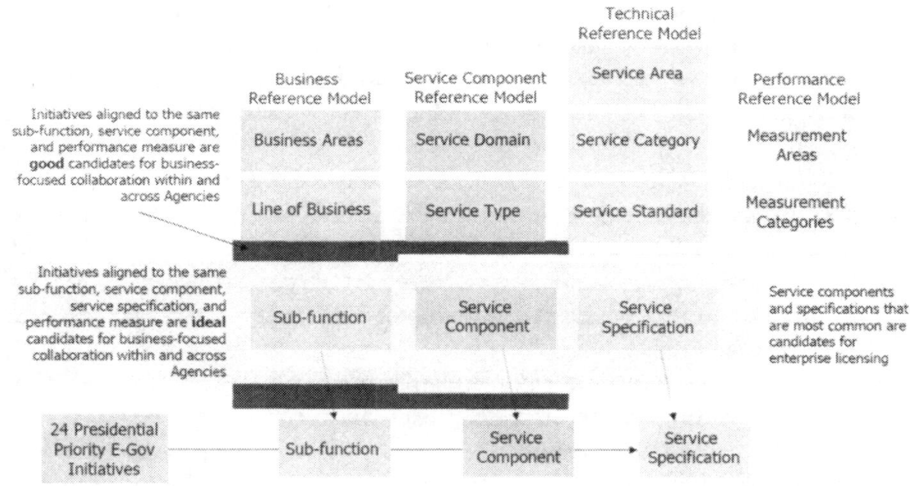

Figure 5.3 FEA reference model integration. (*From:* [22]. © 1992 FEA Program Management Office. Reprinted with permission.)

interoperable commercial/government-off-the-shelf (COTS/GOTS) products to be reused throughout government.

The FEAF is a good example of an enterprise approach used to decrease the overall size of the IT footprint within government with associated huge operations and maintenance costs. The real key is governance and enforcement of compliance plus the establishment of effective cross-government cooperation.

The FEAF report concludes with a discussion of returns, risks, and costs of enterprise architecture, with an analysis of typical costs and cost savings quoted from Larry English.

The CIO Council also published a *Practical Guide to Federal Enterprise Architecture* [23]. This provides guidance on how to plan and manage a federal enterprise architecture project using the FEAF. But it is inadequate if used as the sole source for enterprise architecture guidance because it does not provide any assistance with methods for defining the various artifacts or models in each cell. That is the purpose of this chapter.

5.3.2 Relating the FEAF to the Zachman Framework

Both the federal enterprise architecture framework and Spewak enterprise architecture planning are well-defined approaches to planning and managing enterprise architecture in large complex environments. We discussed in Chapter 1 that the Zachman framework is a rigorous approach to thinking about and managing the design and construction of complex enterprises. But we should note an important point in relation to the FEAF [22]:

> There is little direction or advice provided by the FEAF or by the Spewak EAP—and only broad guidance from John Zachman—on the detailed methods for implementing enterprise architecture.

We will now discuss in more detail within this chapter how the FEAF can be used to map to the Zachman framework. We will start with Figure 5.4, which broadly maps business architecture (initiation and business modeling) to row 1 (Planner) and row 2 (Owner). The implementation strategy in Figure 5.5—plus the current systems and technology—both address row 3 (Designer). The technology architecture maps to row 4 (Builder), row 5 (Subcontractor), and to the actual system.

It is only at Spewak EAP layer 3 (see Figure 5.2) that there is any clear focus on the data architecture, applications architecture, and technology architecture. As discussed earlier, these architectures map to the What [C1], How [C2], and Where [C3] columns, respectively, and also address part of row 2 (Owner). Much rigor is needed in these columns, which is the focus of EAP layer 3 for business transformation enablement.

We will see later that rigor is also important for the Who [C4], When [C5], and Why [C6] columns. Insufficient effort—except at initiation in layer 1—is made in the FEAF or EAP to address these columns. Yet we discussed that Why [C6] is a key column to address if needs for the future are to be considered. We discussed that a focus only on operational processes still used today will inhibit our ability to change in the future.

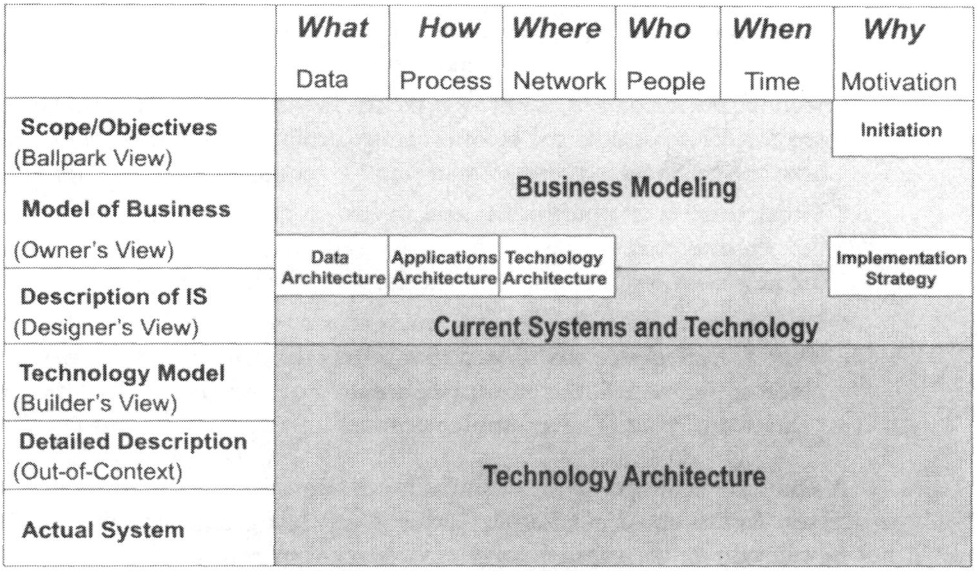

What Data
How Process
Where Network
Who People
When Time
Why Motivation

Scope/Objectives (Ballpark View)
Model of Business (Owner's View)
Description of IS (Designer's View)
Technology Model (Builder's View)
Detailed Description (Out-of-Context)
Actual System

Initiation
Business Modeling
Data Architecture
Applications Architecture
Technology Architecture
Implementation Strategy
Current Systems and Technology
Technology Architecture

Figure 5.4 Broad mapping of Spewak EAP and FEAF to the Zachman framework. (*From:* [24]. © 2005 Robert Weisman, CGI. Reprinted with permission.)

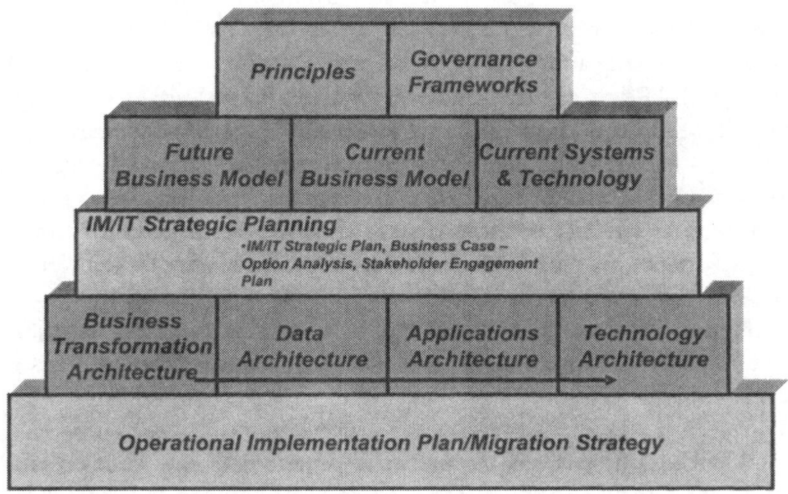

Figure 5.5 The Enterprise Architecture Method (EAM), the copyright which is a CGI extension to Spewak's EAP. (*From:* [25]. © 2005 CGI. Reprinted with permission.)

As people have applied the FEAF and EAP to real-life projects, some difficulties due to a lack of guidance in these areas have become apparent. For example, Figure 5.5 shows a modified version of Spewak's EAP that led to the creation of the Enterprise Architecture Method (EAM) developed and used by CGI [24]. There are four major differences between the two methods:

- First, the CGI EAM assumes that a CEO does not want to build or optimize an information technology infrastructure based on current business processes. It assumes that the enterprise architecture is part of an overall and ongoing corporate business transformation process.

- Second, the terms and use of architecture are not addressed until layer 4 in Figure 5.5. This includes the business transformation architecture that deals with how the business is going to adapt and leverage the new technology.
- Third, there is an operational and an earlier strategic planning phase included that ensures that the business transformation effort is aligned with and drives the new data, applications, and technology architectures.
- Last, a focus on governance frameworks has been added to Spewak's EAP layer 1. Experience has shown that unless the governance frameworks are in place in Figure 5.5, the enterprise architecture effort will founder or become "shelfware" that is never implemented.

A common tendency with business modeling at layer 2 is to focus on existing processes. As discussed in Chapter 1, this is very dangerous; today's processes may not be relevant to the rapid change environment of today and tomorrow. Spewak emphasizes that models should be based on *what* the organization does and not *how* it does it. He states that *what* an organization does is more stable over time, whereas *how* it does things can change. He emphasizes that architectures should be built against stable structures.

We will see in Chapter 8 that this emphasis on "what an organization does" suggests a focus on business activities rather than on business processes, which detail "how." It is true that activities are more stable than processes. But the emphasis taken by EAP is still functional: Activities and processes both appear in column 2. We will see in this chapter that a more stable focus addresses why, who, what, and when at a high level to identify potential reusable activities, before defining business processes in detail. If enterprise architecture projects address processes first, an organization's ability to think clearly about opportunities for tomorrow based on its strategic plans may be limited. It may limit its ability to make the changes that are necessary to move to that tomorrow.

Figure 5.5 thus expands layer 2 by changing business modeling to two components: a future business model and a current business model. An analogy will help us here:

> When hacking our way through an impenetrable jungle while on safari, it is hard to see far ahead. We try to plan our direction by standing on tiptoes. But we can see further if we climb a tree. Or better still, when we climb a mountain. Perhaps the best way ahead is not to continue in the direction we are presently moving. There may be more opportunities if we change direction.

This is the reason for strategic planning: to look further ahead; to plan our new direction on what we want to achieve in the future, rather than continue the current direction and processes based on strategic plans that were set 5 or 10 years ago in a less volatile era. Figure 5.5 suggests that the future business model should be defined *before* the current business model, so as not to inhibit our thinking for the future.

Notice also in Figure 5.5 that IM/IT strategic planning is applied before layer 3, which also includes business transformation architecture. This takes into account the business transformation that may be required to transition from the current business model to the planned future business model.

With refinements, the FEAF and Spewak EAP have served government departments well, not only in the United States but also in many other government departments throughout the world. It has also been used by defense departments.

5.4 Department of Defense Architecture Frameworks

This section discusses how enterprise architecture has been used by many defence forces throughout the world. We will see how the U.S. Department of Defense, the Canadian Department of National Defence (DND), the Australian Defence Organisation (ADO), and the U.K. Ministry of Defence all based their enterprise architecture approaches on the Zachman framework. They modified it for their highly complex environments, to achieve their objectives of *joint force interoperability.*

I will use the spelling *defense* in this section when I am specifically referring to the U.S. Department of Defense (DoD). I will use the other spelling of *defence* when I am referring to all defence organizations, including the United States, Australia, United Kingdom, Canada, and NATO.

5.4.1 Defence Planning Terminology

A point must first be emphasized here on the planning terminology used by defence organizations throughout the world, and the terminology that is also used by commercial and government organizations.

Commercial and Government Planning Terminology

The business planning terminology that we use in Parts I and II is based on widely accepted strategic planning concepts for commercial and government organizations. It defines a hierarchy of plans, as follows:

- *Strategic plans,* which apply at the highest levels of the enterprise;
- *Tactical plans,* which apply at middle management levels of the enterprise;
- *Operational plans,* which apply at the lowest, detailed levels of the enterprise.

This commercial and government business planning terminology has evolved during the last 50 years, from the earliest application of strategic planning methods in the 1950s.

Defence Planning Terminology

In contrast, defence organizations throughout the world have used a different hierarchy for planning and have done so for hundreds of years. The defence planning terminology uses the same words, but they have a different meaning from that used by commercial and government organizations. The defence terminology hierarchy progresses as follows:

- *Strategic plans,* which apply at the highest levels of the enterprise;
- *Operational plans,* which apply at middle management levels of the enterprise;
- *Tactical plans,* which apply at the lowest, detailed levels of the enterprise.

Within this section for defence, I will defer to the defence terminology just listed. Elsewhere in this book I will revert back and use the commercial and government business planning terminology given in the earlier list.

5.4.2 The Need for Defence Interoperability

Command, control, and communications (C3) have been important factors in the success of defence forces throughout history. In the most recent wars, computers have also become critical to warfighting, expanding the factors to C4. From World War I, through all of the wars of the twentieth century and into the twenty-first century, the separate services have increasingly coordinated their warfighting activities, across the army, air force, navy, and marines.

There are two major challenges in defence today when it comes to the new warfighting paradigm. First, there are combined operations whereby similar services from various nations fight together, such as air forces, navies, and armies. This underlies the need for international interoperability. Second, there is the need to fight jointly with dissimilar services such as those operations involving the army, navy, and air force together (see Figure 5.6).

Today most nations have armed forces that use single-service stovepipe systems, from vision through to procurement. In places such as Afghanistan, Bosnia, and Iraq, the nations have to use armed forces that are capable of conducting both joint and combined operations. Major advances have been made but the need for effective

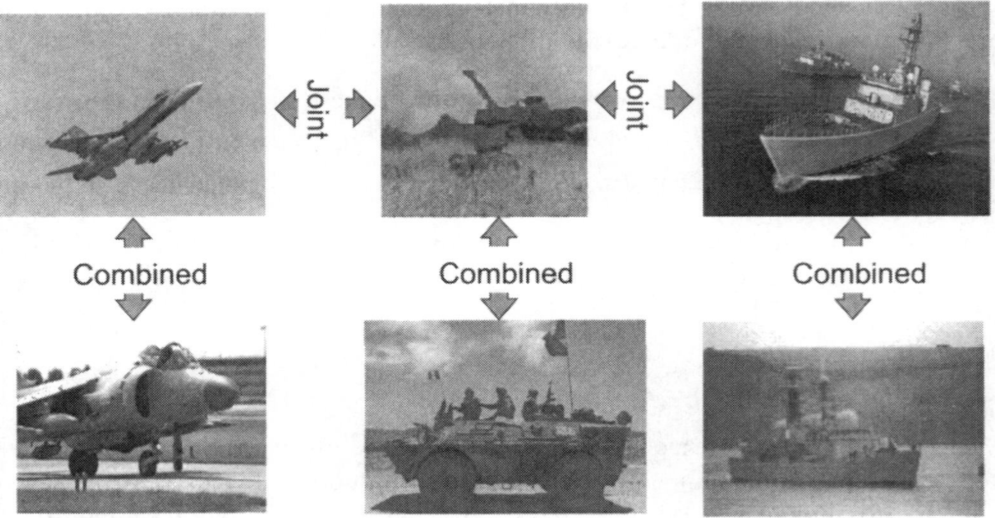

Figure 5.6 Joint and combined defense interoperability is needed. (*From:* [25]. © 2005 Robert Weisman, CGI. Reprinted with permission.)

but flexible enterprise architecture is critical to ensuring that the sophisticated and lethal weaponry employed by these armed forces is only employed when absolutely necessary and then only against legitimate targets of war, instead of friendly, neutral, or disinterested parties. It is hardly surprising to note that the U.S. DoD and other NATO nations have long been involved in the formulation of enterprise architectures to achieve interoperability, which is being increasingly focused on the ability to share information as well as services and equipment.

Another complicating factor is that the nature of future partners in a much wider range of upcoming conflicts is uncertain. In fixed alliances such as NATO, nations always knew their partners. But a move to coalition operations with many potential colleagues and widely varying skills, equipment, military sophistication, and languages have made the effective and safe conduct of military operations very challenging. Additionally there is a need to ensure that information is secure and not accessed by those who are not authorized to access it.

To achieve this security, the DoD enterprise architecture framework was called C4ISR (command, control, communications, computers, intelligence, surveillance, reconnaissance). This has since evolved to the DoD architecture framework (DoDAF). DoDAF will be discussed in more detail shortly.

Interoperability is a critical success factor in warfighting, as becomes clear in the following comments from the U.S. Air Force (USAF) air mobility command (AMC) [26]:

> Interoperability in Defence is the key issue. The United States Department of Defense (DoD) has hundreds of systems that were built at various times with different objectives. These systems were designed to optimize function over the use of standardized data and a common infrastructure. This approach to designing and building systems forced information integration to be accomplished after-the-fact and at the human level versus the computer or machine level. Interfaces to these systems became both complex and difficult to maintain. Changes in any aspect of either data or technology can cause the interface to fail and information to be lost.

The USAF AMC continues with an example of the dangers of a lack of interoperability [26]:

> An approach to interoperability has focused on standardized messaging within the DoD. The United States Message Text Formatting (USMTF) became the standard for transmitting messages that could be machine readable. The standard was implemented in the late 1980's but relied on the aging Automated Digital Network (AUTODIN) messaging system infrastructure.
>
> The rapid build up of troops in the Gulf region in 1991 far exceeded any exercises conducted by the U.S. military in the 1970's and 1980's. The movement of over 500 thousand troops and their associated equipment stressed both the communications and transportation systems. Troops were deployed using commercial charter aircraft and would marry up with equipment that was shipped by either sea or air lift. Backlogs at both the aerial and sea ports were common.
>
> There were documented cases where units were at an air terminal waiting for the remainder of equipment to arrive when two aircraft were in-bound, but only one could land because of ramp restrictions. A decision had to be made on which aircraft to divert. At the time, U.S. Forces were still using the AUTODIN messaging

systems, and it actually took longer to get the message from the debarkation (point in the USA) back to the embarkation (point in the Gulf) than it took for the airplane to fly between locations. As a result, the wrong plane was often diverted—thus complicating the entire process, and causing additional backlogs.

Interoperability issues still plagued the U.S. Military in 1999. During action in 1999 against Serbian air defenses, F-16s had problems with interoperability. On one particular mission a flight of four F-16s were on an air defenses suppression mission. Two of the aircraft had Block 50 counter-radar systems used to identify enemy anti-aircraft radar sites. The two other F-16s were equipped with Block 40 close-air support systems. These two systems could not share information directly. Pilots flying these missions had to share information via radio communications. This added dimension increased risk, took more time, and was less secure. The combatants need interoperability among these sophisticated systems.

Defence departments worldwide are using technology to achieve a revolution in military awareness (RMA). According to the Canadian Department of National Defence [27], the RMA:

> Is a major change in the nature of warfare brought about by the innovative application of new technologies which, combined with dramatic changes in military doctrine and operational and organizational concepts, fundamentally alters the character and conduct of military operations....

The point is that the technological capabilities are outstripping the ability to act on the rapidly changing battlespace knowledge. Near-perfect mission assignment based on enhanced battlespace knowledge and executed by timely precision force that is applied accurately requires a tightly coupled integrated business and technology approach. The threat of an opponent with similar capabilities and possibly a faster mission assignment business process is a definite motivating factor.

Enterprise architecture can assist in specifying an integrated business approach, but the following section will deal with practical solutions to ensure that battle assessment and battlespace knowledge is delivered to commanders so that they can achieve near-perfect mission assignment, whether assisting a non-governmental agency delivering food and medical supplies or annihilating an enemy counterattack.

One of the challenges with enterprise architecture implementation is that there is often no perceived concrete example of the architecture; it appears to be analytical. A common integrated technology (or operating) environment is a clear outcome of an EA exercise. There are several ways to achieve this standardization and much depends on the nature of the business needs and the implementing organization. The following sections discuss several different implementations within defense. Alternative approaches can be used as listed next and discussed in the following paragraphs [28]:

- *Approach 1:* common integrated technology environments;
- *Approach 2:* integrated technology and information environments;
- *Approach 3:* partially integrated technology and information;
- *Approach 4:* federated information and technology environment.

5.4.3 Approach 1: Common Integrated Technology Environments

The obvious way of enabling the rapid and integrated transmission of information to commanders was to have them all use the same systems. Given the nature of joint and combined operations and the thousands of existing systems, this idealistic solution was not practical. Enterprise architecture enabled the establishment of a strategic perspective that facilitated information sharing with: a common representation of shared information—what [C1]; a common process to share information—how [C2]; and a means with which to establish the requisite connectivity—where [C3]; with the right people—who [C4]; at the appropriate time—when [C5]; for the right and authorized reasons—why [C6].

5.4.4 Approach 2: Integrated Technology and Information Environments

The NATO joint operations and intelligence information system (JOIIS) is a good example of where one completely integrated environment supports traditionally separate business functions (namely, operations and intelligence) achieved within a united organizational structure: in NATO operations and used in NATO headquarters. In the integrated HQ, all operations and intelligence staff officers share information and technology perspectives instantaneously. There are no internal system interfaces, just those to external systems. The result is a reduced IT footprint, reduced operations and maintenance costs, and, most importantly, a consistent common operational picture across the two most important staff functions.

One of the other major advantages to a completely integrated system is the common presentation layer that makes transitioning from one staff function to another much easier. In the military where business continuity planning is a way of life, this allows staff officers and commanders to conduct operations and access information in a standard manner in spite of the loss of primary commanders and staff.

5.4.5 Approach 3: Partially Integrated Technology and Information

In large and/or complex organizations with major investments in existing systems, the risk of implementing any change has to be pragmatically managed. One approach is to incrementally implement an ever-increasing common environment. The U.S. defense information infrastructure (DII), illustrated in Figure 5.7, is such an example whereby the standardization process evolved slowly and focused on establishing a common set of functional services/components.

The primary focus of Figure 5.7 is to share information, for which a common information environment evolved based on rapid communications. The common communications environment using standard information interchange and data management functionality resulted in the common operating environment (COE). The individual systems using the DII could focus on the business functions, such as operations and combat support, and would only provide those services and components that were not provided by the DII.

Once these components were proven, then they could be considered for eventual inclusion in the DII. Figure 5.7 illustrates that the defense information infrastructure supports global command and control systems, global combat support systems, and other DII-based systems.

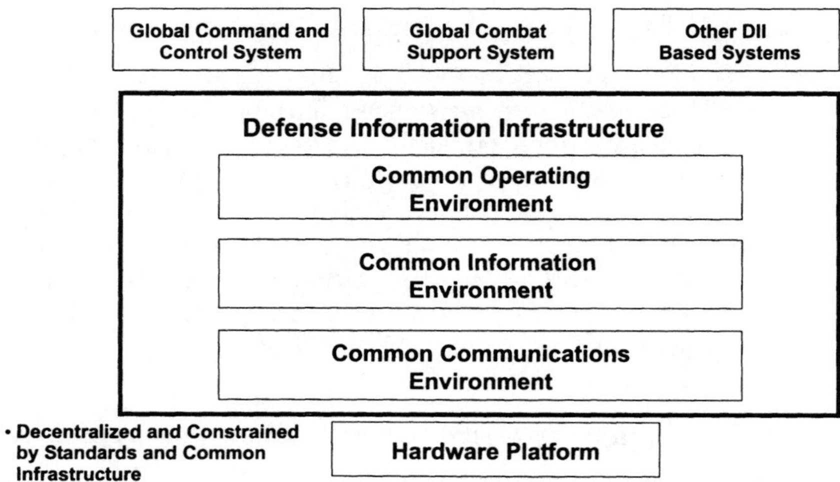

Figure 5.7 Defense information infrastructure. (*From:* [28]. © 2004 Robert Weisman, CGI. Reprinted with permission.)

Figure 5.8 illustrates the complexity of an initial version of the U.S. global command and control system (GCCS). It is indeed an enterprise architecture framework variant with the rows inverted. It shows that business is the underpinning foundation of the technology-based system with a series of proofs of concept and the joint universal data interpreter (JUDI). Although technological innovations such as the JUDI are no longer used, the diagram shows the complexity that just one of the systems using the DII has to address. Other systems are just as complex. Note that the GCCS initially focused on interoperability at the messaging level, using the U.S. Message Text Format and XML-based technologies that we will discuss in Part III.

One of the major features of the U.S. defense information infrastructure, and indeed all of the shared infrastructures, is that they are constantly evolving. As previously stated, the risk of changing to share common components has to be managed

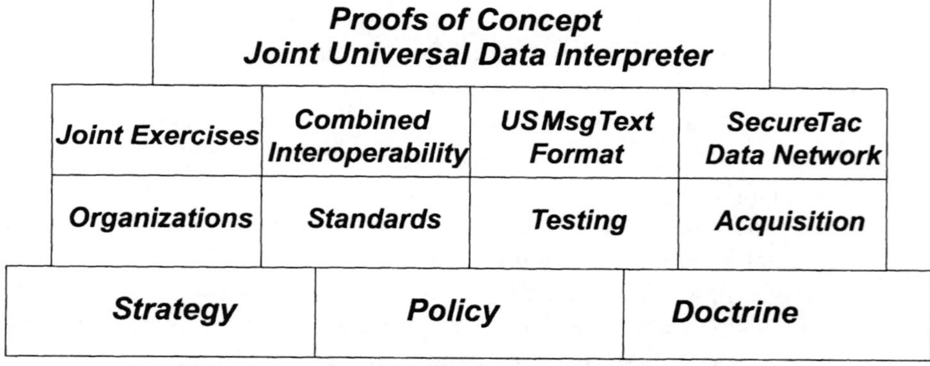

Figure 5.8 U.S. DISA C4I FTW implementation plan for a global command and control system. (*From:* [28]. © 2004 Robert Weisman, CGI. Reprinted with permission.)

and the best way to do it is to go in stages. Figure 5.9 further shows an extremely simplified perspective of the evolution through three stages within the U.S. DoD to a COE: (1) prior to the Gulf War, (2) from 1992 to 1995, and (3) from 1996 to 2000.

One of the major challenges for industry is to keep the acronyms straight and recognize how the concepts are interrelated; these relationships are really critical to ensure that defense clients are optimally supported by contractors. The United States is not the only nation that has a common environment; Figure 5.10 illustrates a very simplified view of the evolution of the U.K. defence environment (which is still converging).

The defence departments in Australia and Canada are following similar paths with their COE and common user core, respectively. Note that the common user core (CUC) term in Canada was specifically conceived to differentiate it from other COE efforts that were initially technology focused. The CUC focused on information sharing and technology harmonization rather than standardization.

A major advantage of sharing information within a COE or a CUC (for the Canadian DND) is the reduction of complexity. Before an information management review in the early 1990s (where information management also included both information holdings and information technology), it was discovered that many of the larger projects were putting in their own wide-area networks. These did not even consider standardization of their information holdings but depended on a system-to-system set of interfaces. The newly formed Defence Information Services Organization (DISO; now called the Defence Information Management Group) standardized the network layer, and the single services each harmonized their information holdings.

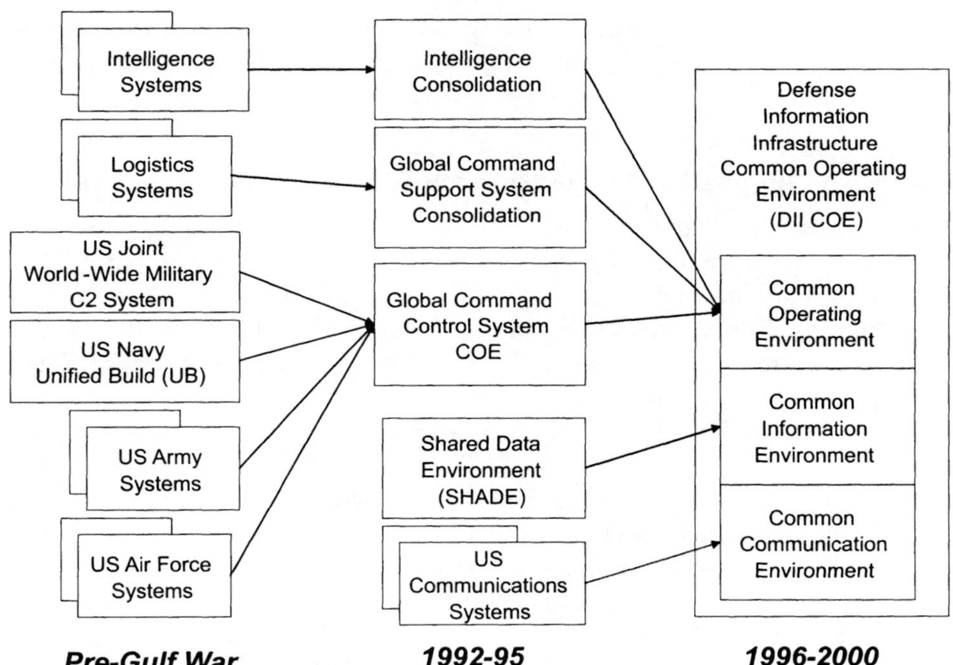

Figure 5.9 Some DoD COE trends. (*From:* [28]. © 2004 Robert Weisman, CGI. Reprinted with permission.)

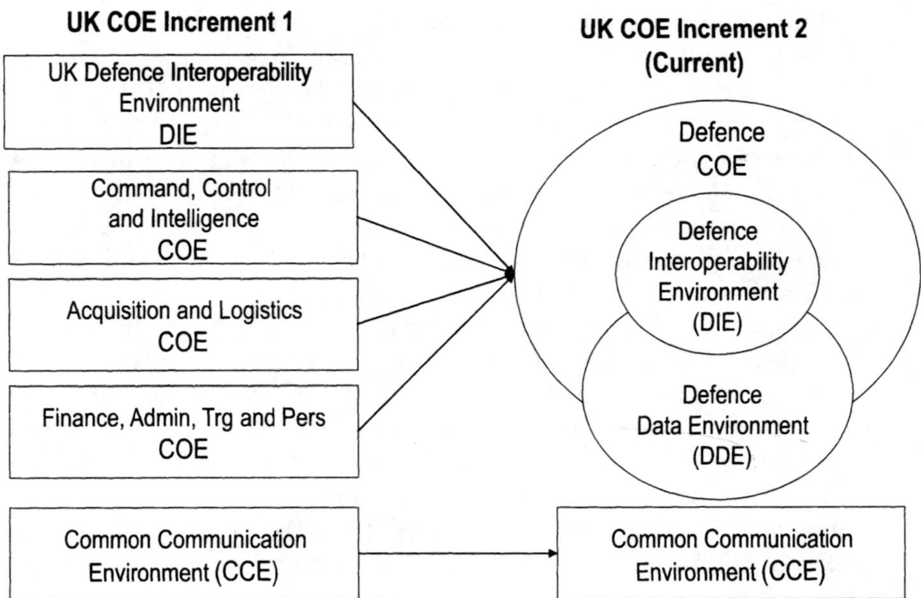

Figure 5.10 U.K. defence COE. (*From:* [28]. © 2004 Robert Weisman, CGI. Reprinted with permission.)

As pathfinder for the Canadian national defence, the army implemented their information management strategy and implemented their initial performance measurement system. This rolled information from the unit up to the national level. It included the use of the emerging army tactical command and control information system (ATCCIS) standard NATO *data feeds* [29]. The first measurement area was operational effectiveness, which was of great interest and relevance to both operational as well as strategic level command and control. This concept is illustrated in Figure 5.11.

5.4.6 Approach 4: Federated Information and Technology Environment

In an alliance, coalition, or any grouping of nations, a flexible approach has to be taken for any potential integration of information or services. Indeed the main focus is to share information and anything else is a bonus. Information security between nations is a major challenge, but the impetus of ongoing allied and coalition operations across the world—with very little warning—has led to significant and pragmatic achievements.

A major example of interoperability efforts is the Army Tactical Command and Control Information Systems (ATCCIS) effort (discussed earlier), which is supported by Supreme Headquarters Allied Powers Europe (SHAPE), a subordinate headquarters to NATO. Many NATO nations cooperated for more than a decade to evolve a data standard for information sharing and accompanying processes. The data model became the NATO Land Command and Control Information Exchange Data (LCCIED) model.

The information exchange data model concept used by NATO is a nonthreatening way to gain acceptance of a data standard without the perception

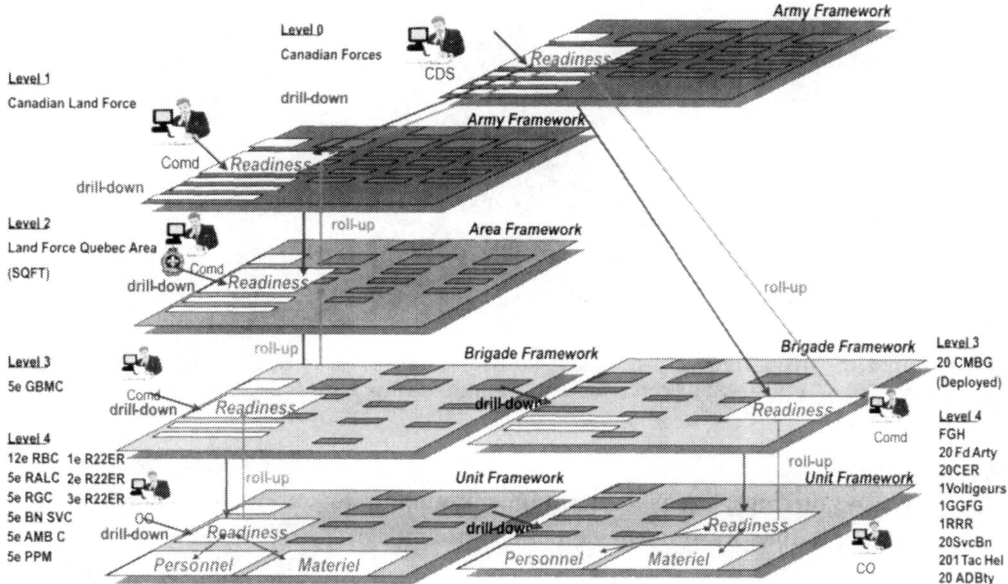

Figure 5.11 Defence drill-down and roll-up functionalities in this Canadian army example. (*Source:* © 2004 Robert Weisman, CGI. Reprinted with permission.)

that its use within national systems is mandatory. However, certain nations have given up trying to integrate their command and control systems and have just used the data model as the basis for a new integrated system. By using the alliance standard data model, it saved the nations millions of dollars in information model development and years of consensus building to gain acceptance. It also saved millions of dollars by making the interfaces to share alliance information trivial through the use of the technologies discussed in Part III.

5.4.7 Evolution of Enterprise Architecture Within DoD

The application of enterprise architecture principles to the DoD coincided also with the definition of the U.S. federal government FEAF, in response to the Clinger-Cohen Act in 1996. As illustrated in Figure 5.12, it was adopted as an improvement over narrative text and capabilities matrices that were dictated by various DoD regulations.

The DoD enterprise architecture work was also based on the enterprise architecture planning approach used by Spewak. The U.S. AMC adopted the Zachman framework as a more precise way to represent requirements and follow the mandated directions of the Clinger-Cohen Act. According to the AMC:

> In the mid 1990s, architectural concepts were being attempted in many organizations within the U.S. Department of Defense community. The joint community was trying to standardize tasks based on the Unified Joint Task List (UJTL):
>
> - The Navy took a more war fighting focus.
> - The Army began standardizing data elements.

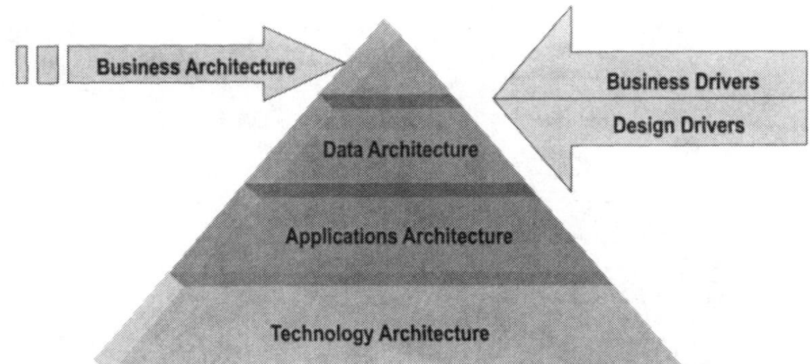

Figure 5.12 The Clinger-Cohen Act was also a starting point for defense enterprise architecture. (*From:* [26]. © U.S. Air Mobility Command. Reprinted with permission.)

- The Air Force began looking at organization-to-organization data exchanges.
- The Marine Corps focused on information flows.

There was no common approach within the Defense community and each service was allowed to pursue its own architectural efforts.

One of the earliest enterprise architecture projects undertaken by the U.S. Air Force was at the air mobility command. The initial AMC enterprise planning effort started in 1994 with a team of U.S. Air Force personnel and contractors working with Steven Spewak. The objectives of the year-long effort were to build a plan that would eventually eliminate stovepipe systems within AMC and improve interoperability, discussed as follows [26]:

> The discovery phases of the project highlighted the extent of the problem within AMC. The EAP team identified 185 automated information systems, 22 communication systems and 9 programs (organizational areas) supporting AMC. These systems were developed as independent programs and used separate hardware, unique software and dedicated communications circuits.
>
> Earlier attempts at addressing the interoperability issue were solution focused. For example, in the 1980s the Ada software development methodology was introduced as a way to unify the software used in weapons systems. However, with reductions in equipment purchases, the demand for Ada support never reached levels originally anticipated. In an effort to continue Ada development, the DoD directed [that] all new software efforts use the Ada software development methodology. However, the limited number of compilers and practitioners restricted its widespread acceptance and use. In addition, new languages that were more suited for client/server and Web applications began to dominate the industry. Other efforts were also attempted in the 1980s.

In 1996, as discussed earlier, the U.S. Congress became active in addressing interoperability issues within the government by passing the Clinger-Cohen Act. This act is also referred to as the Federal Acquisition Reform Act (FARA) or Information Technology Management Reform Act (ITMRA). The act affects many areas of both acquisition and information technology. Specifically, it stipulates that every government agency's CIO is responsible for developing, maintaining, and facilitating the implementation of sound and integrated information technology architecture.

In its implementation of the Clinger-Cohen Act, the Office of Management and Budget published OMB Circular A-130 [30]. The circular requires architectural exhibits for all major programs that are competing for funds, starting with FY04 program objective memorandum (POM) submissions. The impact of Circular A-130 is to ensure that architectures and architectural products are key elements leading to the funding and implementation of all new information systems developed by the U.S. government. The widespread implementation was accomplished in a top-down manner throughout the government and became enforceable by tying it directly to funding and the budget process.

Today, the U.S. Air Force has specific goals for systems integration and interoperability. In August 2002, the air force published the *Air Force Information Strategy*. This document delineates its goals to "... provide seamless integrated, decision quality information to the right people at the right time ... in the right context...." In the same month, the Secretary of the air force wrote in a policy memo that "We believe enterprise architecture is the common enabling foundation that will integrate business and combat support elements with each other and combat operations...."

5.4.8 Defence Architecture Framework

We saw that the key to architecture is the fundamental understanding that the enterprise gains from a focus on architectural elements (primitives). This section discusses how the defence architecture framework has evolved from the Zachman framework, using Spewak enterprise architecture planning as a way to plan for and manage large enterprise architecture projects.

When the Clinger-Cohen Act became law, the DoD introduced the Defense Architecture Framework [31], called the C4ISR framework, where C4ISR is an acronym for command, control, communications, computers, intelligence, surveillance, and reconnaissance. Its focus is on delivery of specific models, called *product deliverables*.

In 2003, the DoD formally adopted C4ISR as the DoD framework. It has evolved through several releases. The latest version was released in February 2004 and is called the *DoD Architecture Framework Version 1.0,* referred to as DoDAF V1.0 [32].

I will refer to the defense architecture framework versions by their respective acronyms: C4ISR and DoDAF. A comment referring to C4ISR is also intended to apply to DoDAF. A comment referring specifically to DoDAF is applicable only to that latest version. Unless a statement is made to the contrary, a DoDAF comment does not also apply to C4ISR.

Figure 5.13 illustrates the components of C4ISR (and also DoDAF). It has three views:

- *Operational view:* This identifies operational relationships and information needs. It captures organizations, functions, information exchanges, scenarios, and logical data.

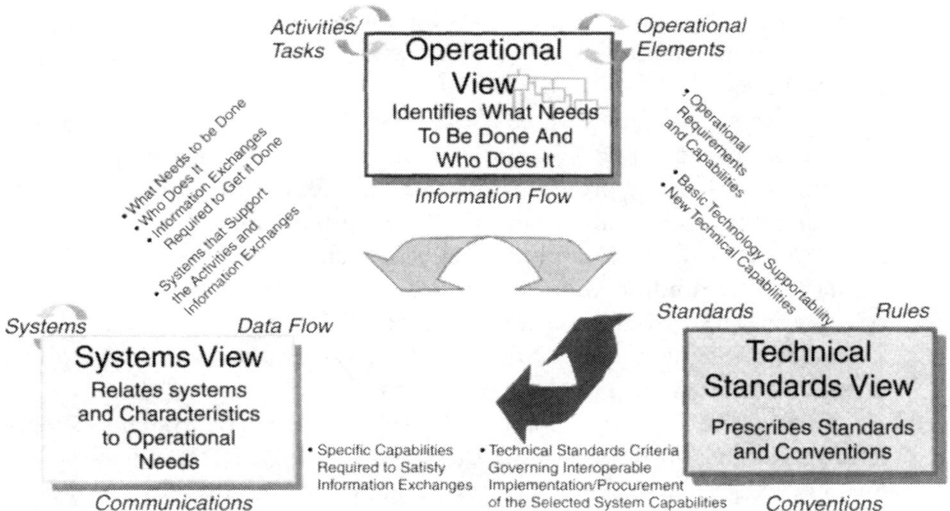

Figure 5.13 DoD operational/systems/technical architecture. (Adapted from the U.S. DoDAF.)

- *Systems view:* This relates capabilities and characteristics to operational requirements. It captures systems relationships, functions, operational support, scenarios, migration paths, technology forecasts, and physical data structures.
- *Technical standards view:* This view prescribes standards and conventions. It captures relevant standards and forecasted standards.

The focus is on collecting the primitive information needed to specify requirements and plan the implementation of systems to support the mission. For example, the primary missions of the air mobility command are air transport and aerial refueling. Returning to the AMC enterprise architecture project [26]:

> In 1994 the DoD Air Mobility Command Enterprise Architecture Plan (EAP) was the largest (EA) project ever attempted. This project proved that EAP could be done for large organizations. It proved that data and information was more stable over time than processes, and that architectures could have a long-term impact on the organization. Enterprise Architecture language is now in common use throughout the AMC.
>
> The AMC conducted a full EAP project from October 1994 to September 1995. During the course of the project the EAP team conducted over 800 interviews with subject matter experts within the Command in both headquarters and field environments. As a result of the interview process, the team identified over 5,000 individual business products and 85 different business functions, which were organized into the business model [called a Mission Analysis in AMC—see Figure 5.14].
>
> The team also identified 210 systems that AMC used in some manner. These systems were catalogued and stored in a database known as the Information Resource Catalogue (IRC) and is still in use today.
>
> Three architectures were developed including a business entity model that included 70 business level entities, an applications architecture that defined 53 candidate applications, and technology architecture. These architectures became the

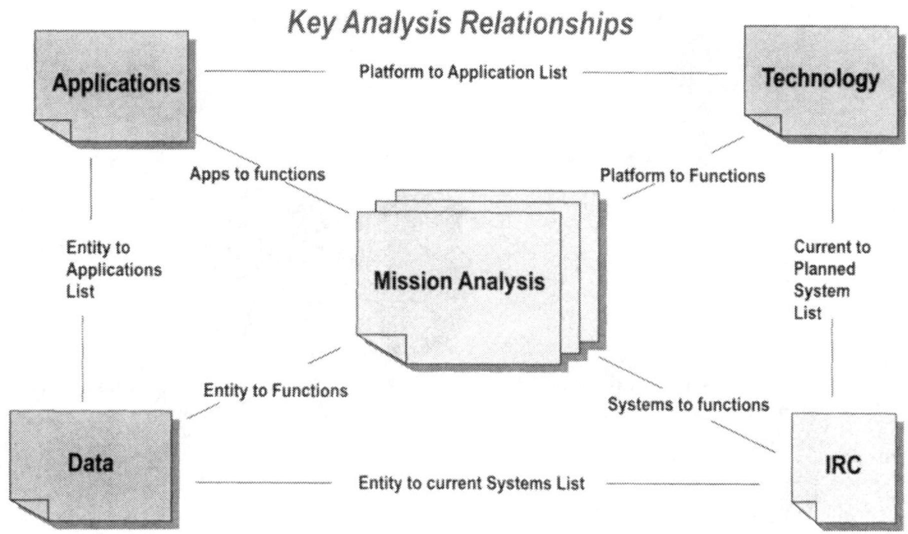

Figure 5.14 Key analysis relationships in C4ISR. (*From:* [26]. © 2004 U.S. Air Mobility Command. Reprinted with permission.)

foundation of the AMC Capabilities Master Plan and have been used as planning guidance and POM submission since they were developed.

Figure 5.14 shows how the air mobility command defined the key analysis relationships in their EAP project, discussed by AMC next [26]:

> This chart shows the key relationships between the architecture, the IRC (Information Resource Catalogue) and Mission Analysis (Business Plan). It depicts the elements and key relationships among the EAP products and also shows the individual primitive elements of information that are shared between each element. It is important to note both the information and the relationships are keys to understanding the total domain of the architecture. Because of the close interaction among these elements, they have to be built in a spiral process in order to keep them synchronized and accurate. After-the-fact integration of these products tends to be a very difficult and tedious task.

The AMC project also defined key planning relationships, as shown by Figure 5.15.

> This chart shows the key planning relationships among the Migration Plan, the architectures, and the IRC. It also depicts the products and primitive information required to develop the implementation plan. Each element in the implementation has a relationship with other elements. For example, you cannot have a functioning database without an infrastructure, and you cannot use data unless the database has been created.

Using the methods described in this book, these relationships can be documented using matrices, as discussed in Chapters 4 and 8.

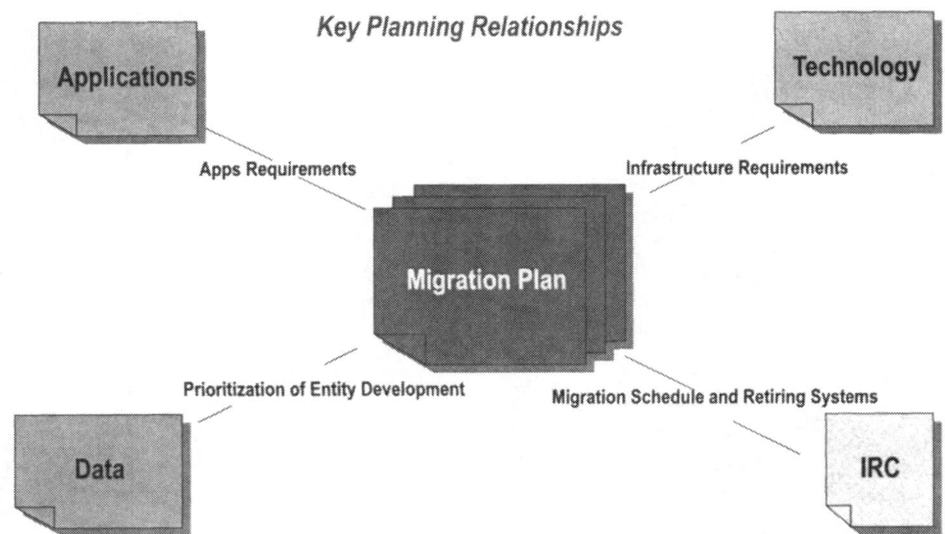

Figure 5.15 Key planning relationships in C4ISR. (*From:* [26]. © 2004 U.S. Air Mobility Command. Reprinted with permission.)

5.4.9 Relating the Zachman Framework to the Defence Framework

The C4ISR framework and DoDAF precisely define the product deliverables to be produced by a defence enterprise architecture project. This section summarizes those deliverables and relates them back to relevant cells in the Zachman framework. As with the FEAF, the C4ISR and DoDAF also use the original Spewak enterprise architecture planning approach, shown in Figure 5.1.

It is important to know how each deliverable maps to the Zachman framework cells. Methods that apply to those cells can then be used most effectively, depending on the relevant interrogative (column), and the relevant perspective (row).

The discussion that follows, on mapping the defense framework to the Zachman framework, is based on work done by CGI in Canada [33], and also independently by the U.S. Air Force AMC [34]. Their contribution to greater understanding of the C4ISR and DoDAF defense frameworks is commended.

Table 5.1 shows the product deliverables involved in the DoD architecture framework. Figure 5.16 shows how product deliverables in the DoDAF framework are related to one another from an "as is" perspective by the AMC. Table 5.1 has been extracted from the *DoD Architecture Framework V2.1 Product Descriptions* PDF document [35]. It summarizes each product deliverable, including its abbreviation and a brief description of its purpose. We will see in Chapter 14 that some of the DoDAF product deliverables can be mapped [36] to business process diagrams using the Business Process Modeling Notation (BPMN) [37].

The key factor to consider with the product deliverables in Table 5.1, and in Figure 5.16 is that they are not independent products: They are separate models that represent different aspects of the architectural problems being solved. In the context of the Zachman framework these product deliverables are not primitives; they are composites.

Table 5.1 DoDAF Architectural Product Deliverables

Applicable View	*Framework Product*	*Framework Product Name*	*General Description*
All Views	AV-1	Overview and Summary Information	Scope, purpose, intended users, environment depicted, analytical findings
All Views	AV-2	Integrated Dictionary	Data repository with definitions of all terms used in all products
Operational	OV-1	High-Level Operational Concept Graphic	High-level graphical/ textual description of operational concept
Operational	OV-2	Operational Node Connectivity Description	Operational nodes, operational activities performed at each node, connectivity and information exchange need lines between nodes
Operational	OV-3	Operational Information Exchange Matrix	Information exchanged between nodes and the relevant attributes of that exchange
Operational	OV-4	Organizational Relationships Chart	Organizational, role, or other relationships among organizations
Operational	OV-5	Operational Activity Model	Operational Activities, relationships among activities, inputs and outputs. Overlays can show cost, performing nodes, or other pertinent information.
Operational	OV-6a	Operational Rules Model	One of the three products used to describe operational activity sequence and timing—identifies business rules that constrain operation
Operational	OV-6b	Operational State Transition Description	One of three products used to describe operational activity sequence and timing—identifies business process responses to events
Operational	OV-6c	Operational Event-Trace Description	One of three products used to describe operational activity sequence and timing—traces actions in a scenario or sequence of events and specifies timing of events
Operational	OV-7	Logical Data Model	Documentation of the data requirements and structural business process rules of the Operational View.
Systems	SV-1	Systems Interface Description	Identification of systems and system components and their interconnections, within and between nodes
Systems	SV-2	SystemsCommunications Description	Systems nodes and their related communications lay-downs
Systems	SV-3	Systems-Systems Matrix	Relationships among systems in a given architecture; can be designed to show relationships of interest (e.g., system-type interfaces, planned vs. existing interfaces, and so forth)
Systems	SV-4	Systems Functionality Description	Functions performed by systems and the information flow among system functions
Systems	SV-5	Operational Activity to Systems Function Traceability Matrix	Mapping of systems back to operational capabilities or of system functions back to operational activities
Systems	SV-6	Systems Data Exchange Matrix	Provides details of systems data being exchanged between systems
Systems	SV-7	Systems Performance Parameters Matrix	Performance characteristics of each system(s) hardware and software elements, for the appropriate timeframe(s)

Table 5.1 (continued)

Applicable View	*Framework Product*	*Framework Product Name*	*General Description*
Systems	SV-8	Systems Evolution Description	Planned incremental steps toward migrating a suite of systems to a more efficient suite, or toward evolving a current system to a future implementation
Systems	SV-9	Systems Technology Forecast	Emerging technologies and software/hardware products that are expected to be available in a given set of timeframes, and that will affect future development of the architecture
Systems	SV-10a	Systems Rules Model	One of three products used to describe systems activity sequence and timing—Constraints that are imposed on systems functionality due to some aspect of systems design or implementation
Systems	SV-10b	Systems State Transition Description	One of three products used to describe systems activity sequence and timing—Responses of a system to events
Systems	SV -10c	Systems Event-Trace Description	One of three products used to describe systems activity sequence and timing—System-specific refinements of critical sequences of events and the timing of these events
Systems	SV-11	Physical Schema	Physical implementation of the information of the Logical Data Model (e.g., message formats, file structures, physical schema)
Technical	TV-1	Technical Standards Profile	Extraction of standards that apply to the given architecture
Technical	TV-2	Technical Standards Forecast	Description of emerging standards that are expected to apply to the given architecture, within an appropriate set of timeframes.

Source: [32].

Next, Figure 5.17 maps the product deliverables from Table 5.1 and Figure 5.16 to the Zachman framework. The abbreviations used in Figure 5.17 are detailed in Table 5.1. Product deliverables that address the scope are highlighted as bold italics. This diagram is evolutionary. It has since been superseded by more precise mapping in the latest DoDAF, which will be discussed shortly.

An important point to remember is that the above mapping to the Zachman framework is not documented in the C4ISR framework document (see the endnotes at the end of the chapter). There is no reference to John Zachman, or any acknowledgment in that document that the C4ISR originated from the Zachman framework. As a result, the power of the Zachman framework as a vehicle for managing large projects for complex defence organizations was completely lost.

The C4ISR framework was a good approach, but its value was diminished. The focus of its authors on detailing each of the product deliverables as composites had lost sight of the real purpose of enterprise architecture: to *clarify and manage complexity*. As a consequence, it was almost impossible for defence staffs that were new to enterprise architecture to see any correspondence between C4ISR and the Zachman framework.

The recently released DoDAF V1.0 rectifies this problem and acknowledges its origin in the Zachman framework. It provides mapping of each product deliverable

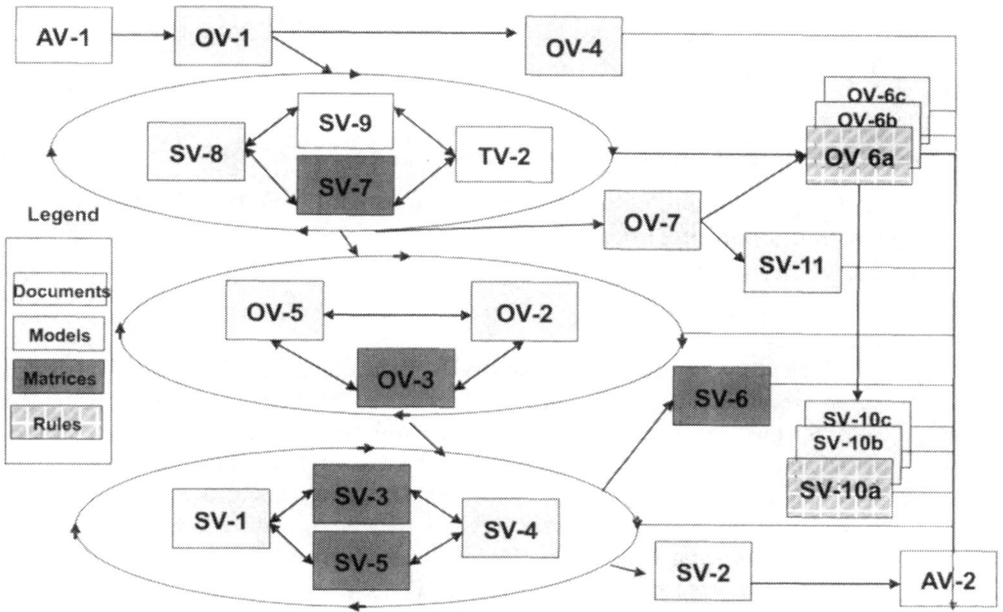

Figure 5.16 The DoDAF framework products ("as is" baseline strategy). See Table 5.1 for the abbreviation references in this figure. (*From:* [34]. © 2004 U.S. Air Mobility Command. Reprinted with permission.)

VIEW	What	How	Where	Who	When	Why
Ops	OV-3 OV-6a OV-7 AV-2	OV-5 AV-2	***OV-1*** OV-2 AV-2	***OV-1*** OV-2 ***OV-4*** AV-2	OV-6b OV-6c AV-2	***AV-1*** OV-6a AV-2
Sys	SV-4 SV-6 SV-10a SV-11 AV-2	SV-5 SV-8 SV-9 AV-2	***SV-1*** SV-2 SV-3 SV-4 AV-2		SV-7 SV-10b SV-10c AV-2	***AV-1*** SV-10a AV-2
Tech	TV-1 TV-2 AV-2	TV-1 TV-2 AV-2				***AV-1*** TV-1 AV-2

Scope *(shown in **Bold Italics**)*

Figure 5.17 C4ISR and DoDAF product deliverables, mapped broadly to the Zachman framework. (*From:* [34]. © 2004 U.S. Air Mobility Command. Reprinted with permission.)

to the relevant Zachman rows and cells of the framework in more detail for DoDAF than is shown in Figure 5.17. Figures showing this mapping are summarized in the DoDAF deskbook [32]. The DoDAF also provides excellent detail about metadata that should be captured in a DoD repository for each product deliverable. The full DoDAF V1.0 documentation is available [32].

5.4.10 Enterprise Architecture Project Results at Defence

Using C4ISR initially and later evolving to DoDAF, the DoD takes a phased approach to building architectures and systems. It develops data models, then infrastructure, and finally applications. For example, the U.S. Air Force comments that [34]:

> The logical data model has been in development for close to 10 years. The development process has been delayed and complicated by the lack of consensus on some parts of the model. According to the Air Mobility Command ... "The concept of location has become a significant issue. The Navy recognizes location as a latitude and longitude while on the high seas. The Air Force recognizes location as the altitude of the aircraft and its radial distance from a known radio beacon. The Army recognizes location as grid coordinates on a map. To all three services, their definition of location is legitimate but to the DoD it is a real quandary." The DoD is now looking at alternate approaches.

A recent development in the data model arena is the concept of communities of interest [34]:

> One example is the transportation community. The community consists of Air Mobility Command, the Surface Deployment and Distribution Command and the Military Sealift Command. These three organizations fall under the operational control of the United States Transportation Command (USTRANSCOM).
>
> The community of interest model is called the Transportation Master Model. The three subordinate commands must submit data elements to USTRANSCOM for approval and inclusion into the Transportation Master Model. Each subordinate command has its own data model such as the AMC Logical Data Model. To be useful, the data models must be implemented in databases that share a common infrastructure.
>
> The DoD has completely restructured the manner in which it arranges for long-haul communication circuits. Ten years ago each new system would arrange for its own communications circuits. Some organizational elements such as weather, intelligence and medical had numerous circuits to meet their needs for teletype, facsimile, and imagery data. As technology changed and capacity grew, the DoD centralized procurement and forced users to share bandwidth. At the base level, fiber optic cable was put in and formed a backbone communication infrastructure up to the building. These changes have allowed for the implementation of major client/server and Web-based applications.

Applications implementations are still governed by the individual services within the DoD. Within the air force, the current focus has moved from individual programs to capabilities. Capabilities are described in high-level concepts of operations (CONOPS) and these documents are made up of a series of architectural products. The architectural products are used to plan systems developments and describe the evolution from the "as is" environment to the new "to be" environment [34]:

Architectural products are now tied to funding within the Federal Government. The Office of Management and Budget (OMB) Circular A-130 requires that each agency create and document an enterprise architecture. Specifically, the Circular calls for the following elements: business processes, information flow and relationship, applications, data descriptions and relationship, and technology infrastructure.

The OMB also requires a capital asset plan and business case (Exhibit 300) for each major program going through the budget submission process. The Air Force submitted 23 Exhibit 300s through the Office of the Secretary of Defense (OSD) during the most recent budget cycle.

Architecture is now considered essential by the U.S. Air Force to achieving its information strategy. According to the air mobility command, it provides [34]:

- On-demand information—what you need when you need it
- Worldwide real-time access—robust infrastructure, always available
- Information assurance—people and technology to protect information
- Robust architectures—establishing the relationship between organizations, processes and the systems that support them
- World-class systems—transformed processes, continuous improvement, leverage the latest technology
- New information technology and best commercial practices—implementing the keys to progress
- Knowledge management—linking expertise in its many forms
- Information empowered—a workforce ready to take maximum advantage of new capabilities
- Responsible stewardship of information technology dollars—visibility, accountability and flexibility

The Air Force has moved from specifying programs to defining capability CONOPS (Concept of Operations). These new concept documents are being developed using architectural tools and concepts. Such capability documents require an enterprise perspective and cannot be effectively produced without architectural support.

Use of architectural discipline will lead to an integrated, interoperable and efficient C4ISR infrastructure. It provides a logical structure for classifying, organizing and relating information that describes and documents the architecture. It provides a model for an integrated architecture including vision, governance, principles, guidance and products. It ensures a common foundation on which to build understanding and enable integration. It also forces adherence to certain basic principles concerning information.

The air mobility command believes in the benefits of enterprise architecture as follows [34]:

There are several basic ideas that must be adhered to if an organization ever hopes to successfully implement an Enterprise Architecture:

- Information must be viewed as a corporate resource and must be managed.
- Information at all levels of the organization must be clearly and consistently defined by the organization.

> - Information must be shared versus distributed for fast, easy access to users.
> - Information must have specified stewards that are accountable for information integrity and accuracy.
> - Information must be protected from unauthorized use and disclosure.
>
> In order to successfully adhere to these tenets, systems must be planned, designed and built from an Enterprise Architecture perspective.

According to the DoD [34]:

> Interoperability is still a key element of any coalition effort to provide agile and lethal force projection anywhere and anytime. Response times are getting shorter, and we don't have time to wire together solutions during the execution phase of an operation. Our adversaries are becoming more sophisticated, and we need complex solutions to counter their threat. Complex sophisticated systems don't just happen—they are planned!

In an expanding global economy we need systems that provide accurate and reliable information anywhere we operate. The world is becoming more and more complex and at an ever increasing rate of change, and we need ways to deal with it.

5.5 The Open Group Architecture Framework

The open group architecture framework (TOGAF) has evolved as an alternative architecture framework that is used by commercial organizations and also by government and defense departments. The TOGAF Web site [38] states that it "is an industry standard architecture framework that may be used freely by any organization wishing to develop an information systems architecture for use within that organization." TOGAF is available in two editions:

- *TOGAF Version 8 (Enterprise Edition):* first published in December 2002 and republished in updated form as TOGAF Version 8.1 in December 2003.
- *TOGAF Version 7 (Technical Edition):* published in December 2001.

The Web site [38] states that TOGAF can be used with FEAF, C4ISR, and DoDAF:

> TOGAF Version 8 uses the same underlying architecture development method that was evolved, with particular focus on Technical Architectures, up to and including TOGAF Version 7. TOGAF Version 8 applies that architecture development method to all the domains of an overall Enterprise Architecture, including Business, Data, and Application Architecture, as well as Technical Architecture....
>
> TOGAF Version 8 Enterprise Edition ('TOGAF 8' for short) is a detailed method and set of supporting resources for developing an Enterprise Architecture. Developed and endorsed by the membership of The Open Group, TOGAF 8 represents an industry consensus framework and method for Enterprise Architecture that is available for use internally by any organization around the world—members and non-members of The Open Group alike—under a free, perpetual license.

As a comprehensive, open method for Enterprise Architecture, TOGAF 8 complements, and can be used in conjunction with, other frameworks that are more focused on specific deliverables for particular vertical sectors such as Government, Defense, and Finance.

TOGAF emphasizes that it provides methodology steps for FEAF, C4ISR, and DoDAF. This is called the TOGAF architecture development method (ADM). We will discuss this further in the following section. A white paper titled "Building Enterprise Architectures with TOGAF" [39] provides an overview of TOGAF and discusses how Popkin (now Telelogic) System Architect can be used with it. System Architect is discussed with modeling tools in Chapter 15.

5.5.1 Role of Enterprise Engineering in FEAF, DoDAF, EAP, and TOGAF

We discussed that methods for the Planner, Owner, and Designer rows of the Zachman framework are the major focus of this chapter. It is important to emphasize that enterprise engineering does not replace FEAF or the defense architecture frameworks C4ISR or DoDAF. It also does not replace Spewak's EAP. Furthermore, it does not replace TOGAF. Instead, enterprise engineering provides additional rapid delivery methods and rigor that enhance these frameworks and methods for enterprise architecture, with rapid delivery technologies using XML, Web services, and SOA, as discussed in Part III. In particular, enterprise engineering methods provide rapid delivery support for the Planner and Owner (rows 1 and 2). These methods strengthen the FEAF and DoD architectures, Spewak EAP, and TOGAF ADM in these rows. They provide for business transformation enablement.

We will examine the enterprise engineering methods and their application to enterprise architecture in detail in later chapters. But first, we need to review project experience in applying enterprise architecture to date.

5.6 Enterprise Architecture Project Experience

There is now a body of experience that has been gained in using enterprise architecture in many large—and small—projects. It has been gained by defence and government organizations; and also by commercial enterprises across most industries. This section summarizes results from these projects, using two project examples.

I will quote John Zachman and Doug Erickson—an enterprise architecture consultant—in this section, adding further comment where relevant. The project summary results that John quotes are based on an enterprise architecture project at the Ohio Bureau of Workers' Compensation, which was undertaken by Doug Erickson of ENTARCO USA Inc. [40]:

> Using a top-down, Enterprise Architecture, enhanced Information Engineering approach with a three-schema data architecture and CASE technology:
>
> - The cost per new data entity (RDBMS table) was reduced from more than $150,000 using traditional systems development methods to less than $10,000 cost per entity.
> - Enterprise data handling labor cost was reduced 50%.

- Development time and cost reductions of more than 50%–90% were subsequently achieved for every succeeding implementation through reuse of database and application components, with no modifications and through effective data and process model management.
- Disk space for data (including history) was reduced by 20%–80% through elimination of data redundancy.

These are typical of the results that are achieved in many other enterprise architecture projects that take a similar top-down model-based approach with automatic code generation.

Table 5.2 summarizes the number of data entities that were identified by the Ohio Bureau of Workers' Compensation for several systems, together with the number of these entities that were reused in later systems and the consequent cost savings.

- The *Rates System* was developed first. The main development method was data modeling based on the ENTARCO Methodology for Enterprise Architecture, together with the AllFusion (formerly called Coolgen and IEF) CASE modeling tool. A total of 1,030 data entities were identified and implemented over 2.5 years.
- The *Benefits Payments* system was developed next and is operational. This system required 720 entities; but 470 had already been developed for the Rates System. They were able to be reused without change.
- The *Retro Rated Billing* system was developed next and is now operational. This required 230 entities, of which 220 were able to be reused.

Table 5.2 Ohio Bureau of Workers' Compensation

System/Time or Cost	*Number of Entities/Time or Cost*	*Number of Reused Entities*
Rates System (operational—2.5 years elapsed time)	1,030	
Benefits Payments (operational)	720	470
Retro Rated Billing (operational)	230	220
Total Elapsed Time: No database failures (never more than 3 data analysts, 3 business analysts, and 10 developers)	4 years	
Health Provider Management (under development)	415	255
Total Cost per Entity: (conservative) Includes legacy data cleansing; all data conversion costs; all interfaces with remaining legacy; no redundancy; complete enterprise alignment and integration	$25,000	
Total Cost Savings: 945 (reused entities) × $25,000	$23,625,000	945

- The total elapsed time for development of these three systems was 4 years. Since these systems went into production, there have been no database changes or failures.
- The *Health Provider Management* system in Table 5.2 was under development when Erickson had quoted these results to Zachman. This system required 415 entities, of which 255 were reused.
- The *Total Cost per Entity* was conservatively calculated as $25,000. This cost includes legacy data cleansing for quality improvement, all data conversion costs, and all interfaces required for access to legacy databases. The results of *no data redundancy* and *complete enterprise alignment and integration* are the objectives and benefits of enterprise architecture using the ENTARCO USA Inc. methodology for Enterprise Architecture (MEA).
- A total of 2,395 entities were required by these systems, but 945 entities were reused. At a cost of $25,000 per entity, this represented a *Total Cost Savings* of $23,625,000.

Table 5.3 shows a comparison of the Ohio Bureau of Workers' Compensation enterprise architecture project results with the development of a similar system for child welfare in another U.S. state. In both cases, AllFusion/Coolgen/IEF was also used as the development tool. But instead of taking an enterprise architecture approach using the ENTARCO MEA, the other state used classic methods for traditional systems development. The results are interesting:

- As we saw in Table 5.2, the Ohio rates system required 1,030 entities. These were fully normalized to eliminate data redundancy. In contrast, the other state's rates system had only 300 entities, which had not been fully normalized.
- The Ohio project took 2.5 years elapsed time for the rates system. The other state took 12 years to develop its system.
- The development cost for the other state project was $42 million, which represents $140,000 cost per data entity. This compares with $25,000 cost per data entity for the Ohio project, as shown in Table 5.2 [41].

Table 5.3 Ohio Project and Another State's Project Comparison

Ohio Project	*Factor*	*Other State Project*
Workers' Compensation Rates System	Application	Child Welfare System
AllFusion/Coolgen/IEF	Same CASE Tool	AllFusion/Coolgen/IEF
ENTARCO MEA (EA based)	Different Methodology	Classic
1,030 (normalized)	Number of Entities	300 (unnormalized)
2.5 Years	Elapsed Time	12 years
(see Table 5.4)	Development Costs	$42 million
$25,000	Cost per Entity	$140,000 (two prime contractors and one local contractor estimated 3 more years needed to enhance or fix)

- Furthermore, even after costing $42 million, the other state's system still required more work. Two prime contractors and one local contractor estimated 3 more years were needed to enhance the system and fix the problems.

The development costs for the Ohio Bureau of Workers' Compensation project were analyzed against three alternatives, as discussed next with reference to Table 5.4. The Ohio project assessed the cost of its development using enterprise architecture as one development alternative. It compared that cost with those of two alternatives: (1) using a package and (2) using traditional systems development methods. The following cost comparisons are summarized in Table 5.4:

- To establish a common base for comparison, a *Recent Package Implementation* cost was calculated based on the number of entities in that package. This provided a *Cost per Entity* of $50,000, compared to $25,000 per entity for the ENTARCO MEA enterprise architecture alternative.
- The package cost per entity in Table 5.4 did *not* include associated costs for data cleansing or data conversions. It included no legacy interfaces, involved added data redundancy, and provided only 60% of the required functionality. All of these costs were included in the $25,000 cost per entity using ENTARCO MEA, which provided 100% of the required functionality.
- *Recent Custom Applications,* which used traditional systems development methods at the Ohio project, but did not use an enterprise architecture, were found to cost from $100,000 to $150,000 per entity.

Applying these alternative costs per entity to the 2,395 entities implemented for the Ohio project, the *Comparative Development Costs* in Table 5.4 are summarized as follows:

Table 5.4 Comparative Costs

Description	*Cost per Entity*	*Total Cost*
Recent Package Implementation: Conservative. No data cleansing, no data conversions, no legacy interfaces, added redundancy and 60% functionality	$50,000	
Recent Custom Applications: Typical legacy, redundant environment	$100,000 to $150,000	
Comparative Development Costs:		
Traditional Application Development Cost: 2,395 entities × $140,000 per entity		$335,300,000
Application Package Implementation Cost: 2,395 entities × $50,000 per entity		$119,750,000
ENTARCO MEA Enterprise Architecture Development Cost: 2,395–945 entities × $25,000 per entity (and enterprise architecture approach is "aligned," with low maintenance)		$36,000,000
Reusable Code:		
In three Operational Systems:	6,128 action blocks	7.0 Average Reuse Factor

- *Traditional Application Development:* 2,395 entities at an average cost per entity of $140,000 totals $335,300,000. This cost would have been outside their budget for funding.
- *Application Package Development:* 2,395 entities at a cost per entity of $50,000 totals $119,750,000.
- *Enterprise Architecture Development:* This approach resulted in 945 entities that were reused of the total 2,395 entities. At a cost per entity of $25,000 for the remaining 1,450 entities, the total cost was $36,000,000.

While there were reusable entities in the ENTARCO enterprise architecture approach, Table 5.4 shows that substantial amounts of program code were also reusable.

- Traditional application development would have required 42,896 subroutines to be coded, tested, and maintained.
- In contrast, the enterprise architecture approach using AllFusion/Coolgen/IEF development tool required the development of 6,128 action block subroutines.
- This represents an *Average Reuse Factor* of 7.0. However, of the action blocks that were reused two or more times, these were reused an average of 17 times. This reuse factor is attributable to the granularity and precision of the data model, as many processes use the same data.

5.6.1 Project Experience Summary

- Approximately four times more entities were defined in the Ohio project. These were fully normalized, compared to the fewer number of unnormalized entities in the example from the other state.
- The Ohio project using highly normalized data resulted in a cost per entity of $25,000 compared to $140,000 per entity for the unnormalized entities.
- The other state took 12 years for a comparable system using AllFusion/Coolgen/IEF but with traditional systems development approaches. The Ohio project took 2.5 years using a very small number of project personnel.
- Entity reuse of 90% saved $23 million.
- The comparative traditional application development cost for the Ohio project would have been $335 million. The application package implementation cost would have been $120 million. The enterprise architecture development cost was less than $36 million.
- In summary, these results showed that enterprise architecture delivered systems in 20% of the time and at 10% of the cost of traditional systems development [42].

The results for the Ohio Bureau of Workers' Compensation enterprise architecture project were dramatic. As stated in the endnote [42], this was largely due to the unusual 12 years' duration of the other state's child welfare project. Most traditional development projects do not take this amount of time.

5.7 Strategies for Enterprise Architecture Implementation

Many strategies are available for implementing enterprise architecture, according to John Zachman. We will discuss three alternative strategies in this section:

- *Strategy A:* Implementation in top-down, rigorous detail;
- *Strategy B:* Selective EA, based on ROI business case;
- *Strategy C:* Deliver progressively in 3-month incremental builds.

We will discuss each of these strategies, with approach and sequence recommendations from Zachman. We will also look at the benefits and limitations of each approach.

5.7.1 Strategy A: Implementation in Top-Down, Rigorous Detail

This is the strategy used by ENTARCO USA, Inc., discussed earlier in Section 5.6. Even the conservatively expressed results in that section's endnote were impressive: Enterprise architecture resulted in systems that were completed in 20% of the time and at 10% of the cost of traditional systems development. This strategy is illustrated in Figure 5.18, with recommendations and sequence quoted by John Zachman. My comments follow as bulleted points.

1. "Survey the business mission, business cycles and organization. Determine products/services/resources."
   - Doug Erickson establishes a high-level definition in row 1 across all columns.
2. "Employ resource life-cycle analysis to define processes."

	What Data	How Function	Where Location	Who People	When Time	Why Future
PLANNER Objectives/Scope	List of Things	List of Processes	List of Locations	Org Structure	List of Events	List of Goals/Obj
OWNER Conceptual	Enterprise Model	Activity Model	Business Logistics	Work Flow	Master Schedule	Business Plan
DESIGNER Logical	Logical Data Model	Process Model	Distrib. Architect.	Human Interface	Process Structure	Business Rules
BUILDER Physical	Physical Data Model	System Model	Technol. Architect.	Presn Interface	Control Structure	Rule Design
SUBCONTRACTOR Out-of-Context	Data Definition	Program	Network Architect.	Security Interface	Timing Definition	Rule Specs
FUNCTIONING ENTERPRISE	Data	Function	Network	Organization	Schedule	Strategy

Figure 5.18 Strategy A—top-down, rigorous detail. (*From:* [44]. © 2002 Zachman International. Reprinted with permission.)

- Erickson uses this to identify and define business processes in column 2 of row 1. Matrices can also be used to represent composites.

3. "Define an enterprise-wide conceptual data model, fully attributed and normalized at an excruciating level of detail."
   - Erickson moves from row 1 to a fully attributed, highly normalized data model at row 2.
4. "Define a logical application architecture at an excruciating level of detail."
   - These process specifications are the result of a business transformation to a "to-be" state.
   - Erickson uses AllFusion/Coolgen/IEF to generate processes, identified by management.
5. "Based on dependency analysis, define segments for implementation."
   - Erickson defines priority processes in complete detail—shown by the vertical sliver starting in column 2, row 3, of Figure 5.18, which is also highlighted.
6. "Transform one segment at a time to physical design and implement the logical data model."
   - Figure 5.18 illustrates vertical slivers defined in excruciating detail in column 1 and column 2 of row 2 (Owner), progressing down through rows 3, 4, and 5 into implementation.

Benefits

- This strategy achieves enterprise-wide data integration with a fully attributed, fully normalized logical data model in column 1, row 2.
- It identifies architecturally normalized business processes before they are submitted for applications design and development as column 2, row 2 deliverables.
- AllFusion/Coolgen/IEF facilitates high reuse of data and code which results in dramatic reductions in development design, construction, and testing costs and time, as discussed in relation to the Ohio project.
- The time and cost savings of this strategy—when compared to traditional systems development methods—are impressive, as discussed earlier.
- Rigorous definition of the Logical Data Model in column 1, row 2 using the ENTARCO MEA can enable applications development to start and run parallel with the data model development.

Doug Erickson emphasizes that the ENTARCO MEA develops the data model so that it can segment "slivers" into "splinters" that can be pushed through to design, construction, test, and implementation in very small increments, all the while working within a nonredundant, highly integrated architecture. He says that it is a management choice and an implementation choice as to when you actually implement a splinter or sliver or a set thereof. He states that: "You may be able to effectively design, construct, and test many splinters and then aggregate them for a 'release' as an implementation package." All the while, ENTARCO demonstrates hard evidence of "components" being developed and successfully user-tested. "As a matter of fact," he says, "we are developing, specifying, designing, developing, testing, and implementing functionality today in time frames of a day, days, a week, or a month depending on the scope, complexity, and points of coordination with relevant business considerations such as availability of resources and scheduling impacts. We are almost always now waiting on the business as the gating factor as to when we implement."

As we will see shortly, Strategy A offers many of the benefits also of Strategy C, the main differentiating factor is that Strategy A is based on the ENTARCO MEA which assumes the use of AllFusion/Coolgen/IEF. As we will soon see, Strategy C achieves similar results but can be used with any development tool, such as those discussed in Section 5.7.3, with rapid delivery into production in 3-month increments.

Doug Erickson achieved impressive results in his use of Strategy A when compared with traditional systems development. Some enterprise architecture projects by others have been less successful. Many projects took Zachman's advice literally. His comments were always intended as guidance, never as absolute dogma. These projects defined each cell rigorously—in an excruciating level of detail, row by row—as shown in Figure 5.19. They suffered from "analysis paralysis," similar to many projects that used traditional methods.

This is a danger of enterprise architecture projects—but not with the ENTARCO MEA. Typically the project team completes each row (Scope, Owner, and Designer, or rows 1–3) in excruciating detail across all columns. The models are passed to Builders (row 4) and Subcontractors (row 5) for implementation. The typical problems that occur after these excruciatingly detailed steps have been as follows:

1. By the time the Designer row was fully defined, the business had changed; the design no longer represented what was needed.
2. The Builders and Subcontractors were not involved earlier in the EA project; they implemented using their tried-and-true traditional

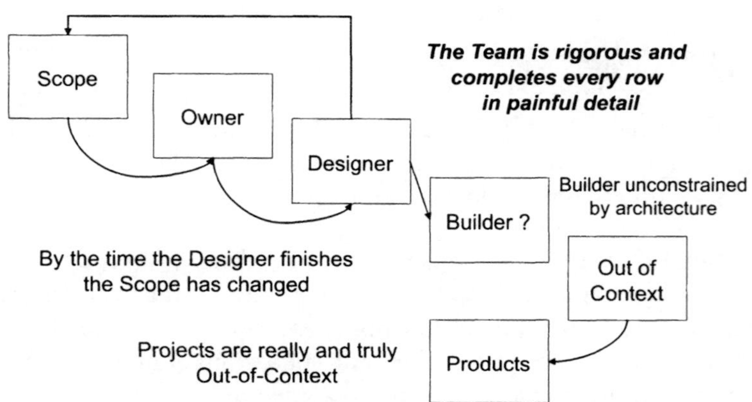

Figure 5.19 Enterprise architecture "analysis paralysis." (*From:* [24]. © 2004 CGI. Reprinted with permission.)

development methods rather than by using enterprise architecture methods.

3. Alternatively, development was outsourced. An even greater disconnect occurred between what had been defined using enterprise architecture and what the Outsourcer built.

5.7.2 Strategy B: Selective EA, Based on ROI Business Case

Strategy B is appropriate if an ROI business case must first be established before a decision is made to introduce an enterprise architecture approach. This is illustrated in Figure 5.20. This is used to whet management interest by identifying "low-hanging fruit" that can provide early ROI benefits. As with strategy A, I've provided John's recommendations and my bullet-point comments.

1. "If you can't make up your mind and you need a business case for proceeding, then try the selective enterprise architecture ROI business case approach. Build out at least the row 1 thing, process, organization and motivation models to a moderate level of detail."
   - Columns 1, 2, 4, and 6 are defined as high-level lists of data, process, organizational structure, and goals and objectives.
2. "Define the relationships between them as matrices."
   - Matrices are defined to relate each of the lists of data to processes; processes to organizational structure; and organizational structure to goals and objectives, respectively, each to the other.
3. "Evaluate legacy applications."

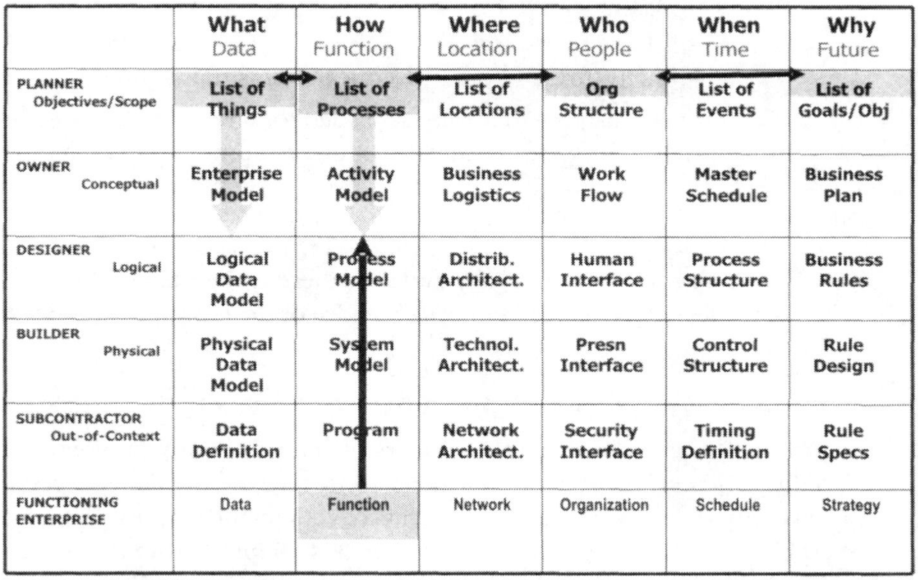

	What Data	How Function	Where Location	Who People	When Time	Why Future
PLANNER Objectives/Scope	List of Things	List of Processes	List of Locations	Org Structure	List of Events	List of Goals/Obj
OWNER Conceptual	Enterprise Model	Activity Model	Business Logistics	Work Flow	Master Schedule	Business Plan
DESIGNER Logical	Logical Data Model	Process Model	Distrib. Architect.	Human Interface	Process Structure	Business Rules
BUILDER Physical	Physical Data Model	System Model	Technol. Architect.	Presn Interface	Control Structure	Rule Design
SUBCONTRACTOR Out-of-Context	Data Definition	Program	Network Architect.	Security Interface	Timing Definition	Rule Specs
FUNCTIONING ENTERPRISE	Data	Function	Network	Organization	Schedule	Strategy

Figure 5.20 Strategy B—selective EA, based on ROI business case. (*Source:* © 2002. John Zachman and Zachman International. Reprinted with permission.)

- Legacy applications (at the bottom of column 2) are evaluated in terms of their ability to support the defined relationship matrices and business needs for the future.

4. "Overlay management values to determine priorities."
   - Management requirements are used to establish priorities based on the previous evaluation of legacy applications.
5. "Identify major systems initiatives."
   - Based on this assessment, major systems are identified for further evaluation.
6. "Develop a business case for proceeding with architecture-based approaches."
   - A business case is developed for these major systems to determine the benefits and trade-offs of using enterprise architecture to achieve business integration.
7. "Assess Enterprise culture for selecting appropriate implementation (methodological) approach."
   - For those major systems that can benefit from enterprise architecture, alternative methods for implementation are selected. The three strategies in this section can assist in this selection.
8. "Commit resources and execute."
   - Allocate required resources and begin enterprise architecture implementation for agreed major systems.

Benefits

- This strategy evaluates the ability of legacy systems to support required data, processes, organizational structure, and business plan relationships.
- It assesses the benefits and trade-offs of enterprise architecture to address the needs for the future and prioritize the systems that should be addressed.
- The business case can then be established for enterprise architecture. The most appropriate enterprise architecture implementation approach can be selected.

Limitation

- With its emphasis on legacy systems, there is the potential for the constraints of the legacy systems to limit the breadth of the required focus for the future.

5.7.3 Strategy C: Deliver in 3-Month Incremental Builds

Figure 5.19 earlier discussed the dangers of analysis paralysis. We saw that strategy A reduces this problem of multiyear projects; the strategy delivers very good results when compared with traditional systems development. But today it is hard to justify even high-return projects if several years must elapse before the major benefits are realized. Most projects today should be capable of delivering priority areas rapidly into production—ideally within 3 to 6 months—so that early results can be achieved without having to wait for full project completion. Figure 5.21 illustrates this concept.

The scope is defined in terms of high-level lists within each column. The Owner row is then defined at a high level to address key business needs, followed by high-level views for these business needs from the Designer, Builder, and Subcontractor perspectives.

This approach leads to incremental implementation of priority areas that are needed first, before other areas that can wait until later. This incremental approach is shown in Figure 5.22. Zachman's recommendations and my bullet-point comments that follow are keyed to numbered sections in the figure.

1. "Do in-depth analysis of the enterprise mission/objectives."
   - Column 6, row 1, identifies goals and objectives in the business plan for the future. This uses strategy analysis as discussed in Chapter 3.
2. "Define the 'things' that have to be managed in row 1."
   - The business plan goals and objectives are used to identify high-level lists of required entities in column 1, row 1. This is discussed in Chapters 6 and 7.
3. "Build an enterprise-wide semantic model to 150–200 entities (column 1, row 2)."
   - A semantic model is also called a strategic model. It is progressively defined in a facilitated modeling session with business experts familiar with the required goals and objectives, based on entities identified in Step 2. The associations between related entities represent strategies from the business plan for key goals and objectives. This is discussed in Chapter 7.
4. "Analyze the semantic model to derive the build sequence for the entire enterprise in about 3-month increments using entity dependency analysis (where the elapsed time for entity dependency analysis is approximately 1 month)."
   - Analysis of each association between entities in the strategic model identifies entity dependencies that can be used to derive project plans, for early

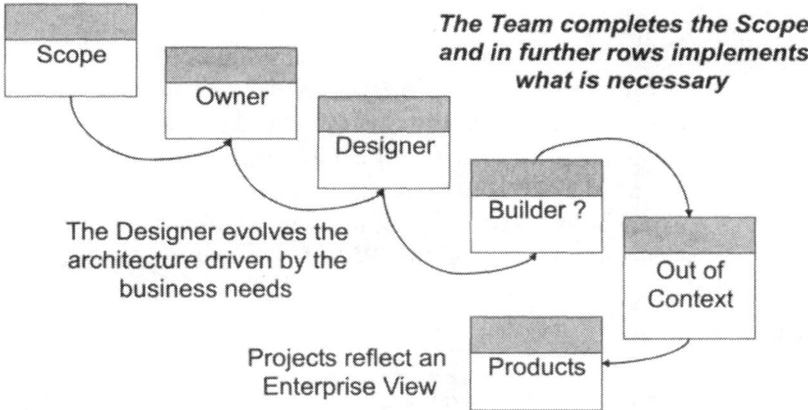

Figure 5.21 Incremental implementation of enterprise architecture. (*From:* [24]. © 2004 Robert Weisman, CGI. Reprinted with permission.)

	What Data	How Function	Where Location	Who People	When Time	Why Future
PLANNER Objectives/Scope	2 List of Things	List of Processes	List of Locations	Org Structure	List of Events	1 List of Goals/Obj
OWNER Conceptual	3 Enterprise Model	4 Activity Model	Business Logistics	5 Work Flow	Master Schedule	Business Plan
DESIGNER Logical	Logical Data Model	Process Model	Distrib. Architect.	Human Interface	Process Structure	Business Rules
BUILDER Physical	Physical Data Model	System Model	Technol. Architect.	Presn Interface	Control Structure	Rule Design
SUBCONTRACTOR Out-of-Context	Data Definition	Program	Network Architect.	Security Interface	Timing Definition	Rule Specs
FUNCTIONING ENTERPRISE	Data 6	Function	Network XML	Organization 6	Schedule	Strategy

Figure 5.22 Strategy C—Deliver enterprise architecture progressively in 3-month incremental builds. (*From:* [44]. © 2004 Zachman International. Reprinted with permission.)

delivery of priority areas as vertical slivers. This is the entity dependency analysis method that Zachman recommends earlier. This method is described in Chapter 7.

5. "Derive the primary business processes from the semantic intersections."
   - Decomposition of many-to-many associations between related entities identifies business activities and business processes in column 2, row 2, from the enterprise model in column 1, row 2. This is also described in Chapter 7. These activities are defined further and used to develop workflow models in column 4, row 2, described in Chapter 8 and processes in Chapter 10.

6. "Begin implementations as resources allow."
   - XML, Web services, and SOA technologies (discussed in Part III) are used for rapid delivery of priority activities and workflows. Column 1 vertical slivers are automatically generated as database definition language (DDL) scripts for priority databases. Column 2 vertical slivers are automatically generated as 70% to 80% of required code from the resulting DDL as discussed in Chapter 15. Column 4 workflows are automatically generated as executable XML-based BPM languages as discussed in Chapter 14.

Benefits

- This approach enables strategic business plans for the future to be defined using the strategy analysis methodology of enterprise engineering in Chapter 3.

- The business plans are used to identify data and information that are required for the future. This is documented in a *strategic model,* which is a high-level enterprise model (column 1, row 2) that achieves enterprise-wide data integration. These high-level entities typically represent 10% of entities that will eventually be defined in the enterprise-wide logical data model in column 1, row 3.
- The strategic model is defined in a facilitated modeling session held over 2 days with business managers or business experts familiar with the strategic business plans. A facilitated modeling session is described in Chapter 7.
- Entity dependency analysis is used to analyze the strategic model. It identifies subsets of the strategic model that represent the vertical slivers that are used for early delivery of priority areas as subprojects. Project plans are also derived from the strategic model for these subprojects using *entity dependency analysis.* This method is described in Chapter 7.
- Past methods for enterprise models left many-to-many associations unresolved between related entities. Strategic modeling decomposes all many-to-many associations. This is used to identify the business activities and business processes that represent vertical slivers in column 2. Management priorities then determine the activity or process vertical slivers to be delivered first in 3-month builds.
- Priority activities are defined further using activity modeling and activity-based costing (ABC), which is used to determine relative costs of current ("as is") and future ("to be") activities so that optimum process improvements are achieved. This is discussed in Chapter 8.
- The priority data slivers, activity slivers, and workflow slivers are then delivered rapidly into production. Priority data slivers are automatically generated as DDL scripts for databases. This same DDL is also used for automatic generation of 70% to 80% of required code in various languages as reusable code patterns based on the DDL database structure. Priority workflows are also automatically generated as executable XML-based code in BPM languages.

Limitations

The following comments are suggestions of how best to implement this strategy. But if these suggestions cannot be utilized, then their absence represents limitations of the strategy.

- Some rework will be required over time with this incremental strategy, with limited but acceptable redundancy.
- The effectiveness of this strategy for 3-month incremental builds depends on the active support of senior management of priority business areas in the enterprise.
- These senior managers should all participate in the two-day strategic modeling facilitated session (see Chapter 7) to provide business direction. This is a large commitment of their valuable time, but it is their direct responsibility; their active involvement is essential for the ultimate success of enterprise architecture. The direction to be taken for rapid delivery of enterprise archi-

tecture will be based on the priorities defined by senior managers during and after this facilitated session.

- Business experts most knowledgeable in the enterprise should also participate in the strategic modeling facilitated session and in later detailed modeling sessions. The accuracy of the strategic model will be compromised if these business experts cannot participate.

5.8 Enterprise Engineering for Enterprise Architecture

Considering the above strategies, we will now discuss methodologies that are used for implementing enterprise architecture. These are based on enterprise engineering, as introduced earlier.

In strategy C, enterprise architecture is progressively delivered in 3-month incremental builds. Priority areas can be delivered rapidly using XML, Web services, and SOA technologies. This strategy uses the six-step approach illustrated in Figure 5.23, and described in the following.

Step 1: Column 6 (Why) is the starting point. This focuses on business plans defined for the future. Although formal strategic planning methods may have originally been used to define these plans at the strategic level, enterprise engineering uses strategy analysis in column 6, rows 1 and 2, to ensure that the plans are also able to be implemented at the tactical and operational levels of the enterprise, with full management accountability. Strategy analysis is discussed in detail in Chapter 3.

Step 2: Strategy analysis uses the organizational structure to identify the managers who are responsible for implementing the business plans. This is defined in column 4 (Who), row 1. Based on priorities identified in the business plans, business

	3	5	6	2	4	1
	What Data	**How** Function	**Where** Location	**Who** People	**When** Time	**Why** Future
PLANNER Objectives/Scope	**List of Things**	**List of Processes**	**List of Locations**	**Org Structure**	**List of Events**	**List of Goals/ Obj**
OWNER Conceptual	**Enterprise Model**	**Activity Model**	**Business Logistics**	**Work Flow**	**Master Schedule**	**Business Plan**
DESIGNER Logical	**Logical Data Model**	**Process Model**	**Distrib. Architect.**	**Human Interface**	**Process Structure**	**Business Rules**
BUILDER Physical	**Physical Data Model**	**System Model**	**Technol. Architect.**	**Presn Interface**	**Control Structure**	**Rule Design**
SUBCONTRACTOR Out-of-Context	**Data Definition**	**Program**	**Network Architect.**	**Security Interface**	**Timing Definition**	**Rule Specs**
FUNCTIONING ENTERPRISE	Data	Function	Network	Organization	Schedule	Strategy

Figure 5.23 Broad enterprise engineering implementation sequence.

experts knowledgeable in these priority areas are also identified in column 4, row 1. Their business knowledge is drawn on through their involvement as enterprise architecture project team members whose participation is scheduled in later implementation steps.

Step 3: The business plans defined in Step 1 are used as a catalyst here, along with the managers and business experts of priority areas that were identified in Step 2. They participate initially in a 2-day facilitated modeling session as described in Chapter 7 to develop a strategic model based on those plans. This strategic model is a high-level enterprise model in column 1 (What), row 2.

Entity dependency analysis is an objective method that is used in this step to derive priority strategic model subsets. These "vertical slivers" can then be implemented as initial priority subprojects for early delivery. Methods used to develop a strategic model and apply entity dependency analysis are described in detail in Chapter 7.

Step 4: Recent enterprise architecture project experience indicates that identification of business events in column 5 (When), row 1, is an important catalyst in identifying reusable business activities in column 2 (How). These events, together with the entity dependency analysis in Step 3, are used to identify reusable business activities that correspond with priority vertical data slivers in column 1 as priority subprojects for early delivery.

Step 5: These priority business activities are defined as activity models that document the inputs, outputs, controls, and mechanisms (resources)—and the associated costs—within these activities that are designed to improve processes. Activity modeling and activity based costing are discussed in Chapter 8.

Step 6: This step, with the identification of strategic model subsets and activity models as vertical slivers based on priorities from Steps 1 and 2, then identifies relevant corresponding locations in column 3 (Where), row 1.

5.9 Summary

The summary is as follows:

- We reviewed the Zachman framework for enterprise architecture, with its six columns that address what, how, where, who, when, and why. The rows of the Zachman framework reflect perspectives of the Planner, Owner, Designer, Builder, and Subcontractor. These questions have to be answered from each perspective, whose input is needed to build an integrated enterprise.
- We examined the U.S. government federal enterprise architecture framework and the U.S. DoD enterprise architecture initiatives: C4ISR and DoDAF. These are all based on the Spewak EAP methodology. We also reviewed the open group architecture framework. We discussed that TOGAF can be used with each of these other frameworks.
- We saw that these approaches offer guidance for managing complex projects, but they provide *little methodology guidance* for the Planner and the Owner rows of the Zachman framework. We discussed that rigorous methods based

on enterprise engineering in these rows are essential to identify both integrated data and reusable processes to achieve business integration.

- To address this, we discussed the strategic methods of enterprise engineering. These methods apply to the Planner and Owner rows of enterprise architecture. They are *strategy analysis*—to define strategic directions; *strategic modeling*—to define integrated data in strategic models; and *entity dependency analysis* to derive project plans for rapid delivery of priority activities.

The chapter concluded with three implementation strategies for enterprise architecture:

- The first strategy showed how enterprise architecture is used conservatively to build systems in 20% of the time and 10% of the cost of traditional systems development. These savings are realized after multiple years, when business integration is achieved in the enterprise.
- The second strategy discussed the development of a ROI business case for enterprise architecture. It can be used with the first and third strategies.
- The third strategy utilized the latest enterprise architecture project experience. It discussed how the strategic methods of enterprise engineering deliver time and cost savings similar to the first strategy, but in 3-month increments. With this strategy, high-priority and high-ROI systems are delivered rapidly for immediate benefit. This third strategy results in steady evolution to an integrated enterprise through progressive business integration, instead of only after multiple years with the first strategy. It can be used by any enterprise architecture project, regardless of also using FEAF, C4ISR or DoDAF, Spewak's EAP, or TOGAF.

We are now ready to move to the detailed methodology chapters. We covered strategy analysis in Chapter 3 to develop business plans that define the future. This is the starting point for enterprise architecture. Chapter 6 discusses business-driven data mapping. Chapter 7 describes how to develop a strategic model for rapid enterprise architecture implementation.

Endnotes

[1] Jackson, M., *Principles of Program Design,* New York: Academic Press, New York, 1975.
[2] Orr, K., *Structured Systems Development,* New York: Yourdon Press, 1977.
[3] Yourdon, E., and L. Constantine, *Structured Design: Fundamentals of a Discipline of Computer Program Systems Design,* Englewood Cliffs, NJ: Prentice-Hall, 1978.
[4] De Marco, T., *Software Systems Development,* New York: Yourdon Press, 1982.
[5] Codd, E., "A Relational Model for Large Shared Data Banks," *CACM,* Vol. 13, No. 6, 1970, pp. 377–387.
[6] Date, C., *Introduction to Data Base, Vols. 1 and 2,* Reading, MA: Addison-Wesley, 1982.
[7] Date, C., *An Introduction to Database Systems,* Vol. 1, 4th ed., Reading, MA: Addison-Wesley, 1986.
[8] Fagin, R., "Normal Forms and Relational Database Operators," *Proc. ACM SIGMOD International Conference on Management of Data,* 1979.
[9] Kent, W., "A Simple Guide to Five Normal Forms in Relational Database Theory," *CACM,* Vol. 26, No. 2, 1983.

[10] Finkelstein, C., *Information Engineering,* six in-depth articles, *Computerworld,* May/June 1981.

[11] Finkelstein, C., and J. Martin, *Technical Report: Information Engineering,* Carnforth, U.K.: Savant Institute, November 1981.

[12] Finkelstein, C., *An Introduction to Information Engineering,* Sydney, Australia: Addison-Wesley, 1989.

[13] Finkelstein, C., *Information Engineering: Strategic Systems Development,* Sydney, Australia: Addison-Wesley, 1992.

[14] Booch, G., *Object-Oriented Analysis and Design with Applications,* 2nd ed., Reading, MA: Addison-Wesley, 1994.

[15] Booch, G., I. Jacobson, and J. Rumbaugh, *The Unified Modeling Language User Guide,* Reading, MA: Addison-Wesley, 1998.

[16] Rumbaugh, J., G. Booch, and I. Jacobson, *The Unified Modeling Language Reference Manual,* Reading, MA: Addison-Wesley, 1998.

[17] Jacobson, I., et al., *The Unified Software Development Process,* Reading, MA: Addison-Wesley, 1999.

[18] Booch, G., J. Rumbaugh, and I. Jacobson, *The Complete UML Training Course,* Englewood Cliffs, NJ: Prentice-Hall, 2000.

[19] Further information about Rational, within IBM, is available from the Rational Web site at http://www.rational.com, or at http://www.imb.com/rational.

[20] The FEAF, Version 1.1, September 1999, is available in PDF format from http://www.itpolicy.gsa.gov/mke/archplus/fedarch1.pdf.

[21] Spewak, S., *Enterprise Architecture Planning: Developing a Blueprint for Data, Applications, and Technology,* New York: Wiley and Sons, 1993.

[22] The federal enterprise architecture program management office at http://www.egov.gov provides extensive reference material on the latest developments for the FEAF reference models. I would like to acknowledge the input and assistance of Robert Weisman of CGI in this section.

[23] CIO Council, *Practical Guide to Federal Enterprise Architecture,* Version 1.0, February 2001.

[24] The Enterprise Architecture Method (EAM)©, developed by CGI, is an extension of Spewak's EAP.

[25] The FEAF and the Zachman framework for enterprise architecture mapping in this section were provided by Robert Weisman and CGI in Ottawa, Canada.

[26] U.S. Air Mobility Command. Much of the material from the USAF AMC has been provided by staff directly involved in the AMC enterprise architecture project from 1994. Further detail is available from Colonel Joseph Butchko (U.S. Air Force, Retired) at Joseph.Butchko@scott.af.mil.

[27] *Canadian Defence Beyond 2010.*

[28] The material for these three defense interoperability approaches was provided by Robert Weisman of CGI. Robert is the enterprise architecture practice manager at CGI Inc. in Ottawa, Ontario, Canada. He can be contacted at robert.weisman@cgi.com. Information about CGI is available at http://www.cgi.com.

[29] ATTCCIS is discussed further, in relation to approach 4 in Section 5.4.6.

[30] The original OMB Circular A-130 is on the White House Web site at http://www.whitehouse.gov/omb/circulars/a130/a130trans4.html. A Word version can be downloaded from http://www.tricare.osd.mil/tmis_new/Policy%5CFederal%5COMB-130. doc. A discussion of OMB Circular A-130 is available at http://www.firstgov.gov/webcontent/documents/a130summary.pdf.

[31] The DoD architecture framework (generally referred to as the C4ISR framework) is a PDF available at http://www.enterprise-architecture.info/Images/Defence C4ISR/Enterprise Architecture Defense.htm.

[32] The DoD architecture framework version 1.0 (DoDAF V1.0) documentation comprises Volume i, Volume ii, and the DoDAF deskbook. These are all located all at http://aitc.aitcnet.org/dodfw.

[33] I would further like to acknowledge the excellent work done by Robert Weisman and CGI in Ottawa, Canada, on defense architectures and on the FEAF reference models.

[34] U.S. Air Mobility Command. I acknowledge the firsthand project experience provided by Joe Butchko (joseph.butchko@scott.af.mil) in relation to the USAF AMC. His comments have been included throughout this chapter. I also acknowledge the work done to map the C4ISR and DoDAF product deliverables to columns of the Zachman framework.

[35] *DoD Architecture Framework, Version 2.1, Volume II —Product Descriptions,* October 2000, includes examples of each product deliverable that is summarized in Table 5.1.

[36] A white paper published by Popkin Software (now Telelogic) titled "Mapping BPMN to the Department of Defense Architecture Framework (DoDAF)" can be downloaded from http://www.telelogic.com.

[37] BPMN can be used to generate executable XML-based code in various BPM languages. These languages include Business Process Execution Language (BPEL) and Business Process Modeling Language (BPML), discussed in Chapter 14. Modeling tools that support BPMN are discussed in Chapter 15.

[38] Further information on TOGAF is available at http://www.opengroup.org/architecture/togaf.

[39] An excellent white paper on TOGAF by Popkin Software (now Telelogic), titled "Building Enterprise Architectures with TOGAF," can be downloaded from the Telelogic Web site at http://www.telelogic.com. It provides an overview of TOGAF and discusses how System Architect can be used with it.

[40] The results in this section are based on the enterprise architecture project undertaken by the Ohio Bureau of Workers' Compensation. These results were quoted by John Zachman, based on information supplied to him by Doug Erickson (e-mail: dataduke@msn.com).

[41] This is a little confusing. The other state system had fewer entities, which were unnormalized (300), whereas the Ohio system had 1,030 normalized entities. The relative cost per entity for the other state system was thus much higher than the Ohio system. A more accurate cost comparison should be based on the relative cost per attribute. However, statistics on the number of *attributes* for each system are not available.

[42] These results are extreme; they reflect the high development cost and long development time (12 years) of the other state system, which was most unusual. A more realistic result expectation for enterprise architecture is 30% of the time and 30% of the cost of traditional development methods.

[43] With rapid business change today, enterprise architecture needs to be delivered faster than by having to spend multiple years. We will see in strategy C that new data modeling methods of *entity dependency analysis* identify priority data model subsets for definition and delivery into production in 3-month incremental builds.

[44] John Zachman uses the results achieved by ENTARCO in Strategy A and discusses Strategies B and C in his "Understanding Enterprise Architecture" seminars that he presents around the world.

CHAPTER 6

Using Business-Driven Data Mapping for Integrated Data

In Chapter 5 we covered enterprise architecture methods. We discussed strategies for rapid delivery of priority enterprise architecture areas into production. In this chapter we will cover business-driven data mapping methods to identify priority data for integration. This is an important method for rapid delivery of enterprise architecture. We will develop these principles further in Chapter 7 to derive project plans from data maps for rapid delivery of priority vertical slivers as discussed in Chapter 5. These methods apply to the What column for the Planner, Owner, and Designer rows [C1R1–C1R3] as illustrated in Figure 6.1.

6.1 Enterprise Architecture Incremental Build Context

This chapter covers data mapping methods for development of data maps from business planning statements. In Chapter 3 we covered strategy analysis to define business plans for the future. This addressed the Zachman framework's Why column for the Planner and Owner rows [C6R1–C6R2]. It uses strategy C from Chapter 5; this is discussed next, with the following steps keyed to Figure 6.2.

- *Step 1:* Strategy analysis in Chapter 3 identified statements for mission, vision, core values, goals, objectives, issues, KPIs, and strategies in the strategic plan.
- *Step 2:* Strategy analysis identified from the organizational structure those managers and business experts responsible for implementing priority areas of the strategic plan.
- *Step 3:* With participation by the identified managers and business experts, over 5 days in a business planning workshop they optionally apply the strategy analysis methodology to define tactical business planning statements to implement strategic plans.
- *Step 4:* Data mapping is used to enable business experts and IT experts to work together to identify data for integration. This begins with a 2-day strategic modeling facilitated session as detailed in Chapter 7. Entities that represent required information and data are listed in the What column for the Planner row [C1R1].
- *Step 5:* The facilitated modeling session continues over 2 days, documenting key entities in a strategic model on a whiteboard. The strategic data map is a high-level enterprise model for the What column in the Owner row [C1R2].

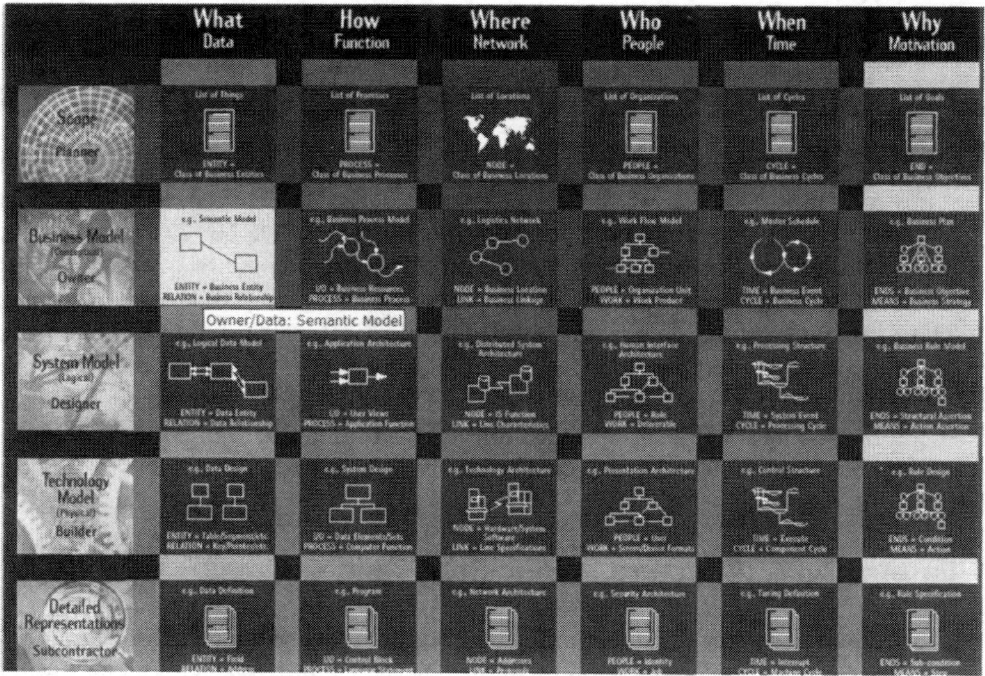

Figure 6.1 Data mapping addresses the Zachman framework's What column [C1R1–C1R3].

	What Data	How Function	Where Location	Who People	When Time	Why Future
PLANNER Objectives/Scope	4 List of Things	List of Processes	List of Locations	2 Org Structure	List of Events	1 List of Goals/Obj
OWNER Conceptual	5 Enterprise Model	Activity Model	Business Logistics	Work Flow	Master Schedule	3 Business Plan
DESIGNER Logical	Logical Data Model	Process Model	Distrib. Architect.	Human Interface	Process Structure	Business Rules
BUILDER Physical	Physical Data Model	System Model	Technol. Architect.	Presn Interface	Control Structure	Rule Design
SUBCONTRACTOR Out-of-Context	Data Definition	Program	Network Architect.	Security Interface	Timing Definition	Rule Specs
FUNCTIONING ENTERPRISE	Data	Function	Network	Organization	Schedule	Strategy

Figure 6.2 Steps 1 through 5 for rapid implementation of enterprise architecture.

These data mapping steps will be used in Chapter 7 to develop a strategic model. We will also use it again in conjunction with business normalization in Chapter 9 for logical data modeling.

6.1.1 Reading Strategy for This Chapter

This chapter introduces data modeling and data mapping concepts. With examples, case study problems, and sample solutions included as additional book material on the accompanying CD-ROM, it shows how to use these methods to develop integrated data models in the What column for the Planner, Owner, and Designer rows [C1R1–C1R3].

The chapter uses IE data modeling notation. If you have used other modeling notations, such as UML class diagrams or IDEF1X, you may find that the concepts in this chapter provide added business-driven skills. If you are an experienced data modeler you will likely want to skim-read the chapter. While doing this, keep alert for notation differences and new concepts that you may not have seen before, including the following:

- Representing time and other complex business rules with association nature;
- The identification of business activities, processes, or systems from a data map;
- The use of structure entities to capture expert rules for knowledge management.

These concepts are used extensively in business-driven data mapping. From your skim-reading of this chapter, you can determine how these business-driven IE concepts also apply to your use of data modeling.

This chapter and Chapter 7 should be read together. Entity dependency analysis methods for data models are introduced in Chapter 7. These methods have not previously been documented elsewhere in the industry. They are used for the manual or automated derivation of project plans and project maps directly from a data map. They are critical methods that are used for the rapid delivery of enterprise architecture.

6.2 Data Modeling Conventions

Data modeling is a major component of systems development and is extensively used by IE. There are two variants of IE, the technical, IT-driven variant and the business-driven variant:

- The IT-driven IE variant was designed so that IT staff could work with users to design information systems that supported the business needs of the 1980s. This variant was documented in the 1981 book titled *Information Engineering* [1]. Many modeling tools today still support this IT-driven IE variant.
- The business-driven IE variant is based on further development from 1983 to support rapid change environments in the 1990s and beyond [2–4], focusing also on the Internet and corporate intranets. This chapter presents the business-driven variant of IE, also called *enterprise engineering* (EE).

The following sections discuss the role of data modeling in the systems development life cycle (SDLC). The basic terminology of entities, attributes, and associations are next defined. The formal conventions that are used for data mapping are then covered.

6.2.1 Business-Driven Enterprise Engineering Phases

Business-driven enterprise engineering supports all phases of the systems development life cycle (SDLC). We discussed in Chapter 1 that the phases above the line in Figure 6.3 are technology independent and focus on the business. These are strategic business planning, data modeling, and function modeling:

- The strategic directions set by management provide input to strategic business planning, as discussed in Chapter 3.
- These plans indicate the information requirements of management and provide input to data modeling, as discussed in this chapter.
- Plans and data models define information usage, as input to function modeling, for activity modeling (Chapter 8) and process modeling (Chapter 10).

6.2.2 Data Modeling Phase

The data modeling phase in Figure 6.3 shows that strategic business planning identifies the information requirements of management and provides input to this phase:

- Strategic business plans provide input to strategic modeling, to develop a strategic model.
- Analysis of the strategic model produces an enterprise architecture portfolio plan (EAPP).

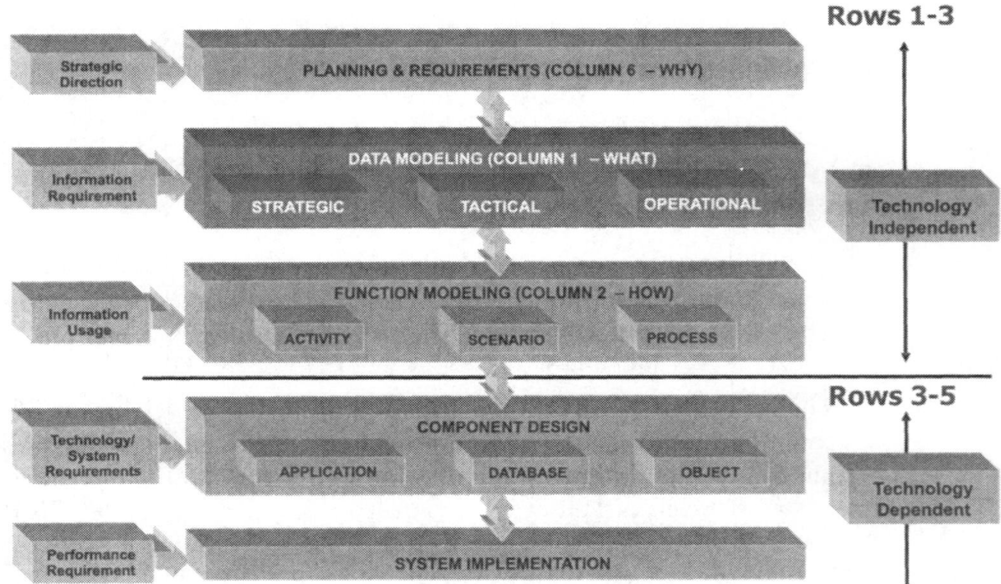

Figure 6.3 Data modeling phase in enterprise engineering.

The strategic model, EAPP, and tactical business plans all provide input to develop tactical data models. These are typically represented as logical data models for the What column and Designer row [C1R3].

The EAPP, tactical data models, and operational business plans all provide input to operational modeling to develop operational data models. These are also shown as logical data models for the What column and Designer row [C1R3].

6.2.3 Definition of Data Modeling

> Data modeling is a process that is used to identify, communicate, and record details about data and the relationships that exist between data, with its own terminology and conventions.

This definition does not assume any prerequisite knowledge of computers, but rather of the business. Enterprise engineering has terminology and conventions so it can be used as a common communication medium between business experts and IT experts.

A business is comprised of organizational units represented in the Who column for the Planner row [C4R1] and business functions or business processes in the How column. We will refer to these collectively as *model views*. We use a terminology of data entities, data attributes, and data associations (or just entities, attributes, and associations) to represent, in a model view, data for part of the business.

A data model includes a schematic representation of entities and associations (called a *data map*—analogous to the street maps in a street directory) and details of entities and attributes (called an *entity list*—analogous to a list of street names and other details in the street directory).

6.2.4 A Simple Data Map

A schematic data map shows each entity as a rectangular box as shown in Figure 6.4 The name of the entity is written within the entity box, in uppercase letters and in the singular for a single occurrence of the entity, such as EMPLOYEE, SKILL, and JOB. There may be many employees, skills, and jobs. However we will use each

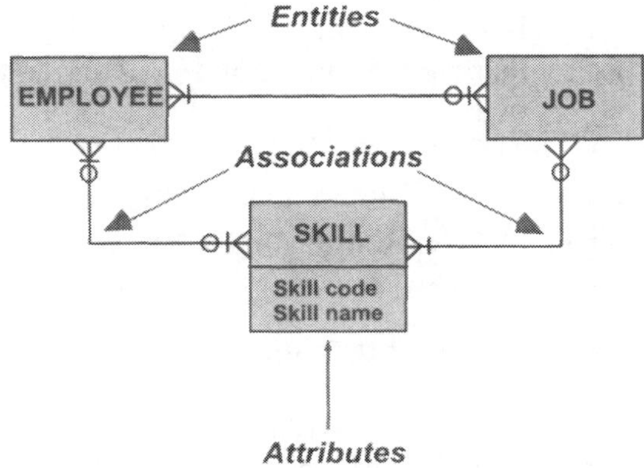

Figure 6.4 Example of a simple data map,

entity box to show the data that we need to know about each employee (to represent all employees), and similarly for each skill and each job, to represent all skills and jobs.

Attributes may optionally be listed within the entity box, as shown in the SKILL entity of Figure 6.4. These are written in lowercase to distinguish them from the entity name. They also are written in the singular, to represent a single occurrence of each attribute.

Two entities that are related in some way are joined by a connecting line that is called an *association*. Symbols drawn on each end of an association line describe the relationship that exists between the two entities. We will discuss these symbols in more detail shortly.

A data map is thus comprised of entity boxes (optionally containing attributes) joined by association lines. It shows data entities of interest and indicates by the associations how those entities are interrelated. Related groups of entities are included in model views for those parts of the organization that are interested in the entities.

This data map notation can be drawn by hand or can be drawn by a *CASE modeling tool* (a computer-aided software engineering software product) that enable data maps to be drawn in different formats. CASE tools are also called *modeling tools* and are discussed in Chapter 15. They allow any changes to be easily made so that all data maps can be kept up to date.

6.2.5 Definition of a Data Entity

> A data entity is something of interest that we may need to refer to later. It is a logical representation of data to be stored in a database in a computer, or in a manual register file or some other storage format if not yet on computer.

We will use the logical term *data entity* (or just *entity*) rather than the more physical term *file* or *record*. When doing logical data modeling, we are not initially concerned with the physical representation of an entity, merely that it does logically exist and will be stored in some way for later reference. It is only during physical database design that we decide how the entity will be physically stored. This depends on the technology that is available, and on the system and performance requirements when implemented.

An entity is always written in the singular, for a single occurrence of the data that it represents. It is also written in capitals to distinguish it from attributes (which are in lowercase). Examples of entities and the data they represent are:

- EMPLOYEE: Data we need to store about each employee.
- JOB: Data we need to store about each job.
- SKILL: Data we need to store about each skill.

6.2.6 Definition of a Data Attribute

> Data attributes are contained in data entities. Attributes provide additional details that describe the entity in which they reside.

We will use the logical term *data attribute* (or just *attribute*) rather than the physical terms *data item, data element,* or *data field.* During later steps in logical data modeling we will define the logical data type of the attribute (text, money, number, and so forth). We will not decide the physical data type and representation of the attribute until physical database design is carried out in [C1R4], when we know more about the systems requirements and the performance requirements for implementation.

An attribute name is always singular, to refer to *one* occurrence of data that it represents. It is also written in lowercase to distinguish it from entities (which are in uppercase).

An attribute should be qualified to avoid any ambiguity, typically by the name of the entity in which it resides. Thus *employee name, employee address,* and *employee phone number* are clearly different from *customer name, customer address,* and *customer phone number.* If we used only *name, address,* and *phone number* it might not be clear whether we were referring to the details of customers or employees.

6.2.7 Definition of Data Associations

> An association is shown by a line joining two entity boxes, to represent a relationship that exists between the relevant entities. It models business rules for those entities.

We will use the term *association* to refer to the logical connection between the related entities, rather than the more physical term *relationship*. During database design, in the physical design phase in the What column and the Builder row [C1R4] we will decide how the association is to be physically implemented. This depends on the database technology that will be used, and also the system and performance requirements when implemented.

A name may optionally be written on an association line to define the meaning of the connection between related entities, as illustrated in Figure 6.5. The association between EMPLOYEE and SKILL is not yet fully defined. However reading from left to right, the data map shows that "employee has skill." Reading from right to left, it shows that "skill is held by employee."

Business-driven data mapping shows only one association line between a pair of entities. If more than one association is drawn between two entities, it generally indicates that more detailed entities exist [5]. These entities should be added to the data map to show more clearly the business rules they represent. IT-driven IE modeling tools allow two or more lines to be shown between a pair of entities. A clearer representation of the business is achieved if only one association is allowed to exist between a pair of entities, and the more detailed entities that are suggested by the other associations are instead added to the data map.

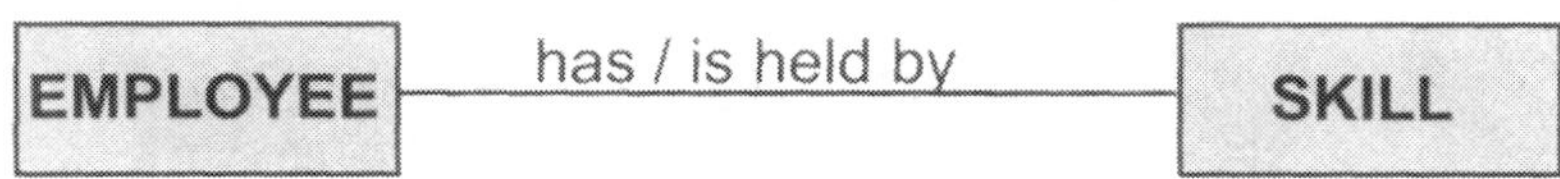

Figure 6.5 A data association in a data map.

6.2.8 Association Degree in Business-Driven Data Mapping

Symbols are added to each end of an association line to indicate the *cardinality,* or *degree,* of the association. In this book we will use the latter term: *degree.*

A "crow's-foot" (also called a "chicken-foot") represents *one or many* occurrences of the entity that it touches, as shown in Figure 6.6. No crow's-foot indicates *one* occurrence of the entity. This convention for *one* is used by the business-driven IE variant.

When reading the meaning of the association, the first entity referenced is always expressed in the singular. The second entity is plural if the association degree is *one or many;* it is singular if the degree is *one.*

The association has now taken on greater meaning. Reading the example in Figure 6.6 from left to right and applying these rules, we can see that "an employee has one or many skills." From right to left it means "a skill is held by one employee." We can now represent business rules and meaning schematically. Other data modeling techniques use different conventions to represent degree. For example IDEF1X is used by many defense departments and uses a solid bullet at the end of an association line to represent *one or many.*

We can now see an important benefit of data modeling. It provides immediate feedback by raising the question "Can a skill be held by one or many employees?" If true, this suggests that the association should be changed from *one* to *one or many* instead at EMPLOYEE.

Other meanings may also apply, such as "teaches/is taught by," or "learns/is learned by." Rather than draw these as additional association lines between the two entities, we will later see that more detailed review of these meanings will help us to identify different types of employees (called subtypes), such as INSTRUCTOR and STUDENT.

6.2.9 Association Degree in IT-Driven Data Mapping

The IT-driven data mapping variant uses a slightly different notation. A "crow's-foot" (also called a "chicken-foot") represents *one or many* occurrences of the entity that it touches. But a different convention for *one* is used by IT-driven modeling tools. This convention uses a bar across the line and no crow's-foot to show *one* occurrence of the entity, as shown in Figure 6.7.

The meaning of the association is still read in the same way. The first entity referenced is always expressed in the singular. The second entity is plural if the association degree is *one or many;* it is singular if the degree is *one.*

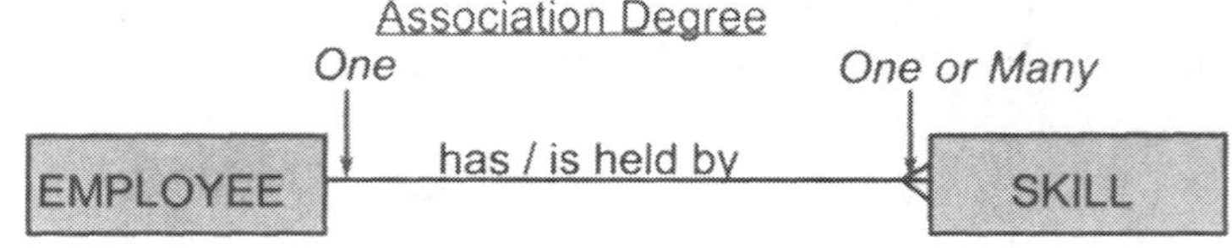

An employee has one or many skills.
A skill is held by one employee.

Figure 6.6 Business-driven association degree of one, and also one or many.

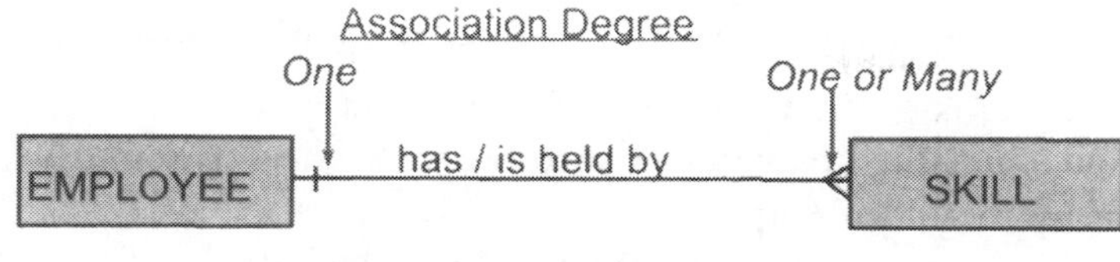

Figure 6.7 IT-driven association degree of *one* and also *one or many.*

As for Figure 6.6, reading the example from left to right and applying these rules to Figure 6.7 we can see that "an employee has one or many skills." From right to left it means "a skill is held by one employee." We can now represent business rules and meaning schematically.

6.2.10 Association Nature in Business-Driven Data Mapping

Other symbols are added to each end of an association line to show *association nature.* In this book we will use the abbreviation *nature.* The notation for nature in Figure 6.8 is used both by business-driven and IT-driven data mapping.

Association nature enables us to provide additional detail in the business rules expressed by the example in Figure 6.8. Reading from left to right—using **bold** for the application of the notation for nature—we can see that "an employee **may** have one or many skills." Reading from right to left means "a skill **must** be held by one employee."

- A "vertical bar" on a line means *mandatory,* and is expressed as *must.*
- A "zero" on a line means *optional,* and is expressed as *may.*

Based on feedback from this interpretation, we may decide to clarify the meaning as shown next in bold: "an employee **may** have *zero,* one or many skills" and "a skill **must** be held by one (**and only one**) employee." This feedback now forces us finally to resolve the question "Can a skill be held by one or many employees?" Does it mean that if we have more than one employee with a skill, all but one must leave? This would be a strange way to run a business! If this interpretation is wrong then the degree must be changed at EMPLOYEE to *mandatory one or many.* This means that "a skill **must** be held by **at least one or many employees.**" This is certainly more realistic.

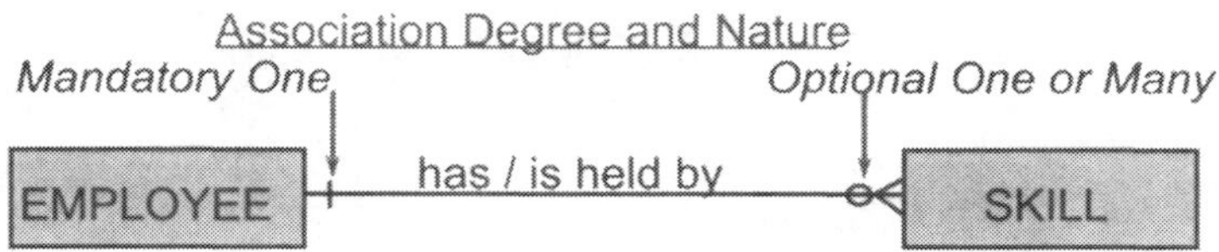

Figure 6.8 business-driven association nature of mandatory and optional.

6.2.11 Association Nature in IT-Driven Data Mapping

When we look at the IT-driven IE notation in Figure 6.9, we see that two bars can exist on a line: the first vertical bar represents a degree of *one,* while the second vertical bar represents a nature of *mandatory.*

Once again, this notation further documents the business rules expressed by the preceding example. As in Figure 6.8, reading again from left to right and showing in bold the application of the notation for nature, we can see that "an employee **may** have zero, one, or many skills." From right to left this means "a skill **must** be held by one employee" [6].

Again based on feedback from this interpretation, we may decide to clarify the meaning as shown next in bold: "an employee may have **zero,** one or many skills" and "a skill **must** be held by one (**and only one**) employee."

6.2.12 Time-Dependent Nature in Business-Driven Data Mapping

We will now see a third notation for nature: using a zero and a bar together—meaning *optional becoming mandatory,* or *will.* This nature enables us to represent more complex business rules. For instance, from the EMPLOYEE entity, the example in Figure 6.10 expresses the rule: "an employee will (eventually) have one or many skills." From the SKILL entity it shows "a skill must be held by only one employee."

Quite independently, as we discussed earlier and in addition to representing the nature of *optional becoming mandatory,* the data map could alternatively show a degree of *mandatory one* or *many* at EMPLOYEE to represent the business rule that "a skill must be held by at least one or many employees." This models the situation where an employee initially has no skills, but will acquire at least one or many skills eventually (i.e., over time). This skill acquisition may occur with formal training, or on-the-job experience gained over time.

Situations that require the use of *optional becoming mandatory* model complex business rules that typically represent business processes. Modeling these processes in more detail may lead to the identification of additional entities, attributes, and associations that should be added to incorporate other business requirements in the data model.

6.2.13 Time-Dependent Nature in IT-Driven Data Mapping

An association nature of *optional becoming mandatory,* or *will,* is not supported for this purpose by the IT-driven data mapping variant. This can limit the ability of IT-driven data maps schematically to represent complex business rules for business

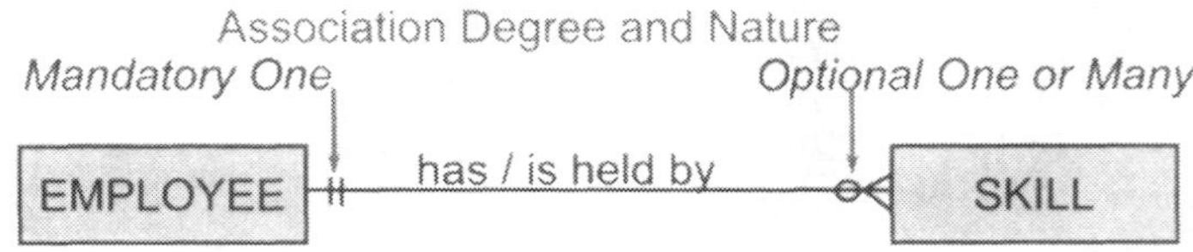

Figure 6.9 IT-driven association nature of mandatory and optional.

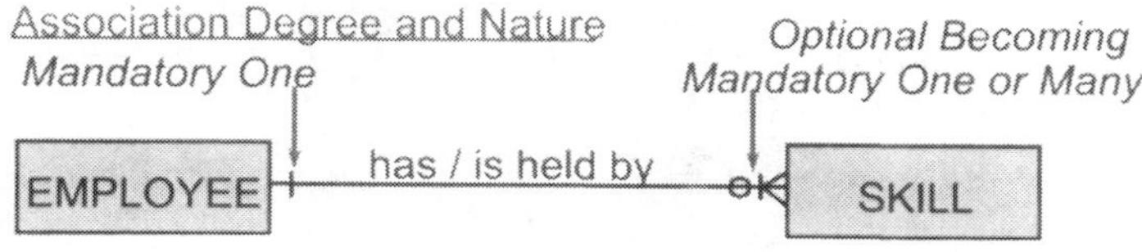

Figure 6.10 Business-driven association nature of mandatory becoming optional.

processes or functions. To overcome this limitation, two alternatives can be employed if using a modeling tool that only supports the IT-driven variant:

1. Use an association name that describes the complex business rule. But most IT-driven modeling tools use association names of limited length. This can constrain their ability to express complex rules.
2. Alternatively, describe the complex rule or process represented by the association by using the IT-driven modeling tool to attach a *purpose description* narrative to the association. Purpose descriptions of associations, and also processes, are discussed later in this chapter.

6.2.14 Summary of Association Degree and Nature

We have now covered the following data mapping concepts:

- An entity box represents data stored for later reference, and is shown in uppercase letters.
- Attributes describe more detail of the entity in which they reside, and are shown in lowercase letters.
- An association is a line showing that the two entities joined by it are related. The association may optionally be named.
- Only one association line is used between each pair of entities.

As summarized in Figure 6.11, an association uses symbols at each end to show the characteristics of association cardinality or *degree,* and *nature* for business-driven data mapping as follows:

- A *crow's-foot* indicates an association degree of *one or many.*
- The *absence of a crow's-foot* indicates a degree of *one.*
- A *bar* across the line always indicates a nature of *mandatory,* and means *"must."*
- A *zero* across the line always indicates a nature of *optional,* and means *"may."*
- A zero and bar always indicate a nature of *optional becoming mandatory* and means *"will."*

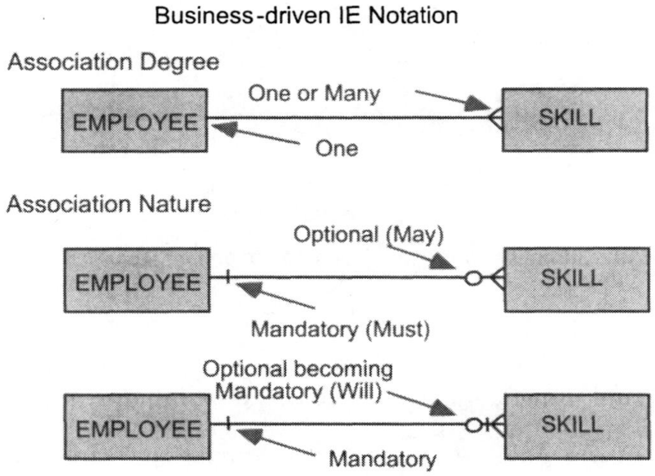

Business-driven IE Notation

Association Degree

EMPLOYEE
One or Many
One
SKILL

Association Nature

EMPLOYEE
Optional (May)
Mandatory (Must)
SKILL

EMPLOYEE
Optional becoming Mandatory (Will)
Mandatory
SKILL

Figure 6.11 Business-driven data mapping notation summary.

6.2.15 Case Study Problem 1

At this stage, it is important to apply the concepts that we have covered to a case study example. This is described in *Box 6.1: Data Mapping Problem 1,* which is included on the accompanying CD-ROM [7]. Please complete this problem now, before reading on. The solution is provided in the *Sample Solutions* section of the CD-ROM as detailed in the case study problems file. Please review that case study sample solution before continuing with the rest of the chapter.

6.3 Data Entity Types

This section now examines the following types of data entities in detail: *principal entity, type entity, secondary entity, intersecting entity, role entity,* and *structure entity.* These entity types enable us to show more clearly the data and information that are used by different business areas and interests within an organization. These entities are used as follows:

- *Principal* (supertype) entities contain common data that are shared throughout an organization.
- *Type* entities are used for project management purposes and typically indicate the existence of more detailed (subtype) entities.
- *Secondary* (subtype) entities contain data that are not to be shared throughout the organization; or where privacy, security, or governance controls are enforced.
- *Intersecting* entities result from decomposition of *many-to-many* associations, and represent potential business activities, processes, or systems.
- *Role* entities are used to define business interrelationships and business roles.
- *Structure* entities are used to capture business knowledge as expert rules for knowledge management.

These entity types allow detailed business knowledge to be represented in data maps, so that business requirements can be more clearly identified.

6.3.1 Principal Entity

A *principal* entity is of interest to many functional areas throughout the organization. As discussed earlier, these functional areas may be organizational units in the Who column and Planner row [C4R1], or business functions or processes in the How column and Planner row [C2R1], collectively called *model views.* Typically principal entities contain common data that are typically shared by many model views.

The concept of a principal entity is also used by IT-driven IE, but is called a *super-type.* It similarly represents common data that are typically to be shared throughout the organization [8].

A principal entity must be uniquely identified by at least one key attribute, called a *primary key.* Primary keys originate in principal entities. We will discuss primary keys in a later section.

The example in Figure 6.12 shows the principal entity EMPLOYEE in the model view HR; that is, it is managed by the human resources (HR) department but shared throughout the enterprise. It contains attributes in an entity list, documented according to the following conventions:

- An entity list contains the name of the entity in uppercase letters.
- Attributes that reside within the entity follow within brackets, separated by commas. These are *employee number, employee name,* and *employee address.*
- Note that *employee number#* is underlined, with suffix "#," which is pronounced "key." This notation indicates that *employee number* is a primary key that is used to uniquely identify each occurrence of an employee, as we will discuss later.

A principal entity, when physically implemented in a database for the What column and Builder row [C1R4], typically becomes a separate database table. The attributes of the entity list in Figure 6.12 become columns of the database table, as shown in Table 6.1 for the EMPLOYEE table. Each occurrence of the entity is implemented as a row in the table. Two employees are shown in this EMPLOYEE

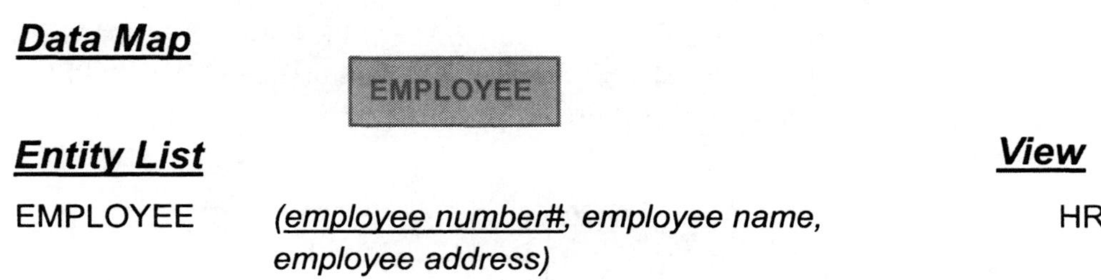

Figure 6.12 A principal entity contains common shared data in an enterprise.

Table 6.1 Example EMPLOYEE Database Table

Employee Number	*Employee Name*	*Employee Address*
1234	John Smith	1 First Street, Anywhere
4567	Jack Brown	2 Second Street, Any City

database table: employee numbers 1234 and 4567 for the fictitious employees "John Smith" and "Jack Brown," respectively.

Because *employee number#* is underlined in the entity list to show that it is a primary key, each employee number in the table must be defined so that it is unique. This uniqueness is clear in Table 6.1. Of course, we are not limited to using numbers for primary keys. We could alternatively use *employee code#* or *employee id#* or any other term that uniquely identifies each employee.

6.3.2 Type Entity

A *type* entity indicates that other entities may also exist for each principal entity. Type entities are used during data mapping for project management purposes. For example, when modeling the example in Figure 6.13 only EMPLOYEE was identified at first.

- The human resources department manages EMPLOYEE details of employee numbers, names, and addresses, but these data are also shared by all other areas.
- The sales department and management services department indicated that there are specific details they need to know about salespersons and managers.
- This indicates the potential existence of additional entities to represent two types of employees: SALESPERSON and MANAGER.
- The entity EMPLOYEE TYPE was added in Figure 6.13 to record the existence of these entities. It is called a *type* entity.

EMPLOYEE TYPE may later be implemented as the database table "Employee Type" in a data warehouse, for example. This can be used to hold derived information that is aggregated from detailed operational data. For instance, management may be interested in the "total number of employees of each type." This is derived by counting the number of employees (i.e., occurrences of the EMPLOYEE entity) who are salespersons and the number of employees who are managers.

The entity EMPLOYEE TYPE indicates that more detailed entities exist for the principal entity EMPLOYEE. These are SALESPERSON and MANAGER and are called *subtype* or *secondary* entities. We will examine SALESPERSON and MANAGER in more detail shortly.

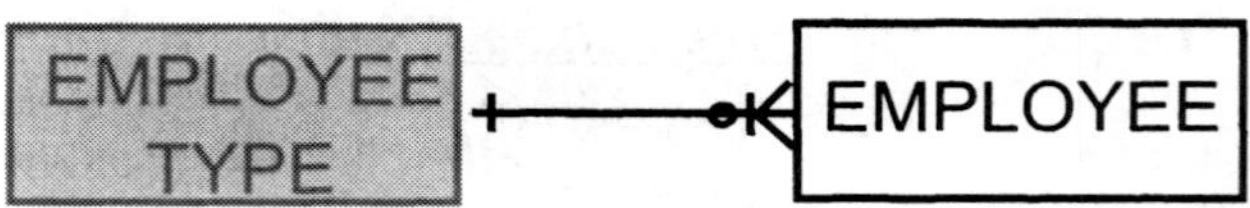

Figure 6.13 A type entity indicates that other entities may also exist.

A *type* entity typically contains the attributes: *(entity-name) type number#* (as a primary key) and *(entity-name) type name* as illustrated in Figure 6.14 for EMPLOYEE TYPE:

EMPLOYEE TYPE (*employee type number#*, employee type name)

The attribute *employee type number#* is also added to the end of EMPLOYEE. Later, in the section on data attribute types we will see that *employee type number#* in this entity is a foreign key. We are not limited only to numbers for employee type. We could use *employee type code#* or *employee type id#* or other terms to identify each employee type.

Employee type number# is a common key that exists in both EMPLOYEE TYPE and EMPLOYEE. It indicates an association exists between the entities; that is, *mandatory one* (at EMPLOYEE TYPE) to *optional becoming mandatory many* (at EMPLOYEE). This is a characteristic association that exists between a type entity and its related principal entity. It is interpreted as "an employee type will (eventually) have one or many employees of that type."

When implemented as an Employee Type table (Table 6.2), we see that the *Employee Type Number* column contains the following values:

- "0" to identify an Employee;
- "1" to identify a Salesperson;
- "2" to identify a Manager.

This concept has been used as a shorthand notation in business for many years. Sometimes codes or numbers become part of the enterprise vocabulary or jargon. For example, a shorthand reference for salespersons might be "code 1" people. Similarly, managers may be called "code 2" people.

The concept of using data fields in a record to indicate the relevant record format has also been used in systems development for many years. For example, the salesperson record may be called a "code 1" record format, with the manager record format called a "code 2" format. This is indicated by a special data field in the record, called a *record type code,* that contains "1" for salesperson records and "2" for manager records.

Other attributes can exist in a type entity, such as required for a data warehouse. The earlier example, "total number of employees of each type," is the attrib-

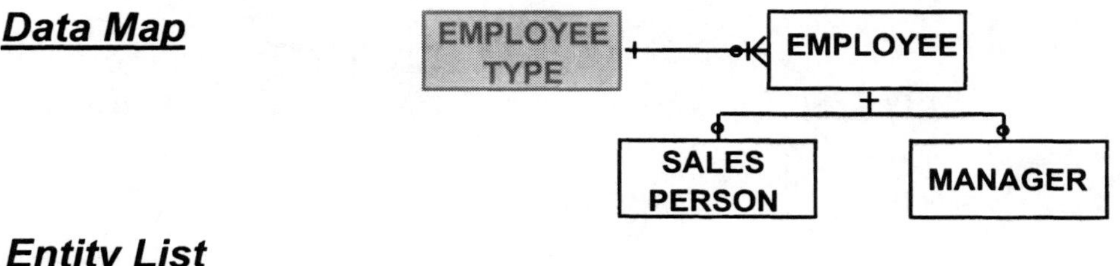

Entity List

EMPLOYEE TYPE (*employee type number#*, *employee type name)*

EMPLOYEE (*employee number#, employee name, employee address, employee type number#)*

Figure 6.14 A type entity data map and entity list.

Table 6.2 Example Database Table: Employee Type

Employee Type Number	*Employee Type Name*
0	EMPLOYEE
1	SALESPERSON
2	MANAGER

ute name. The column name, when implemented, may be "total employees this type."

6.3.3 Secondary Entity

While principal entities are typically shared throughout an organization, some data are of interest only to specific functional areas (i.e., model views). These are called *secondary* entities. IT-driven IE calls these *subtype* entities, but we will use the term *secondary* entity. Secondary entities contain data that are typically not shared throughout the organization, over which privacy, security, or legislative governance controls may be exercised. Secondary entities appear only in those model views that have an interest in privacy, security, or governance authorization for access to the data represented by those secondary entities.

In the example in Figure 6.15, the secondary entities are shaded. They are used to represent specific types of employees.

- We saw earlier that EMPLOYEE is a *principal* (or *supertype*) entity.
- SALESPERSON and MANAGER are *secondary* (or *subtype*) entities. These entities were earlier identified from the *type* entity EMPLOYEE TYPE.
- Secondary entities participate in a characteristic hierarchical association as shown: *mandatory one* association (at the *principal* entity end) to an *optional one* association (at the *secondary* entity end).

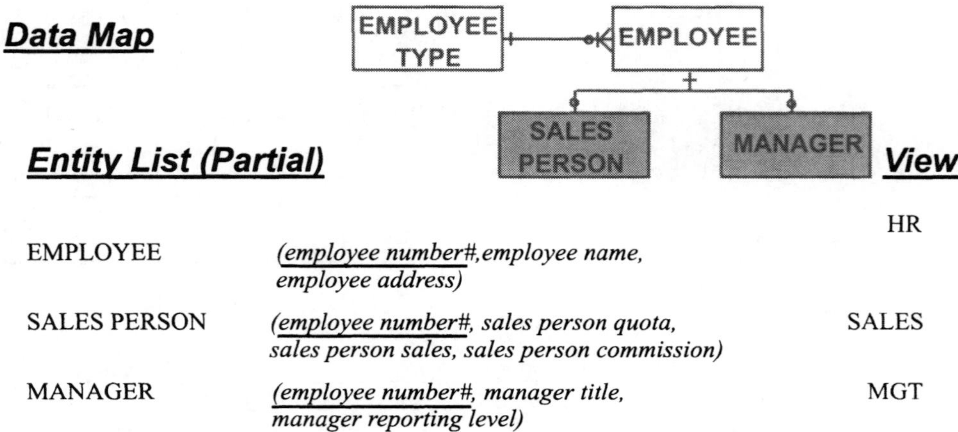

Figure 6.15 A secondary entity data map and entity list.

The entity list for the secondary entities in Figure 6.15 shows attributes that may not be accessible by other model views for privacy, security, or corporate governance reasons:

- SALESPERSON contains the attributes *salesperson quota, salesperson sales,* and *salesperson commission* that are of interest only to the sales department model view. This department exercises privacy and security control over these attributes. They consider these attributes to be sensitive data that are not to be shared by other parts of the business.
- MANAGER contains the attributes *manager title* and *manager reporting level* that are considered of interest only to the management services model view and not to be shared by others.

Notice that both SALESPERSON and MANAGER have the same primary key *employee number#* as has EMPLOYEE. The existence of this common primary key establishes the hierarchical *mandatory one* to *optional one* association between EMPLOYEE and each secondary entity [9]. Other data mapping notations, such as those used by Oracle Designer, use a large entity box for principal or supertype entities, with smaller boxes inside to represent this same hierarchical secondary or subtype representation.

6.3.4 Exclusive Type Entity

An *exclusive type* entity is defined as follows:

An exclusive type entity can be related to only one occurrence of a secondary entity.

We previously discussed the association in the data map in Figure 6.14, namely, *mandatory one* (at EMPLOYEE TYPE) to *optional becoming mandatory many* (at EMPLOYEE). This indicates there *will eventually be one or many* employees for each employee type. However, the *mandatory one* at EMPLOYEE TYPE also indicates that each employee can be of *one (and only one)* employee type. This is called an *exclusive type* entity as illustrated in Figure 6.16.

Expressed more clearly, this exclusive type entity data map in Figure 6.16 indicates (1) an employee who is a salesperson cannot later be promoted to a manager, and (2) an employee who is a manager cannot later be promoted to a salesperson. If the data map in Figure 6.16 correctly models the "promotion" business rules of the organization, it indicates that this enterprise does not promote from within. Instead, it implies that new managers or salespersons are appointed from outside,

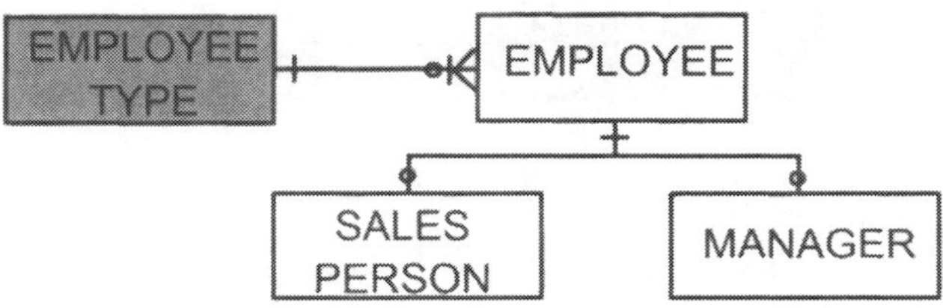

Figure 6.16 An exclusive type entity.

by recruitment. If this data map has been correctly modeled, this would not be a good employer to work for if you were looking for advancement through promotion!

6.3.5 Inclusive Type Entity

An *inclusive type* entity is defined as follows:

> An inclusive type entity can be related to many occurrences of secondary entities.

Contrast the example in Figure 6.16 now with Figure 6.17, which has a modified (highlighted) association, namely, *mandatory one or many* (at EMPLOYEE TYPE) to *optional becoming mandatory many* (at EMPLOYEE).

The *mandatory one* ("Exclusive") at EMPLOYEE TYPE in Figure 6.16 is now a *mandatory one or many* in Figure 6.17. We will also look at the *many-to-many* association between EMPLOYEE TYPE and EMPLOYEE in more detail shortly, when we discuss role entities.

Figure 6.17 shows an inclusive type entity. This indicates that each employee can be of *one or many* employee types *(but at least one)*. The data map now indicates that (1) an employee who is a salesperson can later be promoted to a manager, (2) an employee who is a manager can later be promoted to a salesperson, and (3) an employee can be both a salesperson and a manager at the same time or over time.

If the data map correctly models the "promotion" business rules of the organization, Figure 6.17 now indicates that the organization will promote from within. It allows managers to be salespersons as well. This models a more flexible business rule. We now see more of the power of data mapping: It enables alternative business rules to be evaluated.

Alternatively, Figure 6.17 also enables sales managers to carry a sales quota: as a personal sales quota, or as the aggregate sales quota of all salespersons who report to that sales manager.

6.3.6 Intersecting Entity

An *intersecting* entity is defined as follows:

> An intersecting entity results from the decomposition of a many-to-many association. It indicates the existence of a business activity, business process, or application system.

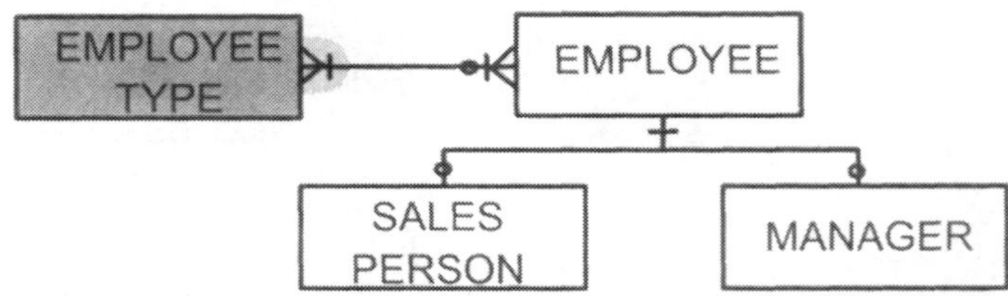

Figure 6.17 An inclusive type entity.

Consider now the next example in Figure 6.18. This is a variation on the solution to Case Study Problem 1 that illustrates the business rule "an employee must have at least one job, but can have many jobs. A job will eventually be filled by at least one or many employees." This data map illustrates a *many-to-many* association. In its present form, it is difficult to determine which jobs an employee has held (over time, or at the same time), or which employees fill (or have filled) a job.

To resolve these questions, a *many-to-many* association must first be decomposed. This results in the addition of an intermediate entity to the data map. This is called an *intersecting* entity [10]. The *many-to-many* association between EMPLOYEE and JOB is decomposed as shown in Figure 6.19.

- A new entity is drawn between the two entities. This is called an *associative* or *intersecting* entity. As discussed in an earlier endnote, we will use the term *intersecting* entity throughout the book.
- The name of this entity typically is based on a combination of the two original entity names. The *intersecting* entity in the example is thus called EMPLOYEE JOB.
- The *many-to-many* association is then decomposed into two *one-to-many* associations.

This introduces a very important principle used in business-driven data mapping for the rapid delivery of enterprise architecture:

An intersecting entity typically indicates the existence of a business activity, business process, or operational system [11].

As we will discuss later in this chapter and in Chapter 7, a business activity comprises one or more related business processes. The preceding example indicates the existence of (1) a potential business activity, called, for instance, an *employee job allocation activity;* (2) a potential business process, called, for instance, an *employee job appointment process,* and (3) a potential operational system, called, for instance, an *employee job assignment system.* This is a powerful characteristic of

Figure 6.18 The importance of many-to-many associations.

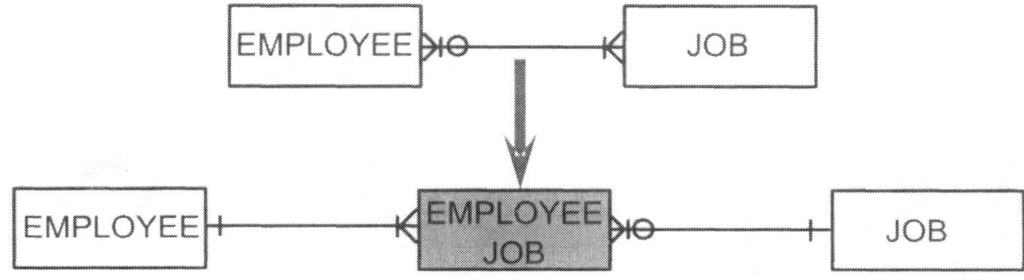

Figure 6.19 Decomposing a many-to-many association.

intersecting entities. The activity, process, or system name that is identified depends on the business needs and terminology. We will see later in Chapter 7 how this principle can be used for the rapid delivery of priority business data and activities, processes, or systems as vertical slivers for What and How.

The steps involved in decomposing a *many-to-many* association are shown in Figure 6.20. For each *many* end of the association:

- An association degree of *one* touches each original entity, and is *mandatory* nature.
- An association degree of *many* touches the intersecting entity.

The nature at the *many* end of the association is then moved across to touch the intersecting entity as shown in Figure 6.20. The implied business rule is then reviewed for validity. It is defined as *optional, mandatory* or *optional becoming mandatory* depending on the business rules that apply to the intersecting entity after decomposition. The interpretation of the business rule for association nature often becomes clearer by considering it from the perspective of the business activity, business process, or system identified by the intersecting entity.

The primary key of an intersecting entity is typically made up of the primary keys of the entities that it joins. The example in Figure 6.21 shows that EMPLOYEE JOB has a combined primary key: *employee number#, job number#*. This is called a *compound primary key*. Compound primary keys are discussed later, in the section on data attribute types.

From the *employee job* physical table in Table 6.3, we can now determine, for a given employee number, all of the jobs held by that person. For example:

- Employee 123 started job 65 on December 12, 2005, at a salary of $30,000.
- Employee 123 started job 89 on January 4, 2006, at a salary of $35,000.

Similarly for a given *job number* we can find all of the employees who have occupied that job. For example:

- Job 65 was held by employee 456 from March 25, 2005 at a salary of $45,000.

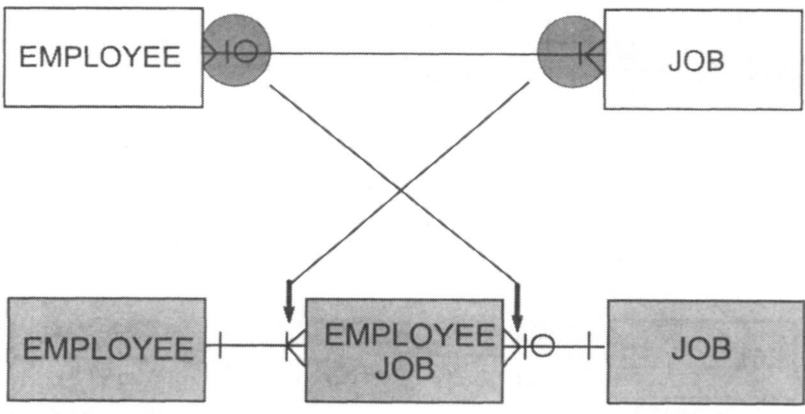

Figure 6.20 Steps in decomposing a many-to-many association.

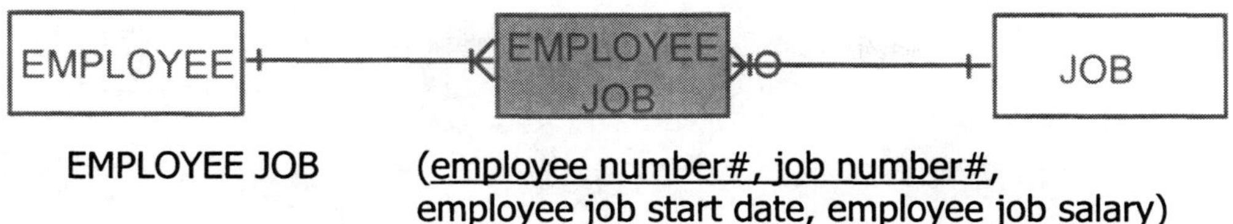

EMPLOYEE JOB (<u>employee number#, job number#,</u> employee job start date, employee job salary)

Figure 6.21 Data map and entity list of an intersecting entity.

Table 6.3 Example Database Table: Employee Job

Employee No.	*Job No.*	*Start Date*	*Salary*
123	65	December 12, 2005	30,000
123	89	January 4, 2006	35,000
456	65	March 25, 2005	45,000

- Job 65 was held by employee 123 from December 12, 2005, at a salary of $30,000.

6.3.7 Role Entity

A *role* entity is defined as follows:

> A role entity decomposes the many-to-many association between a principal entity and an inclusive type entity.

Consider again the example of an *inclusive* type entity in Figure 6.17, where an employee can be both a salesperson and a manager. This is represented by a *many-to-many* association between EMPLOYEE TYPE and EMPLOYEE. It indicates the potential existence of an intersecting entity. This is a special case of the *many-to-many* association rule and results in a *role* entity, as shown in Figure 6.22. It indicates the potential existence of what appears to be an intersecting entity. This entity has been called EMPLOYEE ROLE in that figure. It is a role entity and is a special case of the *many-to-many* association rule when used with an inclusive type entity: A *many-to-many* association between a type entity (e.g., EMPLOYEE TYPE) and a principal entity (e.g., EMPLOYEE) indicates the existence of a role entity.

A role entity specifies the different types (or "roles") that a principal entity can take with an inclusive type entity. As for an intersecting entity, a role entity has a compound primary key: <u>*employee number#*</u>, <u>*employee type number#*</u>. These are from the primary keys of EMPLOYEE and EMPLOYEE TYPE.

Because a *role* entity is a special case of an *intersecting* entity, it indicates the existence of (1) a potential *employee role management activity,* for example; (2) a potential *employee role management process,* for example; and (3) a potential *employee role management system,* for example.

The example in Table 6.4 enables us to record the date each employee started in a role (as a salesperson or as a manager) as well as the performance rating of that employee in each role. Table 6.4 shows that employee 123 started as a salesperson

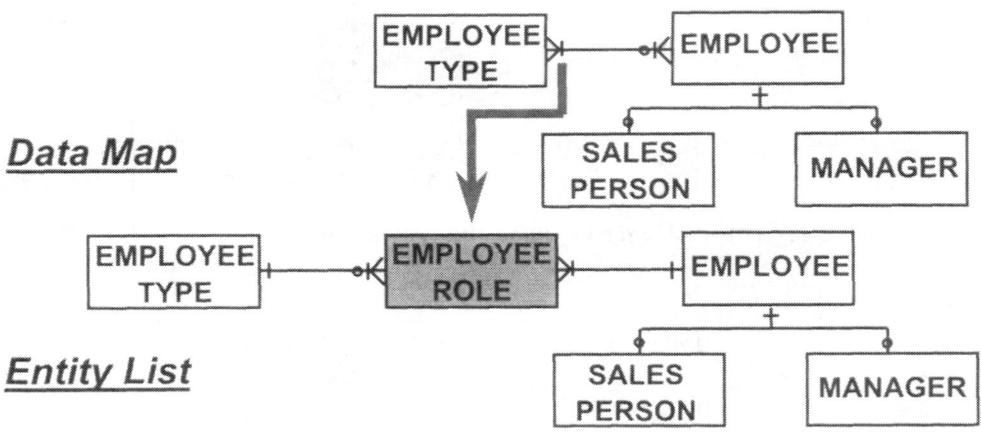

EMPLOYEE TYPE	*(employee type number#, employee type name)*
EMPLOYEE	*(employee number#, employee name, employee address)*
EMPLOYEE ROLE	*(employee number#, employee type number#* *employee role start date, employee role rating)*

Figure 6.22 Data map and entity list of a role entity.

(i.e., Type 1) on December 12, 2005, and had a performance rating of 3. Employee 123 then became a manager (i.e., Type 2) on January 4, 2006, with a rating of 2.

Similarly, employee 456 started as a salesperson on March 25, 2005, with a rating of 2, and then became a manager on April 14, 2004, with a rating of 4. Notice the last line, showing that employee 456 became a salesperson *again,* on May 20, 2005, with a rating of 3. This raises a difficulty:

- EMPLOYEE ROLE has a compound primary key: *employee number#, employee type number#*. We can correctly record details for each employee in each role.
- Employee 456 is a salesperson, twice. This means we can record details of 456 as a salesperson from May 20, 2005, but if we did that, we would then lose history of 456 as a salesperson from April 14, 2005. To correct this problem we need to enable an employee to occupy a role many times.

This capability is provided by making *employee role start date#* also a primary key by adding to the attribute name a suffix "#" (i.e., key), and underlining it to sig-

Table 6.4 Example Database Table: Employee Role

Employee No.	*Type No.*	*Start Date*	*Rating*
123	1	December 12, 2005	3
123	2	January 4, 2006	2
456	1	March 25, 2005	2
456	2	April 14, 2004	4
456	1	May 20, 2005	3

nify it is a primary key. Thus, an employee's rating now depends on the employee number#, the employee type number#, and the employee role start date#.

6.3.8 Case Study Problem 2

We will apply the concepts that we have covered so far to another case study example. This is described in *Box 6.2: Data Mapping Problem 2,* which is included on the accompanying CD-ROM [7]. Please complete this problem now, before reading on. The solution is provided in *Sample Solutions* on the CD-ROM as detailed in the case study problems file. Please next review that case study sample solution before continuing with the rest of the chapter.

6.3.9 Recognizing a Structure Entity

Sometimes we need to show associations between *secondary* entities. Consider secondary entities: CLERK and SUPPORT PERSON.

Figure 6.23 shows a *many-to-many* association between SALESPERSON and MANAGER. It also shows a "recursive" association on EMPLOYEE.

We now know that a *many-to-many* association indicates the potential existence of an *intersecting* entity, such as SALESPERSON MANAGER in Secondary entities.

But what if we had other *secondary* entities, such as CLERK and SUPPORT PERSON—similarly related to all other entities with *many-to-many* associations? We would have to add a number of *secondary* and *intersecting* entities to the data map, such as listed next.

Secondary entities:	CLERK and SUPPORT PERSON
Intersecting entities:	SALESPERSON MANAGER; plus CLERK SALESPERSON and CLERK MANAGER; and also SUPPORT PERSON SALESPERSON and SUPPORT PERSON MANAGER

Considering that any number of secondary entities can exist under a principal entity, to any depth, this approach using intersecting entities adds complexity to the data map. It does not make it easy to represent business knowledge clearly, which should be our main objective.

And what about the other association above: between EMPLOYEE and itself [12]? How should we represent that association?

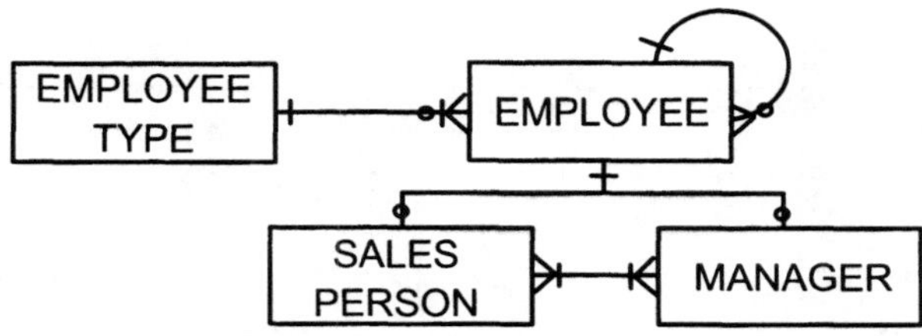

Figure 6.23 Resolving recursive associations, and many-to-many associations between secondary entities.

Figure 6.23 can be modeled much more simply by using a different type of entity, called a *structure* entity and shown in Figure 6.24 by EMPLOYEE STRUCTURE. The *many-to-many* association existing between SALESPERSON and MANAGER, and also the recursive association at EMPLOYEE, have now been replaced by this new *structure* entity.

The name for this entity may use "STRUCTURE" as a suffix (e.g., EMPLOYEE STRUCTURE), or instead may use RELATED EMPLOYEE, for example, or EMPLOYEE RELATIONSHIP. The example shows that structure entities typically exhibit a characteristic *mandatory one to optional many* association between the principal entity and the structure entity. Structure entities enable us to record complex relationships that exist (1) between occurrences of secondary entities, (2) between secondary entity occurrences and also between their related principal entity occurrences, and (3) between different occurrences of a principal entity. These complex interrelationships typically involve expert business knowledge. We will see shortly that a structure entity can be used to represent expert rules for knowledge management.

6.3.10 Structure Entity

A *structure* entity is defined as follows:

> A structure entity is used to represent many-to-many associations between occurrences of secondary entities all under the same principal entity, or to represent recursive associations between occurrences of a single principal or secondary entity.

A structure entity has several possible entity list formats. The numbers in the discussion that follows are keyed to the entity list formats shown in Figure 6.25 [13]:

1. Format 1 uses a compound key: the primary key of the principal entity (*employee number#*), but duplicated to identify related occurrences (as *related employee number#*).

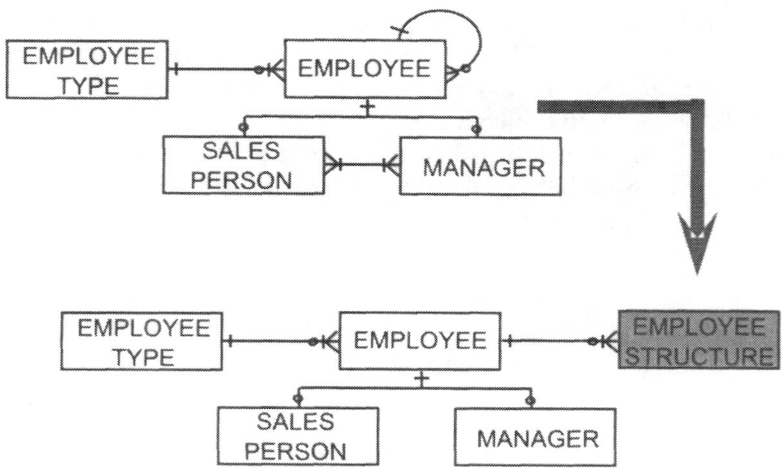

Figure 6.24 Recursive associations and many-to-many associations between secondary entities are resolved by using a structure entity.

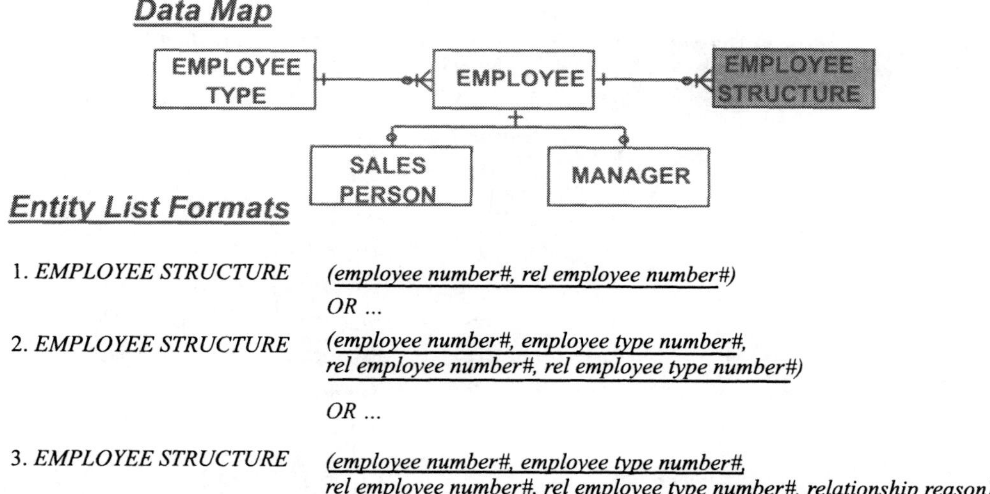

Figure 6.25 Entity list alternatives used by structure entities.

- Format 1 applies when a principal entity is of only one type and can never change. *Employee number#* is all that is needed for identification.

2. Format 2 uses a duplicated compound key: the primary key of the principal entity (*employee number#*), plus the primary key of the type entity (*employee type number#*), duplicated to identify related occurrences (*related employee number#* and *related employee type number#*).
   - Format 2 is used if a principal entity is of many types; *employee number#* and *employee type number#* are both needed for unique identification.
3. As in Format 2, but also indicating the reason for the relationship between entity occurrences (as *relationship reason*).
   - Format 3 provides a reason why the two occurrences are related. It may suggest an expert rule as discussed shortly.

Alternatively, *relationship reason id#* could be used in Format 3 as a foreign key, to establish an association to a separate entity called REASON with the following attributes:

REASON (*relationship reason id#*, reason description)

This now enables any number of reasons to be defined for the relationship between entity occurrences.

6.3.11 Structure Entity Represents a Table

Table 6.5 is based on Format 3 from Figure 6.25. The attribute names become column names in the table. It shows the content of a typical structure table. This table indicates that there can be many reporting relationships, as follows:

Table 6.5 A Typical Structure Table

Employee Number	*Employee Type*	*Employee Number*	*Employee Type*	*Relationship Reason*
1358	Manager	1362	Manager	Manager reporting
		1460	Salesperson	Sales reporting
		1556	Manager	Manager reporting
		1661	Salesperson	Sales reporting
1362	Manager	262	Salesperson	Sales reporting
		1132	Salesperson	Sales reporting
		1441	Salesperson	Sales reporting
1556	Manager	1333	Salesperson	Sales reporting
		1512	Salesperson	Sales reporting

- Manager 1358 manages employees 1362 and 1556 in a *manager reporting* relationship and employees 1460 and 1661 in a *sales reporting* relationship.
- The left to right relationship in the table therefore represents a *manager reporting* relationship, or a *sales reporting* relationship.
- Manager 1362 in turn manages employees 262, 1132, and 1441 in a *sales reporting* relationship.
- Manager 1556 similarly manages employees 1333 and 1512 in a *sales reporting* relationship.

Looking further at Table 6.5 and following the right to left relationship, we can also see that Employee 1441 reports to Manager 1362, who in turn reports to Manager 1358. The right to left relationship therefore represents the *reports to* relationship.

To explain a structure table more clearly, in Tables 6.5 and 6.6, columns with *employee type name* and *related employee type name* have been used for readability instead of *employee type number* and *related employee type number*. In practice, these latter columns with numbers would normally be implemented in a physical table or employee structure—rather than use names for readability as we are doing here.

Table 6.6 A Structure Table with an Expert Rule in the Last Row

Employee Number	*Employee Type*	*Employee Number*	*Employee Type*	*Relationship Reason*
1358	Manager	1362	Manager	Manager reporting
		1460	Salesperson	Sales reporting
		1556	Manager	Manager reporting
		1661	Salesperson	Sales reporting
1362	Manager	262	Salesperson	Sales reporting
		1132	Salesperson	Sales reporting
		1441	Salesperson	Sales reporting
1556	Manager	1333	Salesperson	Sales reporting
		1512	Salesperson	Sales reporting
1441	***Salesperson***	***1512***	***Salesperson***	***ABC Knowledge***

Assume now in Table 6.6 that 1512 is the salesperson responsible for Customer ABC. If 1512 is sick and, hence, absent from work, who is an alternative salesperson to call on ABC?

- Employee 1333 cannot be used. The table shows only that 1333 and 1512 both report to manager 1556. This fact does not indicate at all whether 1333 has any knowledge of Customer ABC.
- However, an additional line has been added at the bottom of the table, shown in ***bold italics***. The last line now shows that 1441 is related to 1512: They both have common knowledge of Customer ABC. This indicates that 1441 can visit Customer ABC, if 1512 is unavailable.

This fact is an example of expert knowledge recorded in the table. It is a powerful characteristic of structure entities: They can be used to capture expert rules. The left to right *manager reporting* and *sales reporting* relationships and the right to left *reports to* relationships are also examples of expert rules for knowledge management. These are rules well known by all employees, but not known at all outside the organization.

The fact that 1441 and 1512 both have common knowledge of Customer ABC was not well known. Previously it was only known by the individuals concerned. Now that the expert rule has been represented in the table, it is available to all who are authorized to access it. Structure entities therefore can implement expert rules so that the knowledge is readily accessible. It also allows changes in that knowledge to be made easily. Chapter 9 will show other examples of the use of structure entities and how they are used to represent expert knowledge as expert rules for knowledge management [14].

6.3.12 Summary of Entity Types

Figure 6.26 summarizes the entity types that are used by business-driven data mapping:

- EMPLOYEE and JOB are *principal* entities and contain attributes shared by all.
- EMPLOYEE TYPE is a *type* entity for project management purposes. *Type* entities often contain aggregate or derived data for data warehouse access.
- SALESPERSON and MANAGER are both *secondary* entities. They typically contain attributes that may not be shared, or where security, privacy, or corporate governance must be exercised.
- EMPLOYEE ROLE is a *role* entity. It shows the roles valid for a *principal entity*. It implements the *many-to-many* association of an *inclusive type* entity.
- EMPLOYEE JOB is an *intersecting* entity to identify potential business activities, business processes, or systems.
- EMPLOYEE STRUCTURE is a *structure* entity. This shows interrelationships between entity occurrences. It indicates expert knowledge that can represent expert rules for knowledge management.

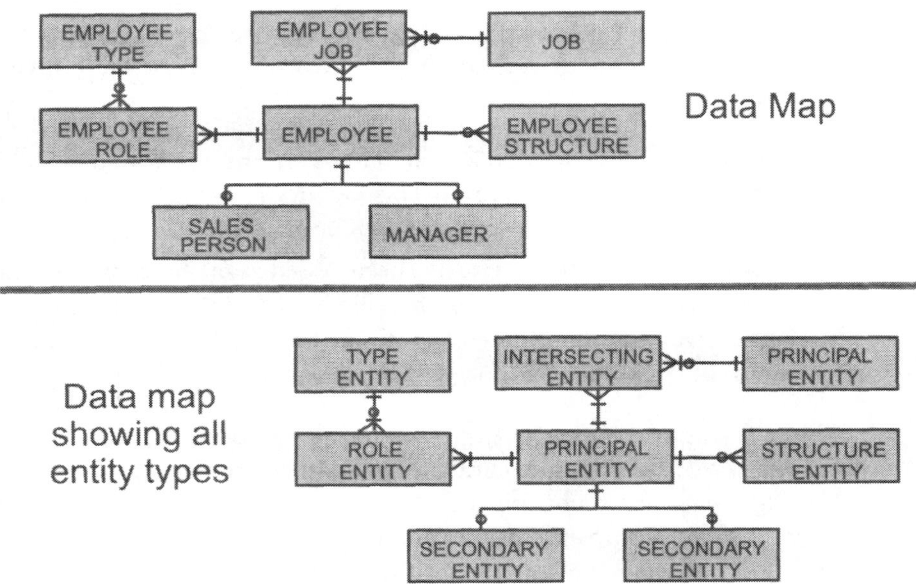

Figure 6.26 Summary of entity types, with examples.

Other entity types are also used by business-driven IE, but are outside the scope of this book. They include *rule* entities, *rule structure* entities, and *condition* entities.

6.3.13 Case Study Problem 3

We will apply the concepts that we have covered so far to another case study example. This is described in *Box 6.3: Data Mapping Problem 3,* which is included on the accompanying CD-ROM [7]. Please complete this problem now, before reading on. The solution is provided in *Sample Solutions* on the CD-ROM as detailed in the case study solutions file. Please review that case study sample solution before continuing with the rest of the chapter.

6.4 Data Attribute Types

This section examines the different types of data attributes in detail. These are *key attributes* and *nonkey attributes.* These data attribute types enable us to show more clearly the detailed attributes that reside in data entities to represent data and information used by different business areas and interests within an organization.

6.4.1 Key Attributes

We first look at *key attributes,* referred to as just *keys.* Several types of keys are covered in the following pages:

- *Primary keys:* Used to identify each entity occurrence, uniquely.
- *Foreign keys:* Identifier in one entity, which is a primary key of another entity.

- *Candidate keys:* Two or more unique identifiers for an entity, all of which are candidates to be chosen as the primary key.
- *Compound keys:* Two or more primary keys, used to establish a unique identifier.

6.4.2 Primary Key, with Examples

A *primary key* is an attribute used to identify one, and only one, occurrence of an entity. An entity must have a unique identifier consisting of one or more primary keys. A primary key can be made up of more than one attribute to establish uniqueness. This is called a *compound primary key* and is discussed shortly.

Two or more occurrences of an entity, all with the same primary key value, cannot be used. Because these key values are all duplicates of the key, the proposed key attribute is not unique and so cannot be used as a primary key. Such an attribute, with nonunique values, instead becomes a *selection attribute* (also called a *secondary key*). This is covered later when we discuss nonkey attributes.

A primary key is written in an entity list with the attribute name underlined, and with a terminating # as shown in Figure 6.27, where it is also highlighted.

No two employees can have the same "employee id"; each "id" is a unique value.

The next example in Figure 6.28 shows *employee number#* underlined: It is a unique primary key. However, notice the following in relation to the example:

- EMPLOYEE uses the primary key *employee number#*. The data map shows that it is a principal entity.
- Both SALESPERSON and MANAGER also use the same primary key *employee number#*. The data map shows these are *secondary* entities.
- This does not violate the uniqueness rule of primary keys: We are not told anything about the *values* of the primary key in the example.

However, we can see from the example that EMPLOYEE, SALESPERSON, and MANAGER all use the same primary key. This is an important concept of data modeling:

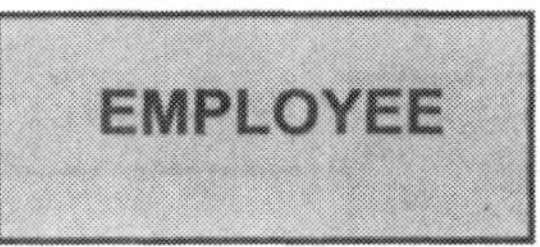

Employee Id #
Employee Name
Employee Salary
Job Title #

Figure 6.27 *Employee Id#* is a primary key.

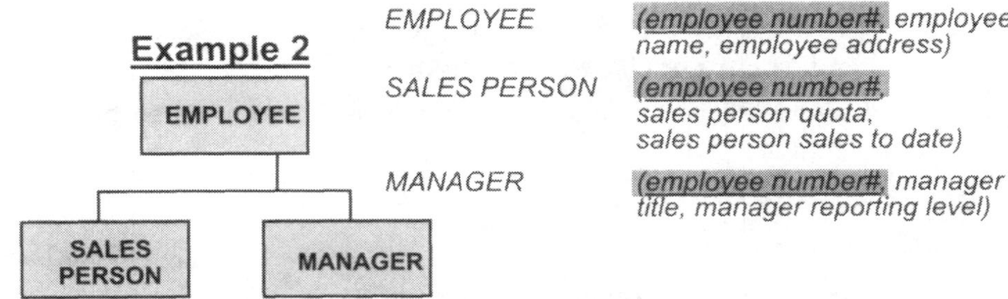

Figure 6.28 The *employee number#* is a common primary key.

A common key that exists in two entities indicates there is an association between those two entities. We will see next that two entities can have common primary keys, common foreign keys, or a mixture of common primary keys and foreign keys.

In fact, it is the common primary key *employee number#* that establishes the implied *mandatory one to optional one* association in the data map in Figure 6.28 between EMPLOYEE and SALESPERSON, and also between EMPLOYEE and MANAGER.

6.4.3 Foreign Key, with Examples

A primary key can be defined in one entity, but can also reside in another entity where it is not a primary key. In this other entity it is referred to as a *foreign key*. Because this key attribute is also a common key, it identifies a potential association between the two entities.

A foreign key is a key attribute and is written in an entity list with a terminating #. But it is not underlined, to distinguish it from primary keys. In the example in Figure 6.29:

- *Job Title#* is a *primary key* in JOB, and so is underlined.
- *Job Title#* is a *foreign key* in EMPLOYEE, and so is *not* underlined.

The common key *Job Title#* indicates an association exists between JOB and EMPLOYEE. The association degree and nature can be determined—in part, fairly automatically:

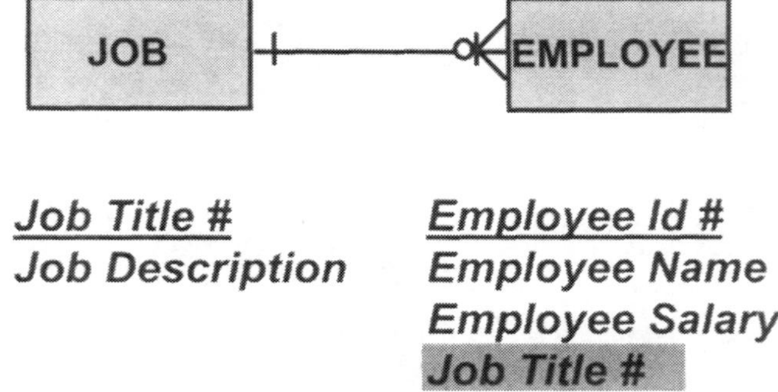

Figure 6.29 *Job Title#* is a common primary and foreign key.

- The association is *mandatory one* where it touches JOB, with *Job Title#* residing as a primary key.
- The association is *many* where it touches EMPLOYEE, with *Job Title#* residing as a foreign key.

However, the association nature at the end with the foreign key (i.e., at EMPLOYEE) cannot be determined automatically from the entity list. It must be determined from business rules:

- *May* a job remain *vacant?* If so, the association nature is *optional* [15].
- *Must* a job *never be vacant?* If so, the association nature is *mandatory.*
- *Will* a job *eventually* be filled? If so, the nature is *optional becoming mandatory.*

In the example shown in Figure 6.30, the foreign key is a key attribute and is written in an entity list with a terminating #. It is not underlined, to distinguish it from primary keys:

- *Employee type number#* is a primary key in EMPLOYEE TYPE and so is underlined.
- *Employee type number#* is a foreign key in EMPLOYEE, and is *not* underlined.

The common key *employee type number#* indicates an association between EMPLOYEE TYPE and EMPLOYEE. Once again, the association degree and nature can be determined—in part, fairly automatically. An association between type and principal entities is characteristically *mandatory one* (at EMPLOYEE TYPE) to *optional becoming mandatory many* (at EMPLOYEE). The association is:

- *Mandatory one* where it touches EMPLOYEE TYPE: *employee type number#* resides in it as a primary key.
- *Many* where it touches EMPLOYEE: as *employee type number#* resides in it as a foreign key.

As before, the association nature at the end with the foreign key (i.e., at EMPLOYEE) cannot be determined automatically from the entity list. It must be determined from business rules [15]:

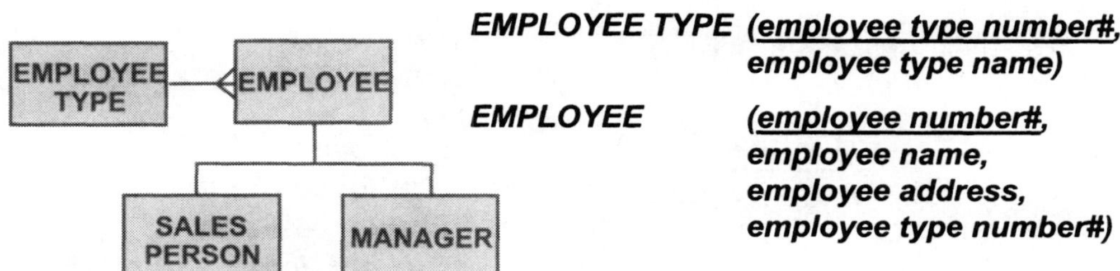

Figure 6.30 *Employee type number#* is a common primary and foreign key.

- *May* there be *no* employees of a particular type? If so, the association nature is *optional.*
- *Must* there be *at least one* employee of each type? If so, the nature is *mandatory.*
- *Will* there *eventually* be an employee of each type? If so, the association nature is *optional becoming mandatory.*

6.4.4 Key Attribute Alias

A key attribute can use alternative names for business meaning. These are called *alias names* and can be used in different parts of an organization in place of the agreed name for the primary key: They exhibit all of the characteristics of the key attribute to which they refer. The example in Figure 6.31 clearly shows this. It illustrates that the foreign key *Current Job#* (in EMPLOYEE) is an alias for *Job Title#* (in JOB). The foreign key *Current Job#* therefore participates as a common key with *Job Title#* in JOB and establishes the association between JOB and EMPLOYEE.

6.4.5 Candidate Keys

An entity can have more than one attribute that is unique and, therefore, can potentially be used as a primary key. Each of these unique attributes is called a *candidate key,* from which is chosen the key attribute that will be used as the primary key. In Figure 6.32, *job title* and *job number* are both unique: There cannot be two or more jobs each having the same *job title* or the same *job number.* Both attributes are thus candidate keys. Either attribute can be chosen to be the primary key of JOB.

6.4.6 Compound Key, with Examples

To establish a unique primary key, it is often necessary to combine two or more primary keys. These are then collectively referred to as a *compound primary key,* often abbreviated to *compound key.* The example in Figure 6.33 indicates the following:

- An employee *must* have at least one or many jobs (over time, and maybe even at the same time).
- A job *will* be filled eventually by one or many employees.

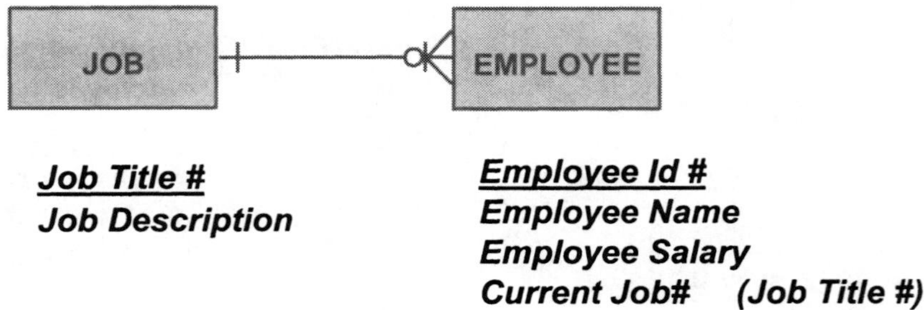

Figure 6.31 *Current Job#* is a foreign key alias for *Job Title#.*

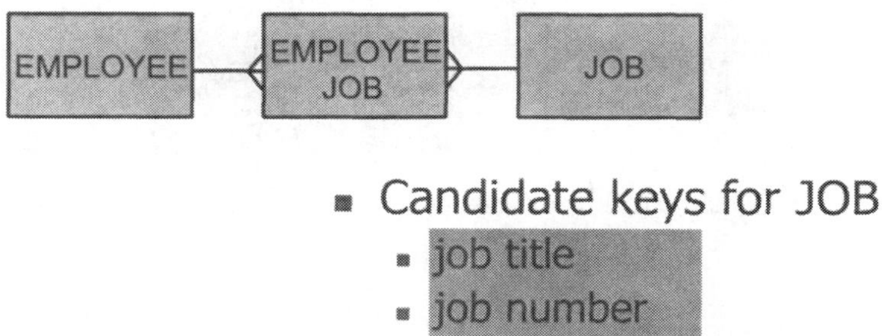

Figure 6.32 The *job title* and *job number* entries are both unique and are candidate keys.

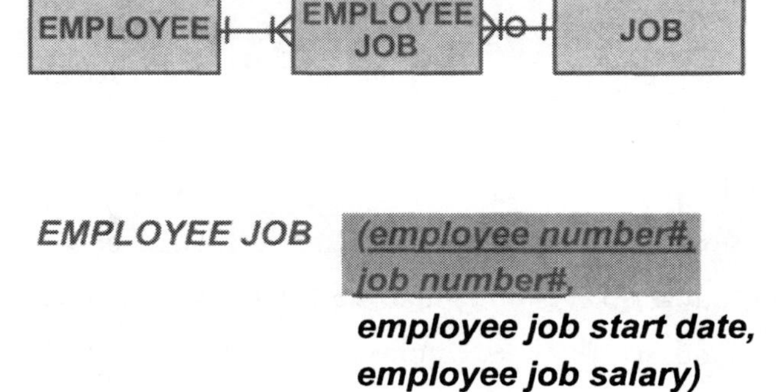

Figure 6.33 Example of compound primary keys.

Because an employee has many jobs, when implemented in an Employee Job table the key value of *employee number#* for an employee exists for each job held by that employee.

Similarly, because a job is filled by many employees, the key value of *job number#* for a job exists for each employee who has filled that job. However, to determine the *start date* of a specific employee in a specific job—and the *salary* of that employee in the job—requires that *both* the *employee number#* and also the *job number#* be known. The attributes *employee job start date* and *employee job salary* depend on the compound primary key *employee number#, job number#*.

The attribute-naming convention that business-driven IE uses—discussed in Section 6.2.6 as "qualifying an attribute name by the name of the entity in which it resides," such as with *employee job start date* and *employee job salary*—also tells us the attributes depend on a compound primary key. Figure 6.34 illustrates that SALARY PAYMENT has a compound primary key:

- Employees are paid on many dates (employees *1001* and *7575* in Table 6.7).
- A pay date pays many employees (see *December 31, 2005,* and also *January 31, 2006,* in Table 6.7).

To determine what amount was paid to a specific employee on a particular date requires *both* the *Employee Id#* and the *Pay Date#*. For example, the Table 6.7 tells us:

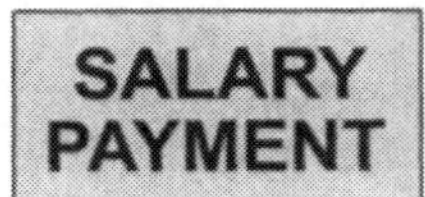

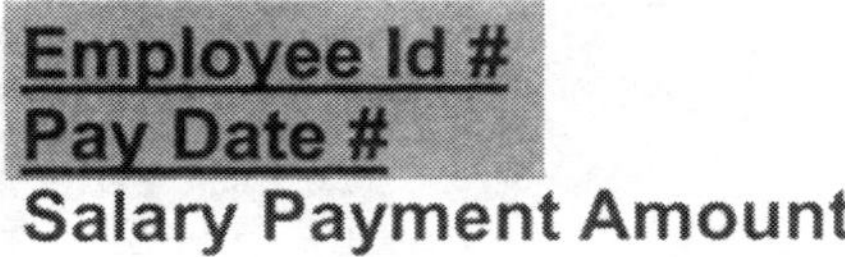

Figure 6.34 Another example of compound primary keys.

Table 6.7 Table of Employee Salaries

Employee ID#	*Pay Date#*	*Salary Amount*
1001	December 31, 2005	1,234.55
1001	January 31, 2006	1,300.00
7575	December 31, 2005	1,300.00
7575	January 31, 2006	1,366.67

- Employee 1001 was paid 1,234.55 on December 31, 2005.
- Employee 7575 was paid 1,300.00 on December 31, 2005.
- On January 31, 2006, employee 1001 was paid 1,300.00.
- On January 31, 2006, employee 7575 was paid 1,366.67.

6.4.7 Nonkey Attributes

We will now cover *no-key attributes,* referred to as *nonkeys*. There are several types of nonkey attributes:

- *Selection attribute:* Unique or nonunique attribute used to refer to, or access, an entity; also called a *secondary key.*
- *Group attribute:* A collective name, used to refer to a group of related attributes.
- *Elemental attribute:* A fundamental attribute that cannot be decomposed any further.
- *Repeating group attribute:* An attribute with many occurrences in an entity.
- *Derived attribute:* An attribute whose value is calculated from other attributes.

These nonkey attribute types are discussed in the following.

6.4.8 Selection Attributes (Secondary Keys)

Employee name is a nonkey attribute that is used to refer to, or select, an employee. We will therefore call it a *selection attribute*. It can be a unique, or a nonunique attribute; for example, there can be many employees with the same name. Written in an entity list as shown in Figure 6.35 the attribute name is surrounded by [square brackets], such as:

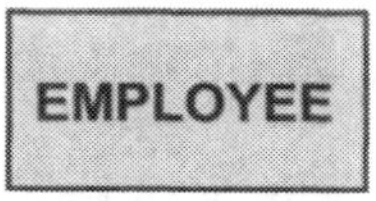

EMPLOYEE (employee number#, [employee name], employee address, [postal code])

Figure 6.35 Examples of selection attributes (secondary keys).

- *[employee name],* which is nonunique. When used as a *selection attribute,* all employees who have the same name can be selected.
- *[postal code],* which is also nonunique. There can be many employees who reside in the same postal area and therefore have the same postcode or zip code.

When the entity is physically implemented as the Employee database table, the attributes *[employee name]* and *[postal code]* can be used to access employees by name or the postal area where they reside. These are not key attributes because they are not unique. More than one employee can have the same name, but each is given a unique employee number to clearly identify each employee. Similarly more than one employee can reside in the same postal area.

Used in this way, a *selection attribute* is often called a *secondary key,* but this is an incorrect attribute categorization [16].

6.4.9 Elemental and Group Attributes

Nonkey attributes represent the data of the organization. They may be elemental or grouped. The following examples highlight the nonkey attributes of EMPLOYEE.

First, the example in Figure 6.36 shows *Employee First Name* and *Employee Last Name.* Each part of the name is explicitly used and its value is captured directly. These are called *elemental attributes*—they are at their atomic level of definition and cannot be decomposed further.

Figure 6.37 shows *(Employee Name)* highlighted. This is called a *group attribute.* Group attributes are written surrounded by a single left and right parenthesis. *(Employee Name)* is an example of a group attribute. It refers to the indented elemental attributes in the figure of *Employee First Name* and *Employee Last Name* for the full name of an employee.

A group attribute name can be used as a collective attribute name to refer implicitly to the component set of elemental attributes in the group that still remain to be explicitly identified and defined.

6.4.10 Repeating Group Attributes

Some attributes can have two or more values for each occurrence of the entity in which they reside. These are called *repeating groups* and are written in an entity list with the attribute name surrounded by ((double parentheses)) as shown in Figure 6.38.

Elemental

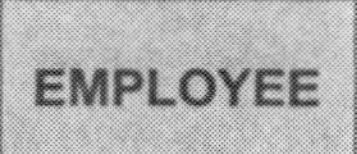

Employee Id #
Employee First Name
Employee Last Name

Figure 6.36 Example of elemental nonkey attributes.

Group

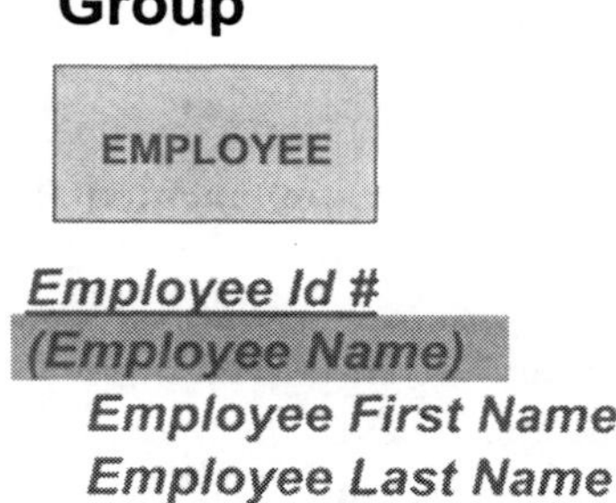

Figure 6.37 Example of group and elemental nonkey attributes.

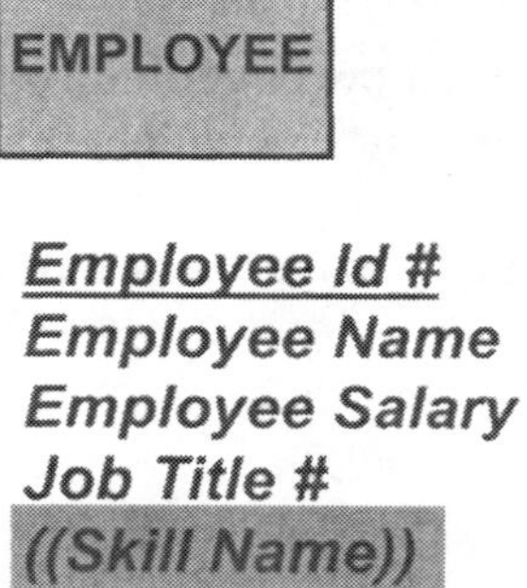

Figure 6.38 Example of repeating group attributes.

An employee can have many skills. Figure 6.38 shows the attribute *((Skill Name))* is surrounded by double parentheses to indicate that it is a repeating group [17]. It may be possible to capture a range of values for a repeating group. For instance:

- Some employee have only one skill (i.e., minimum skills = 1).
- Most employees have four skills (i.e., average skills = 4).
- Some employees have up to 10 skills (i.e., maximum skills = 10).

EMPLOYEE JOB *(employee number#,*
job number#,
((employee job salary code,
employee job start date,
employee job salary amount))

Figure 6.39 Another example of repeating group attributes.

In Figure 6.39, EMPLOYEE has a repeating group surrounded by double parentheses:

((employee job salary code, employee job start date, employee job salary amount))

This indicates that an employee will have more than one salary. Once again, the repeating group indicates the existence of another entity. As mentioned earlier, this is discussed in Chapter 9. In that chapter the repeating group is moved to a new entity as part of the first business normal form rule of business normalization. This new entity most likely would be called EMPLOYEE SALARY HISTORY. Over time, an employee is paid according to different salary codes, which can start to be paid from various dates, and the payment can be for various salary amounts.

6.4.11 Derived Attributes

A *derived attribute* is a nonkey attribute whose value is calculated from other data in the data model. This calculation is defined in a derivation formula that is attached to the definition of the derived attribute, in a data dictionary or repository that is maintained by a modeling tool.

Derived attributes are written in an entity list with the relevant attribute name surrounded by left and right {curly braces}. Figure 6.40 shows the derived attribute *{salesperson sales to date}*. This attribute is derived from *invoice amount* based on the following derivation formula:

salesperson sales to date = Sum of *invoice amount* for all invoices sold by the salesperson in the current period.

This derivation formula implies that an association exists between SALESPERSON and INVOICE.

To enable this calculation to be made, the attribute *invoice amount* must be available. This attribute would typically reside in an entity called INVOICE.

Figure 6.41 is another example, with the derived attribute *{Employee Salary to Date}*. This is derived from the attribute *Salary Gross Pay* based on the following derivation formula:

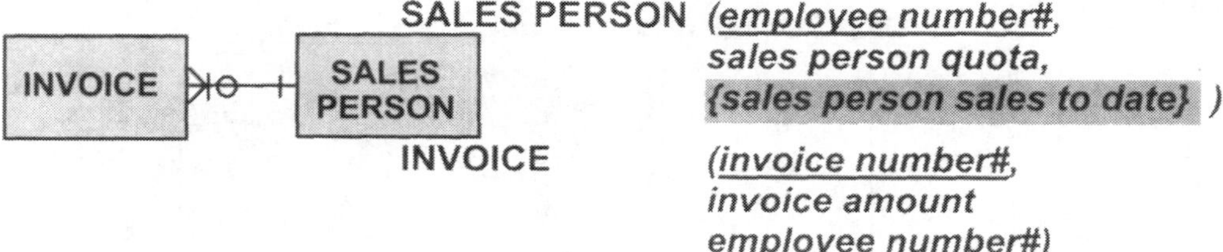

Figure 6.40 Example of a derived attribute.

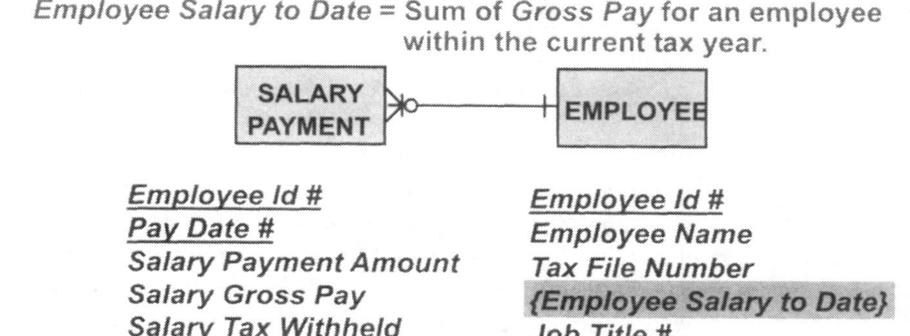

Figure 6.41 Another example of a derived attribute.

Employee Salary to Date = Sum of all *salary gross pay* amounts for an employee within the current tax year.

To enable this calculation to be made, the attribute *Salary Gross Pay* must be available. This resides in the entity SALARY PAYMENT. The derivation formula also implies that an association exists between EMPLOYEE and SALARY PAYMENT.

Whether derived attributes are stored in a database for later reference, or instead derived whenever they are needed, cannot be decided at this stage. This decision depends on several factors: the frequency of reference to the derived attribute, the change volatility of the source attributes used for derivation, the processing needed to derive the attribute, and the response demands. These questions can only be resolved during physical database design in column 1, row 4. In data modeling, the fact that a derived attribute exists is all we know. All derived attributes in an entity, and their derivation formulas, must therefore be recorded for that entity when doing logical data modeling of derived attributes for the What column and the Designer row [C1R3], for use in the physical database design in the Builder row [C1R4].

6.4.12 Optional Attributes

The example in Figure 6.42 illustrates the concept of *optional attributes*. These are attributes that do not have a value for every entity occurrence; that is, their existence is optional. For some entity occurrences they never apply, whereas other occurrences may acquire a value later. The example in Figure 6.42 shows a highlighted optional attribute: *Parking Space Number*. Not all employees have a parking space allocated: only "parking employees." If we include *Parking Space Number* in EMPLOYEE, there would only be a value for parking employees—for those who have been allocated parking spaces. There is no value for "nonparking employees" who have no parking space allocated; that is, a value for the attribute does not exist for them.

Figure 6.42 clarifies the situation. We can see there are two types of employees—these are *secondary* entities: PARKING EMPLOYEE and NONPARKING EMPLOYEE. The attribute *Parking Space Number* is mandatory for a PARKING EMPLOYEE. It does not exist at all for a NONPARKING EMPLOYEE.

Optional attributes generally suggest the existence of *secondary* entities where they must exist, and so are mandatory [18].

6.4.13 Entity List Conventions

To this point, we have used two alternative conventions for documenting the attributes in an entity: We have listed the attributes under the entity name, or we have used the entity list notation, which encloses them in brackets after the entity name. Either is acceptable for manual recording of attributes prior to entering them in a modeling tool. The entity list notation is summarized as follows [19]:

Entity List Notation

- *primary key 1#, primary key 2#,* ...
- [selection attribute 1], [selection attribute 2], ...
- {derived attribute 1}, {derived attribute 2}, ...
- (group attribute 1), (group attribute 2), ...
- ((repeating group 1)), ((repeating group 2)), ...
- optional attribute °, optional attribute °
- nonkey attribute 1, nonkey attribute 2, ...

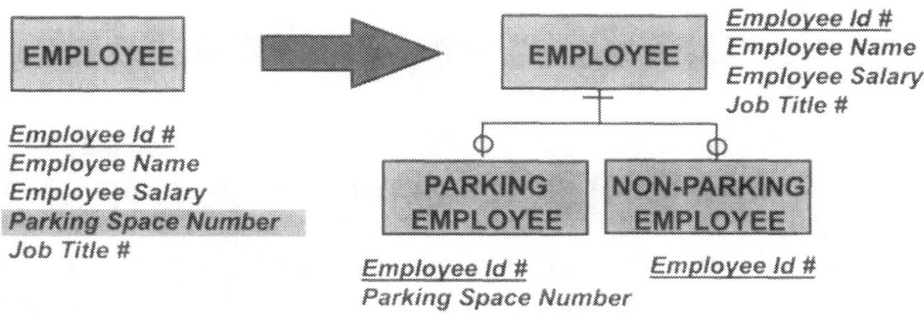

Figure 6.42 Example of optional attributes (shown by the superscript °).

- foreign key 1#, foreign key 2#, ...

The following is an entity list example:

EMPLOYEE (*employee id#*, [employee name], (employee address), [postcode], employee date of birth, {employee age}, ((salary commencement date, employee salary)), department number#)

Note the following about entity lists:

- The entity name is written in uppercase letters and is singular.
- Attributes are written in lowercase, all within the outer brackets, separated by commas.
- Primary keys are listed first, with a suffix # (pronounced "key") and underlined: *employee id#*.
- Selection attributes (secondary keys) have square brackets: *[employee name]*.
- Group attributes are surrounded by parentheses: *(employee address)*.
- Elemental attributes are written with no surrounding symbols: *employee date of birth*.
- Derived attributes have curly braces: {employee age}.
- Repeating Groups have double parentheses: *((employee salary))*.
- Foreign keys are generally listed last, with a suffix # (pronounced "key") but are *not* underlined to distinguish them from primary keys: *department number#*.
- Optional attributes (with a superscript °) can exist with any of the above bracketed conventions.

6.4.14 Entity List for Data Model Examples

The following entity list shows all of the entities that were introduced in the section on data entity types with their attributes now documented in entity list format:

EMPLOYEE TYPE *(employee type number#, employee type name)*

EMPLOYEE ROLE *(employee number#, employee type number#, employee role start date, employee role rating)*

EMPLOYEE *(employee number#, [employee name], (employee address), [postal code])*

SALESPERSON *(employee number#, salesperson quota, {salesperson sales to date})*

MANAGER *(employee number#, [manager title], manager reporting level)*

EMPLOYEE STRUCTURE *(employee number#, employee type number#, rel employee number#, rel employee type number#, relationship reason)*

EMPLOYEE JOB *(employee number#, job number#, employee job start date#, ((employee job salary, employee job commencement date, employee job salary amount)))*

JOB *(job number#, [job title], job standard salary)*

This shows primary keys, foreign keys, selection attributes (secondary keys), group attributes, repeating groups, derived attributes, and elemental attributes as follows:

- Primary keys: *employee type number#*, *employee number#*, and *job number#*.
- Selection attributes: *[employee name], [postal code], [manager title], [job title]*.
- Group attributes: *(employee address)*.
- Repeating groups: *((employee job salary, employee job commencement date, employee job salary amount))*.
- Derived attributes: *{salesperson sales to date}*.
- Elemental attributes: employee role start date, employee role rating, salesperson quota, manager reporting level, relationship reason, employee job start date.
- Foreign keys: *(None shown in Entity List above)*.

6.4.15 Data Map for Data Model Examples

The data map for the preceding entity list is shown in Figure 6.43. Note that each association defined between a pair of entities implements the common keys that exist between those entities:

- EMPLOYEE TYPE–EMPLOYEE ROLE: common key–*employee type number#*.
- EMPLOYEE ROLE–EMPLOYEE: common key–*employee number#*.
- EMPLOYEE–SALESPERSON: common key–*employee number#*.
- EMPLOYEE–MANAGER: common key–*employee number#*.
- EMPLOYEE–EMPLOYEE JOB: common key–*employee number#*.
- JOB–EMPLOYEE JOB: common key–*job number#*.
- EMPLOYEE–EMPLOYEE STRUCTURE: common keys–*employee number# and employee type number#*.

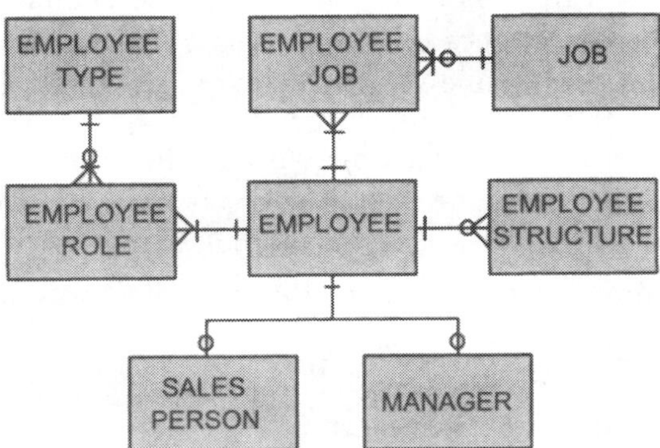

Figure 6.43 Data map of entities for entity list.

Common primary keys and foreign keys in an entity list can be used in this way to derive a data map automatically from an entity list, which illustrates the entities and associations represented by the entity list.

6.4.16 Case Study Problem 4

We will now apply the further concepts that we have covered to another case study example. This is described in *Box 6.4: Data Mapping Problem 4*, which is included on the accompanying CD-ROM [7]. Please complete this problem now, before reading on. The solution is provided in *Sample Solutions* on the CD-ROM as detailed in the case study problems file. Please review that case study sample solution before continuing with the rest of the chapter.

6.5 More About Entities and Attributes

This section provides further details about entities, attributes, and associations. We will first cover documentation of the purpose descriptions for data model entities, attributes, associations, and processes. We will then cover in more detail the following characteristics of entities and attributes:

- *Model View Authority:* for security, privacy, or legislative corporate governance control over entities.
- *Attribute Data Domains:* indicating logical data types, for later implementation as physical data types in databases.
- *Attribute Edit Rules:* which control access to, and change of, attribute values.
- *Attribute Categories:* a summary of attribute types and characteristics.

The following points apply to purpose descriptions of entities, attributes, associations, and processes, collectively called "objects" in the following sections [20].

6.5.1 Purpose Descriptions

Each object must be fully defined to indicate its purpose. A *purpose description* is attached as a narrative to the definition of each object in a data dictionary or repository maintained by a modeling tool. It should enable a clear understanding to be gained of the object because it will eventually become part of the "glossary" (or "language") of the business. It provides the following information:

- It documents what the object is used for in the business, how it is used, and why it is important to the business. It also can include who uses the object, as well as when and where it is used.
- Examples are provided to illustrate the business purpose and uses of the object.
- Business terminology is used in the purpose description to provide a meaningful description of the object.

- While developing a purpose description, the need for other objects and attributes in the data model may become apparent. These are added to the evolving data map and entity list. This expands and stabilizes the data model.

In developing narrative purpose descriptions for objects, follow these guidelines:

- Create a purpose description for every object; it defines its reason for existence.
- Avoid triteness. Do not repeat a name, for example, "an employee type is a type of employee." Instead use, for instance, "Employees can be salespersons, managers or support persons. By knowing the employee type, we can then assign each employee to a relevant job."
- Avoid dictionary definitions. An object name may later need to be changed; if its purpose is still the same, the purpose description should not also have to be changed.

6.5.2 Good Purpose Descriptions

The following statements clearly indicate the purpose of each object. They are examples of good purpose descriptions for entities.

EMPLOYEE TYPE
Purpose: Identifies the categories of individual employees being described. There are three types of employees that the organization is concerned with: salespersons, support persons and managers. Knowing the type of employee enables that person to be assigned to a relevant job.

EMPLOYEE STRUCTURE
Purpose: Used to indicate the employees who are managed by a manager, or the manager that an employee reports to. Also indicates those employees who may have common knowledge, such as expert knowledge of a specific customer.

EMPLOYEE JOB
Purpose: For billing purposes we must identify all of the various employees associated with a job and the number of hours they worked. This information along with the billing rate of each employee allows us to determine the charge to be billed to the customer for the job during any given period.

Do not use the following examples of purpose descriptions—they are poor definitions for entities:

- EMPLOYEE TYPE: "Identifies the types of employees."
- EMPLOYEE STRUCTURE: "Relates one employee to another employee."
- EMPLOYEE JOB: "Indicates an employee's jobs and vice versa."

These purpose descriptions tell us nothing about the relevant entities they define. Contrast them with the good purpose description examples given earlier;

those definitions are more meaningful. Each purpose description clearly tells us what the entity is; how it is used; and why it exists. It can also tell us who, where, and when. Their business meanings are useful.

6.5.3 Attribute Purpose Descriptions

Each attribute must be fully defined to indicate its purpose. A purpose description is attached as a narrative to the definition of each attribute in a data dictionary or repository maintained by a modeling tool. It should enable a clear understanding to be gained of the attribute as it will eventually become part of the "glossary" (or "language") of the business. It should provide the detail as listed bullet points in Section 6.5.1.

6.5.4 Association Purpose Descriptions

Each association must also be fully defined to indicate its purpose. A narrative purpose description is attached to the definition of each association in a data dictionary or repository maintained by a modeling tool. It should provide a clear understanding of the association because it will eventually become part of the "glossary" (or "language") of the business. It follows the same bullet points as listed in Section 6.5.1.

6.5.5 Business Process Purpose Descriptions

We discussed earlier that intersecting entities indicate the existence of business activities, processes, and systems that use those intersecting entities (collectively called *processes*). We document their existence in the Why column and Planner row [C2R1] of the Zachman framework.

A purpose description for each process is defined and attached to the definition of that process in a data dictionary or repository maintained by a modeling tool. It also is attached to, or cross-referenced from, the intersecting entity used to identify it. This should provide an understanding of the process, to become part of the "glossary" (or "language") of the business. It follows the same bullet points as listed in Section 6.5.1.

6.5.6 Entity Model View Authority

It is often necessary to exercise control over an entity. This may be required for security control, privacy control, or corporate governance purposes. This control is implemented by using model views. Figure 6.44 shows model views used to control the entities grouped within them:

- *All (common, shared):* EMPLOYEE TYPE and EMPLOYEE contain attributes that are of interest throughout the organization. No explicit control has been imposed on these entities; they are in a model view that is accessible to all.

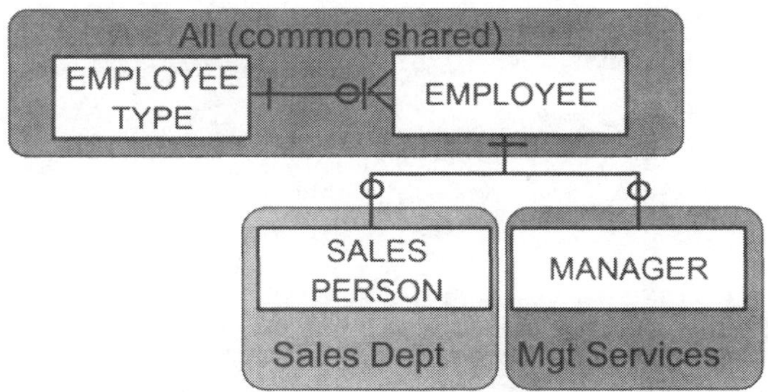

Figure 6.44 Data map showing the concept of model views.

- *Sales Department:* SALESPERSON has attributes that indicate the sales quota and the total sales to date by each salesperson. These attributes are needed by the sales department. Control over these sensitive data is required to be exercised by ensuring that SALESPERSON is only included in the sales department model view and is only accessible by those people given authority to access that model view.
- *Management Services*: MANAGER has an attribute for the manager rating of each manager, as needed by management services. Control over these data is exercised by ensuring that MANAGER is only included in the Management Services model view and is accessible only by those people who are given authority to access that model view.

Principal (supertype) entities are typically used for common, shared use. Secondary (subtype) entities are typically used to manage security control, privacy control, and business control for corporate governance.

6.5.7 Attribute Data Domain

During logical data modeling in the What column for the Designer row [C1R3], the logical value format of data attributes will become apparent. In defining the name and purpose of an attribute, we consider the data values that it will logically contain when implemented in a physical database table. The data values can represent text, numbers, money, codes, or Boolean values such as Yes/No or True/False. These are called *attribute data domains.* They indicate logical data content; not yet expressed as the physical data types for database implementation. The examples in Table 6.8 show logical data domain, length, and decimal precision:

- *Job Title* is Domain: Text, Length: 30 characters.
- *Employment Date* is Domain: Date, Length: N/A (not applicable—predefined).
- *Employee Salary* is Domain: Money, Length: 12 digits, Precision: 2 decimals.

When implemented as columns in physical database tables, they will be translated to physical data types for the database management system to be used, such as:

Table 6.8 Data Values for Data Attributes

Attribute Name	*Domain*	*Length*	*Precision*
Job Title	Text	30	N/A
Employment Date	Date	N/A	N/A
Employee Salary	Money	12	2

- *Job Title*—Character (30).
- *Employment Date*—Date, or Character (8).
- *Employee Salary*—Decimal (12,2).

During logical data modeling there may be many different data domains that should be used. These should each be given an agreed standard logical domain name and purpose, which is documented, such as:

- *Code:* Numeric value of up to 8 digits (say), used for identification or coding purposes;
- *Address:* Variable text to a maximum of, say, 80 alphanumeric characters, for geographic or postal addresses.

6.5.8 Attribute Edit Rules

When defining attributes, the rules for entering or changing values of those attributes should also be defined. These are called *edit rules* and are shown in Figure 6.45. They indicate for each attribute, whether:

- It can be added when the entity in which it resides is first added; that is, *Add Now.*
- It is added later, after the entity where it resides has been added; that is, *Add Later.*
- Once added, the attribute can later be changed; that is, *Modify Later.*
- Once added, the attribute can never be changed; that is, *Cannot Modify.*

Determining these rules is important in logical data modeling for later use when defining detailed editing rules for each attribute in physical database design. It is also important when designing screen layouts and for menu design as discussed in Chapter 10.

6.5.9 Edit Rule Example

Using the edit rules from Figure 6.45 now for the EMPLOYEE example of Table 6.9, we see their purpose:

- Date of birth: Once entered correctly, that date of birth can never change; that is, *Add Now, Cannot Modify.*

	1) When an occurrence of this entity is added, must you assign a value for this attribute? YES	NO
2) Once a value for an attribute has been set, can you later change its value? YES	Add Now, Modify Later	Add Later, Modify Later
NO	Add Now, Cannot Modify	Add Later, Cannot Modify

Figure 6.45 Attribute edit rules.

Table 6.9 Example of Edit Rules Using EMPLOYEE

Attribute Name	*Edit Rule*
Date of Birth	Add Now, Cannot Modify
Termination Date	Add Later, Cannot Modify
Employment Date	Add Now, Modify Later
Employee Name	Add Now, Modify Later
Last Review Date	Add Later, Modify Later

- Termination date: Once employment is terminated, that date can never change; that is, *Add Later, Cannot Modify* (even if a terminated employee is later reemployed).
- Employment date: Following termination, an employee can be reemployed; that is, *Add Now, Modify Later.*
- Employee name: Once entered, an employee's name can later be changed by marriage; that is, *Add Now, Modify Later.*
- Last review date: Changes after each review, to show the date of last review; that is, *Add later, Modify Later.*

6.5.10 Attribute Model View Authority

We saw that we often need to exercise security, privacy, or governance control over an entity. We may need to exercise similar control over attributes. As for entities, attribute control is implemented with model views. In the example in Figure 6.46, a greater degree of control is needed as indicated for the business rules discussed next:

- Read-only: The accounting department can view *Employee Salary*, but cannot change it. The accounting model view does *not* have *update* model view authority for *Employee Salary*.

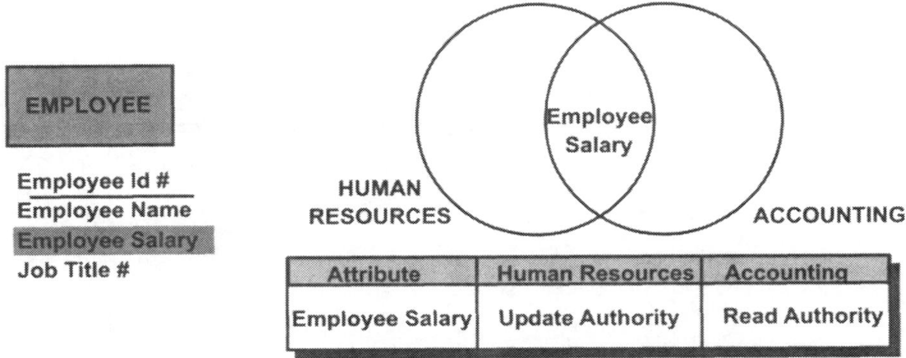

Figure 6.46 Attribute model view authority.

- Update: The human resources department can view *Employee Salary*, and can also change it. The human resources model view has *update* model view authority for *Employee Salary* (which includes *read-only* authority).

Figure 6.46 shows that model views exercise strong control over attributes within entities. Normally the attribute authority matches the model view authority of the entity:

- Modify later: *Update* authority, unless defined as *read-only*.
- Cannot modify: All attributes are *read-only* authority.

Definitions of exceptions to these implicit attribute authorities are important to be able to model business rules correctly. Some attributes may be completely excluded from model views if those parts of the business are not even given *read-only* authority.

6.5.11 Summary of Attribute Characteristics

Figure 6.47 summarizes the characteristics of the attributes that we have covered in this section and list here:

- Common key attributes define associations with other entities. *Employee Id #* is a primary key; it indicates an association with other entities where *employee id#* also exists—as a primary key or a foreign key. *Job Title #* is a foreign key; it indicates that an association exists between EMPLOYEE and JOB, where *Job Title#* exists as a primary key.
- Nonkey attributes represent the detailed data of the organization. This includes any derived attributes.
- *Employee Name* is a nonunique, nonkey group attribute of *first name* and *last name*. It may be defined as a nonunique selection attribute. When implemented in a database, a nonunique index is physically defined for this column in a table, to use *Employee Name* as a secondary key (i.e., selection attribute).

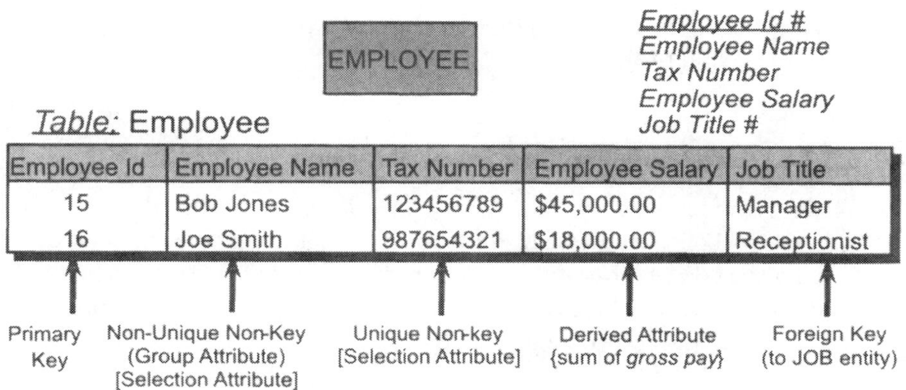

Figure 6.47 Summary of attribute characteristics.

- *Tax Number* is a unique nonkey selection attribute. When implemented in a database, a unique index can physically be defined for this column in a table, to use *Tax Number* as a secondary key.
- *Employee Salary* is a derived, nonkey attribute. Its value is calculated as the Sum of *gross pay* (which exists in another entity, SALARY PAYMENT).

We have now completed many of the concepts used for business-driven data mapping. Before we move to Chapter 7 to learn how to derive project plans from a data model, it is important first to consolidate the data mapping concepts that we have covered. This can be achieved by completing Case Study Problems 5 and 6.

6.5.12 Case Study Problem 5

We will apply all of the concepts that we have covered to a real-life case study example. This is described in *Box 6.5: Data Mapping Problem 5*. This problem will allow you to apply all that you have learned in this chapter. It refers to a clothing manufacturing company that makes ladies' and men's garments. The problem is included on the accompanying CD-ROM [7]. Please complete this problem now, before reading on. The solution is provided in *Sample Solutions* on the accompanying CD-ROM as detailed in the case study problems file. Please review that case study sample solution before continuing with Case Study Problem 6.

6.5.13 Case Study Problem 6

We will now do a more complex case study example. This is described in *Box 6.6: Data Mapping Problem 6*. This problem refers to vehicle accident insurance claims. The problem is based on a process-oriented description of a typical insurance company and is very operational. It documents the operational processes used to resolve and satisfy claims. This problem is included on the accompanying CD-ROM [7]. Please complete this problem now, before reading on. The solution is provided in *Sample Solutions* on the accompanying CD-ROM as detailed in the case study problems file. Please review that case study sample solution before continuing with the rest of the chapter.

6.5.14 Data Modeling Case Study Workshop

A data modeling case study workshop is also discussed on the accompanying CD-ROM [7]. This enables you to test your understanding of data modeling, following the completion of this chapter and Chaper 9. Your solution to this workshop may qualify you to be assessed as a Certified Business Data Modeler (CBM) as discussed on the accompanying CD-ROM.

6.6 Summary

In this chapter we covered data modeling and data mapping methods, focusing on the What column for the Planner, Owner, Designer, and Builder rows [C1R1–C1R4]. We learned the following concepts:

- We discussed the following entity types: *principal* (supertype) entities, *secondary* (subtype) entities, *type* entities, *role* entities, *intersecting* entities, and *structure* entities.
- We saw that *intersecting* entities indicate the existence of business activities, processes, or systems [21].
- We discussed key attributes, such as *primary* keys and *foreign* keys. We covered *candidate* keys, *compound* keys, and *alias* keys.
- We discussed nonkey attributes: *selection (secondary key)* attributes, *group* attributes, *elemental* attributes, *repeating group* attributes, and *derived* attributes.
- We discussed the need for *purpose descriptions* that clearly define *entity* purpose, *attribute* purpose, *association* purpose, and *activity* or *process* purposes. These indicate what the relevant object is, how it is used and why it exists. Who, where, and when are also defined, if appropriate.
- We discussed other characteristics, such as *model view* authority of entities and attributes for *security control, privacy control,* or *governance* purposes.

We are now ready to move to Chapter 7. In that chapter we will apply these concepts to the development of a strategic model. We will identify business activities or processes from the resulting data model, for prioritization and later delivery as subprojects that are the vertical slivers discussed in Chapter 5. We will learn how to derive project plans from a data model to manage these as priority subprojects for rapid delivery. In Chapter 7 we will also review several real-life project examples that have applied the methods covered in this chapter and Chapter 7.

Endnotes

[1] Finkelstein, C., and J. Martin, *Information Engineering,* Carnforth, U.K.: Savant Institute, 1981.

[2] Finkelstein, C., *An Introduction to Information Engineering,* Reading, MA: Addison-Wesley, 1989.

[3] Finkelstein, C., *Information Engineering: Strategic Systems Development,* Reading, MA: Addison-Wesley, 1992.

[4] Finkelstein, C., and P. Aiken, *Building Corporate Portals with XML,* New York: McGraw-Hill, 2000.

[5] We will see that these additional entities are typically *subtype* or *secondary* entities, as discussed later.

[6] Throughout the book we will consistently use the absence of a crow's-foot to mean *one* and a bar across an association line to represent mandatory or **must.**

[7] All case study problems for this chapter are included in the Book Materials folder on the CD-ROM, in the PDF file *Chap-06-Problems.pdf.* The sample solutions for all problems in this chapter are in the PDF file Chap-06-Solutions.pdf in the Book Materials folder.

[8] We will generally use the term *principal entity* in this book.

[9] This hierarchical representation between a principal entity and its related secondary entities is a characteristic of business-driven IE.

[10] Other data modeling methods refer to an intersecting entity as an associative entity.

[11] This very important principle apparently has never been recognized or used by other data modeling methods.

[12] This is a recursive association that is also called a convoluted association by IT-driven IE.

[13] The use of structure entities discussed in this section has not generally been used by other data modeling methods. Only business-driven IE seems to use structure entities to represent expert business knowledge and expert rules as described in this section and in more detail in Chapter 9.

[14] We will discuss other examples of structure entities used to represent expert rules in Chapter 9.

[15] Hence, note the use of *may* in the first bulleted question, *must* in the second question, and *will* in the third bulleted question.

[16] The term *secondary key* has historically been used by database designers (database administrators or DBAs) to refer to what is more correctly called a *selection attribute;* hence, we will use that latter name in preference to *secondary key.* It will typically be implemented as an index to the physical database table.

[17] The existence of a repeating group indicates that further refinement is necessary. A repeating group indicates that another entity exists. This is covered in Chapter 9. The repeating group is moved to a new entity as part of the first business normal form rule of business normalization.

[18] In Chapter 9 we will see that part of the fourth business normal form rule identifies *secondary* (*subtype*) entities based on existence of optional attributes.

[19] This entity list notation is used by business-driven IE to manually record identified data attributes (and their attribute types) for later entry into a modeling tool.

[20] This use of "object" should not be confused with objects in object-oriented methods. It is merely a collective term used here to avoid repetitive text.

[21] These can be prioritized for rapid delivery as subprojects in Chapter 7, which represent the priority vertical slivers discussed in Chapter 5.

CHAPTER 7

Strategic Modeling for Rapid Delivery of Enterprise Architecture

Chapter 6 introduced data modeling and data mapping concepts. Using examples and case study problems, we saw how these methods are used for integrated data models in the What column for the Planner, Owner, and Designer rows [C1R1–C1R3] of the Zachman framework. We will now apply these methods to development of a strategic model in the What column for the Planner [C1R1] and Owner [C1R2] rows (see Figure 7.1). The strategic model is the foundation of the transformed enterprise. This chapter is a key chapter for rapid implementation of enterprise architecture and business transformation.

7.1 Enterprise Architecture Incremental Build Context

This chapter continues data mapping for the rapid implementation of Steps 4 and 5 that we discussed in Chapter 6. We will review these steps—with numbers keyed to Figure 6.2 of Chapter 6.

- *Step 1:* In Chapter 3, we discussed that strategy analysis identifies statements for mission, vision, core values, goals, objectives, issues, KPIs, and strategies in the strategic plan.
- *Step 2:* Strategy analysis identifies from the organizational structure those managers and business experts responsible for implementing priority areas of the strategic plan.
- *Step 3:* During a 5-day business planning workshop, identified managers and business experts optionally apply the strategy analysis methodology to define tactical business planning statements to implement strategic plans. This is Step 3 for rapid delivery of enterprise architecture.
- *Step 4:* Data mapping is used to enable business experts and IT experts to work together to identify data for integration. This begins with a 2-day strategic modeling facilitated session as detailed in this chapter. Entities that represent required information and data are listed in the What column for the Planner row [C1R1].
- *Step 5:* The facilitated modeling session continues over 2 days, documenting key entities in a strategic model on a white board. The strategic model is a high-level semantic model or enterprise model in the What column for the Owner row [C1R2] that represents a "picture of the business" to the partici-

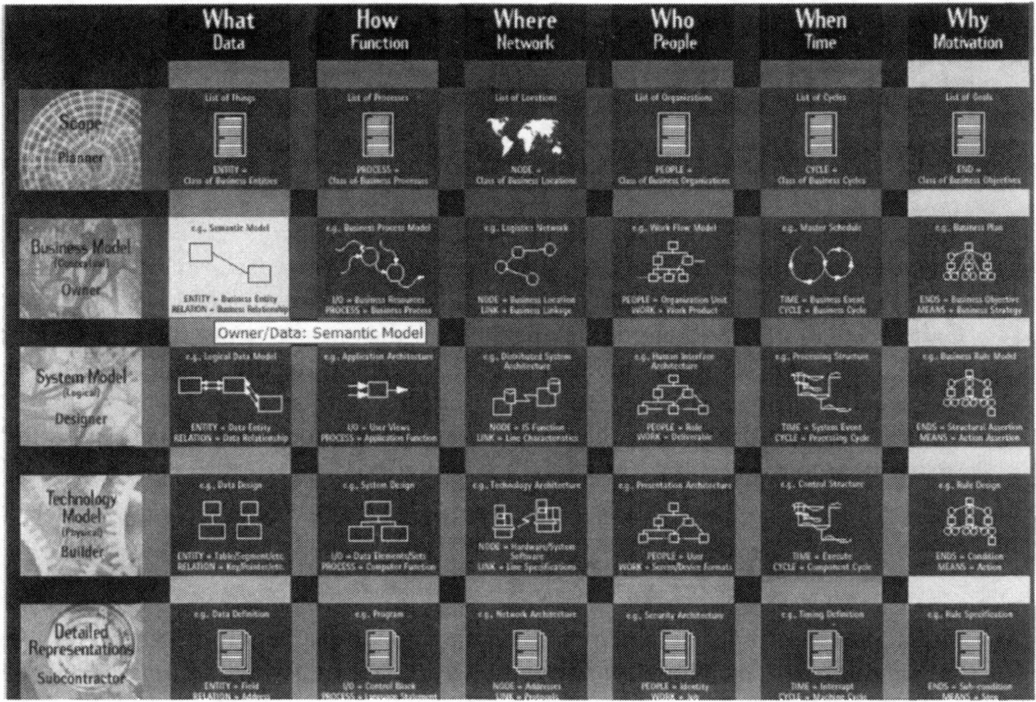

Figure 7.1 Strategic modeling addresses Zachman framework column 1, rows 1 and 2.

pating managers and business experts. Typically 90 to 120 entities are defined in these 2 days.

7.1.1 Reading Strategy for This Chapter

In Chapter 6 we used information engineering notation, but many other data modeling notations could equally well have been used. The concepts presented in that chapter focused on business-driven representation. If you were already experienced in data modeling and IE notation, you may have only skimmed that chapter.

This chapter applies these data modeling concepts to the development of strategic models. It shows how to plan and conduct a business-driven facilitated modeling session. It draws on the knowledge of senior managers and business experts to develop a strategic model that—in their eyes—is a "picture of the business." It identifies business activities and processes from the strategic model, for prioritization by management. These represent vertical slivers for rapid implementation, as discussed in Chapter 5.

We will cover the advanced *entity dependency analysis method* for data models. This has not previously been documented elsewhere in the industry. This and associated methods are used for manual or automated derivation of project plans and project maps from a data model. We will then discuss the results of several real-life projects that used these concepts. The resulting project plans are used to manage the delivery of priority activities as vertical slivers.

Even if you only skimmed Chapter 6, you will want to read this chapter in full detail. It covers the key methods that are used for rapid delivery of enterprise architecture.

7.2 Developing a Strategic Model

As discussed earlier, a strategic model applies to the What column for the Planner [C1R1] and Owner rows [C1R2], where in this latter cell it is referred to as a semantic model or enterprise model as illustrated in Figure 7.1. In this chapter we will apply the data mapping principles we have learned in Chapter 6 to a real-life example [1].

First, we will develop a strategic model based on the example that we started in Chapter 3 for the Project Management Division of XYZ. We will learn how to identify from a data model relevant business activities or processes in the How column for the Planner row [C2R1]. In the final part of the chapter we will cover the entity dependency analysis method, and we will use it to derive project plans and associated project maps from a data model. These will enable activities or processes to be prioritized so they can be used as vertical slivers for rapid delivery of enterprise architecture.

A facilitated modeling session is attended over 2 days by senior managers and business experts of relevant parts of the enterprise, as identified from the organizational structure in the Who column and the Planner row [C4R1]. If the enterprise architecture focus is enterprise-wide, this will include the organization's senior managers. If the focus is on a particular enterprise area only—such as the Project Management Division of XYZ in this example—it will draw on senior managers and business experts of that business unit and other units that interface with it.

7.2.1 Preparing for Strategic Modeling

In Chapter 3 we discussed the content and role of the business planning questionnaire in the section on preparing for strategy analysis. We discussed its use as a catalyst for strategy analysis in a business planning workshop. A template of this questionnaire is discussed in that chapter.

Where it is not appropriate to conduct the business planning workshop, we discussed in Chapter 3 that this same questionnaire can be used as a catalyst for strategic modeling. In this instance, it is renamed the *strategic modeling questionnaire* and is also based on the template on the accompanying CD-ROM [2].

We will now use the responses from Box 3.3 of Chapter 3 as suitable catalysts for strategic modeling. Using strategy analysis, we refined these statements in that chapter. Where it is not feasible to carry out strategy analysis refinement, we can still use raw responses from the questionnaire as catalysts for facilitated strategic modeling. We have an initial set of statements for the initiation and management of projects. The responses from Box 3.3 are repeated here. They will be used in this chapter to illustrate development of a strategic model in a facilitated modeling session.

Repeated from Box 3.3: Policies, Objectives, or Strategies

1. Each project must have a project owner, responsible for allocating and managing the project budget.
2. Each project must have a project manager, responsible for completing the project by the scheduled date, within budget.

3. Projects are only authorized that can achieve project objectives by the scheduled completion date, within budget.

7.2.2 Strategy for the Facilitated Modeling Session

Facilitated modeling draws on expert business knowledge. Two days is a significant amount of time for managers and business experts to allocate. It is important that all participants see the modeling session as an opportunity to identify their business needs and relevant business rules. They should *not* see it as a technical data modeling exercise. The session should focus on developing a picture of the business based on strategic plans and questionnaire responses.

The picture that is built up on a white board does not assume the business participants know any of the data mapping principles that we covered in Chapter 6. Instead, any data mapping should be presented from a business perspective only to help in documenting the business picture.

Unless the managers quickly see that they can directly contribute their business expertise to the evolving picture, they will consider that the session is about computers—that it is for IT staff, and not for them. At the first rest or coffee break they will disappear back to their offices to attend to urgent duties. If this happens, you will not get them back. You will have lost an opportunity to get them actively involved. This opportunity may not easily present itself again. The result will be that your enterprise architecture initiative will become a typical IT project. It will be limited—as for most IT projects—by the difficulty in determining the business requirements [3].

7.2.3 Starting the Facilitated Modeling Session

As we develop the business picture in the following pages, you will see that the relevant data mapping principles are introduced in a nontechnical way to document the business rules that are being represented in the picture. But as it evolves as a strategic model, you will also see that it is in fact a representation of a semantic model or enterprise model in the What column for the Owner row [C1R2].

1. Project Ownership Policy

We will start with the first policy statement from Box 3.3, introduced above—the Project Ownership Policy:

Each project must have a project owner, responsible for allocating and managing the project budget.

The nouns in the above statement are first listed by the facilitator on the white board as listed next. These are potential data entities for the What column for the Planner row [C1R1] as follows:

PROJECT
PROJECT OWNER
BUDGET

PROJECT BUDGET

The first two entities—PROJECT and PROJECT OWNER—are drawn as boxes on the white board as shown in Figure 7.2. The facilitator explains that:

> The PROJECT box is used to represent all of the details that need to be stored about a Project. It is expressed in the singular for a single project. Many projects can exist; each can be represented in the third dimension coming out from the white board. The single PROJECT box that is drawn on the white board will therefore be used to represent all Projects. Similarly the single PROJECT OWNER box that is drawn on the white board will be used to represent all Project Owners.

The facilitator asks if the PROJECT and PROJECT OWNER boxes are related to each other in any way. This question will be answered positively by the business audience. By drawing a line joining them, the facilitator explains that:

> This line will be used to show the business rules that are used to manage Projects and Project Owners. Lines that join boxes also represent business rules for management controls, audit controls, security controls, governance controls, communication paths, or reporting paths.

In this statement the facilitator has explained the concept of association lines in business terms, not technical terms. Next the association degree (cardinality) and the association nature at the end of each line are also defined in business terms, as business rules.

The facilitator asks if a Project can have only one Project Owner. If the audience replies positively, a bar is drawn across the line close to the PROJECT OWNER box. The facilitator explains this by saying that "We will use this bar to represent the business rule you have just confirmed—that a Project **must** have only one Project Owner." If the reply is negative and there are many apparent Project Owners, the facilitator asks if one is nominated as the "responsible owner," or if a Steering Committee acts as the responsible Project Owner.

Next the question is asked for the other end of the line: "Is a Project Owner responsible for only one Project, or for one or many Projects?" If the audience response is "many projects," by holding up three fingers the facilitator introduces the concept of the crow's-foot symbol to represent *one or many,* with a single finger representing *one.* The crow's-foot symbol is added to the end of the line touching the PROJECT box, pointing out that "the one symbol (the absence of a crow's-foot) already

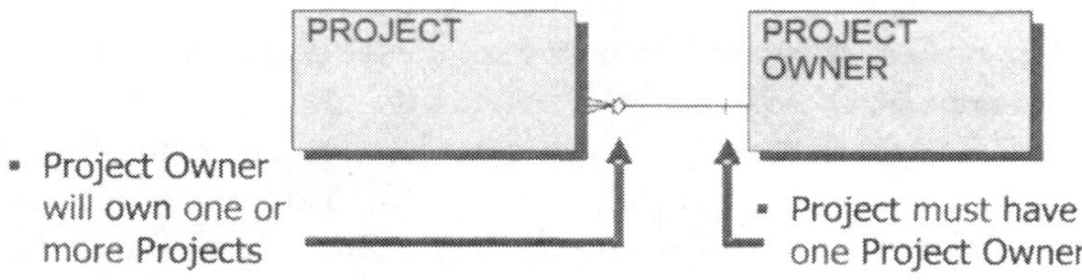

Figure 7.2 The initial strategic model, with business rules shown.

touches the PROJECT OWNER box based on the earlier business rule that you defined." This notation was defined in Chapter 6.

The next question determines the association nature at the PROJECT end of the line, by asking "May a Project Owner have no projects at any time?" For a positive reply, the facilitator adds a zero to the many symbol saying: "This represents the business rule that a Project Owner **may** own zero, one, or many Projects at any time." This notation was also covered in Chapter 6.

On a positive response to "Must a Project Owner have at least one project at any time?" a bar is instead added to the many symbol saying, "This represents the business rule that a Project Owner **must** own at least one or many Projects at any time" (see Chapter 6).

Finally, on a positive response to "Will a Project Owner eventually have at least one or many projects?" a bar and zero are both added to the many symbol saying, "This shows the business rule that a Project Owner **will** eventually own one or many Projects" (see Chapter 6). Figure 7.2 shows the result so far, with PROJECT and PROJECT OWNER documented on the white board. The business rules that have been agreed to by the audience have been written for each end of the line. This is an initial fragment of the strategic model that will eventually be developed for the What column in the Owner row [C1R2].

If an introduction to technical terms is appropriate at this stage, the facilitator continues:

> These boxes are technically called "data entities" or just "entities." Whenever any IT staff refer to "entities," they are talking about these boxes on the white board. They will later be implemented as database tables for reference. At a later time we will also look at details that you need to know about each box. These are called "attributes." These will eventually be implemented as columns of database tables.
>
> The lines that we used to represent business rules are technically called "associations." The **one** and the **one or many** symbols are called association "degree" or "cardinality." The use of **must** for mandatory, **may** for optional, and also **will** for optional becoming mandatory—to further express business rules—are examples of association "nature."
>
> If you later hear IT staff using these terms, you will now know what they mean; but we will continue to use "boxes," "lines," and "business rules." This picture is called a "data map." To ensure that subsequent computer systems that are delivered to you satisfy your business needs, it is very important now that we include in the data map picture of the business all boxes, lines, and business rules that you need, as suggested by the various business planning statements that we will consider.

Referring back to the list of entities above Figure 7.2, BUDGET is added to the white board. On audience confirmation of the business rule that "Projects have Budgets," a line is used to join these two boxes.

The earlier, relevant business rule questions are now asked at each end of the line between BUDGET and PROJECT, with the results added to the white board in Figure 7.3 to show that "a Project must have one or many Budgets" and "a Budget will cover one or many Projects." It is useful also to have a legend of the association degree and nature symbol meanings prominently displayed in the facilitated session, as shown on the left side of Figure 7.3.

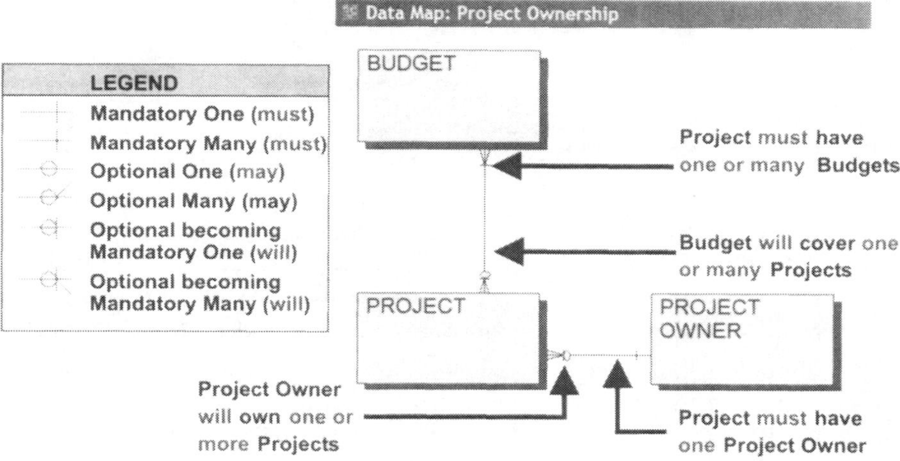

Figure 7.3 Addition of budget and its business rules to the strategic model.

We now need to resolve the representation of the *many-to-many* business rule between BUDGET and PROJECT in Figure 7.4. The facilitator explains in business terms that:

> It is hard to see from this business picture which Budgets relate to which Projects. We need to make this clearer by adding another box between these two boxes. This new box is typically named by combining both words—as in PROJECT BUDGET. In fact the Policy statement that we started with did refer to Project Budgets, although this does not always happen in such a convenient way.

The result of this decomposition is shown in Figure 7.5. The facilitator confirms again the business rules for each crow's-foot (*many*) touching PROJECT BUDGET in the figure, as well as the *mandatory one* rule touching both PROJECT and BUDGET. These are verbally expressed using business terminology as business rules; technical data mapping terminology should not be used, for the reasons discussed earlier.

Notice that PROJECT BUDGET in Figure 7.5 has been arrowed to show that it represents the Project Budget Management Activity. The facilitator explains this principle in business terms by saying, that "whenever we decompose a

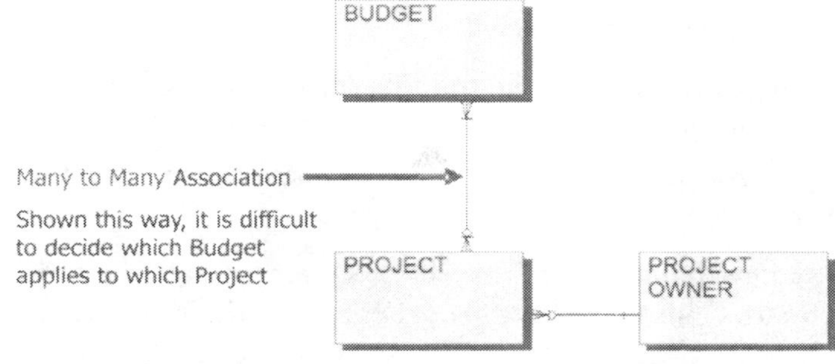

Figure 7.4 Many-to-many rule between project and budget needs resolution.

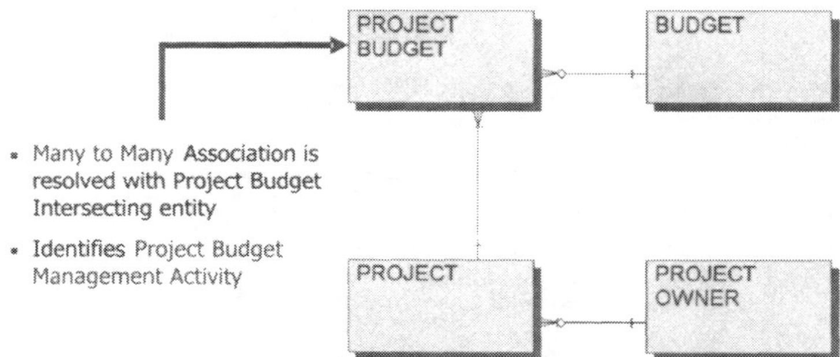

Figure 7.5 Resolution of many-to-many association by adding PROJECT BUDGET.

many-to-many association in this way, we are also focusing on the underlying business activity or business processes that are represented by the intermediate box, which is called an 'intersecting' entity."

In business terms, the facilitator has now introduced broad concepts of business-driven data mapping, as described in Chapter 6. By using nontechnical terms, the managers and business experts in the audience now understand the following:

- Boxes are *data entities* that are stored for later reference as database tables.
- Lines joining related boxes are *associations,* used to represent business rules for management controls, audit controls, security controls, governance controls, communication paths, and reporting paths.
- Symbols on a line touching a box represent business rules that apply to the two boxes joined by the line. They are called association *degree* and *nature.*
- Association *degree* is represented by a crow's-foot symbol for *one or many,* with the absence of a crow's-foot symbol representing *one.*
- Association *nature* is represented by a zero across the line for *optional* or **may,** a bar across the line for *mandatory* or **must;** and a zero and a bar across the line for *optional becoming mandatory* or **will.**
- The result of decomposing a *many-to-many* line is the addition of an intermediate (intersecting) box to the picture, named from the two boxes it joins.
- This intersecting box represents relevant business activities or processes, named initially by adding the suffix "Management Activity" to the intersecting box name.

2. Project Management Policy

The facilitator now moves on to the second policy statement from Box 3.3. This is a statement of the Project Management Policy:

Each project must have a project manager, responsible for completing the project by the scheduled date, within budget.

Any new nouns in the preceding statement are listed by the facilitator on the white board. This is a potential data entity for the What column for the Planner row [C1R1] as follows:

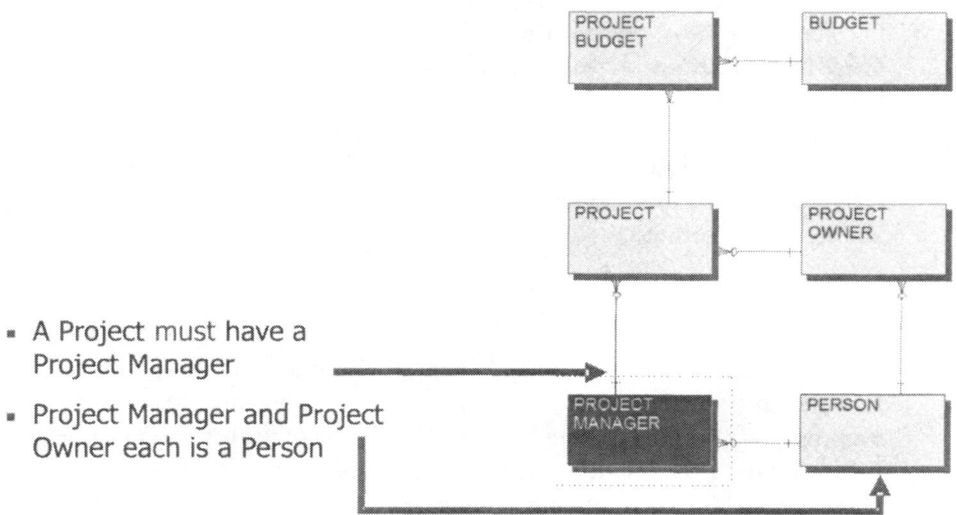

Figure 7.6 Addition of PROJECT MANAGER and PERSON to the strategic model.

- PROJECT MANAGER

The facilitator has listed Project Manager, but not *scheduled date*—because this is descriptive of a Project. It will likely later be identified as an attribute of Project. Attributes are not shown in a strategic data model in [C1R2]. They are defined using business normalization as later discussed in Chapter 9, during more detailed logical data modeling for the What column of the Designer row [C1R3].

Figure 7.6 shows the addition of PROJECT MANAGER to the evolving strategic model. It shows the business rules that "a Project Manager will be responsible for one or many Projects" and "a Project must have a responsible Project Manager." In technical data mapping terminology, this documents the *mandatory one* to *optional many* association between these two entities (see Chapter 6) [4].

Notice that PERSON has also been added for the two implicit business rules, "a Project Manager is a Person" and also "a Project Owner is a Person." Similarly, "a Person may be one or many Project Managers" (most likely over time), and also "a Person may be one or many Project Owners" (again over time).

3. Project Authorization Policy

The third policy statement in Box 3.3 is the Project Authorization Policy:

Projects are only authorized that can achieve project objectives by the scheduled completion date, within budget.

New nouns in this statement are now listed by the facilitator on the white board as follows. These are potential data entities for column 1, row 1, as follows:

- OBJECTIVE
- PROJECT OBJECTIVE

The only new nouns above are OBJECTIVE and PROJECT OBJECTIVE. These two boxes are added to the business picture on the white board, as shown in Figure 7.7.

The *many-to-many* business rule between OBJECTIVE and PROJECT has already been decomposed in Figure 7.7. The intersecting box PROJECT OBJECTIVE is explained by the facilitator as "representing the Project Objective Management Activity."

7.2.4 Continuing the Facilitated Modeling Session

Now that data mapping concepts have been introduced using business terminology and business rules, the business audience can also understand the technical data mapping terminology. Where appropriate, the facilitator can use relevant technical terms, relating the technical terminology back to the equivalent business terms for clarification. This way the business experts will be able to work actively with data administration staff who may lapse into technical data mapping terminology from time to time.

7.2.5 Case Study Exercises for Strategic Modeling

We will now continue to develop the strategic model, using further responses from the strategic modeling questionnaire that was used as the catalyst for strategic modeling. We will use the additional strategic modeling questionnaire responses in Box 7.1 as catalysts [5]. These questionnaire responses will be used to provide input to the case study exercises in the following pages. These exercises will enable you to gain experience in developing a strategic model from such statements. For each of the numbered statements in Box 7.1, carry out the detailed tasks using the strategic model developed to this point and documented next in Figure 7.8.

In practice, in a facilitated modeling session, the facilitator drives the session by using the relevant business statements as catalysts for discussion. But an important

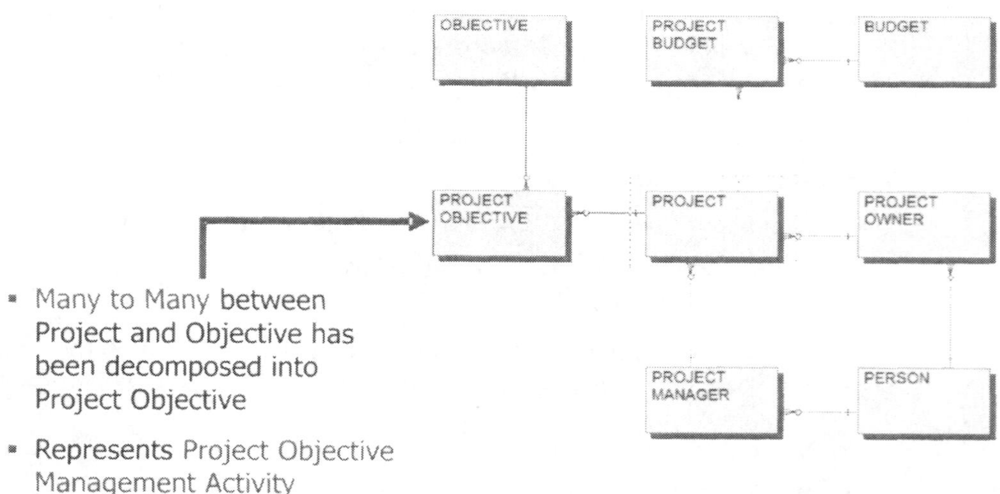

Figure 7.7 Addition of OBJECTIVE and PROJECT OBJECTIVE to the strategic model.

Box 7.1: Strategic Modeling Problems
Problem
POLICY, OBJECTIVE, OR STRATEGY 4. A project may have several project teams. A project team has many people who have the relevant skills needed for each assigned task: to complete it within its allocated time and achieve the project's scheduled completion date. 5. A project comprises many activities. An activity may be unique to a project, but most activities are carried out by many projects. 6. A project and its activities require many skills for their execution and completion. Project team members are allocated to activities based on their specific skills and the skills that are required by relevant tasks. 7. A project requires many resources, which include people, funds, and equipment. The management of project resources is the responsibility of a project manager. 8. Budgets can be related to other budgets. For example, future budgets can be based on related budgets. These related budgets are used to manage expenditures on assets as equipment resources and people as person resources that are used on projects. 9. Projects may be related to other projects. For example, a project may be designed based on an earlier project that used similar activities.
Tasks
Use each of the above numbered statements as a catalyst for strategic modeling. • Using the data map in Figure 7.8 as a starting point, take each statement in turn. List any new nouns in the statement. Add these as new entity boxes to the data map. • Define any associations between each pair of related entities. Decompose all *many-to-many* associations to *one-to-many* associations with an intersecting (associative) entity. Do not define any nonkey attributes. • As each statement is included in the strategic model, check your result with the sample solutions that are included next—before modeling the next statement.

word of warning is needed here: Do *not* be tempted to answer these questions yourself as facilitator based on your knowledge of data modeling. If you do, the strategic model will be viewed by the business audience as *your* solution, not theirs. Under *no* circumstances should you ever let this happen. You should only be a "mirror"—acting to translate their words into a business picture. If you add your ideas to the model on the white board, they will lose interest and they will likely disappear on the next rest break.

During a live facilitated session, you will find that discussions may arise about the correct names to be used in different entity boxes. This is typically because many synonyms are used in most organizations. To resolve this terminology dilemma, each suggested term should be defined precisely by the audience. These definitions should be captured unobtrusively by a scribe at the back of the room, using office automation software (such as Microsoft Word) with a laptop computer for reference later to these definitions. *Synonyms*—different words that all refer to the same thing—can be discussed; a common word can then be agreed to by the business audience. You will also uncover *homonyms*—where the same word is used to refer to different things. Words that are unambiguous can then be chosen.

In Box 7.1 the questionnaire responses are all from the Project Management Division of XYZ. As you are no doubt experienced in project management of IT projects, you can consider yourself a business expert in this discipline. In this situation you will therefore be able to adopt both roles in completing these case study problems: a representative business expert and a facilitator who develops the strategic model on the white board.

In modeling each statement in Box 7.1 you will first adopt your role as a business expert in project management. Then, in your other role as facilitator, add any new entities and associations that you identified as business expert to the strategic model in Figure 7.8. Add association lines and define relevant business rules using association degree and nature symbols. Check each statement solution in turn against the sample solutions that follow. Do not look ahead at solutions for later statements until you have modeled each relevant statement yourself. New entities that are added to this strategic model in Figure 7.8 for each statement in Box 7.1 are highlighted in the following sample solutions by a surrounding box. Review the technical *Discussion of Solution* sections for each statement before moving on to model the next statement.

7.3 Sample Solutions for Strategic Modeling Exercises

7.3.1 Sample Solution for Statement 4: Project Teams

4. A project may have several project teams. A project team has many people who have the relevant skills needed for each assigned task: to complete it

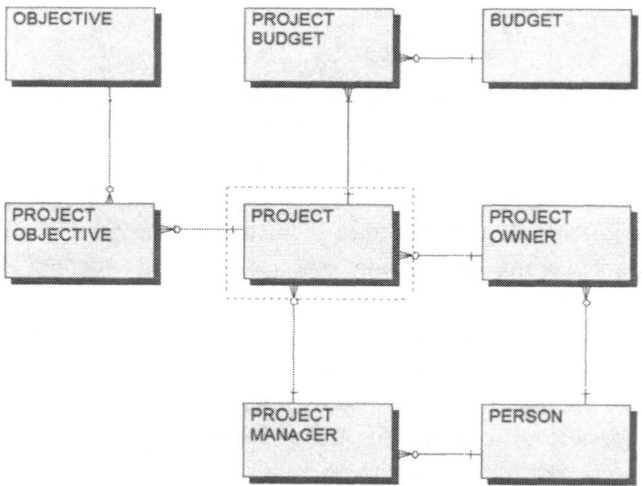

Figure 7.8 Strategic model starting point for use with Box 7.1.

within its allocated time and achieve the project's scheduled completion date.

Discussion of Solution

In the sample solution in Figure 7.9, the following entities were added to the strategic model from Figure 7.8 for the above Project Teams statement:

- TASK and SKILL have been modeled, along with intersecting entities PERSON SKILL and TASK SKILL.
- PROJECT TEAM and PROJECT TEAM MEMBER have been added, with associations to PROJECT MANAGER and PERSON. The intersecting entity PROJECT TEAM MEMBER SKILL has also been modeled.
- There was an extensive discussion about scheduled completion date. Because the focus of this statement is on Tasks and Project Teams, the business experts considered that they needed to represent more than one date. They needed start dates and end dates for Projects and for Budgets; they also needed to represent different periods and also period durations.
- PERIOD was added to represent these. It was needed so the business experts could have details of period start date and period end date. They could then derive period duration, expressed in period unit of measure, which may be in days, weeks, months, or years. PERIOD was related to BUDGET and PROJECT.

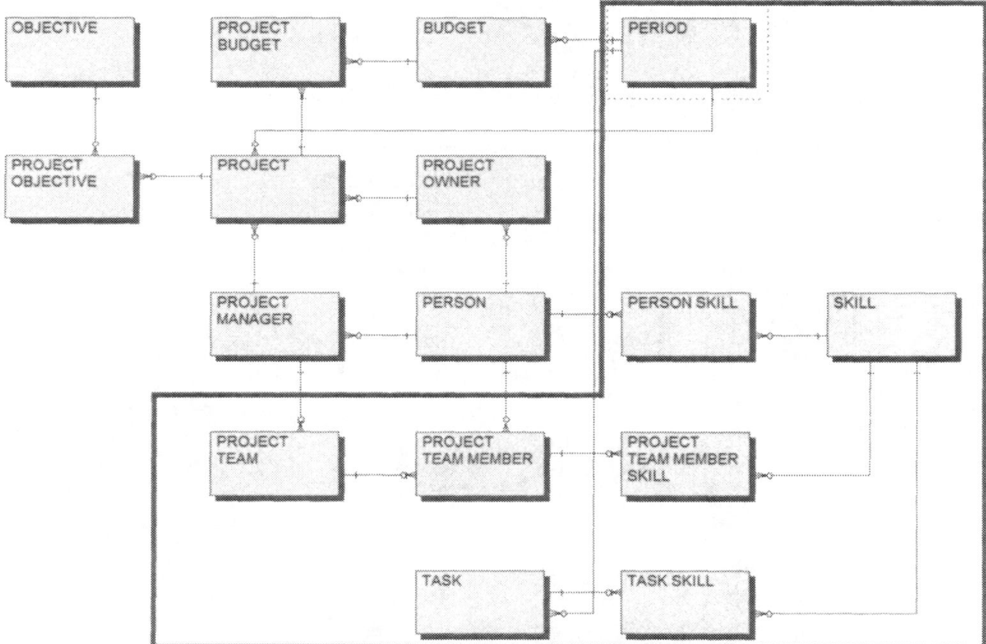

Figure 7.9 Sample solution for project teams in Box 7.1.

7.3.2 Sample Solution for Statement 5: Project Activities

5. A project comprises many activities. An activity may be unique to a project, but most activities are carried out by many projects.

Discussion of Solution

In the sample solution shown in Figure 7.10, the following entities were added to the strategic model from Figure 7.9 for the Project Activities Statement:

- There was considerable discussion from the statement that Projects comprise many Activities. The business experts said Activities indicate what has to be carried out in a Project. They distinguished Activities from Tasks by saying that Tasks define how to carry out the steps in a project. This was a clear distinction between two terms that are often considered synonyms. There was no ambiguity with these business experts.
- ACTIVITY was added, plus PROJECT ACTIVITY, based on this discussion.
- Similarly TASK ACTIVITY was added based on the previous discussion.
- PROJECT TASK may have been identified also at this time, but was not. We will see that this intersecting entity will be identified from the next statement.

7.3.3 Sample Solution for Statement 6: Project Skills

6. A project and its activities require many skills for their execution and completion. Project team members are allocated to activities based on their specific skills and the skills that are required by relevant tasks.

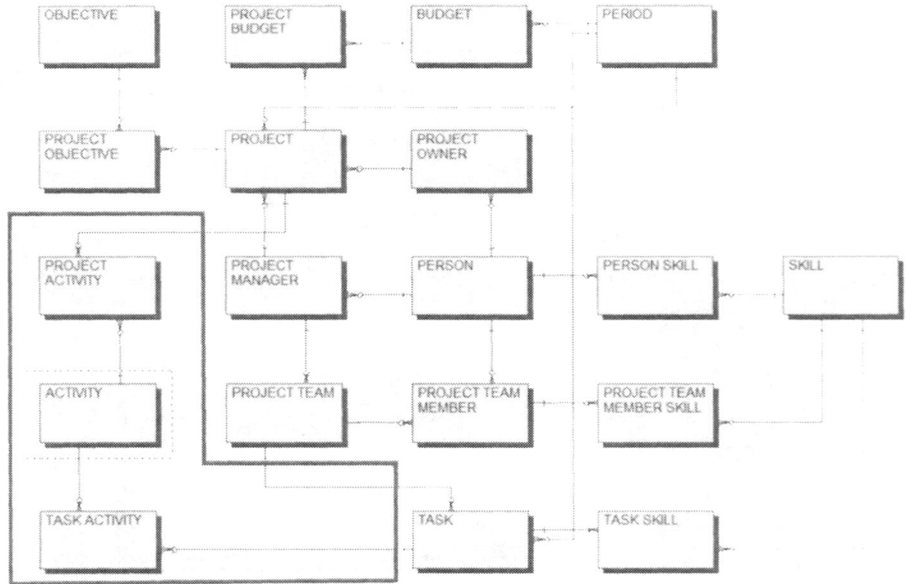

Figure 7.10 Sample solution for project activities in Box 7.1.

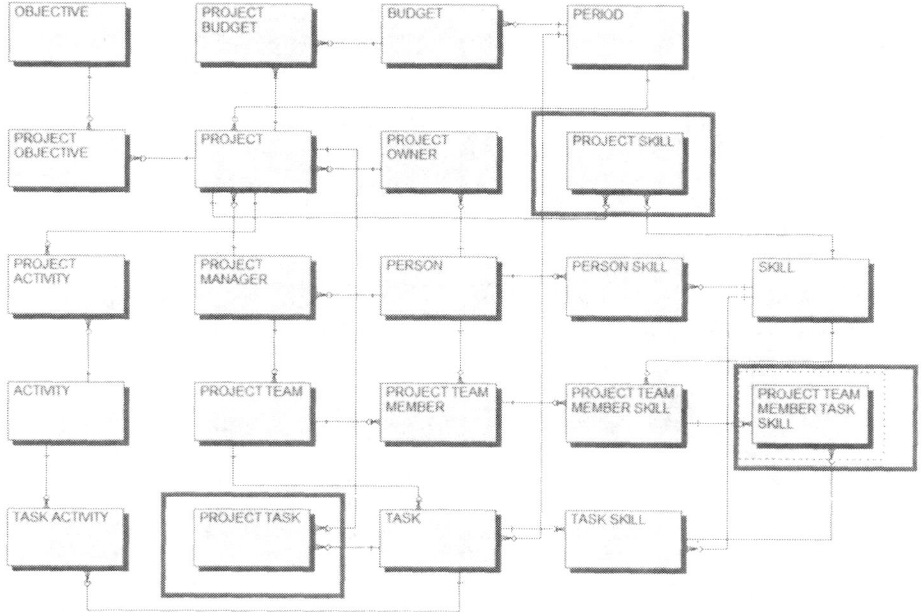

Figure 7.11 Sample solution for project skills in Box 7.1.

Discussion of Solution

In the sample solution in Figure 7.11, the following entities were added to the strategic model from Figure 7.10 for the Project Skills statement:

- PROJECT SKILL was added as the focus of the Project Skills statement.
- Carrying over from the previous statement on Project Activities, there was further discussion of the roles of Activities and Tasks. PROJECT TASK was therefore identified and added at this point.
- Discussing the second sentence in the Project Skills statement, PROJECT TEAM MEMBER TASK SKILL was added as a further intersecting entity to the evolving strategic model.

7.3.4 Sample Solution for Statement 7: Project Resources

7. A project requires many resources, which include people, funds, and equipment. The management of project resources is the responsibility of a project manager.

Discussion of Solution

In the Sample Solution in Figure 7.12, the following entities were added to the strategic model from Figure 7.11 for the Project Resources statement:

- A Resource was discussed as needed to manage various Person Resources, Funds Resources, and Equipment Resources. For example, while details of

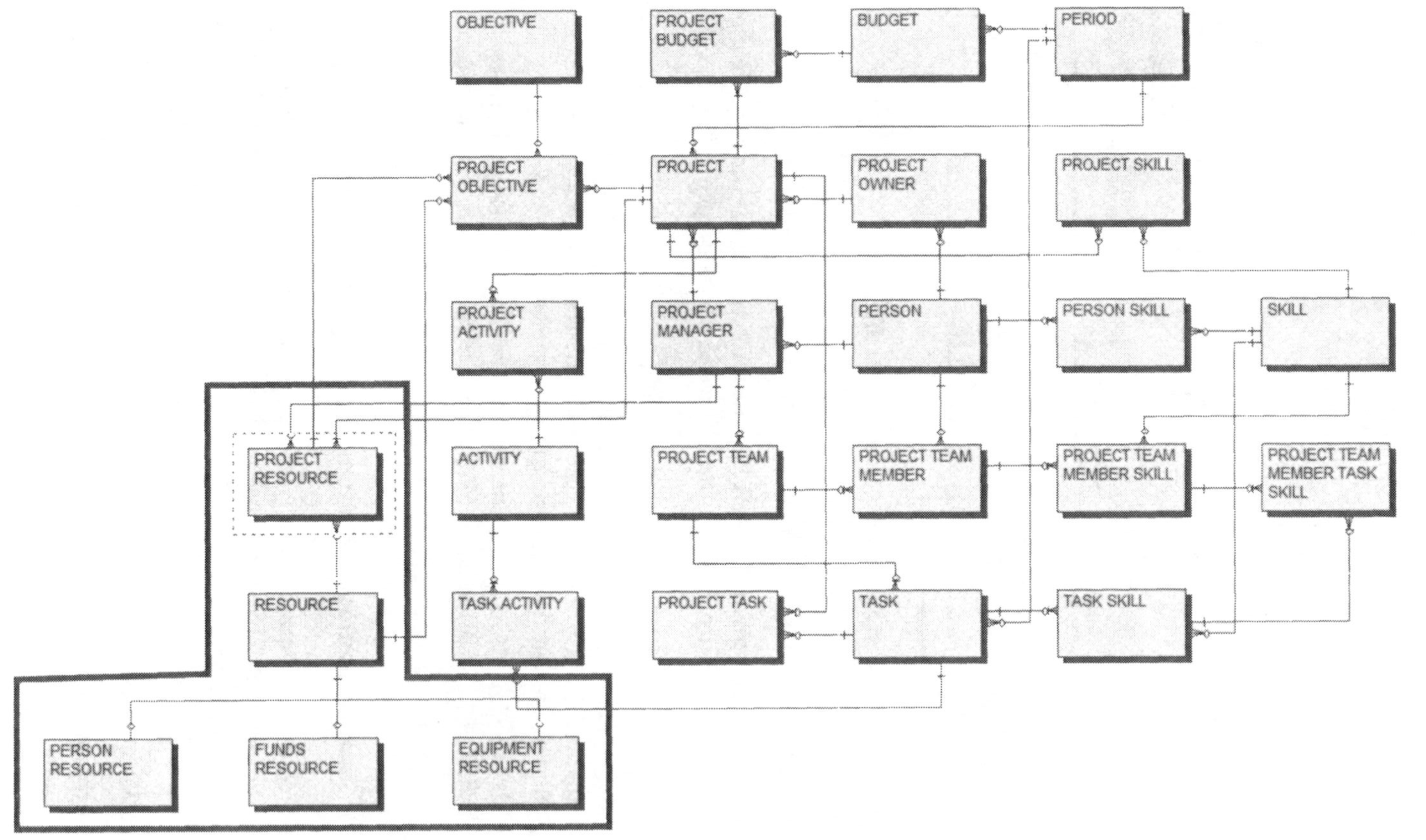

Figure 7.12 Sample solution for project resources in Box 7.1.

each individual person are maintained in Person, the Project Manager needs to know how many systems analysts are available to be allocated as particular Person Resources to a Project. Similarly, Equipment Resources such as workstations are allocated, and Funds Resources are allocated from Budgets.

- RESOURCE was therefore added as a principal (supertype) entity together with the secondary (subtype) entities of PERSON RESOURCE, FUNDS RESOURCE, and EQUIPMENT RESOURCE.
- The intersecting entity PROJECT RESOURCE was added, related to PROJECT, to RESOURCE, and also to PROJECT MANAGER and PROJECT OBJECTIVE.

7.3.5 Sample Solution for Statement 8: Related Budgets

8. Budgets can be related to other budgets. For example, future budgets can be based on related budgets. These related budgets are used to manage expenditure on assets as equipment resources and people as person resources that are used on projects.

Discussion of Solution

In the sample solution in Figure 7.13, the following entities were added to the strategic model from Figure 7.12 for the Related Budgets statement:

- The discussion in the earlier Project Resources statement on Funds Resources being related to Budgets continued here. The business experts said they need to know how specific Budgets are related to other Budgets. RELATED BUDGET was therefore added as a structure entity [6].
- They said these Related Budgets may be Monthly Budgets for a Project, but said they could manage those using the association from PERIOD to BUDGET.
- Related Budgets may be Subproject Budgets as well as overall Departmental Budgets, which were two examples they discussed. Clearly this is suggesting that different subtype Budgets may be of interest, but these have not yet been added to the strategic model.

7.3.6 Sample Solution for Statement 9: Related Projects

9. Projects may be related to other projects. For example, a project may be designed based on an earlier project that used similar activities.

Discussion of Solution

Finally, in the sample solution in Figure 7.14, the following entities were added to the strategic model from Figure 7.13 for the Related Projects statement:

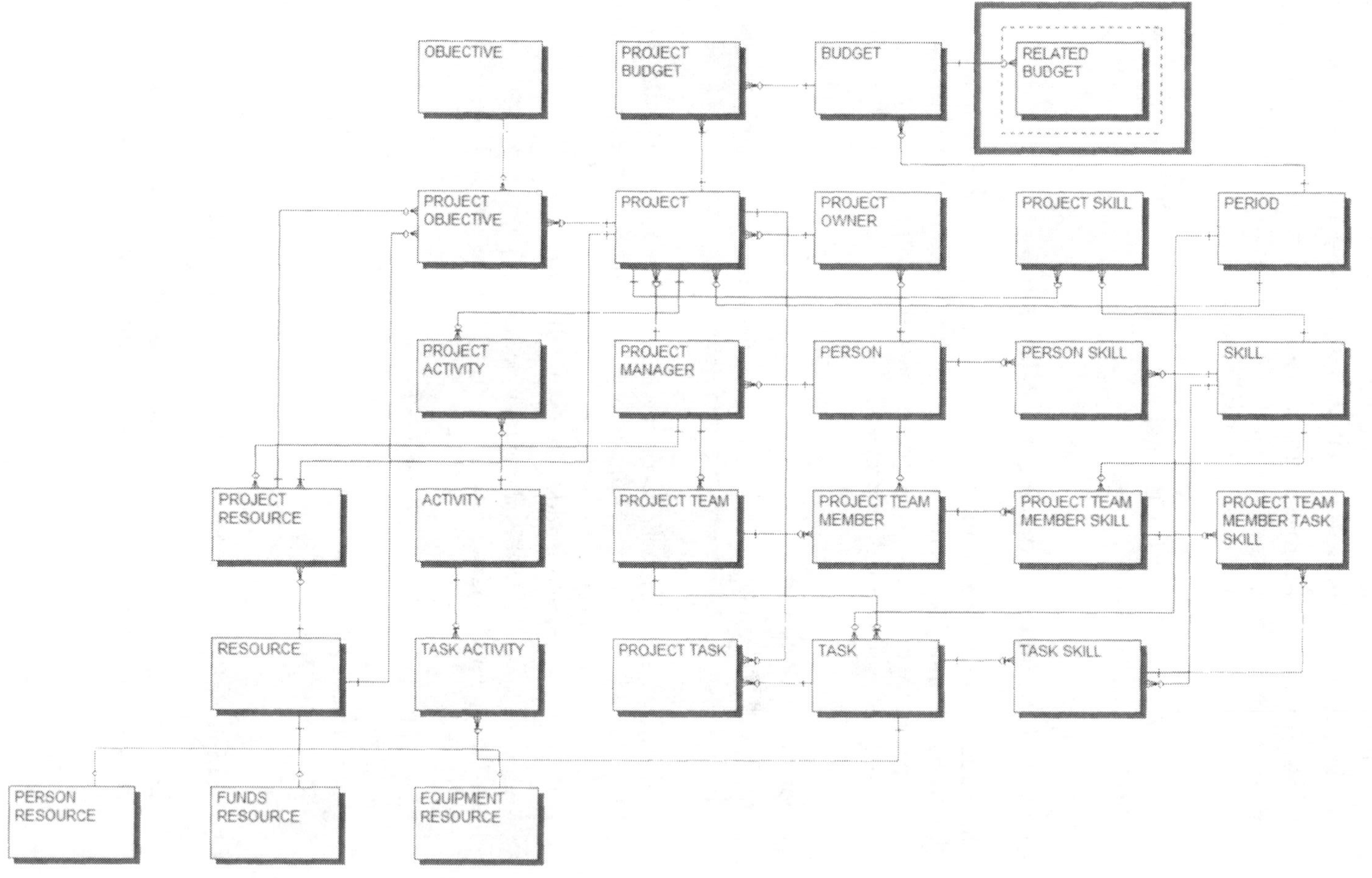

Figure 7.13 Sample solution for related budgets in Box 7.1.

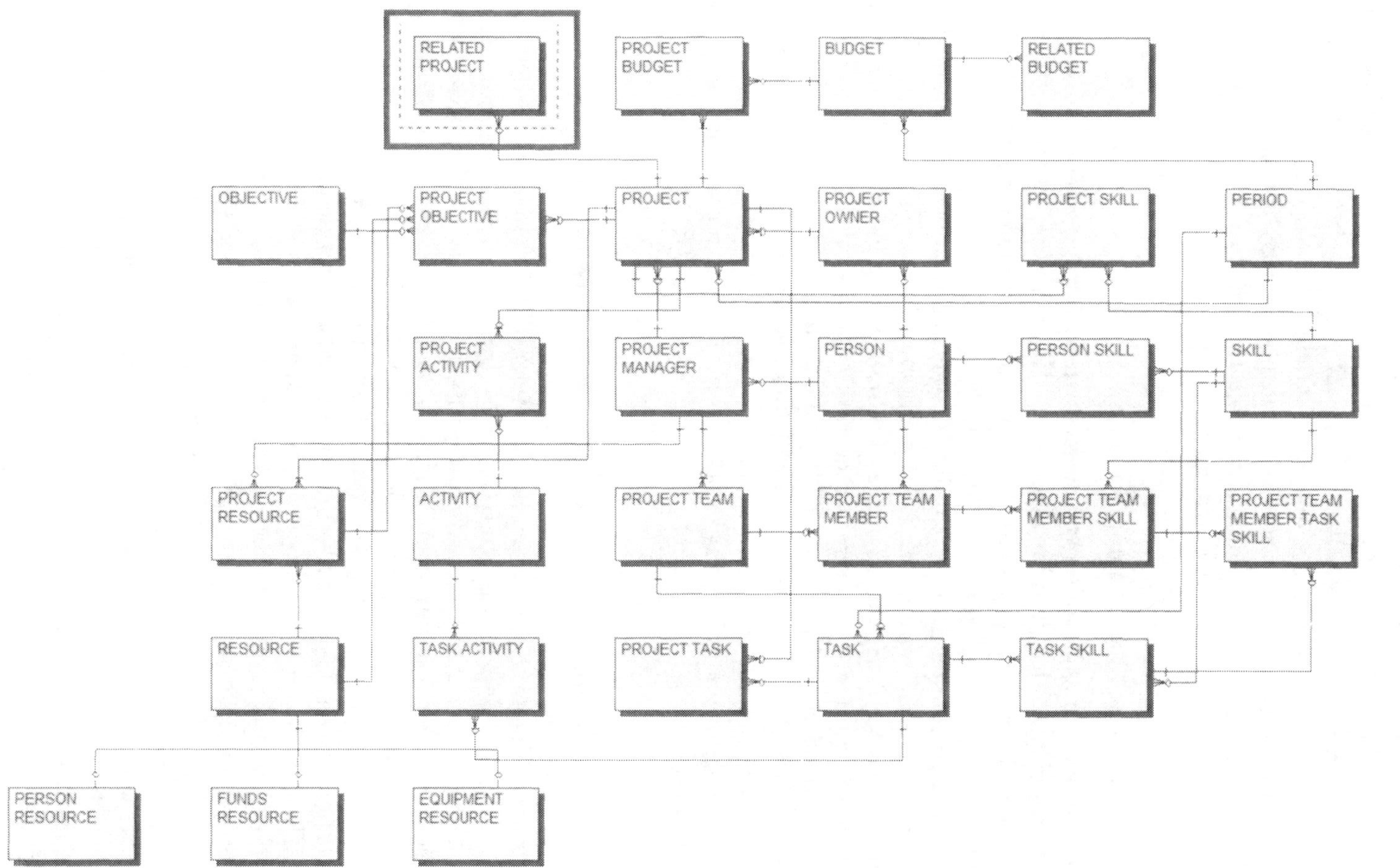

Figure 7.14 Sample solution for related projects in Box 7.1.

- The business experts expressed interest in the ability to use past Projects—with their component Activities and Tasks—as templates for defining new Projects.
- They saw the benefit of using past, completed Projects as the basis for planning new Projects. They said that the Project Activities from a completed Project could be used as templates and tailored to the new Project, with relevant Tasks from that Project further tailored to the new Project. This is, in fact, how they said they go about defining new Projects in practice. RELATED PROJECT was therefore added as a structure entity [6].

7.3.7 Strategic Model Sample Solution

The resulting strategic model from the facilitated modeling session for the case study problems in Box 7.1 is shown in Figure 7.15. This comprises 29 entities; we will analyze it later in this chapter. A larger, more readable version appears in the Problems file on the accompanying CD-ROM [7] as Figure 7.1.

A strategic model from a real-life 2-day facilitated modeling session typically comprises 90 to 120 entities, although some strategic models as large as 150 to 180 entities have been defined. As a rule of thumb, a strategic model contains around 10% of the entities in the overall enterprise. Typically this is 900 to 1,200 entities. When defined in a fully normalized logical data model for the What column in the Designer row [C1R3] [8], some organizations that are more complex than this may even approach 1,500 to 1,800 entities.

We will now use this strategic model as the basis for identifying business activities and processes.

7.4 Identifying Business Activities from a Data Map

We saw in Chapter 6 and earlier in this chapter that the potential existence of business activities and processes can be identified from the intersecting entities in a data map. These entities can be used to identify relevant activity, process, or system names for the How column and the Planner row [C2R1]. By adding the suffix *Management Activity, Process,* or *System* to an intersecting entity name, the relevant column 2 name can suggest itself. Structure entities suggest existence of knowledge bases that can later be used to identify potential expert systems [9].

This identification of activities, processes, or systems defines the list of processes for the How column and the Planner row [C1R1] for prioritization by management. Priority activities or processes can then be used as vertical slivers for rapid delivery of enterprise architecture, based on entity dependency analysis as covered later in this chapter.

We will examine the strategic model sample solution in Figure 7.15. We will use it in the following figures to identify business activity names for later reference. The business activities that potentially exist in the strategic model have been highlighted in Figure 7.16 by surrounding intersecting entities and structure entities in a bold box.

Each surrounding box in Figure 7.16 represents a business activity associated with that entity: named by adding the suffix *Mgt* (for *Management Activity*) for

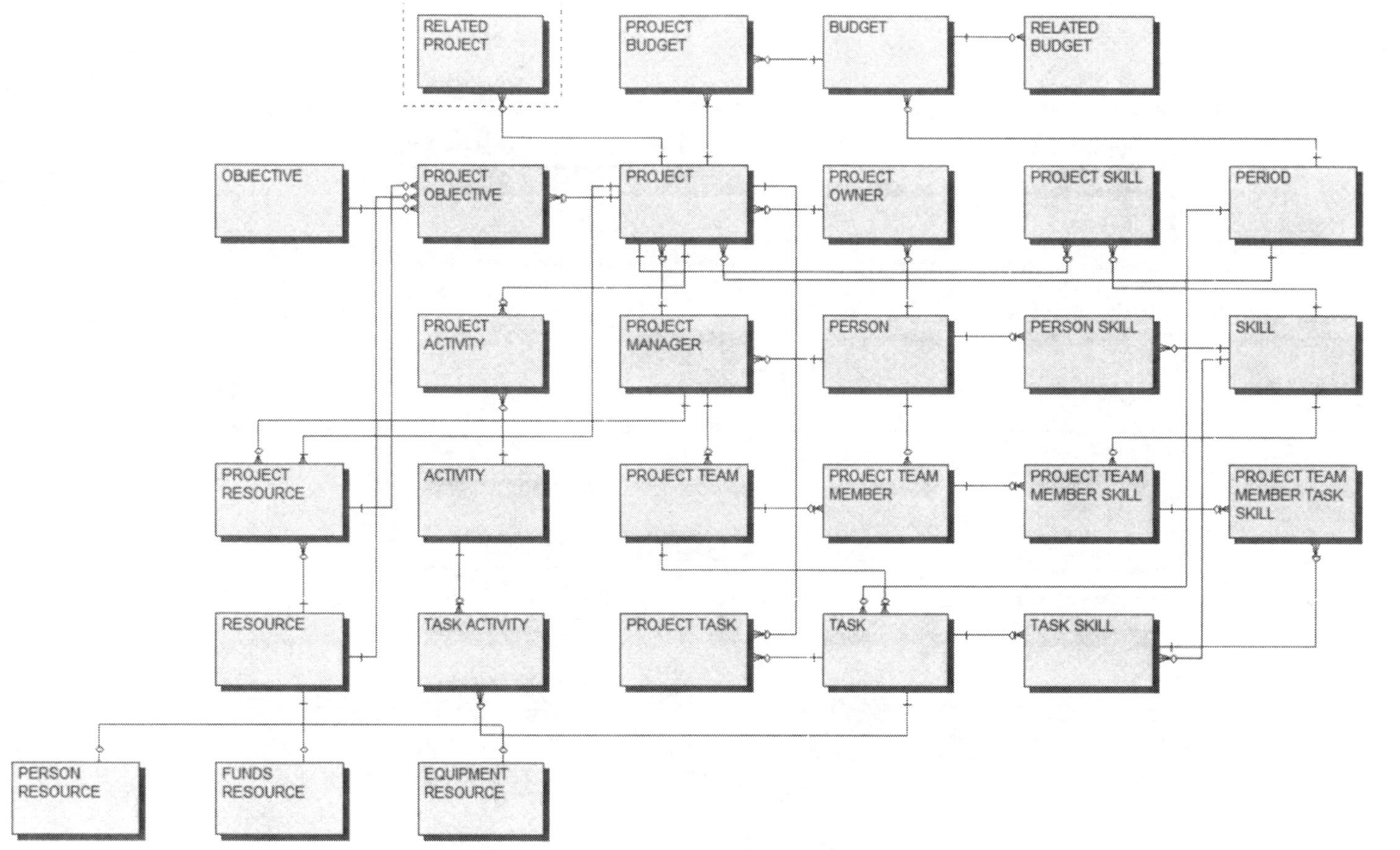

Figure 7.15 Strategic model sample solution for Box 7.1.

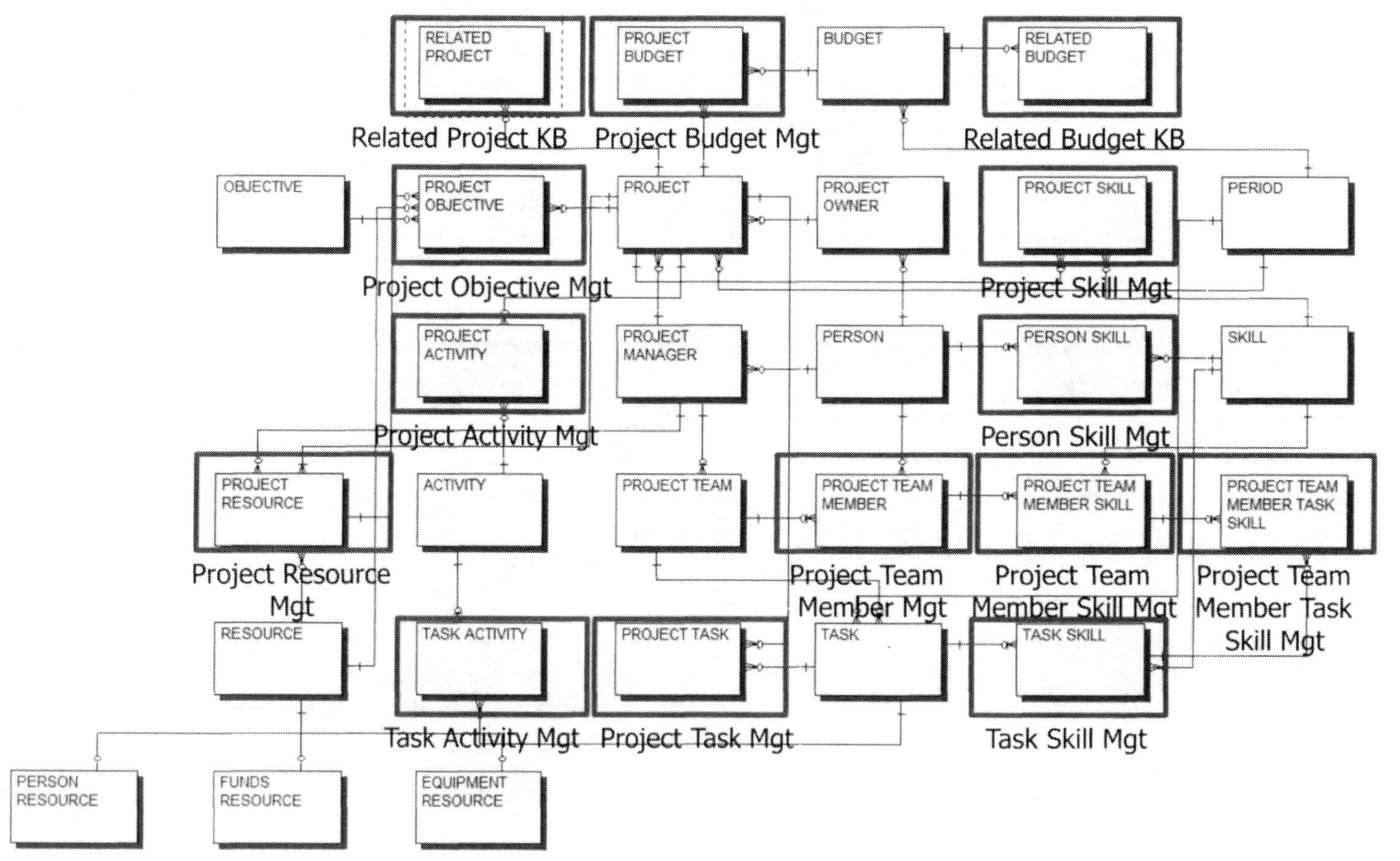

Figure 7.16 Identifying business activities from a strategic model.

intersecting entities or *KB* for knowledge base for structure entities to the relevant entity name. The resulting list of 14 activities is summarized in the following list:

Potential Business Activity

Business Activity 1: Project Budget Management
Business Activity 2: Related Budget Knowledge Base
Business Activity 3: Related Project Knowledge Base
Business Activity 4: Project Objective Management
Business Activity 5: Project Skill Management
Business Activity 6: Project Activity Management
Business Activity 7: Person Skill Management
Business Activity 8: Project Resource Management
Business Activity 9: Project Team Member Management
Business Activity 10: Project Team Member Skill Management
Business Activity 11: Project Team Member Task Skill Management
Business Activity 12: Task Activity Management
Business Activity 13: Project Task Management
Business Activity 14: Task Skill Management

We will now see how a data map can be analyzed to derive project plans. We will see how this analysis is used to extract subsets of data required by activities for detailed data modeling as a logical data model in the What column of the Designer row [C1R3]. This analysis is discussed next.

Using the preceding list of 14 activities, we will briefly overview entity dependency analysis and see how it is used to analyze data maps. We will see how project plans can be derived automatically from a data map. We will use automated analysis first; then we will learn how to do this analysis manually, later in this chapter.

7.5 Deriving Project Plans for Rapid EA Delivery

Figure 7.17 shows the strategic map from Figure 7.8 for the Project Budget Management activity. Notice that a number is written close to each entity box. This indicates the subproject phase number for the Project Budget Management activity, when that entity should be defined in greater detail to identify data attributes in logical data modeling for the What column and the Designer row [C1R3]. These phase numbers have been derived automatically [10]. We will learn shortly how to derive these phase numbers manually. The project phase numbers are derived based on the defined associations and strength of the business rules that join these entities.

Figure 7.17 shows an automatically derived project plan for that activity [11]. This project plan represents a subproject for rapid implementation; it is called a *cluster*. A subproject phase number precedes each entity—separated from the entity name by a right bracket. Each higher phase number is indented one position further

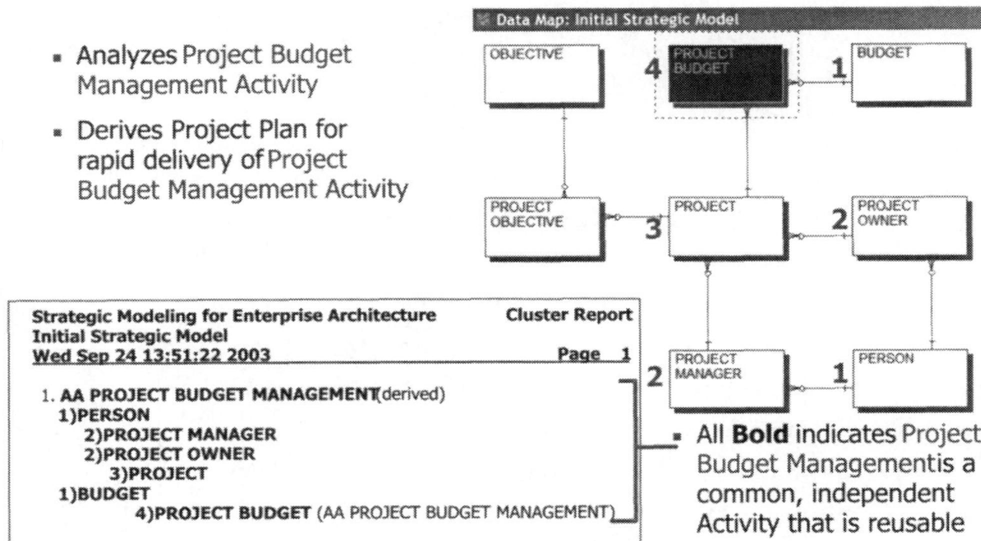

Figure 7.17 Project Budget Management Activity identified from strategic model.

to the right in outline format, so it can be read as a conceptual Gantt chart. Notice also that each of the entity names is **bold**. The comment in Figure 7.17 states that Project Budget Management is a common, independent activity that is reusable. We will see this reuse shortly. Figure 7.18 next illustrates each entity required by the Project Budget Management activity as highlighted. This diagram shows as highlighted the required entities that are needed by the activity. These highlighted entities represent the vertical sliver in [C1] for this activity.

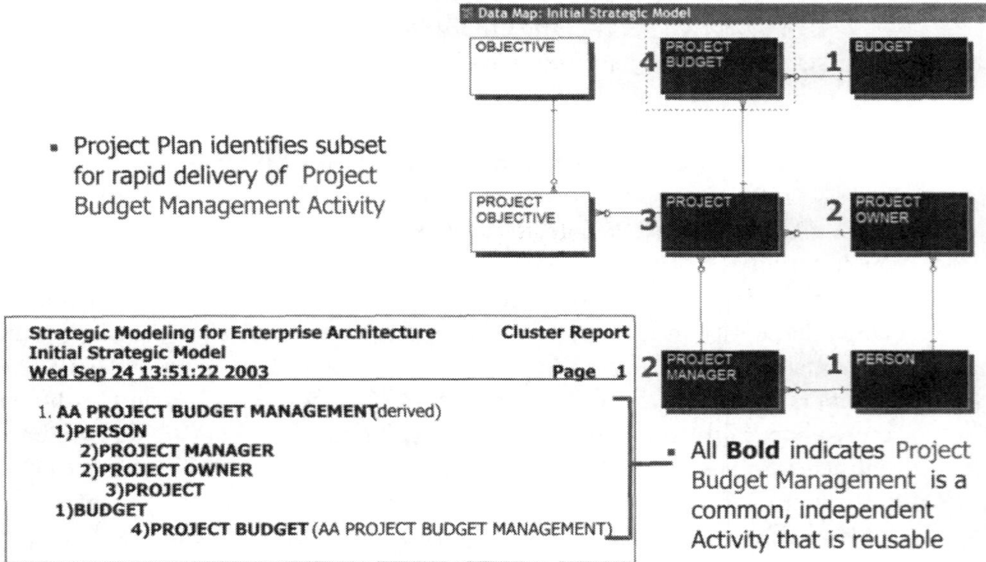

Figure 7.18 Project objective management activity highlighted in strategic model.

Figure 7.19 analyzes the data map further to identify the data entities required by the Project Objective Management activity. Notice that the intersecting entity representing the activity has been highlighted. The project plan for this derived subproject cluster is also included in the figure [12].

Notice that all of the entities listed in the cluster of Figure 7.19 required by the Project Objective Management activity subproject cluster are in **bold,** as we also saw earlier for Figure 7.17. But included in the project plan we also see that BUDGET and PROJECT BUDGET (for Project Budget Management activity) are included, but are not bold. This shows Project Budget Management is a prerequisite reusable activity that is shared. This prerequisite subproject dependency is more apparent in Figure 7.20.

Figure 7.20 shows the Project Budget Management and Project Objective Management subproject clusters both together. We can see now that the Project Budget Management activity has been reused in Project Objective Management. This reflects the mandatory business rule (see Figure 7.5) that a Project must have at least one or many Project Budgets. The analysis has applied this business rule to mean that Project Objectives cannot be managed effectively without also knowing the relevant project budget. This rule certainly is true for most enterprises.

Notice the project map in the bottom section of Figure 7.20. This shows each subproject cluster as a highlighted box. Each box represents all entities and their subproject phases that are contained in the relevant cluster in the top part of the figure. The project map displays the stage in a larger project when the relevant subproject will be implemented. We can see that Project Budget Management is a Stage 1 subproject [13]; Project Objective Management is a Stage 2 subproject [14]. We now know the order in which each subproject should be implemented.

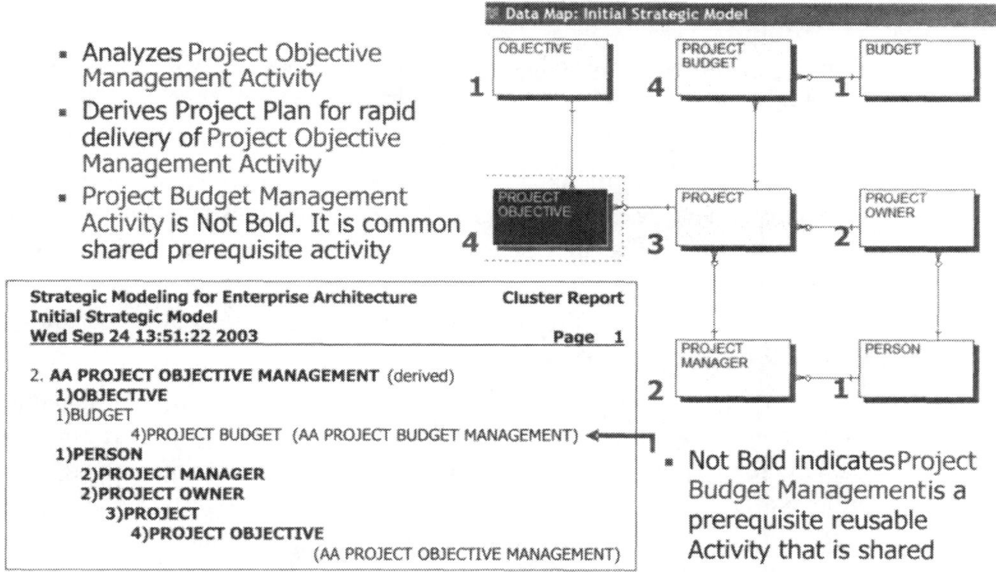

Figure 7.19 Project objective management activity highlighted in strategic model.

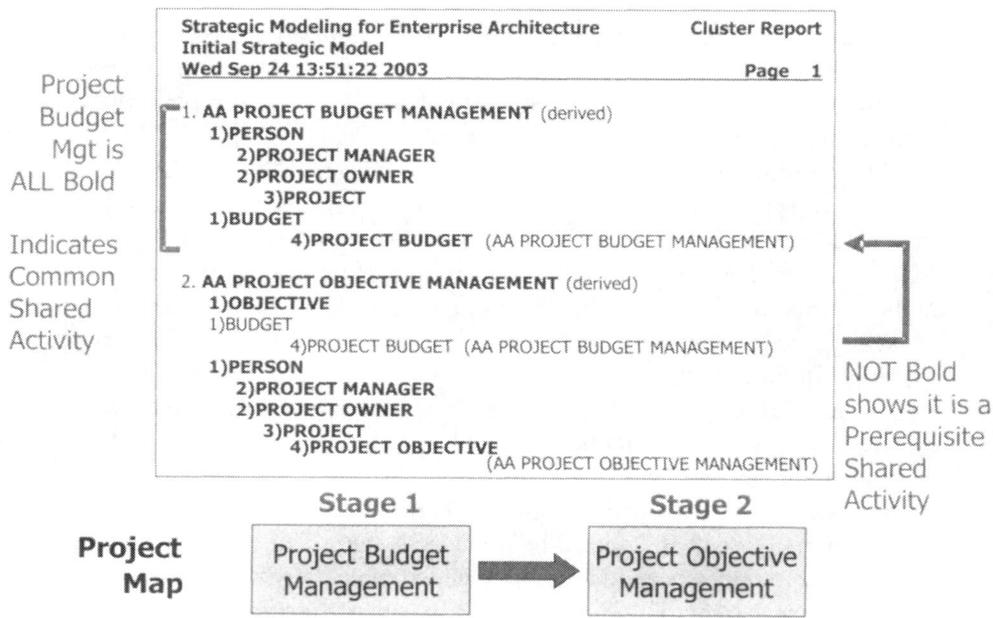

Figure 7.20 Project plans derived from strategic model.

7.5.1 Characteristics of Entity Dependency Analysis

This overview has highlighted some of the benefits of entity dependency analysis:

- Activities are indicated by the existence of intersecting entities that are formed by decomposing *many-to-many* associations.
- Activity names—formed by adding the suffix *Management* to each intersecting entity name—provide the list of processes in the How column for the Planner row [C2R1].
- Project plans can be derived from a data map—using entity dependency analysis—for rapid delivery of priority activities as vertical slivers.
- Each intersecting entity is a separately implementable subproject, called a *Cluster*. This defines the project plan phases for each entity in that cluster.
- The phase numbers in a cluster are derived based on the defined associations and relevant business rules between related entities, using entity dependency analysis (discussed soon).
- A Cluster where all entities are **bold** represents a common independent activity that is reusable. These are potential Stage 1 subprojects.
- A Cluster that references another cluster name that is not bold is dependent on that other cluster as a prerequisite reusable activity that is shared. It is a potential Stage 2 (or higher) subproject, dependent on the not-bold Stage subproject.
- Clusters that contain prerequisite clusters are used to develop a project map. This indicates the Stage numbers for implementation of the subprojects represented by each of those clusters.

We will now examine the rules for entity dependency. We will use these rules to derive project plans manually from a data map, as clusters for separately implementable subprojects. This derivation can also be done automatically by some modeling tools [15].

7.5.2 Entity Dependency Rules

Entity dependency uses several rules to determine the ownership of two related entities. These rules decide ownership by the strength of the business rules represented by the association degree or cardinality—and the association nature—at each end of the association line. We will first examine Entity Dependency Rule 1. This addresses the rule for association degree or cardinality. It is defined next.

Rule 1: Association Degree (or Cardinality) Rule

This rule indicates that an association degree of *One* is stronger than an association degree of *Many:*

- One (—-) is stronger than Many (——<)

Rule 1 is the strongest rule; it overrides the two other association nature rules that will be described shortly. It is illustrated in Figure 7.21. Apply this rule now to the association joining each pair of entities in Figure 7.21. Identify the Owner—entity A or entity B—of the two entities in each pair before reviewing the answers in the following discussion.

Discussion of Entity Dependency

- The first example in Figure 7.21 indicates that A is the Owner. A is related to many B, but each B is related to only one A—which therefore owns each B.
- The second example indicates that B is the Owner. B is related to many A, but each A is related to only one B—which therefore owns each A.

The second entity dependency rule addresses *association nature*—in two parts. The first of these rules is Rule 2a Mandatory Rule, as defined next.

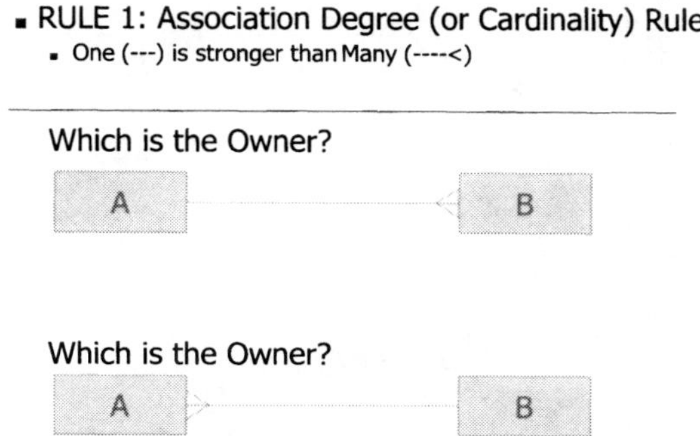

Figure 7.21 Entity Dependency Rule 1 for association degree or cardinality.

Rule 2a: Association Nature—Mandatory Rule

- *Mandatory (must) is stronger than Optional Becoming Mandatory (**will**)*

This indicates that an association nature expressed as *Mandatory* (**must**) is stronger than an association nature of *Optional Becoming Mandatory* (**will**). We will examine examples of this rule in Figure 7.22 **without** considering the association degree rule.

Discussion of Entity Dependency

- The first example in Figure 7.22 indicates that B is the Owner. Each B eventually will be related to A. Each A **mandatorily** must be related to one and only one B.
- The second example indicates that A is the Owner. Each A eventually will be related to B. Each B **mandatorily** must be related to one and only one A.

The second part of the association nature rule is Rule 2b: Optional Becoming Mandatory Rule. This is defined as follows.

Rule 2b: Association Nature—Optional Becoming Mandatory Rule

- *Optional Becoming Mandatory* (**will**) *is stronger than Optional* **may**)

This rule indicates that an association nature of *Optional Becoming Mandatory* (**will**) is stronger than an association nature of *Optional* (**may**). We will examine this rule here, **without** also considering the association degree rule.

Discussion of Entity Dependency

- The first example in Figure 7.23 indicates that B is the Owner. Each B may be related to A (or may never be related). But each A will be related to B (eventually)—and so B is the owner.

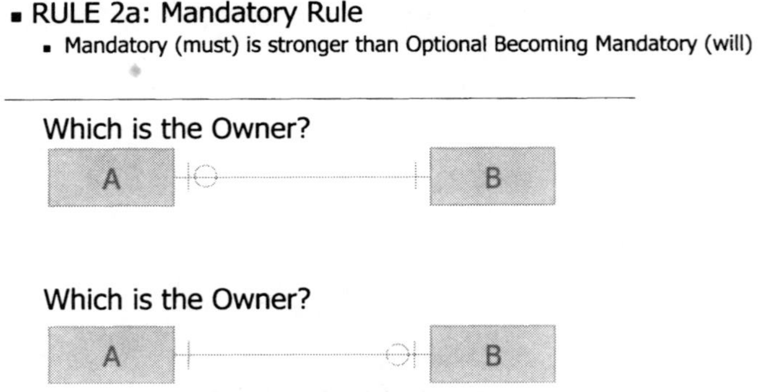

Figure 7.22 Entity Dependency Rule 2a for association nature.

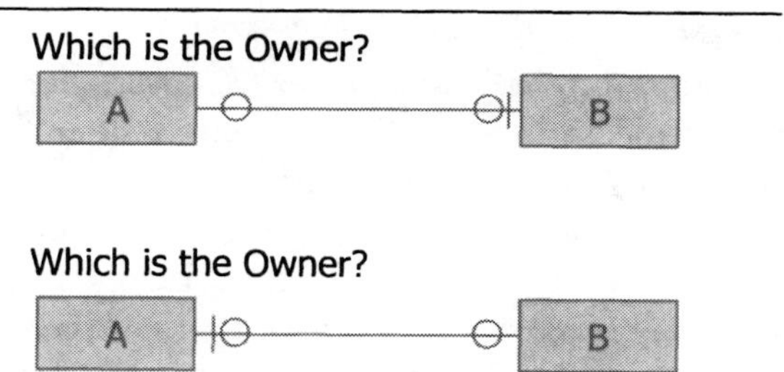

Figure 7.23 Entity Dependency Rule 2b for association nature.

- The second example indicates that A is the Owner. Each A may be related to B (or may never be related). But each B will be related to A (eventually)—and so is the owner.

7.5.3 Entity Dependency Rule Exercises

Figure 7.24 illustrates pairs of entities as practice exercises to apply the three entity dependency rules. Each association in these examples denotes ownership. Write down the owner of each pair—A or B. Next, test yourself by reviewing the following discussion, keyed to the numbered examples in the figure.

Discussion of Entity Dependency

1. There may be many A for each B, but each A is related to one (and only one) B. B therefore is the owner. Notice that it has a *Mandatory One* association touching it. This is the strongest relationship of all; it always indicates ownership.

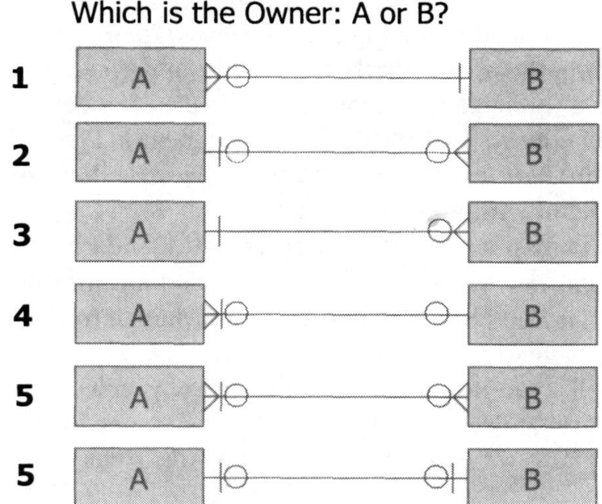

Figure 7.24 Entity dependency examples of ownership.

2. A is the owner: *One* is stronger than *Many,* and will is stronger than *may.*
3. A is again the owner: *Mandatory One* is much stronger than *Optional Many.*
4. B is the owner: *One* at B is stronger than *Many* at A. Notice that the strength of Rule 1 overrides Rule 2a with *will* at A compared to *may* at B. In this example, an *optional one* association usually indicates that more detailed underlying entities are yet to be defined. These are typically secondary or subtype entities. The association is then normally a *mandatory one* association to one or more of those subtype entities, and does not exist **at all** for the other subtype entities (hence, the optionality at the higher principal or supertype entity).
5. We cannot determine ownership from example 5 because of the *many-to-many* association. It must first be decomposed into an intersecting entity, with two *one-to-many* associations to each of these entities—as two owners of the intersecting entity.
6. The *one-to-one* association suggests weak business rules. If this is in fact correct, there is no owner. To resolve this, the two entities should be combined into one entity. If they cannot, more decisive business rules must be defined.

Now that we understand the rules for entity dependency ownership, we will apply these rules to derive project plans from a data map, based on the entity dependency analysis method. Project plans will be derived as clusters of related entities that are separately implementable subprojects. We will use the resulting clusters to develop project maps. These indicate alternative implementation sequences for these subprojects.

7.5.4 Deriving Project Plans and Project Maps

We will use a fragment of a strategic data map as illustrated in Figure 7.25, which is different from the strategic map in Figure 7.14. This was developed in an earlier (separate) facilitated modeling session. This data map comprises entities and associations joining them. No attributes have been defined yet, apart from the (implicit) primary and foreign keys needed to implement the defined associations.

We will now analyze the data map fragment in Figure 7.25. We start by identifying *end-point entities.* These are so called because they have only *many* associations touching them, with no *one* association.

The data map shows that PERSON SKILL and PROJECT RESOURCE are both end-point entities. (PROJECT MANAGER does not **only** have *many* associations touching it; it also has a *one* association touching it from PROJECT RESOURCE. It is called a *prerequisite end-point entity.*)

We will first use the entity dependency rules to identify ownership. This will enable us to derive the project phase sequence for this part of the data map as a project plan. We will apply the following steps to examples in the following figures.

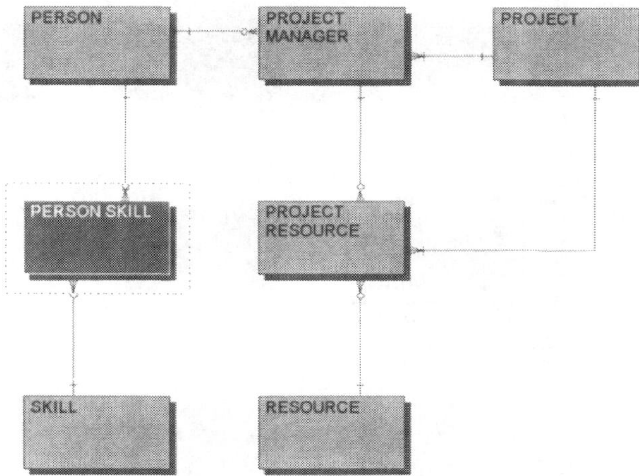

Figure 7.25 Data map to be used for entity dependency analysis.

Entity Dependency Analysis Steps

- *Step 1:* Follow each *many* association back to its related *one* entity. This *one* entity is the owner of the *many* entity. For example, SKILL and PERSON are both owners of PERSON SKILL due to their mandatory *one* associations
- *Step 2:* Continue until an owner entity has all associations touching it that are only *one*. This is marked as *Phase 1*. SKILL and PERSON are therefore both Phase 1.
- *Step 3:* For a Phase 1 entity, follow every association forward to every related *many* entity and increment the phase number of that entity by 1. Based on this step, PERSON SKILL is Phase 2.

We see the application of these three steps in relation to Figure 7.26. The end-point entity PERSON SKILL is named *Person Skill Activity* or *Person Skill Management*. We will document this cluster in outline format based on the steps discussed next.

7.5.5 Steps for Derivation of Project Plans

Based on the *end-point entity*, we will first name the relevant cluster. Applying the preceding three steps, each phase number is written against the relevant entity in Figure 7.26:

- *Step 1:* Follow each *many* association back to its related *one* entity. This *one* entity is the owner of the *many* entity. For example, SKILL and PERSON are both owners of PERSON SKILL.
- *Step 2:* Continue until an owner entity has all associations touching it that are only *one*. This is marked as *Phase 1*. SKILL and PERSON are therefore both Phase 1. Mark them with "1" at the top left of each entity box.

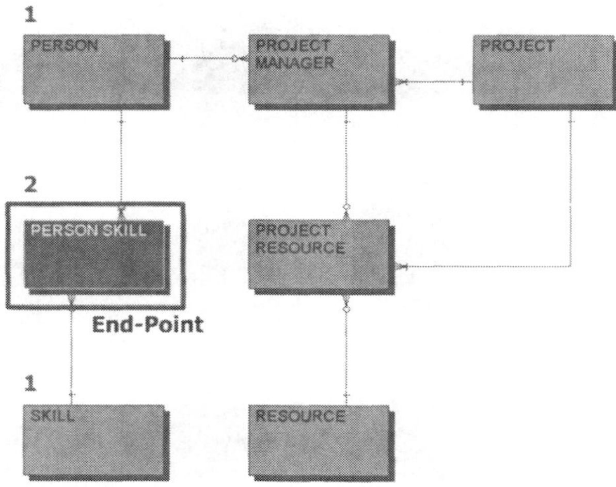

Figure 7.26 Identifying phase numbers for Person Skill Management.

- *Step 3:* For every Phase 1 entity, follow all associations forward to each *many* entity and increment the Phase number of that entity by 1. PERSON SKILL is therefore Phase 2. Mark it with "2" at the top left of the entity box.

The Cluster is then documented in outline format with higher phase entities indented one place to the right for each higher phase number, as shown next. Each directly-related entity is shown in **bold.** This indicates that the end-point entity (PERSON SKILL) in Phase 2 mandatorily requires each of the Phase 1 entities as prerequisites. It represents an independent cluster that can also be reused elsewhere.

PERSON SKILL MANAGEMENT
Phase 1) **PERSON** [16]
Phase 1) **SKILL**
Phase 2) **PERSON SKILL** (Person Skill Management)

We will document this derived cluster in Figure 7.27 now as a *project map.* This illustrates *subproject deliverables*. These are so named because they represent vertical-sliver subprojects that can be delivered early as part of a larger project that requires the relevant activity and associated systems. Figure 7.27 shows the highlighted box PERSON SKILL as a project map for Stage 1. This highlighted box represents the Person Skill Management cluster just shown.

Stage 1

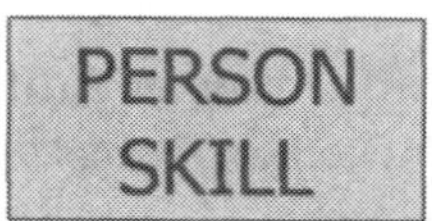

Figure 7.27 Project map subproject deliverables for PERSON SKILL MANAGEMENT.

We will use the term *Stage* to refer to the implementation sequence of vertical-sliver subprojects in a project map, as shown in Figure 7.27. Each subproject in a project map is a highlighted box, named by the end-point entity for a cluster that has been derived from a data map. We will use the term *Phase* to refer to the implementation sequence of entities in a cluster, shown as prefixes with a right-side parenthesis in the cluster represented by Figure 7.27. Each subproject is implemented in a specific Stage of a larger project. Within a subproject, each entity in the associated cluster is implemented in a specific *Phase.*

We saw that the Person Skill Management cluster showed all dependent entities in **bold.** This convention indicates that it is an independent cluster that is reusable. It can therefore be implemented as a Stage 1 subproject that is a deliverable in a more complex project. We will see more complex project maps shortly.

Another part of the data map will now be similarly analyzed as shown in Figure 7.28.

Based on a selected end-point entity, we first name the relevant cluster. For example, the end-point entity PROJECT RESOURCE in Figure 7.28 is named as the cluster *Project Resource Activity* or *Project Resource Management.* From these alternative names, we have decided to name the cluster *Project Resource Management.* We have marked the derived phase numbers on the data map in Figure 7.29. These have been derived based on the steps discussed next.

- *Step 1:* Follow each *many* association back to its related *one* entity. This *one* entity is the owner of the *many* entity. For example, RESOURCE, PROJECT, and PROJECT MANAGER are all owners of PROJECT RESOURCE.
- *Step 2:* Continue until an owner entity has all associations touching it that are only *one*. This is marked as *Phase 1*. RESOURCE and PROJECT are therefore both Phase 1. Mark these "1" at top left of each entity box.
- *Step 3:* Notice that PROJECT MANAGER—an owner of PROJECT RESOURCE—has two *many* as well as a *one* association touching it. It is therefore called a *prerequisite end-point entity* [17].

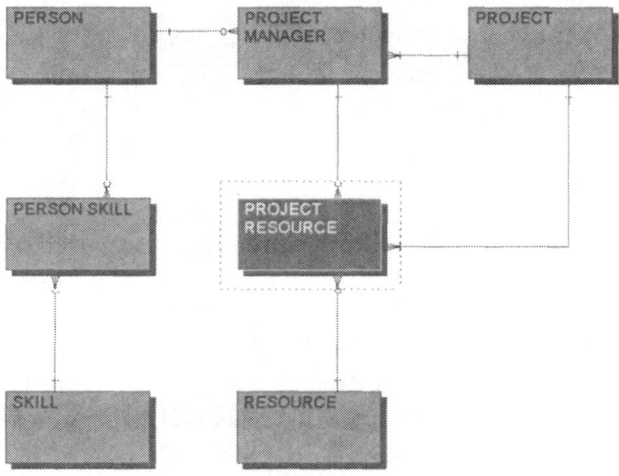

Figure 7.28 End-point PROJECT RESOURCE for entity dependency analysis.

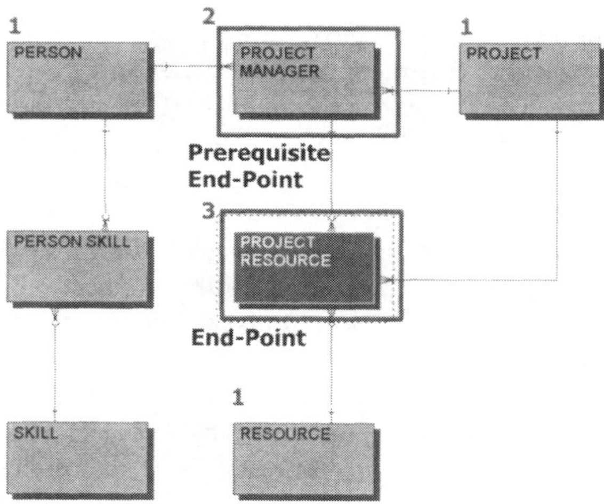

Figure 7.29 Identifying phase numbers for Project Resource Management.

- *Step 4:* Follow each association from PROJECT MANAGER back to its related *one* entity. We see that PROJECT and PERSON are both owners at Phase 1. Mark these "1" at top left of each entity box.
- *Step 5:* For each Phase 1 entity, follow every association forward to each *many* entity and increment the Phase number of that entity by 1. PROJECT MANAGER is therefore Phase 2. Mark this "2" at the top left of each entity box.
- *Step 6:* Continue until the end-point entity is reached. PROJECT RESOURCE is therefore Phase 3. Mark this "3" at the top left of each entity box.

Although we have completed our analysis of Figure 7.29 at Step 6, in many cases we also need to apply some additional steps. These are shown next as Steps 7 and 8; they will be used shortly.

- *Step 7:* Next identify any *one* entity with *mandatory one–to–mandatory many* associations to any other related entities. PROJECT and PROJECT MANAGER are so related.
- *Step 8:* Repeat Steps 4 and 5. PROJECT and PERSON are owners of PROJECT MANAGER at Phase 1. Mark these "1" at the top left of each entity box. PROJECT MANAGER is Phase 2. Mark this "2" at the top left of that entity box.

We will document this Cluster in outline format based on the steps discussed.

PROJECT RESOURCE MANAGEMENT
- Phase 1) **RESOURCE** [18]
- Phase 1) PERSON
  - Phase 2) **PROJECT MANAGER** (Project Management)
- Phase 1) **PROJECT**
  - Phase 3) **PROJECT RESOURCE** (Project Resource Management)

Discussion of Cluster Derivation

Notice in the preceding cluster that PROJECT RESOURCE is directly dependent on each entity above it; it has a lower phase number and is shown in **bold.** PERSON however is *not bold* because it depends only on PROJECT MANAGER, not on PROJECT RESOURCE. Because it is only indirectly dependent on PROJECT RESOURCE, it is therefore shown as *not bold.*

If the association from PROJECT MANAGER to PROJECT RESOURCE did not exist, then PROJECT MANAGER would not be an owner of PROJECT RESOURCE. It would therefore not be included in the cluster at all. However the *mandatory one–to–mandatory many* association from PROJECT to PROJECT MANAGER (in Step 7) **mandates** for each Project that we **must** know the Project Manager. PROJECT MANAGER would then still be a prerequisite end-point and PERSON must therefore still be included. PROJECT MANAGER is a Prerequisite Cluster called *Project Management.* It is indirectly dependent on PROJECT RESOURCE and so would also be shown as *not bold.*

We will add this latest derived Cluster to the project map from Figure 7.27. The result is the project map in Figure 7.30.

Discussion of Project Map

We can see in Figure 7.30 that Project Management is a Stage 1 subproject. Project Resource Management is dependent on it—indicated by the arrow—and so is a Stage 2 subproject. We earlier saw that Person Skill Management is also a Stage 1 subproject. Project Resource Management is not connected to it by an arrow, because it is not dependent on Person Skill Management at all.

This project map now illustrates separate subproject deliverables. Both of these Stage 1 subprojects can be implemented concurrently, as neither depends on the other. However, Project Resource Management is implemented in Stage 2 only after Project Management has been implemented in Stage 1. Separate subproject deliverables, and the order of their implementation, are now clear. We will later see examples where two subprojects in Stage 1 are interdependent and so must be implemented together.

The documentation of subproject deliverables in project maps illustrates implementation sequence alternatives. Entity dependency analysis is used in this way to

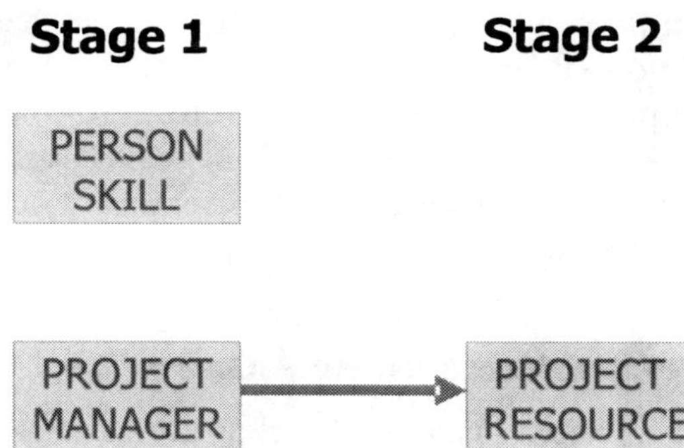

Figure 7.30 Project map subproject deliverables for Project Management and Project Resource Management.

derive separately implementable subprojects as clusters representing vertical slivers. Project maps show subproject deliverables and alternative sequences for implementation of priority clusters. These are the vertical sliver alternatives that we discussed in Chapter 5. Together, the clusters enable precise project management of priority vertical slivers for rapid delivery. They can alternatively be illustrated in Gantt format, such as shown in Figure 7.32.

7.6 Case Study Entity Dependency Problems

We will now apply what we have learned to derive project plans as clusters from the strategic model that we have developed so far. These are included as case study problems on the accompanying CD-ROM. After completing these problems and reviewing the sample solutions, return to this chapter for additional material on real-life strategic modeling project examples that have used entity dependency analysis.

PLEASE COMPLETE CASE STUDY PROBLEMS NOW [19].

On completion of the case study problems and after reviewing your solutions against the sample solutions given on the CD-ROM, you now have developed valuable project plans as do-it-yourself constructions kits for the enterprise. This is discussed next.

7.7 Project Maps Are Do-It-Yourself Construction Kits

The Swedish furniture manufacturer IKEA has furniture showrooms in cities throughout the world. Its furniture is sold in kit form—for "do-it-yourself" (DIY) construction. With the enclosed diagram and instructions, the supplied components can be assembled into the finished furniture item.

Previously in systems development we have built systems in a manner that was like putting together pieces of a jigsaw puzzle—but without a jigsaw picture. We now have that jigsaw picture. This is the strategic data model; it shows us how all data entities "fit together." We also have many clusters derived from a data map, which show us the phase sequence of entities to build each subproject. And we now have project maps that show us how the subprojects can be progressively built in stages. We now see that these project maps and derived clusters provide the unique DIY construction kit for your enterprise that has previously been missing.

Using the project maps and derived clusters, priority subproject clusters can be identified and resources allocated for rapid delivery using the technologies in Part III (see Figure 7.31). Clusters that are of a lower priority can be implemented later only when they are needed.

7.7.1 Using Project Management Packages

In addition to project maps, each subproject cluster that is derived using entity dependency analysis can also provide input for entry into a project management software package such as Microsoft Project. Each entity in a derived cluster is

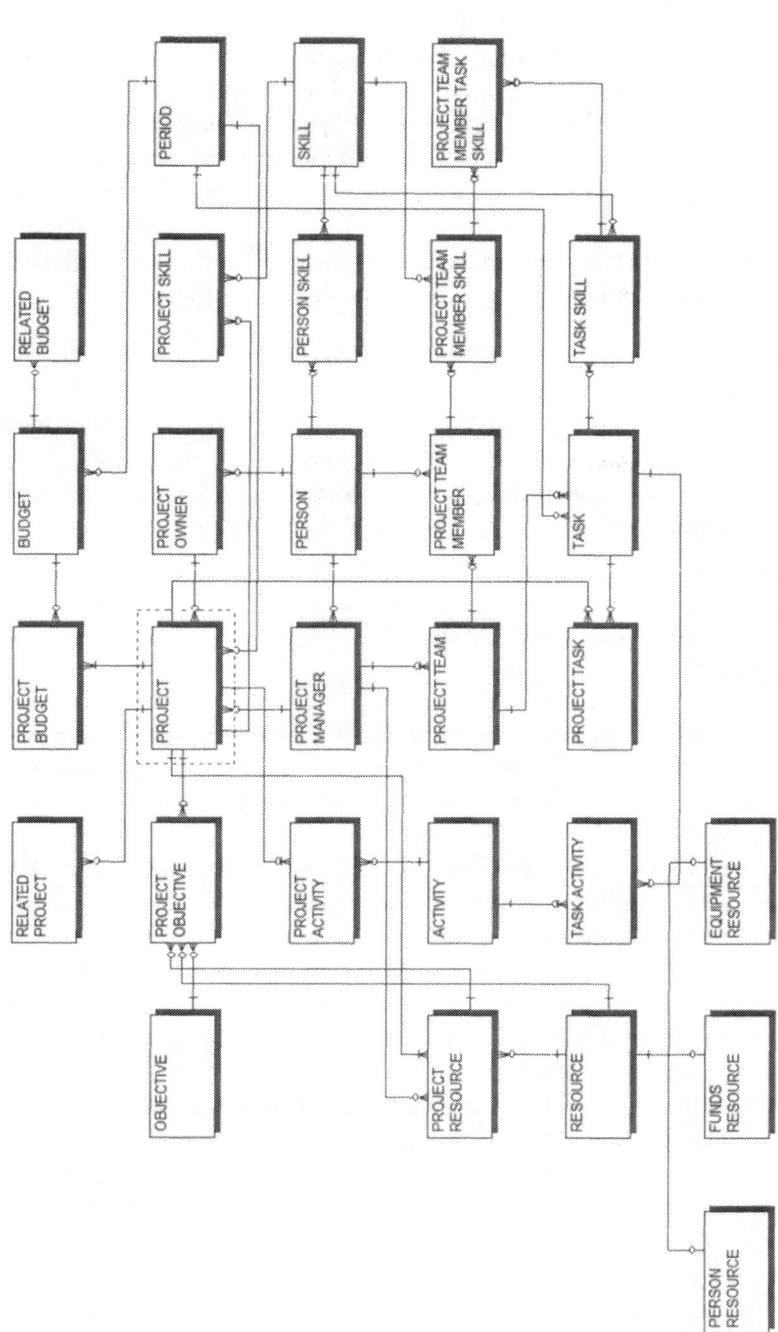

Figure 7.31 This strategic map will be analyzed manually in Case Study Problem 2 on the CD-ROM to derive project plans for subprojects.

entered as a minor task for the relevant derived phase in a larger subproject task. Minor tasks can be collapsed into parent subproject tasks, which are related to other subprojects by their relevant project map stage. Using precedence or pert diagrams, subproject dependencies can be easily managed in a larger project.

The duration that is allocated for each task phase is based on the anticipated number of attributes to be identified during later logical data modeling for each phase entity, as discussed in Chapter 9. You can establish "rules of thumb" for calculating time duration for each attribute as discussed next.

One rule of thumb is based on a 6-hour workday with an average of 2 hours for the definition of each attribute, plus 0.5 hour for later review of a previously defined attribute. This attribute definition includes an agreed attribute name, its purpose description, logical data type, and edit rules as detailed in Chapter 6. The time duration of each phase entity can therefore be estimated as follows:

- *Low-complexity entities:* These typically have 3 to 5 attributes. In the earlier case study, a low-complexity entity may be OBJECTIVE. Such entities will take approximately 1 to 1.5 days for definition plus 0.5 day for review.
- *Medium-complexity entities:* These may have 6 to 10 attributes. Based on the preceding rules of thumb, these will take 2 to 3.5 days for definition plus 0.5 to 1 day for review. An example is PROJECT TEAM.
- *High-complexity entities:* These typically have 11 to 18 attributes or more. Examples of these are RESOURCE, PROJECT, and PERSON. These will take 3.5 to 6 days plus 1 to 1.5 days for review, based on the preceding rules of thumb.

These rules of thumb can be refined based on actual experience within your organization. Definition of entities and attributes that involve technical or political complexity may need more time than this; other situations will require less time.

By using the resource planning capability of Microsoft Project, or by using a spreadsheet, the attribute complexity counts can be easily adjusted and relevant complexity criteria codes can be defined. The time-duration rules of thumb given earlier—for definition and review of attributes—can also be refined as needed. The result is the calculation by Microsoft Project, or by the spreadsheet, of estimated task durations for entry into the software package for close project management during later logical data modeling.

Subprojects can be expanded using Microsoft Project with a Gantt chart that shows their component tasks. They can alternatively be collapsed to show only the higher level subprojects in the Gantt chart. This high-level subproject format may provide a clearer visual representation of subproject stage dependencies than the project map diagram format that was used in this chapter to introduce the concept of project map stage dependencies.

We will now discuss the application of these principles in four real-life projects that used strategic modeling and entity dependency analysis. The first is a public sector project: a large federal government department. The second—a private-sector project—is for a medium-sized regional bank. The third is for a medium-sized government department project. The fourth project is for another large government department. All projects used strategic modeling. We will start with the first government department project.

7.7.2 Large Government Department Project Example

This government department [20] delivers a number of services nationally to persons who make up the population of the country. This population is referred to as their "customers." They focus strongly on identifying the needs of each customer, so that they can provide the most relevant services to address the needs of each person.

The project started with a facilitated strategic modeling session over 2 days, attended by very senior managers in the department and using as a catalyst their strategic plans defined for the 1995–2005 period. The strategic model was developed on white boards and then entered into a modeling tool for analysis and development of a strategic information systems plan (SISP). This strategic modeling project took a total of 3 weeks. Project maps for progressive delivery of priority activities are discussed shortly.

The services that are offered to customers depend on the roles that a person can take. A person role may be as an active customer, as a past customer who is now inactive, or as a potential customer. The department is also interested in the dependents of persons who are customers. These persons, their dependents, and person roles are managed by PERSON STRUCTURE as a Related Persons Knowledge Base.

The cluster identified as the Person Role Management Activity is a prerequisite of the Customer Needs Management Activity, as shown in Figure 7.32. This figure shows a Person Role Management Activity subproject box in Stage 1, with a Customer Needs Analysis Activity subproject box in Stage 2. The phases for entities in the cluster are shown as a Gantt chart for project management purposes.

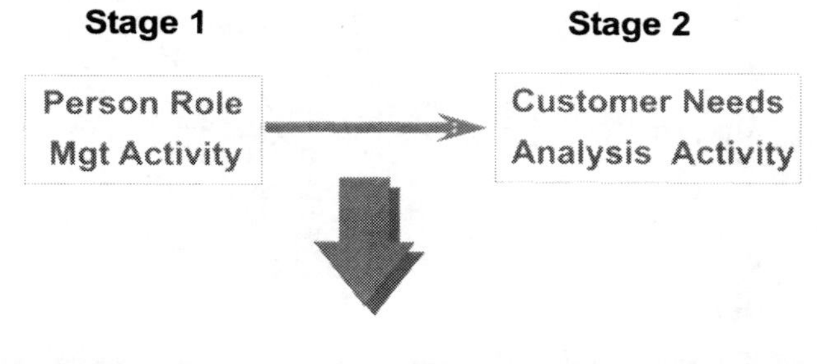

Cluster Content — Project Phase :	1	2	3	4	5	6
1) PERSON TYPE	■					
1) PERIOD	■					
3) PERSON ROLE (Person Role Mgt Activity)			■			
1) SEX	■					
2) PERSON		■				
3) CUSTOMER			■			
1) NEED TYPE	■					
2) NEED		■				
4) CUSTOMER NEED (Cust Needs Analysis)				■		

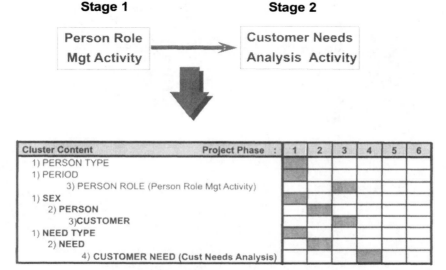

Figure 7.32 Gantt chart for Customer Needs Analysis Activity. (*From:* [20]. © 1997 DSS. Reprinted with permission.)

Figure 7.33 shows a project map for this government project. Person Role Management Activity and Related Persons Knowledge Base represent the National Person Index. This is a fundamental starting point for implementation; it appears in Stage 1 of the summary project map in Figure 7.34 that has been developed from Figure 7.33.

Potentially concurrent subprojects for Service Management, Financial Management and Decision Early Warning [21] are shown in the large boxes in Figure 7.33. We can see from the summary project map in Figure 7.34 the overall implementation sequence.

The large boxes for Person Management, Customer Management, and Service Delivery in Figure 7.33 can be seen as Stage 3 subprojects in Figure 7.34. Finally, Performance Monitoring subprojects in Figure 7.33 are all Stage 4 subprojects in Figure 7.34.

7.7.3 Regional Bank Project Example

The private-sector example was a project for an innovative regional bank in South Korea [22]. Since 1994 this bank had used banking systems implemented using dis-

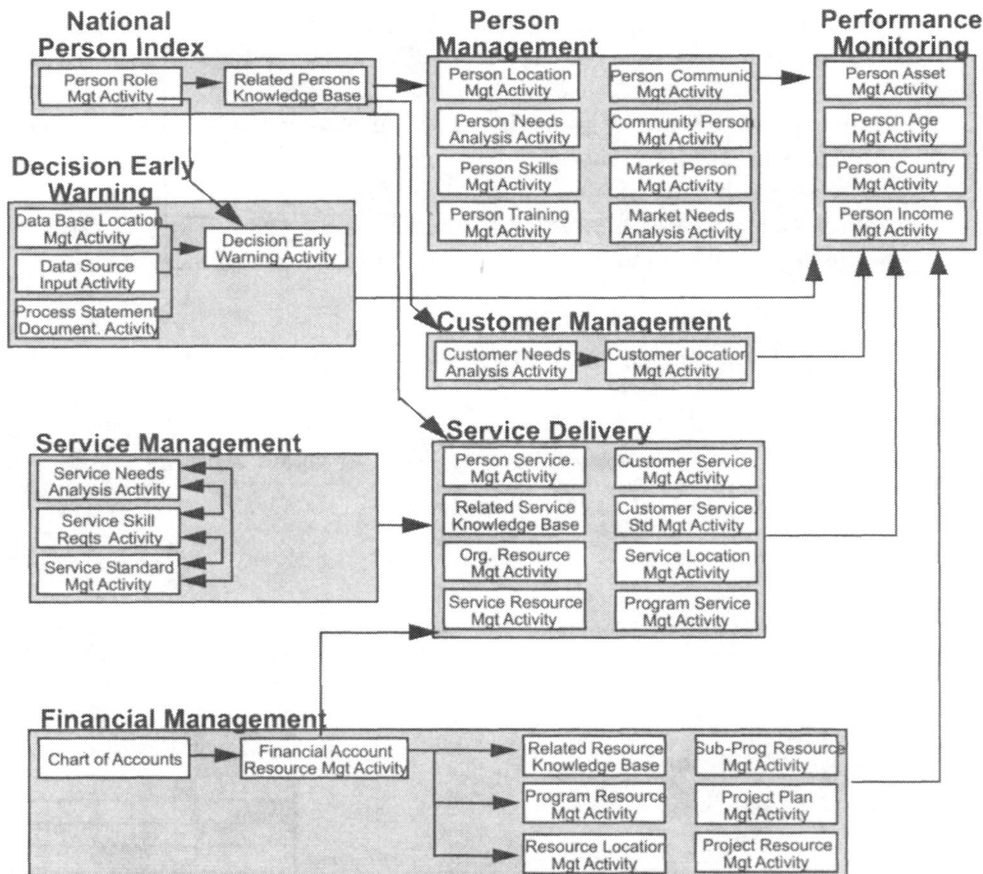

Figure 7.33 Project map for large government department. (*From:* [20]. © 1997 DSS. Reprinted with permission.)

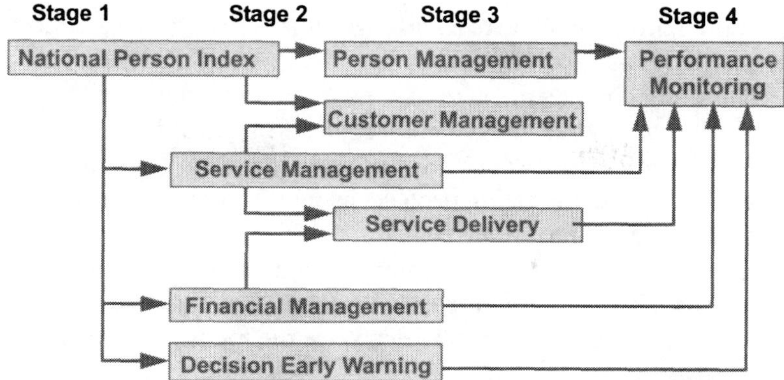

Figure 7.34 Summary project map for government department. (*From:* [20]. © 1997 DSS. Reprinted with permission.)

tributed client/server technologies. A project was initiated in 1997 to redevelop these systems for electronic banking. This was a large project that used strategic modeling to develop project maps to manage the progressive implementation for rapid delivery of priority systems.

The project team comprised banking experts as well as IT experts. The strategic model was first developed over 2 days in a facilitated strategic modeling session. It was entered into a modeling tool for entity dependency analysis and documentation, and then formally presented to managers and their business experts in another day, for review.

Following analysis and review, a summary project map was developed as shown in Figure 7.35. This summarizes more detailed project maps such as that

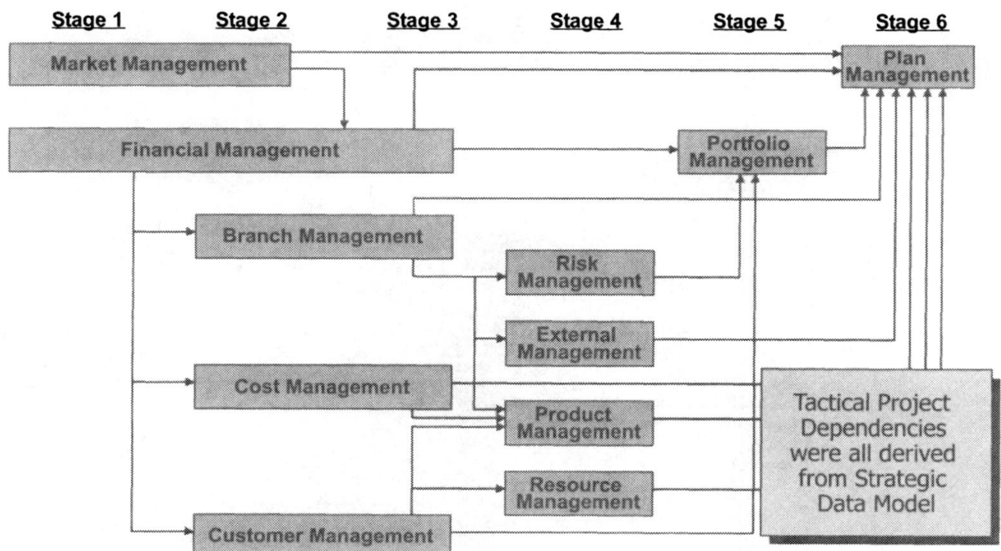

Figure 7.35 Summary project map for regional bank. (*From:* [22]. © 1997 Kwangju Bank. Reprinted with permission.)

shown in Figure 7.36. The total elapsed time for this strategic modeling project was 4 weeks.

The senior management review examined the summary project map in Figure 7.35, the Customer Management Project Map in Figure 7.36, and other project maps to identify priority activities for early delivery. These activities were the focus of later logical data modeling projects using the methods described in Chapter 9, followed by implementation in Java.

Figure 7.36 shows the Customer Management Project Map. This was identified as the highest priority area for management. The Customer Management and Customer Risk Management subprojects were the focus for priority logical data modeling subprojects.

7.7.4 Medium Government Department Project Example

This was a strategic modeling project for enterprise architecture in a new government department [23] that had been established to manage the introduction of manufacturing industries into the country. When this project was undertaken in 2000, a strategic business plan had not yet been completed. However, the legislative articles of law that defined the department were precise. These articles were therefore used as the catalyst for the facilitated strategic modeling session, as illustrated in Figure 7.37.

Figure 7.38 shows a matrix with articles of law (from the Why column [C6] of the Zachman framework) listed as rows, with organization units (from the Who column [C4]) shown as columns. One column has been highlighted to show the subset of law that applies to that organizational unit [24].

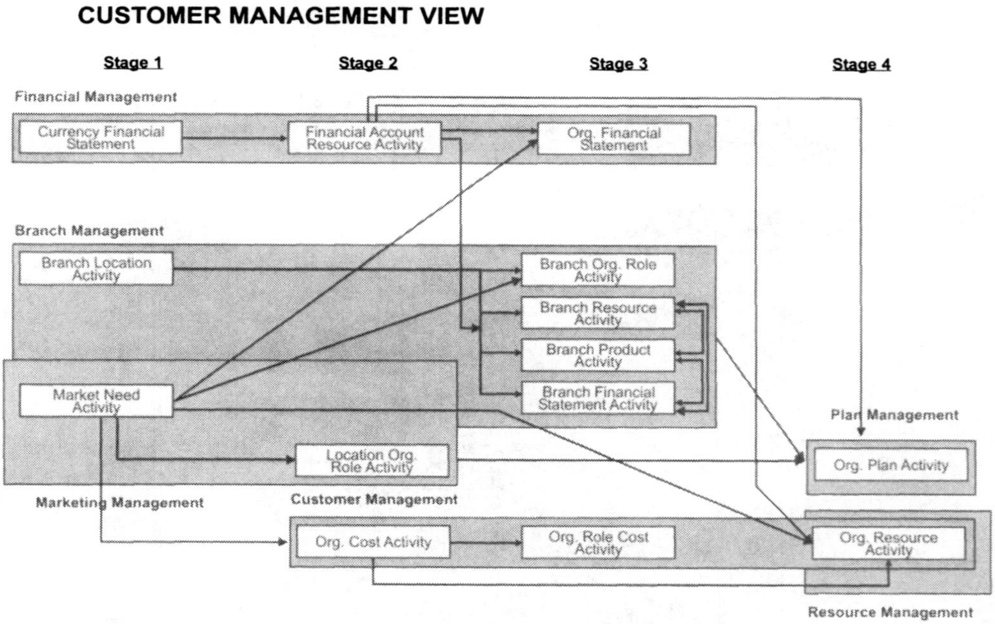

CUSTOMER MANAGEMENT VIEW

Stage 1
Stage 2
Stage 3
Stage 4
Financial Management
Currency Financial Statement
Financial Account Resource Activity
Org. Financial Statement
Branch Management
Branch Location Activity
Branch Org. Role Activity
Branch Resource Activity
Branch Product Activity
Market Need Activity
Branch Financial Statement Activity
Plan Management
Location Org. Role Activity
Org. Plan Activity
Marketing Management
Customer Management
Org. Cost Activity
Org. Role Cost Activity
Org. Resource Activity
Resource Management

Figure 7.36 Customer management project map. (*From:* [22]. © 1997 Kwangju Bank. Reprinted with permission.)

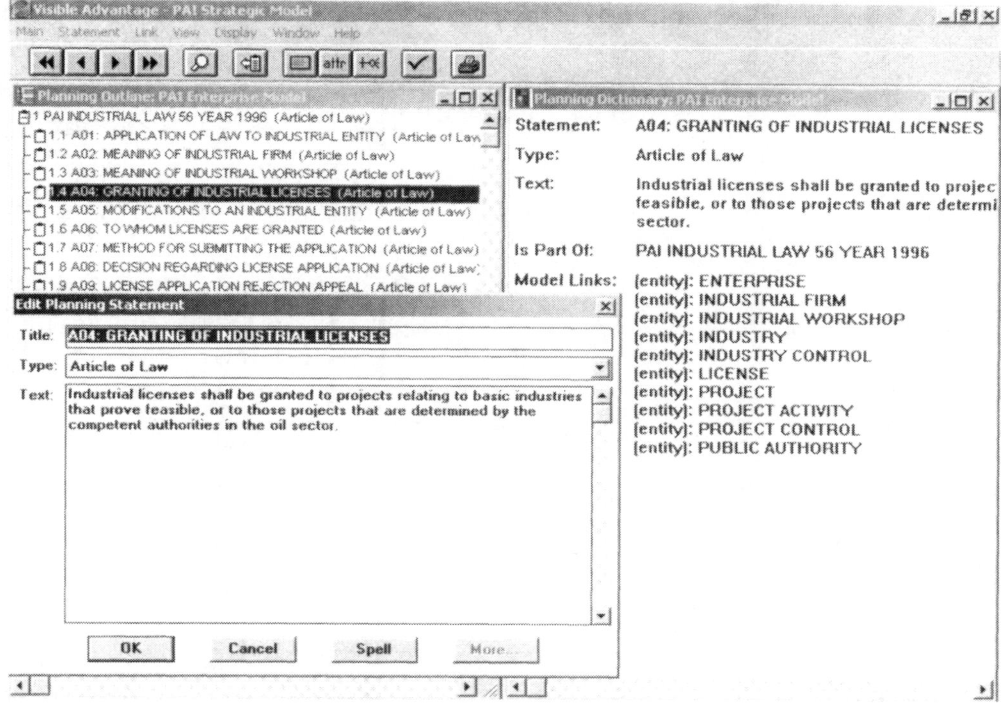

Figure 7.37 Articles of law used as strategic modeling catalyst. (*From:* [23]. © 2000 PAI. Reprinted with permission.)

We will see further examples of this and other matrices in Chapter 8. We will see how these matrices are used to align models across Zachman columns. This government department manages the introduction of new manufacturing industries as projects, with various activities and subactivities as shown in Figure 7.39.

The content of the highlighted ACTIVITY entity on the right is displayed in the left window. Any associations that are shown dimmed on the left are defined outside the organizational unit that is the focus of these two windows. The capabilities of this and other modeling tools are discussed in Chapter 15 [25].

The strategic model in Figure 7.39 was analyzed automatically using entity dependency analysis. Part of this analysis is shown in Figure 7.40. We can see clearly from the cluster report in the top part of Figure 7.40 the subproject dependencies in the project map for delivery of priority activities and associated systems.

This strategic modeling project took 3 weeks for the development and analysis of the strategic model, with its documentation as an EAPP report [26].

7.7.5 Large Government Department Project Example

This fourth project was for a very large government department that provides services to the population [27]. This strategic modeling project was driven by senior management at the highest levels of the department. It was undertaken in 2002.

The catalyst for the strategic modeling facilitated session was the strategic business plan, and also major business events that determine the services that the depart-

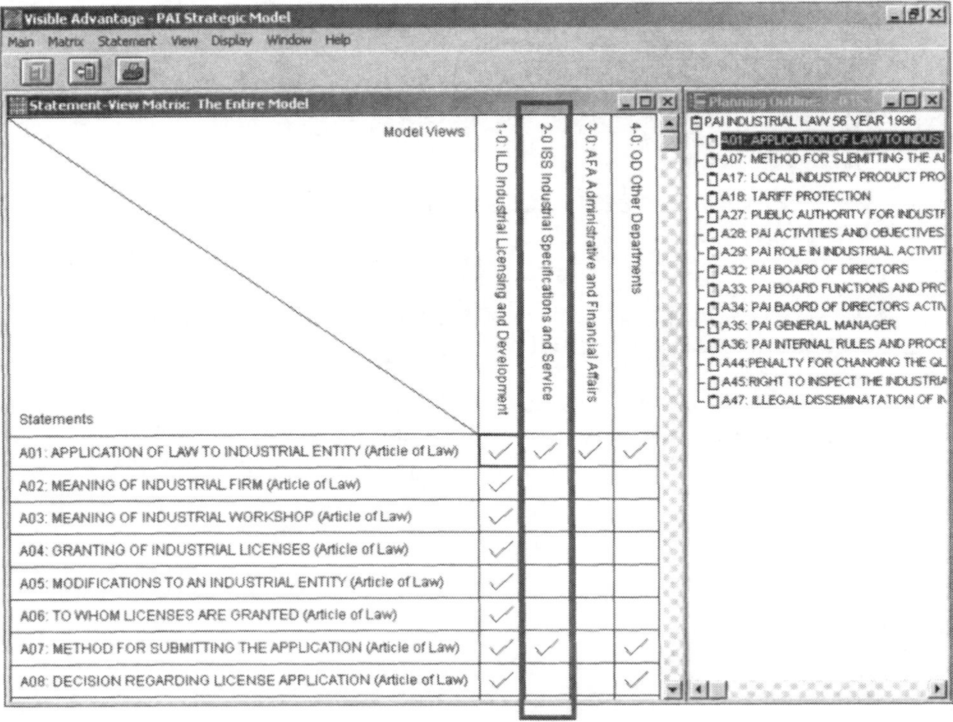

Figure 7.38 Subset article rows for organizational unit columns. (*From:* [23]. © 2000 PAI. Reprinted with permission.)

ment delivers. They call these *life events* as shown in Figure 7.41. They apply to the When column [C5] of the Zachman framework.

This focus on business events in [C5] had a major impact on potential future directions that could be taken by the department. Each event had previously been implemented as a separate stovepipe system. The focus on business events identified reusable business activities that could be potentially shared across many of these stovepipe systems: using activity modeling (see Chapter 8) for further analysis, with implementation using the latest technologies discussed in Part III. The strategic model also resulted in the definition of integrated data models that could be implemented as integrated databases.

There is the potential for significant time and cost savings in the redevelopment of these stovepipe systems. Each activity can be implemented as a common, shared system that can be reused by any relevant life events. In addition to development time and cost savings, there are also potential savings based on access to common shared databases from the potential elimination of data redundancy, as discussed in Chapter 1.

This project had a deadline of 55 days for initial enterprise architecture strategic modeling [28]. This period included 20 days for development and analysis of the strategic model, with a number of consultants in the 55 days also defining activity models of priority activities of interest. We discuss the concepts of activity modeling in Chapter 8.

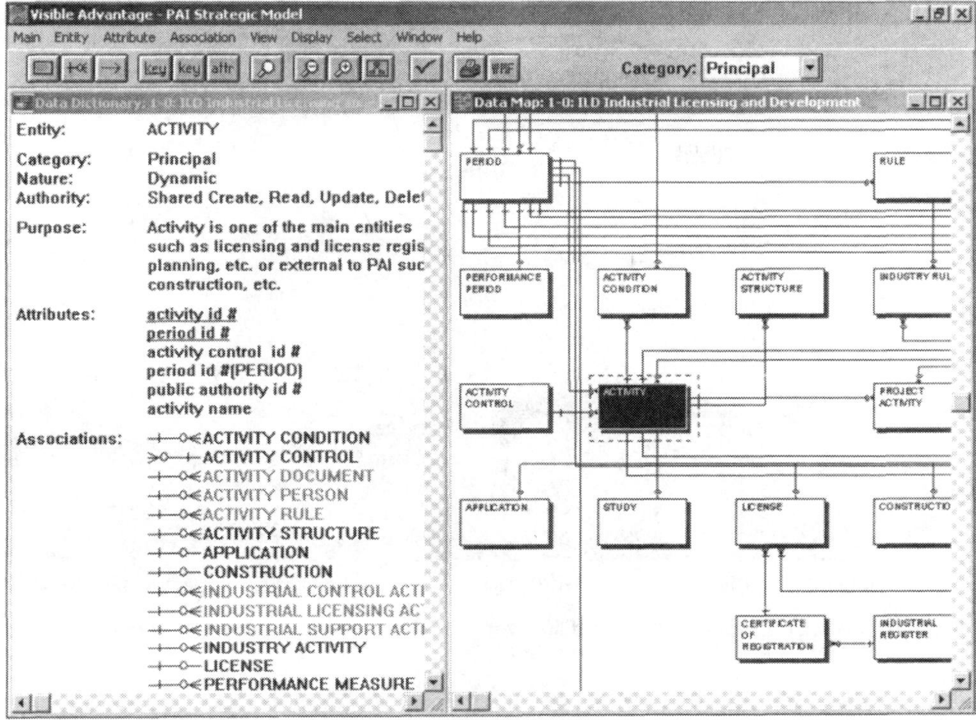

Figure 7.39 Strategic data map developed from articles of law. (*From:* [23]. © 2000 PAI. Reprinted with permission.)

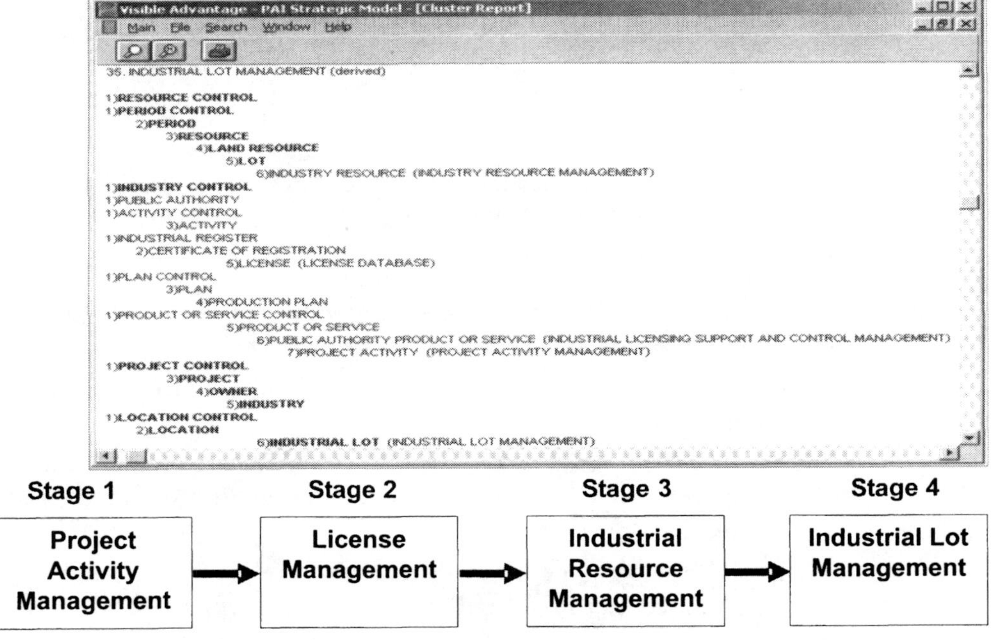

Figure 7.40 Project map from automatically derived clusters. (*From:* [23]. © 2000 PAI. Reprinted with permission.)

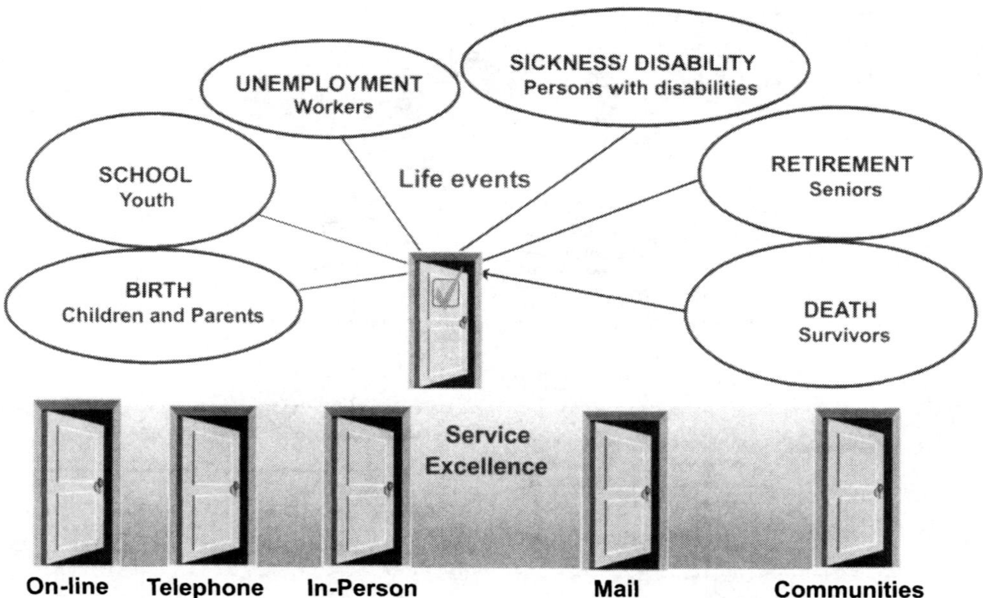

Figure 7.41 Strategic plans and life events used as catalysts for strategic modeling. (*From:* [27]. © 2002 HRDC. Reprinted with permission.)

These four real-life projects are typical of many strategic modeling projects throughout the world that have used the principles covered in this chapter. As discussed, these projects typically take 20 elapsed days for strategic modeling [29]. This includes the 2-day facilitated modeling session, with entity dependency analysis of the strategic model and documentation of the results in an EAPP. This EAPP is used for rapid delivery of priority enterprise architecture areas.

7.8 Summary

In this chapter we covered methods for rapid delivery of enterprise architecture, focusing on the What column for the Planner [C1R1] and Owner rows [C1R2]. We reviewed the following methods:

- We discussed the planning for and the conduct of a facilitated modeling session with senior management and business experts.
- We progressively developed a strategic model on a white board, using business plans and business rules as catalysts.
- We expanded the initial strategic model in a series of case study exercises. You completed these as a business expert experienced in project management and also as a facilitator.
- We learned the entity dependency rules that are used to determine ownership of entities based on the strength of associations defined by business rules.
- We used these entity dependency rules to carry out entity dependency analysis of a data map.

- We analyzed a strategic data map and derived separately implementable clusters that represent management activities or knowledge bases.
- We learned how to analyze these derived clusters to develop project maps. These define the implementation sequence of subprojects represented by each cluster, in a larger project.
- We reviewed four real-life strategic modeling projects for different organizations. In each case strategic modeling was completed in 20 days or less.

We are now ready to move to Chapter 8, where we will cover detailed methods that apply to the definition of activity models in the How column for the Planner [C2R1] and Owner rows [C2R2]. Our focus will be on activity modeling and activity-based costing methods that apply to this column.

Endnotes

[1] If you skipped Chapter 6, but do not understand data mapping methods, the basic concepts will first be introduced from a business perspective in this chapter in Section 7.2 titled "Developing a Strategic Model." You may then want to go back and read Chapter 6 fully.

[2] A strategic modeling questionnaire template is included on the accompanying CD-ROM in the Book Materials folder as the Microsoft Word file *Chap-07-Questionnaire.doc.*

[3] Please note that this does not imply a "greenfield, start-from-scratch approach." As we saw in Chapter 1, the resulting strategic model will be fully integrated, eliminating the data redundancy that occurs in most enterprises so that integrated data model subsets for priority business activities or processes can be implemented and delivered rapidly. The metadata from these integrated data model subsets can be used in Part III in conjunction with XML and Web services to achieve the required integration.

[4] In this chapter, we will later see that this is a very weak business rule that introduces ssevere business problems. In the exercise problems on the CD-ROM, we will later strengthen this business rule to avoid these business problems.

[5] The strategic modeling questionnaire template is provided in the Book Materials folder on the accompanying CD-ROM as the Microsoft Word document *Chap-07-Questionnaire.doc.*

[6] See Chapter 6 for a discussion of structure entities, used to capture expert knowledge for knowledge management.

[7] This larger strategic model is Figure 7.1 in the file *Chap-07-Problems.pdf* in the Book Materials folder of the accompanying CD-ROM.

[8] We will discuss this as part of business normalization in Chapter 9.

[9] Structure entities were discussed in Chapter 6, together with their use in expert systems.

[10] The phase numbers were derived using Visible Advantage, a modeling tool that is discussed in Chapter 15. This modeling tool is provided on the CD-ROM included with the book.

[11] This project plan was also derived using Visible Advantage.

[12] This project plan was also derived using Visible Advantage.

[13] All the entities in the cluster are **bold**, indicating that they are not dependent on anything else. This fact signifies that Project Budget Management is a Stage 1 subproject.

[14] Some of the entities in Figure 7.20 for Project Objective Management are not bold. This signifies that it is a Stage 2 subproject, dependent on Project Budget Management, which we saw is a Stage 1 subproject.

[15] As we have already seen using Visible Advantage, as discussed in this just completed overview.

[16] The **Phase** prefix shown here has been added for initial clarity. It is normally omitted, leaving only the phase number and right parenthesis preceding the relevant entity name.

[17] We will later see in the sample solutions to the entity dependency problems on the accompanying CD-ROM that prerequisite end-points can be separated into their own clusters, called *designated clusters*, for project maps, using Visible Advantage capabilities. Prerequisite end-point entities represent early milestone deliverables. Visible Advantage is discussed in Chapter 15.

[18] Once again, the **Phase** prefix shown here has been added for clarity. It is normally omitted, leaving only the phase number and right parenthesis preceding the relevant entity name.

[19] The case study problems are in the PDF file *Chap-07-Problems.pdf* in the Book Materials folder of the accompanying CD-ROM. The sample solutions are in the PDF file *Chap-07-Solutions.pdf,* also in the Book Materials folder.

[20] This strategic modeling project was for the Department of Social Security (DSS) in Canberra, Australia. DSS provided social security services for the population of Australia when this project was undertaken. DSS has since been subsumed into Centrelink, a larger Australian federal government department.

[21] The concepts and development of decision early warning systems are covered in Finkelstein, C., *Information Engineering: Strategic Systems Development,* Sydney, Australia: Addison-Wesley, 1992.

[22] This project was for Kwangju Bank, in the city of Kwangju, 40 minutes flight south of Seoul, South Korea.

[23] The Public Authority for Industry (PAI) in Kuwait was the focus of this strategic modeling project in 2000. This defined the enterprise architecture for PAI, which was the basis for later development of a data warehouse and an enterprise portal.

[24] Most organizations already have a strategic plan that is used as a catalyst for strategic modeling, or the strategic modeling questionnaire is used, as discussed earlier in this chapter.

[25] The modeling tool used in this project was Visible Advantage, to automatically derive clusters as project plans. This product is discussed in Chapter 15 and is included on the accompanying CD-ROM.

[26] An Enterprise Architecture Portfolio Plan (EAPP) Report is the documentation deliverable from a 20-day strategic modeling project. See http://www.ies.aust.com. Click on the Projects link.

[27] This strategic modeling project in 2002 was for Human Resources Development Canada (HRDC), a very large Canadian federal government department located in Ottawa. This project defined the enterprise architecture for potential redevelopment of many HRDC stovepipe systems. HRDC is now called Social Development Canada (SDC) and Human Resources Skills Development Canada (HRSDC).

[28] Visible Advantage was also used for this project, for automated entity dependency analysis and development of the EAPP. See Chapter 15 for further discussion of this and other modeling tools. This product is also included on the accompanying CD-ROM.

[29] A strategic modeling project can be tailored to address your organization's needs and can be conducted on your premises by Clive Finkelstein. Refer to the IES Web site at http://www.ies.aust.com. Click on the Projects link for more details. Use the Contact Us link to contact him at cfink@ies.aust.com to discuss your environment and requirements.

CHAPTER 8

Strategic Alignment, Activity and Workflow Modeling, and Business Rules

This chapter discusses strategic alignment matrices for business transformation that are used to document relationships between columns in the Zachman framework for management of the transformed enterprise. We discussed the need in Chapter 4 for these matrices for governance analysis. Each matrix defines the alignment that exists between business plans (column 6), people (column 4), data (column 1), activities (column 2), time (column 5) and location (column 3).

The chapter also covers activity modeling and activity-based costing. These methods are used to evaluate alternative activities for priority delivery and apply to the How column and the Planner [C2R1] and Owner rows [C2R2] of the Zachman framework in Figure 8.1. The activities identified in Chapters 6 and 7 are defined here in greater detail. We will also see how activity models and project maps provide input to define workflow models, which are used for the automatic generation of executable code in XML-based BPM languages in Chapter 14. We will also discuss the definition of business rules for use with these BPM languages.

8.1 Enterprise Architecture Incremental Build Context

In Chapter 7 we analyzed the strategic model using the entity dependency analysis method in Steps 4 and 5 of Figure 8.2. Management priorities from business plans in column 6 are used to establish initial priorities for identified activities. These priorities indicate the vertical slivers in the What, How, and Who columns [C1, C2, and C4] that will need to be delivered first.

We will first review Steps 1 through 5 of Figure 8.2 from earlier chapters. Continuing the steps involved with rapid implementation of enterprise architecture, in this chapter we will define matrices in Step 6 of Figure 8.2. Activity models are defined in Step 7, whereas workflow models and business rules are defined in Step 8. These are discussed next, keyed to the numbered arrows in Figure 8.2.

- *Step 1:* In Chapter 3, we discussed that strategy analysis identifies statements for mission, vision, core values, goals, objectives, issues, KPIs, and strategies in the strategic plan.
- *Step 2:* Strategy analysis identifies from the organizational structure those managers and business experts responsible for implementing priority areas of the strategic plan.

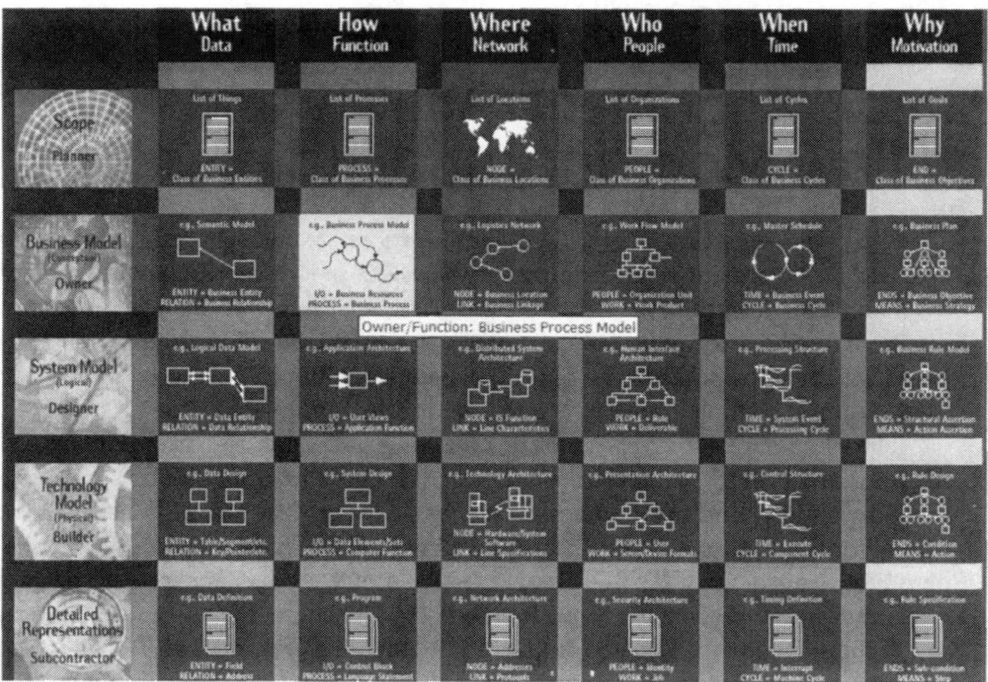

Figure 8.1 Activity modeling addresses column1, rows 1 and 2, of the Zachman framework.

	What Data	How Function	Where Location	Who People	When Time	Why Future
PLANNER Objectives/Scope	**4 List of Things**	**6 List of Processes**	**List of Locations**	**2 Org Structure**	**7 List of Events**	**1 List of Goals/Obj**
OWNER Conceptual	**5 Enterprise Model**	**7 Activity Model**	**Business Logistics**	**8 Work Flow**	**Master Schedule**	**3 Business Plan**
DESIGNER Logical	**Logical Data Model**	**Process Model**	**Distrib. Architect.**	**Human Interface**	**Process Structure**	**Business Rules**
BUILDER Physical	**Physical Data Model**	**System Model**	**Technol. Architect.**	**Presn Interface**	**Control Structure**	**Rule Design**
SUBCONTRACTOR Out-of-Context	**Data Definition**	**Program**	**Network Architect.**	**Security Interface**	**Timing Definition**	**Rule Specs**
FUNCTIONING ENTERPRISE	Data	Function	Network	Organization	Schedule	Strategy

Figure 8.2 Steps 6, 7, and 8 for rapid implementation of enterprise architecture.

- *Step 3:* During a 5-day business planning workshop, the identified managers and business experts optionally apply the strategy analysis methodology to define tactical business planning statements to implement strategic plans. This is Step 3 for rapid delivery of enterprise architecture.

- *Step 4:* In Chapter 6 we saw that data mapping is used to enable business experts and IT experts to work together to identify data for integration. This begins with a 2-day strategic modeling facilitated session as detailed in Chapter 7. Entities that represent required information and data are listed in the What column for the Planner row [C1R1].
- *Step 5:* In Chapter 7 we saw that the facilitated modeling session continues over 2 days, documenting key entities in a strategic model on a white board. The strategic model is a high-level semantic model or enterprise model in the What column for the Owner row [C1R2] that represents a "picture of the business" to the participating managers and business experts. Typically 90 to 120 entities are defined over the course of these 2 days.
- *Step 6:* This step defines strategic alignment matrices in row 1 for key columns. We will cover this and Steps 7 and 8 in this chapter. These matrices are shown as double-headed arrows in Figure 8.2 between these columns and their relevant artifacts with other key columns. Key strategic alignment matrices that are important are listed next and are described in this chapter.
  - Column 6 to column 4: showing people responsible for key planning statements;
  - Column 6 to column 1: showing the data supporting key planning statements;
  - Column 2 to column 1: showing the data required by key business activities;
  - Column 6 to column 2: showing activities supporting key planning statements.
- *Step 7:* In Step 7, the strategic model (see Chapter 7) or business events in the When column and Planner row [C5R1] can be used to identify activities in the How column and Planner row [C2R1]. These are typically common, reusable activities that deliver cost savings and benefits when implemented. Priority activities are defined as high-level activity models in column 2, row 2. Activity-based costing is used to determine the relative cost of alternative activities.
- *Step 8:* Priority activity models from Step 7 are used to develop workflow models in the Who column and Owner row [C4R2]. These workflow models are based on final, agreed-on activity models and business rules that indicate how processes will be invoked. This development of workflow models and definition of business rules are described in this chapter.

8.1.1 Reading Strategy for This Chapter

We first discuss the matrices used for strategic alignment. We saw in Chapter 4 that these alignment matrices are used for governance analysis. We will complete case study problems on the CD-ROM that build on solutions developed in earlier chapters. You will most likely want to read this section in detail. It will help us to determine the strategic alignment of our evolving case study solutions.

We will then cover the concepts of activity modeling and activity-based costing (ABC). If you are already familiar with IDEF0 activity modeling principles, you may wish to skim-read this section of the chapter.

In the final section we will learn how workflow models can be developed from activity models and project maps. We will also see how business rules are defined. Workflow models and business rules can later be delivered as executable code that is generated using the SOA products discussed in Chapter 14.

8.2 Step 6: Define Strategic Alignment Matrices

Before we discuss strategic alignment matrices in detail, we should first understand the relationships that exist between business plans in the Why columns [C6], data in the What column [C1], and also activities and processes in the How column [C2].

8.2.1 Relationship Between Business Plans, Data, and Activities

In Chapter 3 we discussed business plans. We saw that a typical strategic business plan in [C6] includes a mission statement and vision statement. We looked at examples of policies, goals and objectives, and strategies and tactics. These are related to the What and How columns [C1 and C2] as follows:

- *Policy statements* are defined as qualitative guidelines that establish boundaries of responsibility. They define the scope of that part of the enterprise. We saw in Chapters 6 and 7 that policies identify groups of related data entities in [C1].
- *Goals and objectives* are defined as quantitative targets for achievement, with measure, level, and time. Goals are typically long term; objectives are short term. The measures for goals and objectives are implemented as attributes in data entities. We discussed attributes for the What column [C1] in Chapter 6; we will cover them in more detail in Chapter 9.
- *Strategies and tactics* are used to define activities and processes. Strategies in the Why column [C6] indicate what has to be done to achieve goals or objectives. They equate in the How column [C2] to activities that also define what has to be done, but not how. Tactics in [C6] indicate how to carry out relevant strategies. Similarly, processes in [C2] define how to carry out various process steps to implement relevant activities.

In this chapter we will learn how to define and document activities in [C2] that equate to strategies in [C6]. In Chapter 10 we will learn how to define and document processes in [C2] that equate to tactics in [C6].

8.2.2 Aligning Business Plans to Organizational Structure (Column 6–Column 4)

We will start by discussing the alignment of business plans to organizational structure. This is represented in a matrix showing business plans [C6] listed on the left as rows, with organizational units for the organizational structure [C4] as column headings. This is an important matrix: It shows organizational units that are involved in each planning statement and, hence, defines why the unit is needed. The matrix indicates the organizational units that are responsible for managing different planning statements. It answers the key questions of "Who?" and "Why?" We saw an example of this earlier as the function–strategy matrix in Chapter 3 (Figure 3.6).

In Figure 8.3 we can see a typical matrix of business plans and organizational structure in the left window. The planning statements listed as rows of the matrix are the policy statements we used for the case study problems in Chapter 3 and in Chapter 7. The first three rows list policy statements from Chapter 3: P1 Project Ownership, P2 Project Management, and P3 Project Authorization (see Box 3.3). The other rows list policies from Chapter 7: P4 Project Team, P5 Project Activities, P6 Project Skills, and P7 Project Resources (see Box 7.1). These statements were used as catalysts for the strategic modeling facilitated session in Chapter 7. You may wish to review these policy statements before reading any further; they are all conveniently listed in Box P8.1 in the case study problems file on the accompanying CD-ROM [1].

The column headings of the matrix are based on the organizational structure displayed in the right window of Figure 8.3. It shows that the strategic model includes the project management division of XYZ, which has three functional areas: Financial Management, Resource Management, and Schedule Management.

Each policy row in the matrix of Figure 8.3 has a tick in each column where the relevant organization unit has some management responsibility for the statement. By reading across a row, all of the organizational units that are involved in a planning statement can be clearly seen. By reading down a column for a specific organizational unit, all of the policy statements that apply to it are ticked; this is a subset of the policies that apply to the relevant unit.

8.2.3 Case Study Problems for Strategic Alignment Matrices

We will now complete other strategic alignment matrices as case study problems. We will use the strategic data map from Figure 7.14 in Chapter 7, which is included as Figure P8.1 on the accompanying CD-ROM. We will use the policies and activi-

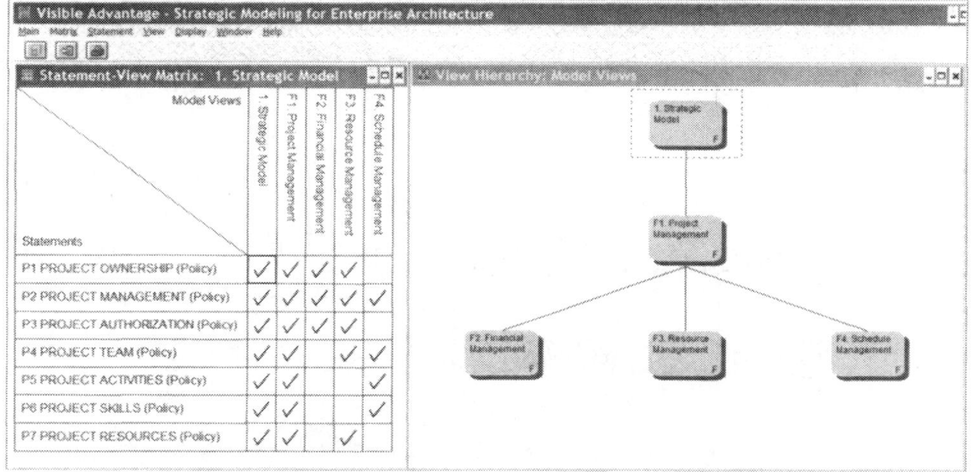

Figure 8.3 Alignment matrix of plans (column 6) to organizational structure (column 4). This matrix shows who is involved and why they are needed.

ties in Box P8.1 for completion of Case Study Problems 1 through 3 [2], documented in Boxes P8.2 through P8.4. After completing these problems, compare your solution with the sample solutions file also on the accompanying CD-ROM [3].

8.3 Step 7: Activity Modeling Concepts

Activity modeling is based on the IDEF0 technique as developed by the U.S. Department of Defense. It is used to transform activities listed in column 2, row 1, into activity models in column 2, rows 2 and 3. But first, we need to understand the differences between functions, activities, and processes.

8.3.1 Differences Between Functions, Activities, and Processes

In Chapter 7 we briefly discussed functions and functional areas. We saw that functional areas are used to manage related functions within an enterprise. A functional area is part of the organizational structure in the Who column and Planner row [C4R1]—it groups related functions for management purposes. In turn, functions group related activities in column 2 as illustrated in Figure 8.4.

Figure 8.4 is an important figure for understanding the essential differences between activities, tasks, and processes. It shows that Business Function A is responsible for activities A1, A2, and B1. Business Function B is responsible for activities B1, B2, and B3. Both Business Function A and B share activity B1, which is a common, reusable activity.

Each activity has component tasks that are separately executable. For example, Figure 8.4 shows that activity A1 has tasks A11 and A12; A2 has tasks A21 and A22; and activity B1 has tasks B11 and B12. Similarly, activity B2 has tasks B21 and B22; and B3 has tasks B31 and B32. However, tasks within activities are not executed until they are explicitly invoked by processes.

Notice that Figure 8.4 shows two processes: Process A and Process B. These invoke executable tasks within activities as shown by the arrows, which identify the

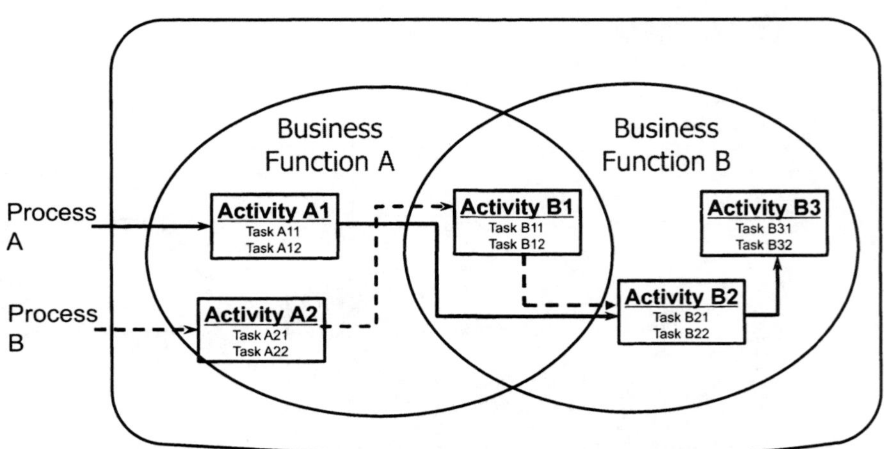

Figure 8.4 Functions group related activities. Activities show what is to be done. Processes show how tasks are executed.

sequence of task invocation for execution. For example, Process A is shown by the solid arrows in the figure; it first invokes tasks that reside in activity A1, B2, and finally B3. Process B is shown by the dashed arrows; it invokes tasks that reside in activity A2, B1, and finally B2.

By defining activities, we establish what has to be done. Depending on the technologies to be used for implementation, separately executable tasks can be defined with activities. The execution sequence defines how these tasks are to be executed by the path that a process takes. Many processes may take different execution paths, each sharing common activities and reusable tasks.

In Chapter 14 we will draw on these principles. We will see how defined activity models, workflow models, and process models are used with SOA technologies and products in Chapter 14, for rapid delivery of enterprise architecture.

8.3.2 Role of IDEF0

We can now discuss activity modeling concepts. IDEF0 is a graphical documentation technique that is used to define an activity model [4]. It shows the relationships between activities. It supports ABC and other economic analyses for process improvement. These include simulations, workflow analysis, and benchmarking.

Activities are the building blocks for business process improvement. For this reason, it is important to analyze and understand business activities before any business process improvements can be determined. By using ABC, activities and their relationships can be defined, as well as the costs associated with those activities.

Activity-based costing (ABC) is used to decide between process improvements for existing activities—called *As-Is* activities—and proposed alternative future activities—called *To-Be* activities. This is illustrated in Figure 8.5. Each activity can be attached to multiple cost centers, with the associated costs for each activity specified for each cost center. Using ABC, costs can be calculated automatically or costs can be overridden if desired.

The As-Is model represents the current state of the organization that is modeled, without any specific process improvement included. It establishes a baseline for later business process improvement actions or programs.

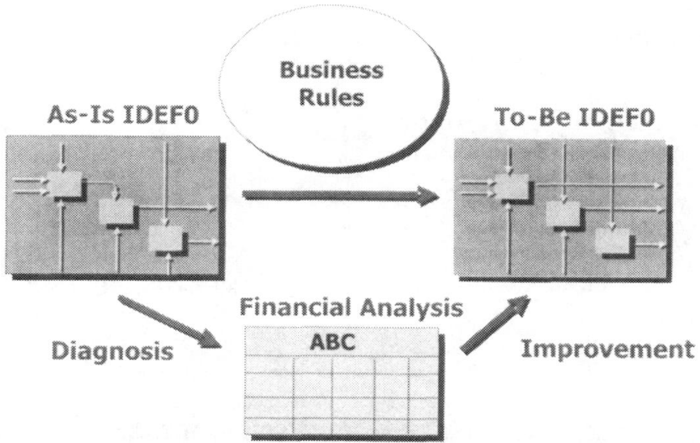

Figure 8.5 Activity models and ABC are used for process improvement.

Unless there is a clear need to compare the costs of To-Be and As-Is activities with each other, activity modeling projects mostly focus on alternative To-Be activities using various technologies. Often, they do not analyze As-Is activities at all. Instead they use business experts with knowledge of the As-Is activities to define alternative To-Be activities. Once implemented, these To-Be activities then become the baseline As-Is activities for cost comparison in the next activity modeling process improvement cycle.

The To-Be activity model is the result of applying process improvement opportunities to current As-Is business processes. Just as a hierarchical outline of business plans in column 6 shows the relationships that exist between different planning statements, so also can an activity hierarchy in column 2 be viewed in a detailed mode as an activity map that shows the components of a specific activity. These components are *subactivities*. An example of an activity model is shown in Figure 8.6.

Two diagrams are used to show relationships that exist between and within activities. Figure 8.6 shows a small activity hierarchy window. The larger window shows the associated activity map. Together they represent an activity model for human resources recruiting. The activity hierarchy list shows the relationship between various activities at different hierarchical levels; the activity map shows the relationship between activities at one level. Most modeling tools that offer support

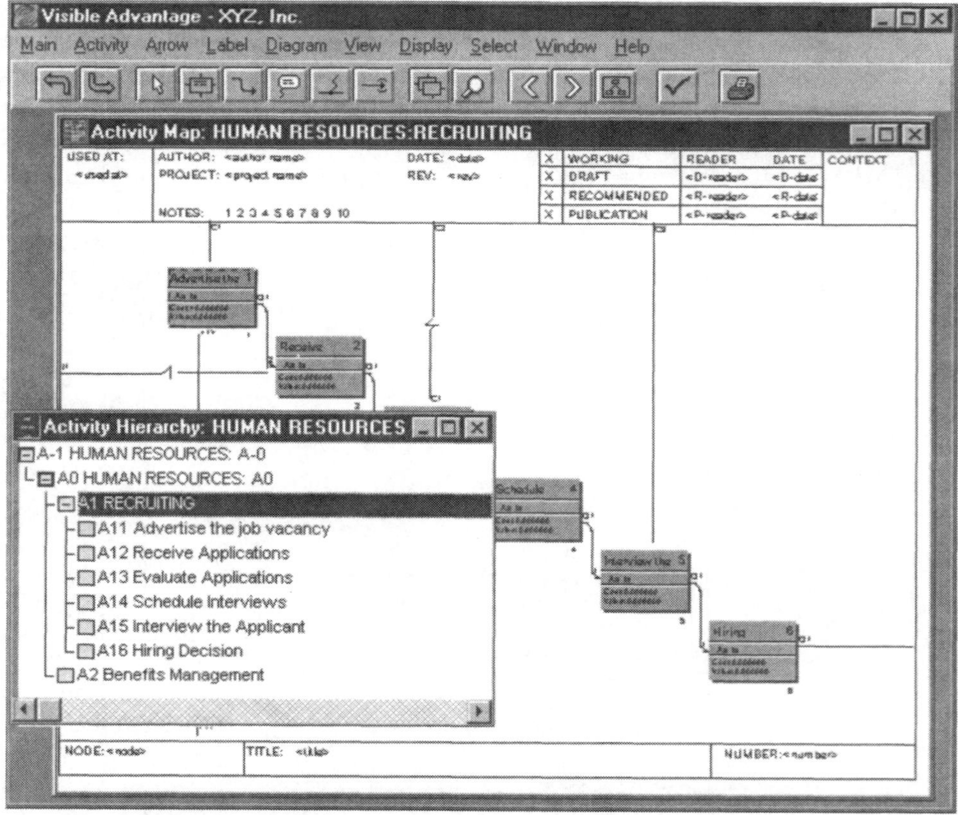

Figure 8.6 Activity model for human resource recruiting.

for IDEF0 activity modeling synchronize these two diagrams; a change in one diagram results in automatic updates also being made to the other diagram.

An activity describes the way an enterprise employs its time and resources to implement its strategies and achieve goals and objectives for its mission. Each activity is named and must be able to be defined. We discussed in Chapters 6 and 7 how activities can be identified and named from a data model.

Other more detailed activities may also exist that have not yet been represented as data in a data model. If activities are defined and added to an activity model, they should be documented in an activity description. This description becomes a catalyst for modeling sessions that expand the data model to incorporate data required by the new activities.

Activities are not based on organizational structure; instead, they implement defined strategies. They are executed repeatedly in an enterprise. An activity defines a beginning and an ending point, expressed in terms of inputs and outputs. It consumes resources to transform the inputs into relevant outputs and so takes an amount of time. Resources use physical, mechanical, or electrical energy and have associated costs. These costs are used by ABC to evaluate various activities that implement alternative strategies.

8.3.3 IDEF0 Model Components

Activity modeling uses IDEF0 models. An IDEF0 model uses several diagrams as listed next and illustrated in Figure 8.7:

- A context diagram that defines the scope of an activity at the highest level;
- A node diagram or activity hierarchy diagram that shows the hierarchical relationship between activity levels;

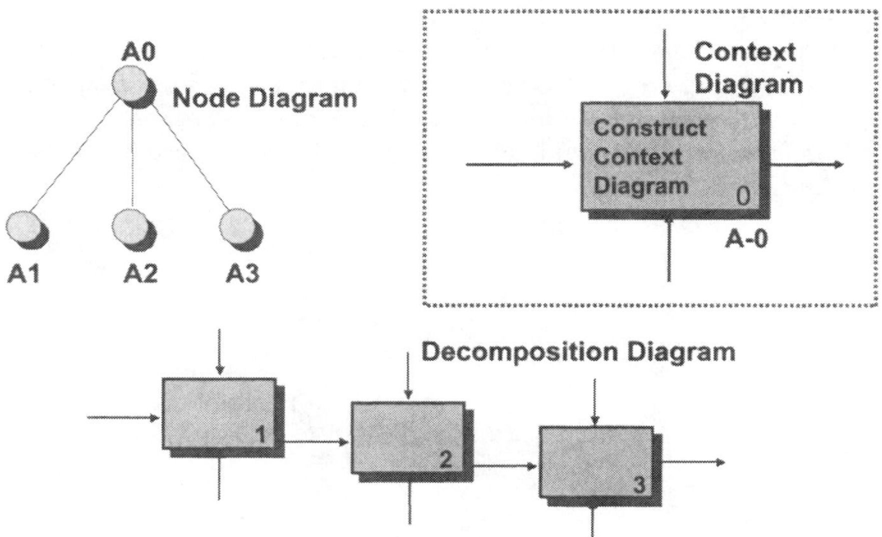

Figure 8.7 IDEF0 activity model diagrams. The context diagram shows the overall scope of an activity at the highest level.

- Decomposition diagrams such as activity maps that show the relationship between all activities at one hierarchical level;
- Explanatory text that documents the activity purpose in an activity description.

8.3.4 Context Diagram

The context diagram presents the environmental context or scope of an activity model. It provides a top-level overview of the activity. It comprises one activity and the inputs, outputs, and other objects that are related to it. It establishes the boundaries for the activity model, representing the scope of a subproject to define that activity in more detail.

Because it represents the highest level of the activity, it is called the A0 activity as shown in Figure 8.7. As a context diagram, it documents all inputs, outputs, material, and other information that relate to the A0 activity. IDEF0 activity models are also called ICOM diagrams. ICOM is an acronym that stands for input, control, output, and mechanism, as shown in Figure 8.8.

ICOM arrows are always placed at right angles to the activity box. There are never any diagonals or curved arrows. An ICOM can be a person, place, thing, concept, or event. It is material or information that is consumed, used, constrained, or produced by the activity.

8.3.5 Reading a Context Diagram

Using the ICOM notation, context diagrams—or activity maps at lower hierarchical levels—can be easily read as shown in Figures 8.9 and 8.10. Using the guiding text in Figure 8.10, we can easily transform the context diagram in Figure 8.9 to the *activity statement* documented next:

Activity Statement

When we *Maintain Organization Property*, we transform the *Work Requests, New Property* and *Property to be Maintained* into the *Accepted Property, Work Performance Receipt* and *Recommended Procedure Changes* under the control of the *Maintenance Budget* and *Organization Policy*, performed by the *Maintenance Personnel* and *Contractors*.

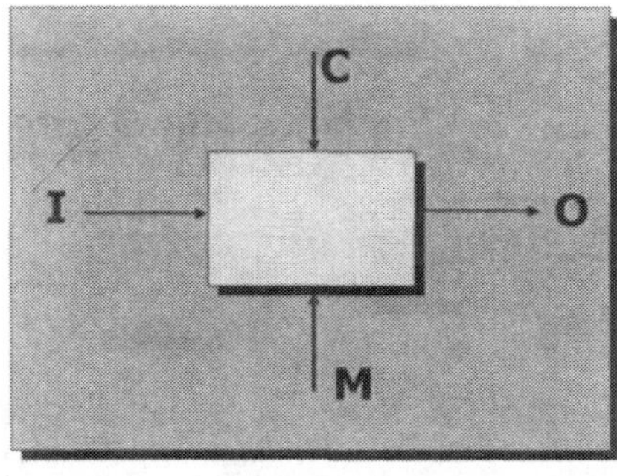

Input to activity
Control over activity
Output from activity
Mechanism performing activity

Figure 8.8 ICOM is an acronym for input, control, output, and mechanism.

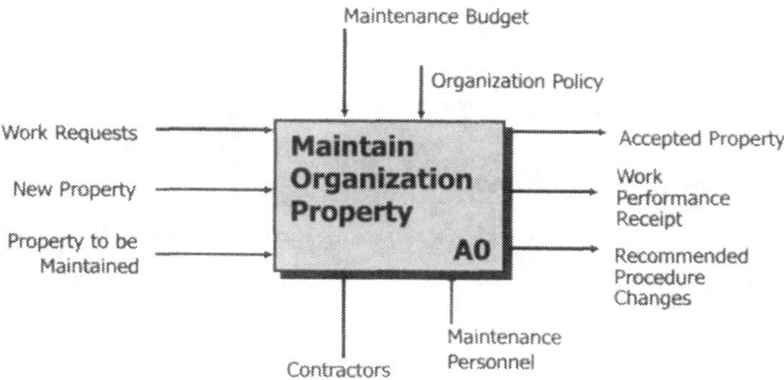

Figure 8.9 A typical context diagram.

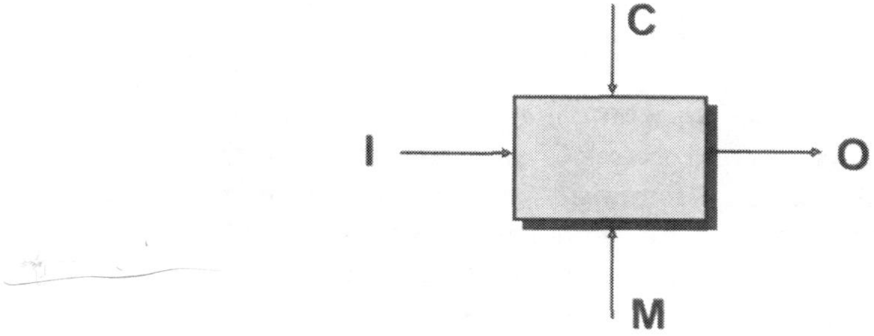

Figure 8.10 Reading high-level context diagram, or lower level activity maps.

We will use this approach to read all context diagrams. This convention can also be used to describe decomposition diagrams such as activity maps. We will discuss each of the component ICOM arrows next.

8.3.6 ICOM Input Arrow

An ICOM input arrow represents the information or material that is provided as input, to be used by the activity or transformed into relevant outputs. An activity generally—but not always—has input. The input arrow always points to the left side of the activity box as shown by Figure 8.10.

If the output produced by the activity is tangible, the input must be tangible as well. Inputs may also represent intangibles, such as ideas. Although inputs are considered optional, they do trigger the activity so it is best to show them on the diagram.

For service-related activities, the differentiation between input and output is more difficult. For example, consider the activity *Process Patient Application*. The input provides details of a patient and the output provides other details of a patient. The input is transformed or consumed. A better identification of the input may be *Patient Data* with the output being defined as, for example, *Updated Patient History*. Modifiers—"patient data" and "updated patient history"—in the ICOM names provide differentiation. Activity maps provide a visual documentation method that can be used effectively with strategy maps (from Chapter 2) to document key activities to be used in a strategy.

8.3.7 ICOM Control Arrow

An ICOM control arrow represents a governance or other constraint on the operation of an activity. These can be policies, business rules, regulations, or other things that guide or regulate the activity. A control arrow always points to the top of the activity box as shown in Figure 8.10. Every activity must have at least one control. An ICOM is considered a control in these situations:

- It shows when to produce an output.
- It shows how to produce an output.
- It dictates which output to produce.

Controls govern how, when, and if an activity is performed. These can be used to illustrate governance controls (see Chapter 4) that are associated with key activities. Controls are expressed as policies, standards, procedures, or regulations and typically are defined in the Why column and Owner row [C6R2] as planning statements. A control is really a special type of input. An activity may have no input, but it must have a control; this is mandatory.

8.3.8 ICOM Output Arrow

An ICOM output arrow represents a result of an activity. It always points away from the right side of the activity box as shown in Figure 8.10. An output is an end of a chain of events. There must be at least one output to an activity.

An output is a purpose of the activity; it is mandatory that at least one output must exist. If an activity is identified that does not have any output, it is definitely a candidate for elimination. From a purely IDEF0 perspective, an activity cannot be modeled if it does not have an identifiable output that is distinct from the input.

8.3.9 ICOM Mechanism Arrow

An ICOM mechanism arrow represents resources, such as people, equipment, or machines, that are needed to perform or support an activity. A mechanism arrow always points to the bottom of an activity box as shown in Figure 8.10.

Mechanisms are the *nonconsumable* resources used to do the actual processing of the activity. Consumable resources are usually identified as input. An activity uses resources to transform inputs into outputs under the constraints imposed by controls.

Mechanisms form the basis of activity-based costing and the various economic analyses that are associated with ABC. We will discuss mechanisms and their use by ABC later in the chapter. They are included to assist in measuring costs associated with an activity.

8.3.10 Activity Maps as Decomposition Diagrams

Decomposition diagrams such as activity maps show the partitioning of a modeled parent activity at a higher level into its component subactivities at the next lower level. Activity maps cover the same topics as the parent activity but in greater detail, as highlighted in Figure 8.11. They can be used to document the interrelationships between activities at any level of detail. They can be used to identify strengths and deficiencies in the As-Is model. They can also be used to specify improvement opportunities in the To-Be model.

Decomposition diagrams such as activity maps are mandatory in an activity model. They comprise three to nine (with an average of six) activities on one page, showing subactivities for the relevant parent activity. The syntax used for activity maps specifies that fewer than three subactivities may not need to be decomposed; they can be included at a higher level. There are exceptions, of course, such as an improvement opportunity, or a special interest or request that may suggest the need for a lower level activity map. As a guideline to avoid complexity, no more than nine subactivities should be specified in the decomposition diagram page.

Activities are shown as boxes that are sequenced logically from upper left to lower right. The position of the boxes does not indicate sequencing or timing but rather how outputs from one activity can become inputs for other activities as shown in Figure 8.11.

8.3.11 Activity Map Feedback Loops

An activity map shows the activities in a logical sequence. There may be times when there is an interruption, such as when an activity is repeated or is skipped altogether. In addition to outputs from one activity becoming inputs for another activity, they can also be used in feedback loops as shown in Figure 8.12.

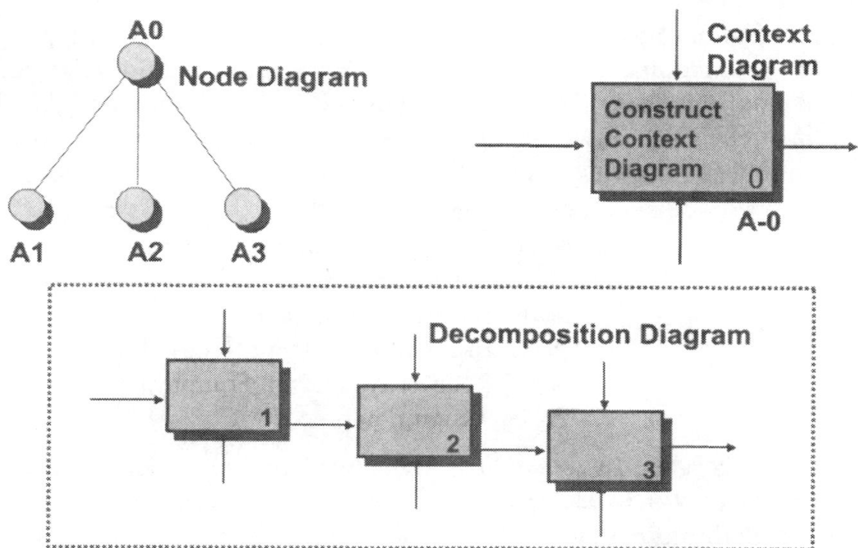

Figure 8.11 IDEF0 activity model diagrams. An activity map is a decomposition diagram that shows the relationship between activities at the same level.

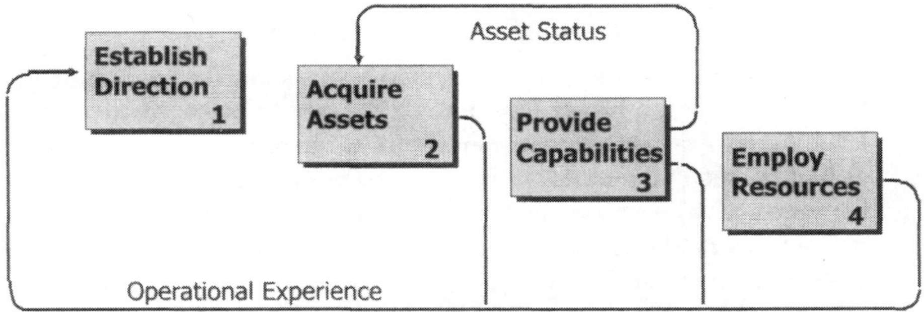

Figure 8.12 Feedback loops originate as outputs. They can feed back as inputs, controls, or mechanisms.

A feedback loop always originates from the right side of an activity box, as an output. It turns backward and indicates that the output of one activity becomes an input, a control or a mechanism to another activity. The example in Figure 8.12 shows the following:

- A2, A3, and A4 all generate an output of *Operational Experience* that feeds back to A1 as an input.
- A3 generates an output of *Asset Status* that feeds back to A2 as a control.

A control feedback is shown as "up and over." An input feedback is shown as "down and under." This same "down and under" convention is also used for a mechanism feedback.

8.3.12 Node Diagram or Activity Hierarchy

A node diagram or activity hierarchy diagram graphically represents the parent–child relationships between nodes of an IDEF0 model, as shown in Figure 8.13.

The node diagram shows complex hierarchical relationships between parent and child activities. Each activity is labeled by the relevant hierarchy level number suffixed by a subactivity number. Activities on the same level are therefore peers to each other as shown in Figure 8.13. Another format is shown here:

A0 Maintain Organization Property
  A2 Provide Maintenance Resources
    A21 Provide Maintenance Equipment
      A211 Schedule Equipment
      A212 Evaluate Equipment Requirements
      A213 Request Additional Equipment
      A214 Assign Equipment

This is called an *activity hierarchy*. It is based on a hierarchical format such as that used by Windows Explorer, with the ability to expand and collapse hierarchical levels. In this format, it can communicate hierarchical levels to any depth, while providing ample room to display a meaningful name for each activity that has been expanded.

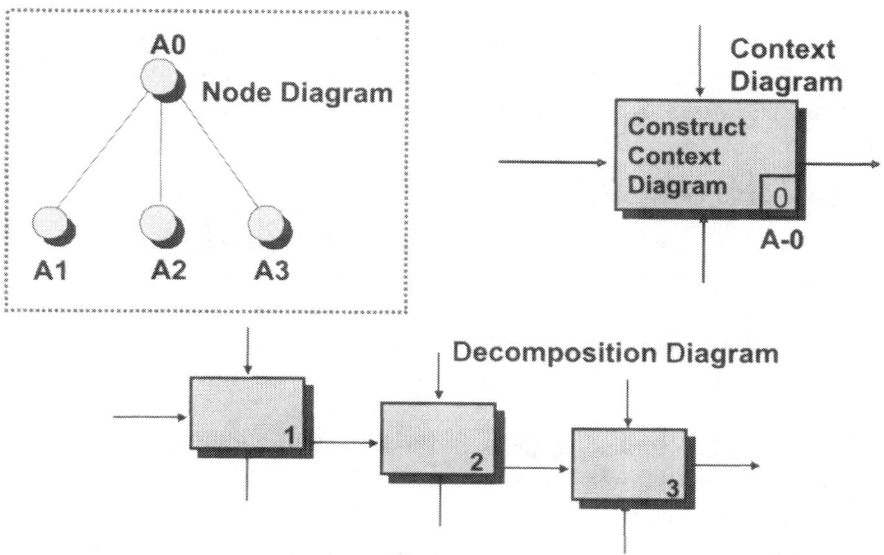

Figure 8.13 IDEF0 activity model diagrams. A node diagram shows hierarchical relationships between activities at different levels.

8.4 Step 7: Activity-Based Costing

Once activity models have been defined as discussed earlier, they can be analyzed for cost-effectiveness. This is Step 7 as discussed in Section 8.1. Activity-based costing is a technique that is used for activity cost accounting. Cost and performance data of activities can be gathered using ABC for further analysis. The application of different technologies can help identify alternative or innovative approaches.

To improve profitability and performance, it is critical to understand where an organization's time is spent and, in detail, what the organization does and how it does it. ABC is used to achieve this, through the following steps:

- Build an activity model of relevant activities.
- Establish cost and performance measures.
- Identify and eliminate nonvalue-added activities.
- Simplify, integrate and streamline value-added activities.
- Emphasize reuse of assets.

Activity cost and performance data provide information that is used to identify accurate product costs, waste in activities, improved business process opportunities, cost drivers (factors causing costs), business strategies, and tactical and operational plans.

Process improvement using ABC results in increased effectiveness (i.e., improvements in quality) and efficiency (i.e., improvements in productivity), typically accompanied by a corresponding reduction in resource requirements and, consequently, lower costs.

Activity-based costing is an accounting technique that helps determine the actual costs associated with each product and/or service produced by the organization, without regard to the organizational structure.

8.4.1 Comparison to Traditional Financial Accounting

Traditional financial accounting breaks down management of an enterprise to specialized units with a division of responsibility. It measures cost performance by comparing costs incurred to budgeted cost, *but has limited information available on the causes of the cost.* There is an underlying assumption in financial accounting that an organization is successful—and so is profitable—if the actual costs do not exceed the budgeted costs.

Costs are applied to parts of the enterprise based on organizational structure, not based on customer, product, or services used. Traditional accounting tracks cost expenditure historically, but does not help determine the cause of the cost. This is emphasized by the advertising manager's complaint that "Only half of what I spend on advertising is effective; the trouble is that I don't know which is the effective half."

Traditional cost accounting allocates overhead costs based on head counts or labor salary relationships. This distorts the assignment of costs to products. The problem is that overhead costs do not necessarily vary in the same way that labor costs do. Some products require more customer service, more parts, more purchasing activity, or more sophisticated and costly equipment.

On the other hand, with activity-based costing most support costs or nonmaterial costs do not vary directly with labor volume. They vary instead with product diversity and operational complexity. Because of this, many existing product costs do not represent the true consumption of the resources that are used to produce them.

Activity-based costing provides managerial accounting and decision-making information. It presents a cost model allocated to activities that assists in the identification of areas for improvement. It provides a baseline for comparison of alternatives. Alternatives may be solutions based on different technologies or realignment of activities, workflows, job descriptions, and so forth. Most frequently, a comparison of alternatives using ABC supports the acquisition or use of different IT solutions.

8.4.2 Steps of Activity-Based Costing

This section provides steps to be used in performing activity cost analyses. These steps should be used as an overall guide to forming a specific approach that is tailored to fit your organization. Five steps are involved in the application of ABC:

ABC Step 1: Analyze activities.

ABC Step 2: Analyze costs.

ABC Step 3: Establish measures.

ABC Step 4: Calculate activity costs.

ABC Step 5: Analyze activity costs.

ABC Step 1: Analyze Activities

This step determines the scope of the activity analysis. It identifies and defines the activities, and then builds and classifies activity models. Many books on activity modeling and activity-based costing are available [5–7]. As defined by James Brimson and John Antos in their book [8]:

> Activities are a combination of people, technology, supplies, methods, and environment that produce a given service. Activities describe what the enterprise does; that is, the way time is spent and the outputs of the process.

This step focuses on developing and documenting the activity models, either the As-Is models, the To-Be models, or both. The activity modeling concepts discussed earlier in this chapter form the basis for ABC Step 1.

ABC Step 2: Analyze Costs

This step identifies the cost elements of each activity and subactivity. The cost basis that is to be used is determined, recasting costs from a departmental or expense-type base to an activity base; it traces all significant costs to activities and determines total resource consumption by activity or subactivity. If an exact tracing of costs to activities is not feasible, costs that cannot be directly linked to an activity are allocated in the best way possible. Once the costs are known, the measures can be established.

ABC Step 3: Establish Measures

Activity measures and performance measures are determined and classified in this step. An activity measure is a measure of the volume of the activity. A performance measure is a measure of how well the activity is performed. These are shown in Figure 8.14, which illustrates inputs, outputs, and resources for the *Pay Invoice*

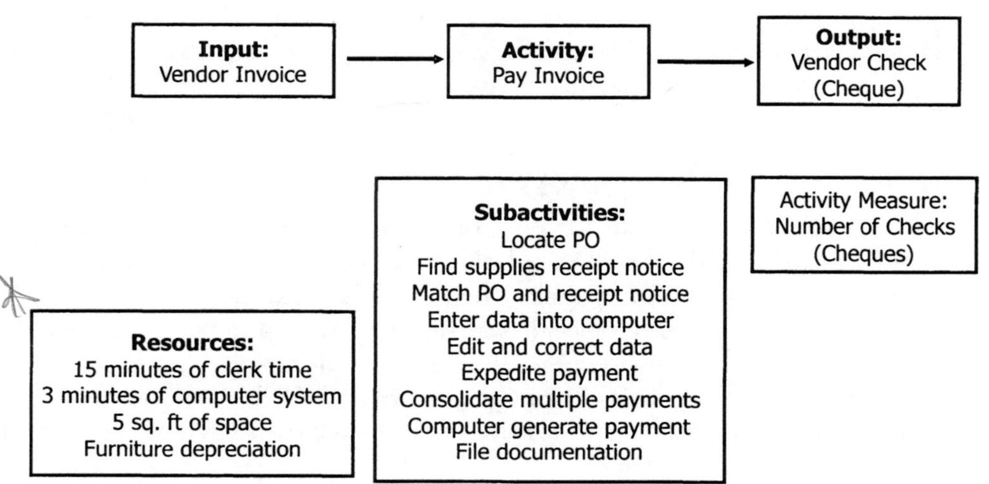

Figure 8.14 Example of an output measure for an activity.

activity. This uses a Vendor Invoice as an input to the activity, with the output being a Vendor Check (Cheque) for payment. The activity has a number of subactivities as listed in the figure. A data entry clerk enters vendor invoice details into a computer for processing, calculation, and payment of the invoice. The *activity measure* in this figure is determined to be the number of checks (cheques) that are produced in a specific period, such as a day.

The cost analysis from Step 2 indicates that each vendor invoice takes 15 minutes of data entry time, plus 3 minutes of computer system time. The clerk's desk occupies 5 square feet of office space; it also has a cost associated with it in the form of a furniture depreciation cost.

These resource costs are calculated and allocated to relevant subactivities in the figure. For example, the daily cost of the clerk's time is based on salary, while the computer time is based on the hardware and software daily costs. If these were purchased, this may be a depreciation cost; if leased, this would be the effective daily lease cost. The cost of office space includes office rental and other overhead costs, calculated on a per-day basis. This daily cost for the total office area can be apportioned to 5 square feet for the clerk's desk. The cost of the desk can also be determined as the daily depreciation cost for that piece of furniture.

By determining all of these resource costs for one day, the total daily cost of the activity can be calculated based on the cost of each subactivity. With the activity measure being the number of checks (cheques) that are produced for payment in a day, the performance measure determines how efficiently these checks can be produced using different technologies. If more invoices and checks can be processed in a day, the cost of each is reduced. We will return to this example shortly to discuss the impact of different technologies on these activity costs.

The activity measure is validated for reasonableness by examining the consumption of resources in a direct ratio to the volume of output. A causal relationship must exist between the volume of the activity and its costs, and the level of the activity driver. An activity measure is homogeneous when each output is the same type as other outputs. In other words, the output has consistent cost behavior patterns. For example, consider the use of the number of processed purchase orders as an activity measure. The problem here is that some purchase orders are complex, with more than 100 line items; others are very simple, with only 1 line item. Therefore, a purchase order is *not* homogeneous; instead it would be better to use the number of line items processed as the activity measure.

ABC Step 4: Calculate Activity Costs

Once the activity measure has been determined, the total cost for the activity can then be calculated. The allocated portion of the nontraceable costs is added to the activity cost. The sum of each activity's costs is multiplied by the activity's frequency—the number of times the activity is performed relative to a single execution of the parent activity—to obtain the total cost for that activity.

The total volume of the activity measure is divided into the total activity cost to obtain the cost per activity measure. This provides the basis for analysis of the activity costs in the next step.

ABC Step 5: Analyze Activity Costs

In analyzing costs, the emphasis is to decide which activities add value, which activities incur the highest cost, and what drives that high cost. From this, an analysis can be done to determine what will streamline, improve, delete, or automate the cost driver. Part of the rationale for identifying cost drivers is to consider elimination or changes in activities.

The understanding obtained in this step will be used to make recommendations regarding changes to the current activities and the business processes that invoke them. The most important information determined during this analysis is the identification of nonvalue-added activities. A nonvalue-added activity may be one that is performed due to nonconformance to standards or policies, or used to correct or revise some form of deficiency. The cost drivers may be responsible for the nonvalue-added activities. Nonvalue-added activities introduce nonvalue-added costs.

The costs gathered during this analysis are presented in worksheet format. Subactivity costs are "rolled up" into parent activity costs, which sum the child activity costs. The data provided in the worksheet can also be used for additional analyses including projections of future costs.

Cost control is achieved by implementing improved methods of performing an activity—by benchmarking or best practices; or by eliminating waste, such as nonvalue-added activities. A by-product of cost analysis is identification of new or improved performance measures. The information from this analysis can be used by operational managers, work teams, and quality circles. This is where alternative technology solutions are considered.

8.4.3 Forming Activity Alternatives

Alternatives consider the effect of changes made to one or more components of an activity model. These alternatives include the following:

- *A different input:* Costs may be reduced by simplifying an input or changing an input's properties while retaining form, fit, and function.
- *A different control:* A revised regulation or specification may relax a process tolerance, thus causing a cost decrease.
- *A different by-product:* An improved process may reduce or eliminate waste so a by-product can be reused. For example, in a wood process mill, the sawdust waste can be used to produce other types of wood products such as in the manufacture of particle board.
- *A different mechanism:* Changing the skill level of the resources may reduce the time and cost to execute a task; or automating a process may reduce cost by displacing a manual activity—offset by the process automation investment cost.
- *A different set of activities:* Changing activities can eliminate nonvalue-added activities.

A nonvalue-added activity is identified when the cost of an activity exceeds its value. Unless the activity is required for regulatory, legal, or other control reasons, its continued use may waste time, money, and other resources. *These nonvalue-added activities are candidates for elimination or consolidation.*

The elimination of a nonvalue-added activity, or its replacement by an alternative activity, results in changes to the baseline cost worksheet. These changes are reflected in both the investment costs and the recurring costs, typically with a decrease in recurring costs and/or an increase in investment costs. Removing nonvalue-added activities may also produce cost savings without an associated increase in investment costs.

For example, organizations such as Wal-Mart and The Gap have successfully eliminated their need to maintain inventories in their warehouses. Instead they use suppliers who offer just-in-time delivery of goods directly from the delivery truck to the shelf, as needed. Electronic commerce technologies such as EDI have enabled them to eliminate inventory activities. For them, warehouse inventory is considered a nonvalued-added product.

Another example arises with analysis of the subactivities needed to pay vendor invoices, as discussed for Figure 8.14. By using enterprise application integration (EAI) and Web services technologies (see Part III), invoices are delivered electronically in XML instead of by mail or fax. Because electronic invoices are machine readable, mail delays and the volume-dependent data entry costs are instead replaced by real-time Internet delivery and EAI software investment costs. Using XML, the data entry clerk's cost—along with office space and furniture depreciation costs in Figure 8.14—can be eliminated with little or no volume-dependent recurring costs. The use of EAI or Web services to replace manual reentry activities can have a dramatic effect on activity costs.

8.4.4 Monitoring the Benefits

The result of activity analysis is that ABC is an ongoing management tool that compares actual costs to projected costs for continual process improvement. Variance tracking is also used to track the difference between projected and actual costs. This should include a "tolerance band" for costs and performance measures. If the results are not within the tolerance band, the alternative should be reevaluated and perhaps a new improvement opportunity identified. When an activity alternative is selected, it then becomes the new functional baseline for the activity. This results in an ongoing reengineering or process improvement.

We will return to the enterprise architecture incremental build context. It is appropriate now to discuss Step 8 in Section 8.1, for workflow modeling.

8.5 Step 8: Workflow Modeling

This section shows us how to derive workflow models from priority activity models and project maps. Workflow models are represented in the Zachman framework by the Who column and Owner row [C4R2] cell as shown in Figure 8.15.

In Chapter 14 we discuss how SOA technologies and BPM languages are used for generation of XML-based BPM code from workflow models. The result is automatically generated code that is directly executable. This is very productive. With

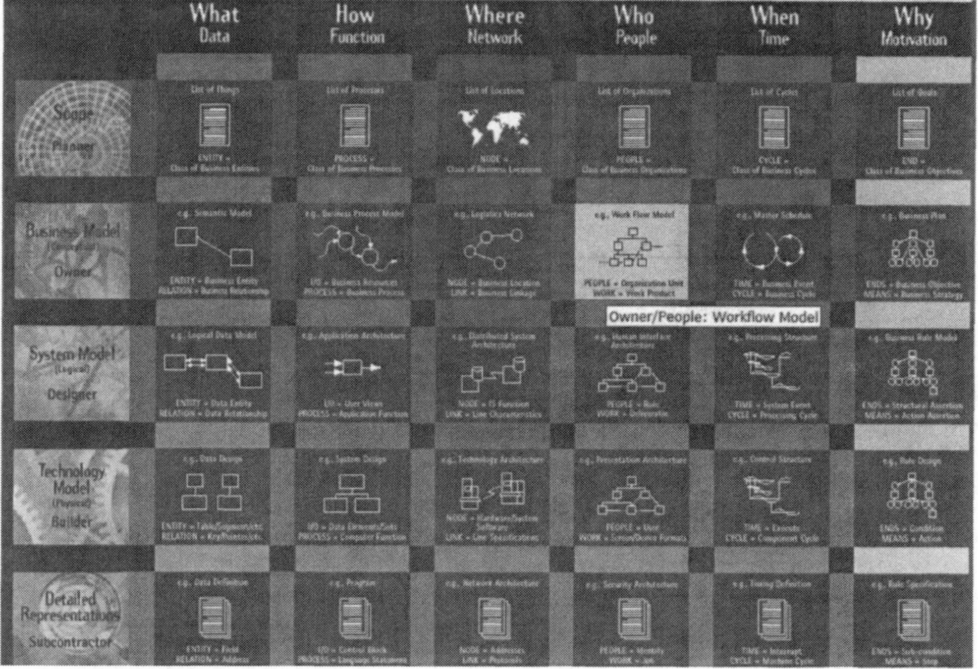

Figure 8.15 Workflow modeling addresses Zachman framework column 4, row 2.

this technology, priority workflows can be rapidly implemented. We will now see how workflow models can be derived using project maps and activity maps.

8.5.1 Using Project Maps for Workflow Modeling

We will use the data map in Figure 8.16 to illustrate how we can use project maps and activity models to derive workflow models. This is a very simple data map, but it will serve our purpose to derive a workflow model. We will use the entity dependency analysis method from Chapter 7 to identify activities in the data map and derive subproject clusters and then a project map, as discussed in the following paragraphs and associated figures.

Figure 8.17 uses a surrounding dashed-dotted line to highlight the first end-point entity: JOB SKILL. We can see this is an intersecting entity, formed by the decomposition of the *many-to-many* association that otherwise would exist between SKILL and JOB. It represents the activity that is called *Job Skill Management* in this example.

Using entity dependency analysis with the highlighted data map subset in Figure 8.17, we can derive the following project plan for implementation of this activity as a subproject cluster. This cluster is also called *Job Skill Management*.

1 JOB SKILL MANAGEMENT (derived)
    1) **JOB**
    1) **SKILL**
        2) **JOB SKILL** (JOB SKILL MANAGEMENT)

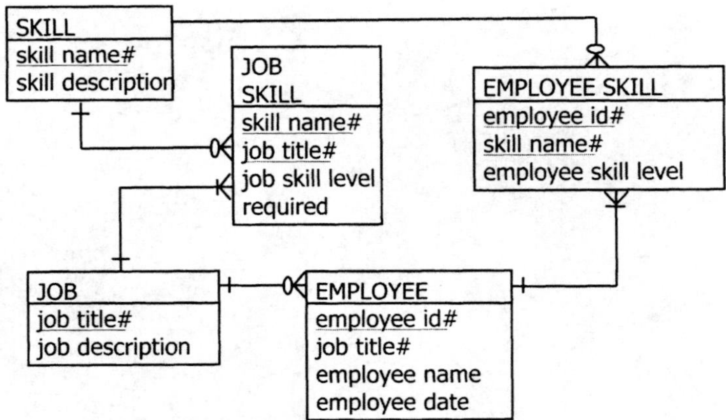

Figure 8.16 Data map to be used for derivation of a workflow model.

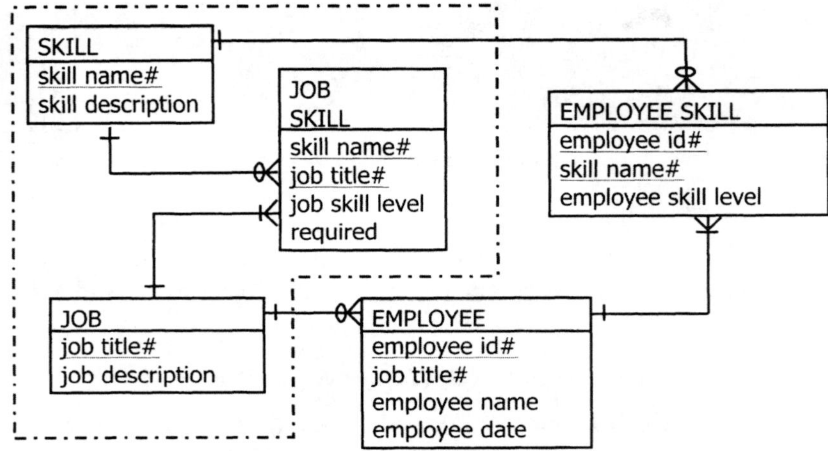

Figure 8.17 Job Skill Management cluster in the data map.

The other end-point entity in Figure 8.17 is EMPLOYEE SKILL, shown outside the dashed-dotted line. This represents the activity called *Employee Skill Management.* Using entity dependency analysis again, the cluster for Employee Skill Management follows:

2 EMPLOYEE SKILL MANAGEMENT (derived)
- 1) **JOB**
  - 2) **EMPLOYEE**
  - 2) JOB SKILL (JOB SKILL MANAGEMENT)
- 1) **SKILL**
  - 3) **EMPLOYEE SKILL** (EMPLOYEE SKILL MANAGEMENT)

Notice that all entities are bold, except for JOB SKILL. This is included in the cluster because of the *mandatory one–to–mandatory many* association between

JOB and JOB SKILL. From this analysis we see that *Job Skill Management* is a prerequisite, shared subproject. The project map derived from these two subproject clusters is shown in Figure 8.18.

8.5.2 Derivation of Activity Models from Project Maps

The project map derived from the data map gives us insight into the possible relationship that also exists between the two activities represented by these subprojects. This makes sense, because a *Job Skill Management* activity determines skills needed for a job, whereas an *Employee Skill Management* activity indicates employees with required skills.

The output from the *Job Skill Management* activity is a list of required skills. This provides input to the *Employee Skill Management* activity. The project map therefore is a starting point to develop activity maps.

The data map in Figure 8.16 suggests that an employee who does not have required skills for one job may instead be assigned to another job. The result is an embryonic activity map with a feedback loop as shown in Figure 8.19.

Using activity modeling as described in this chapter, subactivities can now be defined for these two activities. For example, in Figure 8.20 we can see that Job Skill Management requires three tasks as subactivities: *Develop job description, Compare applicant skills to job,* and *Increase job skill levels.* Similarly, Employee Skill Management has three tasks as subactivities: *Develop employee training log, Determine work assignment,* and *Document additional training.* Figure 8.20 shows these activities and their subactivities in a decomposition diagram that shows the activity hierarchy.

8.5.3 Derivation of a Workflow Model from Activity Maps

We can now start to define a workflow model from the activity decomposition hierarchy in Figure 8.21, which illustrates an activity flowchart in the bottom part of the figure that has been derived from the activity decomposition hierarchy diagram above it. This flowchart is a transitional activity hierarchy diagram that illustrates a potential process sequence for execution of the various tasks in the activity.

Figure 8.21 does not consider external tasks that may also have to be carried out during execution. When these are considered as shown in Figure 8.22, the external tasks are added to the transitional activity flowchart. The result is now a workflow diagram.

Figure 8.22 adds the external tasks *Post open job* and *Receive job application.* When applicant skills are compared to required job skills, a decision is made for any qualified applicants to carry out the external task of *Conduct job interview.*

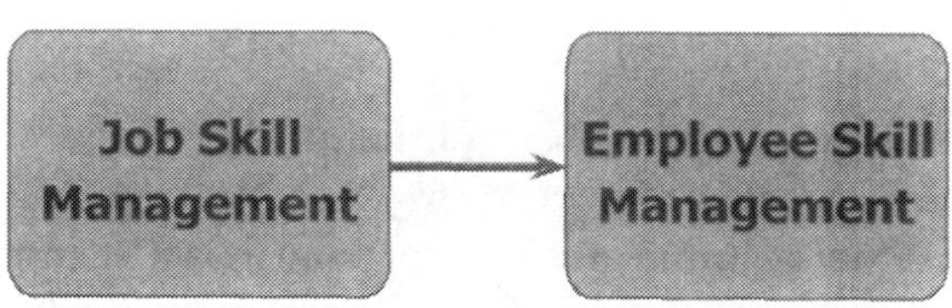

Figure 8.18 Project map for subproject clusters in Figure 8.17.

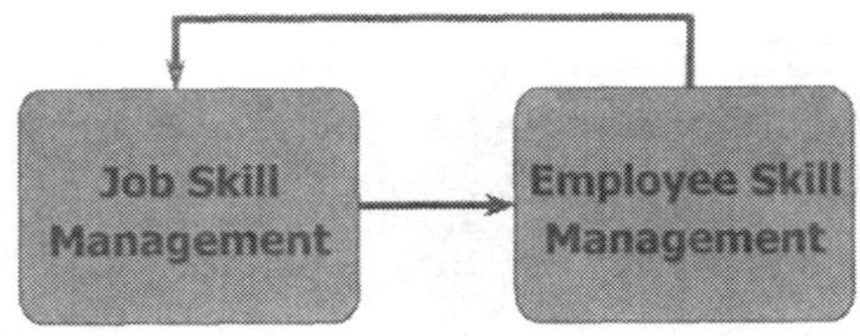

Figure 8.19 Activity map from project map, showing a feedback loop.

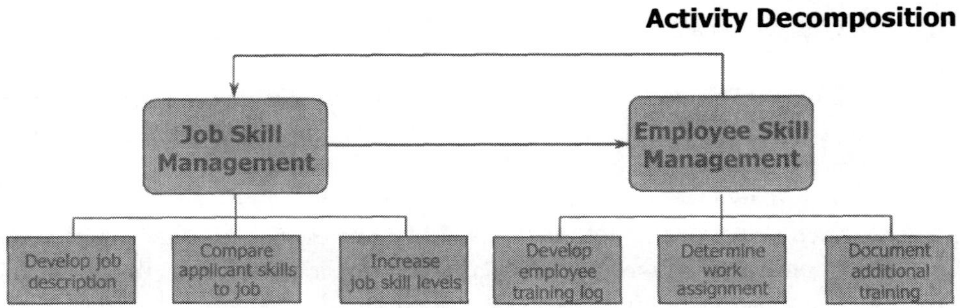

Figure 8.20 Activity map from project map, showing decomposition hierarchy.

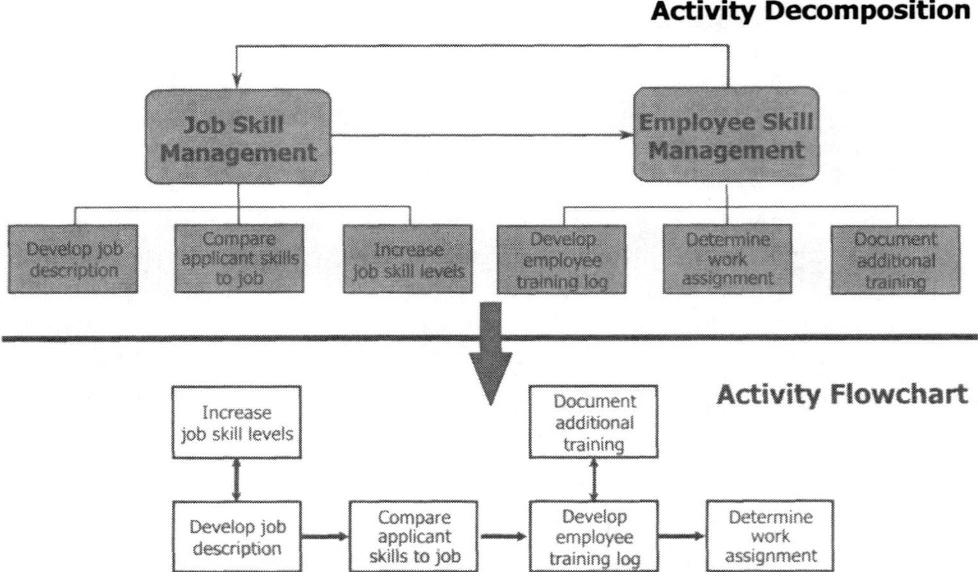

Figure 8.21 Activity flowchart derived from activity hierarchy diagram, showing potential execution sequence.

This workflow diagram example is further refined with additional activities and external tasks as needed. The resulting workflow model is an example of a Zachman framework Who column and Owner row [C4R2] model as illustrated in Figure 8.15. We will see in Chapter 14 that workflow models can be used with BPM lan-

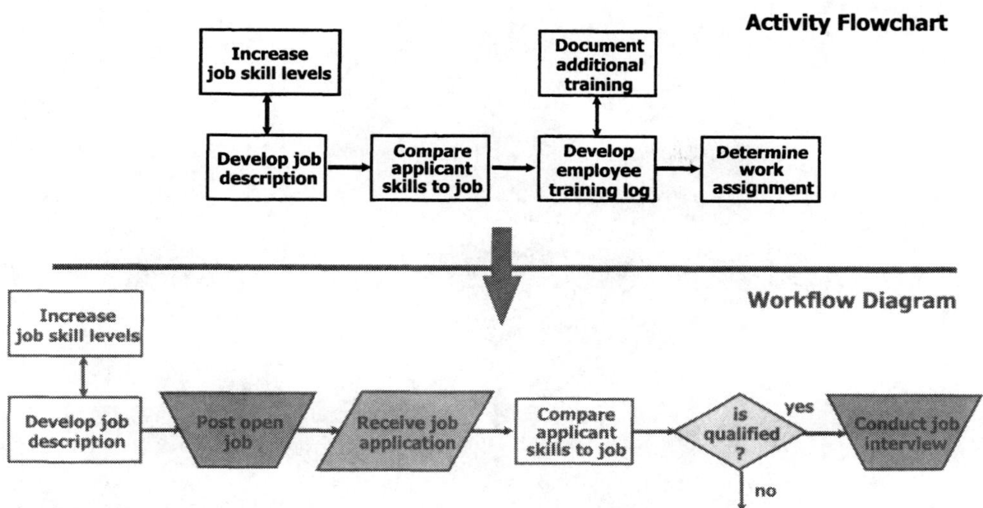

Figure 8.22 Workflow diagram derived from activity flowchart, with external tasks also added.

guages to generate executable XML-based BPM code automatically for rapid delivery into production.

8.6 Step 8: Business Rules for Workflow Modeling

Step 8, as discussed in Section 8.1, is covered in this section. In Chapter 6 we saw that that business rules apply to the Why column and the Designer row [C6R3]. The Builder row [C6R4] covers rule design and [C6R5] for the subcontractor row addresses rule specification. These are shown in Figure 8.23 with [C6R3] highlighted.

Most enterprises have many hundreds or thousands of rules. Previously these have been hard-coded as program logic in programs. The same rule was coded in every program that implemented the logic, resulting in *rule redundancy*. When these rules changed, relevant program logic had to be changed in every affected program, also redundantly.

With business rules in enterprise architecture, each rule is ideally defined once. Rules may be potentially implemented in a *business rule engine* separately from program code [9]. The business rules are defined in the Why column and the Designer row [C6R3]. The rule design (in [C6R4]) can ensure that each rule is designed to be implemented once, yet able to be reused wherever needed. Depending on the rule specification (in [C6R5]) and the rule engine that is used, these rules can be implemented once only, yet shared throughout the enterprise. If a rule changes later, only its specification need be changed. That change is applied automatically wherever it is used throughout the enterprise.

Business rules are defined by Business Rule Solutions [10] as follows [11]:

> A business rule is a directive that is intended to influence or guide business behavior. Such directives exist in support of business policy, which is formulated in response to risks, threats or opportunities.

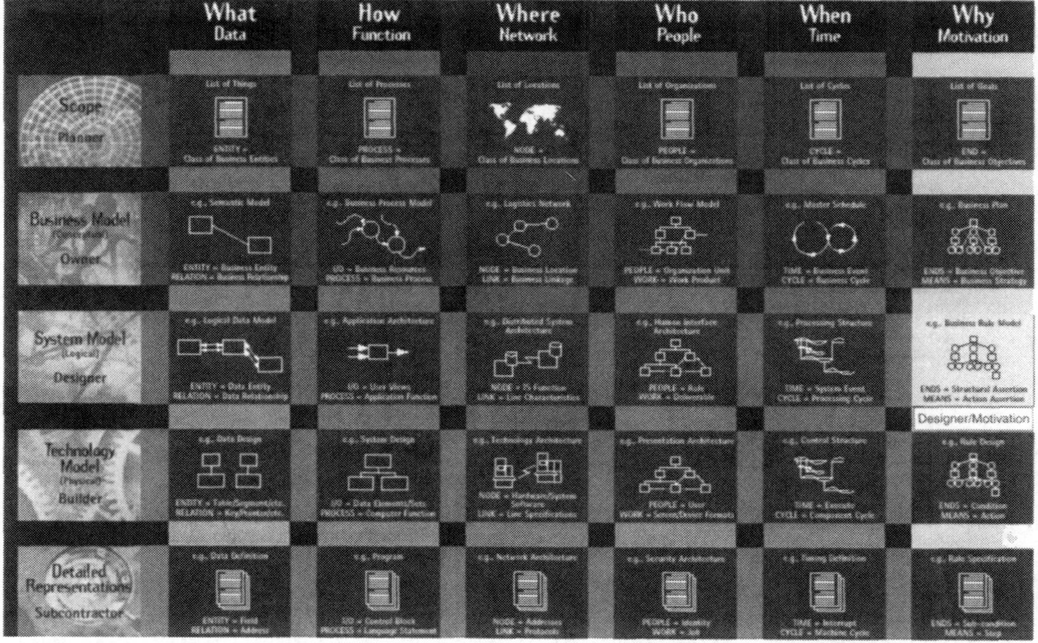

Figure 8.23 Business rules apply to column 6, row 3; rule design is row 4; rule specification is row 5.

Business Rule Solutions has developed BRS Proteus [12, 13]. This methodology is used for the definition, management, and implementation of business rules. A technique to express business rules in a consistent, well-structured manner is the *BRS RuleSpeak Practitioner Kit.* The company has an automated tool, *BRS RuleTrack,* that is used for recording and organizing business rules. It also has the *BRS Conceptual Rule Management MetaModel* and the *BRS Detailed Rule Management MetaModel* [14].

The rest of this section provides an overview of BRS Proteus.

8.6.1 Mapping BRS Proteus to Enterprise Architecture

The BRS Proteus methodology includes support for the Zachman framework, as shown in Figure 8.24. Notice that BRS Proteus supports most cells of the Zachman framework, particularly column 6, rows 1–5. It can be used for detailed definition of business plans in rows 1and 2, where row 1 is *Mission & Goals* and row 2 is *Policy Charter* in Figure 8.24.

BRS Proteus can be used for rows 1 and 2 following strategy analysis. Regardless of whether strategy analysis is used or not, the business planning questionnaire that is discussed in Chapter 3, or the strategic modeling questionnaire in Chapter 7, are still required by later chapters. Consequently, it is strongly recommended that one of these questionnaires be used as discussed earlier, for later input as a catalyst for strategic modeling in Chapter 7.

BRS Proteus also addresses the What column for all rows [C1R1–5] in Figure 8.24. It is used to define *core business concepts* in row 1; develop a high-level enter-

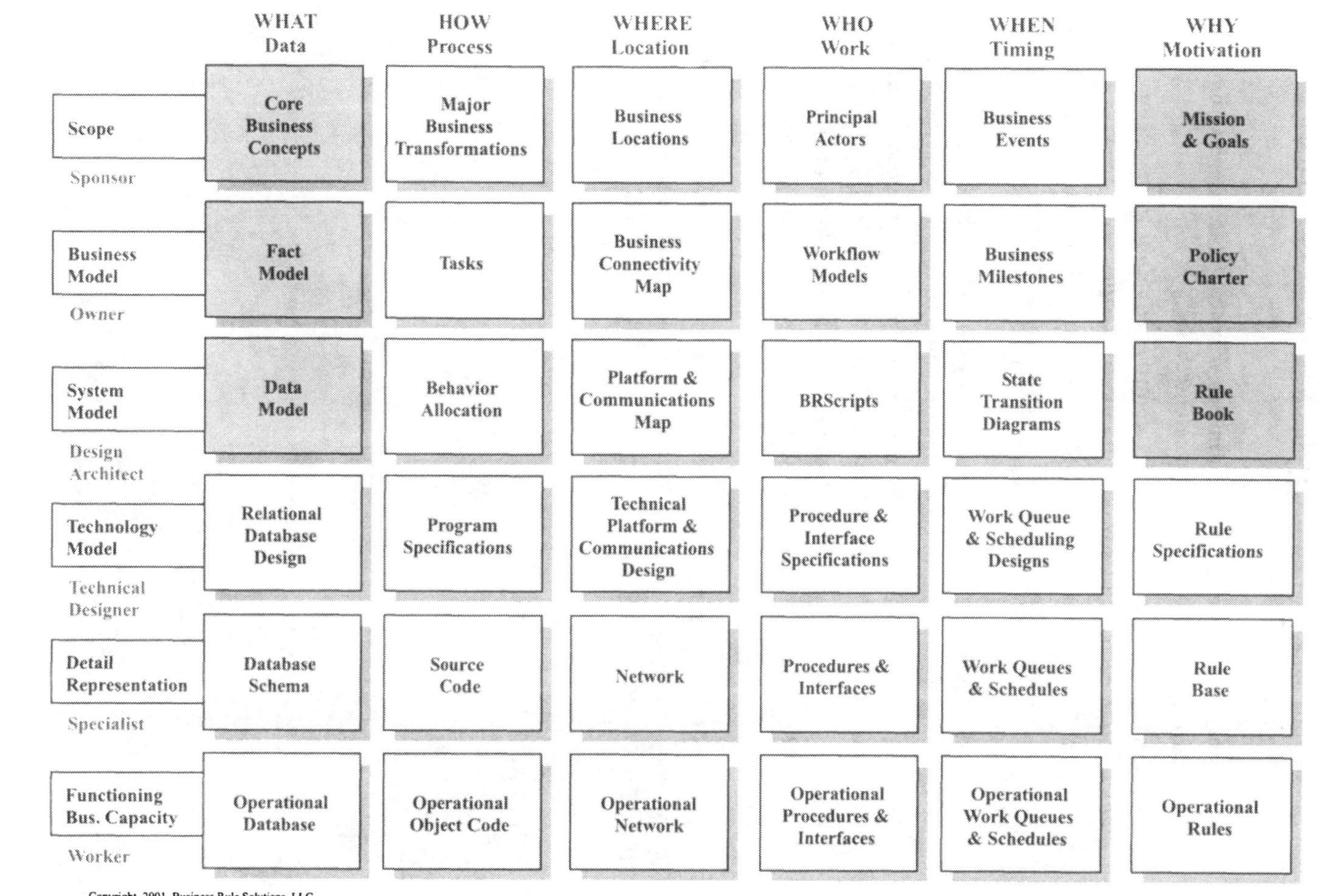

Figure 8.24 BRS Proteus support for Zachman framework. (*From:* [14]. © 2005 Business Rules Solutions, Inc. Reprinted with permission.)

prise model as a *fact model* in row 2; and develop a logical *data model* in row 3. We will review these data modeling steps in BRS Proteus, but we cover detailed data modeling methods in Chapters 6 and 9.

In summary Figure 8.24 illustrates that BRS Proteus uses columns 1 through 6 in rows 1 through 3 as follows:

- Column 6 (Why) uses row 1 to define *mission & goals;* row 2 to define the *policy charter;* and row 3 to develop a *rule book.*
- Column 4 (Who) uses row 1 to identify *principal actors;* row 2 to define *workflow models*; and row 3 to define *BRScripts.*
- Column 1 (What) uses row 1 to define *core business concepts;* row 2 to develop an enterprise model as a *fact model*; and row 3 to develop a *data model.*
- Column 5 (When) uses row 1 to identify *business events*; row 2 to determine *business milestones;* and row 3 to define *state transition diagrams* for timing.
- Column 2 (How) uses row 1 to identify *major business transformations*; row 2 to define *tasks*; and row 3 to define *behavior allocation.*
- Column 3 (Where) uses row 1 to identify *business locations*; row 2 to define the *business connectivity map*; and row 3 to define a *platform & communications map.*

Notice that the columns just listed are in the *enterprise architecture implementation sequence* as recommended in Chapter 5. We will briefly review the BRS Proteus steps in the following pages, in conjunction with Figure 8.25.

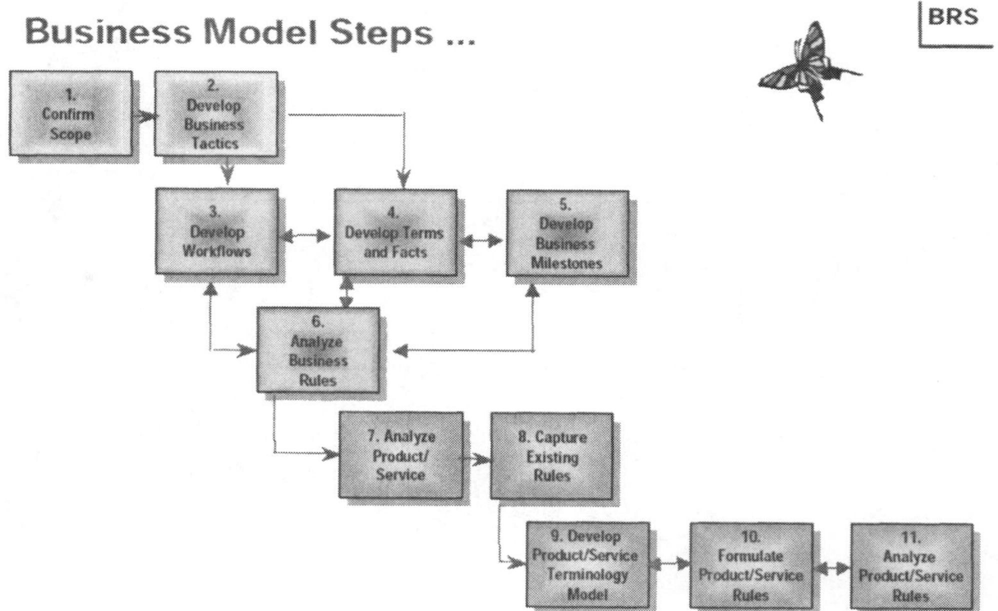

Figure 8.25 Developing the business model. (*From:* [14]. © 2005 Business Rules Solutions, Inc. Reprinted with permission.)

8.6.2 Definition of Business Rules Using BRS Proteus

The steps used by BRS Proteus to develop the business model are illustrated in Figure 8.25. These steps are summarized as follows, with full details given in [15]. Each substep in the following list is referenced to the relevant Zachman framework cell in Figure 8.24 as noted in (parentheses):

- *BRS Step 1:* This first identifies the scope using mission and goals (column 6, row 1) and identifies business events (column 5, row 1). It identifies principal actors (column 4, row 1), core business terms (column 1, row 1), major business transformations (column 2, row 1), and finally identifies business locations (column 3, row 1).
- *BRS Step 2:* This step focuses on column 6 for business tactics. It prepares for business tactics capture, defines high-level tactics, and then identifies risks. It defines business tactics to address the risks and formulates the policy charter (column 6, row 2).
- *BRS Step 3:* This focuses on workflows in column 4 and events in column 5. It identifies scenarios for initiating workflow events; develops As-Is workflows covering tasks, actors, and events; develops To-Be workflows; and defines tasks. The To-Be workflow is revised and enhanced for a variety of scenarios, actors, and roles.
- *BRS Step 4:* This focuses on column 1, row 2. Existing terms and definitions are captured in a high-level data model, called a *fact model.* Data entities are called *terms,* and the relationships between them are called *facts.* The As-Is data model of terms and facts is reviewed. Concrete terms are identified, together with abstract terms, to develop the fact model with a precise business-oriented definition for each term. This fact model is validated for correctness and completeness, and then existing rules are reviewed to ensure that all relevant terminology is represented in the fact model.
- *BRS Step 5:* Business milestones are determined in column 5. Terms for milestone analysis are identified by reviewing the fact model. The stages or states for relevant terms are identified; basic rules are defined to coordinate relevant milestones.
- *BRS Step 6:* The evolving business rules (in column 6) are evaluated and decomposed to their atomic form. Relevant properties are specified for each rule: categorizing rules or relating rules to other rules or to other business model items. The rule set is evaluated collectively and potential rule exceptions are identified.
- *BRS Step 7:* At this point, products and services of the enterprise are reviewed to identify knowledge-intensive components, decision points, and terms essential to understanding, categorizing, and organizing relevant products or services.
- *BRS Step 8:* All relevant sources are determined for existing product or service rules, together with governing rules. All relevant explicit and tacit operating rules are captured. Automated operating rules are extracted as source code statements from automated systems.

- *BRS Step 9:* The product and service terminology model is identified, with names and code structures. A product/service terminology model is developed, with standard categories. Standard names and codes are created at the instance level. Category rules and conversion rules are identified.
- *BRS Step 10:* The evolving product/service rules are formulated and evaluated to eliminate those rules that are obsolete, redundant, ineffective, or out of scope. Operating rule gaps are identified in automated rules within program code statements and/or tables. Governing rules are analyzed to address gaps or missing product/service rules.
- *BRS Step 11:* Finally, any complex product/service rules that remain are analyzed and decomposed into their atomic form. The information or properties describing each rule are specified. Assumptions are challenged for validity. The rule set is finally evaluated for duplications, conflicts, exceptions, and other criteria.

The definition of the business model by BRS Proteus in Figure 8.25 is a prerequisite to the development of the system model. These steps are discussed next, with full details available for download from the Business Rule Solutions Web site [15].

A completeness check for the business model defined in Figure 8.25 is first carried out. This checks completeness as follows (with Zachman framework columns in parentheses): the fact model (column 1), the business process model (column 2), the business connectivity map (column 3), the organizational work model (column 4), business milestones (column 5), and the policy charter (column 6). The rule book and decision points that were defined in the business model are also checked for completeness. All provide input for development of the system model.

Further details on the use of business rules for enterprise architecture are available from the references in the endnotes.

The business rule principles and steps in this section can be used with workflow models developed earlier in this chapter, or with the development of processes as discussed in Chapter 10. These business rules for workflow models and process models can be used with SOA and BPM products as described in Chapter 14. For example, Microsoft BizTalk Server includes a business rule engine so each business rule is defined once. Rules can be changed easily, with automatic updates of each workflow or process that references it, for automatic generation of executable XML-based BPM code. This is discussed further in Chapter 14.

8.7 Summary

In this chapter we discussed strategic alignment matrices. We covered the following alignment principles:

- Columns of the Zachman framework should be aligned across each framework row. This is achieved by using key strategic alignment matrices for columns 6, 4, 1, 2, 5, and 3, as summarized next.
- Using matrices, business plans in column 6 should be aligned with people in column 4, data in column 1, functions in column 2, time in column 5, and

locations in column 3. They apply to each planning statement, each organizational unit, each data entity, each activity, each business event, and each location. These matrices answer the questions why, who, what, how, when and where.

- Activities in column 2 correspond to strategies in column 6. Both specify what has to be done. Processes in column 2 correspond to tactics in column 6. These specify how the tactics are implemented.
- Functional areas in column 4 are organizational units that manage functions in column 2. In turn, these functions group related activities; several functions can share common reusable activities.
- These matrices can also be used for governance analysis as discussed in Chapter 4.

We covered activity modeling and activity-based costing as follows:

- Activities group related tasks; these tasks are invoked by processes that execute required tasks in specific sequences based on business rules.
- Activity modeling uses IDEF0 diagrams: the context diagram, node or activity hierarchy diagrams, and functional decomposition activity maps. Together, these activity modeling diagrams document what has to be done by each activity.
- An activity model documents the transformation of inputs into outputs, based on controls such as business rules or constraints. Resources for this transformation are provided by mechanisms.
- Costs are associated with resources used as mechanisms. These resources can be used to calculate activity costs, by using activity-based costing.
- ABC is used to evaluate activity costs and identify opportunities for process improvements, improved efficiency, or reduced cost.
- ABC forms the basis for economic analyses that is used to evaluate the feasibility of alternatives to the current activities. These alternatives can utilize different technologies to achieve required process improvements or cost reductions.
- The definition of alternative activities may also include the development of new or enhanced data models, as well as activity models.

We covered workflow modeling and business rules as follows:

- Project maps, developed from data maps using entity dependency analysis in Chapter 7, are used to derive activity maps, activity hierarchy diagrams, and workflow models.
- We discussed methods in column 6 that are used for business rules. These identify the mission and goals in row 1 and the policy charter in row 2.
- We discussed the BRS Proteus business rules methodology in row 3 to identify business rules in a rule book. This is used also for rule design in row 4 and rule specification in row 5.

- The result of using the BRS Proteus methodology is the definition of all cells of column 6, and major definition of many cells in the other columns, down to row 3.

We can now move to Chapter 9 where we will cover methods for detailed definition of logical and physical data models in column 1, rows 3 and 4. Our focus will be on business normalization and physical database design for these Zachman framework cells.

Endnotes

[1] The case study problems are in the PDF file *Chap-08-Problems.pdf* in the Book Materials folder on the accompanying CD-ROM.

[2] These problems are in the PDF file *Chap-08-Problems.pdf* in the Book Materials folder on the accompanying CD-ROM.

[3] The sample solutions are in the PDF file *Chap-08-Solutions.pdf* in the Book Materials folder on the accompanying CD-ROM.

[4] IDEF0 is widely used for activity modeling by the U.S. Department of Defense. Other diagramming techniques could also be used, such as activity diagrams in UML. We will use IDEF0 in this chapter.

[5] Cokins, G. *Activity-Based Cost Management: An Executive's Guide.*

[6] Daly, J. L., *Pricing for Profitability: Activity-Based Pricing for Competitive Advantage.*

[7] Brimson, J., *Activity Accounting: An Activity-Based Costing Approach.*

[8] Brimson, J., and J. Antos, *Activity Based Management for Service Industries, Government Entities, and Nonprofit Organizations.*

[9] A business rules engine is a software product that analyzes defined business rules and executes them as conditional logic.

[10] Details about Business Rule Solutions and its methodologies, software tools, and consulting and education services are available at http://www.brsolutions.com.

[11] The leading practitioner of business rules today is Business Rule Solutions, Inc., located in Houston, Texas. Ron Ross and Gladys Lam are cofounders. Ron Ross is considered the father of business rules, with many books published on this subject.

[12] Ross, R., *The Business Rule Book,* 2nd ed., Houston, TX: Business Rule Solutions, 1997.

[13] Ross, R., *Principles of the Business Rules Approach,* Reading, MA: Addison-Wesley, 2003.

[14] Overviews of BRS Proteus and BRS RuleSpeak are available for download at http://www.brsolutions.com. Details of BRS RuleTrack, the BRS Conceptual Rule Management MetaModel, and BRS Detailed Rule Management MetaModel are also available from the same Web site.

[15] Full details describing steps for defining the business model and the system model using BRS Proteus are available from the Business Rule Solutions Web site at http://www.brsolutions.com.

CHAPTER 9

Using Business Normalization for Future Business Needs

This chapter introduces business normalization. This is a business-driven method that is used to identify data needed for future requirements. An advanced logical data modeling method, it is used with data mapping (see Chapter 6) to develop data models with greater entity and attribute detail. Together, these methods expand the strategic model developed in Chapter 7 from the What column and the Owner row [C1R2] of the Zachman framework into a logical data model in the Owner row [C1R3] as illustrated in Figure 9.1.

9.1 Enterprise Architecture Incremental Build Context

We discussed the incremental build sequence for enterprise architecture in Chapter 5. Logical data modeling using business normalization is carried out at this stage in Step 9 of Figure 9.2 as follows (with the earlier steps in the figure also included):

- *Step 1:* In Chapter 3, we discussed that strategy analysis identifies statements for mission, vision, core values, goals, objectives, issues, KPIs, and strategies in the strategic plan.
- *Step 2:* Strategy analysis identifies from the organizational structure those managers and business experts responsible for implementing priority areas of the strategic plan.
- *Step 3:* During a 5-day business planning workshop, the identified managers and business experts optionally apply the strategy analysis methodology to define tactical business planning statements to implement strategic plans.
- *Step 4:* In Chapter 6 we saw that data mapping is used to enable business experts and IT experts to work together to identify data for integration. This begins with a 2-day strategic modeling facilitated session as detailed in this chapter. Entities that represent required information and data are listed in the What column for the Planner row [C1R1].
- *Step 5:* In Chapter 7 we saw that the facilitated modeling session continues over 2 days, documenting key entities in a strategic model on a white board. The strategic model is a high-level semantic model or enterprise model in the What column for the Owner row [C1R2] that represents a "picture of the business" to the participating managers and business experts. Typically 90 to 120 entities are defined in these 2 days.

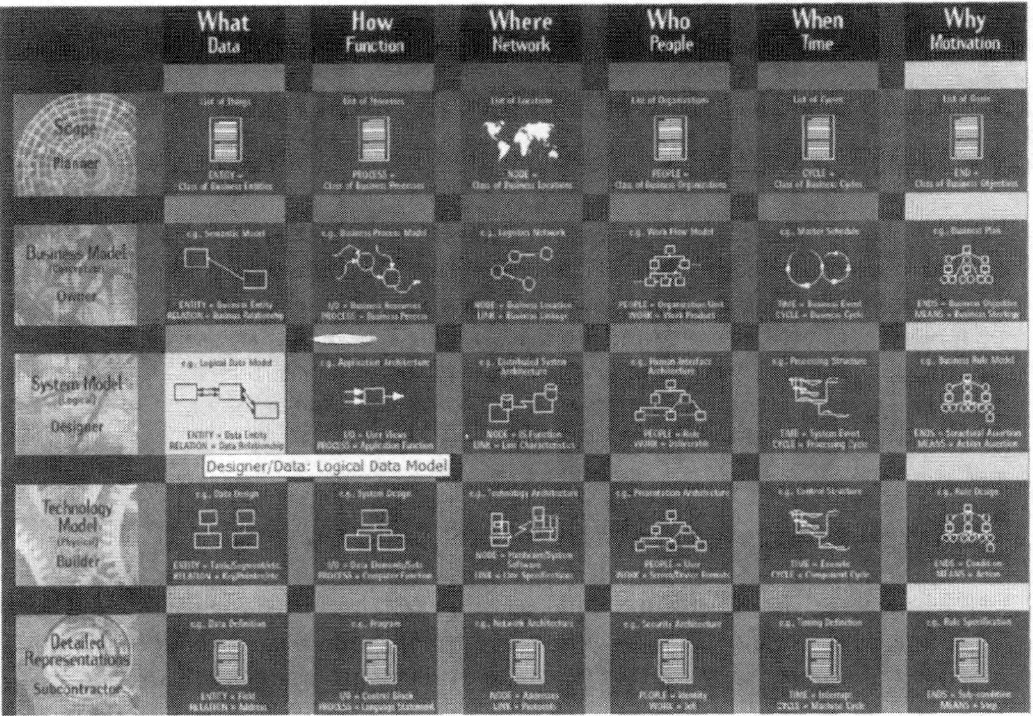

Figure 9.1 Logical data modeling addresses Zachman framework column 1, row 3

- *Step 6:* This step next defines strategic alignment matrices in row 1 for key columns. We covered this in Chapter 8. These matrices are shown as double-headed arrows in Figure 9.2 between these columns and their relevant artifacts with other key columns. Key strategic alignment matrices that are important are listed below and were described in Chapter 8.
  - Column 6 to column 4: showing people responsible for key planning statements;
  - Column 6 to column 1: showing the data supporting key planning statements;
  - Column 2 to column 1: showing the data required by key business activities;
  - Column 6 to column 2: showing activities supporting key planning statements.
- *Step 7:* In Step 7, the strategic model (see Chapter 7) or business events in the When column and Planner row [C5R1] can be used to identify activities in the How column and Planner row [C2R1]. These are typically common, reusable activities that deliver cost savings and benefits when implemented. Priority activities are defined as high-level activity models in column 2, row 2. In Chapter 8, activity-based costing is used to determine the relative cost of alternative activities.
- *Step 8:* Priority activity models from Step 7 are used to develop workflow models in the Who column and Owner row [C4R2]. These workflow models

	What Data	How Function	Where Location	Who People	When Time	Why Future
PLANNER Objectives/Scope	4 List of Things	6 List of Processes	List of Locations	2 Org Structure	7 List of Events	1 List of Goals/Obj
OWNER Conceptual	5 Enterprise Model	7 Activity Model	Business Logistics	8 Work Flow	Master Schedule	3 Business Plan
DESIGNER Logical	9 Logical Data Model	11 Process Model	Distrib. Architect.	10 Human Interface	Process Structure	Business Rules
BUILDER Physical	Physical Data Model	System Model	Technol. Architect.	Presn Interface	Control Structure	Rule Design
SUBCONTRACTOR Out-of-Context	Data Definition	Program	Network Architect.	Security Interface	Timing Definition	Rule Specs
FUNCTIONING ENTERPRISE	Data	Function	Network	Organization	Schedule	Strategy

Figure 9.2 Logical data modeling for 3-month incremental builds.

are based on final, agreed-on activity models and business rules that indicate how processes will be invoked. This development of workflow models and definition of business rules were described in Chapter 8.

- *Step 9:* The high-level strategic model from the Owner's perspective (in column 1, row 2) is expanded to greater detail in this step, transforming it into a fully attributed logical data model from the Designer's perspective (in column 1, row 3). This uses data mapping (described in Chapter 6) together with business normalization, which is the subject of this chapter.

Project plans derived in Chapter 7 using entity dependency analysis are used to schedule participation in logical data modeling sessions of business experts who have detailed business knowledge of required data entities. They apply their expertise in these modeling sessions, participating actively with IT staff to expand the strategic model to the logical data model detail in column 1 row 3.

Priority data subsets are expanded to column 1, row 3, as vertical data slivers in Figure 9.2. Details of all defined entities, attributes, associations, and relevant business rules are entered concurrently into a modeling tool. This generates a physical database design for the target database management system (DBMS) product selected by the project team. It transforms the logical data model vertical sliver into a physical data model sliver in column 1, row 4, for the Builder. The modeling tool also generates the relevant data definition language (DDL) script as a vertical data sliver in column 1, row 5, for database implementation of that priority data sliver.

9.1.1 Reading Strategy for This Chapter

Business normalization is intended for use by business experts and IT experts, working in a design partnership. If you are experienced in normalization, you will note with business normalization that these definitions focus on how to apply the rule, rather than on the formal technical definitions.

You may want to skim-read through to third normal form. You will find that the normalization cross-check that follows the Third Business Normal Form extends traditional normalization. When used by business experts, it helps identify future business needs.

You can skim-read the Fourth Business Normal Form also, but you should read the section on the Fifth Business Normal Form fully. It discusses the treatment of recursive associations and shows how expert knowledge is captured as expert rules for business intelligence purposes.

9.2 Introduction to Normalization

Normalization was developed in the late 1960s by Dr. Edgar (Ted) Codd, while working on relational theory as a research fellow at the IBM San Jose Research Laboratory. He applied mathematical set theory as a formal discipline to identify and structure data in relational databases. Normalization, defined by him from this research activity, applied a formal set of rules to data. These rules reflected an academic emphasis in the early 1970s. In the mid-1970s, normalization evolved in two directions, one with a technical focus and the other with a business focus.

Normalization evolved further in the 1980s into two clear variants: traditional normalization [1] and business normalization [2, 3]. The first is used by data administrators (DAs) and database administrators (DBAs) to design databases, but business users find it technical and difficult to apply. In contrast, business normalization can be used both by business experts and computer experts.

We will cover business normalization in detail in this chapter. Refer to [1, 2] for information on traditional normalization.

9.2.1 Business Normalization

Business normalization is used by business managers and business staff, as well as by IT computer staff. It depends on knowledge of the business, rather than of computers. Both variants of normalization define five normal form rules: First Normal Form (1NF) to Fifth Normal Form (5NF) for traditional normalization; and First Business Normal Form (1BNF) to Fifth Business Normal Form (5BNF) for business normalization. The qualifier "Business" and the prefix "B" are used to differentiate business normalization from traditional normalization as shown in Table 9.1.

Table 9.1 Normalization Rules

Traditional Normalization	*Business Normalization*
First Normal Form (1NF)	First Business Normal Form (1BNF)
Second Normal Form (2NF)	Second Business Normal Form (2BNF)
Third Normal Form (3NF)	Third Business Normal Form (3BNF)
Fourth Normal Form (4NF)	Fourth Business Normal Form (4BNF)
Fifth Normal Form (5NF)	Fifth Business Normal Form (5BNF)

- 1BNF to 3BNF produce the same results as 1NF to 3NF, except that the rules for business normalization focus on "how" to apply each rule, rather than on the academic correctness of the rule definition as with traditional normalization.
- 4BNF is similar to 4NF, in that each approach defines the existence of supertype and subtype entities. There is more business emphasis on representing detailed business knowledge with 4BNF than with 4NF.
- 5BNF is quite different from 5NF. 5NF is sometimes called "Project-Join" normal form. In contrast, 5BNF represents expert business knowledge as expert rules in tables as data. In this form, knowledge can be changed rapidly to reflect the dynamic nature of expert business rules and knowledge in today's changing business environment.

We will now address the reasons for normalization, which are based on good forms and database design. We will start by considering typical forms design problems.

9.2.2 Resolution of Forms' Design Problems

Normalization is used to structure data so that relevant details can be accessed and required changes can be made more efficiently. For example, the employee register form shown in Figure 9.3—where a separate form for each employee is filed in sequence by employee number—is not designed very efficiently. Consider the following problems that occur when making changes to employee details:

- If we know the employee number, it is easy to turn to a specific employee's form to change that person's address. This change presents no problem.
- However, if we change a job name of "Clerk" to "Records Administrator" the task is more difficult. We must examine each employee's form to identify who has a job as a Clerk, and then change that job name to Records Administrator. We only finish when we have examined every employee form in the Employee Register.
- Similarly, to change a skill name from "Clerical" to "Records Administration" skill, we must examine every skill held by an employee and change every

EMPLOYEE REGISTER
Number:
Name:
Address:
P/Code:
Skill No Skill Name Skill Level
Sales Quota:
Manager Title:
Job Name:
Salary:

Consider This Problem:
- The Employee Register is kept in Employee Number sequence.
- Given Employee Number, how would you change:
  Employee Address?
  Job Name?
  Skill Name?

Figure 9.3 Problems that can occur with the employee register form.

Clerical skill to a Records Administration skill. We are only finished when we have examined all skills for every employee in the Employee Register.

These typical problems have already been solved in business. In practice, the Employee Register is structured differently than in Figure 9.3, as illustrated next. The concept of normalization in business is not new. In fact, its principles have been used by business informally for forms design and record management since the early twentieth century. When applied by business experts, these principles are based on business normalization.

Problems associated with the preceding changes for Figure 9.3 are resolved as shown in the following figures. For example, details for each employee are typically moved to a separate employee details form as illustrated in Figure 9.4.

Each employee is uniquely identified by an *employee number*. Employee name, address, and *postcode* further describe the employee. Each employee who is a salesperson has a *sales quota*. Each employee who is a manager has a *manager title*. Each employee has a specific *job name* and receives a *salary*. (Changes in *job name* will be discussed later.) Thus, the details describing an employee can be easily changed, given the employee number of the relevant employee.

The employee register form provides space only for seven skills per employee. This is very limiting. If an employee has more than seven skills, then additional pages of the form are needed to record those extra skills. But this is not ideal either; it is not good forms design or records management practice.

Instead each skill row in an employee register form, showing the level of that skill held by the employee, is moved to a separate employee skill details form. Any number of forms can thus be used: one for each skill held by an employee. The previous constraint of only seven skills per employee register form is thus resolved in Figure 9.5.

There is nothing unusual about this way of recording employee skills. This approach has been used by business for decades. It is an example of efficient records management practice. But this does not resolve the problem of a change in skill name. There may be many employees with the same skill. Each employee skill details form must still be examined to change the skill name of all employees with the relevant skill.

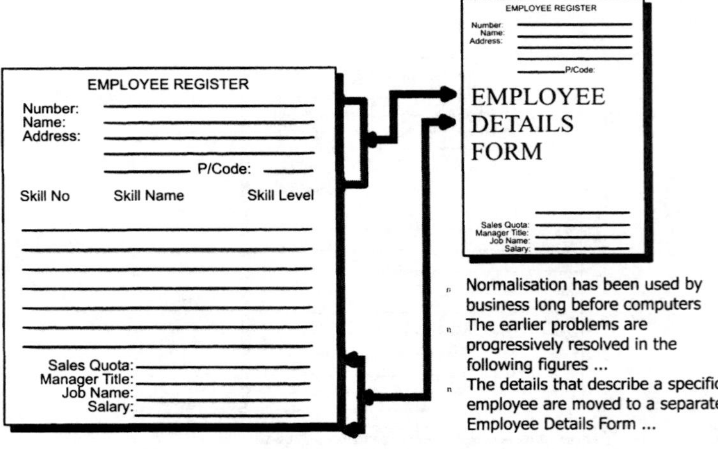

Figure 9.4 Employee details are moved to an employee details form.

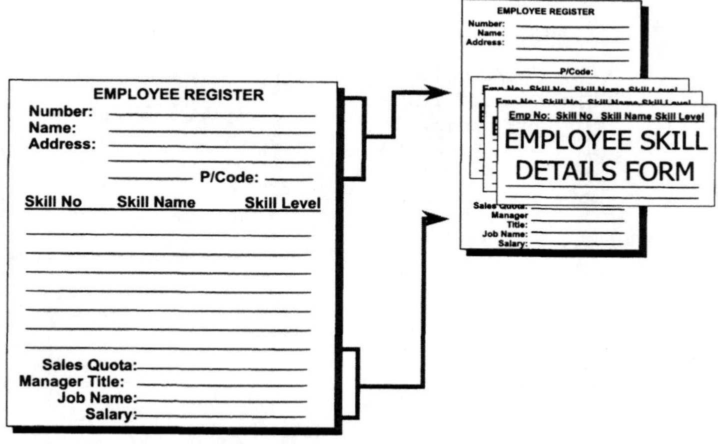

Figure 9.5 Employee skills are moved to an employee skill details form.

Figure 9.6 resolves the problem of changing skill names. Each skill is given a unique *skill number*. This *skill number* is included in the employee skill details form in place of the *skill name*. Each *skill name* is identified by this unique *skill number* in a separate *skill details form*, where it can be changed easily. In this form, skill number 38 has a skill name: "Clerical." This can be easily changed to "Records Administration." Note that the employee *skill details form* is not affected. *Skill number* 38 in that form now automatically refers to the changed *skill name*. The problem of changing the name of a skill has been resolved.

A similar principle is used to accommodate a change of *job name*. A separate job details form is used, with a unique *job number* used to identify each *job name* as shown in Figure 9.7. The *job name* in the employee register form, which was earlier moved to the employee details form without change, is now replaced by a *job number*, which is used to identify the *job name* in the job details form.

Now a *job name* can be changed without requiring any change to the employee details form. For example, *job number* 25 is *job name* "Clerical." It can now be

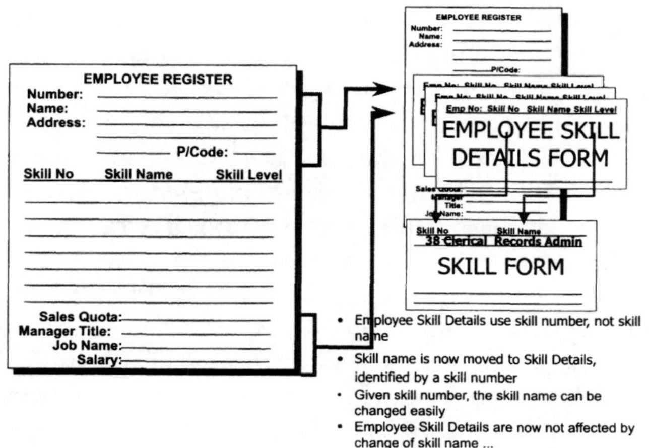

Figure 9.6 Skills are moved to a skill details form.

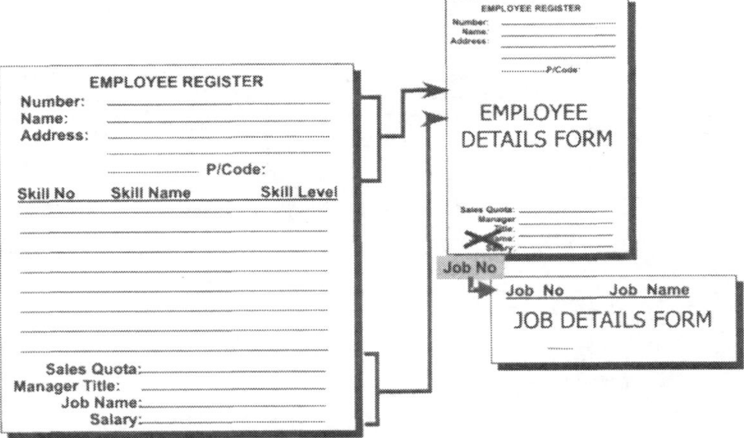

Figure 9.7 Job name is moved to a job details form.

changed to a new *job name:* "Records Management." Note that the employee details form is not affected. Each employee who has *job number* 25 is now automatically changed to the Records Management job. The problem in changing the name of a job has also been resolved.

9.2.3 Resolving Database Design Problems

The principles used to resolve the employee register form design problems above can also be used for good database design. For example, the employee details form in Figure 9.3 is implemented as a single row for each employee in an employee database table. This has the advantage of bringing all of the details for an employee together in one place, where they are easier to reference or access. Achieving this advantage is one of the reasons for normalization.

Similarly, the employee skills form in Figure 9.4 is separated out as an employee skill form and a separate skill form, for a manual system, or as an employee skill table and a separate skill table in a database for automated systems. The reason for this change is that it is now easier to record any number of skills for an employee by using the employee skill table. Each row of that table relates to a skill held by a specific employee, and gives that employee's skill level. It also enables the name of a skill to be changed directly in the skill table given the *skill number*. This changes all references of that skill to the new *skill name:* by using the *skill number* in the employee skill table to link to that *skill number* row in the skill table. These advantages are further reasons for normalization: Restructuring of the data in this way enables changes to data to be made very efficiently.

The three tables in Figure 9.8 are EMPLOYEE (for Employee Details), EMPLOYEE SKILL, and SKILL. These table names are shown in capitals because they are physical tables implemented from logical entities: the EMPLOYEE entity; the EMPLOYEE SKILL entity; and the SKILL entity. We can see that each table contains a number of rows, each row holding details for a single employee, for one skill of an employee, or for one skill.

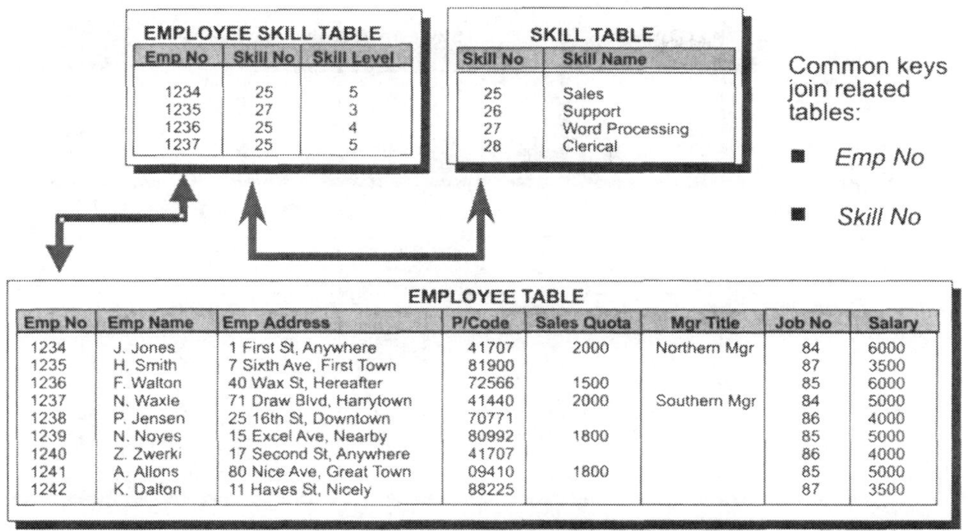

EMPLOYEE SKILL TABLE

Emp No	Skill No	Skill Level
1234	25	5
1235	27	3
1236	25	4
1237	25	5

SKILL TABLE

Skill No	Skill Name
25	Sales
26	Support
27	Word Processing
28	Clerical

EMPLOYEE TABLE

Emp No	Emp Name	Emp Address	P/Code	Sales Quota	Mgr Title	Job No	Salary
1234	J. Jones	1 First St, Anywhere	41707	2000	Northern Mgr	84	6000
1235	H. Smith	7 Sixth Ave, First Town	81900			87	3500
1236	F. Walton	40 Wax St, Hereafter	72566	1500		85	6000
1237	N. Waxle	71 Draw Blvd, Harrytown	41440	2000	Southern Mgr	84	5000
1238	P. Jensen	25 16th St, Downtown	70771			86	4000
1239	N. Noyes	15 Excel Ave, Nearby	80992	1800		85	5000
1240	Z. Zwerki	17 Second St, Anywhere	41707			86	4000
1241	A. Allons	80 Nice Ave, Great Town	09410	1800		85	5000
1242	K. Dalton	11 Haves St, Nicely	88225			87	3500

Figure 9.8 The EMPLOYEE, EMPLOYEE SKILL, and SKILL tables use common keys for cross-reference.

9.2.4 Tables Related by Common Keys

Notice that the tables in Figure 9.8 are joined by common keys. *Emp No.* (in EMPLOYEE) is a common key that joins with EMPLOYEE SKILL, thus identifying all of the skills held by each employee with a unique *Emp No. Skill No.* (in EMPLOYEE SKILL) is a common key that joins with SKILL, thus allowing the *Skill Name* for each *Skill No.* to be determined. For example, the following keys refer to values in rows of these tables:

- Employee: 1234 is J. Jones, who has Skill: 25 (Sales) at Skill Level: 5.
- Employee: 1235 is H. Smith, with Skill: 27 (Word Processing) at Skill Level: 3.
- Employees who have Sales skills (Skill No: 25 in SKILL) are 1234 (J. Jones), 1236 (F. Walton), and 1237 (N. Waxle) in EMPLOYEE SKILL and EMPLOYEE.

We use common keys between tables to help us locate information naturally. Similarly, the *Job Name*—which we moved in Figure 9.7 to the Job Details form—is separately implemented in a database table called JOB in Figure 9.9. We replaced *Job Name* in EMPLOYEE with Job No.; we use *Job No.* to obtain the relevant *Job Name* from JOB.

By implementing *Job Name* in a JOB table, it is now possible to change the name of a job without having to change the name of that job in EMPLOYEE for all employees working in the changed job. Provided *Job No.* is not changed, that job number in each row for employees in the job will now refer to the relevant row in the JOB table for that *Job No.*—and hence automatically use the new job name. This restructuring of the EMPLOYEE table with a separate JOB table enables changes to a job name to be made more efficiently. This is another reason for normalization.

EMPLOYEE SKILL TABLE

Emp No	Skill No	Skill Level
1234	25	5
1235	27	3
1236	25	4
1237	25	5

SKILL TABLE

Skill No	Skill Name
25	Sales
26	Support
27	Word Processing
28	Clerical

JOB TABLE

Job No	Job Name
84	Sales Manager
85	Sales Representative
86	Support Engineer
87	Word Processor

Job No **is a common key**

EMPLOYEE TABLE

Emp No	Emp Name	Emp Address	P/Code	Sales Quota	Mgr Title	Job No	Salary
1234	J. Jones	1 First St, Anywhere	41707	2000	Northern Mgr	84	6000
1235	H. Smith	7 Sixth Ave, First Town	81900			87	3500
1236	F. Walton	40 Wax St, Hereafter	72566	1500		85	6000
1237	N. Waxle	71 Draw Blvd, Harrytown	41440	2000	Southern Mgr	84	5000
1238	P. Jensen	25 16th St, Downtown	70771			86	4000
1239	N. Noyes	15 Excel Ave, Nearby	80992	1800		85	5000
1240	Z. Zwerki	17 Second St, Anywhere	41707			86	4000
1241	A. Allons	80 Nice Ave, Great Town	09410	1800		85	5000
1242	K. Dalton	11 Haves St, Nicely	88225			87	3500

Figure 9.9 We can extract *Job Name* from the JOB table based on *Job No.*

Let us summarize how these tables are implemented. We can see from Figure 9.9 that the JOB and EMPLOYEE tables are now joined by a common key: *Job No.* The JOB table identifies the relevant *Job Name* for the specific *Job No.* that is recorded in the EMPLOYEE table for each employee. Given a *Job No.,* the *Job Name* for that job can be directly changed in the JOB table. All of the employees who are employed in that job (from *Job No.* in the EMPLOYEE table) now automatically refer to the changed *Job Name* in the JOB table.

Using the preceding details in each table, we can extract the following information:

- Job No.: 84 is "Sales Manager," with Sales Managers 1234 (J. Jones) and 1237 (N. Waxle).
- Job No.: 85 is "Sales Representative." These Sales Representatives are 1236 (F. Walton), 1239 (N. Noyes), and 1241 (A. Allons).
- Employees: 1238 (P. Jensen) and 1240 (Z. Zwerki) are Support Engineers (Job No.: 86).
- Employees: 1235 (H. Smith) and 1242 (K. Dalton) are Word Processors (Job No.: 87).

Once again, we used common keys in the tables above to extract this information. This is a natural way to work with tables, using common keys to identify related information.

We have now learned an important principle of normalization: *The relationships between tables are established by common keys,* as shown in Figure 9.10. Tables are joined using these common keys. This is how we naturally extract related information from tables, as we saw with the preceding examples.

Referring back to the concepts of primary, compound, and foreign keys covered in Chapter 6, these common keys are:

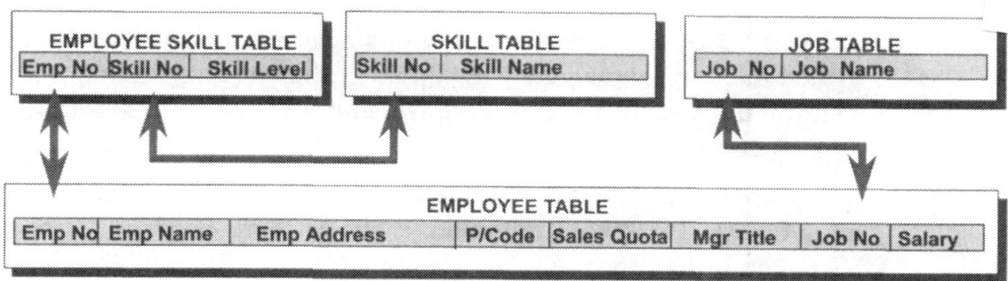

Figure 9.10 All tables are related by common keys for cross-reference.

- Primary keys: *Emp No#* (in EMPLOYEE), *Skill No#* (in SKILL), *Job No#* (in JOB).
- Compound primary keys: *Emp No#, Skill No#* (in EMPLOYEE SKILL).
- Foreign keys: *Job No#* (in EMPLOYEE)—note that this key is not underlined, because it is a foreign key.

Although not advisable, for business reasons the content of a primary key, compound key, or foreign key sometimes may change. This can have a negative performance impact on databases. Database management system (DBMS) software products implement these common keys as indexes, so that related information can be accessed and retrieved rapidly. If the values of these keys change, all affected indexes must be updated to reflect the new key values. This is called *index maintenance* and is carried out automatically by the DBMS. To minimize the impact that index value changes have on performance, a *surrogate key* [4] is used. For example, if the *Emp No* value of an employee might change, we should instead use, say, *Emp Id#* as a surrogate primary key as follows. We can then ensure that *Emp Id#* can never be changed.

EMPLOYEE (*Emp Id#, Emp No, Employee Name,* and so forth)

Emp No can now be changed as needed for business purposes. But because *Emp Id#* is a surrogate key and *never* changes, the problem of index maintenance on performance no longer arises.

9.2.5 Benefits of Business Normalization

Business normalization goes beyond efficient forms design and record management. Traditional normalization is complex and is very difficult for business experts to use. In contrast, business normalization is designed so that it can easily be used by business experts. It provides the following benefits:

- It is based on formal rules designed to be used by business experts and also by computer experts, working together in a design partnership.
- It consolidates the redundant data versions that exist in an organization into shared, integrated data resources that are readily available for use by all staff who are authorized to access that data.

- Because they exist in only one place, whenever data are updated, those integrated data are immediately available in the latest up-to-date version. Information derived from that data version is thus accurate throughout the organization.
- When applied by business experts, business normalization results in the design of databases that can accommodate the business needs of users of the data throughout the enterprise.
- Business experts use business normalization to identify potential future business changes. Databases are designed to enable those changes to be easily applied.
- This results in development of higher quality databases and systems to support current business needs; and to support future business needs as they arise.

9.2.6 Normalized Tables and Rules

We will now review some of the basic relational rules relating to tables, postulated by Ted Codd. In his research work with IBM he developed *relational theory,* the foundation of relational database management systems (RDBMS) used today. These are discussed based on the example Employee table shown in Table 9.2.

- Each column name in a table is unique, and the order of the columns in a table has no bearing on its meaning. This ensures that there is no ambiguity in identifying a relevant column within a table. Business normalization recommends that each column (i.e., attribute) have a unique name in the enterprise to avoid any ambiguity with homonyms, that is, other columns that have the same name, but that represent different data.
- Each row in a table has a unique primary key value, and so is a unique row. The Employee table shows that *Employee Number* is unique, which thus makes each Employee row unique.
- Notice that *Employee Number* in the table is in ascending sequence. This orders the rows for access purposes, but this order has no effect on the meaning of each row.

Table 9.2 Employee Table

Employee Number	*Employee Name*	*Employee Address*	*Post Code*	*Sales Quota*	*Manger Title*	*Job No.*	*Salary*
1234	J. Jones	1 First St, Anywhere	41707	2000	Northern Mgr	84	6000
1235	H. Smith	7 Sixth Ave, First Town	81900			87	3500
1236	F. Walton	40 Wax St, Hereafter	72566	1500		85	6000
1237	N. Waxle	71 Draw Blvd, Harrytown	41440	2000	Southern Mgr	84	5000
1238	P. Jensen	25 16th St, Downtown	70771			86	4000
1239	N. Noyes	15 Excel Ave, Nearby	80992	1800		85	5000
1240	Z. Zwerki	17 Second St, Anywhere	41707			86	4000
1241	A. Allons	80 Nice Ave, Great Town	09410	1800		85	5000
1242	K. Dalton	11 Haves St, Nicely	88225			87	3500

- The order of rows can be changed based on the values in specific columns of the table, by defining database indexes on those columns. Again, this ordering is for access purposes only; it has no effect on the meaning of the rows.

These relational rules are fundamental to relational database theory, to business normalization, and to traditional normalization.

9.2.7 Identifying Data as a Business Resource

Data represent a valuable business resource at all levels of a business: at the operational level, at middle management (tactical) levels, and at senior management (strategic) levels. The same data can exist in different redundant versions throughout an organization. If one version of the data is updated, all versions of the same data must be similarly updated if the data are to be accurate and consistent throughout the organization.

Information needed at middle and senior management levels is typically derived from the operational data. But if redundant versions of data are not all at the same level of update, information derived from these versions will be inconsistent. The problem with inconsistent information leads to a lack of credibility: Managers may ask which is the correct version; that is, which is derived from the correct data?

Business normalization resolves redundant data and inconsistent information problems. It identifies the data resource needed by the business. Redundant versions are combined as an integrated, nonredundant version. When updated, information derived from it is accurate and consistent and is available to all who are authorized to access it.

Business normalization uses 1BNF to 3BNF to identify data as a business resource, and to structure it in a nonredundant form where it can be shared throughout the business.

A number of case study problems follow that will enable you to test your understanding of the role of primary keys. We will then introduce the rules that are used for 1BNF to 3BNF, along with examples and problem exercises. Later sections will refine the data we identify to include greater business knowledge.

9.2.8 Case Study Problems 1 to 6

We will reinforce the principles discussed so far in six case study problems [5]. A discussion of the solution is provided in the Solutions file [6].

9.3 First Business Normal Form (1BNF)

The rule for 1BNF is expressed as follows.

First Business Normal Form (1BNF) Rule

1BNF Step 1: Identify and remove repeating group attributes to another entity.

1BNF Step 2: The primary key of this other entity is made up of a compound key, comprising the primary key of the entity in which the repeating group originally resided together with the repeating group key itself, or instead another unique key based on business needs.

1BNF Step 3: The name of the new entity initially may be based on a combination of the name of the repeating group and the name of the entity in which the repeating group resided.

1BNF Step 4: It may later be renamed according to its final attribute content after business normalization is completed.

This rule addresses repeating group attributes. The entity list notation introduced in Chapter 6 showed repeating groups surrounded by double parentheses, such as: ((repeating group)), which makes their identification easy. 1BNF involves the four steps just listed:

- Step 1 moves repeating groups into another entity.
- Step 2 determines the primary keys of that new entity.
- Steps 3 and 4 then determine the name of that new entity.

To illustrate the application of business normalization, we will use an example based on the unnormalized entity (with Legend) shown in Figure 9.11 as follows.

EMPLOYEE (*employee number#*, [name], (address), [postcode], ((skill number#, [skill name], skill level)), sales quota, [manager title], job name, salary)

LEGEND
primary key#, [selection attribute], (group attribute), {derived attribute}, nonkey attribute, ((repeating group)), foreign key#

Using entity notation (see the legend in Figure 9.11), the primary key of EMPLOYEE is *employee number#*. Selection attributes (secondary keys) are defined for *[name]*, *[postcode]*, *[skill name]*, and *[manager title]* A group attribute is defined for *(address)*, while a repeating group exists of *((skill number#, [skill name], skill level))*.

As you may remember from Chapter 6, to avoid ambiguity, attributes should be qualified by the name of the entity in which they reside. This has not been done yet in Figure 9.11. The unqualified attribute names will be used to illustrate some of the

EMPLOYEE (employee number#, [name], (address), [postcode], ((skill number#, [skill name], skill level)), sales quota, [manager title], job name, salary)

LEGEND

primary key#, [selection attribute], (group attribute), {derived attribute}, non-key attribute, ((repeating group)), foreign key#

Figure 9.11 Unnormalized entity, used as an example for business normalization.

problems that can arise. We will resolve this naming issue later in the chapter with a normalization cross-check to clarify the full attribute business meaning.

This unnormalized entity is typical of data that exist at operational business levels. We will use this example to show how the rules of business normalization can be used to identify required data attributes that need to be recorded about employees.

The entity from Figure 9.11 is also drawn as a data map in Figure 9.12. There is only one entity; the data map thus contains only one entity box—EMPLOYEE [7]. As we normalize, we will draw a data map that shows progressive normalization for each business normal form. We will see that each entity exists in two forms: as an entity list of attributes in entities and as a data map of associations between entities.

9.3.1 Example of First Business Normal Form

Applying the 1BNF rule to the unnormalized entity in Figure 9.11, the repeating group is highlighted and is moved out into a new entity, leaving EMPLOYEE below. The repeating group is *((skill number#, [skill name], skill level))*. It has a key of *skill number#*. The repeating group identifies skills of an employee. This key is combined with the original primary key, *employee number#*. The new entity is called EMPLOYEE SKILL. We can use a different business name for this entity if we wish, as discussed in Chapter 6. Entity names should always be singular.

EMPLOYEE (*employee number#*, [name], (address), [postcode], sales quota, [manager title], job name, salary)

EMPLOYEE SKILL (*employee number#*, *skill number#*, [skill name], skill level)

The original entity has now expanded into two entities; both are shown in the data map in Figure 9.13. As *employee number#* is a common key to both entities, an association line is drawn joining them. At the EMPLOYEE end, *employee number#* is the entire primary key; the association degree and nature is therefore drawn as *mandatory one,* touching EMPLOYEE.

At EMPLOYEE SKILL, *employee number#* is part of a compound key; the association degree is thus *many*. Definition of the association nature now depends on

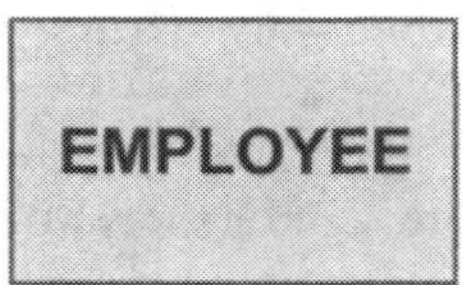

Figure 9.12 Data map of unnormalized entity.

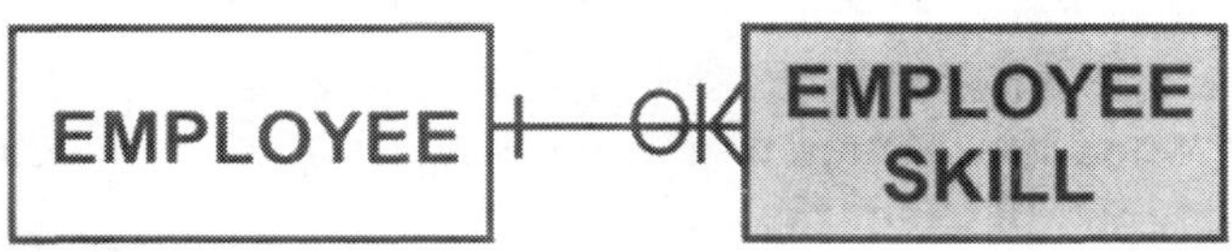

Figure 9.13 Data map of 1BNF entities.

business rules. Here, the data map shows the rule of *optional becoming mandatory many*, to represent the business rule that "skills **will** eventually be gained by many employees (such as through training)."

The entities and data map are now said to be "in First Business Normal Form (1BNF)."

9.3.2 Case Study Problem 7: Normalization Preparation and 1BNF

We are now ready to do Case Study Problems 7 and 8. Problem 7 analyzes an existing document—a restaurant receipt—to prepare it for normalization. Problem 8 normalizes the result to 1BNF [8].

9.4 Second Business Normal Form (2BNF)

The rule for 2BNF is shown next.

Second Business Normal Form (2BNF) Rule

> *2BNF Step 1:* Identify and remove to another entity those attributes which are only partially dependent on the primary key and also dependent on one or more other key attributes, **or** ...
>
> *2BNF Step 2:* which are dependent on only part of the compound key and possibly one or more other key attributes.

This rule addresses the partial dependency of attributes on the primary key:

- Step 1 identifies attributes that depend on the primary key—and also on other key attributes. It moves those attributes into an entity where *all* of those key attributes comprise the entire compound primary key.
- Step 2 examines attributes that reside in entities with a compound primary key, but where the attributes depend on only part of that compound key—and also perhaps on other key attributes—and moves those attributes into an entity where *all* of those key attributes comprise the entire compound primary key [9].

The application of this 2BNF rule is often achieved by first identifying all compound key entities and then applying Step 2 to those compound key entities. Step 1 is then applied by looking at entities with only one primary key.

9.4.1 Example of Second Business Normal Form

We will start with EMPLOYEE in 1BNF. Applying the 2BNF rule, we will use Step 2 first to examine the compound key entity: EMPLOYEE SKILL earlier, after IBNF. We will look at each of the attributes in turn.

- *Skill level* is the level of a skill held by an employee. It is dependent on both key attributes and does not satisfy the 2BNF rule. It remains in EMPLOYEE SKILL.

  EMPLOYEE SKILL (*employee number#*, *skill number#*, skill level)

- *Skill name* depends only on *skill number#*. It is not at all dependent on *employee number#*. It satisfies the 2BNF rule and so is moved into a new entity SKILL.

  SKILL (*skill number#*, [skill name])

- Other attributes in EMPLOYEE also satisfy the first part of the 2BNF rule (in particular *salary*). We will make a deliberate error and overlook *salary* in this 2BNF example. This can happen unintentionally in real life. Later in this chapter we will see how we can detect this deliberate "error" and correct it.

EMPLOYEE SKILL now contains only attributes that depend on the entire compound primary key, and so is in 2BNF. The 2BNF result is shown next.

EMPLOYEE (*employee number#*, [name], (address), [postcode], sales quota, [manager title], job name, salary)

EMPLOYEE SKILL (*employee number#*, *skill number#*, skill level)

SKILL (*skill number#*, [skill name])

9.4.2 Second Business Normal Form Data Map

EMPLOYEE is in 2BNF above. We will develop this as a 2BNF data map in Figure 9.14, in which there are three entities. We draw three entity boxes in a row. The compound key entity EMPLOYEE SKILL is named as the center entity. The left entity is named EMPLOYEE; the right entity is named SKILL.

- EMPLOYEE and EMPLOYEE SKILL have a common key: *employee number#*. These two entities are therefore joined with a line to represent an association. *Employee number#* is the entire primary key of EMPLOYEE, so the degree and nature at EMPLOYEE is *mandatory one*. Because *employee number#* is part of the EMPLOYEE SKILL compound key, the association degree at EMPLOYEE SKILL is *many*. Its nature depends on business rules: We will use *optional becoming mandatory* to show that "an employee who has no skills will eventually gain, or learn, skills through training."

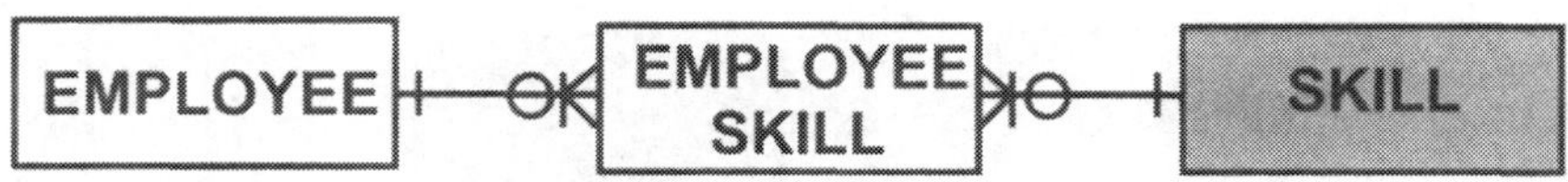

Figure 9.14 2BNF EMPLOYEE, EMPLOYEE SKILL, and SKILL entities.

- Similarly, SKILL and EMPLOYEE SKILL have a common key (*skill number#*) and so are joined. *Skill number#* is the primary key of SKILL so the degree and nature at SKILL is *mandatory one*. *Skill number#* is part of the compound key of EMPLOYEE SKILL, so the association degree at EMPLOYEE SKILL is *many*. Its nature depends on business rules: We will use *optional becoming mandatory* to show "a skill will be gained, or learned, by employees through training."

9.4.3 Alternative Normalization Approaches

Consider now how we developed data maps in Chapter 6. Using the top data map shown in Figure 9.15, the EMPLOYEE to SKILL *many-to-many* association is decomposed to an intersecting entity EMPLOYEE SKILL with two *one-to-many* associations as shown in the bottom data map.

We can now see that the decomposition of a *many-to-many* association is a schematic application of the first two rules of normalization. The intersecting entity EMPLOYEE SKILL resolves the *many-to-many* association, and is graphically analogous to:

- Moving out a repeating group of attributes to EMPLOYEE SKILL (1BNF);
- Moving out partially dependent attributes into another entity—SKILL (2BNF).

Data mapping and business normalization, used together in logical data modeling, become a powerful combination that is used to identify and structure data as a business resource:

- After business normalization, all normalized entities are drawn in a data map.
- Each end of an association is evaluated for business rules: whether *one* or *many* in degree; and *mandatory* or *optional* or *optional becoming mandatory* nature.
- Any *many-to-many* associations are resolved by adding an intersecting entity.
- Other attributes of this entity are then identified, added, and further normalized.

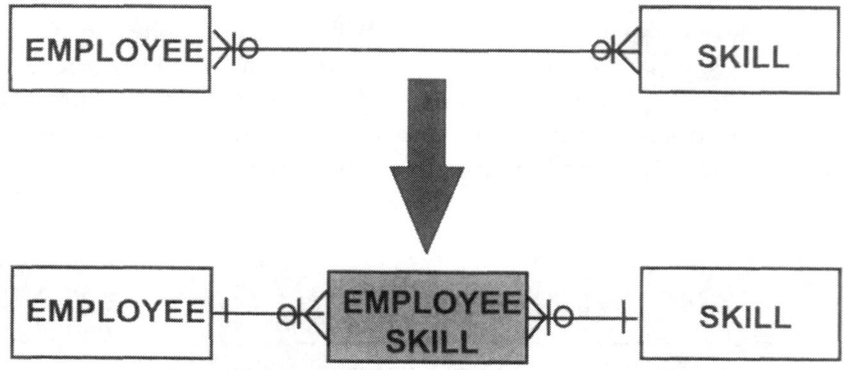

Figure 9.15 Decomposition of many-to-many applies to 1BNF and 2BNF.

Later in the chapter we will see how these complementary steps of data mapping and business normalization are used to structure data that are needed by the business now. We will also see how they are used to identify data potentially needed for the future, based on anticipated business changes. *This will enable us to design for the future.*

We were graphically able to normalize the EMPLOYEE and SKILL data map in Figure 9.15 because we knew of the existence of both entities and the *many-to-many* association between them. But what if we only knew of the SKILL entity? Data mapping would not have helped us to identify the existence of employees.

Business normalization helps us in this instance:

1. We must first identify all of the attributes of SKILL:

   SKILL (*skill number#*, [skill name], ((employee number#, employee name, skill level)))

2. In 1BNF, we move the repeating group to a new entity:

   EMPLOYEE SKILL (*skill number#, employee number#,* employee name, employee skill level)

3. This leaves behind the attributes of SKILL:

   SKILL (*skill number#*, [skill name])

4. The data map of these two entities, SKILL and EMPLOYEE SKILL, is now shown in Figure 9.16.

The association degree and nature at SKILL is *mandatory one,* because it has only a single primary key: *skill number#*. The association degree at EMPLOYEE SKILL is *many,* because *skill number#* is part of a compound primary key. The nature is *optional becoming mandatory,* based on the business rule that "skills will eventually have employees trained in them."

Developing this SKILL example further, we now apply 2BNF:

5. We identify attributes in the compound key entity EMPLOYEE SKILL that depend on only part of the compound key (Step 2 of 2BNF):

   EMPLOYEE SKILL (*skill number#*, *employee number#*, employee name, employee skill level)

6. For example, employee name depends only on *employee number#*; it is not at all dependent on the other part of the primary key, *skill number#*. We therefore will move it to a new entity, called EMPLOYEE:

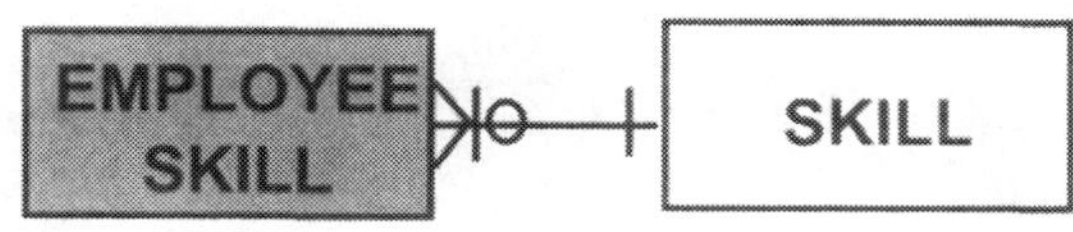

Figure 9.16 Applying the 1BNF Rule to SKILL.

EMPLOYEE (*employee number#*, employee name)

7. This leaves behind the remaining attributes of EMPLOYEE SKILL:

   EMPLOYEE SKILL (*skill number#*, *employee number#*, employee skill level)

8. We add this entity EMPLOYEE also to the data map as shown in Figure 9.17.

- The association degree and nature at EMPLOYEE is *mandatory one*, because it has only a single primary key, *employee number#*.
- The association degree at EMPLOYEE SKILL is *many*, because *employee number#* is part of a compound primary key. The nature is *optional becoming mandatory*, based on the business rule that "an employee will eventually be trained in skills."

We now see another powerful characteristic of business normalization:

- *It does not matter where we start;* we will always achieve the same result if we have access to expert business knowledge of the meaning of the data. Additional EMPLOYEE attributes (both qualitative and quantitative) can then be identified.

But haven't we overlooked an important principle? You will remember in Chapter 6 that we discussed how attribute names are qualified by the name of the entities in which they reside. We did not question the attribute names in this example. We accepted attribute names as defined in the original unnormalized entity. For example, *name* and *address* might previously have been (incorrectly) assumed to refer to the customer that each employee is responsible for, and interpreted to mean the *customer name* and *customer address*. We would not even have been aware of this erroneous assumption, because there have been no questions about the meaning of any attributes. By applying the attribute qualification principle just discussed, the attribute names have now been changed as follows:

EMPLOYEE (*employee number#*, [employee name], (employee address), [employee postcode], employee sales quota, [employee manager title], job name, salary)

EMPLOYEE SKILL (*employee number#*, *skill number#*, employee skill level)

SKILL (*skill number#*, [skill name])

The EMPLOYEE attributes are all prefixed by *employee*. It is now clear that we are referring to *employee name* and *employee address*, not a customer. We are also

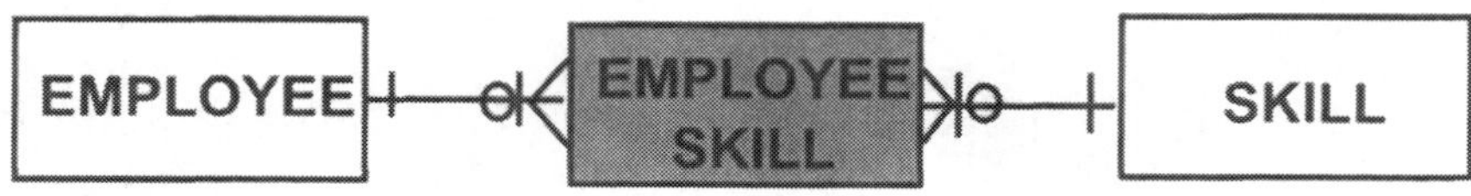

Figure 9.17 Applying the 2BNF Rule to SKILL.

interested in the *employee skill level* in EMPLOYEE SKILL. But we deliberately have not yet changed *salary* to *employee salary*. We will examine *salary* in more detail next.

9.4.4 Identification of Homonyms and Synonyms

We will now see how the attribute qualification rule helps us to identify several attributes based on *salary*. We will ask a number of questions that help us to resolve its meaning:

- What does *salary* in EMPLOYEE represent?
  - If it is *employee salary,* it belongs in EMPLOYEE, defined as:

    The salary that is paid regularly to an employee for work performed.
  - But if it is *job salary,* it belongs in a new entity, JOB, defined as:

    The salary that is paid regularly to any employee for work performed in a specific job.
  - If it is *employee job salary,* it belongs in another new entity, EMPLOYEE JOB, defined as:

    The salary that is paid regularly to an employee for work performed by that employee in a specific job.
  - If it is *employee skill salary* or even *employee skill level salary,* both of these belong in EMPLOYEE SKILL, defined as:

    The salary that is paid regularly to an employee for work performed based on the skills (and the level of those skills) held by that employee.

This attribute qualification rule uncovers homonyms and also synonyms, defined as follows:

- *Homonym:* The same name used to refer to different data;
- *Synonyms:* Different names used to refer to the same data.

We can see that this naming rule helps us to clarify the meaning of the attribute, place it in an entity where it is wholly dependent on the entire primary key, and then qualify that attribute with the name of the final entity in which it resides.

It also helps us identify the possible existence of other entities that we previously had not considered, such as JOB and EMPLOYEE JOB. We will look at these possibilities next.

In fact, by applying the attribute qualification rule to *salary* in EMPLOYEE, we can identify *14 homonyms*. The first 7 of these homonyms are as follows:

- *employee salary ...* in EMPLOYEE;
- *job salary ...* in a new entity called JOB;
- *employee job salary ...* in a new entity called EMPLOYEE JOB;
- *skill salary ...* in SKILL;
- *job skill salary ...* in a new entity called JOB SKILL;

- *employee skill salary* ... in EMPLOYEE SKILL;
- employee skill level salary ... in EMPLOYEE SKILL.

This rule also uncovers another seven *salary history* homonyms that are also dependent on time:

- *employee salary history, job salary history,* or *employee job salary history* in EMPLOYEE HISTORY, JOB HISTORY, or EMPLOYEE JOB HISTORY entities.
- *skill salary history* or *job skill salary history* in SKILL HISTORY or JOB SKILL HISTORY entities.
- *employee skill salary history* or *employee skill level salary history* in the entity EMPLOYEE SKILL HISTORY.

This has identified entities and possibilities for the future that we had not considered. At this stage we will not decide which of these *salary* attributes are required. We will let it remain as *salary* and consider it again during the cross-check later in the chapter.

9.4.5 Case Study Problem 9: 2BNF

We will now do another exercise based on the restaurant receipt example that we used in earlier case study problems. Take a moment to review again the receipt form in the diagram associated with Case Study Problem 7. We normalized this to 1BNF in Case Study Problem 8. We will normalize it to 2BNF in Case Study Problem 9 [10].

9.5 Third Business Normal Form (3BNF)

The rule for 3BNF is shown next:

Third Business Normal Form (3BNF) Rule

- *3BNF Step 1:* Identify and remove into another entity those attributes which are dependent on a key other than the primary (or compound) key.

The 3BNF rule identifies attributes that are not at all dependent on the primary key of the entity in which they reside. It identifies those attributes that were originally placed in the wrong entity. This may have been because the meaning of the attribute was not clear from the original attribute name. These attributes should therefore be moved to other entities where they are wholly dependent on the entire primary key. If necessary, the attributes should be renamed, perhaps by qualifying them with the new entity name in which they reside, so that their meaning is clear.

The following examples illustrate the application of this 3BNF rule.

9.5.1 Example of Third Business Normal Form

We will continue with the EMPLOYEE entity. We earlier left it in 2BNF as follows:

EMPLOYEE (*employee number#*, [employee name], (employee address), [employee postcode], employee sales quota, [employee manager title], job name, salary)

We now examine each of the attributes in turn, to decide if each attribute wholly depends on the primary key *employee number#*.

- The attributes [employee name], (employee address), [employee postcode], employee sales quota, and [employee manager title] all describe the employee. They are wholly dependent on *employee number#* and so do not satisfy 3BNF.
- But what about *job name?* Is it dependent on *employee number#?*
- No; a job is not named because of the specific employee in that job. In fact it is not at all dependent on *employee number#*. It thus satisfies the 3BNF rule. It is wholly dependent on *job number#* and so is moved into a new entity JOB:

  JOB (*job number#*, job name)

However, so that we still know the job held by each employee, we must replace *job name* in EMPLOYEE now with a foreign key to JOB; that is, *job number#* in **bold** next:

EMPLOYEE (*employee number#*, [employee name], (employee address), [employee postcode], employee sales quota, [employee manager title], **job number#,** salary)

EMPLOYEE and JOB are now joined by the common key *job number#*.

9.5.2 Third Business Normal Form Data Map

We will now add the new entity to the 2BNF data map, producing the 3BNF data map shown in Figure 9.18.

- EMPLOYEE and JOB both have a common key, *job number#*. This is the primary key of JOB. It is a foreign key in EMPLOYEE.
- JOB is thus placed close to EMPLOYEE. An association line joins them.

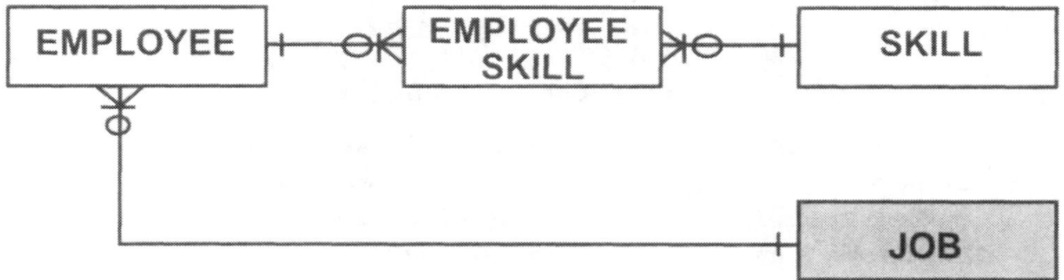

Figure 9.18 Example data map in 3BNF.

- The association degree and nature at JOB is shown as *mandatory one*—because job number# is the primary key of JOB.
- The association degree at EMPLOYEE is shown as *many*—because *job number#* is a foreign key of EMPLOYEE.
- The association nature at EMPLOYEE depends on the business rules:

  May a job remain vacant? If so, the association nature is *optional.*

  Must a job always be filled? If so, the association nature is *mandatory.*

  Will a job eventually be filled? If so, the association nature is drawn as *optional becoming mandatory*. We chose this rule for the data map.

The result is a data map that represents the 3BNF entities. The entity list and data map are both therefore said to be in 3BNF.

9.5.3 Case Study Problem 10: 3BNF

We will now do the final exercise in this section. This is based on the restaurant receipt example that we used earlier in Case Study Problems 7, 8, and 9. Take a moment again to review the receipt form in Case Study Problem 7.

We have already normalized the receipt to 1BNF and 2BNF. We will normalize it to 3BNF [11].

9.6 Identifying Current and Future Business Needs

This section refines the Third Business Normal Form entities we have identified so far. It evaluates whether current business needs are supported by the data that have been uncovered. It uses business normalization to anticipate potential future business needs [12].

- A *normalization* cross-check is applied to the entities normalized to 3BNF, to confirm the accuracy and business flexibility of normalization to this point.
- The *Fourth Business Normal Form (4BNF)* rule is then introduced to uncover additional business meaning. This identifies subtype and supertype entities.
- We will later refine these business entities further—by capturing expert business knowledge using the *Fifth Business Normal Form (5BNF).*

We will now use a normalization cross-check to identify current and future business needs.

9.6.1 Normalization Cross-Check of Employee

With the Employee entities in 3BNF, we now apply a cross-checking step. This examines the accuracy of normalization. It assesses the flexibility to support future business needs. *It helps the organization to design for the future.*

To this point we have applied each business normalization rule in turn to all entities. The normalization cross-check now applies *all three rules* to *each attribute* in turn. We will examine attributes in the 3BNF EMPLOYEE entity to illustrate its application:

> EMPLOYEE (*employee number#*, [employee name], (employee address), [employee postcode], employee sales quota, [employee manager title], job number#, salary)

We will start by cross-checking normalization of the *employee name* attribute.

We apply the 1BNF, 2BNF, and 3BNF rules all in turn to this attribute. The relevant questions are asked below and then discussed:

- Is *employee name* a repeating group (i.e., 1BNF)?
- Is *employee name* only partially dependent on *employee number#* (2BNF)?
- Is *employee name not* dependent at all on *employee number#* (3BNF)?

Each question is repeated below. Answers for 1BNF, 2BNF, and 3BNF rules, applied in turn to the *employee name* attribute, are then discussed.

- Is *employee name* a repeating group (i.e., 1BNF)? For example, a name can be changed by marriage. We can update to the new name, but do we also need to keep previous names in a separate EMPLOYEE NAME entity? Do we need a record of other changes also for the employee? These would all be held in EMPLOYEE HISTORY, with a compound primary key of, say, *employee number#*, *date of change#*.
- Is *employee name* only partially dependent on *employee number#* (2BNF)? For example, who is employee 75? If *employee number#* is unique, we need no other information. But if we must also know the branch office for the employee, it is unique only to each branch office. *Employee name* is moved to BRANCH EMPLOYEE with the keys *employee number#*, *branch office#*. We also need a BRANCH OFFICE entity.
- Is *employee name not* dependent on *employee number#* at all (3BNF)? This is unlikely, but if it is correct then *employee name* is moved from EMPLOYEE to another entity—where it depends on the entire key of that entity.
- If the preceding answers do apply for the future, after this normalization cross-check we may need to add the following new entities:

  EMPLOYEE NAME and/or EMPLOYEE HISTORY

  BRANCH OFFICE and BRANCH EMPLOYEE

Continuing our normalization cross-check of the EMPLOYEE entity:

> EMPLOYEE (*employee number#*, [employee name], (employee address), [employee postcode], employee sales quota, [employee manager title], job number#, salary)

We will now apply all three rules to the next attribute, *employee address*.

- Is *employee address* a repeating group (i.e., 1BNF)? For example, do we need the home address and one (or more) work addresses for each employee?
- Does employee address partially depend on *employee number#* (i.e., 2BNF)?
- Can more than one employee reside at the same address? Is this an important fact to know?
- Is *employee address not* dependent on *employee number#* at all (i.e., 3BNF)?

These same questions also apply to *[employee postcode]* as part of *employee address* but it is defined as a selection attribute (secondary key). This will permit later access of the EMPLOYEE database table by postcode or zip code. The various answers to these cross-checking *address* questions are discussed next:

- Is *employee address* a repeating group (i.e., 1BNF)? For example, do we need the home address and one (or more) work addresses for each employee? If *employee address* is a repeating group we will need a new entity EMPLOYEE ADDRESS with a compound primary key: *employee number#, address id#,* for instance.
- Does *employee address* partially depend on *employee number#* (i.e., 2BNF)?
- If *employee address* depends on *employee number#* and *date#,* for instance, do we need a history of past addresses for an employee?
- If so, we will need a new entity: EMPLOYEE ADDRESS HISTORY with a compound primary key of *employee number#, address id #, date#*.
- Is *employee address* not dependent on *employee number#* at all (i.e., 3BNF)? For example, if a branch manager has a company-provided house, this address is known and would be an attribute of BRANCH: It does not depend at all on *employee number#*. Because a manager is an employee, we must copy the company house address (while at that branch) also to the manager's *employee address* in EMPLOYEE. Employee address is still required.
- Can more than one employee reside at the same residence?
- If so, we would need EMPLOYEE ADDRESS with a compound primary key of *employee number#, address id#*.
- Therefore, the new entities identified from this cross-check are:

  BRANCH OFFICE, EMPLOYEE ADDRESS, EMPLOYEE ADDRESS HISTORY

We continue our normalization cross-check of the EMPLOYEE entity further:

EMPLOYEE (*employee number#,* [employee name], (employee address), [employee postcode], employee sales quota, [employee manager title], job number#, salary)

We will cover *employee sales quota* and *[employee manager title]* later in this section, so we will defer any discussion of them here. We now apply all three rules to the foreign key attribute of *job number#:*

- Is *job number#* a repeating group (i.e., 1BNF)? For example, can an employee have more than one job at a time?
- Does *job number#* depend on *employee number#* and something else (i.e., 2BNF)? For example, can an employee have several jobs *over time*?
- Is *job number# not* at all dependent on *employee number#* (i.e., 3BNF)?

The various answers to these questions are considered next. Continuing our cross-check of *job number#* in EMPLOYEE:

- Is *job number#* a repeating group (i.e., 1BNF)? For example, can an employee have more than one job at a time? If *job number#* is a repeating group, we will need a new entity EMPLOYEE JOB, with *employee number#, job number#* as a compound primary key.
- Does *job number#* depend on *employee number#* and also something else (i.e., 2BNF)? For example, can an employee have several jobs over time? If *job number#* is dependent on both *employee number#* and *date#,* do we need a record of previous jobs for each employee in Employee Job History? If so, we will need a new entity: EMPLOYEE JOB HISTORY with *employee number#, job number#, date#* as the compound primary key.
- Is *job number# not* dependent at all on *employee number#* (i.e., 3BNF)? This is unlikely, because it provides information about each employee, in this case the current job for the employee with the relevant *employee number#.*
- Therefore, the new entities identified from this cross-check are:

  EMPLOYEE JOB and EMPLOYEE JOB HISTORY

We now see the power of this normalization cross-check: *It raises many questions that we may not previously have asked.* It forces us to decide whether the new entities we identified should be added to support our needs now or to support our needs in the future. If they are relevant, we can accommodate these current or future needs in the data models that we develop now, to support database needs for today and tomorrow.

From the cross-check, the most obvious refinement is that an employee can have many jobs—over time, and perhaps also at the same time. That is, the foreign key *job number#* is a repeating group. It is, therefore, moved to a new entity EMPLOYEE JOB:

EMPLOYEE (*employee number#,* [employee name], (employee address), [employee postcode], employee sales quota, [employee manager title], salary)

EMPLOYEE JOB (*employee number#, job number#*)

JOB (*job number#,* job name)

The common key *employee number#*—between EMPLOYEE and EMPLOYEE JOB—thus allows us, for a given employee, to determine all jobs held by that employee.

We normally would immediately add the new entity EMPLOYEE JOB to the data map of 3BNF Employee entities. We will do that shortly. First we will finish cross-checking the remaining EMPLOYEE attributes.

9.6.2 What About Future Salary Needs?

The final EMPLOYEE attribute to be cross-checked is *salary.* In our earlier discussion of *salary,* we identified 14 homonyms (see Section 9.4.4). This identified the seven homonyms [13] as follows:

- *employee salary, job salary, employee job salary, skill salary, job skill salary, employee skill salary, employee skill level salary.*

This rule also uncovers another seven *salary history* homonyms dependent on time:

- *employee salary history, job salary history,* or *employee job salary history.*
- *skill salary history* or *job skill salary history.*
- *employee skill salary history* or *employee skill level salary history.*

We deferred making an earlier decision about these homonyms. Now is the time for such a decision. We will see that even if we missed some homonyms then, we would identify them now, as part of the normalization cross-check.

9.6.3 Accommodating Employee Job Salary

Applying the normalization cross-check to *salary,* we realize it is a repeating group (i.e., 1BNF). It was erroneously not shown with double parentheses as ((*salary*)) in the original unnormalized entity. We have now identified that omission from the cross-check:

> EMPLOYEE (*employee number#,* [employee name], (employee address), [employee postcode], employee sales quota, [employee manager title], job number#, ((salary)))
>
> JOB (*job number#,* job name)

The homonyms that were discussed also suggested this error. Which are relevant?

- If each job has a standard salary, this would be *job salary.* We should add this as a new attribute to JOB:

  JOB (*job number#,* job name, job salary)

- The salary may not be fixed for all employees in the same job; that is, it may vary—based on an employee's age, skill, or seniority—as *employee job salary.* We also should add this as a new attribute to EMPLOYEE JOB. If it may change over time, we should add *date#* as part of the compound primary key:

EMPLOYEE JOB (*employee number#*, *job number#*, *date#*, employee job salary)

The entity EMPLOYEE JOB exists between EMPLOYEE and JOB. It is clear that *job name* and *salary* in the original unnormalized EMPLOYEE entity were both repeating—as ((*job name, salary*)). *Job name* later became *job number#,* but should have been a repeating foreign key: ((*job number#*)). *Salary* became *job salary* and *employee job salary*. The normalization cross-check has corrected these errors. We can see that EMPLOYEE JOB is an intersecting entity.

9.6.4 Result of Business Normalization Cross-Check

We removed the repeating foreign key of ((*job number#*)) from EMPLOYEE. We then added attributes to EMPLOYEE JOB and JOB. These entities are now:

EMPLOYEE (*employee number#*, [employee name], (employee address), [employee postcode], employee sales quota, [employee manager title])

EMPLOYEE JOB (*employee number#*, *job number#*, *date#*, employee job salary)

JOB (*job number#*, job name, job salary)

We will now add EMPLOYEE JOB to the 3BNF data map developed in Figure 9.18. This entity has a compound primary key of *employee number#*, *job number#*. It is shown as EMPLOYEE JOB between EMPLOYEE and JOB. The result is shown in Figure 9.19.

- *Employee number#* is the common key in EMPLOYEE and EMPLOYEE JOB. An association line is drawn with *mandatory one* at EMPLOYEE (for the single primary key) and *many* at EMPLOYEE JOB (for the compound key). The degree is shown as *optional becoming mandatory,* for the business rule that "an employee will eventually be allocated a job after training."
- *Job number#* is the common key between JOB and EMPLOYEE JOB. The association is *mandatory one* at JOB (for the single primary key) and *many* at EMPLOYEE JOB (for the compound key). It is *optional becoming mandatory* to show the rule that "a job will eventually be filled by an employee after training."

Figure 9.19 3BNF data map after normalization cross-check.

9.6.5 Summary for Third Business Normal Form

An easy and memorable summary of 3BNF can be stated as:

> An attribute is moved to an entity where it is dependent on the key, the whole key, and nothing but the key, so help me, Codd.

Business normalization applies business knowledge to ensure that each attribute resides in an entity where it is *wholly dependent on the entire primary key* of that entity. The following conditions must all be satisfied:

- No attribute in the entity can be a repeating group (i.e., 1BNF).
- No attribute can depend on only part of a compound primary key, or on any other key attributes in addition to the entire primary key (i.e., 2BNF).
- No attribute can depend on a key other than the primary key (i.e., 3BNF).

Therefore to be in 3BNF, all the attributes in each entity must all be wholly dependent on the entire primary key of that entity.

9.6.6 Case Study Problem 11: Normalization Cross-Check

After this *Close Encounter of the Third Business Normal Form,* we are now ready to apply the normalization cross-check to the restaurant receipt entities in the case study problems. This is covered in Case Study Problem 11 [14].

9.7 Fourth Business Normal Form (4BNF)

We are now ready to consider the next normalization rule: 4BNF. This is defined as follows:

Fourth Business Normal Form (4BNF) Rule

> *4BNF Step 1:* An entity is said to be in Fourth Business Normal Form when it is in Third Business Normal Form, and its attributes depend not only on the entire primary (compound key), but also on the value of the key, or on 4BNF Step 2.
>
> *4BNF Step 2:* when an attribute has been relocated from an entity where it is optional, instead to an entity where it is wholly dependent on the key and must exist, and so is mandatory.

This rule helps us to identify detailed entities that include greater business meaning.

- The first part of the 4BNF rule identifies attributes that are dependent only on certain values of the primary key. This is called *value dependency.* An example of value dependency was used many years ago in banking. One block of account numbers was allocated for savings accounts while a different block of account numbers was allocated for checking (i.e., trading) accounts. The type of account could only be determined from the account number value.

- The second part of the 4BNF rule identifies optional attributes. This occurs often and is a useful starting point for identifying 4BNF entities.

The 4BNF rule enables us to identify subtype entities and supertype entities, which are discussed next.

9.7.1 Example of Fourth Business Normal Form

We will illustrate 4BNF using EMPLOYEE (3BNF):

EMPLOYEE (*employee number#*, [employee name], (employee address), [postcode], employee sales quota, [employee manager title])

Using Step 2 of 4BNF first, we examine each attribute. We ask if each attribute applies to some (but not all) employees; that is, if it is *optional.* Two attributes satisfy this question:

- An *employee sales quota* exists only for employees who are *salespersons.* This attribute is therefore moved into a new entity SALESPERSON:

  SALESPERSON (*employee number#*, salesperson quota)

- An *employee manager title* exists only for employees who are *managers.* This attribute is also moved into a new entity MANAGER:

  MANAGER (*employee number#*, [manager title])

- The primary key is *employee number#* for each entity. The two attribute names have also been changed so they are qualified by their new entity names.

Because we have identified two types of employees, we must also add the Type entity EMPLOYEE TYPE:

EMPLOYEE TYPE (*employee type number#*, employee type name)

- *Employee type number#* must also be added to EMPLOYEE as a foreign key:

  EMPLOYEE (*employee number#*, [employee name], (employee address), [postcode], *employee type number#*)

The completed 4BNF entity list is shown as follows:

EMPLOYEE TYPE (*employee type number#*, employee type name)

EMPLOYEE (*employee number#*, [employee name], (employee address), [postcode], employee type number#)

SALESPERSON (*employee number#*, salesperson quota)

MANAGER (*employee number#*, [manager title])

9.7.2 Fourth Business Normal Form Data Map

The data map for the 4BNF EMPLOYEE entities just discussed is shown in Figure 9.20. Because [Employee name], (employee address), and [postcode] exist for all employees:

- EMPLOYEE is drawn first. EMPLOYEE TYPE is drawn to its left, and joined by a line because of the common key *employee type number#*. The association degree is *mandatory one* at EMPLOYEE TYPE and *optional becoming mandatory many* at EMPLOYEE.
- Referring back to Chapter 6, it is now clear that:

  EMPLOYEE is, in fact, a *principal* entity.
  EMPLOYEE TYPE is, in fact, a *type* entity.
- SALESPERSON and MANAGER are then drawn below EMPLOYEE. Because *employee number#* is a common primary key to these three entities, the degree and nature of the association is *mandatory one* at EMPLOYEE. It is *optional one* at SALESPERSON and also at MANAGER. It is therefore now clear that SALESPERSON and MANAGER are both secondary entities
- Secondary entities are called *subtypes;* principal entities are called *supertypes.*

Additional attributes may also be needed for the new entities. These may in turn lead to the identification of further secondary (subtype) entities to be added to the 4BNF data map.

9.7.3 Case Study Problem 12: 4BNF

We have already normalized to 3BNF in Case Study Problem 10. We did the normalization cross-check in Case Study Problem 11. But we will not use the additional entities identified in that cross-check; we will instead utilize the 3BNF entities from Case Study Problem 10 and then normalize to 4BNF [15].

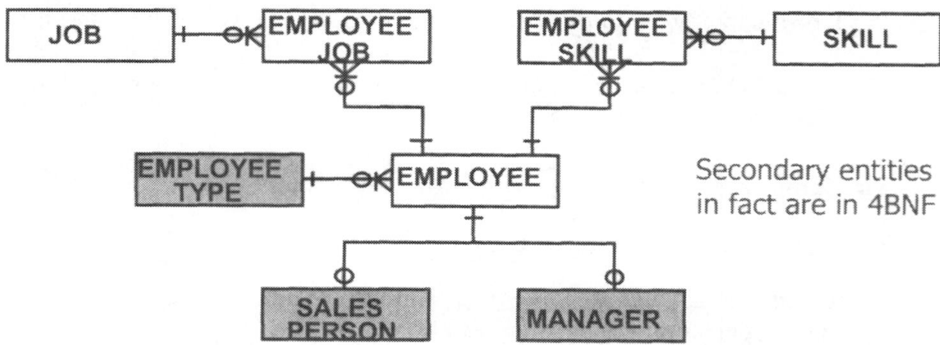

Figure 9.20 4BNF data map for 4BNF entities.

9.8 Capturing Expert Business Knowledge

This section covers the capture of expert business knowledge in a data model using Fifth Business Normal Form (5BNF). The 5BNF rule is first introduced to show its format and use for recording expert business knowledge. Several 5BNF examples are discussed, showing how 5BNF can be used to represent expert knowledge efficiently for a number of business applications. Finally, an exercise problem on 5BNF allows you to test your understanding.

9.8.1 Fifth Business Normal Form (5BNF)

5BNF is quite different from 5NF as used by traditional normalization. 5NF is also called "Project-Join" normal form. In nontechnical terms, 5NF ensures that if each attribute is separated out into an individual entity, these entities can later be joined again to produce the original entity. 5BNF is different. It enables expert business knowledge to be identified and captured so that it can be stored, managed, and accessed efficiently for business benefit. The definition of 5BNF follows:

Fifth Business Normal Form (5BNF) Rule

- *5BNF Step 1*: Identify any principal entity that has a recursive association to itself.
- *5BNF Step 2:* Identify any principal entity that has secondary entities related to each other in *one-to-many* or *many-to-many* associations
- *5BNF Step 3:* Add a structure entity, with a *one-to-many* association from the principal entity to the structure entity, named from the principal entity with an added prefix of "Related" or a suffix of "Structure."

This rule helps us to identify expert business knowledge. It shows how knowledge is captured in a data model for later database access. We earlier saw that 1BNF through 4BNF dependencies apply to *every* occurrence of *all* related entities. In contrast, 5BNF identifies dependencies or relationships that exist between only *some occurrences* of the same entity or entity type. Where they exist, these dependencies or relationships may be due to common related factors outside the scope of the data model. This is generally due to expert knowledge held by individuals or groups of people, or instead due to expert rules that apply.

The 5BNF rule enables us to identify *structure* entities, which are discussed next.

9.8.2 Example of Fifth Business Normal Form

You no doubt remember the format of *structure* entities, which we earlier covered in Chapter 6 [16]. Three alternative formats were introduced in that chapter. We will consider the most flexible format for EMPLOYEE STRUCTURE, as shown next:

EMPLOYEE STRUCTURE (*employee number#*, *employee type number#*, *rel employee number#*, *rel employee type number#*, relationship reason)

This Employee Structure format shows that an employee with an *employee number#* and *employee type number#* is related to another employee who has the same, or a different *related employee number#*, with the same, or a different *related employee type number#*. The relationship between these employee occurrences is based on a common factor, as indicated by *relationship reason*.

A further alternative with even greater flexibility uses a separate REASON entity, as shown in Figure 9.21. This uses *reason id#* as a foreign key in EMPLOYEE STRUCTURE.

EMPLOYEE STRUCTURE (*employee number#*, *employee type number#*, *rel employee number#*, *rel employee type number#*, reason id#)

REASON (*reason id#*, relationship reason)

This format enables any number of *relationship reason*(s) to be used in the separate REASON entity, each identified by *reason id#* and referenced by *reason id#* as a foreign key in EMPLOYEE STRUCTURE.

EMPLOYEE STRUCTURE is shown as a 5BNF entity in the data map of Figure 9.21, also including REASON [17]. This clearly shows that the structure entities we discussed in Chapter 6 are in fact 5BNF entities.

Alternatively we may use RELATED EMPLOYEE as the entity name. This may be a more meaningful name than EMPLOYEE STRUCTURE. In addition, notice in Figure 9.21 that only one association line is drawn between principal and structure entities in a data map. As can be seen by *relationship reason* (or *reason id#*) in the EMPLOYEE STRUCTURE entity, this single line represents far more relationships than can be drawn as multiple association lines on a data map.

9.8.3 Examples of 5BNF Entities: Employee Structure

EMPLOYEE STRUCTURE is best discussed by using typical employee values. The complete 5BNF table will be developed over the next few figures to illustrate. It is established from the EMPLOYEE STRUCTURE format as shown in Figure 9.22.

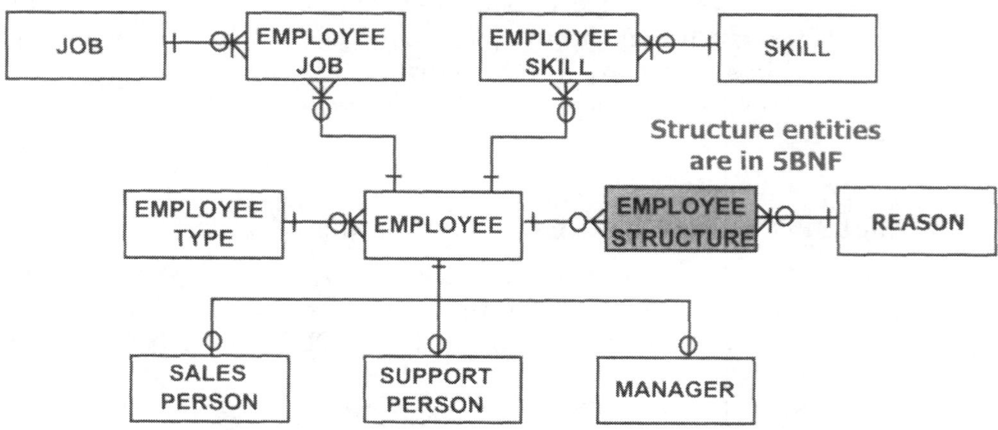

Figure 9.21 Data map showing a typical 5BNF entity.

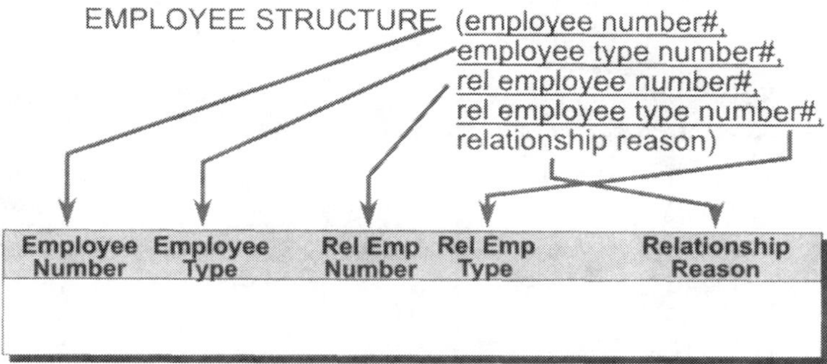

■ For readability, we will use *Employee Type Name* and *Rel Emp Type Name*, rather than *Employee Type Number* and *Rel Employee Type Number*

Figure 9.22 Format of EMPLOYEE STRUCTURE 5BNF entity.

- *Employee number#* is the first column of the table—Employee Number.
- *Employee type number#* is the second column of the table—Employee Type. However as discussed in Chapter 6 we will use *Employee Type Name* values instead. Rather than show an actual value of "2" in *Employee Type Number,* we will instead show it as if it were *Employee Type Name* with a corresponding value of "Manager." The table will be more readable as an example in the following discussions.
- *Rel employee number#* is the third column of the table—Rel(ated) Emp(loyee) Number.
- *Rel employee type number#* is the fourth column—Rel(ated) Emp(loyee) Type, but is shown in the table (also for readability purposes) as if it were *rel employee type name.*
- *Relationship reason* is the fifth column—Relationship Reason. As discussed, in practice *reason id#* would be a foreign key to the table REASON as discussed for Figure 9.21.

Each row of EMPLOYEE STRUCTURE [18] shows reporting relationships for managers and staff. While well known within an organization, this is expert knowledge outside the enterprise.

- Examining *Employee Number* in Figure 9.23, we can see that Employee 1358 is a Manager, who manages 1362 (also a Manager) in a *General Management* relationship. 1358 also manages Employee 1556 (a Manager), but manages Employees 1460 and 1661 each in a *Sales Management* relationship. From *Rel Emp Number,* we see that all of these employees *report to* 1358.
- Similarly, 1362 is a Manager of 262, 1132 and 1441 for Sales Management, and of 1088 in a Support Management relationship. And Manager 1556 manages 1333 and 1512 (Sales Mgt) and 1495 (Support Mgt).
- The figure shows that these employees all *report to* managers 1362 and 1556.

Continuing our discussion using actual examples of the EMPLOYEE STRUCTURE table, we will next examine the *Sales Support* relationship.

Manages

Employee Number	Employee Type	Rel Emp Number	Rel Emp Type	Relationship Reason
1358	Manager	1362	Manager	General Mgt
		1460	Sales	Sales Mgt
		1556	Manager	General Mgt
		1661	Sales Person	Sales Mgt
1362	Manager	262	Sales Person	Sales Mgt
		1088	Support	Support Mgt
		1132	Sales Person	Sales Mgt
		1441	Sales Person	Sales Mgt
1556	Manager	1333	Sales Person	Sales Mgt
		1495	Support	Support Mgt
		1512	Sales Person	Sales Mgt

Reports to

Figure 9.23 Employee structure 5BNF *Manages* and *Reports to* relationships.

- We can see in Figure 9.24 that Employee 1088 is a Support person, who *supports* Salespersons 1460, 1661, 1132, and 1441 in a *Sales Support* relationship.
- 1495 also *supports* Salespersons 1460, 1661, 1333, and 1512 in a *Sales Support* relationship.
- From *Rel Emp Number,* we see from Figure 9.24 that all Salespersons are now *supported by* 1088 or 1495.

We can now use the content of EMPLOYEE STRUCTURE to answer questions relating to *Sales Support* relationships from the table content:

1. Which Salespersons are supported by Support Person 1088?
   Using the column *Employee Number* we see that 1088 *supports* Salespersons 1460, 1661, 1132 and 1441 in a *Sales Support* relationship (see Figure 9.25).
2. Which Salespersons are supported by Support Person 1495?

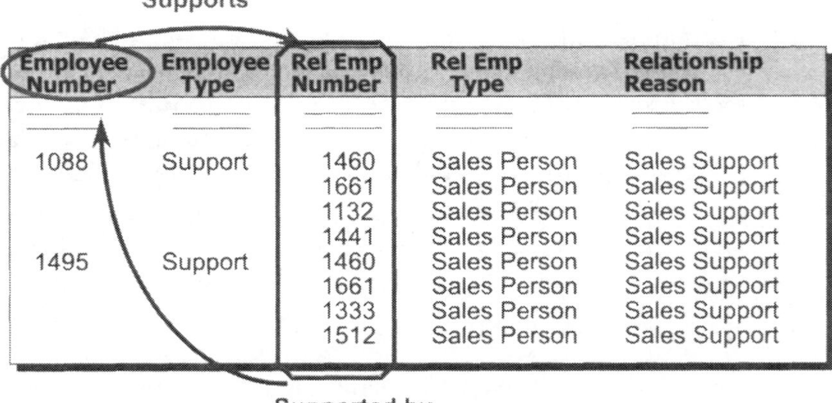

Supports

Employee Number	Employee Type	Rel Emp Number	Rel Emp Type	Relationship Reason
1088	Support	1460	Sales Person	Sales Support
		1661	Sales Person	Sales Support
		1132	Sales Person	Sales Support
		1441	Sales Person	Sales Support
1495	Support	1460	Sales Person	Sales Support
		1661	Sales Person	Sales Support
		1333	Sales Person	Sales Support
		1512	Sales Person	Sales Support

Supported by

Figure 9.24 Employee structure *Supports* and *Supported by* relationships.

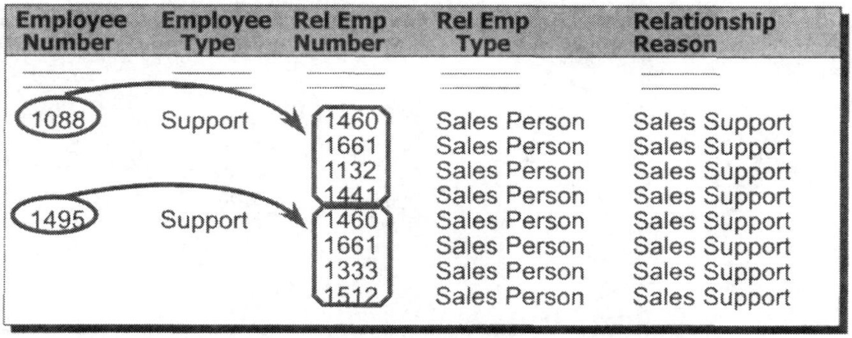

Employee Number	Employee Type	Rel Emp Number	Rel Emp Type	Relationship Reason
1088	Support	1460	Sales Person	Sales Support
		1661	Sales Person	Sales Support
		1132	Sales Person	Sales Support
		1441	Sales Person	Sales Support
1495	Support	1460	Sales Person	Sales Support
		1661	Sales Person	Sales Support
		1333	Sales Person	Sales Support
		1512	Sales Person	Sales Support

- **1. Which Sales Persons does 1088 support?**
- **2. Which Sales Persons does 1495 support?**

Figure 9.25 Answers to Questions 1 and 2 on *Sales Support* relationships.

Once again, using the column *Employee Number* we see that 1495 supports Salespersons 1460, 1661, 1333, and 1512 in a *Sales Support* relationship (see Figure 9.25).

While these support relationships may be well known by the people involved, this information may not be known outside their immediate work groups. The format and content of the EMPLOYEE STRUCTURE table now enables these facts to be easily determined by others with the relevant access authority, who have a need to know.

From the other perspective, we can also use EMPLOYEE STRUCTURE to determine which Support Persons support specific Salespersons. Let us consider other questions:

3. Who supports Salespersons 1333 and 1512?
   Using the third column *Rel Employee Number,* we can clearly see that 1333 and 1512 are both supported by Support Person 1495 (see Figure 9.26).
4. Who supports Salespersons 1460 and 1661?

Again using the third column *Rel Employee Number,* we see that 1460 and 1661 are both supported by two Support Persons: 1088 or 1495 (see Figure 9.26).

While these *Supported By* relationships may be well known by the people involved, the format of the EMPLOYEE STRUCTURE table enables this reverse information to be found by others with appropriate authority—without additional data or extra knowledge being required.

To this point, the EMPLOYEE STRUCTURE table has shown well-known relationships between Managers and their staff, and between Support staff and the people they support. We will now use it to provide expert knowledge that is not well known. Consider the following questions.

5. If Support Person 1088 is sick, who supports Salespersons 1460 and 1661?
   Using the third column *Rel Employee Number,* we see that 1460 and

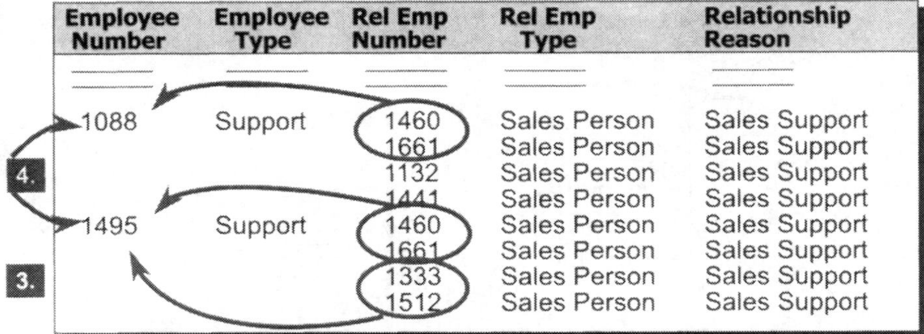

Employee Number	Employee Type	Rel Emp Number	Rel Emp Type	Relationship Reason
1088	Support	1460	Sales Person	Sales Support
		1661	Sales Person	Sales Support
		1132	Sales Person	Sales Support
		1441	Sales Person	Sales Support
1495	Support	1460	Sales Person	Sales Support
		1661	Sales Person	Sales Support
		1333	Sales Person	Sales Support
		1512	Sales Person	Sales Support

- **3. Who supports Sales Persons 1333 and 1512?**
- **4. Who supports Sales Persons 1460 and 1661?**

Figure 9.26 Answers to Questions 3 and 4 on *Sales Support* relationships.

1661 are both supported by Support Person 1495—if 1088 is absent (see Figure 9.27).

6. But if Support Person 1088 is sick, who supports 1132 and 1441?
   There is no backup support allocated for these Salespersons. They are left with no support at all if 1088 is absent (see Figure 9.27). *Who should they turn to for support?*

We now see a new row (in bold italics) has been added at the end of EMPLOYEE STRUCTURE in Figure 9.28. It shows that Support Person 1495 supports Support Person 1088. The *Relationship Reason* is *Backup Support.*

7. In Figure 9.28, we see that if Support Person 1088 is sick, 1495 can provide backup support to the Salesperson clients of 1088: 1460, 1661, 1132, and 1441.

In this case, further data—the last row (in bold italics) of the table in Figure 9.28—enabled us to answer Question 6. This extra row represents expert knowledge that was not previously available: the fact that 1495 has the skills needed to provide backup support for 1088. The reverse may not necessarily also be true: 1088 may have only a subset of the skills of 1495 and so may be unable to provide backup support to Salesperson clients of 1495.

9.8.4 Example of 5BNF: Product Structure

We will look at other examples of 5BNF structure entities. Our next example considers Product *Bills of Material,* which are used in the manufacturing industry to determine the component parts or items used to manufacture a product. The 5BNF data map for PRODUCT STRUCTURE is shown in Figure 9.29.

The data map in Figure 9.29 indicates that a PRODUCT can be an ASSEMBLY, SUBASSEMBLY, COMPONENT ITEM, or an ALTERNATIVE ITEM. PRODUCT STRUCTURE is a 5BNF structure entity, used to show relationships between these secondary entities.

Employee Number	Employee Type	Rel Emp Number	Rel Emp Type	Relationship Reason
1088	Support	1460	Sales Person	Sales Support
		1661	Sales Person	Sales Support
		1132	Sales Person	Sales Support
		1441	Sales Person	Sales Support
1495	Support	1460	Sales Person	Sales Support
		1661	Sales Person	Sales Support
		1333	Sales Person	Sales Support
		1512	Sales Person	Sales Support

5. ??
6. ??

- **5. If 1088 is sick, who supports 1460 and 1661?**
- **6. If 1088 is sick, who supports 1132 and 1441?**

Figure 9.27 Answers to Questions 5 and 6 on *Sales Support* relationships.

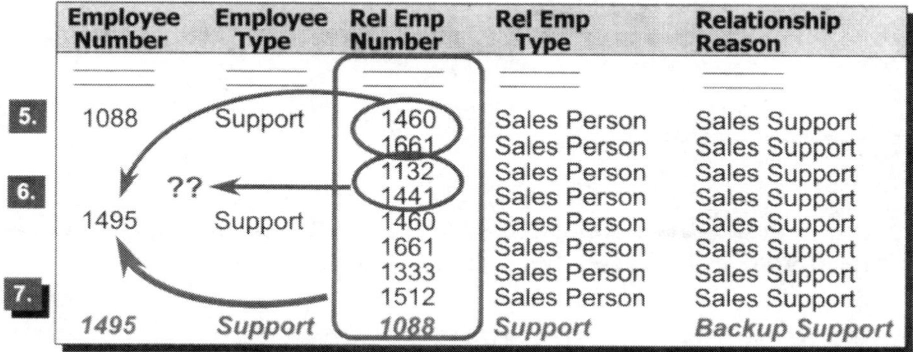

Employee Number	Employee Type	Rel Emp Number	Rel Emp Type	Relationship Reason
1088	Support	1460	Sales Person	Sales Support
		1661	Sales Person	Sales Support
		1132	Sales Person	Sales Support
		1441	Sales Person	Sales Support
1495	Support	1460	Sales Person	Sales Support
		1661	Sales Person	Sales Support
		1333	Sales Person	Sales Support
		1512	Sales Person	Sales Support
1495	*Support*	*1088*	*Support*	*Backup Support*

- **5. If 1088 is sick, who supports 1460 and 1661?**
- **6. If 1088 is sick, who supports 1132 and 1441?**
- ***7. If 1088 is sick, 1495 provides support to all.***

Figure 9.28 Effect of expert knowledge *Backup Support* relationship.

PRODUCT STRUCTURE shows a <u>*product no#*</u> of a specific <u>*product type no#*</u> that requires a <u>*rel(ated) product no#*</u> and <u>*rel(ated) product type no#*</u>. The *sequence no* in which it is used to manufacture other related products is specified, as well as the *quantity* for this current related product. A further attribute—say, *product use*—offers a similar function to *relationship reason* in EMPLOYEE STRUCTURE. We will not include *product use* here.

PRODUCT STRUCTURE (<u>*product no#*</u>, <u>*product type no#*</u>, <u>*rel product no#*</u>, <u>*rel product type no#*</u>, sequence no, quantity)

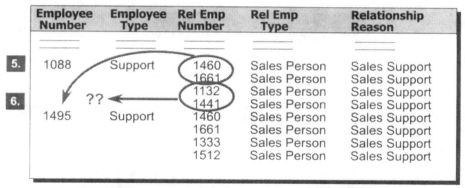

As we saw earlier, a 5BNF PRODUCT STRUCTURE can be implemented for very high database access efficiency—because all of the keys are numeric. We will see in the following figures that a 5BNF PRODUCT STRUCTURE with the format at the top of Figure 9.30 provides very flexible *Bill of Material* support for manufac-

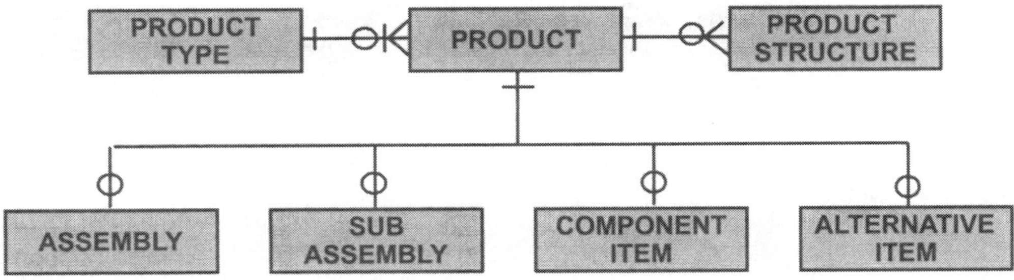

Figure 9.29 5BNF Data Map for PRODUCT STRUCTURE.

PRODUCT STRUCTURE (<u>product no#, product type no#, rel product no#, rel product type no#,</u> sequence no, quantity)

How are Assemblies Manufactured?

Assembled From

Prod No	Prod Type	Rel Prod No	Rel Prod Type	Seq No	Qty
4358	ASM	4362	SUB	1	2
		4460	ITEM	2	4
		4556	SUB	3	2
		4664	ITEM	4	6

Figure 9.30 High-level PRODUCT STRUCTURE *Bill of Material* table.

turing. We will further see that this PRODUCT STRUCTURE format can also be used for *Where-Used* applications, which are used to identify which COMPONENT ITEM or ALTERNATIVE ITEM can be used to build a specific ASSEMBLY or SUBASSEMBLY.

The PRODUCT STRUCTURE table specifies part of a *Bill of Material* as shown in Figure 9.30. We will use this to answer a number of questions.

- *Product No* 4358 is an Assembly (*ASM*) whose manufacture is documented by the four rows of the PRODUCT STRUCTURE table (part shown in Figure 9.30).
  - *Product No* 4358 is assembled first (*sequence no* = 1) from a *quantity* of 2 of *Product No* 4362, which is a Subassembly (*SUB*).
  - *Product No* 4460—a Component Item (*ITEM*)—is assembled next (*sequence no* = 2), for which a *quantity* of 4 is needed.
  - *Product No* 4556 (a *SUB*) is next assembled (*sequence no* 3), using a *quantity* of 2.
  - *Product No* 4664 (an *ITEM*) is finally assembled (*sequence no* 4), for a *quantity* of 6.

These relationships between occurrences of products of different types are represented easily using the 5BNF PRODUCT STRUCTURE format. In Figure 9.31 we will examine the manufacture of the Subassemblies, *Product No* 4362 and 4556.

- We saw that *Product No* 4358 is an Assembly (*ASM*). It is assembled first from the Subassembly (*SUB*) *Product No* 4362, for which a *quantity* of 2 is needed
- *Product No* 4362 is itself assembled from the Component Items (*ITEM*) shown by rows 5–7 of the table in Figure 9.31. (Figure 9.30 covered rows 1–4, which specify the manufacture of *ASM* 4358.)
    - Row 5 shows that *SUB* 4362 is assembled from ITEM 1262 (*sequence no* 1), for which a *quantity* of 4 is needed.
    - Row 6 specifies *SUB* 4362 is next assembled from ITEM 4432 (*sequence no* 2), using a *quantity* of 6.
    - Finally (*sequence no* 3), row 7 specifies a *quantity* of 4 of ITEM 4460 is to be used in the manufacture of *SUB* 4362.

The PRODUCT STRUCTURE table in Figure 9.31 also specifies the *Bill of Material* for the other Subassembly. This is shown in Figures 9.32 and 9.33.

- We saw that *ASM* 4358 is also assembled from Subassembly (*SUB*) *Product No* 4556, for which a *quantity* of 2 is needed.
- Product No 4556 is assembled from the Component Items (*ITEM*) shown by rows 8–10 of the table. (The earlier figures covered rows 1–4 for *ASM* 4358 and rows 5–7 for *SUB* 4362.)
- Row 8 shows that *SUB* 4556 is assembled from ITEM 4333 (*sequence no* 1), for which a *quantity* of 2 is needed, as illustrated in Figure 9.33.
- Row 9 specifies *SUB* 4556 is next assembled from ITEM 4495 (*sequence no* 2), using a *quantity* of 6.
- Finally (*sequence no* 3), row 10 specifies a *quantity* of 4 of ITEM 4460 is to be used in the manufacture of *SUB* 4556.

Prod No	Prod Type	Rel Prod No	Rel Prod Type	Seq No	Qty
4358	ASM	4362	SUB	1	2
		4460	ITEM	2	4
		4556	SUB	3	2
		4664	ITEM	4	6
4362	SUB	1262	ITEM	1	4
		4432	ITEM	2	6
		4460	ITEM	3	4
4556	SUB	4333	ITEM	1	2
		4495	ITEM	2	6
		4460	ITEM	3	4
4495	ALT	4088	ITEM	-	-

Figure 9.31 Manufacture of Subassembly 4362 in PRODUCT STRUCTURE.

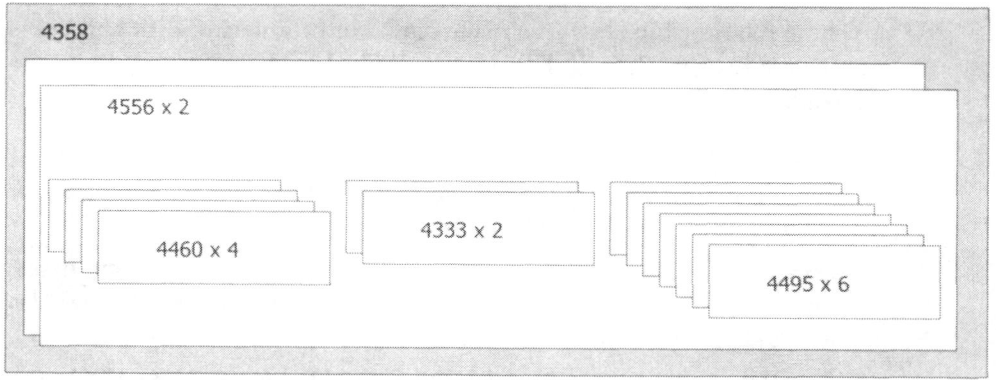

Figure 9.32 Quantities used for physical assembly of *SUB* 4556 for *ASM* 4358. (*Source:* [19]. Robert Weisman, CGI. Reprinted with permission.)

Prod No	Prod Type	Rel Prod No	Rel Prod Type	Seq No	Qty
4358	ASM	4362	SUB	1	2
		4460	ITEM	2	4
		4556	SUB	3	2
		4664	ITEM	4	6
4362	SUB	1262	ITEM	1	4
		4432	ITEM	2	6
		4460	ITEM	3	4
4556	SUB	4333	ITEM	1	2
		4495	ITEM	2	6
		4460	ITEM	3	4
4495	ALT	4088	ITEM	-	-

Figure 9.33 Manufacture of Subassembly 4556 in PRODUCT STRUCTURE.

The manufacture of Assembly 4358 and Subassemblies 4362 and 4556 have all now been succinctly defined by the PRODUCT STRUCTURE table. All rows of the PRODUCT STRUCTURE table are shown in Table 9.3. The complete *Bill of Material* for the manufacture of *ASM* 4358 is summarized next, where the Row No. column is not part of the PRODUCT STRUCTURE table but is used as a key to the discussion that follows:

- *Product No* 4358 is an Assembly (*ASM*). It is assembled first (*sequence no* = 1) from a *quantity* of 2 of *Product No* 4362—a Subassembly (*SUB*).
- *Product No* 4460—a Component Item (*ITEM*)—is next assembled (*sequence no* = 2), for which a *quantity* of 4 is needed (see row 2 of Table 9.3).
- *Product No* 4556 (a *SUB*) and 4664 (an *ITEM*) are then used (*sequence no* 3 and 4), with a *quantity* of 2 and 6, respectively (see Table 9.3).
- Similarly, *Product No* 4362—the Subassembly used for 4358 above—is itself assembled from Component Items 1262, 4432, and 4460 (see rows 5–7). A

Table 9.3 Completed PRODUCT STRUCTURE Table

Row No.	*Product Number*	*Product Type*	*Rel Product Number*	*Rel Product Type*	*Sequence Number*	*Quantity*
1	4358	ASM	4362	SUB	1	2
2		4460	ITEM	2	4	
3		4556	SUB	3	2	
4		4664	ITEM	4	6	
5	4362	SUB	1262	ITEM	1	4
6		4432	ITEM	2	6	
7		4460	ITEM	3	4	
8	4556	SUB	4333	ITEM	1	2
9		4495	ITEM	2	6	
10		4460	ITEM	3	4	

quantity of 4, 6, and 4 of these respective items are needed, assembled in that *sequence*.

- Also *Product No* 4556—the other Subassembly used for 4358 above—is itself assembled from Component Items 4333, 4495, and 4460. A *quantity* of 2, 6, and 4 of these respective items is needed, assembled in that *sequence* as shown in Figure 9.32 (see rows 8–10 of Table 9.3).

But what if there is an insufficient quantity of ITEM 4495, which is used in the manufacture of *SUB* 4556. Can Subassembly 4556 be built, and also Assembly 4358? Figure 9.34 provides expert knowledge that assists us.

- The last row of the table in Figure 9.34 now offers expert knowledge that was not known earlier: ITEM 4495 has an Alternative Item (*ALT*)—ITEM 4088. It tells us that ITEM 4088 can be used in place of ITEM 4495 wherever it is required. No values for *quantity* or *sequence no* are relevant for this row, however.
- Manufacture of Subassembly 4556 and Assembly 4358 is therefore completed using ITEM 4088, based on expert knowledge from the last row of the table.

9.8.5 Using Product Structure for "Where-Used"

The PRODUCT STRUCTURE table has so far been used to specify *Bills of Material* for the manufacture of *ASM* 4358. We will use the same information to satisfy another manufacturing application, called "*Where-Used.*" This shows—for component items, alternative items, and subassemblies—where each unit is used (hence the term "*Where-Used*") and the quantities required by each use in the manufacture of subassemblies or assemblies.

The following question shows how a 5BNF PRODUCT STRUCTURE table that is used for *Bills of Material* can also be used to support *Where-Used* queries:

We have only 20 units of ITEM 4460 in stock. Where is this item used, and how many subassemblies and assemblies can we manufacture from these 20 units?

But what if Component Items not available?

Prod No	Prod Type	Rel Prod No	Rel Prod Type	Seq No	Qty
4358	ASM	4362	SUB	1	2
		4460	ITEM	2	4
		4556	SUB	3	2
		4664	ITEM	4	6
4362	SUB	1262	ITEM	1	4
		4432	ITEM	2	6
		4460	ITEM	3	4
4556	SUB	4333	ITEM	1	2
		4495	ITEM	2	X
		4460	ITEM	3	4
4495	**ALT**	**4088**	**ITEM**	-	-

Figure 9.34 Expert knowledge of Alternative Item 4088 in PRODUCT STRUCTURE.

We will now use the *Rel Product No* column in Figure 9.35 to identify all rows where ITEM 4460 is used, and the quantities required for each of those uses. It is often more effective to start from the bottom of the table, examining the rows relating to Subassemblies first, working from the bottom up to the top of Table 9.3:

- From *Rel Product No*, we see that ITEM 4460 is in row 10. It is used in the manufacture of *SUB* 4556, for which a quantity of 4 units of 4460 is required.
- ITEM 4460 is also used in row 7 in the manufacture of *SUB* 4362, for which a further quantity of 4 units of 4460 is required.
- Finally, ITEM 4460 is used in row 2 in the manufacture of *ASM* 4358, for which an additional quantity of 4 units of 4460 is needed.
- Because 2 units of *SUB* 4362 and of 4556 are each used for *ASM* 4358, each of which uses 4 units of 4460, we can build 1 unit of *ASM* 4358 from 20 of 4460. (Two units of *SUB* 4362 use 8 units of 4460. Two units of *SUB* 4556 also use 8 units of 4460. *ASM* itself uses another 4 units, for a total of 20 units of 4460.)

9.8.6 Example of 5BNF: Organization Relationships

We will now discuss an example in Figure 9.36 that utilizes a 5BNF structure entity to capture expert market knowledge. The data map documents the business rule that:

An organization participates in many markets. A market also has many organizations that do business in it.

This data map shows two entities: ORG (for Organization) and MARKET.

- The association from ORG to MARKET is *mandatory one–to–mandatory many*, because an organization *must* participate in at least one market.
- The association from MARKET to ORG is *mandatory one–to–optional becoming mandatory many:* A market *will eventually* have at least one organization operating in it, to be considered a market.

ITEM 4460 has only 20 units. What can we make?

Prod No	Prod Type	Rel Prod No	Rel Prod Type	Seq No	Qty
4358	ASM	4362	SUB	1	2
		4460	ITEM	2	4
		4556	SUB	3	2
		4664	ITEM	4	6
4362	SUB	1262	ITEM	1	4
		4432	ITEM	2	6
		4460	ITEM	3	4
4556	SUB	4333	ITEM	1	2
		4495	ITEM	2	6
		4460	ITEM	3	4
4495	ALT	4088	ITEM	-	-

Figure 9.35 Example of "Where-Used" with PRODUCT STRUCTURE.

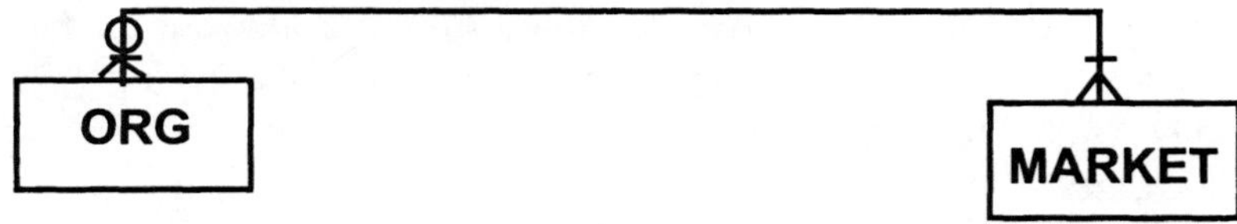

Figure 9.36 5BNF high-level example of ORGANIZATION STRUCTURE.

We are also told that an organization may be a public-sector organization (such as a government department) or a private-sector organization (such as a company). We will also need to know how each of these organizations is structured, both for ourselves (for this example, we will assume the name of XYZ Corporation) and for other organizations who are of interest, such as customers and suppliers.

The data map in Figure 9.37 has been expanded to represent the previous statements:

- We see in that ORG is a principal (supertype) entity, with ORG TYPE as a type entity. There are also three secondary (subtype) entities below ORG:
  - PRIVATE ORG—for a private-sector organization such as a company;
  - PUBLIC ORG—for a public-sector government organization;
  - UNIT—for a business unit of an organization, such as ourselves (XYZ) or business units of any private- or public-sector organization of interest.
  - Secondary entities (subtypes) have also been added below UNIT (which is thus a *typed secondary* entity) and UNIT TYPE is added:

    The 4BNF entities below UNIT are for business units: DEPT (department), DIVN (division), and AREA (business area).

We could instead link ORG TYPE to UNIT, with a *mandatory one-to-optional becoming mandatory many* association between ORG TYPE and UNIT. We will

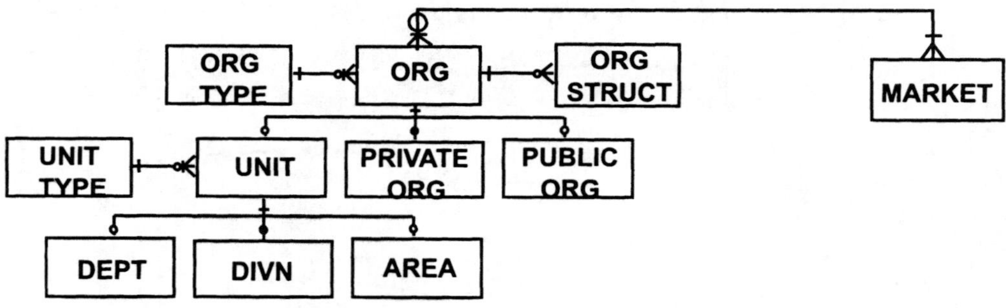

Figure 9.37 5BNF and 4BNF examples of ORGANIZATION STRUCTURE.

see shortly that there are many interrelationships between occurrences of these secondary entities, which satisfy the 5BNF rule. The data map thus includes:

- ORG STRUCT—for the 5BNF Organization structure entity.

We now need to resolve the *many-to-many* association between ORG and MARKET. This will require the addition of an intersecting entity, as is done in Figure 9.38. This may be ORG MARKET, but we are told by business experts of XYZ that:

> An organization has many roles in a market: as a customer, supplier, or competitor. Customers can be grouped (as "retail customers," "wholesale customers" or "high-volume customers") and Suppliers can also be grouped (as "just-in-time suppliers").

From this, a relevant name for the entity is ORG ROLE (for Organization Role).

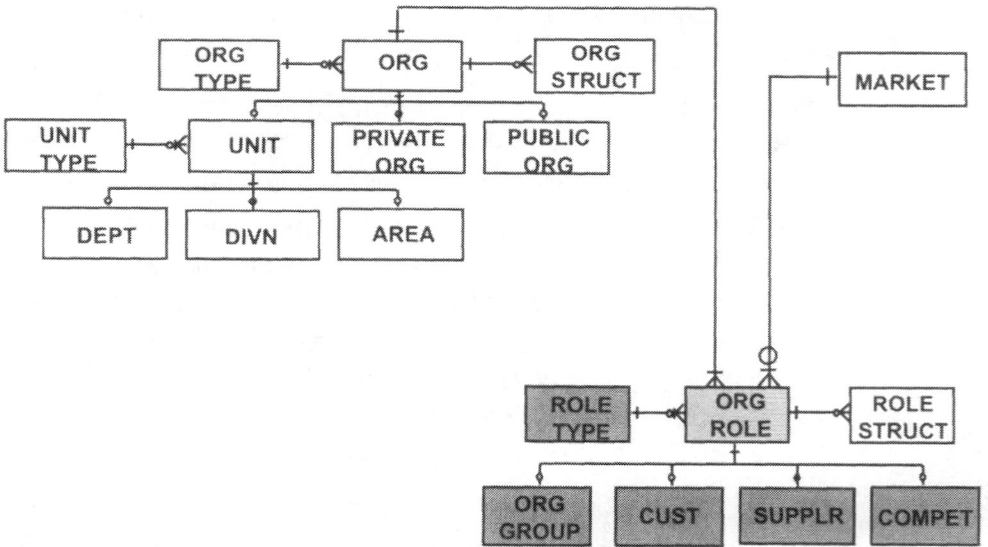

Figure 9.38 Resolution of *many-to-many* association with ORG ROLE.

Because we are clearly interested in different types of organization roles, we will show ORG ROLE as a principal (supertype) entity, with ROLE TYPE as a type entity. We will also show the following secondary (subtype) entities:

- CUST—for an organization role of Customer;
- SUPPLR—for an organization role of Supplier;
- COMPET—for an organization role of Competitor.
- ORG GROUP—for an organization role of Organization Group.

Because we are interested in interrelationships between customers *(retail, wholesale,* or *high-volume)* and suppliers *(just-in-time),* the data map in Figure 9.38 also shows:

- ROLE STRUCT—a 5BNF Organization Role structure entity.

9.8.7 5BNF Example: Organization Role Structure

The data map in Figure 9.39 will now be used in the following pages to show the power of 5BNF. We will see how 5BNF records the complexity of business in real life: with interrelationships that exist between organizations, and between the roles that organizations can take in different market environments. We will examine the following 5BNF tables in this figure:

- ORG STRUCT is used to show the business unit structure of XYZ (or of any organization), as well as interrelationships between organizations.
- ROLE STRUCT allows organization roles to be defined as a customer, supplier, or competitor. It specifies groups of related organizations: as customers (retail, wholesale, high-volume); or related suppliers (just-in-time); or competitors.

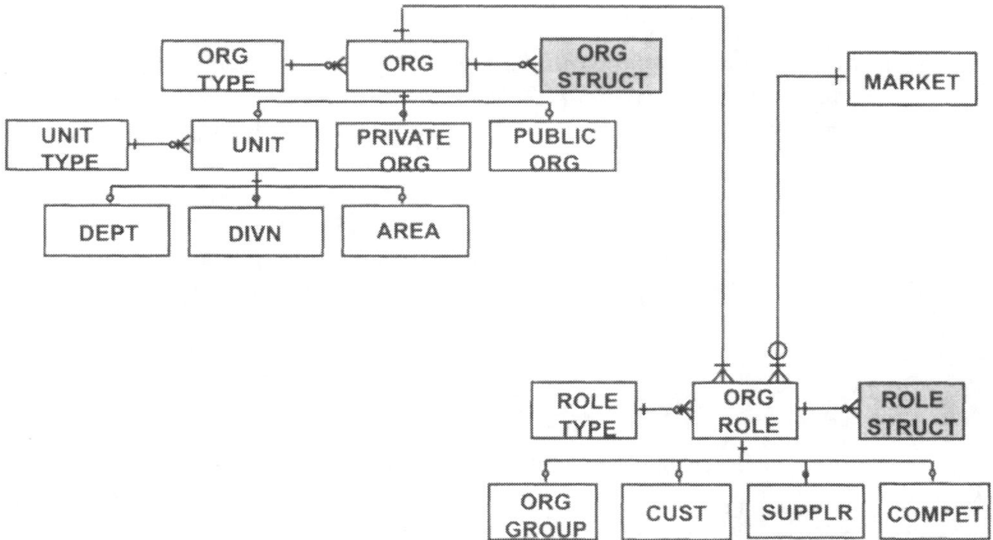

Figure 9.39 5BNF data map showing ORG STRUCT and ROLE STRUCT.

Figure 9.40 shows typical content for a 5BNF Organization Role Structure table, ROLE STRUCT:

- *Org No* XYZ has *Org Role Type* of "Supplier" to:
  Rel Org No KLM, which therefore has *Rel Org Role Type* of "Customer";
  Rel Org No MNO, which has *Rel Org Role Type* of "Customer";
  Rel Org No PTC, which also has *Rel Org Role Type* of "Customer."

This is well-known to staff who work in the Sales Department, but is not at all known by any staff who work outside Sales. Examining the table further, we see that:

- *Org No* XYZ also has *Org Role Type* of "Customer" to:
  Rel Org No Brink, which has *Rel Org Role Type* of "Supplier";
  Rel Org No PMM, which also has *Rel Org Role Type* of "Supplier."

This information is well known by the staff people who work in the Purchasing Department, but is not known by staff people who work outside Purchasing. The final part of the table then shows:

- *Org No* XYZ additionally has *Org Role Type* of "Competitor" to:
  Rel Org No MPP, which thus has *Rel Org Role Type* of "Competitor";
  Rel Org No PXM, which has *Rel Org Role Type* of "Competitor";
  Rel Org No Brink, which also has *Rel Org Role Type* of "Competitor."

Once again, this information is known by staff people who work in the Marketing Department, but it is not known by any staff who work outside Marketing. But now we see some interested facts when we examine this table more closely in Figure 9.41.

- *Brink is both a Supplier and a Competitor.* This was not known before. XYZ adds a clause in its *Supplier Purchase Agreement* that prevents Brink from withholding supply from XYZ for competitive advantage.

ORGANISATION ROLE STRUCTURE			
Org	**Org Role**	**Rel Org**	**Rel Org Role**
XYZ	Supplier	KLM	Customer
		MNO	Customer
		PTC	Customer
XYZ	Customer	Brink	Supplier
		PMM	Supplier
XYZ	Competitor	MPP	Competitor
		PXM	Competitor
		Brink	Competitor

Figure 9.40 5BNF ROLE STRUCT table showing typical content.

ORGANISATION ROLE STRUCTURE			
Org	Org Role	Rel Org	Rel Org Role
XYZ	Supplier	KLM	Customer
		MNO	Customer
		PTC	Customer
XYZ	Customer	Brink	Supplier
		PMM	Supplier
XYZ	Competitor	MPP	Competitor
		PXM	Competitor
		Brink	Competitor

What does this mean?

Figure 9.41 5BNF ROLE STRUCT table shows important facts about Brink.

This is an example of expert knowledge that was not previously known by XYZ. Now that it has been discovered, this knowledge enables more effective Supplier Management for Sarbanes-Oxley internal control reporting (see Chapter 4).

9.8.8 5BNF Example: Organization Structure

Looking now at content of the 5BNF Organization Structure entity, ORG STRUCT, the table in Figure 9.42 provides additional facts.

- *Org No* XYZ has *Org Role Type* of "Unit," specifying an internal structure of:

  Rel Org No "Finance," which has *Rel Org Role Type* of "Department";

  Rel Org No "Marketing," which has *Rel Org Role Type* of "Department";

  Rel Org No "Sales," which also has *Rel Org Role Type* of "Department."

This is well known to all staff people who work for XYZ, but it is not known outside XYZ. We also see from the table that XYZ Corporate Department has added other relationships that are of interest to it: those between parent and subsidiary organizations. We will see shortly how information about these relationships is used.

- *Org No* ABC has *Org Role Type* of "Parent" to:

  Rel Org No KLM, which has *Rel Org Role Type* of "Subsidiary";

ORGANISATION STRUCTURE			
Org	Org Type	Rel Org	Rel Org Type
XYZ	Unit	Finance	Department
		Marketing	Department
		Sales	Department
ABC	Parent	KLM	Subsidiary
		MNO	Subsidiary
		PTC	Subsidiary
		Brink	Subsidiary
PXM	Parent	MPP	Subsidiary
		PMM	Subsidiary
MNO	Shareholder	PXM	Parent

Figure 9.42 5BNF ORG STRUCT table shows additional facts.

Rel Org No MNO, which has *Rel Org Role Type* of "Subsidiary";
Rel Org No PTC, which has *Rel Org Role Type* of "Subsidiary";
Rel Org No Brink, which has *Rel Org Role Type* of "Subsidiary."

- *Org No* PXM has *Org Role Type* of "Parent" to:
  Rel Org No MPP, which has *Rel Org Role Type* of "Subsidiary";
  Rel Org No PMM, which has *Rel Org Role Type* of "Subsidiary."
- *Org No* MNO has *Org Role Type* of "Major Shareholder" to:
  Rel Org No PXM, which has *Rel Org Role Type* of "Parent."

These shareholder relationships are typically all reported annually by public companies in countries throughout the world, and so are in the public domain.

9.8.9 5BNF Expert Knowledge: Market Intelligence

We will now examine both of these 5BNF structure tables together: ROLE STRUCT and ORG STRUCT in Figure 9.43. We will see the expert knowledge that they now contain:

1. KLM, MNO, PTC, and Brink are all sister organizations (see ORG STRUCT).
2. But KLM, MNO, and PTC are customers of XYZ (see ROLE STRUCT).
3. And Brink, their sister organization, is a Competitor (see ROLE STRUCT).
   - What if they share with Brink (XYZ's competitor) information about XYZ that they learn as our customers? Brink would then have a competitive advantage.
   - Now that we have knowledge of this close relationship, it would be wise to include a restraint clause in their Sales Agreements with XYZ—to prevent them sharing sensitive information with their sister company, XYZ's competitor Brink. This would be a competitive threat to XYZ.

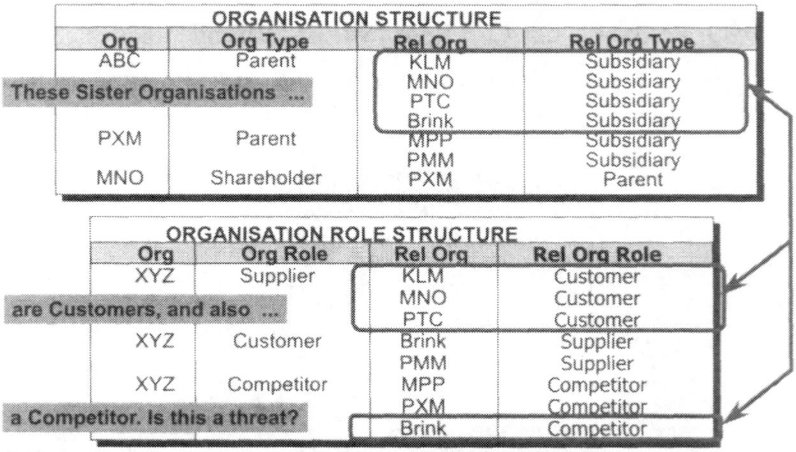

ORGANISATION STRUCTURE

Org	Org Type	Rel Org	Rel Org Type
ABC	Parent	KLM	Subsidiary
		MNO	Subsidiary
		PTC	Subsidiary
		Brink	Subsidiary
PXM	Parent	MPP	Subsidiary
		PMM	Subsidiary
MNO	Shareholder	PXM	Parent

These Sister Organisations ...

ORGANISATION ROLE STRUCTURE

Org	Org Role	Rel Org	Rel Org Role
XYZ	Supplier	KLM	Customer
		MNO	Customer
		PTC	Customer
XYZ	Customer	Brink	Supplier
		PMM	Supplier
XYZ	Competitor	MPP	Competitor
		PXM	Competitor
		Brink	Competitor

are Customers, and also ...

a Competitor. Is this a threat?

Figure 9.43 Both 5BNF tables are used together to obtain market intelligence.

This knowledge is often called *market intelligence*. While it may well have been known by experienced staff before, this 5BNF table brings this knowledge together so that it is clearly apparent. It can now be acted on directly for marketing, purchasing, sales, and other management purposes, such as Sarbanes-Oxley (see Chapter 4).

Referring back to ORG STRUCT, we also see in Figure 9.44 that:

1. PXM (who is a Competitor) is the parent of MPP and PMM—who are therefore subsidiaries of PXM.
2. The first of these subsidiaries is MPP, which is another Competitor. But the second subsidiary is PMM, which is a Supplier.
3. What if PXM (its Parent), asks PMM (a Supplier) to withhold supply from XYZ for the competitive benefit of MPP (a Competitor subsidiary of PXM)? This would be a competitive threat to XYZ. It may be possible to avoid it by a competitive restraint clause in the Supplier Purchase Agreement for PMM.

We now see that 5BNF tables can provide an enormous amount of useful expert knowledge. It is important to be aware of this if we are to manage customers and suppliers efficiently and compete effectively.

Finally, referring again to ORG STRUCT, we also see in Figure 9.45 that:

1. MNO, a Customer of XYZ ...
2. is also a shareholder of PXM.
3. But PXM is a Competitor of XYZ.
4. This is a competitive threat.

MNO could use knowledge it learns about XYZ as its customer and can share that knowledge with its PXM subsidiary (an XYZ Competitor). This is a competitive threat to XYZ. It may require a restraint clause in the MNO Sales Agreement to prevent this happening.

Of course, legal restraints discussed in this and the earlier figures offer no guarantee that these competitive threats will not arise. This knowledge is normally held

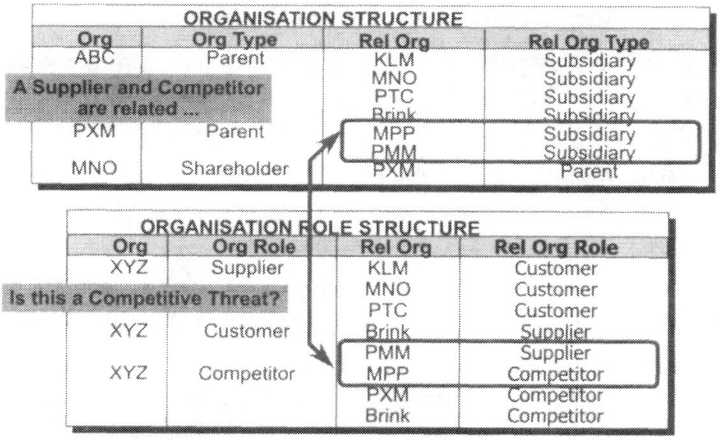

ORGANISATION STRUCTURE

Org	Org Type	Rel Org	Rel Org Type
ABC	Parent	KLM	Subsidiary
		MNO	Subsidiary
		PTC	Subsidiary
		Brink	Subsidiary
PXM	Parent	MPP	Subsidiary
		PMM	Subsidiary
MNO	Shareholder	PXM	Parent

A Supplier and Competitor are related ...

ORGANISATION ROLE STRUCTURE

Org	Org Role	Rel Org	Rel Org Role
XYZ	Supplier	KLM	Customer
		MNO	Customer
		PTC	Customer
XYZ	Customer	Brink	Supplier
		PMM	Supplier
XYZ	Competitor	MPP	Competitor
		PXM	Competitor
		Brink	Competitor

Is this a Competitive Threat?

Figure 9.44 Further market intelligence from these 5BNF tables.

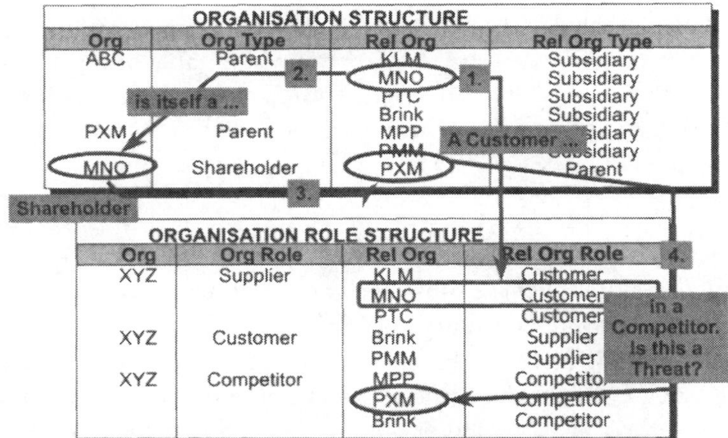

Figure 9.45 Still further market intelligence from these 5BNF tables.

by experienced staff. But these examples show how this expert knowledge is now more accessible in 5BNF structure entities.

9.8.10 Case Study Problem 13: 5BNF

We are now ready to do the 5BNF exercise, Case Study Problem 13 of this chapter [20].

9.9 Summary

The rules of business normalization can be summarized as follows:

- 1BNF moves repeating groups into a new entity.
  The repeating group key, plus the primary key of the entity where the repeating group resided, both become part of the compound key of this new entity. This entity is typically an *intersecting* entity.
- 2BNF moves partially dependent attributes to a new entity. This entity has a compound key: with the partially dependent component of the original key, plus other key attributes on which that attribute wholly depends.
- 3BNF moves out attributes not dependent at all on the key. These attributes are moved to an entity where they depend on the whole key.
- 4BNF moves out value-dependent attributes, or optional attributes. They are moved to *secondary* (subtype) entities where they are mandatory, with the same primary key as the original entity, a *principal* (supertype) entity.
- 5BNF shows relationships between specific occurrences of keys. A 5BNF table is used to store predefined knowledge, or expert rules, so that it is readily accessible by authorized people.

9.9.1 Summarized Benefits of Business Normalization

We have now almost completed the chapter. The benefits of business normalization are now clearly apparent:

- *Uncontrolled data redundancy is eliminated.* Each nonkey attribute can reside in only one entity, where it is wholly dependent on "the key, the whole key, and nothing but the key." Homonyms or synonyms are clearly identified, appropriately named, and reside in their relevant entities.
- *Redundant data maintenance processes are minimized.* Because data redundancy has been eliminated, redundant processes needed to keep those redundant data up to date are also eliminated. Each normalized entity is maintained by only one set of relevant create, read, update, and delete data maintenance processes.
- *Data are more stable and able to accommodate business change.* Business processes can change often, to reflect changed business conditions. In contrast, data are more stable and generally change only when the nature of the business changes. For example, new data entities and new or changed attributes may be needed to support new business directions.
- *Future business data needs are identified by the normalization cross-check.* A normalization cross-check, as we saw, enables future needs to be determined. The entity list and data map, which together comprise a data model, can thus be modified to easily incorporate these future business needs.
- *The logic for processing 5BNF structure entities is generic.* Because every structure entity has a similar format, the logic that is developed for processing a structure entity is generic and reusable. This is important, because it means that this common logic can be used for processing expert rules in any 5BNF entity.

Endnotes

[1] Date, C., *An Introduction to Databases,* Reading, MA: Addison-Wesley, 1988, and later editions. This covers traditional normalization in detail.

[2] Finkelstein, C., *An Introduction to Information Engineering,* Reading, MA: Addison-Wesley, 1989. This covers both normalization variants briefly.

[3] Finkelstein, C., *Information Engineering: Strategic Systems Development,* Reading, MA: Addison-Wesley, 1992. This covers business normalization in detail.

[4] A surrogate key is a unique identifying key, which is used for this purpose because its value can never be changed.

[5] Case Study Problems 1 through 6 are in the PDF file *Chap-09-Problems.pdf* in the Book Materials folder on the accompanying CD-ROM.

[6] The sample solutions are in the PDF file *Chap-09-Solutions.pdf* in the Book Materials folder on the CD-ROM.

[7] Attributes can be optionally displayed within the entity box, in a data map.

[8] Case Study Problems 7 and 8 are in PDF file *Chap-09-Problems.pdf* in the Book Materials folder on the CD-ROM.

[9] If you are aware of the Boyce-Codd Normal Form for compound key entities, which is used in traditional normalization with 3NF, the 2BNF rule has productively resolved the problem that the Boyce-Codd Normal Form does not address until after 3NF.

[10] Case Study Problem 9 is in the PDF file *Chap-09-Problems.pdf* in the Book Materials folder on the CD-ROM.

[11] Case Study Problem 10 is in the PDF file *Chap-09-Problems.pdf* in the Book Materials folder on the CD-ROM.

[12] This normalization cross-check is not formally required by traditional normalization, but has been applied intuitively by very experienced data modelers. It is a formal requirement of business normalization, because it helps identify data that are needed for the future.

[13] Refer to the earlier definitions for each of these salary homonym attributes in Section 9.4.4.

[14] Case Study Problem 11 is in the PDF file *Chap-09-Problems.pdf* in the Book Materials folder on the CD-ROM.

[15] Case Study Problem 12 is in the PDF file *Chap-09-Problems.pdf* in the Book Materials folder on the CD-ROM.

[16] The definition of a structure entity from Chapter 6 is as follows: "A structure entity is used to represent many-to-many associations between occurrences of secondary entities all under the same principal entity, or to represent recursive associations between occurrences of a single principal or secondary entity." The 5BNF rule definition tells us how to identify and represent a structure entity in a data map.

[17] REASON can contain other attributes also, such as for matrix resource purposes.

[18] EMPLOYEE STRUCTURE contains all numeric values. When physically implemented as a database table, each numeric value will occupy 4 bytes; each row will occupy 20 bytes. This results in high-performance 5BNF database processing.

[19] This figure was provided by Robert Weisman of CGI to clarify this product Bills of Material example.

[20] Case Study Problem 13 is in the PDF file *Chap-09-Problems.pdf* in the Book Materials folder on the CD-ROM.

CHAPTER 10

Menu Design, Screen Design, Performance Analysis, and Process Modeling

In the first part of this chapter we will briefly discuss menu structures and screen designs. These address the human interface architecture in the Who column and Designer row [C4R3], and the presentation architecture in the Who column and Builder row [C4R4] of the Zachman framework. We will see how menu structures and screen designs can initially be defined from data models, based on the entity dependency analysis method described in Chapter 7. We will see how menu structures and screen designs are used for systems design in the How column and Builder row [C2R4], as part of prototype implementation. We will see how a physical database design in the What column and the Builder row [C1R4] is optimized for transaction performance analysis in a distributed systems architecture and technology architecture in the Where column for the Designer [C3R3] and Builder rows [C3R4].

Process models, as described in this chapter, address the How column for the Designer [C3R3] and Builder rows [C2R4] as highlighted in Figure 10.1. We cover process modeling in the second part of the chapter. Process models using the language-independent process notation that is described can be implemented in Java, C, C++, C#, or any object-oriented or procedural language. They can be used as workflow models or process models for the SOA BPM languages discussed in Chapter 14.

Taken together, the methods and techniques covered in this chapter progress from columns 1, 2, 3, and 4 through row 3 for the Designer, down to row 4 for the Builder of Figure 10.1.

10.1 Enterprise Architecture Incremental Build Context

We discussed the incremental build sequence for enterprise architecture in Chapter 5. The human interface menu design and presentation interface screen design are carried out in Step 10 of Figure 10.2, with process modeling in Step 11, as discussed in the following list; the previous steps also included, for context:

- *Step 1:* In Chapter 3, we discussed that strategy analysis identifies statements for mission, vision, core values, goals, objectives, issues, KPIs, and strategies in the strategic plan.

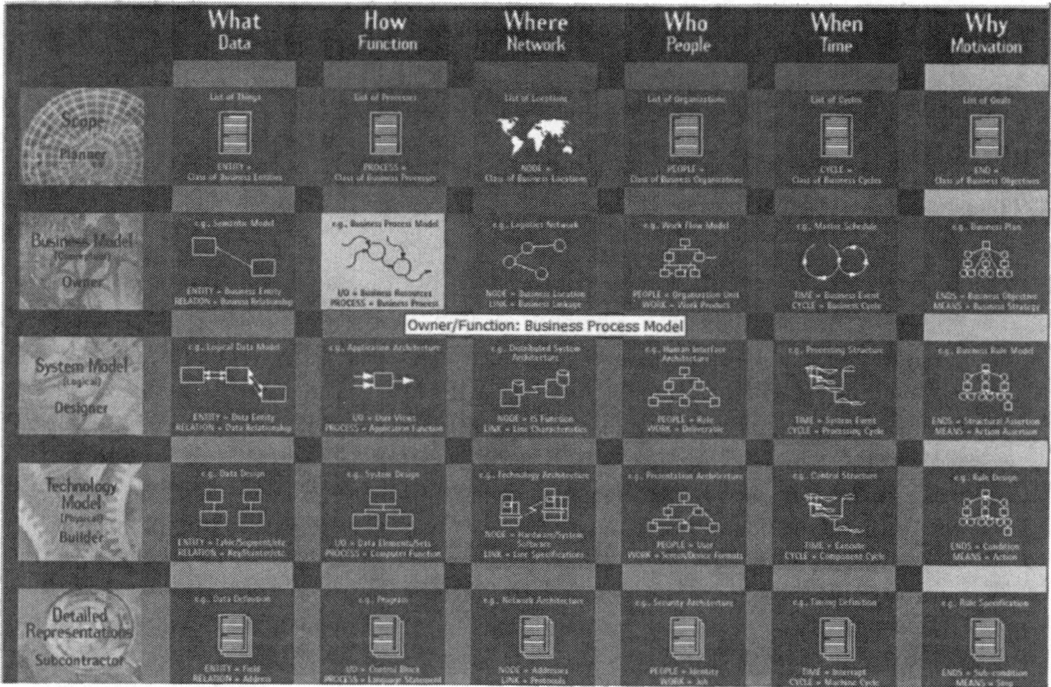

Figure 10.1 Process models address Zachman framework column 2, rows 2 and 3.

	What Data	How Function	Where Location	Who People	When Time	Why Future
PLANNER Objectives/Scope	4 List of Things	6 List of Processes	List of Locations	2 Org Structure	7 List of Events	1 List of Goals/Obj
OWNER Conceptual	5 Enterprise Model	7 Activity Model	Business Logistics	8 Work Flow	Master Schedule	3 Business Plan
DESIGNER Logical	9 Logical Data Model	11 Process Model	Distrib. Architect.	10 Human Interface	Process Structure	Business Rules
BUILDER Physical	Physical Data Model	System Model	Technol. Architect.	Presn Interface	Control Structure	Rule Design
SUBCONTRACTOR Out-of-Context	Data Definition	Program	Network Architect.	Security Interface	Timing Definition	Rule Specs
FUNCTIONING ENTERPRISE	Data	Function	Network	Organization	Schedule	Strategy

Figure 10.2 Menus, screens, and processes are defined for columns 4 and 2.

- *Step 2:* Strategy analysis identifies from the organizational structure those managers and business experts responsible for implementing priority areas of the strategic plan.

- *Step 3:* During a 5-day business planning workshop, the identified managers and business experts optionally apply the strategy analysis methodology to define tactical business planning statements to implement strategic plans.
- *Step 4:* In Chapter 6 we saw that data mapping is used to enable business experts and IT experts to work together to identify data for integration. This begins with a 2-day strategic modeling facilitated session as detailed in Chapter 7. Entities that represent required information and data are listed in the What column for the Planner row [C1R1].
- *Step 5:* In Chapter 7 we saw that the facilitated modeling session continues over 2 days, documenting key entities in a strategic model on a white board. The strategic model is a high-level semantic model or enterprise model in the What column for the Owner row [C1R2] that represents a "picture of the business" to the participating managers and business experts. Typically 90 to 120 entities are defined in these 2 days.
- *Step 6:* This step next defines strategic alignment matrices in row 1 for key columns. We covered this in Chapter 8. These matrices are shown in Figure 10.2 as double-headed arrows between these columns and their relevant artifacts with other key columns. Key strategic alignment matrices that are important are listed next and were described in Chapter 8:

  Column 6 to column 4: showing people responsible for key planning statements;
  Column 6 to column 1: showing the data supporting key planning statements;
  Column 2 to column 1: showing the data required by key business activities;
  Column 6 to column 2: showing activities supporting key planning statements.
- *Step 7:* In Step 7, the strategic model (see Chapter 7) or business events in the When column and Planner row [C5R1] can be used to identify activities in the How column and Planner row [C2R1]. These are typically common, reusable activities that deliver cost savings and benefits when implemented. Priority activities are defined as high-level activity models in column 2, row 2. In Chapter 8, activity-based costing was used to determine the relative cost of alternative activities.
- *Step 8:* Priority activity models from Step 7 are used to develop workflow models in the Who column and Owner row [C4R2]. These workflow models are based on final, agreed-on activity models and business rules that indicate how processes will be invoked. This development of workflow models and definition of business rules were described in Chapter 8.
- *Step 9:* The high-level strategic model from the Owner's perspective [C1R2] is expanded to greater detail in this step, transforming it to a fully attributed logical data model from the Designer's perspective [C1R3]. This uses data mapping (described in Chapter 6) together with business normalization, which was covered in Chapter 9.
- *Step 10:* The logical data model, defined in Chapter 9 for [C1R3], is used as initial input for the definition of menu structures and screen designs. Project plans, derived in Chapter 7 as clusters using entity dependency analysis, are

used to define the menu structure as part of the human architecture in [C4R3] (see Figure 10.2). Screen design—part of the presentation architecture in [C4R4]—can be defined based on logical data model entities, associations, and attributes. In this chapter we will also discuss physical database design and distributed systems design strategies to optimize transaction response times for local and networked transaction access performance analyses.

- *Step 11:* Process models are defined in this step for early delivery of priority activities that were identified in Chapter 8. Process models expand business rules—defined in Chapter 8 for [C6R3] of Figure 10.2—into conditional logic in processes. Business rules are also shown as data model associations in [C1R2–3] (see Chapters 6 and 9). These process models are language independent: They permit the detailed definition of logic for later implementation by using procedural, object-oriented, or workflow-based BPM languages.

10.1.1 Reading Strategy for This Chapter

The chapter does not cover menu design or screen design in detail. Nor does it address in detail physical database design and transaction performance analysis for distributed systems design. Many excellent books on these topics are available that will offer you much more comprehensive assistance than this chapter provides. Instead the emphasis is to show how guidance for these design tasks is provided from the use of data models and clusters in the What column, derived using entity dependency analysis as described in Chapter 7. The first part of the chapter also illustrates the rapid delivery of prototyped systems using prototyping tools. For these reasons you may want to read these pages in detail to see how guidance is provided from data models for menu design, screen design, and transaction performance analysis.

The process modeling notation in the second part of the chapter is intended for use by business experts and IT experts working together in a joint design partnership. The notation can be used to model processes that will be implemented in any object-oriented or procedural language. It can also be used to model workflow-based logic using Web services, SOA, and BPM languages as discussed in Chapters 13 and 14.

If you use UML, you may want to skim-read the process modeling notation in the second part of the chapter. If you see new approaches beneficial to your present methods, you can decide to read these pages in more detail, with the objective of incorporating these approaches into your present UML modeling methods.

10.2 Initial Menu Structure from a Data Model

We saw that entity dependency analysis in Chapter 7 uses business rules, represented as data model associations, to derive clusters. This derivation is based on the relative strength of the associations using the three entity dependency rules that were discussed in Chapter 7. Each cluster becomes a separately implementable subproject, represented in Figure 10.2 by the vertical sliver for Step 9 in column 1. The next pages show how these clusters also provide insight into the likely menu structure needed to navigate the physical databases that will later be implemented from a logical data model. Menu design represents part of the human interface in [C4R3].

10.2.1 Simple Menu Structure Design for Person Skill

We will use the data map fragment in Figure 10.3 to illustrate these concepts. Applying the entity dependency analysis method described in Chapter 7, we see that the data map on the left side of Figure 10.3 results in the derivation of Person Skill Management as the cluster to the right. This represents the existence of a potential business activity or process in [C2R2–3].

This cluster helps us determine the potential menu structure, where the phase number in the cluster indicates the menu depth. For example, a Phase 1 entity [1] indicates that it is a first-level menu item, while each higher phase number indicates the existence of a next-level menu item. From Figure 10.3 we can derive the potential menu structure, shown in Figure 10.4.

The menu structure at the top right of Figure 10.4 shows that *Person ...* is a menu entry point [2]. This is illustrated by the arrow touching PERSON in the data map at the left. We see that a phase number of 1 from the cluster in Figure 10.3 has become a first-level menu entry point in Figure 10.4.

Person Skill is a Phase 2 entity in Figure 10.3. In the menu structure at the top right of Figure 10.4, it is indented one position to the right to show that it is a second-level menu item. This is illustrated in the data map at the left by the arrow from PERSON to PERSON SKILL.

Similarly, SKILL is a Phase 1 entity in Figure 10.3. It is shown as a menu entry point by the arrow touching SKILL in the data map in Figure 10.4 and by *Skill ...* as the first-level menu item in the menu structure at the bottom right of the figure. PERSON SKILL is a Phase 2 entity. *Person Skill* is therefore indented one position to the right, indicating that it is a second-level menu item, illustrated by the arrow from SKILL to PERSON SKILL.

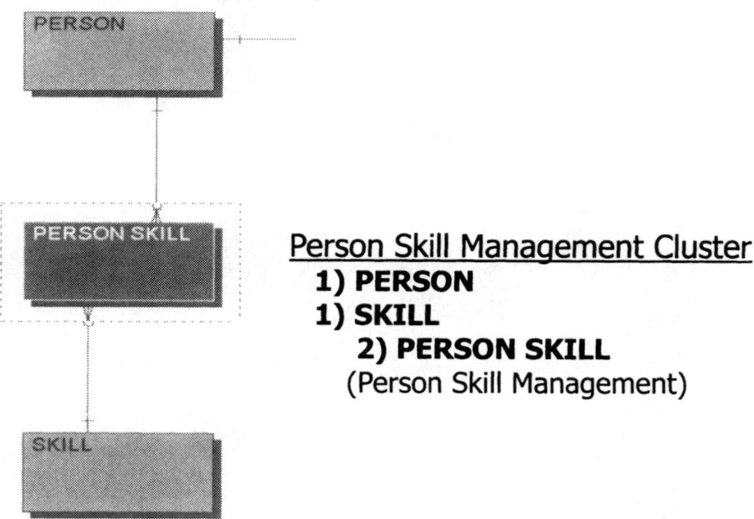

Figure 10.3 Data map fragment to be used for menu structure design.

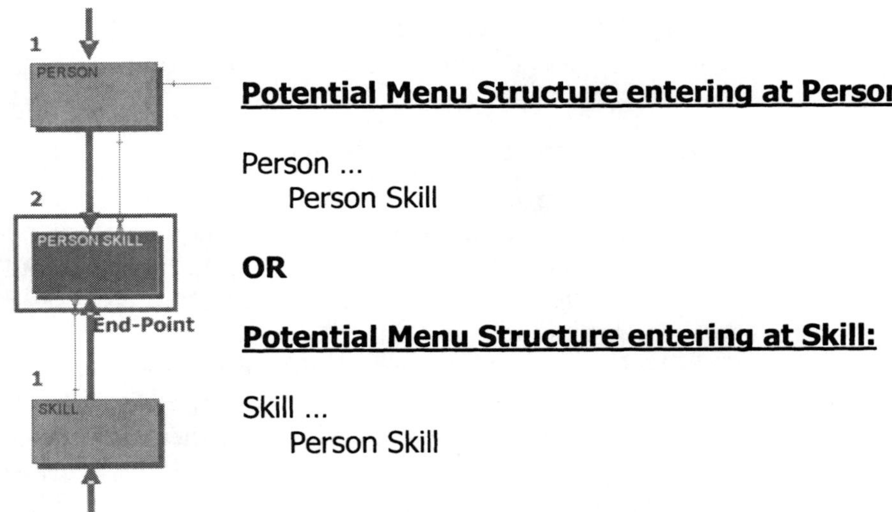

Figure 10.4 Menu structure design from a data map fragment.

10.2.2 Tabbed Menu Structure Design for Project Resource Management

We will use a more complex data map to discuss other menu structure design examples that can be derived from entity dependency clusters. For this purpose we will use the data map and cluster shown in Figure 10.5 to derive a tabbed menu structure for Project Resource Management. From this data map, the derived cluster is shown to the right of the figure. The end-point entity PROJECT RESOURCE in the data

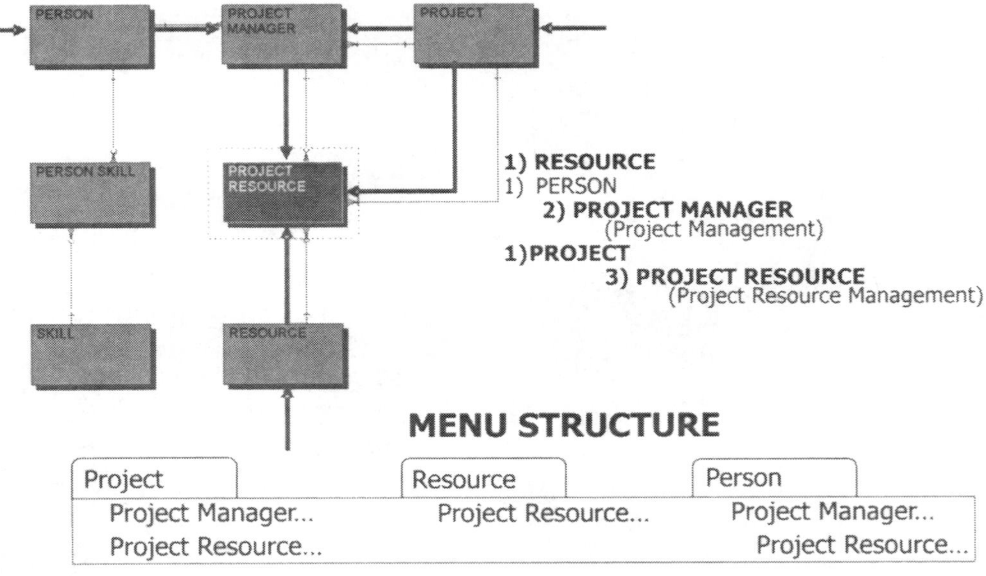

Figure 10.5 Project Resource Management menu structure design.

map is the focus of this cluster. It appears as the last line in the cluster, representing Project Resource Management.

We see that PROJECT RESOURCE in Figure 10.5 is directly dependent on RESOURCE and on PROJECT, as shown by the *mandatory one* association to each of these entities. Each entity has a *mandatory one* association touching it, so each is a Phase 1 entity in the cluster.

PROJECT RESOURCE is directly dependent on PROJECT MANAGER; but this entity is also dependent on PROJECT, which is Phase 1. PROJECT MANAGER is thus a Phase 2 entity, which means that PROJECT RESOURCE is a Phase 3 entity in the cluster.

PROJECT MANAGER is also dependent on PERSON, which is thus a Phase 1 entity. It also appears in the cluster. It is shown *not bold* because it does not have a direct association with PROJECT RESOURCE. Because each of the other entities in the cluster does have a direct association with PROJECT RESOURCE, they are all shown as **bold.**

At the bottom of Figure 10.5 is a potential tabbed menu structure that is suggested by the cluster. Each of the Phase 1 entities represents menu item entry points. These are shown as tabs on the menu and as entry-point arrows in the data map.

We will first use the menu tab at *Project*, which is Phase 1 in the cluster. PROJECT MANAGER is Phase 2, so *Project Manager* appears indented as a menu item in the menu under *Project.*

PROJECT RESOURCE appears as Phase 3 in the cluster, so *Project Resource* would potentially be further indented in the menu under *Project Manager.* However, the direct association from PROJECT to PROJECT RESOURCE in the data map suggests instead that *Project Resource* can appear in the tabbed menu under *Project* at the same level as *Project Manager.*

Compare this now with the *Person* menu tab in Figure 10.5. *Project Manager* is indented under the *Person* tab, while *Project Resource* is further indented under *Project Manager.* This indent to the third level is correct, because we can see from the data map that PERSON does not have a direct association with PROJECT RESOURCE.

Finally, we see from the data map that RESOURCE has a direct association only with PROJECT RESOURCE. Therefore, the *Resource* menu tab has only one indented menu item: *Project Resource.*

From these examples, we can see that the derived clusters from a data map offer insight into potential menu structure dependencies for menu design.

10.3 Preliminary Screen Designs from a Data Model

We can also gain some insight into preliminary screen designs from an examination of data model entities, associations, and data attributes. In Chapter 9 we saw transformation of a strategic model in [C1R2] into a logical data model in [C1R3]. We defined the data attributes that are needed in each data entity to represent the current and future business needs. These data attributes are implemented as data fields in screen designs. The design of screens is part of the presentation interface in [C1R4].

10.3.1 Typical Screen Design for a Single Entity

Following the definition of attributes in the logical data model [C1R3], each entity is later implemented as a separate table when installed as part of a physical database. The attributes within the entity become columns of the table and the entity occurrences become rows of that table.

When the table is later used in production, its values will change during processing. Data maintenance changes needed to keep each column and row value up to date require create, read, update, and delete (CRUD) processing. Screen designs for this CRUD processing can be derived from the definition of each entity in the logical data model.

Two typical screen designs are derived from a logical entity definition: a columnar screen or a tabular data grid screen. A *columnar screen design* shows the attributes of a single entity occurrence (implemented as columns of a single row of a table) as data fields, listed under each other on the screen. A *tabular data grid screen* shows occurrences of the entity in a spreadsheet format as rows, with the attributes as columns of the spreadsheet grid. A columnar screen design example is shown in Figure 10.6.

Figure 10.6 shows an order entry data map (with attributes displayed in each entity) at the top left of the figure. The cluster beside it (at the top right of the figure) has been derived from this data map using entity dependency analysis. The bottom left shows *Customer...* as a first-level menu item. The columnar screen design at the bottom right has been derived from the logical definition of the entity CUSTOMER. Each attribute name within the entity becomes a data field label that precedes a screen area, used to display the field on the screen for visual processing. We will discuss this and other examples further in a later section on prototyping from a data

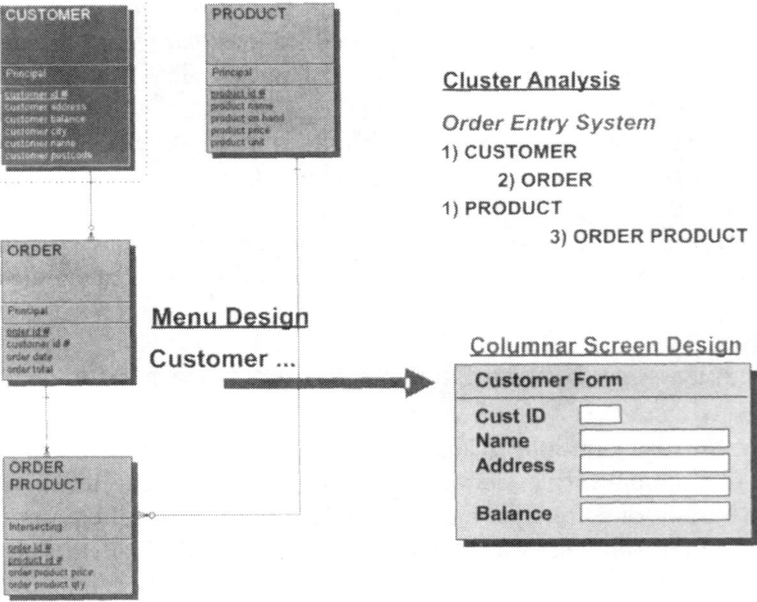

Figure 10.6 Typical columnar screen design from an entity.

model (Section 10.5). We will see that some prototyping tools can automatically generate these screen designs.

10.3.2 Typical Screen Design for *One-to-Many* Associations

The top part of Figure 10.7 shows the data map that we developed in Chapter 6. We can see that the access path along the *one-to-many* association from JOB to JOB SKILL has been highlighted. This suggests that—following access to a specific JOB—all of the JOB SKILLS for that JOB can be displayed.

The bottom part of Figure 10.7 shows the relevant access logic and preliminary screen design. We can see that a *one-to-many* association in the data map suggests a potential Master–Detail screen design.

Similarly, the highlighted access path from SKILL to JOB SKILL in Figure 10.8 suggests that—following access to a specific SKILL—all occurrences of the JOB SKILLS for that SKILL should be displayed. This is shown by the preliminary Master–Detail screen at the bottom right of that figure.

The data fields that are displayed in the screen designs of Figure 10.8 are based on the data attributes defined in the logical data model in [C1R3]. We can see in the Master–Detail screen design at the bottom left of the figure that *Job No* and *Job*

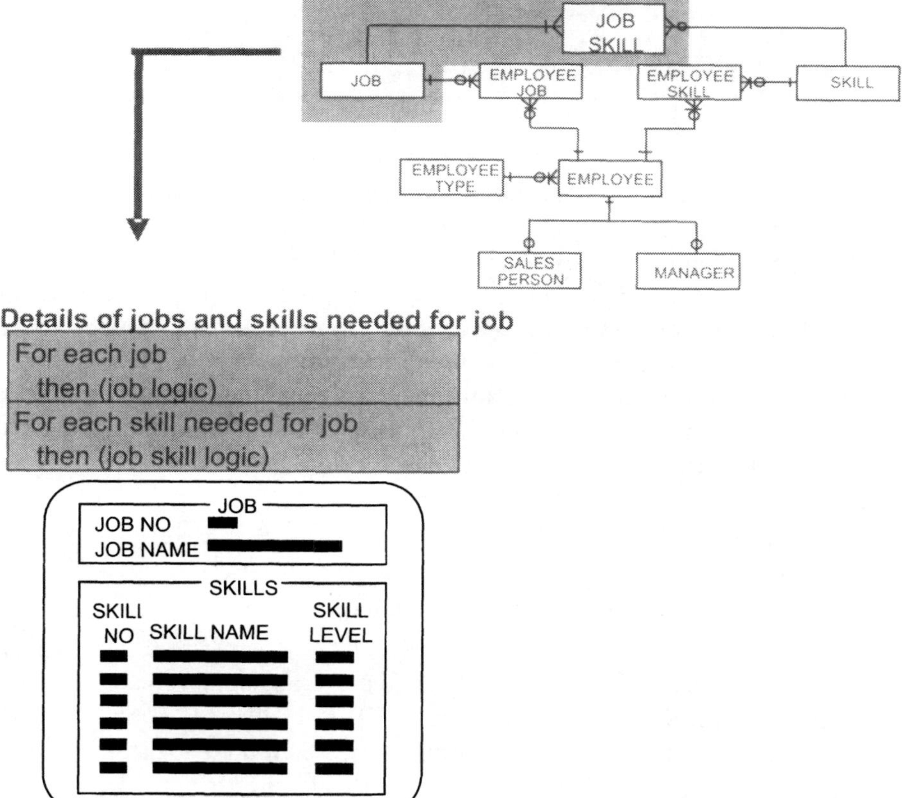

Figure 10.7 *One-to-many* associations suggest Master–Detail screen designs.

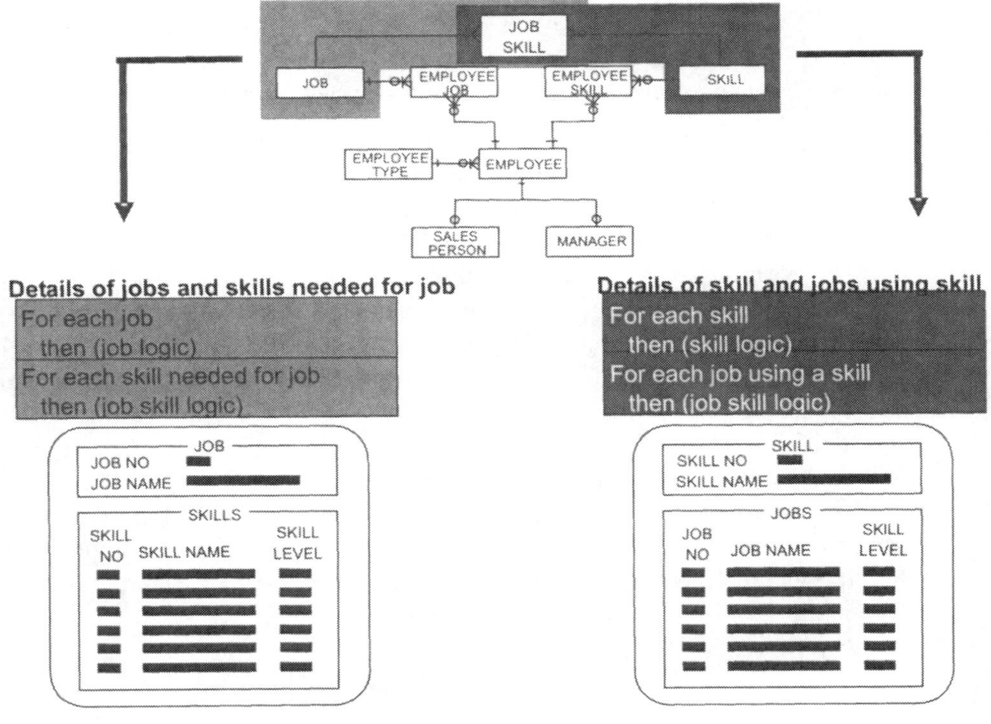

Figure 10.8 The entry point is the Master, in a Master–Detail screen design.

Name fields in the Job Master section were extracted from those attributes in JOB. Similarly, the *Skill No* and *Skill Level* fields in the Skills Detail section were extracted from those same attributes in JOB SKILL.

However the *Skill Name* field in the Skills Detail section does not exist in JOB SKILL. As the data model was previously normalized in Chapter 9 to 3BNF (in fact, 4BNF), we find that the *Skill Name* attribute exists in SKILL. This tells us that merely examining the associations in a data map does not give us all of the information we need for screen design. We must also understand the attributes in the other (Owner) entities that exist in the relevant data map clusters.

1) JOB
1) SKILL
   2) JOB SKILL (Job Skill Management)

JOB SKILL is Phase 2 in the *Job Skill Management* cluster shown here. This is directly dependent on both JOB and SKILL, as Phase 1 entities in the cluster. The reference to *Skill Name* in the Skills Detail section (see bottom left of Figure 10.8) requires an access to SKILL. Similarly the reference to *Job Name* in the Jobs Detail section at the bottom right of Figure 10.8 requires an access to JOB.

10.4 Database Capacity Planning and Transaction Performance

The logical data model in [C1R3]—fully attributed in Chapter 9—is transformed to [C1R4] as a physical database design for implementation by the target DBMS. This physical database design is typically generated automatically by a modeling tool. These tools are also used to automatically generate the DDL scripts that are needed for database installation in [C1R5]. We will discuss the capabilities of various modeling tools in Chapter 15.

As part of the physical database design, most modeling tools optimize the resulting design according to the target DBMS product that will be used for database installation. Some tools may also assist with database capacity planning. The next section discusses manual methods for database capacity planning.

10.4.1 Database Capacity Planning from a Logical Data Model

We will use the same data map from Figure 10.8 to calculate database sizes for capacity planning of servers or workstations. This is illustrated in Figure 10.9. We will also use this same data map later in the chapter for calculation of potential transaction response times and for distributed database transaction performance analyses.

Figure 10.10 shows the data map with the number of row occurrences displayed above the relevant entity box as a number in italics. This is called the *data volume*. It is also used to calculate the frequency of occurrence along each association and is shown as a number in brackets at the *many* end of each association in the data map. For example, Figure 10.10 shows that there will be *100* rows in the JOB entity, when this entity is implemented as a physical database table called JOB. There will be *1000* rows in the physical JOB SKILL table and *50* rows in the physical SKILL table.

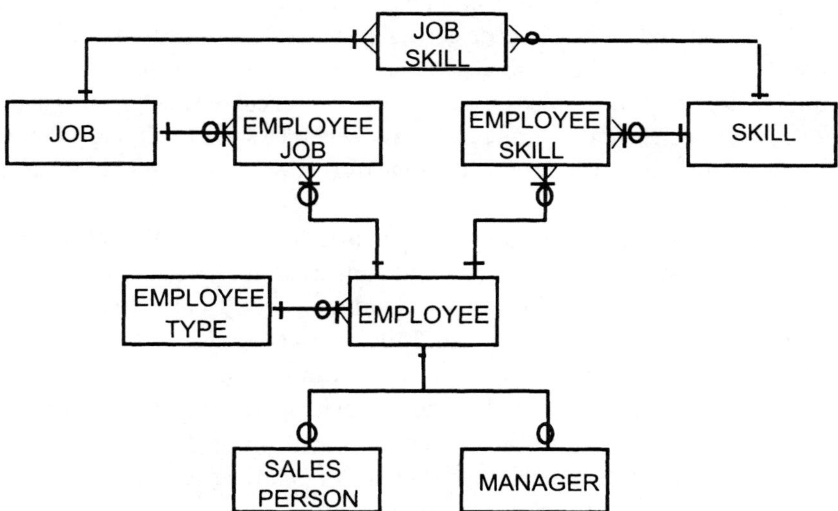

Figure 10.9 Data map used for database capacity planning, for transaction response time analyses, and for distributed transaction performance analyses.

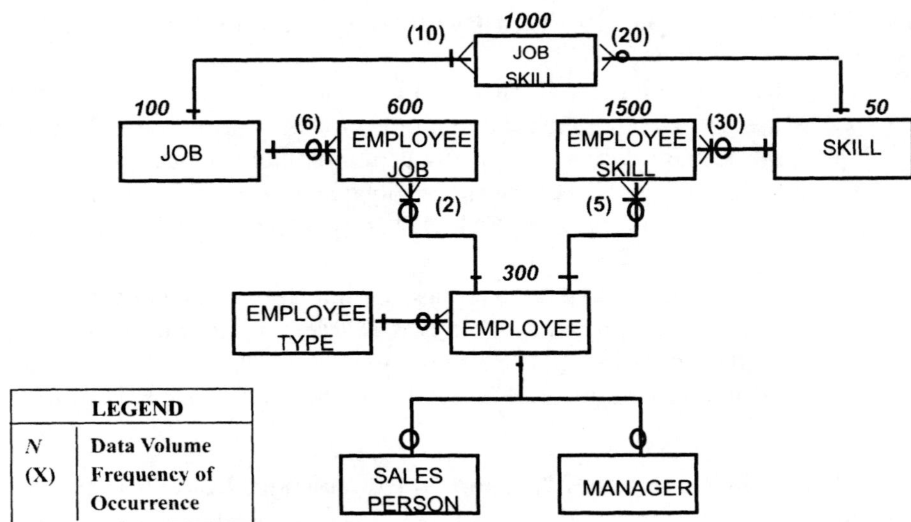

Figure 10.10 Data map showing data volumes and association frequencies of occurrence.

From these row occurrences, the average frequency of occurrence of each association can be calculated. For example, we can see that there is an average of (10) Job Skills for each Job and an average of (20) Job Skills for each Skill [3].

As part of logical data modeling in [C1R3], the logical data type of each attribute is defined. This will later be used to implement each attribute as a column of the relevant physical table for that entity [4]. This definition is typically carried out automatically by the modeling tool, based on *logical data type to physical data type* transformation rules specified by the data modeler, or the DBA. This physical data type specification also indicates the actual number of bytes needed to implement each column.

Based on the physical row structure and format used by the target DBMS, the length of each row of a table can be calculated. This is the sum of the actual number of bytes needed to implement each physical column in that table. A spreadsheet is used to carry out these calculations, multiplying the calculated row length by the data volume of the table, expressed as row occurrences as shown in Figure 10.10. The result is the total number of bytes needed to store each physical table. For capacity planning, the total database size is thus the sum of the size of each physical table in the database.

The same spreadsheet can also be used to calculate the frequency of occurrence along each association. This is based on the respective data volumes for the two entities joined by the association. For example, we discussed earlier that there are an average of (10) Job Skills for each Job and an average of (20) Job Skills for each Skill [3]. Additionally, if minimum and maximum data volume row occurrences are available, the same calculation can be used to determine minimum and maximum association frequencies of occurrence.

We will use the calculated frequency of occurrence to determine transaction performance response times as discussed next.

10.4.2 Logical Transaction Performance Analysis

We will now analyze the performance of a logical transaction that accesses the database tables represented by the data map in Figure 10.10 to answer the following query:

For each Job, first identify all of the Job Skills required by that Job. For each of these Skills, next identify each Employee who has the relevant Skills and determine each Employee's name.

The resolution of this query requires a number of logical accesses to the data map that is shown in Figure 10.11. Each logical access will be calculated in the following pages as physical I/O accesses for transaction performance analysis, when the data model is later implemented as a physical database.

We will calculate the performance of a single query transaction, as well as an average of 5 query transactions per hour. These transactions are shown by the arrow entering the data map at JOB in Figure 10.11 with the numbers "*1 (5)*" under the arrow touching JOB, where the number in parentheses is the total number of transactions per hour. Table 10.1 uses the association frequencies of occurrence from Figure 10.10 to calculate the logical references [5] made by a single Job query transaction, and the total logical references made by 5 transactions per hour.

This access to JOB is shown in the first detail row of Table 10.1; it appears as *Entry : JOB* in the second column of that row, under the heading *Access Path*. The third column of the row indicates that the *Type of Access* is a *Read (R)* access. The fourth column is headed *Association Frequency of Occurrence (Assoc. Freq.)* and shows the association frequency as *1*, for access to a single Job. The fifth column shows that this single Job query requires *Number of Logical References (Logical Refs.)* also of *1*. The sixth (and final) column shows the *Total References per Hour* (Total Refs.) to the data map is *(5)* [6].

The arrow in the data map of Figure 10.11 from JOB to JOB SKILL is labeled 1, to identify this as access path 1. The logical accesses for this access path are shown

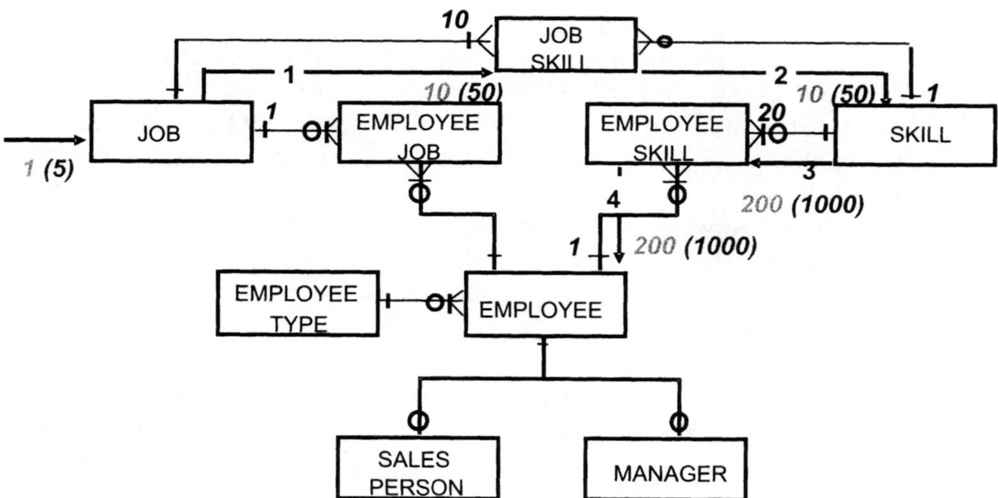

Figure 10.11 Logical transaction performance analysis data map.

Table 10.1 Logical Transaction Performance Analysis

Path No.	*Access Path*	*Type of Access*	*Assoc. Freq.*	*Logical Refs.*	*Total Refs.*
	Entry : JOB	R	1	1	(5)
1.	JOB : JOB SKILL	R	10	10	(50)
2.	JOB SKILL : SKILL	R	1	10	(50)
3.	SKILL : EMPLOYEE SKILL	R	20	200	(1,000)
4.	EMPLOYEE SKILL : EMPLOYEE	R	1	200	(1,000)
	TRANSACTION TOTAL			421	(2,105)

as JOB:JOB SKILL for access path 1 of Table 10.1. The *Assoc. Freq.* of 10 for this row is multiplied by the *Logical Refs.* in the preceding row, to calculate the *Logical Refs.* for row 2, This results in a value of 10 in the fifth column and (50) *Total Refs.* in the sixth column. The arrowhead for access path 1—touching JOB SKILL in the data map—shows the numbers *10 (50)*. This indicates that each access to a JOB requires a logical access to each of the 10 Job Skills for that JOB, with total logical accesses in an hour to 50 Job Skills.

The next arrow in the data map—from JOB SKILL to SKILL—is labeled 2 and is shown as access path 2 in Table 10.1. The logical accesses for this access path are shown as JOB SKILL : SKILL in access path 2 of the table. The *Assoc. Freq.* of 1 for this row is multiplied by the *Logical Refs.* in the preceding row of 10, to calculate the *Logical Refs.* for row 3. This results in a value of 10 in the fifth column and (50) *Total Refs.* in the sixth column. The arrowhead for access path 2—touching SKILL in the data map—also shows numbers *10 (50)*. This indicates that each access to a JOB SKILL requires a logical access to each of the 10 Skills for that Job Skill, with total logical accesses in an hour to 50 Skills.

Similarly, access path 3 in Table 10.1 identifies the path from SKILL to EMPLOYEE SKILL; this is access path 3 of the table for the *Access Path* SKILL:EMPLOYEE SKILL. The *Assoc. Freq.* of 20 at EMPLOYEE SKILL for each of the 10 separate accesses to SKILL in path 3 results in 200 *Logical Refs.* to EMPLOYEE SKILL in path 3—with (1,000) *Total Refs.*

In turn, access path 4 in row 5 of Table 10.1 calculates logical accesses for EMPLOYEE SKILL : EMPLOYEE. The *Assoc. Freq.* of 1 at EMPLOYEE in path 5, multiplied by each of the 200 separate accesses to EMPLOYEE SKILL in path 4, results in 200 *Logical Refs.* to EMPLOYEE in row 5—together with (1,000) *Total Refs.*

We will now sum the *Logical Refs.* column and the *Total Refs.* column for all rows in Table 10.1. The last row of the table indicates that the *Transaction Total* for each transaction is 421 logical references, with 2,105 total references based on 5 transactions per hour.

These logical references do not yet represent physical I/O accesses to database tables. We cannot use these logical reference totals in their present form to calculate anticipated transaction response times for transaction performance analysis. We first must consider physical database design alternatives. These are discussed in the following topics.

10.4.3 Physical Transaction Performance Analysis—Not Optimized

To calculate anticipated transaction response times for transaction performance analysis, we will discuss the performance impact of various physical database design strategies. We will first consider a database design where each logical data entity is implemented as a separate physical database table. Each logical reference will therefore require a physical I/O access to the relevant table.

Figure 10.12 illustrates this example. The data map shows each of the referenced entities highlighted to represent physical I/O accesses. The legend assumes an I/O access time of 10 ms. This is also shown as an added *Access Time* column in Table 10.2, where each row expresses this 10-ms access time as 0.010 second.

Notice that the last column is now headed *I/O Time*. This is the product of the value in the *Access Time* column, multiplied by the value in the *Logical Refs.* column for each row. This calculates the actual I/O time needed to access the physical table for that row.

Each of the rows in Table 10.2 shows the I/O time that has been calculated for each referenced entity. This represents the physical I/O time that is needed to access each physical table. The *Transaction Total* in the last row shows a total of 421 *Logical Refs.* as before, but now the *I/O Time* column shows a total of 4.21 seconds—representing a calculated *Transaction Response Time* of 4.21 seconds. This is not a long duration for a response time, but if possible a faster response time would certainly be preferred.

The physical database design strategy that was used in this example—with each logical entity implemented as a separate physical table—has not been optimized to improve the transaction response time performance. Several alternative physical database design strategies exist that we can use to improve on this response time as discussed next.

10.4.4 Physical Transaction Performance Analysis—Database Clustering

Most DBMS products today enable a DBA to specify that child entities—participating in a *one-to-many* association—be stored physically close to the parent entity to minimize I/O access. This parent is the owner entity of the association. For example,

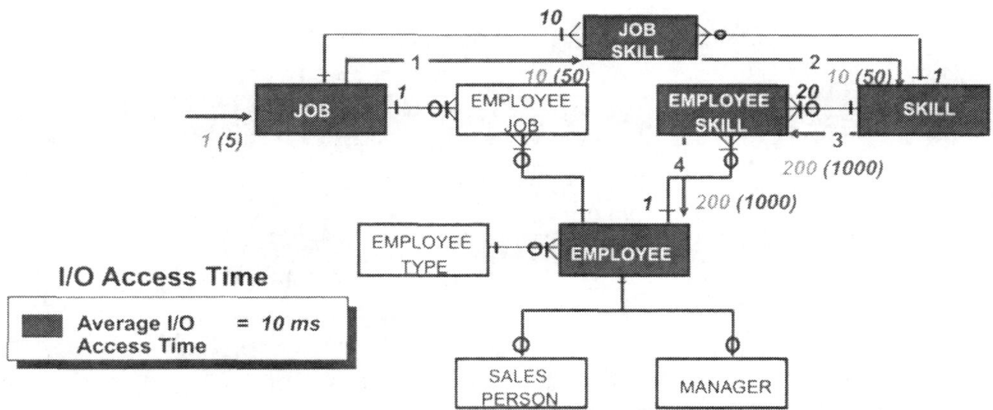

Figure 10.12 Physical transaction performance analysis data map—not optimized.

Table 10.2 Physical Transaction Performance Analysis—Not Optimized

Path No.	*Access Path*	*Access Time*	*Type of Access*	*Assoc. Freq.*	*Logical Refs.*	*I/O Time*
	Entry : JOB	0.010 sec	R	*1*	1	0.01 sec
1.	JOB : JOB SKILL	0.010 sec	R	10	10	0.10 sec
2.	JOB SKILL : SKILL	0.010 sec	R	*1*	10	0.10 sec
3.	SKILL : EMPLOYEE SKILL	0.010 sec	R	20	200	2.00 sec
4.	EMPLOYEE SKILL : EMPLOYEE	0.010 sec	R	*1*	200	2.00 sec
	TRANSACTION TOTAL				421	4.21 sec

in Figure 10.13 we can see that JOB SKILL (at the *many* end of the *one-to-many* association between JOB and JOB SKILL) is owned by JOB (which is at the *one* end of the association). Similarly EMPLOYEE SKILL is owned by SKILL. Each entity is a child of the respective parent (owner) entity.

When implemented as physical tables in a database, the DBA can specify to the DBMS product that each child table should be physically stored close to the parent table. The DBMS then stores all related rows together in the same I/O page (or pages). With this physical database design strategy, the parent and all related child table row occurrences can be retrieved together in the same I/O access. This database design strategy is called *database clustering* [7].

In the Figure 10.13 data map, we see the specifications for database clustering at the left. It indicates that JOB SKILL is clustered with JOB, and EMPLOYEE SKILL is clustered with SKILL. The *Clustered Access Time* legend shows the average I/O access time is 10 ms as before. It also shows that the buffer access time (in DBMS I/O page memory) is assumed to take 1 ms.

When there is a reference to JOB, the DBMS accesses the relevant JOB row with an I/O access that takes an assumed 10 ms. With this I/O access for JOB, all of the related row occurrences of JOB SKILL for that JOB are automatically retrieved by the DBMS at the same time. When each related JOB SKILL is requested, the DBMS finds that it is already in its I/O page buffer. No further I/O access is needed. A memory reference to the buffer is used instead, which takes only 1 ms for each reference.

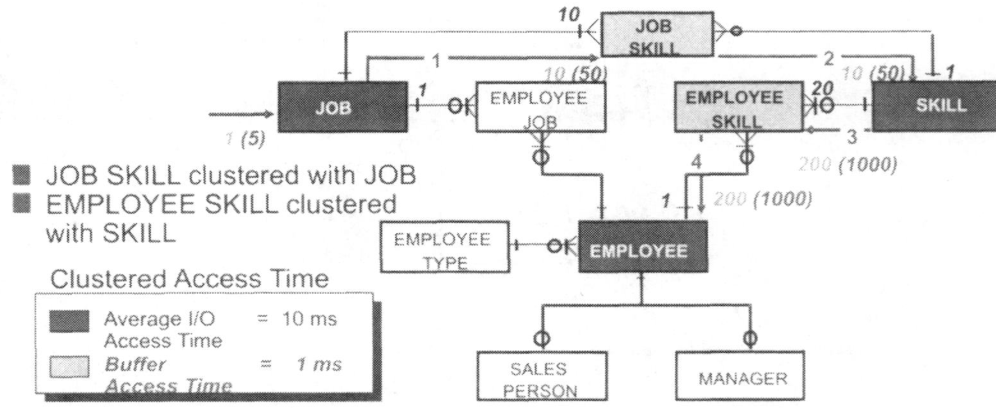

Figure 10.13 Physical transaction performance analysis data map—database clustering.

The performance impact of database clustering becomes apparent when we examine Table 10.3. Notice that the *Access Time* column for the JOB : JOB SKILL row and the SKILL : EMPLOYEE SKILL row contains a value of 0.001 sec (for 1 ms) in each row. When this *Access Time* value is multiplied by the relevant *Logical Refs.* value, the *I/O Time* value for that row is much lower than the corresponding values in Table 10.2.

More importantly, notice also the *Transaction Total* in the *I/O Time* column. This shows that the estimated physical transaction response time has now been calculated as 2.32 seconds, compared to 4.21 seconds before database clustering. Most DBMS products offer the use of database clustering, along with other design strategies, to optimize physical database design for improved transaction response time performance in this way.

It is not the purpose of this chapter to develop these physical database design strategies further. But we will see that other design strategies can be used to optimize distributed database design and transaction response times across a network. These strategies are addressed in the following pages. They are part of the distributed systems architecture and technology architecture in the Where column for the Designer [C3R3] and Builder rows [C3R4] of Figure 10.1.

10.4.5 Distributed Database Design—Not Optimized

The data map in Figure 10.9 that we have used for transaction performance analysis to this point has assumed that all tables are directly accessible locally in the physical database implemented from that data map. This centralized database assumption meant that we only needed to optimize for database I/O access performance, discussed in relation to Tables 10.2 and 10.3.

In practice, tables in the database could be distributed across the local-area network (LAN) of an enterprise, or across the Internet—on network servers as illustrated in Figure 10.14. This shows a distributed database example where the tables for JOB SKILL, SKILL, and EMPLOYEE SKILL are physically installed on network servers in each branch office. Each branch server holds these details only for employees at the relevant branch, along with their Employee Skills and the associated Job Skills required at that branch. The other tables continue to be physically stored on a centralized mainframe server.

This means some of the accesses that we discussed earlier now need to be across the LAN or Internet, with associated network communication delays. We can

Table 10.3 Physical Transaction Performance Analysis—Database Clustering

Path No.	*Access Path*	*Access Time*	*Type of Access*	*Assoc. Freq.*	*Logical Refs.*	*I/O Time*
	Entry : JOB	0.010 sec	R	*1*	1	0.01 sec
1.	JOB : JOB SKILL	*0.001 sec*	R	10	10	0.01 sec
2.	JOB SKILL : SKILL	0.010 sec	R	*1*	10	0.10 sec
3.	SKILL : EMPLOYEE SKILL	*0.001 sec*	R	20	200	0.20 sec
4.	EMPLOYEE SKILL : EMPLOYEE	0.010 sec	R	*1*	200	2.00 sec
	TRANSACTION TOTAL				421	2.32 sec

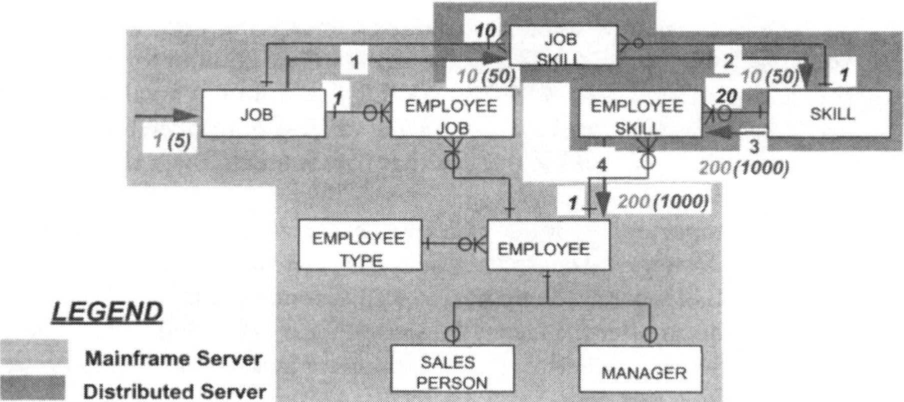

Figure 10.14 Distributed database design data map—not optimized.

clearly see that access path 1—from JOB (on the mainframe) to JOB SKILL (on the branch server)—involves communication across the network. Similarly access path 4—from EMPLOYEE SKILL (on the branch server) to EMPLOYEE (on the mainframe)—involves network communication as well. The access time along these two access paths needs to consider network propagation and transmission delays. We must take this network delay impact into account when calculating distributed transaction performance analysis, which is discussed next.

10.4.6 Distributed Transaction Performance Analysis—Network Impact

In Figure 10.15 we will assume that the typical network access time is 1 second. The actual access time across the network, of course, will vary in practice from this assumption. It depends on network traffic volume and communication speed (sometimes called network capacity or bandwidth), network design and associated propagation delays, and many other factors. Without complicating the example with these real-life considerations, we will assume a network access time of 1 sec as shown in the legend in Figure 10.15—this is a convenient assumption.

The distributed database design in Table 10.4 assumes that the DBA has specified to the branch server DBMS that it must generate an index on *Job Number* to JOB SKILL. This will be used as an entry point at the branch server to access the Job Skills required by a specific Job.

Obtaining the relevant *Job Name* will require an access from JOB SKILL to JOB across the network. This is the reverse direction for access path 1 than would be used with the completely centralized database discussed in Tables 10.2 and 10.3. Similarly, given the Skills required by the Job, each Employee Skill occurrence for those Skills will require a network access from EMPLOYEE SKILL to EMPLOYEE to obtain each *Employee Name*.

Table 10.4 shows an *Access Time* value of 1 second for network access paths 1 and 4. The product of network access time multiplied by the *Logical Refs.* for each row (shown in *italics* in the table) results in an I/O time of 10 seconds for access path 1 and 200 seconds for access path 4. The *Transaction Total* in the last row shows the *I/O Time* is now 212.11 seconds, an unacceptable transaction response time of

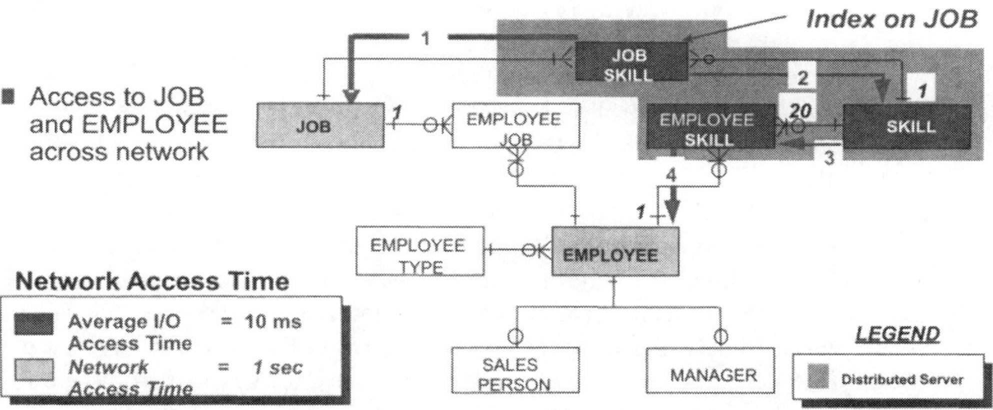

Figure 10.15 Distributed transaction performance analysis data map—network impact.

Table 10.4 Distributed Transaction Performance Analysis—Network Impact

Path No.	*Access Path*	*Access Time*	*Type of Access*	*Assoc. Freq.*	*Logical Refs.*	*I/O Time*
Index	Entry : JOB	0.01 sec	R	*1*	1	0.01 sec
1.	JOB SKILL : JOB	*1.00 sec*	*R*	*10*	*10*	*10.00 sec*
2.	JOB SKILL : SKILL	0.01 sec	R	*1*	10	0.10 sec
3.	SKILL : EMPLOYEE SKILL	0.01 sec	R	*20*	200	2.00 sec
4.	EMPLOYEE SKILL : EMPLOYEE	*1.00 sec*	*R*	*1*	*200*	*200.00 sec*
	TRANSACTION TOTAL				421	212.11 sec

around 3.5 minutes—reflecting the impact of the time delays associated with network access.

10.4.7 Distributed Transaction Performance Analysis—Data Replication

We can improve this unacceptable network access transaction response time by using some distributed database design considerations. The only reason that access is made across the network for each of access paths 1 and 4 is to obtain, respectively, *Job Name* and *Employee Name*. These columns are wholly dependent on *Job Number* in JOB and *Employee Number* in EMPLOYEE. For normalization to 3BNF we must leave both of these columns positioned in those tables. But what if we also positioned them in JOB SKILL and EMPLOYEE SKILL? This would be redundant, but what is the impact?

In fact, this would completely eliminate the need for any access across the network! If *Job Name* is stored redundantly in JOB SKILL and *Employee Name* is stored redundantly in EMPLOYEE SKILL, this would certainly violate 3BNF. But in this case, the data redundancy is called *data replication*. It would create a negative performance impact if these columns were volatile and hence changed frequently. They would then need to be updated often across the network to reflect their latest values, which would impact negatively on overall performance.

However, in practice these columns are not typically volatile. A *Job Name* changes only infrequently in most organizations; *Employee Name* changes even less frequently—such as by marriage—and so is even less volatile. The redundant presence of these columns also in the JOB SKILL and in EMPLOYEE SKILL tables, stored in the branch server, obviates any need to access the network at all. Figure 10.15 shows the impact of this Replication database design strategy.

Table 10.5 illustrates what happens if we eliminate access paths 1 and 4 from the table, shown as strike-through text. We see that the previous access time across the network of 1 second for these two access paths in Figure 10.15 has now changed instead to a buffer access time of 1 ms. This results in I/O times of 0.01 second for path 1 and 0.20 second for path 4. The *Transaction Total* in the last row for *I/O Time*, previously unacceptable at approximately 3.5 minutes, has now been reduced to a more reasonable response time of 2.32 seconds.

We have seen through this example that a distributed systems architecture in [C3R3] can use reasonable design assumptions for replicated physical database design and, hence, can have a significant impact on network performance. There are, of course, many other network design optimization opportunities that present themselves in specific enterprise situations. These can improve distributed performance even further, but they are outside the scope of the book.

In the next section, we apply the menu design and screen design concepts covered in this chapter to a prototyping example.

10.5 Prototyping from a Data Model

We now develop a prototype using a typical sales and distribution data model as illustrated in Figure 10.16, which is based on operational data models defined for order entry, purchasing, marketing, and product development. We will use this for the derivation of project plans, with the definition also of menus and screen designs directly from this data model. This will be based on DDL generation using the Visible Advantage modeling tool together with Microsoft Access. This modeling tool is discussed in Chapter 15 and included on the accompanying CD-ROM.

The order entry data map, with all of its attributes displayed, is shown in greater detail in Figure 10.17. We will use this data map for automatic prototype generation.

Table 10.5 Distributed Transaction Performance Analysis—Data Replication

Path No.	*Access Path*	*Access Time*	*Type of Access*	*Assoc. Freq.*	*Logical Refs.*	*I/O Time*
Index	Entry : JOB	0.01 sec	R	*1*	1	0.01 sec
~~1.~~	~~JOB SKILL : JOB~~	*0.001 sec*	*R*	*10*	*10*	*0.01 sec*
2.	JOB SKILL : SKILL	0.01 sec	R	*1*	10	0.10 sec
3.	SKILL : EMPLOYEE SKILL	0.01 sec	R	*20*	200	2.00 sec
~~4.~~	~~EMPLOYEE SKILL : EMPLOYEE~~	*0.001 sec*	*R*	*1*	*200*	*0.20 sec*
	TRANSACTION TOTAL				421	2.32 sec

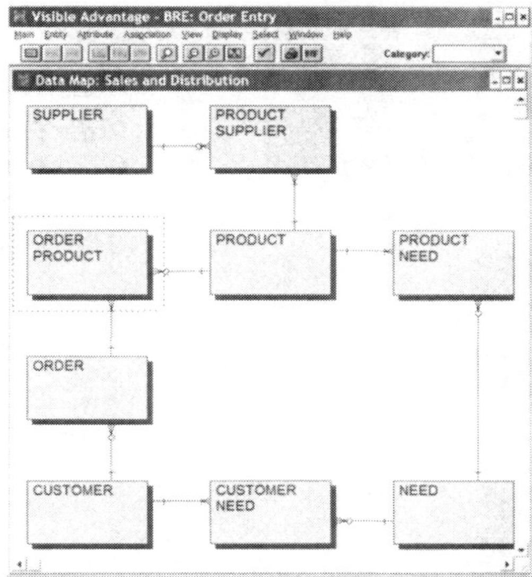

Figure 10.16 Typical sales and distribution data model, to be used for prototyping.

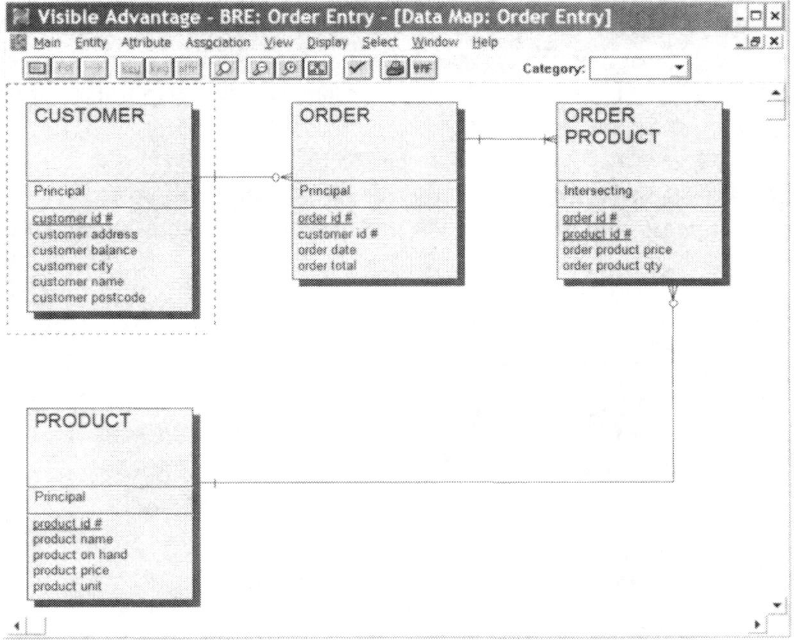

Figure 10.17 The order entry data map, with all attributes displayed.

10.5.1 Menu Design and Screen Design from the Order Entry Data Map

The cluster analysis project plan from the order entry data map shown in Figure 10.17 is now displayed in Figure 10.18. This shows a hierarchical menu structure at the bottom left of the figure, with each menu level indented based on the project phase numbering in the cluster at the top right.

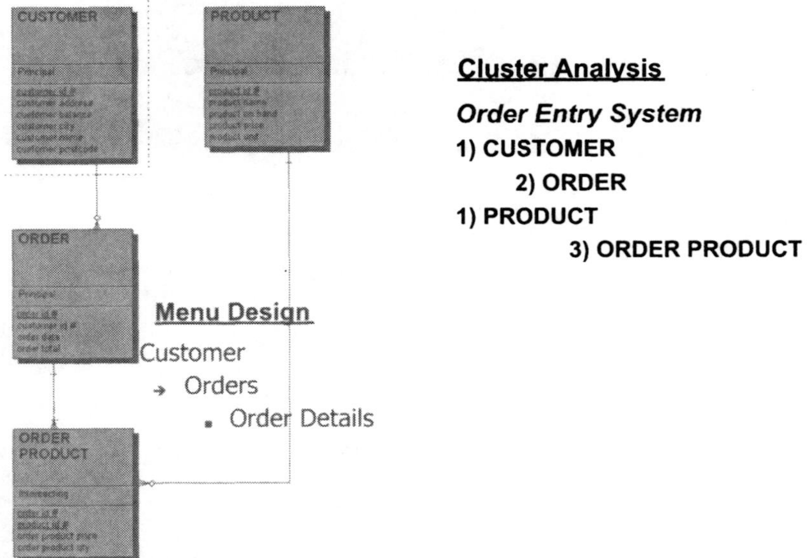

Figure 10.18 Cluster analysis and menu design of order entry data map.

The CUSTOMER entity in Phase 1 of Figure 10.19 is highlighted, to focus on the screen design of the customer form. This is shown by the top-level menu item of *Customer* ... at the left and the columnar screen design at the bottom right of the figure.

In Figure 10.20 we see that the ORDER entity in Phase 2 is now highlighted in the data map to address the screen design of the order form. This is the second-level menu item of *Order* ... at the left and the Master–Detail screen design at the bottom

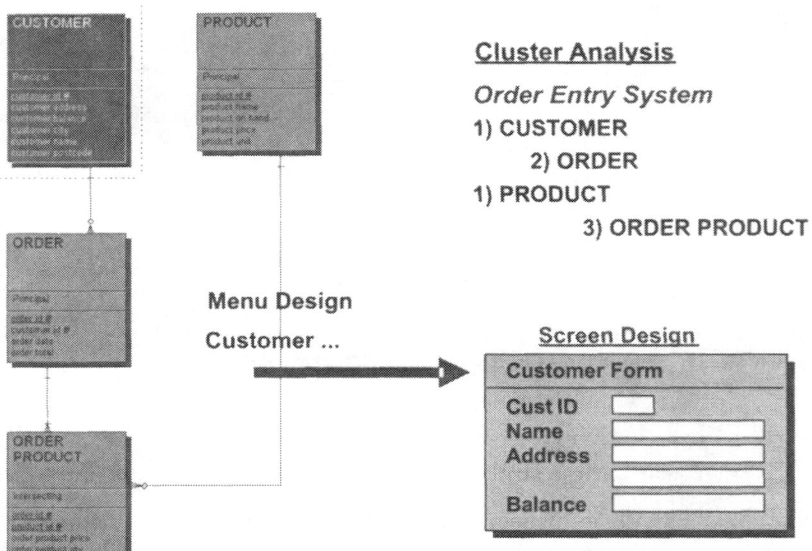

Figure 10.19 Screen design of the customer form from the CUSTOMER entity.

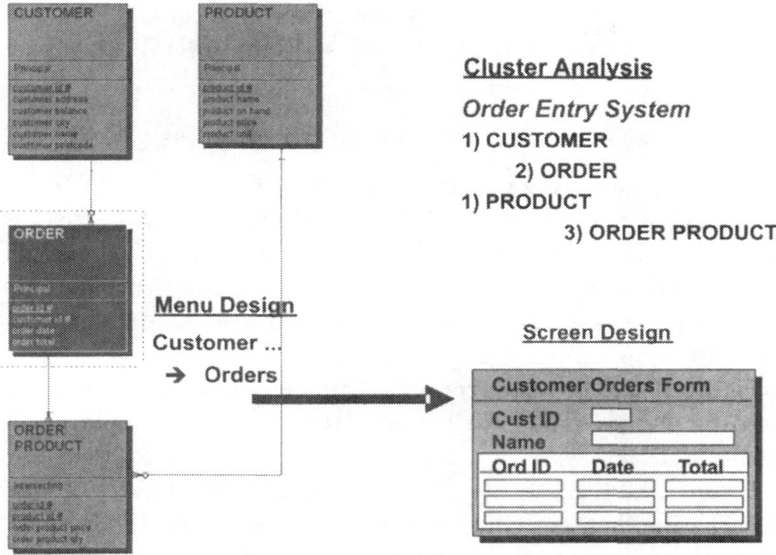

Figure 10.20 Screen design of the order form from the ORDER entity.

right of the figure. We can see that a Phase 2 entity results in a Master–Detail screen design.

The ORDER PRODUCT entity is an intersecting entity in Figure 10.21. It is dependent on PRODUCT also, so both entities are highlighted in the data map of this figure. We can see that a Phase 3 entity typically represents a Master–Detail–Detail design, as shown at the bottom right of the figure.

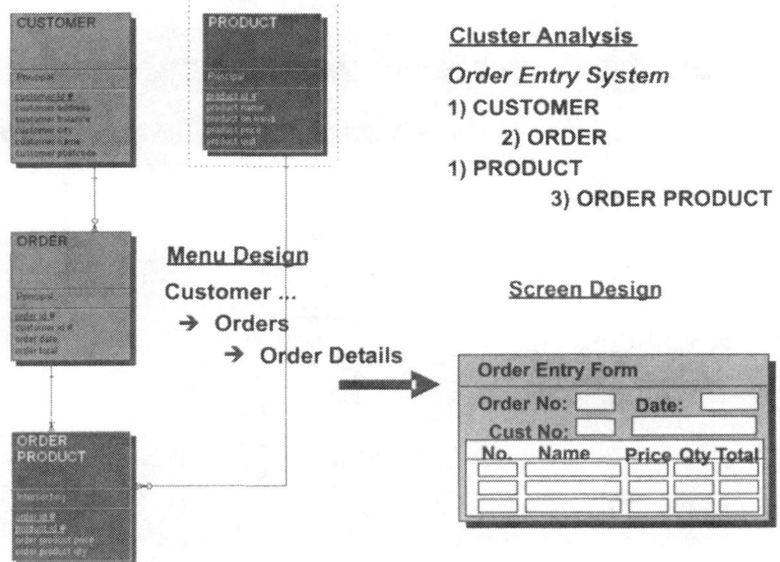

Figure 10.21 Screen design of the order details form from ORDER PRODUCT.

We will next use a modeling tool to automatically generate the physical database design [C1R4] and the DDL SQL script in [C1R5] [8].

10.5.2 Tables and Relationships in Microsoft Access

Figure 10.22 shows the physical database design and the DDL for the order entry data model automatically generated for Microsoft Access. It shows the DDL SQL CREATE TABLE statements, along with the primary and foreign key constraints generated for each physical table. These constraints physically implement the business rules represented by the associations in the logical data model for order entry in Figure 10.17.

Figure 10.23 shows the resulting data model, when the DDL file is imported into Microsoft Access. The entities and relationships are displayed using Access data model notation.

Figure 10.24 shows the CUSTOMER table in Phase 1 of Figure 10.19, which has been generated as a columnar table. Or instead it could have been generated as a data sheet grid format. Either generation option can be completed in less than a minute using the Wizards within Access. The Phase 1 PRODUCT entity and each of the other tables can also be similarly generated as columnar tables.

The Phase 2 ORDER entity in Figure 10.20 can be designed using Access as a Master–Detail form. Before designing a Phase 3 order details form on ORDER_PRODUCT, the dependency of ORDER_PRODUCT on PRODUCT must be specified as a Join Query between these two entities. A Master–Detail–Detail Form for ORDER_PRODUCT can then be designed.

10.5.3 Reusing Screen and Menu Designs

We will now see how we can reuse the previously designed screens from Figure 10.19. With entry from PRODUCT for a specific Product Number, Figure 10.25

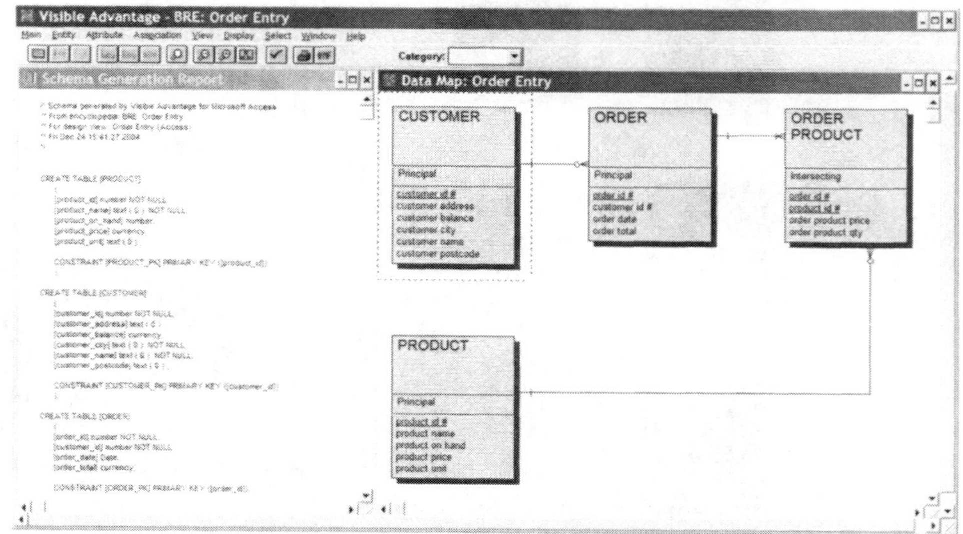

Figure 10.22 Physical database design and DDL generated for Microsoft Access.

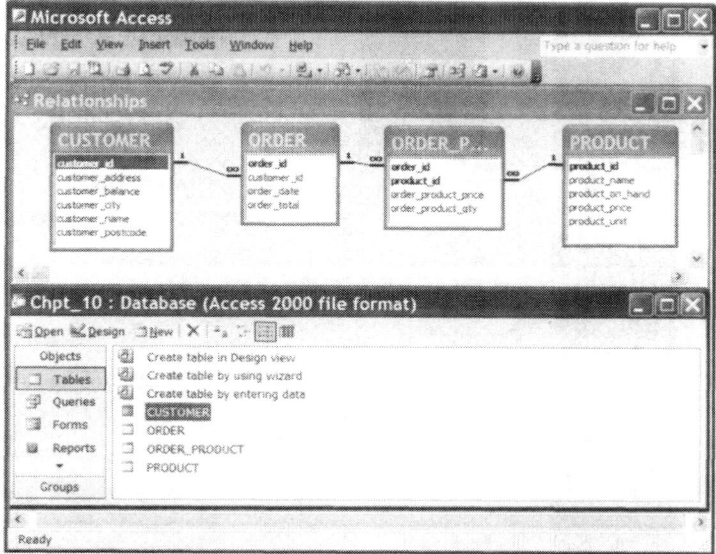

Figure 10.23 Generated DDL opened as a data model in Microsoft Access.

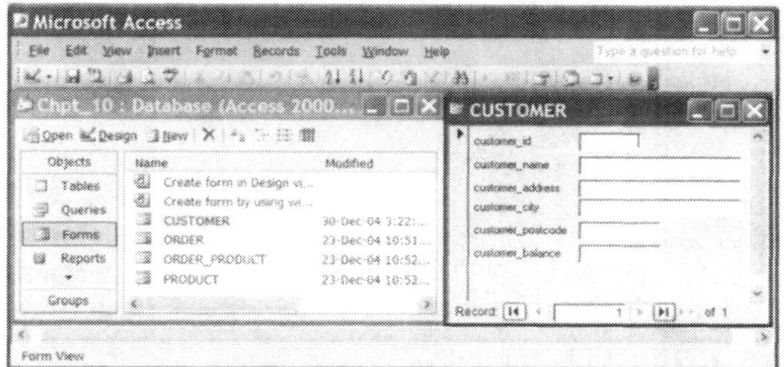

Figure 10.24 CUSTOMER in Phase 1 is generated as a columnar table.

shows how the Master–Detail–Detail form, designed in Figure 10.21, is reused to select an Order Number from all of those listed for the relevant product.

The data map in Figure 10.25 shows the selected order row highlighted in the form, with the ORDER entity highlighted also in the data map to show the navigation that is conceptually occurring as we reuse the form. Figure 10.26 then shows how the customer form for that selected Order is displayed. The relevant navigation is again shown conceptually on the data map by the highlighted CUSTOMER entity.

10.6 Process Modeling

We will now cover the process modeling methodology. This transforms activity models in the How column and Owner row [C2R2] to process models in the Owner and Designer rows [C2R3], as shown earlier in Figure 10.1.

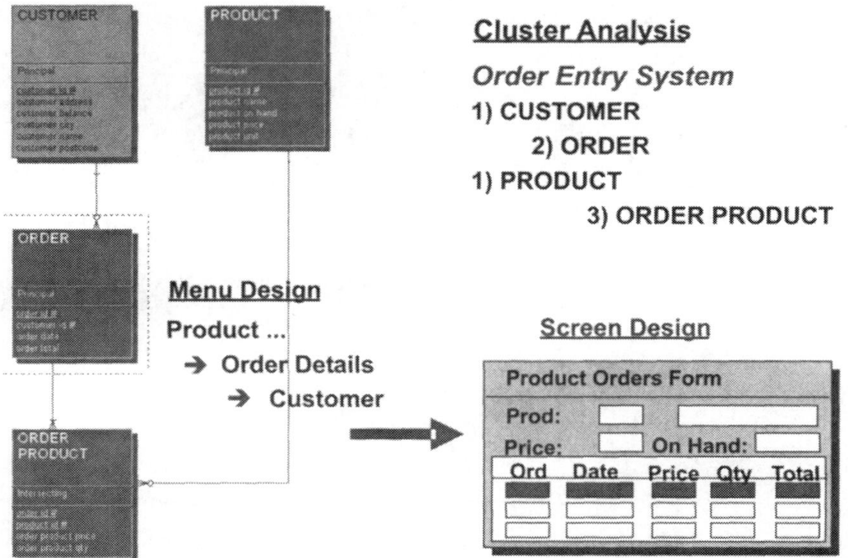

Figure 10.25 Reuse of menus and screens with entry from PRODUCT.

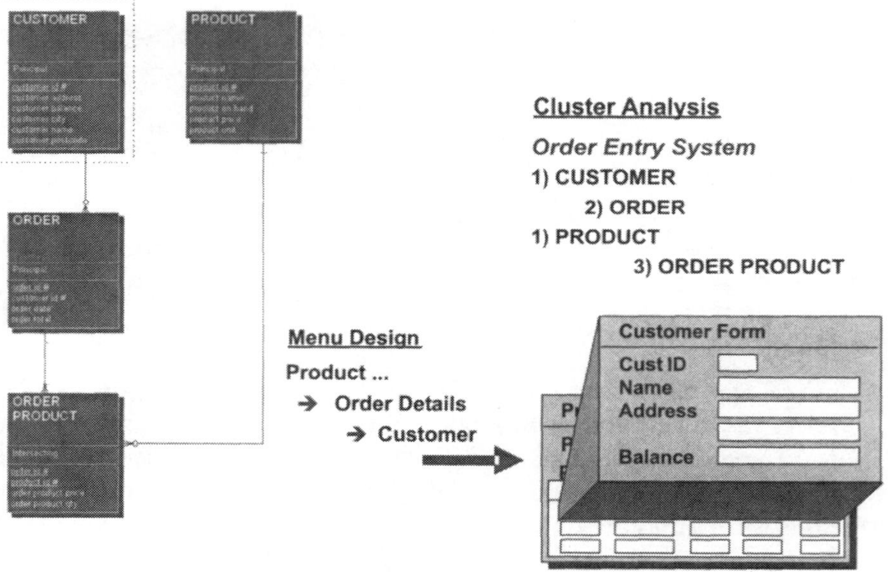

Figure 10.26 Reuse of CUSTOMER form with entry from PRODUCT.

Many methods are used for process modeling. These include data flow diagrams (DFDs), based on the structured methods of software engineering as documented by Ed Yourdon [9], Tom De Marco [10], and Ken Orr [11]. These methods also include the object-oriented unified modeling language (UML) as advocated by Booch [12, 13], Rumbaugh [14], and Jacobson [15, 16]. I will not cover these methods in this book because they are well documented in the provided endnotes.

Instead, in this section I will only provide an overview of the process modeling method used by enterprise engineering. This is a technology-independent method that is used for precise definition of process logic for serial execution of processes. It is used also for the definition of logic for concurrent execution of parallel processes. This method is based on automatic generation of object-oriented process logic from data models—as database code patterns [17].

The concepts for automatic generation of code from database code patterns are used in code generators that can generate 80% to 90% of executable code in various languages from the DDL scripts that define the database structure. These code generators are discussed in Chapter 15 [18].

10.6.1 Differences Between Functions, Activities, and Processes

In Section 8.3.1, also titled *Differences Between Functions, Activities, and Processes,* we discussed the roles of functions, activities, and processes using Figure 8.4. You may wish to review the discussion of Figure 8.4 in Chapter 8. We saw there that an activity has component tasks that are separately executable. These tasks may be elemental data access processes, or instead may be reusable processes, as discussed earlier.

Figure 10.27 shows these DAPs as executable tasks invoked by business processes. It illustrates that a business process explicitly invokes these tasks or reusable processes in an appropriate execution sequence.

10.6.2 Relationship Between Activity Modeling and Process Modeling

It is important now to discuss how activity models and process models are related. The top half of Figure 10.27 illustrates the components used for activity modeling,

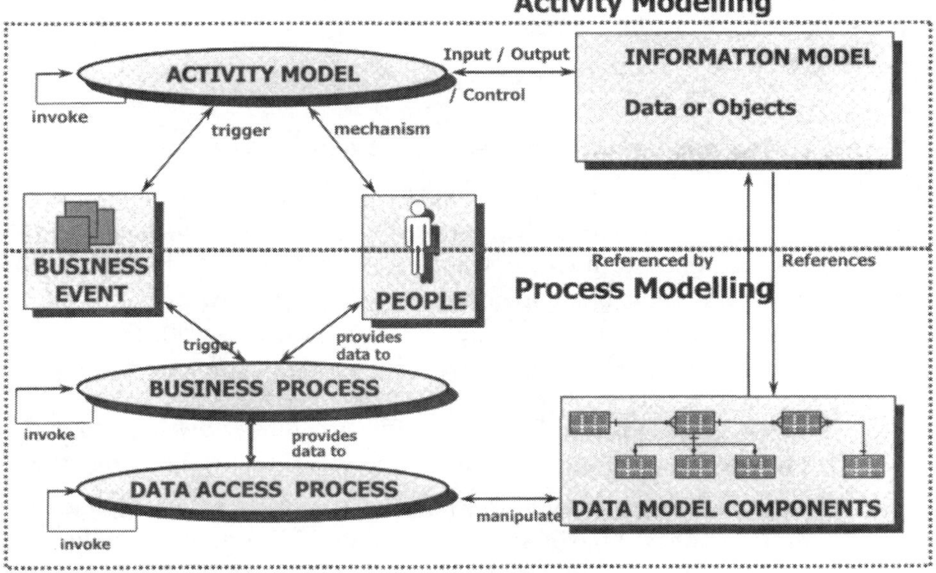

Figure 10.27 Relationship between activity modeling and process modeling.

as discussed in Chapter 8. An *activity model* is represented by the ellipse in the top left of the figure. An activity model can invoke other activity models. The activity model *input, output,* and *control* components—represented by the *Information Model* at the top right of the figure—utilize *mechanisms,* represented by *people,* and triggered by *business events.*

The bottom half of Figure 10.27 illustrates the components used for process modeling. A *business process* is also triggered by a *business event.* It accepts input from, or provides output to, *people.* A business process can invoke other business processes, but cannot directly access data in databases, represented at the bottom right of the figure by *data model components.* Instead, a business process provides data to, or requests data from, *data access processes* (DAPs).

A DAP represents logic that can invoke other DAPs and manipulate data in databases, represented by the data model components at the bottom right of the figure. However, a DAP cannot itself communicate directly with the outside world. It can only respond to invocation requests from business processes. This DAP logic represents the *method* logic used in UML and other object-oriented approaches, while the data model components represent object-oriented data such as those in UML class diagrams.

Process modeling in enterprise engineering is based on the fact that each entity in a data model has an absolute total of four DAPs: These are the O-O *create, read, update,* and *delete* methods—memorably called *CRUD* [19].

The top-down approaches from the Planner and Owner perspectives that are used in this book directly result in reusable activities and reusable business processes. It has been very difficult to identify reusable processes based on bottom-up approaches—from the Subcontractor, Builder, and Designer perspectives—that have been used by many O-O approaches. Instead, reusable activities are identified from the top down using entity dependency analysis in Chapter 7, with activity modeling in Chapter 8. These are then implemented as reusable business processes in process models as described in this section. With this separation of business processes and DAPs, reusable methods can be generated automatically from data models. Each DAP method is generated once, but can be shared by many business processes.

10.6.3 The Role of Business Events in Activities and Processes

A *business event* is defined as a component of a business function that documents some stimulus that occurs either internally or externally to the enterprise, to which the enterprise must respond in some predefined manner. In the Zachman framework, business events relate to column 5, row 1. We saw in Figure 10.27 that business events trigger both business activities and business processes.

The components of a business event for activities and processes are as follows:

- *Business event name:* The name serves as a reference for managing and using a business event. It must be unique and is written in the simple present tense.
- *Business event purpose:* The purpose is a clear, business-language statement that describes a business event. It answers the questions *what, how, where, who, when,* and *why* and must be meaningful to the business participants.

- *Business event frequency:* The frequency is the specified number of occurrences of a stimulus within a given time frame that initiates a business event.

10.6.4 Elemental Process Modeling Logic Commands

A *data access process* is defined as an atomic, reusable set of process steps that is used to accomplish one specific type of data access on an entity. It enforces explicit referential integrity rules for that entity. A DAP passes data between business processes and the data model. It can be initiated by either a business process or another DAP and enforces data integrity within the data model.

A *process step* is a component of a process model that accomplishes a single command within the framework of a business process or data access process, as illustrated by Figure 10.28.

There are four groups of process step commands: *external interface, data access, invocation,* and *decision control*—with a total of 11 commands in these four groups. Taken together, these 11 process step commands establish a technology-independent process modeling schematic notation and pseudo-code language that can be used to define any process logic. For example, in Chapter 14 we will discuss SOA and BPM languages. The process modeling notation discussed in this section can be used to represent process logic for subsequent automatic generation of BPM languages described in that chapter.

Referring again to Figure 10.28, we now describe each of these commands.

External Interface Commands

This group of three commands describes the input and output steps of a process:

- *ACCEPT*: Accept input for a process. This input can be from a computer terminal or some other external device.
- *PRESENT*: Provide output from a process. This output can be to a computer terminal or some other external device.
- *CHOOSE:* Provide output to and accept input for a process. This output and input can be from, and to, a computer terminal or some other external device.

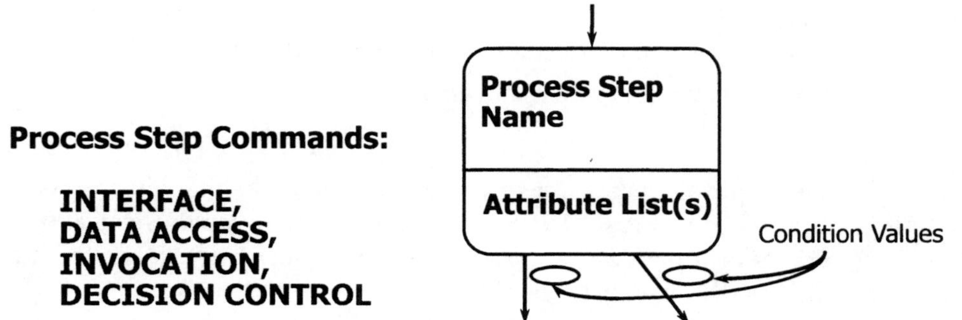

Figure 10.28 A process step may be one of four process step commands.

Data Access Commands

This group of four commands implements process logic associated with the DAPs that exist for every entity. These commands establish and maintain referential integrity logic based on the entity dependency analysis rules discussed in Chapter 7:

- *CREATE:* Create an occurrence of an entity. This data access logic establishes explicit data integrity that the entity has on its owners, typically defined using methods similar to the entity dependency analysis approach.
- *READ:* Read an occurrence of an entity. This data access logic maintains data integrity with the entity's owners, established when the entity was created.
- *UPDATE:* Update an occurrence of an entity. This data access logic maintains data integrity with the entity's owners, established when the entity was created.
- *DELETE:* Delete an occurrence of an entity. This data access logic maintains data integrity with the entity's owners, established when the entity was created.

Invocation Commands

There is one invocation command in this group: DO. This is used to invoke execution of a data access process or a business process as follows:

- *DO:* Invoke a data access process, such as DO CREATE CUSTOMER; DO READ ORDER; DO UPDATE ORDER.
- *DO:* Invoke a business process, such as DO Add New Customer; DO Retrieve Customer Order; DO Update Customer Order

Decision Commands

Three commands can be used to express any decision logic and take an execution path based on that value, as illustrated by the alternative paths at the bottom of Figure 10.28:

- *EXAMINE:* This examines a condition value and then takes a relevant execution path based on that value.
- *EVALUATE:* This evaluates an expression to determine a condition value. It then takes relevant execution paths based on the truth or falsity of that value.
- *NEXT:* This equates to a null condition value, so that the next in-line process step is executed.

An example of a process map and process hierarchy that illustrates this process logic is provided by Figure 10.29. A *process map* is a graphical depiction of a business process or a data access process. A *process hierarchy* shows the hierarchical relationships that exist between these process maps [20].

Process map logic is read top to bottom. The Accept command shown after the Start icon at the top of the left window of Figure 10.29 accepts input for a PERSON

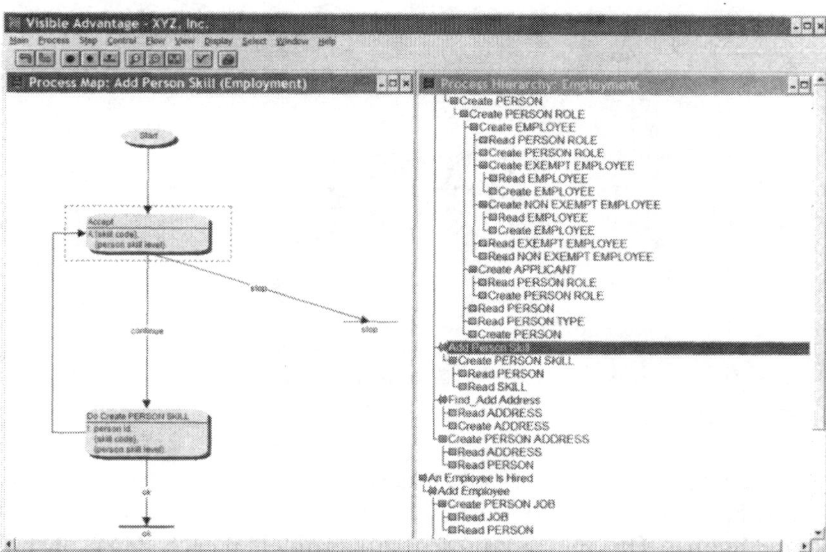

Figure 10.29 A process map for the business process: Add *Person Skill* in the Employment function.

(identified by *person id*). This input is the *skill code* and the *person skill level* values for each SKILL held by that PERSON. These attributes become the *Initiation List* used in the next process step.

The next step creates a PERSON SKILL object occurrence for each skill; shown by the *Do Create PERSON SKILL* process step that invokes that DAP. The Do Create step then loops back to the Accept step. This iterative execution continues until all skills have been accepted, as shown by the execution path after the Do Create to *OK*, or when stopped earlier, as shown by the branch after the Accept to *Stop*.

The right window of Figure 10.29 shows part of the process hierarchy that is initiated by the business event "an application is received" for the Employment function. A business event is represented in a process hierarchy by a single-headed broad arrow; however, no business events are presently visible in this figure.

A business process is represented by a double-headed broad arrow; this is highlighted in the right window as *Add Person Skill*. DAPs are represented by a rectangle; these DAPs are shown beneath the business process as Create PERSON SKILL, Read PERSON, and Read SKILL. We will see the logic derived for these DAPs shortly, but first we need to discuss how parallel logic is represented in process maps.

10.6.5 Definition of Parallel Logic in Process Maps

Figure 10.30 shows four process steps, identified as A, B, C, and D. The notation in this figure can be used to show serial execution as well as parallel (concurrent) execution. Serial execution is used when each process step is executed sequentially in turn. Each step must fully complete before the next process step commences. For serial execution, Figure 10.30 is read top to bottom, left to right. Process Step A is executed first. On its completion Step B is next executed, then Step C, and finally Step D—in that sequence. In this example, the total execution time is the sum of the separate execution times for all four process steps.

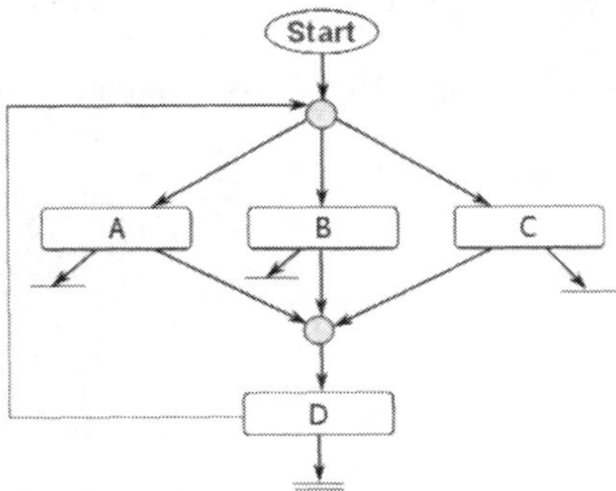

Figure 10.30 Representation of serial or parallel logic in a process map.

Such serial logic is typically implemented in single-task-execution operating systems. However, serial execution can involve processing delays as each step is executed in turn. This may not present any problem if each step is of short duration and all execution can be carried out locally on the same machine. But it may present a severe performance problem if these steps must execute on other machines across a LAN, on the corporate intranet, or across the Internet. In this case parallel execution is often needed to achieve acceptable execution performance, as discussed next.

Two solid circle connectors follow the Start icon in the process map in Figure 10.30. The first connector above the three steps A, B, and C indicates the start of parallel execution. The second circle connector below these steps indicates the end of parallel execution: All three steps must complete before step D can commence execution.

In this parallel processing example, the execution time for process steps A–C is the longest time to completion of any of these concurrently executed processes. The

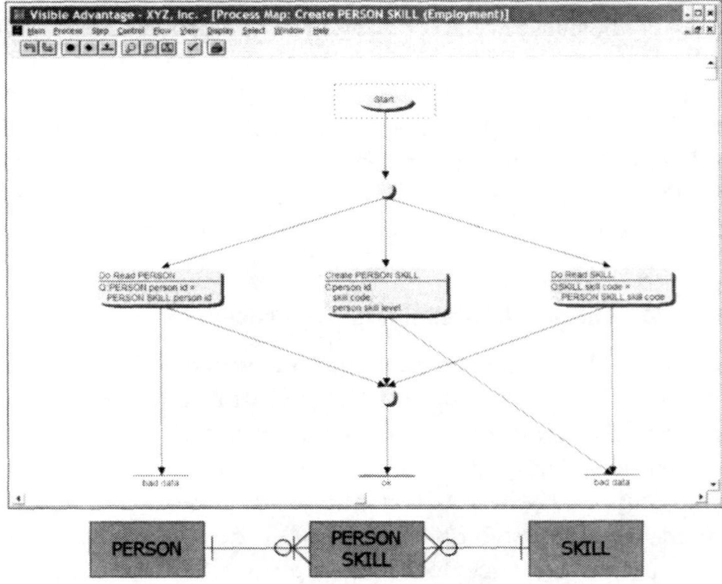

Figure 10.31 This parallel logic has been automatically generated for the DAP *Create PERSON SKILL* from the data map shown at the bottom of this figure.

total execution time then adds the execution time of step D. The result is faster execution than for the earlier serial execution example. We will now see how these principles apply to a real example in the next section.

10.6.6 Derivation of Logic for Database Code Patterns

Figure 10.31 shows the parallel process logic for the DAP *Create PERSON SKILL*. This DAP is invoked by the *Do Create PERSON SKILL* process step at the bottom of the left window in Figure 10.29. It is shown in the right window of that figure by DAP rectangles beneath the highlighted *Add Person Skill* business process as Create PERSON SKILL, Read PERSON, and Read SKILL.

The purpose of the DAP is to create an occurrence of the entity PERSON SKILL. Applying entity dependency analysis, as described in Chapter 7, we know that this intersecting entity is dependent on both of its owners: PERSON and SKILL. For referential integrity purposes, each PERSON SKILL occurrence that is created must be for a valid PERSON and a valid SKILL.

Notice that the left process step *Do Read PERSON* validates that the *person id* primary key of PERSON equals the *person id* of the compound primary key of PERSON SKILL. This qualification statement has been automatically generated by the modeling tool from the primary keys of both entities. If both keys are equal, the conditional path is taken to the parallel logic completion circle. If both primary keys are not equal, the *bad data* error conditional path is taken.

In the right process step, *Do Read SKILL,* the qualification statement is also automatically derived by the modeling tool. It validates that the *skill code* primary key of SKILL equals the *skill code* of the compound primary key of PERSON SKILL. Once again, if both keys are equal, the conditional path is taken to the parallel logic completion circle. But if these primary keys are not equal, the *bad data* error conditional path is taken.

Concurrently with these two referential integrity validation steps, the central DAP process step *Create PERSON SKILL* is executed, using the attributes *person id, skill code,* and *person skill level* that were provided as the *Initiation List* when invoked by the *Do Create PERSON SKILL* step at the bottom of the process map in the left window of Figure 10.29. If no I/O error occurs when writing these data, the conditional path is taken to the parallel logic completion circle. But if an unrecoverable I/O error occurs, the conditional path is taken to *bad data*.

If no validation or I/O errors occurred during execution, following convergence of these conditional execution paths at the parallel logic completion circle, the valid completion of the DAP is represented by the double line, also shown by *ok*. This is the same logic that is automatically applied by RDBMSs to maintain referential integrity based on primary and foreign key constraints defined by the DBA. An RDBMS automatically issues a *Commit* command to signify valid execution completion. However, if any *bad data* errors occurred as discussed earlier, no *Commit* command is issued. Instead the PERSON SKILL occurrence that was created in error is removed; it is said to be "rolled back" to ensure that referential integrity is always observed.

We have now covered the main concepts of process modeling [21].

10.7 Summary

In this chapter we saw how data models provide guidance for menu design and screen design.

- We learned that *entity dependency analysis* can be used to define clusters that provide guidance for menu structure design. We discussed the design of simple hierarchical menus as well as tabbed menu structures.
- We discussed concepts for design of screen formats, guided by a data model. We saw that a single entity can be implemented either as a columnar screen format or a data sheet (spreadsheet) grid format.
- We saw that a *one-to-many* association between two entities is implemented as a Master–Detail screen format. This is typically used as the screen format for an intersecting entity.
- We analyzed a data model for physical database design and capacity planning.
- We learned that we could use the access paths taken through a data model by a transaction to calculate the transaction performance response time.
- We saw that we could optimize this transaction response time by using different physical database design strategies for local access. We also learned how to optimize the response time for remote, distributed access.
- We then applied these menu design and screen design concepts to prototype an order entry application. We used a modeling tool to generate DDL SQL scripts for installation of the generated tables using Microsoft Access.
- We used Access Wizards and design tools to automatically generate screen forms to be used to prototype execution of this order entry application.

We gained an overview of the process modeling method used by enterprise engineering for enterprise architecture.

- Process modeling uses a business-driven, language-independent schematic and pseudo-code notation for business processes. Process models defined using this notation can be implemented in any object-oriented or procedural language.
- We discussed the relationship between activity models and process models and saw that both are initiated or triggered by business events.
- A business process defines the process steps that are involved in creating, reading, updating, or deleting data in response to a business event. A business process can invoke other business processes to reuse a set of specified logic for multiple purposes.
- A business process invokes DAPs for create, read, update, or delete occurrences of data model components.
- We discussed the 11 process step commands that can be used schematically to implement any process logic constructs. We saw an example of process maps for business processes and for DAPs using these commands.

- We discussed the automatic derivation from a data model of parallel logic, shown in process maps for data access processes.
- We learned that these concepts are used today by code generators that generate 80% to 90% of executable code in various languages from the DDL scripts that define the database structure. Code generators are discussed in Chapter 15.

We have now reached the end of Part II on enterprise architecture methods. We are ready to move to Part III, where we will discuss the rapid delivery technologies that can be used with these methods to deliver priority business activities and business processes into production in 3-month increments.

Endnotes

[1] We discussed in Chapter 7 that a Phase 1 entity has only *mandatory one* associations, and no *mandatory many* associations, touching it.

[2] A menu entry point is the highest-level menu item that can be invoked in a menu of commands.

[3] Calculated from 1,000 Job Skill rows divided by 100 Job rows = 10 frequency of occurrence, and by 1,000 Job Skill rows divided by 50 Skill rows = 20 frequency of occurrence.

[4] The logical data type of each attribute may be defined as logical domains such as text, money, and number, which are later converted to the relevant physical data types (domains) of varchar, decimal (12,2), integer as supported by the DBMS to be used for physical database implementation.

[5] A logical reference refers to a potential logical access to an entity in a logical data model. It does not equate to a physical access to a physical database table; this depends on the physical database design strategy that is used, as discussed in the following pages.

[6] *Total References per Hour* sums the *Logical References per Hour* for each access path row in Table 10.1.

[7] Note that a database cluster has no relationship at all to an entity dependency cluster, which is derived from a data map as described in Chapter 7. These are two completely different concepts. Database clustering enables the DBMS to retrieve a referenced row of the parent table and, in the same I/O access, also to retrieve all related child rows for the parent row. The result is improved database access performance and transaction response time performance, as we will see shortly.

[8] This prototyping and automatic generation of Access DDL is based on the use of Visible Advantage and Visible Analyst, which are discussed in Chapter 15 and included on the accompanying CD-ROM.

[9] Yourdon, E., and L. Constantine, *Structured Design: Fundamentals of a Discipline of Computer Program Systems Design,* Englewood Cliffs, NJ: Prentice-Hall, 1978.

[10] De Marco, T., *Software Systems Development,* New York: Yourdon Press, 1982.

[11] Orr, K., *Structured Systems Development,* New York: Yourdon Press, 1977.

[12] Booch, G., *Object-Oriented Analysis and Design with Applications,* 2nd ed., Reading, MA: Addison-Wesley, 1994.

[13] Booch, G., I. Jacobson, and J. Rumbaugh, *The Unified Modeling Language User Guide,* Reading, MA: Addison-Wesley, 1998.

[14] Rumbaugh, J., G. Booch, and I. Jacobson, *The Unified Modeling Language Reference Manual,* Reading, MA: Addison-Wesley, 1998.

[15] Jacobson, I., et al., *The Unified Software Development Process,* Reading, MA: Addison-Wesley, 1999.

[16] Booch, G., J. Rumbaugh, and I. Jacobson, *The Complete UML Training Course,* Englewood Cliffs, NJ: Prentice-Hall, 2000.

[17] Process modeling, as described in this section, is fully supported by the Visible Advantage modeling tool, which is included on the accompanying CD-ROM.

[18] Visible Developer, discussed in Chapter 15, is an example code generator that uses database code patterns. This software product is also included on the accompanying CD-ROM.

[19] Visible Advantage (see Chapter 15) automatically generates all DAPs (CRUD) for every entity in a data model.

[20] The screen shot in Figure 10.29 shows part of the process map and process hierarchy for the XYZ sample encyclopedia repository that is supplied with the Visible Advantage modeling tool. This modeling tool is included on the accompanying CD-ROM (see Chapter 15). A PDF Tutorial and the User's Guide (installed with the software) provide an overview of this tool and details of the process modeling notation and method that are described in this section.

[21] Refer to the accompanying CD-ROM for more information in the Tutorial and User's Guide on Process Modeling for the Visible Advantage modeling tool that is also supplied with this book.

PART III

Enterprise Integration Technologies

The chapters in this part cover the technologies and vendor products that can be used to deliver into production the priority databases, activities, and processes identified in Part II. Each separate technology is introduced fully in a chapter, followed by representative vendor products that use the technology together with a discussion of relevant vendor strategies in a Product Descriptions file on the CD-ROM.

Chapter 11: Enterprise Application Integration Concepts. This is the first of the technology chapters. It introduces the basic concepts of enterprise application integration (EAI) that are used throughout this part. The CD-ROM discusses a number of software products that are offered by EAI vendors, together with their use of EAI technologies.

Chapter 12: Enterprise Portal Technologies for Integration. This chapter introduces the concepts and technologies used by enterprise portals. It discusses their use for rapid delivery of priority information and content resources in enterprise integration projects. Several enterprise portal vendors and their product strategies are discussed on the CD-ROM.

Chapter 13: Web Services for Real-Time Integration. Web services concepts and technologies are introduced in this chapter, along with the evolution of Web services. It describes the technical foundations of Web services that are used for enterprise integration in this part. It discusses their use in enterprise portals with Web services for remote portals. A number of Web services vendors and their software products and strategies are discussed on the CD-ROM.

Chapter 14: Service-Oriented Architecture for Integration. The technologies used by SOA and BPM languages are discussed. Four BPM languages are described: Business Process Execution Language for Web Services (BPEL); Web Services Choreography Interface (WSCI); Business Process Modeling Language (BPML); and Business Process Specification Schema (BPSS) for ebXML. These offer the potential to transform systems development in twenty-first-century enterprises, with XML-based BPM languages automatically generated as executable code directly from workflow models or process models. The chapter also covers Business Process Modeling Notation (BPMN), an emerging standard for modeling business processes. SOA strategies being used by vendors of EAI products, enterprise portals, Web services, and SOA are discussed, along with a number of representative SOA and BPM products from these vendors on the CD-ROM.

Chapter 15: Managing and Delivering Enterprise Architecture. This final chapter brings together the methodology and technology parts of the book. It discusses the use of modeling tools that can be used to capture the business models for enterprise architecture as described in Part II. It discusses several modeling tool vendors and their products on the CD-ROM. It covers the directions that are being taken by operating system software and DBMSs in moving toward the virtualization of hardware. The chapter concludes with a summary of the main methodology and technology messages from the book.

Note that all product descriptions for each chapter are included as PDF files named *Chap-xx-Products.pdf,* where xx = chapter number, in the Book Materials folder on the accompanying CD-ROM.

CHAPTER 11

Enterprise Application Integration Concepts

This chapter introduces the concepts of XML and enterprise application integration. EAI applies both to integration of applications within an enterprise (intraenterprise) as well as between enterprises (inter-enterprise). A good understanding of these EAI concepts is fundamental to appreciating the opportunities presented by some of the latest integration technologies used by enterprise architecture. We will first examine business-to-business (B2B) integration issues and B2B business drivers. We will look at trading communities and XML messaging standards.

11.1 Technologies for Enterprise Integration

Very effective technologies are now becoming available for enterprise integration. These achieve technology integration, based on the use of XML (Extensible Markup Language), EAI, and Web services. We will briefly introduce XML here.

A prerequisite for the effective use of XML is data modeling: to define the metadata that XML requires. Many data modeling tools automatically generate XML definition files from defined metadata.

We discussed XYZ Corporation in Chapter 1. Consider now two other organizations: ABC Inc. and DEF Enterprises who buy products from XYZ. In doing business with its customer ABC Inc., XYZ carries out the following business activities:

- The XYZ Sales Department accepts sales orders from customer ABC to be processed by the XYZ Order Entry Department. This is carried out by the Order Entry Management activity.
- Before an order can be processed, the XYZ Credit Control Department first checks the available credit for its client ABC based on the current values of *client account balance* and *client credit limit*, and the total amount of the requested order. This activity is called Credit Control Management to authorize order entry processing.
- After the Order Entry Department has fully processed the order, the Accounts Receivable section in the XYZ Finance Department uses the Customer Invoice Management activity to issue an invoice. This increases the *debtor account balance* of its debtor ABC by the total amount of the order.
- The new *debtor account balance* is used to update the redundant versions of the same amount due to XYZ: the *customer account balance* for customer

ABC in the Sales and Order Entry Departments; and the *client account balance* for client ABC for the Credit Control Department. This is required for data maintenance synchronization of these redundant versions of *account balance*. This is the responsibility of the Accounts Receivable Management activity.

Because of the different terminology and identification used by each area of XYZ, it is not always clear that they are dealing with the same organization: ABC. For example, customers of XYZ are identified in the Sales and Order Entry Departments by *customer number*: ABC has a unique Customer Number. Clients are identified in the Credit Control Department by *client id*, with a unique Client ID for ABC. Debtors are identified in the Finance Department by *debtor code*, again with a unique Debtor Code for ABC. But due to the lack of business integration, ABC Inc. now appears to XYZ as three quite separate organizations: as a customer; as a client; and as a debtor. Let us examine how XML handles this situation.

11.1.1 Basic XML Concepts

XML indicates the context of relevant data by surrounding that data with *tags* that define its meaning. For example, sales orders from ABC appear in XML as shown next:

<Customer>ABC Inc.</Customer>

where *<Customer>* is a start tag and *</Customer>* is an end tag. These XML tags surround and identify relevant data content. Clearly ABC Inc. is a customer

But the Credit Control and Finance Departments use different terminology. They only recognize ABC by their relevant terms:

<Client>ABC Inc.</Client> for the Credit Control Department
<Debtor>ABC Inc.</Debtor> for Accounts Receivable in the Finance Department

The start and end tags clearly indicate the terminology that is used in each department. We can see from these XML data fragments that each department is dealing with the same enterprise: ABC.

11.1.2 Business Documents

Let us now discuss the relevant activities and the corresponding business documents that are exchanged between Customer ABC and its Supplier XYZ.

- The ABC purchasing activity produces purchase orders that are sent to XYZ as its supplier. These purchase orders can be sent by mail or fax.
- When received by the XYZ Order Entry Department, they are manually entered as sales orders by the XYZ Order Entry Management activity, as mentioned earlier.
- On sales order acceptance after Credit Control Management processing by the XYZ Credit Control Department, XYZ sends an order acknowledgment back

to ABC, followed later by a delivery advice or advance shipping notice (ASN). These documents are received by the ABC Purchase Order Acceptance activity.

- Finally the Accounts Receivable section in the XYZ Finance Department sends a customer invoice to its debtor: ABC. It is received by the ABC Accounts Payable activity in their Finance Department as a supplier invoice from its supplier XYZ.

All of these documents are exchanged between the two companies: the purchase order originating the order at ABC; the order acknowledgment of receipt by XYZ, sent back to ABC; the delivery advice or ASN; and later the invoice that is sent by XYZ to ABC. Each of these documents must be manually reentered by XYZ or by ABC staff into relevant XYZ or ABC processing systems.

11.1.3 Electronic XML Documents

An example of the purchase order (PO) that is exchanged between both companies is shown in Figure 11.1. This PO is issued by *Smith and Co,* a subsidiary of ABC. It is a PO expressed in XML. We will use this PO to discuss some of the basic concepts of XML [1], documented as a summary in Box 11.1.

11.1.4 The Need for XML Transformation

Consider now that Smith and Co is no longer a subsidiary of ABC Inc., but is a subsidiary of DEF Enterprises. The purchase order instead would use the XML PO format that is utilized by DEF. This is shown in Figure 11.2, side by side with the same PO in the XML format that is used by ABC. This purchase order is *OrderNo: 1234.*

We see that the DEF PO format on the left shows the order number as an attribute of *<PurchaseOrder OrderNo="1234">*. On the right it is shown as an XML element *<OrdNo>1234</OrdNo>*.

ABC PO Format - Smith and Co

```
<PurchaseOrder >
  <Party Type="Buyer">
  <Reference>AB24567</Reference>
    <Name>Smith and Co</Name>
    <Street>123 High St</Street>
    <Town>Epping Forest</Town>
    <PostCode >E15 2HQ</ PostCode >
  </Party>
  <Party Type="Supplier">
    ...
  </Party>
  <OrdNo >1234</ OrdNo >
  <OrderItem >
    ...
  </OrderItem >
  <Tax Type="VAT" Percent="17.5">
    ...
  </Tax>
  ...
</PurchaseOrder >
```

Figure 11.1 Example of an XML purchase order. (*Source:* © 2001 Software AG. Reprinted with permission.)

Box 11.1: Basic XML Concepts

XML is text, in any written language. It is human readable and machine readable. Each start tag, such as <Name>, is an XML element. It must be followed by an end tag, such as </Name>. Both tags surround the data content. Figure 11.1 shows that this content is "Smith and Co."

A tag or XML element is a single word with no spaces, where the first character of the tag is a letter or an underscore; it cannot be a number or any special character other than an underscore. Distinct from HTML, which is case-insensitive, XML is case-sensitive. For this reason <NAME>, <Name>, and <name> are three different XML elements or tags.

An XML element start tag can also contain XML attributes, separated from the start tag and each other by a space. Each attribute name is followed by an "=" and then a value surrounded by single or double quotes. For example, <Party Type="Buyer"> in Figure 11.1 or <Tax Type="VAT" Percent="17.5"> are XML attributes of the <Party> and <Tax> XML elements.

DEF PO Format – Smith and Co

```
<PurchaseOrder   OrderNo ="1234">
  <Buyer  BuyerNo ="AB24567"
     Name="Smith and Co">
    <Address1>123 High St</Address1>
    <Address2>Epping Forest</Address2>
    <Zip>E15 2HQ</Zip>
  </Buyer>
  <Supplier>
    ...
  </Supplier>
  <OrderItem >
    ...
  </ OrderItem >
  <Tax>
    <TaxType >VAT</ TaxType >
    <TaxPercent >17.5</ TaxPercent >
    ...
  </Tax>
  ...
</ PurchaseOrder >
```

ABC PO Format - Smith and Co

```
<PurchaseOrder  >
  <Party Type="Buyer">
  <Reference>AB24567</Reference>
    <Name>Smith and Co</Name>
    <Street>123 High St</Street>
    <Town>Epping Forest</Town>
    <PostCode >E15 2HQ</ PostCode >
  </Party>
  <Party Type="Supplier">
    ...
  </Party>
  <OrdNo >1234</ OrdNo >
  <OrderItem >
    ...
  </ OrderItem >
  <Tax Type="VAT" Percent="17.5">
    ...
  </Tax>
  ...
</ PurchaseOrder >
```

- ***Different organizations can define same data in different ways***
- ***Enterprise Application Integration uses XML to resolve differences***

Figure 11.2 A purchase order in two different XML formats. (*Source:* © 2001 Software AG. Reprinted with permission.)

The Buyer Number identification and name on the left for DEF are shown as attributes of Buyer: *<Buyer BuyerNo="AB24567" Name="Smith and Co">*. On the right for ABC each is an XML element: *<Reference>AB24567</Reference> <Name>Smith and Co</Name>*.

On the right the address is *<Street>123 High St</Street> <Town>Epping Forest</Town> <PostCode>E15 2HQ</PostCode>*. On the left the address uses quite different element names: *<Address1>123 High St</Address1> <Address2>Epping Forest</Address2> <Zip>E15 2HQ</Zip>*.

Finally we can see that XML attributes for *<Tax>* are used by ABC on the right, as *<Tax Type="VAT" Percent="17.5">*. In contrast, the format on the left uses child elements of *<Tax>*. These are *<TaxType>VAT</TaxType>* and *<TaxPercent> 17.5</TaxPercent>*, surrounded *by <Tax> ... </Tax>* as their parent element.

From Figure 11.2 we see that these purchase order formats in XML are quite different from each other, yet both contain exactly the same PO data content. Both ABC and DEF are customers of XYZ, which likely uses a different XML format for its sales orders. As noted in the figure, different organizations can all define the same data in different ways. Each of the customers of XYZ may have quite different PO formats.

So what should XYZ do? Should it require every customer to use a standard format, such as the XYZ sales order format? This would be very convenient for XYZ. But it would not be convenient for its customers. Rather than change their PO formats so they could buy from XYZ, it would easier for them not to buy. Instead they can buy from a supplier other than XYZ. If XYZ mandated that only its XML sales format be used, it would quite likely lose many customers and their orders.

Because each customer most likely has its own PO format in XML, to attract their continued business XYZ must be able to accept every different format. It therefore must be able to transform each format into its own sales order XML format. This is one of the advantages of XML: It is very easy to do data transformation using XML. Extensible Style Language Transformation (XSLT) [2] is used to transform from one XML format to another [3].

Each document to be exchanged between XYZ and ABC previously had to be printed and then mailed or faxed, as discussed earlier. It is then manually reentered by the receiving company into its relevant system for processing.

However, this manual reentry step changes with XML. Each document is intercepted before printing and is instead converted to an XML electronic document. This is then transmitted across the Internet, or within the corporate intranet, as text in XML.

Using XML, the manual reentry step is bypassed. These electronic documents are sent automatically as XML messages between the relevant XYZ and ABC systems.

XML messaging allows these enterprise applications to be integrated. Not surprisingly, this is called *enterprise application integration*. EAI is used across enterprise boundaries between XYZ and ABC as inter-enterprise application integration. Used within an enterprise, such as in XYZ, it is called intra-enterprise application integration.

A transformation front end is added to each system for EAI between the various systems. In normal processing workflow, these systems are ABC Procurement, XYZ Order Entry, XYZ Order Acknowledgment, XYZ Advance Shipping Notice, ABC PO Acceptance, ABC Advance Shipping Notice, XYZ Customer Invoicing, and ABC Accounts Payable. An example of an XSLT engine used for transformation of data formats is illustrated in Figure 11.3 for Microsoft BizTalk, which is discussed later in this chapter in the Product Descriptions on the accompanying CD-ROM.

11.2 B2B Cost-Effective Business Drivers

Some of the reasons for the rapid acceptance of e-business are due to its cost effectiveness: It realizes dramatic cost savings. The savings from e-business can be best

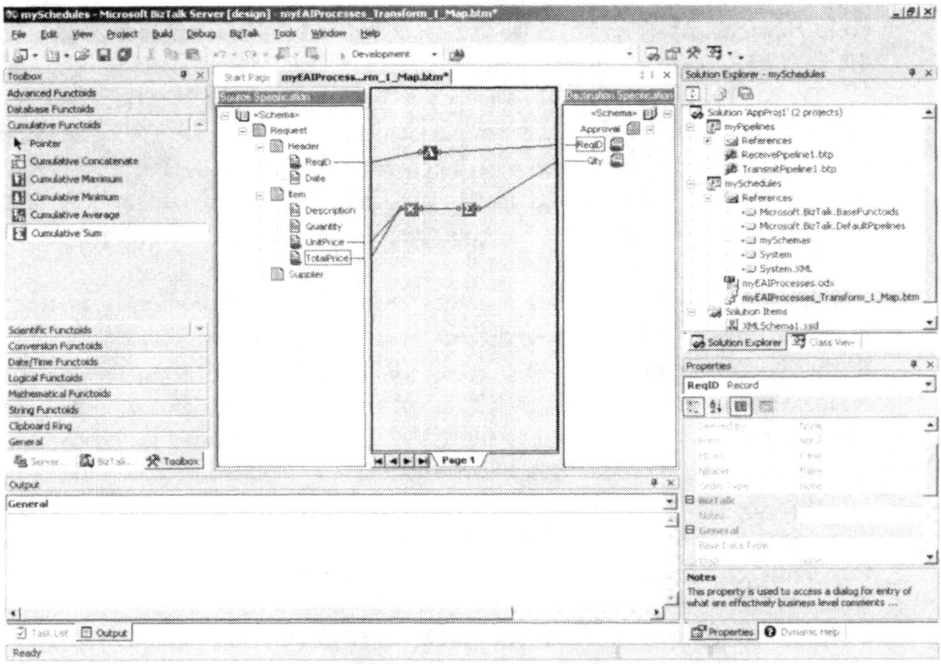

Figure 11.3 Example of the XSLT transformation engine used by BizTalk Data Mapper. (*Source:* © 2004 Microsoft Corporation. Reprinted with permission.)

understood by looking at the associated costs for purchasing and invoicing in enterprises.

According to Gartner Group, a typical purchase order, with approvals, costs around \$100 to \$150. This transaction processing cost is static. There is no difference whether the item purchased is a \$5,000 computer, a \$5 million piece of equipment, or a \$5 box of pens. In each of these cases, the \$100 to \$150 transaction processing cost remains the same. Gartner Group has found that 75% of items in a typical purchase order or invoice cost less than \$1,000. So this processing cost makes up a significant proportion of the cost of each item.

The transaction processing cost applies regardless of the currency that is involved. For example, the same \$100 to \$150 transaction cost applies whether expressed as \$USD in the United States; \$CND in Canada; \$AUD in Australia; or as £UK in England. The cost has nothing to do with country exchange rates; rather, it depends on the cost of living in each country. This is due to the manual processing that is required: to key the details of all items in a purchase order, to correct any data entry or other errors, to authorize the purchase order, and to mail or fax it to a supplier for fulfillment. All of these manual steps have been required historically, as we discussed in Chapter 1.

Similar costs are incurred when the purchase order is received as a sales order by the supplier. As we discussed earlier, details of the sales order must be manually entered into an order entry system for processing; any data entry or other errors must be corrected and each ordered item must be checked for available inventory and pricing.

On acceptance of the sales order, an ASN [4] is then printed to be mailed or faxed back to the customer. An invoice is also printed to be mailed or faxed to the customer. We now see why this manual data entry and processing typically costs $100 to $150 for purchase orders. A similar cost is also incurred with manual reentry and processing of sales orders and invoices.

We discussed earlier that manual data entry and correction steps can be bypassed by transmitting electronic XML purchase orders and invoices between customers and suppliers across the Internet. These XML documents can be transformed for automatic entry into the order entry system and other relevant systems without the need for manual reentry and processing. This has a dramatic effect on the costs that are incurred.

Using EAI as discussed in this chapter, according to Gartner, this cost drops to $8 to $10 for transaction processing. These cost savings are enjoyed by both of the enterprises in a customer–supplier trading relationship.

Using EAI, delays previously associated with manual data entry—for the correction of errors with related manual processing, followed by mailing or faxing—all disappear with electronic XML document transmission. The previous manual delays are reduced to minutes, even seconds. EAI enables processing to be completed in near real time.

Furthermore, an Aberdeen Group survey has indicated the complete manual purchase requisition cycle lasts on average 7.3 days while this data entry, correction, and related manual processing is completed. But an automated buy-side e-commerce system using Electronic Data Interchange (EDI) messaging typically reduces this time to 2 days, as the manual cost for reentry of transactions is avoided also by using EDI.

11.2.1 The Growth of Trading Communities

Let us examine further the impact that the Internet is having on business. With the easy interconnection offered by Internet technologies, any enterprise can now communicate instantly with any other enterprise anywhere in the world—as buyers and suppliers for B2B e-business.

The major problems associated with e-business are connecting everyone together and finding buyers and suppliers. The Internet offers the ability to easily interconnect buyers and suppliers in real time—and worldwide.

11.2.2 Connecting Enterprises

Trading communities (also called *trading networks*) have sprung up during the last few years to take advantage of the dramatic cost savings discussed earlier that are available from e-business. These enable enterprises to do business with other enterprises anywhere in the world, using a variety of messaging formats and protocols. These formats include RosettaNet, BizTalk, EDI, ebXML, and others as illustrated in Figure 11.4. We will discuss these messaging formats later in this chapter.

Trading communities utilize the technologies of EAI and XML. A trading community can be horizontal across many industries, or vertical within a single industry. An example of a vertical trading community is *Covisint,* established in the

Figure 11.4 Trading communities accept a variety of XML message envelope formats, automatically converting from one to the other. (*Source:* © 2002 CommerceOne. Reprinted with permission.)

United States between automobile manufacturers GM, Ford, Daimler/Chrysler, Nissan, and more than 60,000 suppliers, with more than $240 billion in purchases per year.

We discussed earlier—with XYZ Corporation, ABC Inc., and DEF Enterprises—that organizations use different terminology and message structures as they do e-business together. We saw that there is a need for transformation between different terminology (as XML metadata tags) and different XML message formats; EAI is an important enabler of this transformation. Enterprises can interconnect in several ways across the Internet, as discussed next.

Figure 11.5 shows the simplest way in which two enterprises can connect for e-business: via a Web browser. In this example, if Company 1 places an order with Company 2, it has to print out this order directly from the Web form used to order products online from Company 2. It must then manually reenter that online order as a purchase order into the back-end procurement system of Company 1. With this manual data entry, Company 1 does not benefit from any of the cost and time savings that we discussed above.

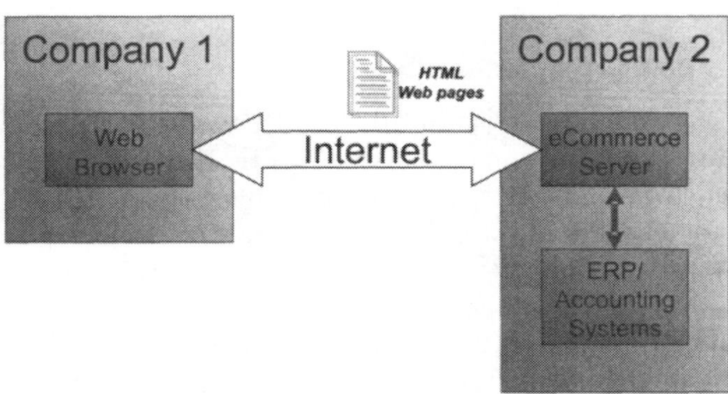

Figure 11.5 Using a Web browser, Company 1 can connect easily to Company 2 to purchase goods and services. (*Source:* © 2002 CommerceOne. Reprinted with permission.)

Similarly Company 2 may also have to print out all sales orders received online, such as from Company 1. If it does not have its online order acceptance system integrated with its back-end order entry system, it must also manually reenter those sales orders into the order entry system, With this manual data entry, Company 2 also does not benefit from any of the cost and time savings we saw earlier.

While this browser-based approach is inexpensive to implement, it does not result in the dramatic cost and time savings that can be achieved from bypassing manual reentry, by using electronic order entry through e-business.

In contrast, another approach is shown in Figure 11.6. This enables Company 1 (ABC, for example) to authorize a purchase order in its back-end supplier procurement system. This PO is not printed out and mailed or faxed to Company 2 (XYZ, for example) as has traditionally been done. The PO is transformed instead into an XML purchase order, which is transmitted electronically over the Internet to Company 2 (XYZ).

On receipt, the XYZ order acceptance system receives the PO sent by ABC now as a sales order. This sales order is transferred electronically—without requiring manual reentry as in Figure 11.5—into its integrated back-end sales order entry system. Both of the companies in Figure 11.6 are now engaged in e-business: Their online e-commerce systems are now closely integrated with their back-end processing systems.

The approach in Figure 11.6 bypasses the cost and delays previously associated with manual reentry. It enables dramatic cost savings to be achieved as discussed earlier. A typical static purchase order transaction processing cost of $100 to $150 that occurs with manual reentry is now typically reduced to $8 to $10 (for both Buyer ABC and Supplier XYZ), by using an electronic XML PO as illustrated.

As we discussed earlier, Company 1 and Company 2 (ABC and XYZ) must agree on the format of the ABC purchase order—received by XYZ as a sales order. We will call this agreed format *PO Type 1*, as shown in Figure 11.7. Both ABC and XYZ will each need to transform between this agreed PO Type 1 format and its own internal enterprise format, based on each company's own defined enterprise metadata.

In dealing with Company 1 and Company 3, Figure 11.7 shows that another format may also be needed: *PO Type 2*. Similarly other PO formats may need to be

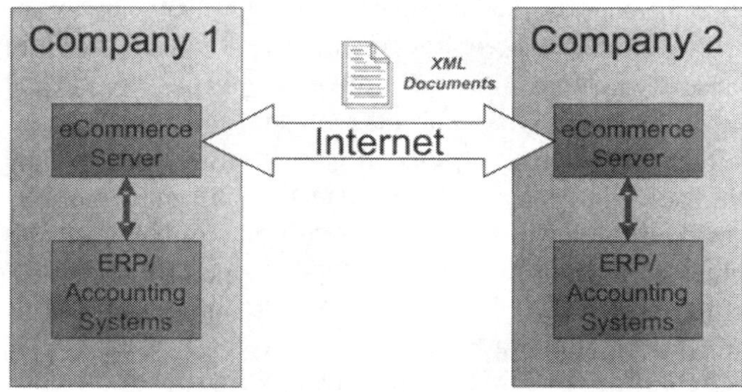

Figure 11.6 Company 1 and Company 2 both use XML electronic purchase orders directly from or to back-end systems. (*Source:* © 2002 CommerceOne. Reprinted with permission.)

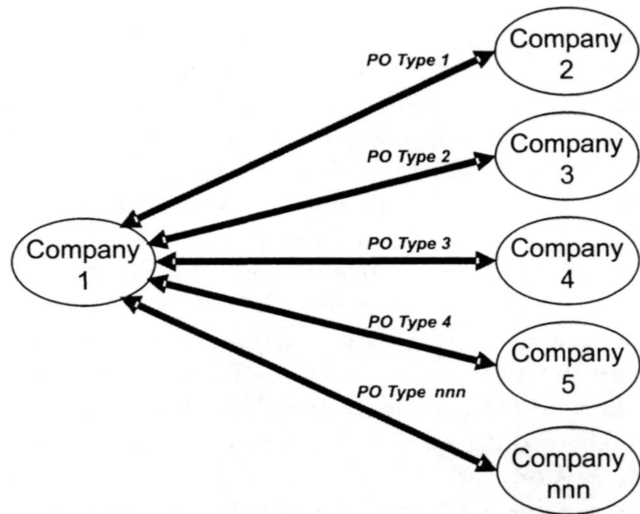

Figure 11.7 There are many possible XML formats for document interchange between organizations. (*Source:* © 2002 CommerceOne. Reprinted with permission.)

agreed between each buyer and supplier pair. But Company 1 may have 1,000 different suppliers—each with a different PO format. And each of those may also have 1,000 other companies that they do business with—again each with a different PO format. These companies, doing business with many other companies, result in 1 million separate transformation formats.

It is clear that this approach of *many-to-many* transformation pairs does not scale.

XML alone is not a complete answer. We discussed that the example shown in Figure 11.2 uses exactly the same data but with two different XML PO formats. These are only two of the million PO format pairs discussed in relation to Figure 11.7.

To address this problem of *many-to-many* transformations, common document formats are being defined in XML for each industry [5], as illustrated in Figure 11.8. This shows a standard purchase order format, specified to address typical PO data as used in many industries. Because of the extensibility of XML, industry extensions can be defined easily to tailor a standard PO format for each industry, addressing their particular requirements.

Figure 11.8 shows the addition of travel industry PO extensions—and also auto industry PO extensions—to address the specific needs of companies in those industries. These PO formats for each industry can be used as a PO standard by all companies that do business with each other in that industry.

In effect, the *many-to-many* transformation problem that we discussed earlier has been resolved to a *many-to-one* transformation: from each company's enterprise metadata to the relevant industry standard. Similarly, on receipt of this standard PO, each receiving company can do the corresponding *one-to-many* transformation: converting the received PO to each company's own sales order format based on its own enterprise metadata [6].

This solution of XML format transformation is usually based on a defined industry markup language that specifies common metadata and XML document

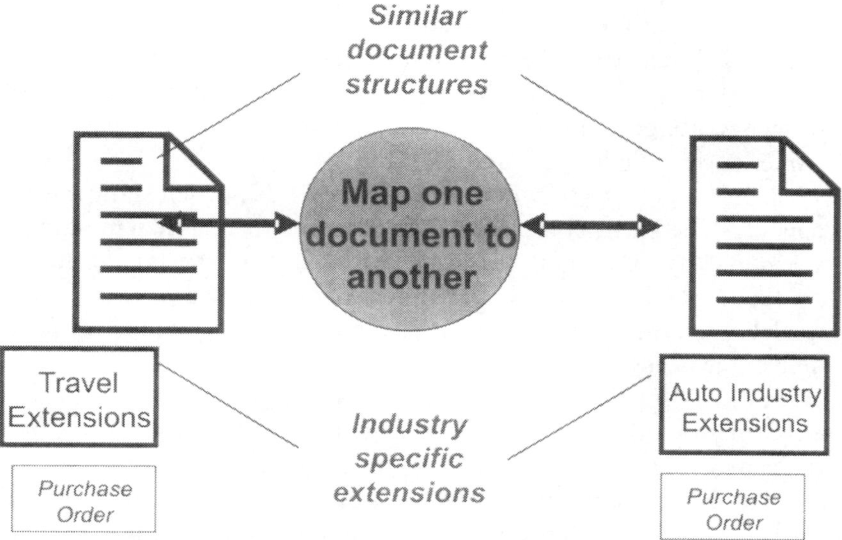

Figure 11.8 A common XML purchase order format can easily be extended using XML to address different industry requirements. (*Source:* © 2002 CommerceOne. Reprinted with permission.)

formats [7]. These are used for business communication and data interchange between companies doing business together in an industry. Each company now only needs to convert to and from the agreed industry-standard XML format and its own enterprise metadata. This principle (of *many-to-one* and also *one-to-many* document transformation) is the basis of standard XML format transformation for industry markup languages in most industries [8].

We now need to consider the problem of document delivery. In the real world, a purchase order is printed by a buyer, then inserted in an envelope and mailed to a supplier as shown in Figure 11.9. On receipt, the supplier opens the envelope and delivers it to its order entry section for data entry and processing as a sales order.

Figure 11.9 Real-world document delivery. (*Source:* © 2002 CommerceOne. Reprinted with permission.)

Mail delivery is fairly reliable: The mail is almost always delivered correctly. However, it is slow: It can take days; sometimes even weeks for delivery of a mailed envelope. If fast, guaranteed delivery is required, a courier service is often used. This service is offered by the postal service in many countries, as well as by shipping companies such as FedEx, UPS, or DHL.

Contrast Figure 11.9 now with Figure 11.10, which shows electronic document delivery. The XML document can be attached to an e-mail message and transmitted electronically. But e-mail messages can be lost, or the same message may be delivered multiple times. To avoid problems of lost messages—or of multiple e-mail copies delivered from the one message—a more reliable method of electronic document delivery is needed.

UPS, DHL, FedEx, and post offices use particular document formats for the envelopes that they use. If electronic documents are to be transmitted between computer programs, common formats are also needed for electronic envelopes.

Trading communities—such as CommerceOne and Ariba, and also message broker middleware products for a similar trading function—have emerged to address problems of reliable electronic document delivery and common envelope formats in XML. These transform documents between standard XML message envelope formats, automatically.

Using this approach, an XML message sent by one company, which uses one standard XML message envelope, is transformed by a trading community or message broker to the specific envelope message format used by another company with which it does business. For example, CommerceOne automatically transforms message envelope formats to and from its own metadata language: xCBL (XML Common Business Language). In this way, messages that use standard XML formats, such as RosettaNet [9], EDI, ebXML (EDI in XML), BizTalk (from Microsoft), OAG (Open Application Group), or OBI (Open Buyers Interchange), are all automatically converted by trading communities or message brokers from one XML message format to any of the other XML formats. In addition to these benefits of support for XML message envelope formats with automatic XML document translation, they also provide a reliable electronic "postal system" that guarantees delivery, with no lost or repeated messages, as shown in Figure 11.10.

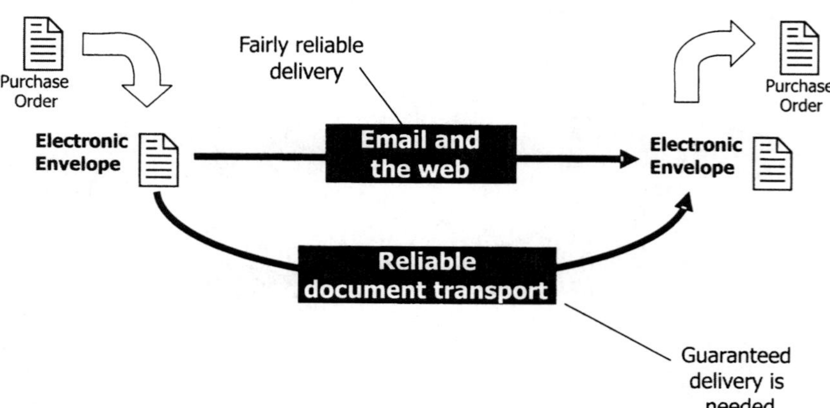

Figure 11.10 Electronic document delivery. (*Source:* © 2002 CommerceOne. Reprinted with permission.)

11.2.3 Finding Buyers and Suppliers

A further consideration is the location of buyers and suppliers. Using standard Internet search engines to locate trading partners on the Internet is not comprehensive enough. To address the problem of locating buyers and suppliers on the Internet, most trading communities allow suppliers to "advertise" the products and services that they offer. Using XML they register and display on the trading community the products and services that they want to sell. Buyers can then visit the trading community and use XML to search for the products and services that they want to buy.

Alternatively, buyers use XML to register their tenders, requests for information (RFIs), requests for quote (RFQs) or requests for proposal (RFPs) with the trading community. Suppliers then use the XML search facilities offered by the trading community to locate each tender, RFI, RFQ, or RFP issued by relevant buyers to whom they want to respond.

Many trading communities have emerged in recent years. Trading communities survive by attracting many buyers and suppliers to trade with each other. A trading community typically generates revenue by taking a small percentage of the value of each trading transaction. So its ability to match buyers with suppliers is vital in generating future revenue for the trading community.

To survive, the multitude of trading communities that exist today will likely consolidate into one or two large communities in each industry or community group. Size, geographic scope, and industry visibility are key factors in the survival of trading communities.

Figure 11.11 illustrates the Global Trading Web (GTW), established worldwide by CommerceOne. Separate trading communities are hosted by large telecommunications authorities in many countries, such as Japan, Singapore, Germany, the United Kingdom, Latin America, and elsewhere. The CommerceOne software and facilities are commonly used by all, so that a buyer in one country can trade easily with a supplier in any other country, by using the GTW to communicate seamlessly.

Buyers and suppliers—using this approach through trading communities—can only find and do business with other companies that also use the same trading community. Any companies that do not use the same trading community are excluded.

What is needed is an electronic "Internet Yellow Pages." This is similar in concept to the Yellow Pages printed directories in most cities and countries throughout the world: listing businesses under different categories for products and services that they provide. We will consider solutions to this problem in this and later chapters, when we look at Internet Yellow Pages facilities based on ebXML and XML Web services.

We now discuss the concepts associated with XML messaging standards in more detail.

11.3 XML Messaging and Repository Standards

XML messaging requires standards for XML envelope formats, as well as standards for XML business documents within those envelopes. As we briefly discussed earlier, there are many XML message envelope standards. Some also include business

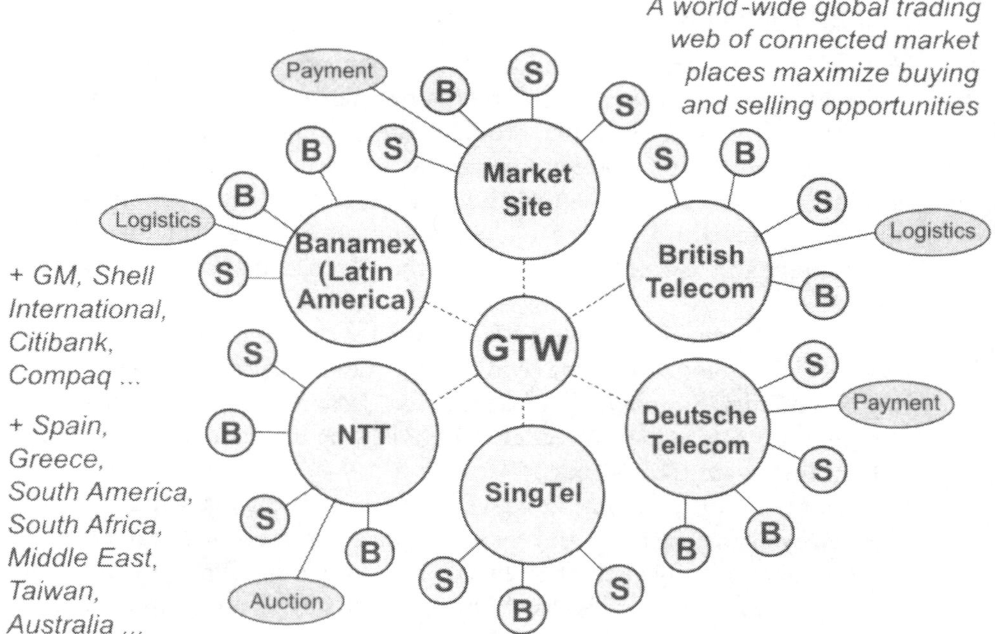

Figure 11.11 CommerceOne has established a Global Trading Web using large telephone companies across many countries. (*Source:* © 2002 CommerceOne. Reprinted with permission.)

document formats for particular industries. The major envelope format standards follow:

- RosettaNet [10]: Used by the information technology and electronic components industries, RosettaNet defines XML message envelope standards and business document standards. The RosettaNet Web site also includes a repository of RosettaNet document formats freely available as XML Document Type Definition (DTD) files and XML Schema Definition (XSD) files. We will discuss RosettaNet later in this chapter.
- BizTalk [11]: Microsoft BizTalk Server is widely used in many industries. It defines an XML message envelope format for guaranteed message delivery. It does not specify business document standards, but includes a repository of many XML document formats. These are also freely available as DTD files and XSD files, defining common XML business documents for use with BizTalk. We will discuss BizTalk later in this chapter in the Product Descriptions on the accompanying CD-ROM.
- ebXML [12]: Electronic Business XML extends the decades of experience with EDI to XML. The Organization for the Advancement of Structured Information Standards (OASIS) together with UN/CEFACT [13] are the standards bodies involved in the ebXML specifications for use with EDI. Like BizTalk, ebXML is a message envelope format, but it also includes a registry as an Internet Yellow Pages directory, as discussed earlier. The ebXML Web sites in the endnotes include repositories that hold definitions of common XML document formats available for free use by other organizations considering ebXML

and EDI interchange. We will look at ebXML in more detail later in this chapter.

- UDDI [14]: Universal Description, Discovery and Integration (UDDI) defines an XML registry for an Internet Yellow Pages similar to the ebXML.org registry. It is used with Web services defined using Simple Object Access Protocol (SOAP) and Web services Description Language (WSDL). While UDDI provides much of the same functionality of ebXML, its focus is much broader than for use with EDI. We will discuss Web services, SOAP, WSDL, and UDDI in detail in Chapter 13.

11.3.1 Industry Markup Vocabularies

As we discussed briefly earlier, many industries have defined industry markup vocabularies for XML document interchange and metadata communication. These vocabularies define various business document formats used in each industry and, hence, become industry standards. Examples of some industry markup vocabularies [15] include the following:

- Banking and finance [16]: A cooperative banking and finance industry effort has defined industry markup languages among major financial institutions—and the service providers and information technology vendors—plus their customers in small business and consumer markets. Some of these languages include IFX (Interactive Financial eXchange), OFX (Open Financial eXchange), and FpML (Financial Products Markup Language). See the endnotes for a list of Web sites.
- Audit and financial reporting [17]: Defined as a universal language for financial information, reporting, and analysis, the eXtensible Business Reporting Language (XBRL) addresses the problem of a lack of financial reporting standards. It resolves the problem of ineffective communication with investors, of inefficient aggregation and analysis, and of inefficient creation of financial statements. XBRL standards bodies exist in many countries, including XBRL USA, XBRL Australia, XBRL Canada, XBRL UK, and others.
- Health care [18]: HL7 (Health Level 7) defines standards for exchange, management, and integration of data that supports clinical patient care and the management, delivery, and evaluation of health care services. HL7 standards are defined for message interchange, software components, medical logic, and document and record architectures.

We will now discuss some of the concepts that are associated with the above major XML messaging standards in more detail.

11.3.2 RosettaNet

RosettaNet is a complete specification for XML messaging. It defines message envelope formats, business document formats, and processes for the IT and electronic component (EC) industries. It was cooperatively defined from 1999 by several hundred companies in these industries, with some listed in Table 11.1.

Table 11.1 List of Organizations That Contributed to the Development of RosettaNet

IT Industry		
3Com	Federal Express	NEC*
American Express	GSA	Netscape
Arrow*	Hewlett-Packard	Office Depot
Avnet*	IBM*	pcOrder
ntblCisco*	Ingram	Quantum
Computacenter	Insight	Siemens
Compaq	Intel*	Solectron*
CompUSA	Lucent*	Tech Data
Dell	MicroAge	UPS
	Microsoft	
EC Industry		
Agilent	Hitachi	Philips
Altera	IBM*	Pioneer
AMD	Intel*	Samsung
Arrow*	Kemet	Solectron*
Avnet*	Lucent*	ST Microelectronics
AVX	Micron	Texas Instruments
Bourns	Molex	Toshiba
Cisco*	Motorola	Tyco (Amp)
FCI	National	VEBA
Future	NEC*	Xilinx

* = in both IT and EC industries.

RosettaNet is based on the concepts of partner interface processes (PIPs). A PIP is defined as follows:

> A PIP depicts activities, decisions, and interactions that fulfill a business transaction between two partners in the supply chain.

PIPs are fundamental to the operation and use of RosettaNet. Not only does RosettaNet define one of the most complete industry markup vocabularies; it also extends beyond IT and EC common interchange XML document formats and industry terminology to defined infrastructure for messaging. It has established a legal foundation for B2B e-business that also benefits other industries. Many middleware tools support RosettaNet.

The relationship between the concepts of a PIP and EDI are shown in Table 11.2. While a PIP focuses on processes and so is process-centric, EDI focuses on data in messages and is message-centric. A PIP involves real-time, dynamic processing while EDI addresses batch processing of large volume EDI files.

EDI is used for around 10% of the B2B processes between large trading partners, while a PIP addresses 100% of the processing of IT and EC B2B processes. EDI has been in use for decades, based on expensive, leased lines used as value-added networks. In contrast, RosettaNet is designed for inexpensive use of the Internet.

Table 11.2 Comparison Between RosettaNet PIP and EDI

PIP	*EDI*
Process-centric	Message-centric
Real time	Batch
100% of B2B processes	10% of B2B processes
Internet-enabled	VAN-enabled
XML	X12/EDIFACT/JECALS
Global	Regional
All businesses	Large businesses
Standard industry dictionaries	Custom industry dictionaries

EDI is based on defined standards (X12, EDIFACT, or JECALS), whereas a PIP is based on the use of XML. EDI is intended for regional use by large trading partners, whereas a PIP can be used globally. In fact, because of complexity and cost, EDI is used by large businesses with custom industry metadata dictionaries. In contrast, a PIP is used by all businesses through standard industry metadata dictionaries.

Some of the PIP categories in RosettaNet, with [square brackets] indicating the number of PIPs defined in that category, are listed in Table 11.3.

For example, the characteristics of *PIP 3A4: Manage Purchase Order* are shown in Table 11.4. This PIP covers specifications for PO request, PO acceptance, PO change, and PO cancellation. These processes are used by ABC and DEF as customers of XYZ—their supplier—if these companies all operate in the IT or EC industries. Using PIP 3A4 specifications, a company is identified by its GTIN (Global Trade Identified Number) or by its defined DUNS [19] number.

Important performance criteria are defined for each RosettaNet PIP. For example, *PIP 3A4: Manage Purchase Order* in Table 11.4 defines that a supplier must acknowledge receipt of a 3A4 message within 2 hours; it must respond and agree or decline to act on the request within 24 hours, for which authorization is required. Secure transport, digital signature, and SSL security are all required.

Note that the specification indicates that nonrepudiation is required. This is an important principle of RosettaNet. The definition of the RosettaNet specifications also established the legal nature of electronic documents, so that they have the same force in law as do paper documents. For example, when a customer sends a paper purchase order to a supplier requesting specific products or services for fulfillment, and that PO is accepted by the supplier, a legal agreement is implicitly entered into by both parties. By mutual acceptance, the supplier has agreed to supply the requested products or services at the agreed price by the agreed date; by request the customer also implicitly agrees to pay that price when the requested products or services are provided by the supplier on that date.

The same legal principles also apply to RosettaNet electronic documents. For example, when a customer issues an electronic XML PO request for specific products or services to a supplier and the supplier responds with an electronic PO acceptance message, a legal agreement has been entered into between both parties. The

Table 11.3 List of RosettaNet PIPs

Partner/Product Review
Partner review [3]
Product/service review [3]
Product Information
Preparation for distribution [8]
Product change notification [6]
Marketing Information Management
Lead management [3]
Promotion management [6]
Design win management (EC) [5]
Order Management
Quote and order entry [7]
Transportation and distribution [9]
Product configuration [16]
Returns and finance management [4]
Inventory Management
Price protection [5]
Collaborative forecasting [2]
Inventory allocation and replenishment [2]
Inventory and sales reporting [10]
Ship from stock and debit/credit (EC) [6]
Service and Support
Warranty management [1]
Asset management [TBD]
Technical support and services [4]

PO request and PO acceptance are now legally binding on both parties. This is shown by specifying *Non-Repudiation Required: YES.*

RosettaNet, with its PIPs, message envelope formats, and business document formats, is a full solution for e-business in the IT and EC industries. Other more general solutions are available through software products such as Microsoft BizTalk Server and also ebXML software products from many vendors. These address message delivery with envelope formats as discussed next.

11.4 ebXML

Electronic Business XML is called ebXML [20]. It defines the evolution of EDI applications and messages to XML. It is a joint effort by UN/CEFACT (the United Nations body for Trade Facilitation and Electronic Business) and OASIS.

ebXML is a worldwide standardization of XML business specifications to migrate EDI to XML. It defines a technical framework that enables XML to be utilized in a consistent manner for the exchange of all electronic business data.

Table 11.4 Content of RosettaNet *PIP 3A4 Manage Purchase Order*

Manage Purchase Order
Messages Guidelines/XML Schemas (DTDs) for PIP 3A4
PO Request
PO Acceptance
PO Change
PO Cancellation
Significant Data
haGTIN (Global Trade Identifier Number)
DUNS
Performance Criteria
Time to Acknowledge Receipt: 2 hours
Time to Respond to Action: 24 hours
Authorization Required: Yes
Non-Repudiation Required: Yes
Secure Transport Required: Yes
Digital Signature Required: Yes
SSL Required: Yes

The ebXML specification phase involved more than 3,000 organizations worldwide, meeting quarterly. It ran over an 18-month period from November 1999 through May 2001. The ebXML Specifications were first released in May 2001; they document ebXML for use by EDI and middleware software vendors. We will see on the CD-ROM that BizTalk uses the BizTalk Orchestration Designer to define process logic and workflow. The ebXML specifications originally assumed that business process logic would instead be defined in UML diagrams. These UML diagrams were to be used automatically to generate executable XML-based code in Business Process Specification Schema (BPSS) [21]. We will discuss BPSS in Chapter 14.

ebXML was designed in part for use by large enterprises who use EDI. It was designed for use also by smaller companies, as discussed shortly. Large trading partners will likely continue to use their EDI software middleware vendors. But the advantage ebXML offers them is the low-cost capability of the Internet for message transfer, rather than the high-cost leased lines previously required for EDI. Conversion between EDI and ebXML is automatically provided by EDI software middleware vendors.

The ebXML message structure is very similar to that used for BizTalk messages. ebXML specifies an ebXML header envelope and an ebXML payload envelope as illustrated in Figure 11.12. The header envelope contains the ebXML header document, with a manifest and details of the header, similar in concept to BizTalk [22]. The payload envelope contains the actual XML document(s), called the *payload documents* by ebXML. BizTalk uses synonymous terms: business document in the body of the message.

As discussed earlier, ebXML was also designed for use by small and medium enterprises (SMEs). Large EDI trading partners already do business with each other,

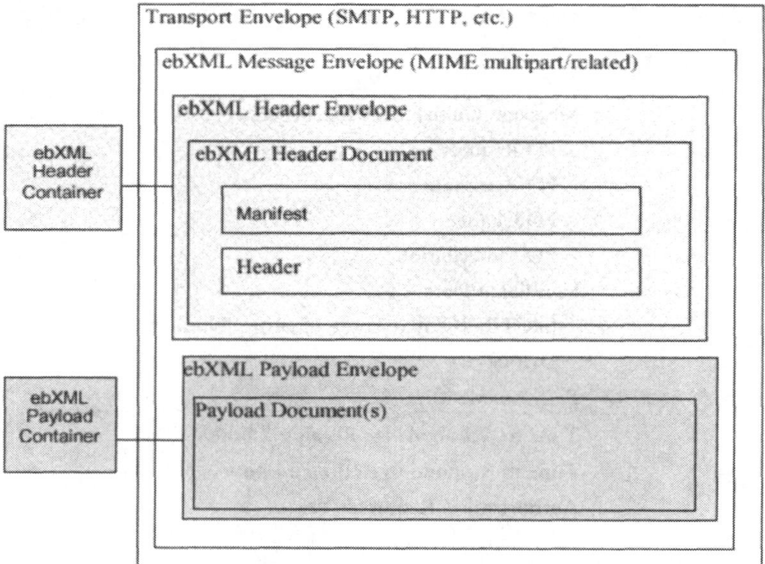

Figure 11.12 ebXML message envelope format. (*From:* [20]. © 2001 ebXML.org. Reprinted with permission.)

but SMEs may not know of other SMEs with whom they want to trade. Figure 11.13 shows how they can find each other.

Figure 11.13 shows typical use of ebXML by Company A and Company B. Company A decides that it wants to publish the availability of its products and services for online purchase using ebXML. For discussion purposes, we will assume

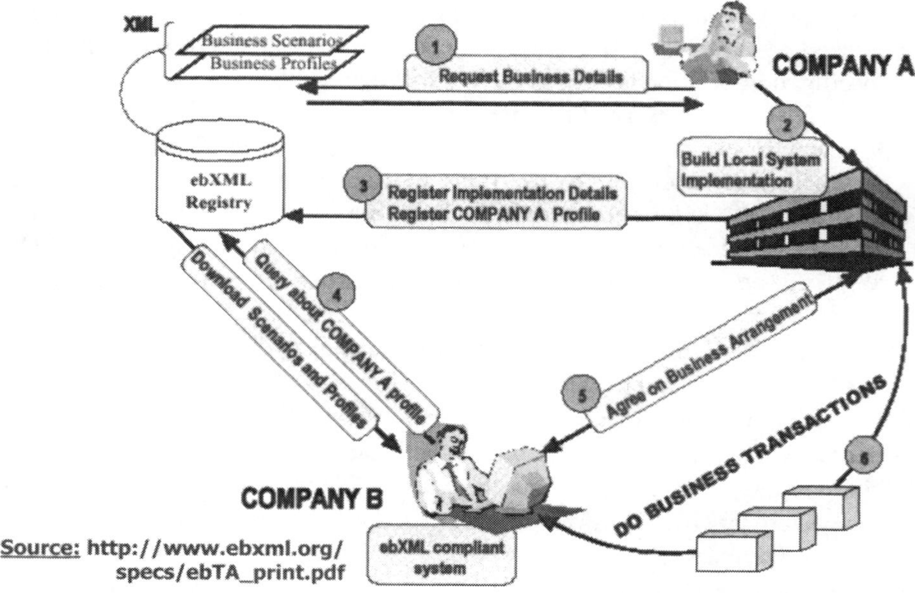

Figure 11.13 Steps in using the ebXML repository. (*From:* [20]. © 2001 ebXML.org. Reprinted with permission.)

that Company A is a bank (Bank A) that wants to offer its credit card authorization and processing services via ebXML. We will also assume that Company B wants to use ebXML for credit card authorization and processing from a bank. We will use the earlier example of XYZ, which now wants to implement an online store for its customers to visit. The XYZ online store decides that it wants to use ebXML for credit card authorization and payment. The steps described below are referenced to Figure 11.13 using (parentheses).

- Bank A (Company A) requests ebXML specification details from ebXML.org: the ebXML registry and repository (1). These specifications are sent by ebXML.org and are used by Bank A (2) to develop its credit card authorization and processing service details, for publishing to ebXML.org (3).
- The XYZ online store (Company B) may be located anywhere in the world. It decides that it wants to find out if any bank offers a credit card authorization and processing service using ebXML. It queries the ebXML.org registry. It receives back details of all banks that have registered to provide those services (4).
- The XYZ online store selects Bank A and contacts it to exchange Collaboration Protocol Agreements (CPAs) (5), based on the Bank's ebXML definition. The XYZ online store prepares its credit card authorization and processing service ebXML transaction requests based on the format and specifications published by the bank. Through specific development based on the Bank A specifications, the XYZ online store tightly binds itself to the bank. This was initially supported by ebXML with *compile-time binding;* more recently ebXML has also specified support for *run-time binding* as with Web services [23]. Both companies commence business transactions together (6), having established a valid business relationship based on the ebXML Specifications.
- The steps in Figure 11.13 are as documented in the ebXML specifications. By using an ebXML middleware product, the bank supplies relevant details and BPSS code in XML for publication of the credit card authorization and processing service on ebXML.org; see steps (1) and (2). The middleware package then publishes those specifications (3). Similarly, also by using an ebXML middleware product, the online store asks the middleware product to "find" relevant suppliers of credit card authorization and processing services. Based on the response for all banks (4), and using the package to download the relevant BPSS XML code of interest, the XYZ online Store contacts Bank A to enter into a collaboration protocol agreement (CPA) (5).

As discussed earlier, the ebXML BPSS XML code was intended to be automatically generated from UML diagrams to define the collaboration and coordination of business processes in achieving a physical business interchange between parties [24].

11.4.1 XML Integration Server Concepts

We will now discuss the concepts and use of integration servers (also called *interaction servers*). These concepts are used by trading communities and also message broker software products to direct XML messages to the appropriate software code modules or programs, for processing relevant XML messages. The numbered steps in Figure 11.14 are keyed to the following discussion for XYZ Corporation. Figure 11.14 illustrates processing involved in XML messages received across the firewall of an enterprise. On receipt, each XML message is examined by an integration server—such as that used by message brokers or trading communities—to determine the content of the message and the application program or code module that is required to process it.

The XML document (1) is first located in a document repository. This indicates the relevant workflow steps (2) that are needed to process the received XML message. The XYZ document repository also specifies the data transformations (3) that are required to convert the XML message format to the input data format structure and data types expected by enterprise systems, for processing by the receiving application program or code module (4).

The concepts associated with integration servers are best described using an example based on XYZ and ABC, as discussed earlier. Figure 11.15 illustrates the relevant workflow steps to be followed by the XYZ order entry system on receipt of a purchase order sent by a buyer: ABC. The following steps are keyed to Figure 11.15, where ABC uses the Open Application Group (OAG) PO XML message format.

We can see in Figure 11.15 that on receipt of the XML message (A), if the total value of the PO is less than $10,000, the business rule used by XYZ is to immediately accept the order (B). But if the total value of the PO is $10,000 or greater (C), the business rule requires the credit status of the buyer to be checked first (D) to determine whether the PO should be accepted or rejected (E). The buyer is then notified of acceptance or rejection by an XML message sent in response to the PO (F).

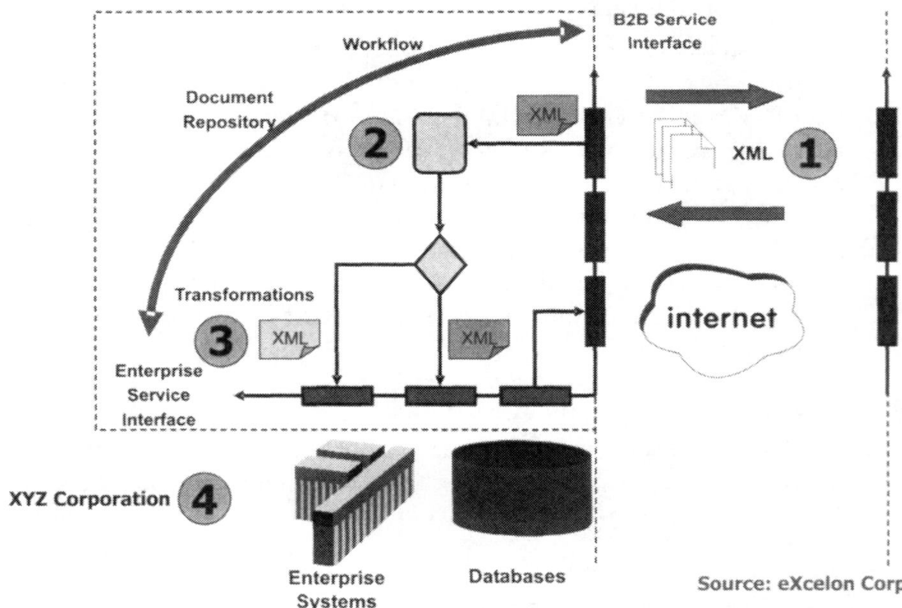

Figure 11.14 XML messages are examined for content and process workflow. They are transformed to the format expected by back-end enterprise systems. (*Source:* © 2001 Sonic Software. Reprinted with permission.)

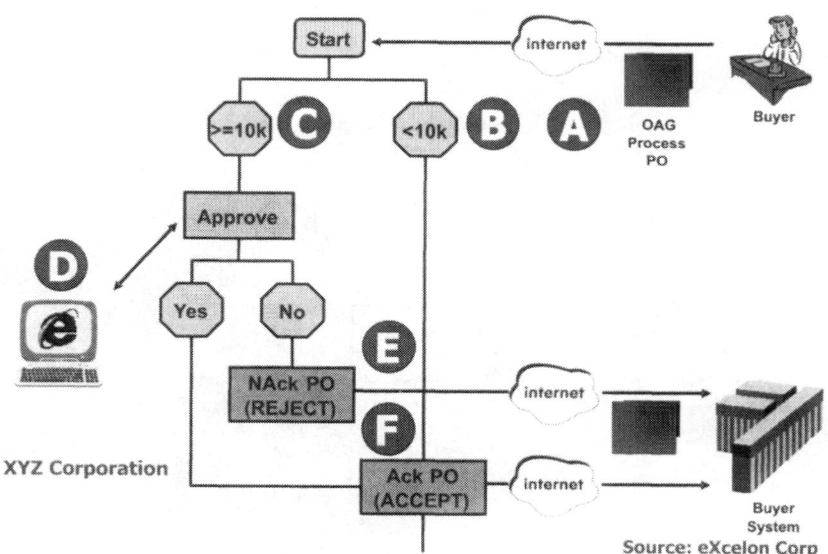

Figure 11.15 XYZ workflow steps to accept an XML PO sent by ABC. (*Source:* © 2001 Sonic Software. Reprinted with permission.)

For accepted purchase orders to be processed as sales orders, Figure 11.16 shows that the quantity of each ordered item in inventory is checked by XYZ (G). If insufficient quantity is available to fulfill the ordered quantity, XYZ may need to order sufficient quantities of each out-of-stock item from its own suppliers to replenish its inventory (H).

When these items are received into inventory (I), or if sufficient quantity is already available, the buyer's PO (from ABC) is processed (J). An ASN is sent back to the buyer (K), together with a customer invoice (L), for the items that are supplied in satisfaction of the ABC purchase order.

Let us now look at the workflow processing for Buyer ABC in Figure 11.17, with numbered steps now, keyed to the following discussion.

Following transmission of the PO to XYZ earlier, the workflow engine at ABC examines each later received XML message and then carries out the steps detailed next.

1. The first message received by ABC is the delivery advice or ASN, which is transmitted by XYZ in confirmation of processing the PO earlier sent by ABC to XYZ (1). This ASN message is directed to the Purchase Order Acceptance System for ABC processing (2). The XML message indicates the date when the ordered items in the PO will be delivered into ABC inventory, and the agreed price between ABC and XYZ for each item. The copy of the PO that was saved originally by ABC is therefore updated accordingly with the ASN details (3).
2. Later, the customer invoice transmitted by XYZ in XML is received by ABC as a supplier invoice (4). This XML message is directed to the ABC Accounts Payable System for processing (5), which examines the supplier invoice to determine that (a) the referenced PO is valid, (b) the ordered

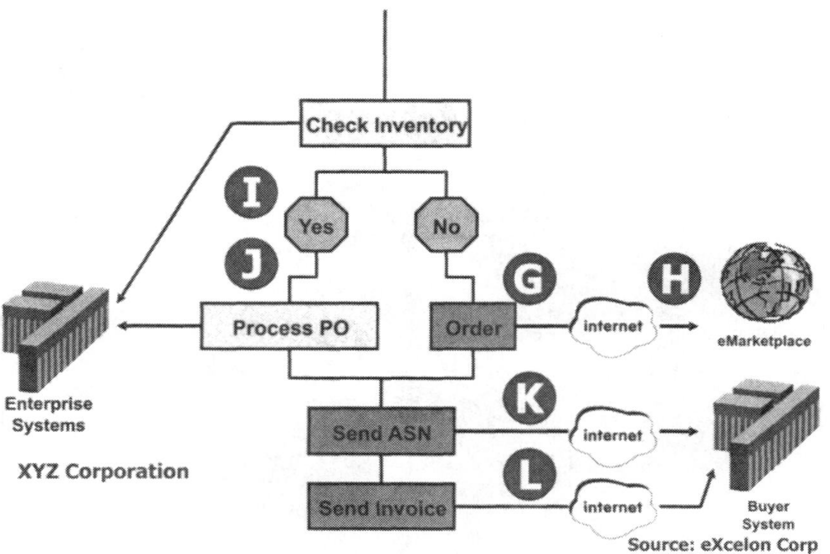

Figure 11.16 XYZ workflow steps to process an XML PO that was sent by ABC. (*Source:* © 2001 Sonic Software. Reprinted with permission.)

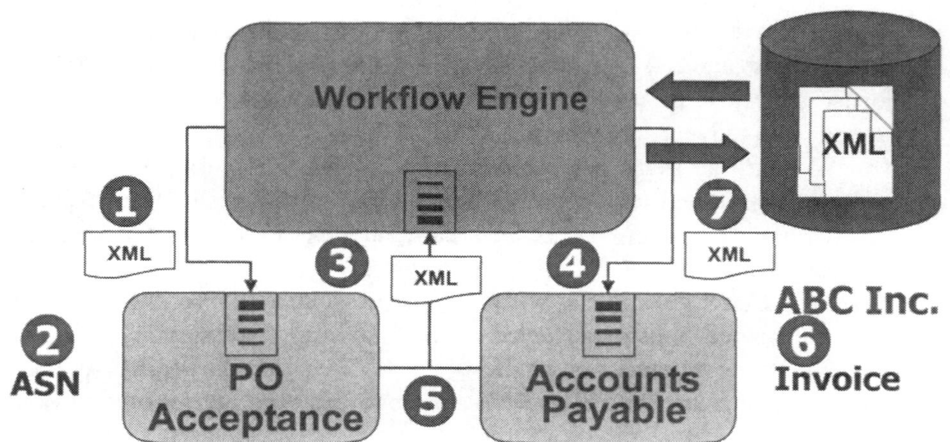

Figure 11.17 ABC workflow steps for receipt of the ASN and supplier invoice from XYZ. (*Source:* © 2001 Sonic Software. Reprinted with permission.)

items have been delivered by XYZ, and (c) they have been received into inventory by ABC. The items are checked to confirm that (d) the correct items were delivered in the correct quantity, (e) they are in good order, and (f) they are priced correctly (6).

3. If the supplier invoice is correct as discussed in Step 2, the ABC accounts payable system authorizes payment of the total amount of the supplier invoice to XYZ (7). This is typically achieved by sending a wire transfer request message in XML to ABC's bank, authorizing the automatic

transfer of the invoiced amount due from the ABC bank account directly to the nominated XYZ bank account.

The workflow process logic for each XML message is documented diagrammatically in a workflow diagram. In the past this workflow diagram would then be printed so that a programmer could manually code the relevant process logic using various programming languages [25].

Distinct from this past manual coding approach, most of today's EAI workflow tools first provide facilities to test that the diagrammed logic in the workflow diagram is correct. This is similar to what we will discuss in relation to the Microsoft BizTalk Orchestration Designer in the Product Descriptions section on the accompanying CD-ROM. In the same way, after correcting identified logic errors in the diagrammed chart—instead of printing the diagram for manual coding—today's EAI workflow tools automatically generate executable logic directly from the diagram, without requiring any manual programming.

The result is fast implementation with no coding errors or "bugs." Furthermore, if any changes are later required to be made to the defined workflow, these changes can now be made at the diagrammatic level. The changed workflow diagram is tested again, and once more it is automatically regenerated as executable code. We will discuss these concepts further, when we cover SOA in Chapter 14.

11.4.2 Redundant Data Update Using EAI

We will now revisit the problem that was introduced in Chapter 1, with redundant data versions in the enterprise. We saw that data such as a *Customer Address* may exist in other versions also, such as *Client Address* and *Debtor Address*—as used by the Sales Department, the Credit Department, and the Accounting Department. If a customer is also a supplier, we discussed that the *Supplier Address* and *Creditor Address* would also be redundant.

Figure 11.18 considers that each redundant address version must be kept up to date if any one version of these data changes. For example, if the *customer address* is changed in the order entry system, an address change notification form is printed and sent by internal company mail (or by fax) to each part of the organization where the address exists redundantly. The relevant change address data maintenance transaction is then used to manually reenter the new address, thus updating the previous version of the address to the new, changed address.

The manual data maintenance activity in Figure 11.18, which is needed to keep each redundant data version up to date, involves redundant data entry of the changed address, updating the *client address* in the credit control system and the *debtor address* in the invoicing system for accounts receivable in the Finance Department. This is redundant work, with redundant staffing to do this redundant data entry. Also the address change transaction used by each redundant data maintenance system may not use the same operating procedure or screen design for data entry; this will also require redundant training of staff to do this redundant data maintenance processing.

The redundant work, redundant staffing, redundant processing, and redundant training are very expensive, time consuming, and error prone. This is the high-cost

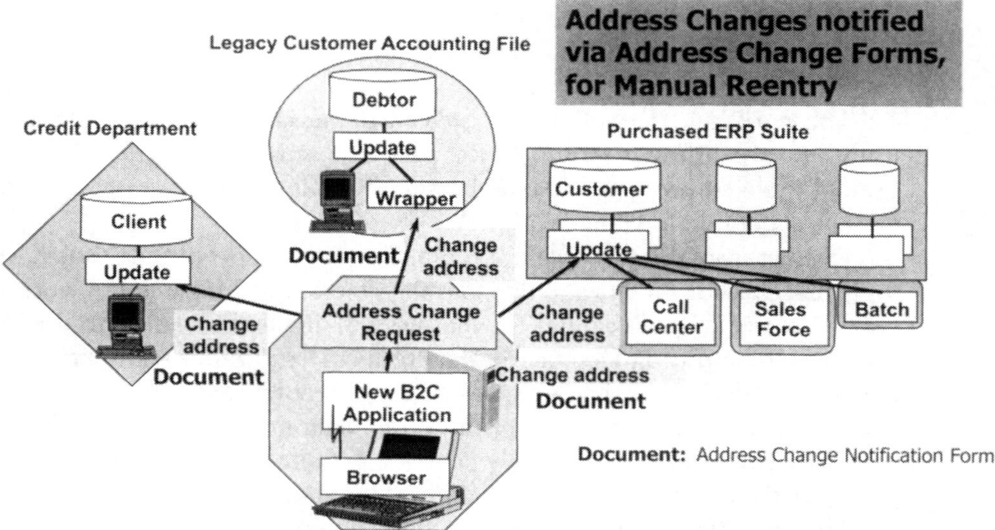

Figure 11.18 Address change notification form with manual reentry. (*After:* Gartner Group.)

operational consequence of redundant data. EAI now addresses this problem very efficiently and inexpensively, as discussed next in relation to Figure 11.19.

With EAI, rather than print then mail or fax the address change notification form to parts of the enterprise, in Figure 11.19 it is output as an XML address change notification message. This XML message is transmitted electronically to data maintenance address change systems throughout the organization using EAI middleware products such as BizTalk or ebXML middleware products. The XML address change notification message can be delivered electronically and transformed

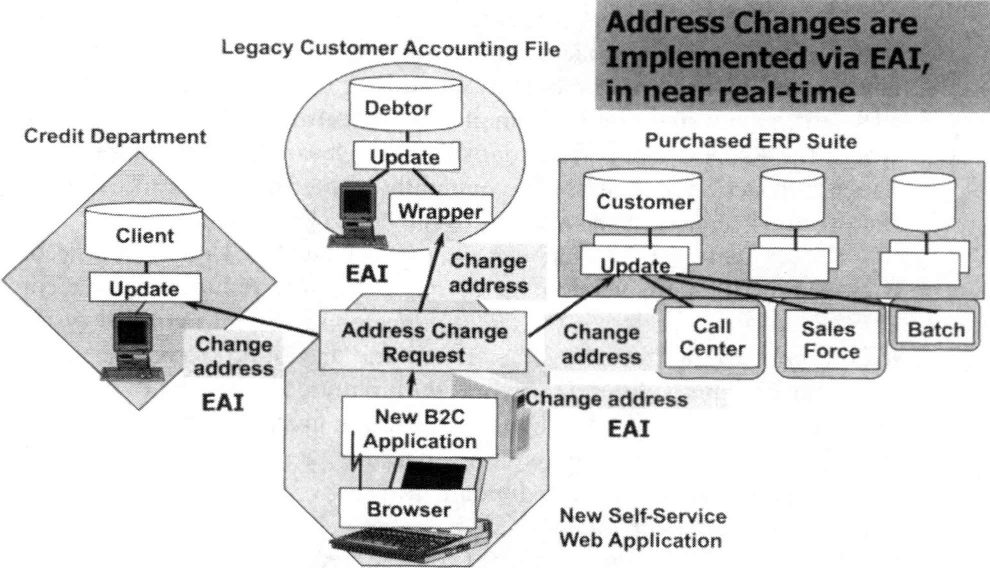

Figure 11.19 Address change notification using EAI alleviates the need for manual reentry. (*After:* Gartner Group.)

to the input data format required by each address change system for direct input, without requiring any manual reentry.

The electronic XML address change notification message is transmitted automatically in *near real time*. The result is inexpensive data maintenance synchronization, with no errors introduced—a problem often experienced with the previous manual data entry approach, as discussed.

Using EAI methods and middleware products in this way, the redundant data version problem is addressed very efficiently and inexpensively. It converts the many redundant versions of the same data (which is bad), now to "replicated" data (which is good). This replicated data are now maintained and synchronized electronically in near real time, so that it is always kept up to date.

We will also revisit this same problem of redundant data again in Chapter 13, when we discuss Web services.

We have covered many of the concepts and technologies behind EAI. We will now finish this chapter by looking at the EAI support provided by webMethods. This vendor provides the EAI infrastructure used by other EAI vendors: by trading networks, by B2B vendors, message brokers, message delivery vendors, and other EAI middleware vendors. Many of these vendors license EAI technology from webMethods. They license EAI, B2B, reliable message delivery, and envelope translation functionality needed for EAI. In fact, webMethods is the major EAI infrastructure vendor.

11.5 EAI Vendors and Products

The various software products from EAI vendors discussed in this chapter are included as the PDF file *Chap-11-Products.pdf* in the Book Materials folder on the accompanying CD-ROM. These products include the following:

- Microsoft BizTalk Server;
- EAI using webMethods;
- IBM EAI Products;
- SeeBeyond EAI Products;
- Vitria EAI Products;
- Tibco EAI Products.

11.6 Summary

We complete this chapter with a brief summary of the EAI concepts that we have covered:

- *Cost reduction:* The typical cost of manual entry and processing of a purchase order is \$100 to \$150, independent of the value of the items purchased. This cost typically drops to \$8 to \$10 using EAI for transaction processing. This is a powerful business driver for EAI.

- *Buyers and suppliers:* Trading communities (trading networks) help customers and suppliers to find each other, so they can do business together. This is most cost effective when both organizations can eliminate the manual reentry of documents, and instead connect their back-end systems to each other automatically through EAI.
- *Document delivery:* Trading communities connect customers, suppliers, and business partners to each other across the Internet—with reliable, guaranteed electronic document delivery. A variety of envelope formats and message protocols are used, with automatic transformation between them.
- *Message formats:* The major message formats include RosettaNet (for the IT and EC industry), with envelope formats based on BizTalk (from Microsoft) or ebXML (for use by large and small enterprises, via EDI and XML).
- *Graphical process models:* With BizTalk, we first saw graphical process models that are used for BPM. This enables business logic to be defined by business users as workflow diagrams, tested for correct logical execution, and then compiled for automatic execution—without further programming.
- *Industry markup vocabularies:* These have been defined for most industries and include XBRL (for audit and financial reporting); IFX, OFX, and FpML (for banking and finance); and HL7 (for health care). Other industry markup vocabularies are listed in the XML Catalog at OASIS (http://www.xml.org).
- *Internet Yellow Pages:* ebXML.org and UDDI.org both offer an Internet Yellow Pages capability, so that organizations that want to do business together can find each other easily. This will be covered in more detail in Chapter 13.
- *XML integration servers:* We looked at some concepts involved in XML message interchange, as carried out by integration servers. These concepts are based on workflow processes, and also data transformation between different XML document formats.
- *EAI for redundant data:* We saw how EAI can be used to keep redundant data versions up to date, using XML documents to synchronize data changes throughout the enterprise in near real time.
- *webMethods:* On the CD-ROM we briefly mentioned the EAI support provided by webMethods. We used this vendor to introduce technologies that are required for EAI, as an example of the support that EAI middleware vendors need to provide. We saw that webMethods supports the capabilities of:
    - *Business Process Modeling,* for the development of graphical workflow models for business process management.
    - *System Integration,* with support for adapters to access ERP packages, databases, mainframe legacy systems, messaging middleware, and flat file, e-mail and other interfaces. A discussion of Web services support within EAI middleware products was deferred to Chapter 13.
    - *Business Process Monitoring,* with support for real-time monitoring and maintenance of business processes, was also discussed.
    - *Business Process Optimization,* with support for real-time metrics that allow process optimization during normal EAI operation.

- *Other EAI vendors:* We finished the chapter on the CD-ROM with a review of other Enterprise Application Integration middleware vendors, including IBM WebSphere Business Integration Server, SeeBeyond Business Integration Suite, Vitria BusinessWare Business Process Integration, and TIBCO BusinessWorks.

We will now move to Chapter 12, where we will discuss the use of enterprise portals for enterprise integration.

Endnotes

[1] Introductory articles and white papers on XML can be found at the World Wide Web Consortium (W3C) Web site at http://www.w3c.org and the Organization for Advancement of Structured Information Standards (OASIS) at http://www.xml.org.

[2] Extensible Style Language Transformation (XSLT) and Extensible Style Language (XSL) specifications and white papers are available from W3C at http://www.w3c.org, and from OASIS at http://www.xml.org.

[3] The XSLT language specifies in XML the transformation that is to be carried out, processed by an XSLT processor, which is called an *XSLT transformation engine,* as shown in Figure 11.3.

[4] An advanced shipping notice (ASN) typically provides confirmation of acceptance by a supplier of a purchase order issued by a customer, and advises the price and planned date for delivery of the order to the customer.

[5] This is discussed shortly, in Section 11.3.1, Industry Markup Vocabularies.

[6] This comment on *many-to many* transformations has no correspondence to the concept of *many-to many* associations that we discussed in Chapters 6 and 7.

[7] Integration problems are still encountered by cross-industry enterprises, such as government departments or diversified companies that may not have agreed common document formats.

[8] To find out the Industry Markup Languages that have been defined in your industry, visit the OASIS Web site at http://www.xml.org. Click on the XML Catalog button in the left frame. Scroll down the XML Catalog industry list displayed alphabetically in the right frame to locate your industry and follow the links.

[9] This is an XML format used by the information technology and electronic components industries. We will discuss RosettaNet shortly.

[10] Further information on RosettaNet is available from http://www.rosettanet.org.

[11] Further information about BizTalk is available from http://www.microsoft.com/biztalk and also from the BizTalk Web site at http://www.biztalk.org. BizTalk is discussed in *Chap-11-Products.PDF* on the accompanying CD-ROM.

[12] Detailed information on ebXML is available from OASIS at http://www.xml.org and also from http://www.ebxml.org.

[13] UN/CEFACT is the United Nations body for Trade Facilitation and Electronic Business.

[14] Information on UDDI is available from OASIS at http://www.xml.org and also from http://www.uddi.org/. Information on SOAP and WSDL is at http://www.w3c.org. Web services are covered in detail in Chapter 13.

[15] If you need to find specific industry markup vocabularies, visit OASIS at http://www.xml.org. Click on the XML Catalog link to display an alphabetical list of industries with links to details on their relevant industry markup vocabularies.

[16] Information on banking and finance industry markup languages is available from their Web sites: IFX at http://www.ifxforum.org, OFX at http://www.ofx.org, and FpML at http://www.fpml.org.

[17] Information on XBRL is available from http://www.xbrl.org. This includes the use of XBRL for financial statements, general ledgers, journal entry reporting, credit reporting,

risk reporting, regulatory filings, assurance schedules, tax filings, and for "business" reporting.

[18] Further information on HL7 for health care is available at http://www.hl7.org.

[19] A DUNS number is an identifier that Dunn and Bradstreet uses to identify individual companies for creditworthiness inquiries. Refer to the Dunn and Bradstreet Web site at http://www.dnb.com.

[20] The current ebXML specifications are available from http://www.ebxml.org. Further details on ebXML are also available from OASIS at http://www.xml.org.

[21] We will see in Chapter 14 that BPSS 2.0 specifications now refer to the use of Business Process Modeling Notation (BPMN), rather than UML, to define business process logic. BPMN is covered in Chapter 14.

[22] See the product description of BizTalk in the PDF file *Chap-11-Products.pdf* in the Book Materials folder on the accompanying CD-ROM.

[23] The initial specification of ebXML was tightly coupled based on *compile-time binding:* with code based on the specifications of the ebXML service provider. In contrast, ebXML now—and Web services—are based on loosely coupled *run-time binding*: with dynamic binding carried out in real time, as discussed in Chapter 13.

[24] As discussed in an earlier footnote, BPSS 2.0 now contemplates the use of BPMN to define business process logic. This is discussed further in Chapter 14.

[25] We used to joke that it was the programmer's job to code in the "bugs"!

CHAPTER 12

Enterprise Portal Technologies for Integration

This chapter covers the concepts, product categories, features, and benefits of *enterprise portals*, also called *corporate portals* or *enterprise information portals.* It shows how an enterprise portal (EP) is a gateway to the structured data and unstructured data resources of an organization. It shows how these resources are accessed from an enterprise portal, along with execution of business processes and application systems. This technology is important for integration, because it provides easy access to resources where access was often difficult before. The chapter includes case study examples of real-life enterprise portals and introduces three portal categories: collaborative portals, business intelligence portals, and integration portals. On the CD-ROM several portal products in each category are discussed.

12.1 The Evolution of Enterprise Portals

The term *enterprise information portal* (EIP) was used in a November 16, 1998, Merrill Lynch report [1]. They commented that EIP systems provide companies with great competitive advantage. They identified a new category for integration of systems in an EIP—with "integrated applications that combine, standardize, index, analyze and distribute targeted, relevant information that end users need to do their day-to-day jobs more efficiently and productively." They identified benefits that include lowered costs, increased sales, and better deployment of resources. In a few short years, a large number of products came onto the market. This chapter discusses the current status of the enterprise portal market, and the use of enterprise portals for enterprise integration.

12.1.1 Definition of an Enterprise Portal

As mentioned earlier, an EIP is also called an enterprise portal (EP) or a corporate portal (CP). We will use the term *enterprise portal* in this chapter. These three equivalent terms are defined as follows:

> A single gateway via the network to relevant workflows, application systems, and databases, tailored to the specific job responsibilities of each individual.

An enterprise portal can appear in different forms, depending on the job responsibilities of each person accessing the portal. For example, an *employee portal* is defined in this way:

> A single gateway that enables all employees to access the processes, systems, workflows and databases via the network to carry out their relevant job responsibilities, with full security and firewall protection.

Another example is a *customer portal,* defined as follows:

> A single gateway via the network to details about products and services, catalogs, and order and invoice status for customers, tailored to the unique requirements of each customer.

Because of this tailoring, a customer portal offers great opportunities for one-to-one customer personalization and management for the Customer Relationship Management (CRM) function. Similarly, an enterprise portal that offers personalization and management for the Supply Chain Management (SCM) function is a *supplier portal* and is defined as follows:

> A single gateway to the purchase orders and related status information for the suppliers of an enterprise.

An enterprise portal as a *partner/shareholder portal* is similarly "a single gateway for business partners or shareholders."

12.1.2 Structured and Unstructured Data Resources

Data warehouses and information systems provide access to structured data in the databases and data files of an enterprise. These data and information resources typically represent only 10% to 30% of the total knowledge resources in most enterprises today. The structured data are generally managed reasonably well, although (as we discussed in Chapter 1) we do need to integrate the data better—a focus of this book.

In contrast, unstructured data resources exist as documents, reports, e-mail, graphics, images, audio, and video. These unstructured data sources represent the remaining 70% to 90% of the knowledge resources of an enterprise. They are typically inaccessible from data warehouses and information systems. Unstructured data are generally *not managed well*, and definitely are *not integrated*: They exist in many different versions scattered throughout the enterprise and in different file formats: Microsoft Word, Excel, PowerPoint or Outlook; Adobe Acrobat PDF files; and different image, graphics, audio, and video formats.

An advantage of enterprise portals is that they enable structured and unstructured data to be integrated (often by using XML) and made accessible through a portal interface that is tailored to the unique data, information, knowledge, workflow, business processes, and systems that are required by each individual.

12.1.3 Basic Architecture of an Enterprise Portal

An enterprise portal is a Web-enabled, distributed environment with a single, common, managed user interface to information supporting all categories of end users. It facilitates and supports e-commerce, e-business, enterprise resource planning (ERP), CRM, and SCM, along with browser-enabled access for customers, suppliers, business partners, and employees. It supports operations such as virtual integration, knowledge-enabled processes, and cross-function delivery of applications.

A key characteristic of enterprise portals is support of a single sign-on function: enabling qualified users to sign on once to the portal and be automatically signed on to each application or resource that they are authorized to access for relevant sites in the enterprise network.

An enterprise portal facilitates sharing and distribution of information, and permits virtual teams to operate in a distributed environment. It reduces administrative and operational costs, replaces hardcopy with electronic documentation, and ensures security of sensitive information with rapid response to business challenges.

An enterprise portal is typically based on Web server technology, with import/export interfaces to decision processing systems (data warehouses), collaborative processing systems (Lotus Notes or Microsoft Exchange), and many other corporate and external systems. A search engine capability is typically included, with metadata crawlers that access data imported from these various databases and systems—to make the data and information available for access and for processing. Figure 12.1 illustrates the architecture of a typical enterprise portal.

A business information directory is used to provide details about all data, information, and knowledge resources, as well as relevant metadata (descriptions and definition of those resources) and the workflows, processes, and systems that are managed by the portal. It also provides information about each user's contact and security details and profiles, defining who can access the portal and what degree of access is authorized for them.

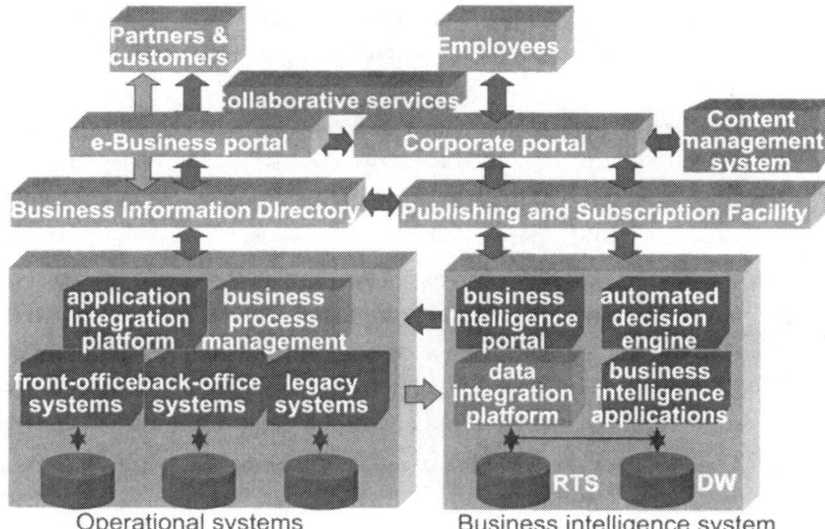

Figure 12.1 Typical enterprise portal architecture. (*From:* [2]. © 2005 BI Research, Inc. Reprinted with permission.)

Finally, an enterprise portal provides a publishing facility that indicates what resources are available through the portal, and a subscription facility that allows each individual to tailor their access to the portal uniquely to meet their specific needs.

The architecture of an enterprise portal is designed to provide a single point of content delivery and management (see Figure 12.1) [2]. It supports access to a variety of structured and unstructured information, including databases, spreadsheets, text documents, e-mail messages, news feeds, Web pages, audio files, video streams, and business applications. An enterprise portal uses a personalized interface, with shared service access for queries, reports, scheduling, alerts, notification of events, and integration with business intelligence tools. It supports central administration of the user environment, including the assignment of authorities, roles and responsibilities, privileges, permissions, security, and authorization from a single point of control.

Content management is supported from many data sources, with automatic recognition by some portal products of multiple data types within a single data source. Distributed management of the repository catalog is typically supported, including the ability to review, approve, or delete content. Access to objects in the repository can be restricted by object, person, or folder. Many portal products can scale to support hundreds of thousands of users, including provision for multiple Web servers and application servers

Typical portal configuration options include definition of access privileges, assignment of roles and privileges to individuals, connection to available applications, management of the desktop and screen areas, and the rule database behind the product. Administration options include the ability to reconfigure access based on roles and privileges, add or delete resources to a role, assign users to roles, and switch users between roles.

Some of the functions supported by a portal follow. Many functions are implemented as servers configured by the portal administrator, as summarized next:

- *Authentication server:* This is used to define user identify profiles in the portal repository. It maps data, content, and people to a defined user—automatically or contextually.
- *Security server:* This provides support for single sign-on, encryption, and also for various security technologies, such as Kerberos or HTTP/SSL.
- *Search engine:* This server capability supports ad hoc searching across both structured and unstructured data sources, either within or outside the portal.
- *Content management server:* This scans, filters, and catalogs content from disparate data and resources. It often supports Web crawlers on the Internet and intranet.
- *Business analysis server:* This is used for built-in decision support functions, such as ad hoc queries, reports, graphs, analyses, and links to external BI tools.
- *Connections server:* This provides real-time connections to many source data systems, including legacy, ERP, DBMS, e-commerce, e-business, and so forth.
- *Collaboration Server:* This allows users to interact with individuals, groups, teams, and experts to share data and solve problems.

- *Events/alerts server:* This controls notifications and alerts by time or database events, including a personal broadcaster.
- *Designer:* This provides the capability to design the end-user interface so that the desktop "real estate" can be managed effectively, with dynamic configuration of resources and mode of interaction.
- *Administrator:* The administration server supports management of role-based content delivery to users, groups of users, or groups of groups.

12.1.4 Integration Using an Enterprise Portal

An enterprise portal provides easy access to structured and unstructured data sources, as we discussed earlier. The portal "desktop," presented through a browser, is a number of independent windows that deliver views of the underlying data resources assigned to each relevant window. Figures 12.2 through 12.4, shown in the next section of this chapter, illustrate what typical portals look like.

An enterprise portal appears to deliver integration across many data sources presented in the separate windows. But this is deceptive; each window is typically independent of all others. The windows are *not* integrated. Furthermore, we discussed in Chapter 1 that redundant data versions also exist throughout the enterprise, at different levels of update. These data versions also are not integrated.

An enterprise portal that provides a view to one of these redundant versions sees only those values for the relevant version. Hopefully these are up to date. But if they are out of date, that version must be synchronized with more recently updated versions that exist elsewhere in the enterprise. This is a very important point.

A portal presents an appearance of integration. It supports presentation integration. But the underlying data themselves must first be integrated. Access through a portal to nonintegrated, out-of-sync data is irresponsible and is the ultimate exercise in futility. This is also highly dangerous because the data will appear to be integrated, but are not.

We saw in Chapter 11 how redundant data versions can be synchronized in near real time through enterprise application integration. The examples in Figures 11.18 and 11.19 used XML address change notification forms that were sent via EAI to update the customer, client, debtor, supplier and creditor addresses. Such an EAI approach will ensure that all data versions are synchronized throughout the enterprise when any redundant data value changes. If this is achieved, then any version of that data value will be at the same level of update. The enterprise portal then can provide easy access to integrated data.

A data warehouse offers *read-only* access to historical information extracted as periodic snapshots from operational databases and systems. Enterprise portals can access data warehouse and also operate against databases and collaborative systems for read-only access. However, most portal products today also support CRUD (update) access for relevant information, based on each individual's specific access and authority profiles. This is also important: A CRUD capability enables an enterprise portal to initiate immediate execution of application systems and business processes from the portal.

In Chapter 11 we discussed the use of business process management as used by EAI middleware tools. These support business process modeling, integration, monitoring, and optimization. Many enterprise portal products now enable middleware tools to be invoked from the portal. This not only integrates data as discussed earlier, but it also integrates business processes within and between enterprises. This is very important.

BPM middleware products in a portal provide very flexible integration capabilities. They offer rapid implementation with real-time monitoring and optimization.

We will leave this topic now. Other aspects of integration from enterprise portals will be discussed when we look at BPM again in conjunction with Web services and SOA in Chapters 13 and 14, respectively.

To illustrate the use and application of enterprise portals, we will review three enterprise portal case studies. The different portal categories will be discussed. On the CD-ROM we will examine a number of portal products that are available in each of these categories. We will conclude the chapter with a summary of the main characteristics that you should look for when assessing the ability of each product to satisfy your particular portal requirements.

12.2 Enterprise Portal Case Studies

The three portal case study examples in this section were the winners of DCI's Annual Portal Excellence Awards [3]. We will use entries submitted by Herman Miller, Ford Motor Company, and General Motors Corporation [4] with descriptions of their respective portals from their award submissions. These will be used to introduce some of the products and technologies that are associated with enterprise portals.

12.2.1 Herman Miller B2B E-Business Portal

Clicks-and-bricks retailer Herman Miller does most of its business selling high-end, preassembled office furniture. To accomplish this, Herman Miller deployed an e-business integration portal called MySIGN (Supplier Information Global Network) to create a supplier value chain. The MySIGN portal serves as a personal webtop, providing every party throughout the company's value chain with real-time information from the enterprise's ERP applications and databases. This sharing of information gives Herman Miller and its suppliers a competitive advantage, helping them stay "in sync" with customer demands, changes to internal schedules, and intercompany receipts and payments.

With a global presence in more than 40 countries and nearly $2 billion in revenue during fiscal year 2000, Herman Miller used the TopTier e-Business Integration Portal as a key component of an aggressive 5-year plan to double the revenue of its business [5].

By streamlining operations and compressing time-to-market, Herman Miller planned on doubling its throughput without the need for additional materials planners, trucks, or square feet of warehouse space. Herman Miller and TopTier won the E-Business Portal category in DCI's Annual Portal Excellence Awards.

By choosing TopTier as the portal vendor to help them create MySIGN, Herman Miller increased its speed and reliability in supporting a streamlined supplier relationship. Because most of the company's raw materials come from 600 suppliers around the world, it desperately needed to streamline communications and payment procedures with them. This best-in-class supplier value chain closed the loop between demand forecasting and supplier-managed inventory with an online supplier source. This provided up-to-date information on demand, supply, exception orders, invoices, delivery schedules, and lag times—with all critical business intelligence synchronized on one computer screen.

"No one is going to lead in this industry without leading in technology," said Michael Volkems, the CEO of Herman Miller. From the senior executives down, Herman Miller decided that it would connect its suppliers and customers. Everything tied into that corporate strategy, and the company made a key commitment to do so. In the previous 5 years, Herman Miller had invested in technologies to improve internal and external business processes. These investments, which included deploying the portal, have enabled it to raise its reliability from 75% to more than 95% in on-time shipments.

Herman Miller had two main requirements in building the portal. One was to have two-way communication: back-and-forth collaboration with suppliers. The second was to give suppliers a real-time look at Herman Miller's business. The portal was designed to help suppliers in two areas: on the *financial* side, suppliers can look at prices to make sure they are in sync, as well as invoices; on the *planning* side, suppliers can look at Herman Miller's manufacturing lead times and engineering data—such as materials requirements, drawings, and revision letters.

Some people at Herman Miller were afraid suppliers would feel that the company was putting the burden on the suppliers. However, the reception was very positive, since the benefits for suppliers more than made up for any burden. In the past suppliers had to make decisions based on limited information, so they were often making assumptions in shipping materials. The portal eliminates the need to call three people at Herman Miller to get information, which is a big time-saver. The portal has shifted the old purchasing model of "the more information you had and the less your supplier had, the more power you had" to an information-sharing focus, which has been beneficial to all parties involved.

Kelly Nelson, customer service/scheduling representative for Milwaukee-based Mid-States Aluminum, one of Herman Miller's suppliers, says that before using the portal, Mid-States was sending Herman Miller four or five inaccurate deliveries per month (that is, shipping the wrong parts). But in the first 18 months using the portal, 95% of its deliveries to Herman Miller were accurate. "We're much better able to plan our machinery and our people," Nelson later said, adding that the portal had also helped Mid-States cut inaccurate billing by "at least seventy percent." In this way, Herman Miller has become a much more valuable (read "profitable") customer to Mid-States.

Herman Miller initially had more than 500 internal and external users actively employing the portal. Internally, portal users included personnel in various roles such as supply management personnel, material planners, and quality engineers. Suppliers also utilized the portal, with users found in multiple departments, such as management, customer service, scheduling, quality assurance, and finance.

The MySIGN portal is based on integration portal technology, using the TopTier Integration Portal (now called the *SAP Enterprise Portal*). The different enterprise portal categories are discussed later in this chapter on the accompanying CD-ROM. It features patented HyperRelational technology, which allows users to access, interconnect, update, edit, and delete information from multiple software applications and data sources through a simple Drag-and-Relate process. We will look at these two technologies later in the chapter, when we discuss SAP Enterprise Portal in more detail in the Product Descriptions section on the accompanying CD-ROM.

An example of the Herman Miller MySIGN portal is shown in Figure 12.2. This shows that suppliers can click on and drag a payment figure into a section called "Payment Details." This instantly provides information on the different invoices that make up that payment. This Drag-and-Relate technology allowed Herman Miller to connect its Baan ERP system easily with existing legacy applications, eliminating the need to convert all systems into the Baan applications. This integration is versatile—Herman Miller can grow the support over time, enjoying higher levels of functionality and compatibility as they add, change, and develop new enterprise applications. Existing applications do not require extensive changes and can evolve to more integration levels as needed.

Herman Miller's portal took 3 months to develop by three developers. They chose to take a phased approach to the implementation and gradually implemented new functionality. So while the portal was initially only introduced to employees, it was then extended beyond the enterprise to suppliers. Although the portal was developed and maintained by a group of employees who work on multiple projects, the time they spend on maintaining the portal is the equivalent only of one full-time employee.

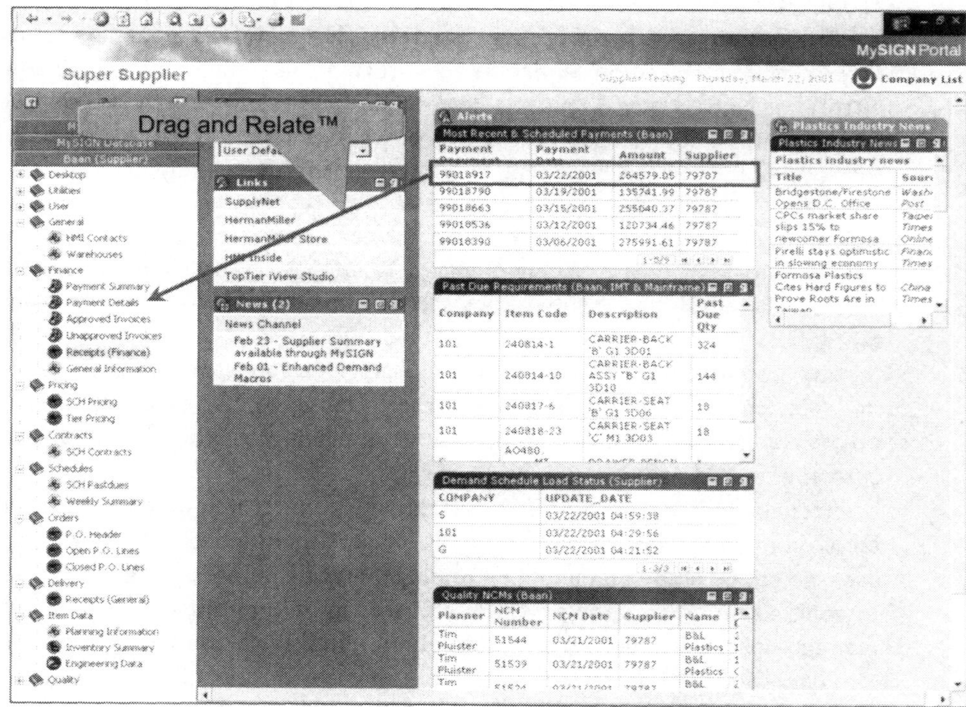

Figure 12.2 Herman Miller MySIGN e-business portal. (*Source:* © 2001 Herman Miller.)

The business result was to move its suppliers from their previous reactive, random supply state to a collaborative environment, in which Herman Miller and its suppliers work together proactively to identify and solve problems and provide predictable supply availability. This has increased the reliability of suppliers, moving from limited visibility to demand and inventory to higher visibility, and from low supplier reliability to high reliability. The result is increased supply and repeat purchases and increased sales. Some comments of the impact that it has also had on Herman Miller's suppliers follow, in their own words:

- "I hope that this technology is the future and that ALL our customers start using it!"
- "We applaud your efforts!"
- "It will be so nice not having to bother other people for information any more!"
- MySIGN "has made life much easier!"

In summarizing reasons for the success of the MySIGN portal, Herman Miller found the following six criteria to be extremely important:

- Business must be a corporate priority.
- The business side *must* drive technology.
- Focus on specific business problems or needs.
- Start small, but aim *big*.
- Don't forget about the infrastructure.
- Change is inevitable—prepare to manage it.

12.2.2 Ford Motor Company B2E Internal Corporate Portal

Ford Motor Company's portal is an example of a business-to-employee (B2E) internal corporate portal. This second case study example won DCI's Annual Portal Excellence Award for the Best Internal Corporate Portal category.

Ford had been investing aggressively in intranet technologies, enterprise applications, and Web services since the early 1980s, but many employees were still struggling to unlock the full potential of these resources for driving growth. As Ford took steps to meet the information needs of its global organization, employees increasingly lagged behind, lost in a maze of complex applications and hundreds of thousands of Web pages. To find the data they needed to do their jobs, Ford employees faced the challenge of navigating the company's many Web-based systems, network file servers, and intranet sites, as well as all of the resources scattered throughout the Internet.

Ford used the *Plumtree Corporate Portal* to implement an expansive framework for its ambitious B2E e-business strategy. The world's second largest automaker chose Plumtree to create a single, simple Web destination for 200,000 employees enterprise-wide to find and share the content and services they need to support customers and speed products to market. The Plumtree Corporate Portal is similar in appearance to a consumer Web portal, but with a directory of links to corporate documents and Plumtree Portal *Gadgets* [6].

Ford deployed the Plumtree Corporate Portal as part of an initiative to modernize the world's largest intranet, hub.ford.com. This intranet was based on 1,500 Web sites for 800 Ford facilities and 150 manufacturing plants worldwide. The Plumtree portal enabled Ford to integrate the hundreds of thousands of Web pages that comprised hub.ford.com in one enterprise-wide Web destination. Figure 12.3 illustrates part of the Employee section of the Ford B2E internal corporate portal.

Information is available through the Ford portal for CRM also: order fulfillment, customer satisfaction, sales and volume tracking, economic assessments, competitive information, and Ford community initiatives. This diverse information is integrated for easy point-and-click access from the Ford portal regardless of how these separate systems and databases are implemented "under the covers."

The Ford portal brings together more than 1 million documents on Ford networks and the Internet in a single, searchable directory of links to files, Web pages, and chapters. Now, Ford employees anywhere can draw on a common base of best practices, market news, product specifications, performance metrics, and policy and procedures for the information they need to make confident business decisions and act quickly on revenue opportunities.

After approximately 8 months of development, testing, and pilots, the Ford portal went into production in April 2000. The portal was initially launched for 11,000 users in the Process Leadership group.

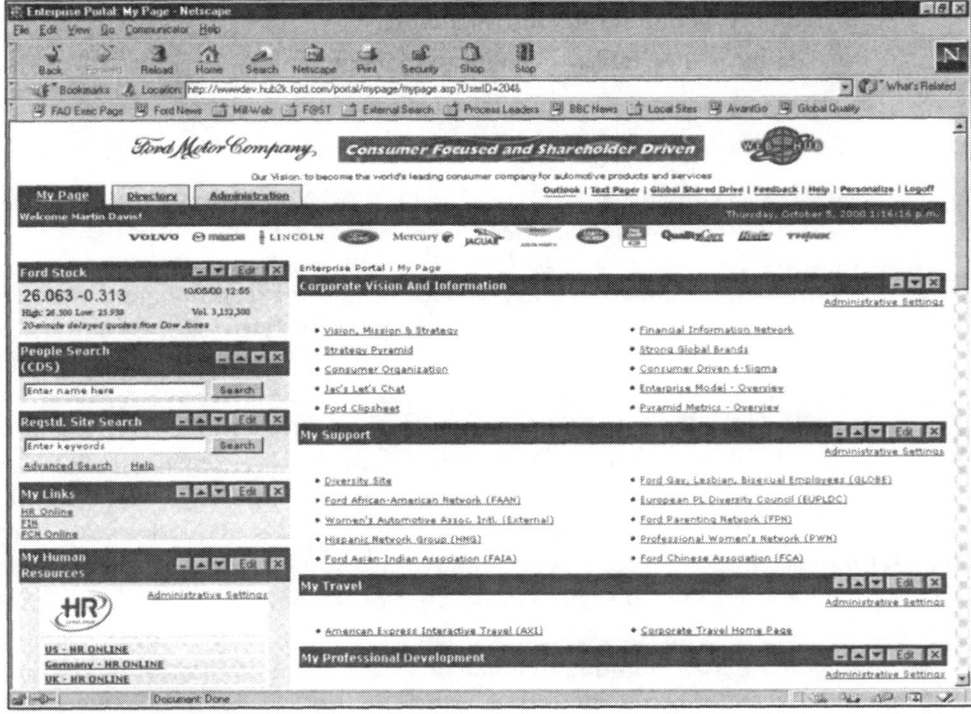

Figure 12.3 Employee section of the Ford B2E portal. (*Source:* © 2002 Ford Motor Corporation. Reprinted with permission.)

For the initial launch, the Ford Portal project team integrated its proprietary Web Single Logon security application into the Plumtree platform, developed custom gadgets (adapters), tailored the portal interface and conducted usability tests, functional tests, and load tests. Portal content is currently structured by a high-level directory hierarchy, which was refined with taxonomies for separate business units as the roll-out proceeded.

The project was called the *Millennium Portal.* The team included a project manager and Plumtree engineer, a two-person Web infrastructure technology team, a three-person enterprise information team, a three-person governance team, and a two-person communications team. An infrastructure planning and support team, a quality assurance and quality control testing team, a technical support team, and a systems integration team provided other assistance.

The Ford portal was deployed for 200,000 employees worldwide. With the phased B2E portal rollout, Ford used strategies to market the portal internally and survey employees to gather feedback. Initially, Ford focused on delivering a portal horizontally across its employee base, but planned also to integrate vertical portals for specific business units such as product development, manufacturing, marketing, and finance. Ford exports portal resources to other platforms and devices using the Plumtree technology via syndicated Gadgets. This distributes up-to-date information to portals of specialists and suppliers worldwide.

By using the Plumtree portal, Ford opened its back-end systems to broader audiences, bridging geographic and functional boundaries with a simple Web experience that reaches from the factory floor ... to the boardroom ... and to the field. Now assembly line workers and executives alike have a single desktop destination for the tools they need to work effectively and collaborate closely to drive sales. With a Web-based document directory for bringing order to corporate intranets, and an open architecture for integrating application and Internet services to popularize their use, the Plumtree platform empowers Ford to realize the full value of existing resources rather than deploying new ones.

We will discuss technical aspects of Ford's use of the Plumtree Corporate Portal shortly, when we cover this product in more detail in the Product Descriptions sections on the accompanying CD-ROM.

12.2.3 General Motors Corporation Employee Portal

General Motors Corporation was the winner of the 2002 DCI Internal Corporate Portal Excellence Award, with the submission of an employee portal called MySocrates.com. It was coincidental that both Ford and GM were each Portal Excellence Award winners in separate years: Their success had nothing to do with the fact that they are both in the automobile industry.

The GM portal is believed to be one of the world's largest employee portals, delivering approximately 4 million pages to more than 240,000 North American and 120,000 international hourly and salaried employees. The GM employee portal eventually grew to nearly 400,000 employees worldwide. A larger example yet again is the winner of the 2003 DCI Portal Excellence Award: the U.S. Army portal with 1.3 million users.

GM sells products in more than 200 countries; has manufacturing operations in 50+ countries; has 388,000 active employees worldwide; and has 450,000 retirees, who along with their families, represent more than 1.2 million lives that are covered by multiple benefits. The portal is targeted to all General Motors employees, both union and nonunion as well as retired GM employees. GM employees were provided access to the portal in late 2001.

It is important to understand the different modes of access for the portal. The portal can be accessed at work, as well as at home. It can be accessed via Web browsers as well as via TV set-top boxes. General Motors conducted an employee survey, which revealed that 30% of GM workers did not have access to a computer either at home or work. To counter this and boost employee use of mySocrates.com, GM provided a subsidized ISP offering of AOL Classic, as well as AOL TV (a product that provides Internet access through a television), to maximize the access to all employees, especially UAW hourly employees who typically do not have desktop computer access at work. GM also planned future implementation of wireless access via cellular and PDA devices to further ease and enhance employee access to MySocrates.com.

The GM portal provided technology, information resources, and content from both internal and external sources for General Motors employees. The server technology used in this solution was Sun Microsystem's iPlanet Portal Server. The iPlanet Portal Server is the basis for Workscape's Employee.com ASP hosted platform and enables the creation of a portal that responds to a person's needs: to present appropriate content, services, and applications based on the user's role and context within the enterprise.

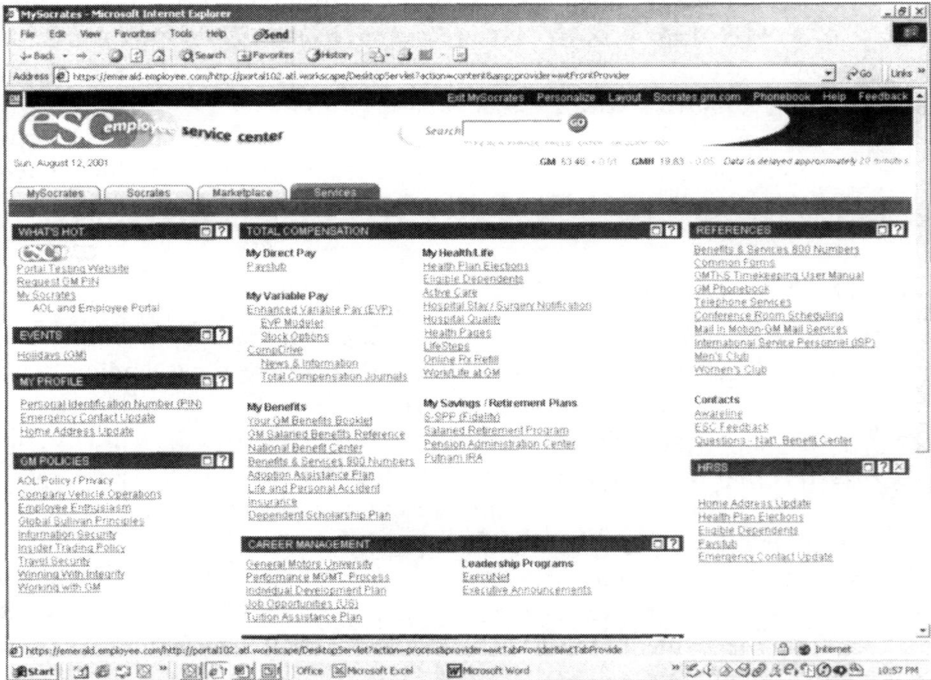

Figure 12.4 General Motors' MySocrates.com employee portal. (*Source:* © 2002 General Motors Corporation. Reprinted with permission.)

MySocrates.com is one of GM's top five global strategic imperatives. MySocrates.com offers GM employees secure self-service access to human resources applications and corporate information. The site includes electronic access to 401K retirement savings account information, electronic copies of pay stubs, online learning courses, and links with dozens of GM's internal and external vendors as illustrated in Figure 12.4. Key aspects are as follows:

- Ensures timely, consistent messages to every GM employee, thereby creating a previously unattainable parity between the salaried and UAW hourly workforces, minimizing the filtering and misinterpretation of communication and information.
- Consolidates and indexes relevant content from hundreds of sources, as well as bringing collaboration and productivity tools to the desktop or TV set-top.
- Eliminates hundreds of previous internal Web sites, consolidating them into one easily accessible portal.
- Provides immediate visibility and access for all GM employees to the e-commerce offerings of GM businesses.

The portal delivers the strategic "One Company" philosophy that drives all GM employee initiatives. General Motors is not only one of the world's largest companies, but they also have a diverse employee base that includes direct staff and union-based workers located in office buildings plus factory locations. Factor in the desire to be seen as the "employer of choice," and the business problems that need to be addressed are enormous.

Strategic business problems solved by the GM MySocrates employee portal include the following:

- GM is now viewed by current and future employees as an "employer of choice." It provides employees with leading edge corporate communication and connection via leading edge tools and technologies.
- GM now connects with all employees in a personalized way, with each perceived as an "audience of one" and ... "one size fits me."
- GM improves the strategic relationship with the UAW by creating information and communication parity between salaried and hourly workforces.
- Immediate, anywhere access available via the portal to information content and tools improves employee satisfaction, morale, and loyalty, leading to increased worker productivity.
- This solution has cost and ROI benefits that are very unique. There are the "standard" employee portal benefits, plus the cost and time savings aspects of a hosted solution.

Of significance due to the size of the GM employee population is the performance and scalability of the architecture, as well as the variety of security measures to ensure sufficient availability (24 × 7 × 365) of this employee portal. Redundancy, load balancing, failover, disaster recovery and backup, performance monitoring, data security, network security, and protection against physical intrusion as well as physical site security and hazard protection all had to pass extremely rigorous GM standards before going into live production.

The solution is "industrial strength" and was able to withstand all tests. Extensive load and stress testing were completed on the GM portal at all points, measuring user session concurrency and activity. The portal supports more than 32,000 concurrent user sessions and more than 1 million "hits" per hour. It can be scaled higher by adding network and server capacity.

The portal has been in production since November 2001. As with all portals, it is an ongoing process to continue to enhance the portal's capabilities as well as improve the return on investment. Phase 1 development included:

- Building the portal infrastructure and hosted environment, with a network, security and hosted data facility.
- Developing access authentication security schema and authorizations based on employee role differences.
- Providing initial employee and manager self-service transactions of name and address change, emergency contact change, electronic pay stub, dependent and beneficiary maintenance, and compensation planning for managers. Each of these applications integrated to GM's back-end systems of record.
- AOL content and AOL/TV integration.
- Content links to more than 1,200 content sites managed by GM, plus syndicated news, stocks and weather content, as well as a special GM "auto" channel.
- Additional productivity and collaboration tools such as search and e-mail.

Later Phase 2 development included:

- Additional "integrated" productivity and collaboration tools such as secure instant messaging (IM), chat, and fully integrated e-mail;
- Further employee and manager self-service applications such as vacation time off, personal benefits statements, employment and wage verification, benefits enrollment, new hire processing, employee onboarding, talent review profile, and a "Leaders' Dashboard" containing most HR-related transactions that managers perform in the course of their role;
- Additional GM marketplace content and SCM opportunities.

12.3 Enterprise Portal Product Categories

As mentioned at the beginning of this chapter, enterprise portals comprise three categories: collaborative portals, business intelligence portals, and integration portals. Portal products are generally categorized based on their predominant focus, but most also offer capabilities in other categories. This section provides a brief overview of the types of enterprise portal products [7].

12.3.1 Collaborative Portal Products

Collaborative portals generally focus on unstructured knowledge resources, and typically offer access to Microsoft Exchange and Lotus Notes. Examples of such resources are documents, reports, e-mail, graphics, images, audio, and video. The Ford B2E internal corporate portal and the GM employee portal discussed earlier are examples of collaborative portals. Collaborative portal products include the following:

- IBM WebSphere Portal from IBM Corporation;
- Plumtree Corporate Portal from Plumtree software (now BEA);
- Microsoft SharePoint Portal Server from Microsoft Corporation;
- Citrix NFuse Elite Portal from Citrix, Inc.

12.3.2 Business Intelligence Portal Products

Business intelligence portals generally focus on structured knowledge resources, with access to data warehouses and information system databases. These structured resources are accessed via business intelligence (BI), online analytical processing (OLAP), and other tools. Most data warehouse products are evolving into this BI portal category. Some representative BI portal products include:

- Axielle from Ascential Software (now IBM);
- CleverPath Portal from Computer Associates;
- Cognos Upfront from Cognos, Inc.;
- Enterprise Information Portal from Hummingbird.

12.3.3 Integration Portal Products

Integration portals focus on easy integration between structured and unstructured knowledge resources existing in information systems and data warehouse databases, ERP environments, CRM, SCM, and others—within an enterprise via the corporate intranet, or between enterprises via the Internet. The Herman Miller B2B e-business portal (MySIGN) discussed earlier is an example of an integration portal. A popular integration portal product is SAP Enterprise Portal from SAP.

12.4 Enterprise Portal Product Descriptions

The portal products listed in Section 12.3 are discussed in the PDF file *Chap-12-Products.pdf* in the Book Materials folder on the accompanying CD-ROM.

12.5 Summary

In this chapter and in the Product Descriptions on the accompanying CD-ROM, we covered three portal categories: collaborative portals, business intelligence portals, and integration portals. Products were discussed in each category, covering their architecture and the technologies that they use, with their relative strengths. We conclude this chapter with a summary of the desired characteristics that should be exhibited by most portal products.

12.5.1 Summary of Enterprise Portal Characteristics

The general capabilities, features, or facilities of enterprise portals [8] are to:

- Provide a single point of content delivery and management.
- Collect and organize information, making it easy to navigate.
- Provide a customizable, personalized, Web-based user interface.
- Include a content management system that automatically scans, filters, and catalogs content from internal and external sources.
- Provide a capability to easily publish information and subscribe to information tailored to end users' specific needs.
- Include a search engine, content scanner, and Web crawlers to maintain, analyze, and locate information.
- Provide an interactive portal capability, interacting with the underlying corporate applications.
- Provide a role-based portal capability for users to manage and update corporate data.
- Utilize a single sign-on for password and authentication, ideally LDAP-compliant.
- Utilize and attach to the native security of the underlying applications.
- Provide support for and integration of structured and unstructured information.
- Provide integrated access to an enterprise business intelligence system.
- Provide access to query and reporting, spreadsheet, graphs, and OLAP functions.
- Provide integration at the metadata level with ERP, CRM, SCM, e-commerce applications, analytic applications, BI tools, and ETL tools.
- Support a standards-based infrastructure and environment, with support for HTML, HTTP/SSL, XML, LDAP, Java, JavaScript, ActiveX, Web services, and so forth.
- Utilize an architecture that supports XML messaging
- Provide event-driven alerts or notification to users on user-defined events.

The discussion of each product in the Product Descriptions section for this chapter on the accompanying CD-ROM can be used with this list of desirable characteristics to identify those products that you may wish to research in greater detail. More information can be found by visiting each vendor's Web site, as detailed in the endnotes and in the section on the CD-ROM.

In the next chapter, we discuss the concepts of Web services. We will review a number of Web services products and integrated development environments. We will discuss their evolution and use in achieving enterprise integration. We will look at WSRP, a standard specification for plug-and-play adapters to be added dynamically to a portal.

Endnotes

[1] Shilakes, C. C., and J. Tylman, *Enterprise Information Portals,* Merrill Lynch EIP report, New York, November 16, 1998. This report was published in *Infoworld,* February 1998 (see http://www.infoworld.com). It is also referenced in a PDF file at http://www.dkms.com/papers/eipdef.pdf.

[2] I acknowledge the input provided by Colin White of Intelligent Business Strategies, Inc., and BI Research, Inc. His e-mail is cwhite@bi-research.com.

[3] The Digital Consulting Institute (DCI) presents the Portal, Collaboration and Content Management Conference, which is scheduled quarterly in cities throughout the United States. The latest information on enterprise portals is available from http://www.portalscommunity.com. Register to receive an e-mail newsletter.

[4] I acknowledge with thanks the permission given by DCI to use narratives submitted by Herman Miller, Ford Motor Company, and General Motors Corporation, based on their entries in DCI's Annual Portal Excellence Awards.

[5] The company TopTier Software was purchased by SAP in 2001. The product is now known as the SAP Enterprise Portal. We will discuss this product in detail later in the Product Descriptions section of this chapter on the CD-ROM.

[6] *Gadgets* is the trademarked term that Plumtree uses to describe adapters developed for a variety of data sources, including embedded collaboration tools, e-business applications, and Internet services. We will discuss the capabilities of the Plumtree portal product and the role of Gadgets later in this chapter in the Product Descriptions section on the CD-ROM.

[7] I acknowledge the input provided by, and the copyright held in material from, each relevant portal vendor for the products included in this chapter in the Product Descriptions section on the CD-ROM, whether through direct contact and discussion or indirectly from their Web sites. Further information can be obtained by visiting the Web sites, as referenced for each product on the CD-ROM.

[8] I also acknowledge the input of Pieter Mimno, detailing the characteristics and strengths of many of the portal products discussed in this chapter. His e-mail is pmimno@mimno.com.

CHAPTER 13

Web Services for Real-Time Integration

This chapter introduces the concepts and reasons for the rapid growth of Web services, which are key technologies for enterprise integration. The chapter covers the concepts in some technical detail, with a discussion of typical examples and applications that use Web services. We cover the evolution of Web services. The chapter includes details of tools and products from a number of vendors that support this growing field. These are covered in the Product Descriptions section on the CD-ROM.

13.1 Introduction to Web Services

As we discussed briefly in Chapters 1 and 11, each computer program and each software component is still largely hand-coded from scratch. Yet much of the hand-coded logic in most programs is implied by the database structure that the program is designed to use. Code generators today can use standard code patterns to automatically generate 80% to 90% of program code that was previously manually coded. Using these code generators, we are starting to see the automatic generation of programs in a variety of languages. But object-oriented programming has not yet delivered on its promise of interchangeable and reusable code modules. It is true that object-oriented programmers can develop reusable code modules—but it takes considerable time and skill to achieve this result. We discussed in Chapter 1 that this has limited our ability to reuse much code.

Because of different hardware and operating system platforms, we still have considerable problems in integrating code modules within and between enterprises. These different platforms and programming languages use various application program interfaces (APIs). Programs or code modules written in one language with a particular API cannot be easily integrated with other programs or code modules on different platforms. To address this problem, remote procedure call (RPC) technologies that use CORBA (Common Object Request Broker Architecture), COM (Common Object Model), Distributed COM (DCOM), and other Remote Procedure Call (RPC) approaches have enabled tightly coupled integration of code across dissimilar platforms in real time.

But the complexity of RPC approaches for different APIs has meant that code module integration and reuse is still time consuming and difficult. Web services and associated XML technologies have recently been developed to address real-time program and code module integration. We will discuss Web services and related XML technologies in this chapter.

Furthermore, most enterprises have a common problem: Different business processes and procedures are used to do the same thing, where a common standard procedure could be used instead. For example, in Chapters 1 and 11 we discussed problems experienced in updating a changed customer address in each of the different versions of customer data in an enterprise. The customer address may need to be changed in the Customer table (for the Sales and Order Entry Departments), the Client table (for the Credit Control Department), and the Debtor table (for the Accounts Receivable section of the Finance Department). These tables must be changed using special address-change maintenance programs written for each separate department. The same details must be updated in every table where the customer's address exists redundantly. This is redundant work. It also requires redundant staffing to enter these redundant data changes. These programs may each use change procedures that do not all operate the same way. This also means redundant training, if the programs used for address updating all have different data entry operating procedures.

These address data should be able to be updated using a common customer-address-update process, used as a standard process throughout the enterprise. This leads to the design of common, reusable business processes using Web services, and common Web service processes and workflows.

Let us now consider the concepts, components, and potential of Web services in the IT industry.

13.1.1 Concepts and Components of Web Services

Web services emerged to address the problems of software integration just mentioned. Early work carried out independently by various companies from 1999 to 2000 culminated in the submission by IBM, Microsoft, and Ariba of initial Web services specifications for consideration by the World Wide Web Consortium (W3C) in September 2000. Web services are based on XML. Many companies are currently working on specifications for interoperable Web services [1]. The IBM AlphaWorks Web site [2] describes Web services as follows [3]:

> Web services are self-describing, self-contained, modular applications that can be mixed and matched with other Web services to create innovative products, processes, and value chains. Web services are Internet applications that fulfill a specific task or a set of tasks that work with many other Web services in an interoperable manner to carry out their part of a complex work flow or a business transaction. In essence, they enable just-in-time application integration and these Web applications can be dynamically changed by the creation of new Web services. Various applications that are available on the Internet can be accessed and invoked at run time without prior knowledge and programming requirements to enable business processes and decision-making at Web speeds.

This programmatic integration of code modules and applications using language-specific and operating-system-specific APIs has made program integration very difficult in the past. Code modules integrated using RPC technologies such as COM, DCOM, or CORBA interfaces have been used as we discussed earlier, but they are tightly coupled. Because of this tight coupling, a change that is made in one component can affect other components; their level of integration is fragile. While they are effective, these technologies have been very complex and time consuming to use, making them expensive to implement and maintain.

In contrast, application program interfaces can also be defined using XML. An API can be specified in an XML language called SOAP (Simple Object Access Protocol), which offers the advantage that it can be used with any programming language and operating system that understands XML. Because SOAP is a simple language, integrated code modules can be loosely coupled. Changes in one component do not affect other components as we saw with tightly coupled RPC approaches; instead, program integration is more flexible. Because of this, SOAP is less expensive to use and maintain.

The definition of APIs using SOAP is one required component of Web services. The services that can be carried out by the code module or program must also be described. This is specified using another language based on XML, called Web Services Description Language (WSDL). WSDL identifies the SOAP specification that is to be used for the code module API. It identifies the input and output SOAP message formats that are also required for input to and output from the module or program. Each WSDL specification is then used to describe the particular Web services to be accessed via the Internet, or from a corporate intranet, by publishing it to a relevant Internet or intranet Web server.

But SOAP and WSDL alone are not sufficient. Unless Web services are published in an electronic Yellow Pages directory that is accessible within an enterprise (via its intranet) or available worldwide (via the Internet), no one would know of the existence of the available Web services. Another XML language used to achieve this is Universal Description, Discovery and Integration (UDDI). This is used for publication in a UDDI directory, which enables the Web services to be found by others. SOAP, WSDL, and UDDI are related to each other as shown in Figure 13.1.

13.2 Intranet and Internet Web Services for Integration

To understand their power, ease of use, and flexibility, we will look at two examples that illustrate how Web services can be used internally within an enterprise, and externally between enterprises. The first example uses Web services within an enterprise, via the intranet. The second example then considers Web services between enterprises, across the Internet.

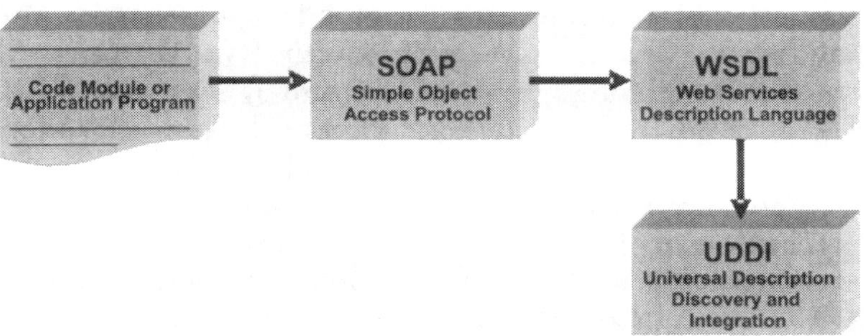

Figure 13.1 Web services are implemented using SOAP, WSDL, and UDDI.

13.2.1 Intranet Web Services Integration Example

To examine intranet Web services, we will use the earlier problem that we discussed in Chapter 11 that arose from changes in data that required us to make changes to each redundant data version. We saw that this resulted in redundant work and redundant staffing to do that work. It also often resulted in redundant training for the staff. These were all manual procedures that were used to make the required data changes. They were slow, error prone, and expensive—and until all required changes were made, other problems were encountered because the different versions of the data were not synchronized.

We saw in Chapter 11 with Figures 11.18 and 11.19 that EAI can assist here. Web services also offer a great deal of benefit. Each data entry maintenance program used to change a redundant table can be defined so that the data changes are expressed as Web services, using SOAP. In this instance, integration with Web services is achieved in real time. For example, a Web service using SOAP—called, for example, *CreateNewCustomer*—invokes the *Create Customer* logic and business rules by the Customer data entry program used in the Sales and Order Entry Departments. *ReadCustomer, UpdateCustomer,* and *DeleteCustomer* Web services can also be defined, to invoke the corresponding *Read, Change,* or *Delete* logic and business rules in the Customer data entry program. Similarly, *CreateNewClient, ReadClient, UpdateClient,* and *DeleteClient* Web services can be defined with SOAP to invoke the corresponding logic and rules in the Client data entry program for the Credit Control Department. Also, SOAP Web services can be defined to invoke the Debtor data entry program logic and rules in the Accounts Receivable section of the Finance Department.

In Chapter 11, in Figure 11.18, we discussed the process of making address changes: When a customer address change was made manually by the Order Entry Department, an address change notification form was also printed. This form was sent to the Credit Control and Accounts Receivable sections; they could make the relevant manual data changes to the Client and Debtor tables that they also maintain (see Figure 11.18). In the past, the only way to avoid this manual updating was to completely replace the separate redundant tables with an integrated table that could be used by all. In addition, all of the previous application programs that used the redundant tables also have had to be replaced by new, integrated programs that used the integrated table. This approach, requiring table replacement and application program redevelopment, is expensive and complex.

Instead, these data changes can be expressed as Web services for each redundant table. Each Web service is specified using WSDL. This identifies the defined SOAP specifications and relevant SOAP input and output messages. When the WSDL specifications are published to the intranet Web server, the address change notification form that was previously printed is replaced by SOAP and WSDL defined Web services. Each WSDL specification identifies the relevant SOAP messages needed to invoke data change logic and business rules in the Customer, Client, or Debtor tables as illustrated in Figure 13.2.

The slow, error-prone manual procedures for data entry are now replaced by real-time, dynamic Web service transactions. These are sent via the intranet as SOAP messages that invoke the relevant Web service in each table needed to keep the redundant data up to date. The result is the immediate synchronization of all

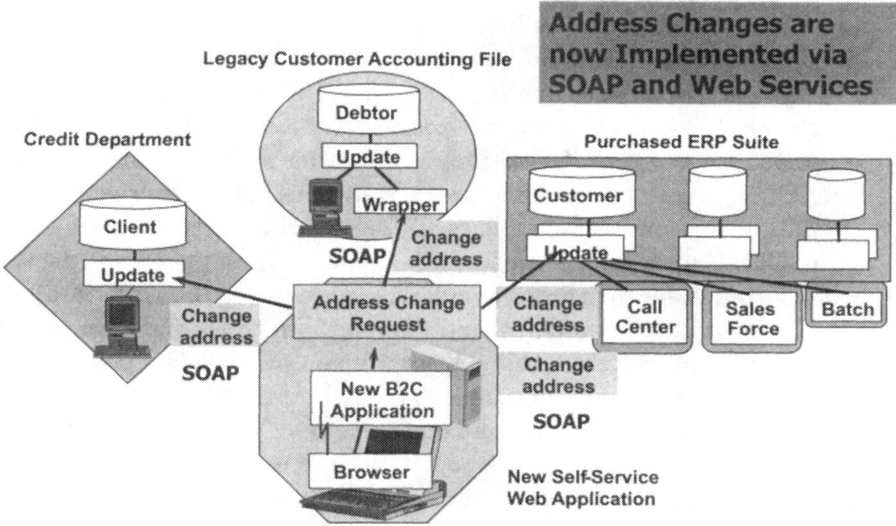

Figure 13.2 Address change notification using SOAP and Web services avoids the need for manual reentry. (*Source:* Gartner Group.)

related data changes to all relevant tables. Using Web services, redundant tables can remain and can continue to be updated by their separate data entry programs. This updating is now done quickly and automatically using SOAP messages and Web services in real time, rather than having the costly redevelopment and replacement of the tables and programs with integrated tables and programs. *The earlier redundant data problem has now been replaced by a replicated data environment that is kept up to date and synchronized in real time.*

13.2.2 Internet Web Services Integration Example

The second Web services example shows their use outside the enterprise. In this case we will look at the ordering of products or services from an online store via the Internet. The store accepts orders online, for payment by credit card. The credit card must first be approved by the relevant bank. If the card is valid and credit is available, payment is credited to the store's bank account. The store then orders the requested products or services from its supplier, and arranges with a logistic (shipping) company for the goods to be picked up from the supplier and delivered directly to the customer. This is called *drop-shipping.*

In the past, this scenario was carried out by the store using mail, phone, or fax to communicate with the bank, the supplier, and the shipping company. This took time and often introduced errors and delays. To improve customer service, the store replaced this mail, phone, and fax communication with online coordination with the bank, the supplier, and the shipping company. But this presented severe problems in the past using RPC technologies. For example, the bank may use CORBA for online credit card authorization and payment, the logistic company may use COM, and the supplier may use yet another RPC approach. These different RPC interfaces added dramatically to complexity and to the time required by the store to implement this online coordination.

Now let us consider this scenario using Web services, as shown in Figure 13.3. The bank defines its *CreditCardApproval* and *CreditCardPayment* Web services as a combined *CreditCardCheck* Web service using SOAP. It publishes these interfaces, plus SOAP input and output message formats, to its Internet Web server using WSDL. It registers these credit card Web services (defined by SOAP and WSDL) using UDDI to the UDDI registry [4]. Similarly the supplier and the shipping company also register their respective Web services using SOAP, WSDL, and UDDI.

To locate banks, suppliers, and shipping companies that offer relevant Web services, the store visits the UDDI registry. It issues UDDI *Find* requests to locate Web services that satisfy its requirements. Using the SOAP, WSDL, and UDDI specifications published by relevant companies, the store prepares the SOAP interface, and input and output messages. It sends these SOAP messages to the URL Internet address of the relevant Web servers, as published in the UDDI registry via UDDI and WSDL by the selected bank, supplier, and shipping company. These standards act together as an integrating technology.

This Web services approach has many benefits. A standard process is used to integrate the Web services of various organizations, regardless of where they are located worldwide. This provides clear advantages of greater simplicity and ease of use, which in turn lead to benefits of faster implementation and lower cost.

The store can select any bank, supplier, and shipping company that meets its needs for Web services. For example, if a customer is located overseas, a supplier and shipping company near the customer can easily be used. This offers the benefit of lower cost—so producing greater profit—or the lower cost can be passed on to the customer as lower prices.

Each of the Web services companies gains benefits also. Web services can be easily published for worldwide access. Depending on the value of a Web service to users worldwide, each Web service can be charged on a per-use basis. Each "per-use"

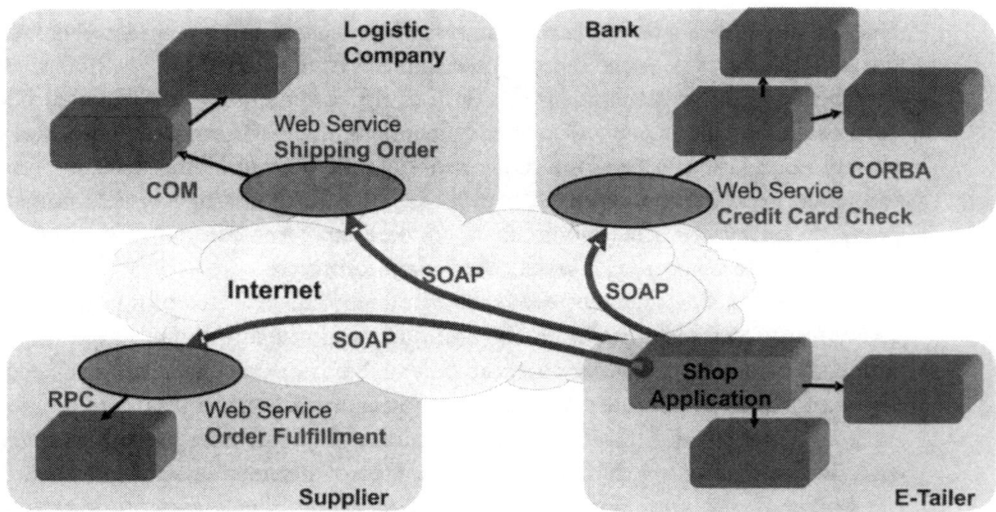

Figure 13.3 Invocation of remote Web services for credit card approval, order fulfillment and shipping using SOAP. (*Source:* © 2001 Software AG. Reprinted with permission.)

price may be a micro-payment of cents or micro-cents, for example. But such Web services—which previously have been inaccessible, often locked away in monolithic legacy application programs—can also generate additional revenue. We will discuss this example further later in the chapter, when we consider transaction recovery and fee paying in Section 13.4, *Web Services Evolution*.

The next section of this chapter discusses the basic concepts of SOAP, WSDL, and UDDI in more detail, and their progress toward standard Web services languages. Other XML markup languages that are also evolving to support Web services are then introduced.

13.3 XML Standards for Web Services

The initial Web services XML markup languages are now in place: SOAP, UDDI, and WSDL. These were defined in the first phase of Web services, in the period from 1999 to 2001. They are listed in Table 13.1 and have now effectively become de facto standards. Each is described in more detail in the following paragraphs.

The following discussion provides an overview of how SOAP, WSDL, and UDDI are both specified and used. This material can be skipped by readers who are not interested in these technical details. Most of the development tools discussed later in this chapter in the Product Descriptions section on the accompanying CD-ROM will automatically generate many of these specifications. However, if you do wish briefly to review this section, you will gain a better appreciation of how these XML protocols are used to define Web services. This understanding may help you to identify new opportunities within your organization where Web services can be utilized to great benefit.

For readability, only a broad description of SOAP, WSDL, and UDDI are provided here. Links are provided to relevant white papers with coding descriptions and downloadable code samples. These will enable you to access greater detail if desired.

We will start by discussing SOAP for messaging between applications. We will next introduce WSDL to define application interfaces in more detail, along with relevant input and output messages. We will then see how services are published to a UDDI registry, for later search and retrieval of relevant services for particular business purposes.

Table 13.1 XML Markup Languages in the First Phase of Web Services

Standard	*Description*
SOAP	*Simple Object Access Protocol:* SOAP is the XML protocol used to specify methods or function calls as Web services in XML, and the message formats for the transfer of SOAP input and output messages between Web services.
WSDL	*Web Services Description Language:* WSDL is the XML protocol that is used to describe Web services. It indicates required SOAP message formats and invocation protocols to use specific Web services.
UDDI	*Universal Description, Discovery and Integration:* UDDI is the XML protocol used to specify Web services to public registries (via the Internet) or private registries (via intranets). It implements the concepts of Internet Directory White Pages (to identify and describe enterprises), Yellow Pages (to describe available Web services), and Green Pages (to define the technical specifications for using Web services).

13.3.1 SOAP Definition

SOAP is an XML specification that defines the format of messages between application programs. It is both language and platform independent [5]. SOAP has since been submitted to W3C for consideration as a recommended standard. It has been widely adopted throughout the IT industry, with many languages and development environments now also providing automatic conversion of existing function calls to SOAP.

SOAP was defined for several purposes. These include XML messages and RPC—as well as one-way and asynchronous messaging—for the invocation of code in any language and development environment on other machines. We will discuss the use of SOAP for XML messaging, which is the exchange of data for RPC between application programs. Figure 13.4 illustrates the structure of a SOAP message envelope [6], which describes SOAP messages and their structure in more detail.

The first element in a SOAP message is the envelope. This identifies the XML document as being a SOAP message and includes the SOAP header and SOAP body of the message. It defines the version information of the message, and the rules to be followed by the relevant applications that process that SOAP message. Name spaces are defined that point to details of the relevant version and rule definitions. Within and immediately following the envelope, a SOAP message can contain a SOAP header element. This is optional; it can be used to extend the message syntax independent of any applications that process the message. This extension could include authorization or transaction information, for example.

The SOAP body element contains application-specific data. This may include RPCs to methods to be executed on receipt of the message. The syntax used to encode data in the body can be defined in encoding rules. The body element can hold any XML data that an application needs to receive or send as XML messages. In general, SOAP messages are not written directly by programmers. They are translated from program function calls in various languages to SOAP messages automatically by Web services development tools or IDEs, which are discussed later in this chapter on the accompanying CD-ROM.

SOAP messages do not dictate either a transport or convention. SOAP supports many transport protocols, via HTTP, MSMQ, MQ Series, SMTP, and TCP/IP. It has been implemented on different hardware and software platforms; in fact, more than 30 SOAP implementations are currently available. Most SOAP usage is for

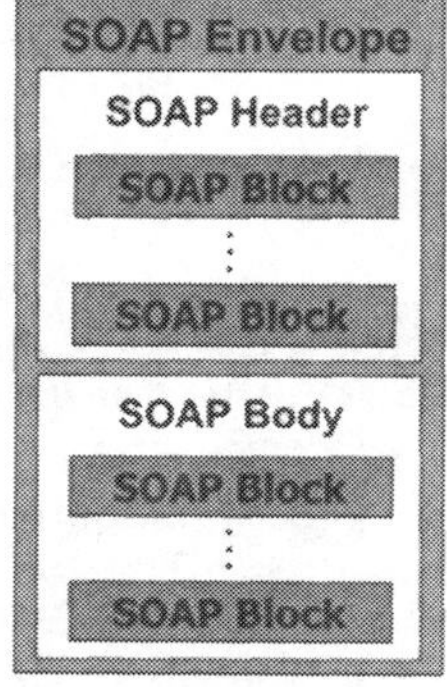

Figure 13.4 SOAP message envelope structure. (*From:* [6]. © 2001 W3C.org. Reprinted with permission.)

delivery of messages for RPCs over HTTP via the Internet or intranet. This is indeed our focus for Web services: using SOAP messages for RPC over HTTP. However, SOAP also supports document/literal messaging [7], as used for EAI (see Chapter 11). This enables inclusion of the address change notification form in a SOAP message as we discussed for Figure 11.19 in Chapter 11.

13.3.2 WSDL Definition

WSDL was defined to address the following questions in relation to Web services:

- What business services are offered online by an organization?
- How can these business services be invoked online?
- What information does a business service require from a Service Requester, when the service is invoked?
- How is this information to be provided, and in what format?
- How will the service send information back to the Service Requester, and in what format?

Authoring in WSDL involves four steps to describe a service. Steps 1 through 3 first define the specifications of the Web service interface and required input and output messages. These result in the preparation of a WSDL interface file for the included Web services. Step 4 describes the definition of the WSDL implementation file. These are illustrated in Figure 13.5.

When published to a UDDI registry by the owner of the Web services (the *Service Provider*), the WSDL implementation file provides information needed by a user of the Web service (the *Service Requester*) to locate the WSDL interface file on the Web server of the service provider.

By following the steps as described and illustrated in the WSDL specifications [8], you will see that the WSDL interface file and the WSDL implementation file

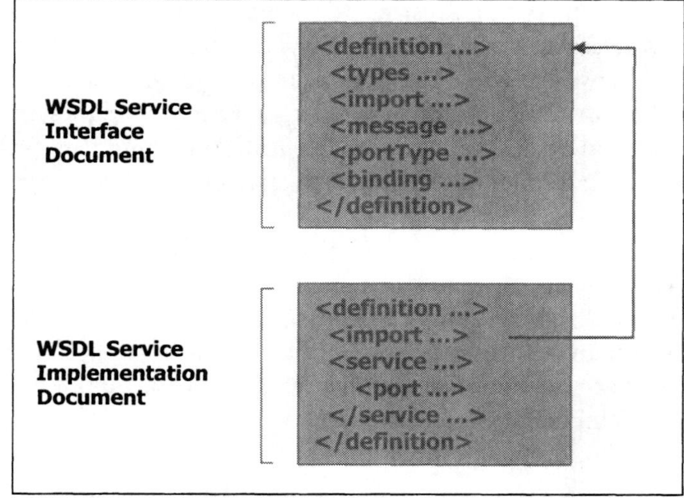

Figure 13.5 Structure of WSDL interface and implementation files. (*From:* [8]. © 2001 IBM Corporation. Reprinted with permission.)

provide the required information needed to describe the SOAP interface and the SOAP input and output messages for each Web service.

After reading this section, you will recognize that once each Web service is named, with each named input and output message, the coding of the WSDL interface file and WSDL implementation file could potentially be automatically generated. This is exactly what is discussed later in this chapter, when we cover the Web service development tools and products offered by different software vendors in the Product Descriptions section on the accompanying CD-ROM.

13.3.3 UDDI Definition

UDDI specifies how to describe, publish, and discover information about Web services in a UDDI registry [9]. The structure and use of UDDI is analogous to a printed *Yellow Pages Directory*. Three components are used:

- *Yellow Pages,* with industrial categorizations based on service taxonomies for an industry. For example, a bank may register its credit card processing Web services in the category of *Credit Card Services* and also *Banking Services.*
- *White Pages,* which include the name, contact details, and other identifiers of the enterprise. For example, these detail the name, address, phone numbers, fax numbers, and Web site URLs of the bank. They describe the credit card processing Web services that are offered, and reference the credit card WSDL specification files.
- *Green Pages* detail the technical information about services exposed by the enterprise. These also include URLs to the WSDL specifications. In turn, these reference the Web service SOAP specifications on the bank's Web server.

The UDDI Yellow Pages are analogous to categories in the printed directory; the White Pages are analogous to detailed entries in the directory, referenced from the categories. Green Pages are also used, similar to details in a printed directory, and link to the WSDL files and from there to the SOAP specifications.

Details such as those just mentioned are published to a UDDI registry, describing the Web services that are offered by the enterprise. Such an organization is called a Service Provider, while the organization managing the UDDI registry is called a Service Broker. Other organizations (called Service Requesters) use the UDDI registry to locate the details of services (Yellow and White Pages) that address a specific business use, and then locate the technical details (Green Pages) for specific services that are required.

The definition of Web services in a UDDI registry [10] is illustrated in Figure 13.6. The < BusinessEntity> element provides White Pages information about a Service Provider organization or business. It contains one or more elements that define each separate <BusinessService> that defines the Yellow Pages details. A <BusinessService> contains specifications of one or more <BindingTemplate>. Each <BindingTemplate> references a <tModel> element, defining the Green Pages technical model (tModel) specifications for a service.

Figure 13.7 shows how a WSDL implementation file uses the <service> element to point to a UDDI <BusinessService> element and WSDL <port> elements to point

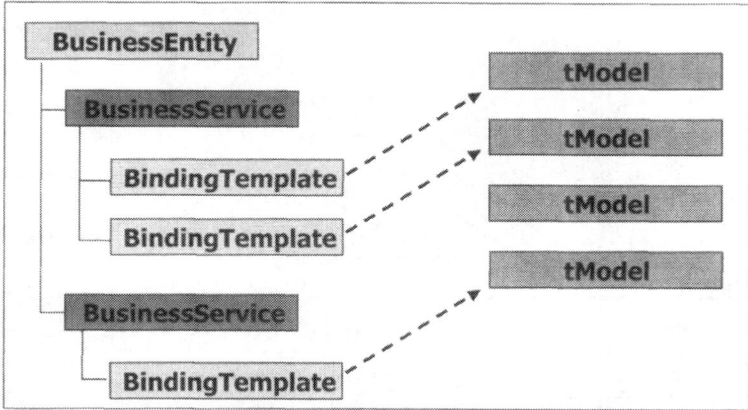

Figure 13.6 Structure of a UDDI definition. (*From:* [10]. © 2001 IBM Corporation. Reprinted with permission.)

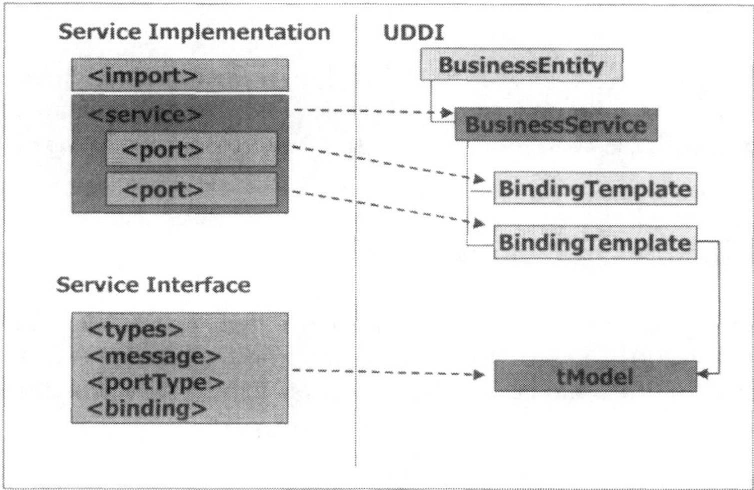

Figure 13.7 Relationship between WSDL files and a UDDI definition. (*From:* [10]. © 2001 IBM Corporation. Reprinted with permission.)

to UDDI <BindingTemplate> elements. The WSDL interface file points to UDDI <tModel> (Green Pages) technical specifications.

Figure 13.8 illustrates how UDDI, WSDL, and SOAP are used, with the following description keyed to the figure. A Service Provider uses UDDI and WSDL to publish specifications for its Web services—as Yellow Pages (1)—to a Service Broker. This may be a private registry, or a public UDDI registry such as the one at http://www.uddi.org (2). A Service Requester searches the UDDI registry later, to discover available Web services for a specific business purpose (3). The Service Broker returns relevant UDDI and WSDL specifications for that business purpose, as earlier published by each Service Provider (4).

The Service Requester in Figure 13.8 selects the most relevant Web services to address its needs (3). It uses the returned UDDI and WSDL specifications from the

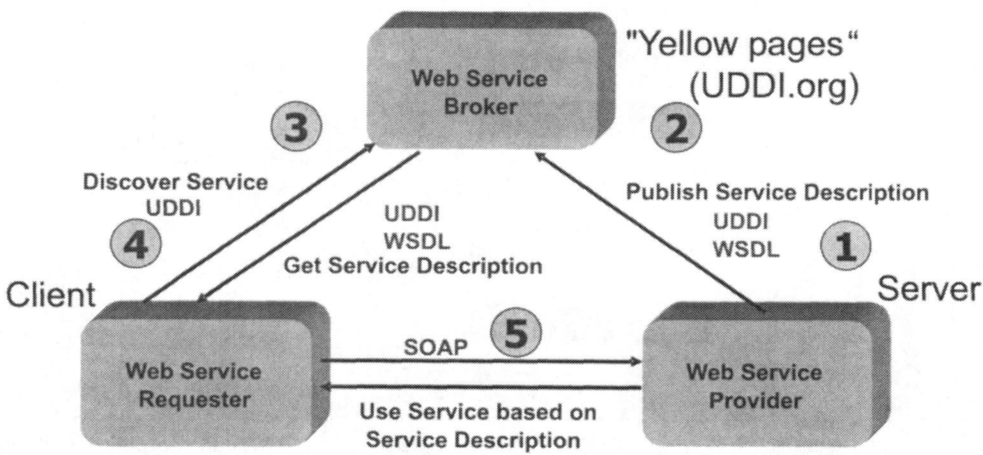

Figure 13.8 Publishing and discovering Web service using UDDI, WSDL, and SOAP. (*Source:* © 2001 Software AG. Reprinted with permission.)

Service Broker UDDI registry to prepare its Client Service Requests. These are then sent as SOAP input messages (5) to the SOAP server nominated by the Service Provider, with the Web service processing results returned as SOAP output messages.

13.4 Web Services Evolution

Web services evolution has been defined in three phases. We refer to the period from 1999 to 2001 as *Phase 1* and the period from 2002 to 2004 as *Phase 2*. The current period of 2005 and beyond is *Phase 3* of Web services evolution.

13.4.1 Phase 1 Evolution: 1999–2001

With development tools for SOAP, WSDL, and UDDI now available from Microsoft, IBM, Sun, Software AG, and many others, the development of Web services tools is now complete. Phase 1 has been the focus of the chapter to this point.

13.4.2 Phase 2 Evolution: 2002–2004

In 2002 business Web services began to appear in large numbers, with business-to-consumer (B2C) access to mass consumer-oriented Web services. An example of such B2C Web services is *My Services* from Microsoft (code named Hailstorm). These are part of Microsoft .NET, discussed on the accompanying CD-ROM.

Private UDDI registries support private exchanges. Public registries also emerged to support public exchanges, with government use of Web services accelerating sharply. Some of these public registries offered free access to Web services, but most became available on a fee-paying basis. We will discuss some implications of fee-based Web services in the following section.

A number of XML-based languages have been defined for Phase 2, as summarized in Table 13.2. Some of these are discussed further now.

For Web services to be able to deliver fast, seamless integration of business partners on an enterprise scale during Phase 2, a number of issues were addressed. These included quality of service (QoS), network reliability, transaction recovery, real-time messaging, security, and billing mechanisms. Some of these issues are discussed in the following paragraphs.

Web services networks between service providers and service requesters must handle end-point authentication between partners, and must provide security, data encryption, and nonrepudiation of transactions. Web services network vendors will also need to offer both synchronous and asynchronous messaging; the latter enables a *Client Service Requester* to carry out other tasks while waiting for a response from a *Service Provider*. Network-quality monitoring, error management, and data-compression schemes help improve network scalability and reliability.

Web service network vendors that have emerged to address these issues include Grand Central, Flamenco Networks, and Kenamea. Of these, Grand Central Communications [11] uses a centralized hub topology for reliable, secure Web services message delivery, whereas Flamenco [12] uses a server proxy for a multipoint network approach. Both focus on transactional stability, with network monitoring on a server-to-server basis. On the other hand, Kenamea [13] specializes in last-mile network delivery to a broad range of device types, such as for supply chains.

Transaction recovery is very important, particularly with Web services transactions that involve concurrent database changes carried out by Web services delivered by more than one service provider. In the Internet Web services integration example discussed earlier for Figure 13.3, three service providers were involved: the bank, the supplier, and the shipping (logistic) company. In this example, performance issues associated with Internet transmission latency and message traffic delays demand that asynchronous messaging be used to communicate with these three service providers. But errors can often occur:

1. The bank may decline to accept credit card payment for purchase because the customer's credit limit has been exceeded or the card number is incorrect.
2. The supplier may find that some or all of the requested products are out of stock and so must be back-ordered, with credit card payment adjusted to pay only for products that can be delivered.

In these situations, if error 1 occurs, the complete order placed with the supplier—as well as the pickup to be made by the logistics company—must both be canceled. While error 2 is less serious, because of the backorder the credit card payment amount with the bank must be adjusted to the correct value for the actual products to be shipped.

The three Web service transactions are in fact interdependent; each Web service can only commit its database processing when it is certain that all related Web services have completed successfully. But if complete failure occurs—such as for error 1—all database changes by each Web service must be completely rolled back. We see that Web service transaction recovery in a multiple-enterprise example such as

Table 13.2 XML Markup Languages Used in Phase 2 of Web Services

Specification	*Description*
SOAP-DSIG	*SOAP Digital Signatures:* This is an XML protocol developed by IBM for digitally signing and securing SOAP messages. (*Resource:* W3C at http://www.w3c.org/TR/SOAP-dsig)
WSIL	*Web Services Inspection Language:* WSIL complements UDDI by facilitating the discovery of available Web services on Web sites that may not yet be listed in a UDDI registry. This is important for locating internal Web services within an enterprise. (*Resource:* http://www-106.ibm.com/developerworks/webservices/library/ws-wsilover)
WSFL	*Web Services Flow Language:* WSFL is an XML protocol developed by IBM for BPM. WSFL defines workflow logic for the integration of Web services and immediate execution of business process logic. WSFL and XLANG (from BizTalk; see later entry) have been incorporated into BPEL (see later entry). (*Resource:* http://www-3.ibm.com/software/solutions/webservices/documentation.html)
WSCM	*Web Services Component Model:* WSCM is being defined by OASIS for the composition and presentation of Web services. (*Resource:* OASIS at http://www.xml.org)
ebXML	*Electronic Business XML:* This specifies the XML protocol for EDI. It defines ebXML registry entries (similar in concept to UDDI), with ebXML message envelope formats, business process definitions, and other process invocation details. Products supporting ebXML need to interoperate with Web services and BizTalk (see next entry). We discussed ebXML in Chapter 11. (*Resources:* OASIS at http://www.xml.org and also http://www.ebxml.org)
BizTalk	*BizTalk Server:* Microsoft BizTalk supports XML messaging and B2B integration. It uses the BizTalk message envelope format, *Business Orchestration,* and XML *Data Mapping* definitions. We discussed BizTalk in Chapter 11 on the CD-ROM. BizTalk initially generated XLANG for business process logic execution. With BizTalk Server 2004, XLANG and WSFL (see earlier entry) were both incorporated into BPEL, now automatically generated (see next entry). (*Resources:* http://www.microsoft.com/biztalk and also http://www.biztalk.org)
BPEL4WS (called BPEL)	*Business Process Execution Language for Web services:* BPEL is becoming a de facto standard language for definition of workflow logic in BPM. It brings together automatic generation of process logic from workflow diagrams in BizTalk from Microsoft and WebSphere from IBM, for execution (see Chapter 14). (*Resource:* http://www.xml.org)
HTTPR	HTTPR is a proposal for reliable transport over HTTP. (*Resource:* http://www.w3c.org)
SAML	*Security Assertion Markup Language:* This is a defined OASIS standard for security definition and management. It is used with WS-Security, XML-Signature, XML-Encryption (see later entries). (*Resource:* OASIS at http://www.xml.org)
WS-Security	*WS-Security* is an OASIS standard. It describes enhancements to SOAP messaging to provide message integrity and message confidentiality (through XML-Signature) and message authentication (through XML-Encryption). It provides a general-purpose mechanism for associating security tokens with messages. (*Resource:* OASIS at http://www.xml.org)
XML-Signature	*XML-Signature* specifies digital signatures for message integrity and authentication. WS-Security provides processing rules for XML Signature in SOAP messages. Signature can be applied over part or all of an XML document. (*Resource:* W3C at http://www.w3c.org)
XML-Encryption	*XML-Encryption* specifies the encryption of digital content to ensure the confidentiality of XML information transfers. It allows parts of an XML document to be encrypted while leaving other parts open. (*Resource:* W3C at http://www.w3c.org)
WS-Federation	*WS-Federation* defines mechanisms to allow different security domains to federate by brokering trust of identities, attributes, or authentication between participating Web services. It was proposed by Microsoft, IBM, BEA, and others. (*Resource:* Microsoft at http://msdn.microsoft.com/webservices/understanding/advancedwebservices/default.asp)

this is certainly nontrivial. Full transaction recovery support must be provided by Web services products that offer the functionality used in this example. We will discuss this further in Chapter 14.

Web services authentication and security vendors have developed products to manage authorization credentials for disparate Web services environments; vendors include Netegrity, Oblix, and OpenNetwork. One security-focused product is Microsoft Passport [14].

Once an end user has been authenticated to Microsoft Passport, a user ID is allocated. This single ID identifies that person throughout the Internet; with this user ID other service providers can get information about the user, based only on the specific details that the user has authorized others to see and use. The overriding principle of Microsoft Passport is that the user is always in control. The user has sole authority to make as much, or as little, information as desired available to others. More than 165 million users of Hotmail and MSDN already use Microsoft Passport.

Microsoft announced the addition of Kerberos security support to Passport in 2001. This is a network authentication protocol that adds strong, secret-key cryptography. With Kerberos support, Passport offers interoperability with other Kerberos-compliant protocols, all delivering strong authorization security. With interoperability as an objective, OASIS has defined the Security Assertion Markup Language (SAML). A link to the SAML specifications is provided in Table 13.2, shown earlier.

As we have discussed, Phase 2 of Web services ran from 2002 to 2004. This period focused on the definition of additional Web service standards that were needed: SOAP-DSIG, WSIL, WSFL, and WSCM. Table 13.2 describes these and also includes other related standards and products: ebXML, BizTalk, HTTPR, SAML, WS-Security, XML-Signature XML-Encryption, and WS-Federation. The links in Table 13.2 offer access to more resources. Phase 2 standards provided a dynamic infrastructure for businesses to interoperate using Web services, leading to what IBM refers to as *dynamic e-business.*

13.4.3 Phase 3 Evolution: 2005 and Beyond

We are now in Phase 3. Organizations will change not only their business processes, but also their business models as they move to real-time collaboration and integration of processes both within and between enterprises. While Phase 1 and 2 both addressed the surfacing of Web services previously locked away in current and legacy systems, Phase 3 will see the emergence of new software products and systems that are designed and developed from the outset to be delivered as Web services. These will be used by organizations to find business partners dynamically or to use remote resources, to enable organizations to adapt rapidly to change. However, several challenges present themselves during this period.

13.5 Challenges in Phase 3 Evolution

As this chapter indicates, the adoption of Web services from a technical perspective is not complex. We will see shortly that the SOAP, WSDL, and UDDI specifications are all automatically generated. However, Web services alone cannot solve the data integration problem, because they do not address the information semantics issue.

13.5.1 Importance of Message Semantics: Metadata

Web services provide standards for messaging, interfaces, and discovery as we have discussed. But these standards are silent about definition of message payload metadata—the message content. We saw in Chapter 11 that XML—and thus Web services—is totally dependent on the definition of *metadata*. In that chapter we learned that industry markup vocabularies, which we discussed in Chapter 11, have been defined for most industries. These establish metadata for messages that are exchanged between trading partners. Industry markup vocabularies that we discussed include RosettaNet (for IT and EC industries); IFX, OFX, and FpML (for banking); HL7 (for health care); XBRL (for finance and audit); and ebXML (for EDI) [15].

In Part II we saw that metadata is defined using data modeling methods in Chapter 6 and business normalization methods in Chapter 9. These methods can be used to define the content—and associated metadata—to be exchanged in messages between trading partners. Data models that are produced using these methods define the metadata that are inherent in electronic documents that are exchanged as messages. In Chapter 15 we will see that modeling tools that are used during data modeling to capture these metadata can also generate the relevant XML document type definitions (DTDs) or XML schema definitions (XSDs) that define the message content.

As we have seen in earlier chapters, a lack of agreed metadata meaning is dangerous. The use of data modeling methods and modeling tools to generate metadata has been absent so far in the use of Web services. This book emphasizes the use of metadata for business integration—along with XML and Web services for technology integration—as the solution to the challenge of a lack of message semantics definition [16].

13.5.2 Revenue Models for Web Services

Another challenge is associated with new business models that emerged to support Web services during Phase 2, for wide business use in Phase 3. As IBM indicates [17], several questions need to be addressed:

- What revenue models will be applicable for the service?
- How does the service provider address pricing?
- Does the service provider host their service or outsource the hosting?
- How is billing handled?

New terminology is starting to emerge to describe this new environment. IBM has suggested the terms discussed next [18]. Similar terms are also emerging from Microsoft and others; these are also shown next in [square brackets].

> *Asset owner* is the person or entity that owns a particular Web service and the associated intellectual property pertaining to the software resource. *Hosted service providers* are a type of asset owner. Business entities in this category are usually companies that have a software asset that has been enabled for Web services, who have selected a business-model-like subscription and now need a deployable environment to be hosted and managed. This role is best suited for small ISVs (Independent Software Vendors), who prefer to delegate the actual hosting aspects of the service to an entity that is more adapt at managing the infrastructure and quality of service issues associated with such a role. *Independent service providers* are another type of asset owner. Business entities in this category are usually companies that wish to establish their own environment for Web services and maybe even create a private UDDI node to publish those services to the Web. This role is best suited for enterprise customers.
>
> *Service consumer* is the requesting application or another service provider playing the role of an aggregator that will consume at least one, fee-based software service [function/operation].
>
> *Service broker* is a role that could be addressed by possibly two companies. The first could be any business entity interested in exploring the opportunities around directory services or yellow pages for reusable software components. The second would be a vendor who can provide the necessary UDDI and hosting assets needed to provide a public UDDI service (green pages).
>
> *Service provider* is the person or entity that is actually implementing the hosting environment for the asset owner. The service provider may be the same as the asset owner, as in the case of an independent service provider. A service provider is the entity that is responsible for the deployment environment and provisioning aspects related to making a fee-based Web service available for sale. [Microsoft tends to use the term *service operator*.]
>
> *Software Asset Mall* (SAM) is a business entity that provides deployment and hosting facilities for two or more asset owners (*Hosted Service Providers*). In such a case, the operator of the mall will collect revenue based on a combination of possible (but not exhaustive) service fees: hosting charges, transaction surcharges, and access registration. A utility server is also necessary to meet the deployment and provisioning needs of a SAM.

An extensive list of enabling services associated with the above terminology is suggested by IBM [18]. These address security, key management, transformation, logging, clock, calendar, authorization control, user management, tax calculator, credit check, payment services, account management, billing, fulfillment, order management, currency conversion, service credentialing, and metering service to name a few.

The XMETHODS Web site provides a public list of Web services [19]. This lists several hundred Web services that are available and based on SOAP, with direct links to each asset owner. Each service name link and description provides the full invocation details needed by each SOAP message.

A UDDI browser [20] provides an easy UDDI online search capability, without programming. A service operator can be selected between XMETHODS,

Microsoft, and IBM UDDI test registries. This supports searching for UDDI business names, service names, service types (tModel), SOAP services (tModel), discovery URL, DUNS code [21], ISO 3166 codes, and others. This UDDI browser will enable you to gain an appreciation of some of the many Web services that are becoming available. Both Microsoft and IBM also provide a number of UDDI development tools, including UDDI editors, UDDI publishing tools, WSDL editors, and WSDL generators.

13.6 Web Services Products

Many software vendors are developing products and tools to support Web services. Some of the products or development environments from major vendors are listed next. Several products are described in the Product Descriptions PDF file *Chap-13-Products.pdf* in the Book Materials folder on the accompanying CD-ROM. Products are discussed from the following vendors and environments:

- Microsoft Corporation;
- IBM Corporation;
- Software AG;
- SUN;
- Oracle;
- ERP vendors;
- Borland and Linux.

13.7 Summary

In this chapter we discussed the concepts of Web services and associated XML technologies for real-time program and code module integration that is both language independent and platform independent. Web services are specified in XML using SOAP, WSDL, and UDDI.

- Phase 1 evolution of Web services ran from 1999 to 2001. Phase 2 was from 2002 to 2004, with Phase 3 evolution running from 2005 and onward. Business Web services started to appear in 2002 with B2C access to mass consumer-oriented Web services. Since 2003, UDDI registry adoption has grown rapidly. Organizations are now moving to real-time collaboration and integration of processes both within and between enterprises.
- For Web services to deliver fast, seamless integration of business partners on an enterprise scale, many issues must be addressed. These were discussed in the chapter and include QoS, network reliability, transaction recovery, real-time messaging, security, and billing mechanisms.
- On the CD-ROM we saw that many software vendors are developing products and tools to support Web services as follows:

Microsoft is using .NET to transform the company based on XML and Web services. All .NET languages are built on a common language specification to unify programming models for cross-language integration.

IBM's Web services products are based on WebSphere and Java, with full support and generation of SOAP, WSDL, and UDDI using Java 2 Enterprise Edition (J2EE). WebSphere Application Server is integrated with WebSphere Studio Workbench for the development of Web services.

Software AG offers its Enterprise Legacy Integrator for integration of Web services, Java/EJB, and RPC, with integration adapters for legacy applications, databases, CRM, and ERP environments. The Software AG Centrasite is an SOA repository.

Sun Open Net Environment (Sun.ONE) supports Web services using Sun Forte for Java.

Oracle Application Server supports Java and Web services development with Oracle JDeveloper and Application Development Framework (ADF).

Other Web services software vendors include ERP vendors Oracle, SAP, and PeopleSoft (now part of Oracle), with Web services products also from BEA, Borland, Bowstreet, Cacheon, Cape Clear, iPlanet, Killdara, SilverStream, VelociGen, and others.

- On the CD-ROM we discussed Web services for remote portals through the use of WSRP, and also considered WSRP within applications. This offers a plug-and-play capability for easy inclusion of Web services in any environment.

Chapter 14 continues our discussion of enterprise integration technologies. It builds on the introduction to business process integration products for EAI that we considered in Chapter 11. Chapter 14 uses concepts from Web services to introduce business process management technologies such as BPEL and WSCI. It covers several emerging BPM products.

Endnotes

[1] The Web Services Interoperability Group (WS-I) was founded by IBM, Microsoft, BEA, and others in 2002. Its goal is to achieve seamless Web services interoperability between all vendors in WS-I.

[2] The IBM Alphaworks Web site is at http://www.alphaworks.ibm.com.

[3] IBM's Web Services Toolkit provides a run-time environment as well as demo/examples to design and execute Web service applications to find one another and collaborate in business transactions without programming requirements or human intervention.

[4] The Public UDDI Registry is at http://www.uddi.org, accessible across the Internet from any browser. Private UDDI registries can also be implemented in an enterprise, accessible via its intranet.

[5] SOAP was defined by Microsoft, DevelopMentor, and UserLand to solve some of the problems associated with distributed applications.

[6] The SOAP Message Structure specification is documented at W3C; at http://www.w3c.org/ and also at http://www.w3.org.

[7] Document/literal specifies that a complete electronic XML document is included in the SOAP envelope. This enables XML purchase orders to be included as part of the SOAP message, as for EAI in Chapter 11.

[8] The WSDL interface and WSDL implementation files are discussed in an IBM white paper at http://www-106.ibm.com/developerworks/webservices/library/ws-wsdl.

[9] The definition and evolution of UDDI is now being managed within OASIS, which also is involved in the definition and evolution of ebXML. This augurs well for achieving agreement and interoperability between Web services and ebXML. Visit OASIS at http://www.xml.org.

[10] The UDDI specifications are also discussed in the same IBM white paper referenced earlier for WSDL [8].

[11] Further information on Grand Central Communications is available at http://www.grandcentral.com.

[12] Further information on Flamenco Networks is available at http://www.flamenconetworks.com.

[13] Further information on Kenamea is available at http://www.kenamea.com.

[14] Microsoft Passport was proposed by Microsoft to move security for Web services from the responsibility of each machine to a security layer spanning the Internet instead.

[15] To find out the industry markup languages that have been defined in your industry, visit the OASIS Web site at http://www.xml.org. Click on the XML Catalog button in the left frame. Scroll down the XML Catalog industry list displayed alphabetically in the right frame to locate your industry and follow the links.

[16] The methods discussed in Part II that define the semantics of the message content are even more critical for success with Web services than the technical aspects discussed in this chapter.

[17] IBM has discussed many Web services business alternatives in Phase 3 in a white paper at http://www-106.ibm.com/developerworks/webservices/library/ws-arc5.html.

[18] IBM discusses these services at http://www-106.ibm.com/developerworks/webservices/library/ws-arc6.

[19] The XMETHODS public list of Web services is at http://www.xmethods.com.

[20] A UDDI browser is available at http://www.soapclient.com/uddisearch.html.

[21] The DUNS code is an identifier used by Dunn and Bradstreet to identify companies uniquely worldwide.

CHAPTER 14

Service-Oriented Architecture for Integration

In Chapter 12 we discussed enterprise portals, and Chapter 13 covered Web services. In this chapter we cover concepts of other integration technologies: service-oriented architecture (SOA) and business process management (BPM). We discuss several XML-based BPM languages: BPEL4WS (Business Process Execution Language for Web services), WSCI (Web Services Choreography Interface), BPML (Business Process Modeling Language), and BPSS (Business Process Specification Schema) for ebXML. We also cover Business Process Modeling Notation (BPMN). The chapter ends with an overview of a number of BPM products from various vendors that are included in the Product Descriptions section on the accompanying CD-ROM.

14.1 Importance of Service-Oriented Architecture

Web services technology has now advanced so that functions within existing application programs and suites—as well as functions within ERP, CRM, SCM, and other packages—can be easily and reliably published to an intranet or the Internet for remote execution using SOAP, WSDL, and UDDI. But what has been missing until now is an automated way to invoke available Web services based on business rules. This technology is now becoming available with BPM tools.

The term *service-oriented architecture* has until now been synonymous with *Web services*. In this chapter we will use SOA more precisely to refer to Web services that are implemented with BPM tools. This is an important distinction. SOA is expected to make a significant contribution to the future of systems development technologies as indicated in the following paragraphs.

Before SOA, systems development used workflow diagrams, systems flowcharts, or process models that were drawn and then printed, so that relevant business logic could be coded by hand. These manually coded programs were laboriously tested and eventually deployed for execution. With SOA using BPM tools, this manual coding and testing step is bypassed. Instead, the diagrams are tested for correct logical execution using simulation methods. Once correct, these diagrams are then automatically generated as XML-based BPM languages for immediate execution.

This BPM technology—in conjunction with major support from modeling tools (see Chapter 15)—is a major advance in the productivity of systems development; it is as significant as the development of high-level language compilers in the late

1950s. Through the use of business rules, it becomes easy to execute and invoke Web services anywhere in the world. When business rules change, the relevant logic in the diagrams is changed; these diagrams are then automatically regenerated. This promises to transform totally the way we build systems in the future: from slow, error-prone manual coding to an automated discipline. It will enable enterprises to implement changed business rules in minutes or hours, rather than in months or years. The focus will change from debugging code to performance optimization of automatically generated executable XML-based BPM code. Enterprises will then be able to change direction rapidly ... to turn on a dime, so to speak.

14.1.1 Manual Integration Approaches

Historically, people have conducted business between companies. They have exchanged documents such as purchase orders, advanced shipping notices (ASNs), and delivery advices for ordered products, and finally they have exchanged invoices for payment.

Effectively, through these documents people have acted as the integrators between the processes at each company; that is, between the processes for the buyer and supplier in a typical business trading relationship. These documents have been manually entered by each company into their respective systems for processing. This manual entry and subsequent automated processing reflects the human interface that is part of each automated process. We discussed in Chapters 1 and 11 the problems involved with this approach, with data having to be entered manually into many systems. When those data values change, because much of the data exist redundantly, the changed data must be manually reentered many times to ensure that all redundant data versions are up to date.

We discussed in Chapter 11 that the impact of e-business means that the human operator has been taken out of the feedback loop that exists between supplier and buyer. Instead of a "real-world" event—such as the physical receipt of a mailed order form, or a check, or a telephone enquiry on the status of an account—the real world has migrated to the computer. When the human operator is removed from a process, the computer is no longer modeling real-world events—it has become the real world itself. Through e-business, the process is exposed directly to the outside world.

When viewed in this way, the effect of e-business on the enterprise is significant. The most obvious impact is the need for continuous availability. When the computer becomes the real business, it follows that when it is unavailable business cannot be conducted.

Without the human operator acting as a buffer, business processes are exposed directly to those with whom we conduct business: as a customer, provider, or business partner. So business processes must be examined in a new light: Do they really represent the organization in the way we would wish it to be viewed?

The most important attribute of business processes is that they should be consistent. When a customer carries out a series of online transactions—such as making a payment, followed immediately by initiating a new purchase—a failure to process the payment in real time is unacceptable because it may cause the following purchase transaction to fail a credit check (because the payment for the preceding order has not yet been processed). This means that all transactions necessary to fulfill a specific service have to work together in a coordinated way—without requiring any human interaction. It requires that the application systems for these transactions be well integrated, as we have discussed throughout this book.

There are many examples of how e-business can present problems, which are made more complex if the customer uses different access methods for different transactions depending on what is most convenient at the time. The detailed view of the customer should be the same to a human operator in a main branch as it is via the Web, and it should still be the same if contact is instead made through a telephone support center. For most mature organizations, e-business must coexist with all forms of interaction with the outside world.

Figure 14.1 shows some of the typical problems faced by most organizations in achieving complete business integration. Corporate customers, online stores, retailers, consumers, suppliers, and business partners all communicate with the enterprise and the various systems within the enterprise.

A central *integration platform* is needed as an interface for all of these communications, similar to the central role historically taken by a mail room, which effectively acted as a central registry. Like a mail room, the central integration platform needs to be able to accept all input messages received in envelopes, open them, and then direct them to the relevant area or systems within the enterprise for action. Also like a mail room, all output should also be directed from these areas in a standard envelope through the integration platform to the relevant recipient.

With the central role of the integration platform, all communications should be received and sent in a standard way. Similar to using standard envelopes that contain physical messages for communication, so also are electronic envelopes used to contain electronic messages for transmission, as we discussed in Chapter 11.

Another problem with a central integration platform, as we saw in Chapter 1, is that many databases in most enterprises exhibit a high degree of data redundancy. When a customer address, for example, is changed in the Customer table, all redun-

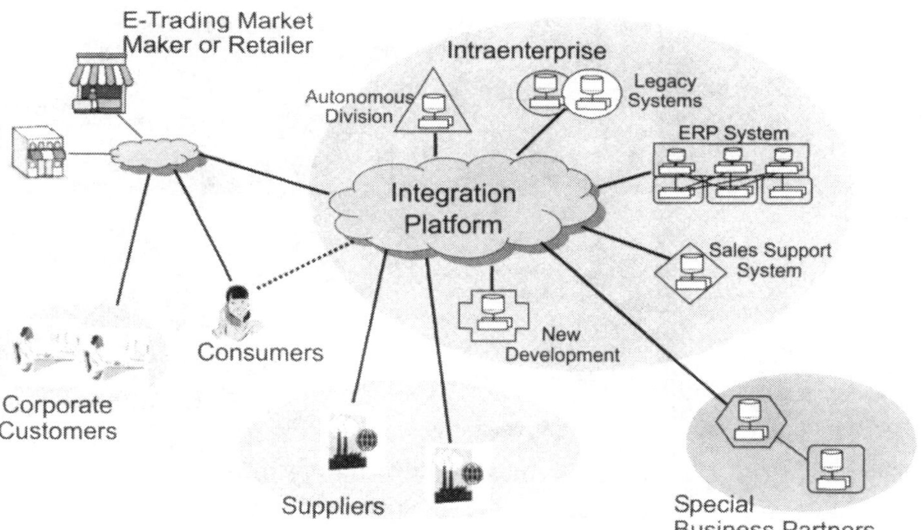

Figure 14.1 Integration platform is for all types of communication. (*Source*: © 2001 Software AG. Reprinted with permission.)

dant versions of that address must also be changed in every other table (Client, Debtor, and so forth), containing the same data version redundantly. We saw in Chapter 11 how EAI assists in resolving this intra-enterprise redundant data integration. We also discussed the use of Web services in Chapter 13 and how they enable this integration to be achieved in real time.

A typical enterprise needs to communicate with not just hundreds, but many thousands of customers, suppliers, and outsourcers. For this reason, to be effective, any integration solution must be able to scale substantially, to support large online transaction volumes.

Many potential errors can occur when applications are executed between enterprises across the Internet, or within an enterprise via the intranet. The resolution of these errors requires coordinated error management between applications, regardless of the applications that are involved.

14.1.2 Coordinated Error Management

In Chapter 13 we discussed an online store that needs to use processes from a bank, a logistic (shipping) company, and a supplier. We considered several RPC protocols that can be used for communication between process components hosted on servers at these different organizations. We saw how services from these processes are made available as Web services across the Internet using standard protocols such as HTTP, SOAP, WSDL, and UDDI.

In the event of errors occurring during execution of these processes, error recovery and management must be coordinated across the systems that are involved. Figure 14.2 shows some of the possible errors that may arise at the:

- *Bank,* due to an invalid credit card number or insufficient credit left in the card;

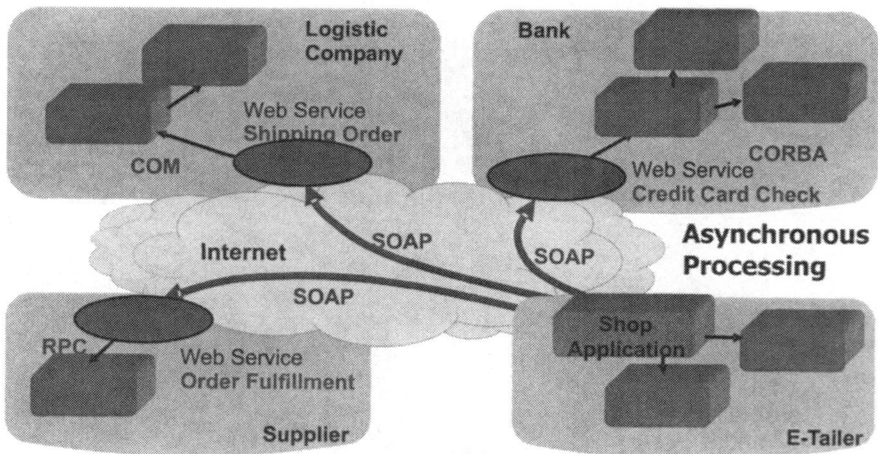

- Bank: Invalid Credit Card or Insufficient Credit?
- Supplier: Out of Stock Products – Backordered?
- Logistics: Supplier or Customer Location?

Figure 14.2 What errors can occur? (*Source:* Software AG.)

- *Supplier,* due to products that are out of stock and so must be back-ordered;
- *Logistics company,* due to a supplier or customer location that is not serviced by the shipping company.

Because of transmission and processing delays across the Internet, it is generally not practical to use Web service requests that operate synchronously (serially). For these performance reasons, most requests generally should operate asynchronously (i.e., concurrently). Several error situations can occur and recovery strategies need to be defined.

In the first situation listed earlier, errors can arise at the bank due to an invalid credit card number or insufficient credit left in the card. Note in Figure 14.2 that the bank uses a compound Web service called *Credit Card Check*. This checks the validity of the credit card. If valid, the card is used immediately by the bank to process payment for the order and deposit it in the online store's bank account. The following error situations and recovery actions can arise:

1. The store invokes the *Credit Card Check* Web service at the bank. The bank validates the card and notifies the store that it has rejected the credit card, due to an invalid card number or credit limit exceeded. No payment is deposited.
2. The recovery action taken by the store is typically to request the supplier to cancel the order if the card is rejected for either reason
3. The customer must then be notified of the reason for cancellation.

And, of course, as we saw earlier, the supplier and logistic company must also be notified to cancel the order and the delivery. In this case the order and associated business are lost.

At the start of this discussion I said that the Web service requests should be carried out asynchronously, for performance reasons. But errors will still arise even if we made each request synchronously. For example, if we waited for validation and processing of the credit card before placing the order with the supplier in Figure 14.2, we would not have to request later cancellation of the order by the supplier for an invalid card as indicated in the previous paragraph. However, synchronous processing would not help us with other errors that can also arise at the same time, as shown by Figure 14.2 and discussed next.

The supplier is Out-of-Stock for some requested products. In this case, the following happens:

1. The store invokes the *Credit Card Check* at the bank, which validates the card and deposits the *Total Order Amount* in the store's bank account.
2. The requested products are ordered from the supplier, but some products are out of stock. We will assume in this example that there is no provision for adjusting the *Total Order Amount*.
3. The recovery action requires that the store invoke a *Credit Card Reversal* Web service at the bank, which processes a credit for the *Total Order Amount*; hence, reversing the payment and deducting that amount from the store's bank account.

4. The customer is then notified of the reason for cancellation and the order is lost.

This situation is equally unsatisfactory. Recovery from the supplier's out-of-stock error has meant that the valid payment received for the order must be completely reversed.

We will now look at an approach that enables these error situations to be accommodated, without losing the order or creating an unhappy customer. Note in Figure 14.3 at the bank that the *Credit Card Check* compound Web service in Figure 14.2 has now been replaced by two component Web services: *Check Card* and *Credit Card Process* in Figure 14.3. This illustrates a more effective approach for processing a partially filled order:

1. The store invokes the *Check Card* Web service at the bank. This verifies that the credit card is valid and the credit limit is sufficient for payment of the *Total Order Amount*. The bank therefore authorizes the use of the credit card for later payment and notifies the store. Full payment for the order is not made yet.
2. The supplier fulfills the order with products that are available. Any out-of-stock products that have to be back-ordered are not charged to the credit card. The *Total Order Amount* is changed to an *Adjusted Total Order Amount*. This pays only for those products that can be fulfilled, less any out-of-stock products that are back-ordered.
3. The store now invokes the *Credit Card Process* Web service at the bank. The bank processes the *Adjusted Total Order Amount* to pay for those products that can be fulfilled. The card was validated for the *Total Order Amount*, so payment for the lower *Adjusted Total Order Amount* can now be processed and deposited into the store's bank account.

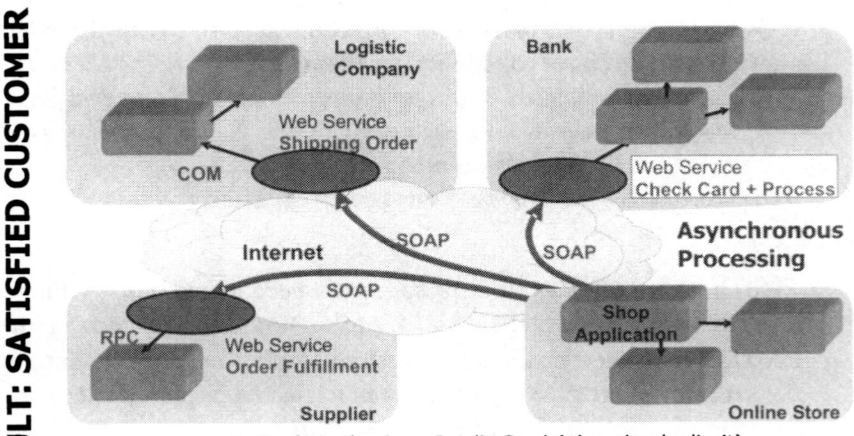

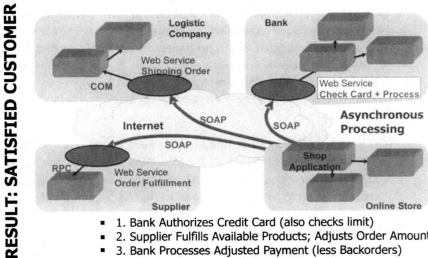

- 1. Bank Authorizes Credit Card (also checks limit)
- 2. Supplier Fulfills Available Products; Adjusts Order Amount
- 3. Bank Processes Adjusted Payment (less Backorders)
- 4. Shipping Order Placed for Supplier Pickup
- 5. Customer Notified of Part Shipment, with Backorders Later

Figure 14.3 Real-time error management. (*Source:* Software AG.)

4. A shipping order is sent to the logistic company, requesting the partial order be picked up from the supplier and delivered to the customer.
5. The customer is notified of the partial shipment and part payment, with the back-ordered products to be shipped separately and paid for at a later date.

The approach just discussed for Figure 14.3 represents an effective recovery process. Because all processing must be completed correctly by the bank, supplier, and logistic company, all processing and recovery steps in this order transaction must be coordinated.

Error situations that can occur between the bank, supplier, and logistic company across the Internet can also occur within an enterprise via the intranet whenever complex Web services transactions are involved that update multiple database tables. We can also see that error situations arise regardless of synchronous or asynchronous processing. These error problems occur because the multiple Web services were dependent on each other. The processes resulted in the interdependent updating of multiple databases: at the bank, supplier, logistic company, and also at the store. They all must execute in a coordinated way, and any errors must be recovered in a coordinated way. This fact is not new. Since the advent of the first computer application systems in the 1950s and 1960s, we have known of the need for coordination of complex, real-time processes and error recovery for multiple database updates.

Any middleware products that wish to provide transaction support for multiple services within or between enterprises for transactions, such as for the order just discussed, *must* provide managed and coordinated full transaction recovery support.

Recognizing the need for coordination of complex transactions, XML specifications have been developed to address these problems. When errors occur with Web services, transaction recovery must be coordinated. This has lead to the definition of specifications for *WS-Transaction* and *WS-Coordination* [1] of Web services, which are used in conjunction with XML-based BPM languages: BPEL4WS, WSCI, or included in BPML. These are discussed in the next section.

14.2 Introduction to Service-Oriented and Event-Driven Architectures

Service-oriented architecture is the term that has emerged to describe executable components, such as Web services, that can be invoked by other programs that act as clients or consumers of those services. As well as the execution of Web services, these services can also be complete modern—or even legacy—application programs that can be invoked for execution as a "black box." A developer does not need to know how the programs work; they need only know the input required, the output provided, and how to invoke them for execution.

The services are loosely coupled to the client program. They can be invoked based on decisions made by business rules. This means that developers can swap one service out and replace it by another service that is designed to achieve the same or enhanced result without having to worry about their inner workings. Today standard parts in a car can be interchanged without having to strip down the whole car and rebuild it. So also with SOA we have similar flexibility, where existing services can be easily replaced by improved services without having to change the internal logic of monolithic application programs as was necessary in the past. Software categories that provide this SOA flexibility are called BPM or business product integration (BPI) products.

A further term also describes these BPM and BPI execution environments: *event-driven architecture* (EDA) [2]. This is an approach for designing and building applications where business events trigger messages to be sent between independent services that are completely unaware of each other. An event may be the receipt by the enterprise of a sales order transaction from a customer for processing. An event may also be a change in a data value that requires a purchase order to be placed with a supplier, when the available quantity of a product in the warehouse falls below a minimum balance threshold.

Because the services in an EDA environment are independent, they are decoupled—as distinct from the loosely coupled services of the SOA-based approach discussed earlier. An event source sends messages to middleware software, which matches the messages against the subscription criteria or business rules of programs or services that want to be notified of these events. Messages are typically sent using the publish-and-subscribe approach because this enables simultaneous delivery to multiple destinations.

We saw in Chapter 11 that BPM is used for workflow modeling and execution by several products for EAI. These were illustrated in the Product Descriptions for Chapter 11 in Figures P11.1 and P11.2 for Microsoft BizTalk, and in Figures P11.4 through P11.7 for the webMethods Business Integrator. IBM, SeeBeyond, Tibco, and Vitria use similar BPM approaches in their EAI products.

To date, most BPM products have used proprietary methods to define process logic in workflow diagrams. To overcome these product-focused solutions, an open architecture approach has been defined for interoperability. Two XML languages have emerged as alternatives: BPEL4WS and WSCI. We will discuss these next. We also consider their roles with the BPML and ebXML BPSS definitions.

The focus in the next section is not to cover each BPM language in detail; we will only discuss the different emphasis that each takes, based on their specifications. We will refer to relevant sections from the specifications, which are shown as indented paragraphs in "quotes" and copyright remains with the relevant authors. Full details are available from the specifications that are summarized with URLs in the endnotes at the end of the chapter.

14.2.1 Business Process Execution Language (BPEL)

Recognizing the complexity of accessing Web services in synchronous and asynchronous environments, in 2002 IBM, Microsoft, and BEA introduced the jointly defined *Business Process Execution Language for Web Services* (BPEL4WS or BPEL or, more recently, WS-BPEL). Its specification is now being managed by OASIS [3].

BPEL combines capabilities of IBM's WSFL and those of Microsoft's XLANG. We were introduced to these briefly in Chapters 11 and 13. BPEL includes WSFL support for graph-oriented processes, together with XLANG support of structural constructs for processes. BPEL is designed to support implementation of any complex business process and to describe interfaces of business processes. The WSCI specifications from Sun and others is an alternative specification to BPEL. We will discuss WSCI shortly.

WS-Coordination (Web services-Coordination) and WS-Transaction (Web services-Transaction) specifications have been defined for use with BPEL. These offer transaction and process coordination and recovery to address typical error conditions as discussed earlier. We will review an example in this section of the use of BPEL, WS-Coordination, and WS-Transaction.

BPEL is a comprehensive workflow definition execution language specified in XML. It can be defined as a programming language and executed directly, but is more likely to be automatically generated from workflow diagrams. The BPEL language commands are called *Activities*. Example Activity constructs include the following [4]:

- Invoke an operation on a Web service (<invoke>).
- Wait for an external message (<receive>).
- Generate a response for input/output (<reply>).
- Wait for some time (<wait>).
- Copy data between locations (<assign>).
- Indicate that an error occurred or something went wrong (<throw>).
- Terminate the entire service instance (<terminate>).
- Do nothing (<empty>).
- Define a sequence of steps to be executed in a specific order (<sequence>).
- Branch using a "case statement" (<switch>).
- Define a loop (<while>).
- Execute one of several alternative paths (<pick>).
- Indicate that steps should be executed in parallel (<flow>).
- Indicate fault logic processing via <throw> and <catch>.
- Define *compensation* for error recovery; implement compensating actions for any irreversible actions in error.
- Fault handling and compensation can be supported recursively by specifying the relevant scope of execution.

Many white papers on BPEL [5] are available from IBM, Microsoft, and OASIS.

BPEL is a comprehensive workflow definition execution language that is specified in XML. It can be written as a programming language and executed directly. But it is mainly intended for automatic generation and execution directly from workflow diagrams. The IBM DeveloperWorks Web site has a white paper [4] that describes two examples: loan processing and the travel agent example in Figure 14.4.

Figure 14.4 shows the integration of reservation Web services from airline, hotel, and car rental partners in a travel itinerary business process. The white paper [4] details how the activities of a business process are externalized as Web services, such as the initial wait for receipt of a customer itinerary request, for example. The coordination activities for multiple Web services within a business transaction are described, together with the dynamic linking to services from multiple providers at run time. This is based on data that are derived from the process flow itself; for

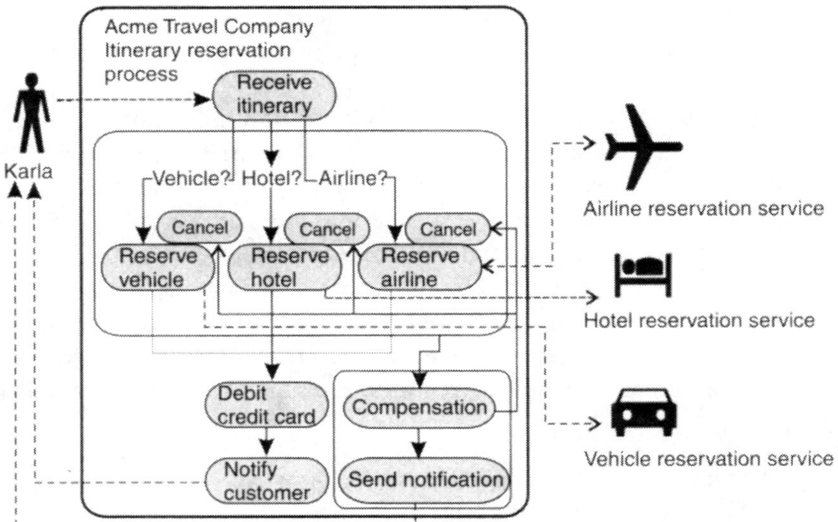

Figure 14.4 A travel agent example using BPEL. (*From:* [4]. © 2002 IBM Corporation. Reprinted with permission.)

example, which airline the customer wishes to use, the preferred car rental company, and a requested hotel. BPEL, WS-Coordination, and WS-Transaction specification [6] describe how they are used together.

WS-Coordination (WS-C) describes an extensible framework for coordinating the actions of distributed applications operating in a heterogeneous environment. WS-C is used to create an environment to propagate an activity to other services and so coordinate their actions or to register for coordination protocols. It defines coordination types that specify a set of coordination behaviors.

WS-Transaction (WS-T) specifies two coordination types used in conjunction with WS-Coordination: *Atomic Transaction* (AT) and *Business Activity* (BA). The AT behavior is used to coordinate activities that have a short duration, whereas BA behavior coordinates activities that are long in duration and so need to apply business logic to handle business exceptions.

Apart from IBM, BEA, and Microsoft products, another third-party product to support BPEL is *ChoreoServer* [7] from OpenStorm Software. Intended for application and trading partner integration, it is fully compliant with the BPEL specifications with a centralized repository for integration logic and business process automation scripts.

Other BPEL-based products are *BPWS4J* and *WebSphere 5.0 Integration Edition* from IBM, and *BPEL Orchestration Server* from Collaxa [8]. This provides comprehensive Web services support for BPEL4WS and BPEL4WS Debugger, monitored execution of business flows through a visual audit trail, console and audit trails, WS-Addressing, XPATH manipulation of XML documents, peer-to-peer conversation patterns, send and receive messages through JMS queues and topics, and native integration with asynchronous Web services using BEA Workshop.

Development of BPEL, WS-C, and WS-T is now managed by the OASIS WSBPEL Technical Committee. Its members include Booz Allen Hamilton, BEA, CommerceOne, E2open, EDS, IBM, Microsoft, NEC, Novell, Oracle, SAP,

SeeBeyond, Siebel, Sun, Sybase, Tibco, Vignette, Waveset, and others. With the strength of these organizations behind its adoption, BPEL is expected to become a major force in XML-based languages for BPM.

We next consider how WSCI addresses similar requirements as a BPM language.

14.2.2 Web Services Choreography Interface (WSCI)

WSCI is an interface description language that is used to define the flow of messages exchanged by Web services participating in coordinated activities with other services. WSCI works in conjunction with WSDL. Whereas WSDL describes a Web service in terms of operations that it supports and the protocols bound to such services, WSCI describes how multiple WSDL operations and related Web services are invoked (choreographed). It defines properties those choreographies expose, such as transaction and correlation. WSCI can work with service definition languages that exhibit the same characteristics as WSDL.

WSCI [9] was submitted to the W3C based on work by BEA, BPMI, CommerceOne, Fujitsu, Intalio, IONA, Oracle, SAP, SeeBeyond, and Sun. Many of these companies are involved in both BPEL and WSCI, and BPMI is also involved in BPML, as discussed later in this chapter.

WSCI describes the behavior of Web services. It works in terms of logical andtemporal dependencies between messages and includes sequencing rules, correlation, exception handling, and transactions similar to BPEL. It describes the collective message exchange among interacting Web services, providing a message-oriented view of the interactions.

WSCI does not address the definition and the implementation of the internal processes that actually drive the message exchange. Instead, it describes the behavior of a Web service through its message-flow-oriented architecture. A Web service is considered to be a "black box" of logic that provides defined output results when provided with the specific input values that are required for processing. The WSCI specifications also use a travel agent example to describe how WSCI works, similar to the example that is used by BPEL and illustrated in Figure 14.4.

Simple services are those services whose behavior does not depend on the scenario in which they are used. These are defined quite adequately by WSDL in terms of interfaces. However, *complex services* are those services that require collaboration between several interactions within or between enterprises. These need more complete definition such as is provided by WSCI or BPEL. Both languages enable the execution of multiple Web services to be coordinated between multiple parties and collaborated between various services. To address this, the WSCI specifications state [9]:

> In a message exchange, any Web service described by WSCI can interact with:
>
> - Other Web services, whose implementation has been derived by their WSCI description;
> - "Hard-coded" software components with internally encoded mechanisms to guarantee the correct sequence of the exchange;

- Or human-controlled software agents where the human determines the sequence of interaction within the constraints of the WSCI description.

WSCI supports *message choreography,* which describes the order in which messages can be sent or received in a given message exchange; the rules that govern such ordering; and the boundaries of a message exchange. These boundaries define when the exchange starts and ends.

Business transactions are defined in terms of *transaction boundaries*, which are also associated with compensating actions to recover from any errors. This describes which operations are performed. It enables the Web service to join a distributed transaction with other services with which it interacts. WSCI does not define a two-phase commit protocol over the Web or how transactions are carried out by Web services. Rather, it allows a Web service to define precisely the transaction boundaries and the externally observable compensation behavior.

When errors occur—as they will eventually—WSCI manages recovery from these errors through *exception handling.* WSCI describes how the Web service will react when any exceptional conditions happen and provides definition of alternative patterns of behavior to manage exceptional situations and faults.

Associated with this, WSCI also defines how concurrent transactions or conversations are supported by using *thread management.* This describes if and how a Web service is capable of managing multiple conversations with the same partner or different partners. It also describes the required relationship among parts of different messages belonging to the same message exchange. Further, WSCI describes relationships among the parts of different messages that collectively guarantee consistency of a message exchange.

A key requirement for SOA is the definition of interfaces between Web services. These are defined by WSCI as *connectors*, which describe how the operations performed by different Web services are actually linked. WSCI enables the mapping of *consume* operations from a Web service to "produce" operations from another Web service, to build a model of the global exchange. By means of the WSCI global model it is also possible to describe how interfaces from different services can be linked to build an end-to-end model of interactions.

WSCI defines the operational context and dynamic participation of Web services in a message exchange. *Operational context* describes how a specific Web service behaves in the context of different message exchanges. *Dynamic participation* describes how the identity of the target service is dynamically selected, based on some criteria that are known at run time and that depend on information such as message components.

The WSCI specifications state that it is *not* a "workflow description language"; it assumes that this role will be covered by some other specification that addresses the description of collaborative processes. This is provided by various BPM products, which are discussed later in the chapter. WSCI can then be used to describe the observable behavior of a Web service that interacts with a workflow, or a system that itself implements a workflow. In a model describing how multiple participants interact, WSCI describes the interface "boundaries" for each participant.

Most business processes rely on collaboration with other processes. An organization can automate these collaborative processes within the same enterprise—as well as between enterprises—to achieve defined business objectives. For this reason, the processes and their collaboration must be carefully modeled.

Later in this chapter we will discuss the ebXML BPSS. This is similar in concept to BPEL and WSCI and is intended for use in defining ebXML applications. At the time of this writing, BPSS was more complete as a specification: It describes how models are used to generate XML-based BPSS definitions. BPSS 1.0 illustrates these XML-generation concepts with UML class diagrams and action diagrams. BPSS does not mandate that only UML be used; any methodology and modeling tool can be used that can achieve similar XML generation for BPSS from process or activity models [10].

Automatic generation of XML-based execution languages from various models is an important principle that we will discuss later in this chapter and Chapter 15, when we consider rapid delivery of priority activities or systems from enterprise architecture [10].

We conclude this section with a brief comparison between WSCI and the contributing technologies to BPEL: WSFL and XLANG.

- IBM's Web Services Flow Language (WSFL) defines a "flow" that involves multiple services as well as the Web services representation of this flow. However, it does not describe how a Web service participates in collaboration to maintain session state, nor does it describe what a Web service can expose to other services with respect to a shared collaboration. In contrast, these interfaces are clearly defined by WSCI.
- Microsoft's XLANG was bound to a specific service interface: BizTalk Orchestration Designer. In contrast, WSCI applies to all services supporting a particular static interface and so can be bound to any static definition language, such as with WSDL. Therefore, WSCI can be used to describe any Web service that exchanges messages, regardless of the way the service was built.

WSCI was defined from its initial introduction as an open architecture environment. With IBM, Microsoft, and BEA as major proponents of BPEL, there was initial industry concern that these large companies would enforce proprietary control over BPEL. That did not happen: Early in the definition of BPEL, IBM and BEA supported the concept of open architecture. Microsoft also recognized there was more for all to gain by ensuring that the use of BPEL was royalty free and hence available to all. BPEL and WSCI are both intended to be open architecture, even though they are alternative approaches.

14.2.3 Business Process Modeling Language (BPML)

WSCI and BPEL are complementary to BPML. Whereas WSCI and BPEL are alternative approaches to define interaction between services deployed across multiple systems, BPML can be used to define the detailed business process behind each service [11]. BPML maps business activities to message exchanges. It can be used for the definition of enterprise business processes, the definition of complex Web services, and the definition of multiple-party collaborations. Some of the organizations that are involved in the definition of the BPML specifications are CSC, Intalio, SAP, Sun, SeeBeyond, and Versata. Its intent is as follows [11]:

> *Business Process Modeling Language (BPML)* is an XML language to define a formal model for expressing executable processes that address all aspects of enterprise business processes. BPML defines activities of varying complexity, transactions and compensation, data management, concurrency, exception handling and operational semantics. BPML provides a grammar in the form of an XML Schema to enable the persistence and interchange of definitions across heterogeneous systems and modeling tools.

BPML is a rich and mature language that can be used to express both simple as well as complex business processes. It builds on the foundation of WSCI for expressing public interfaces and choreographies as discussed earlier. It can also use name spaces to incorporate WSCI activities within BPML processes.

BPML and BPEL share an identical set of idioms and similar syntaxes as block-structured languages. Compared to the activities supported by BPEL as listed earlier in this chapter, BPML syntax supports activities and activity types, processes, properties, signals, schedules, and exceptions. To illustrate, simple and complex BPML activity types are listed and discussed next.

Simple BPML Activity Types

A *simple activity* is any activity that may lead to the execution of multiple activities, specifically the *action, call, compensate,* and *spawn* activities. However, a simple activity does not by itself define the context for the execution of other activities. Differentiating between these further, the following language summary illustrates that BPML includes all of the logic constructs of a rigorous programming language [11]:

- *action:* Performs or invokes an operation involving the exchange of input and output messages.
- *assign:* Assigns a new value to a property.
- *call:* Instantiates a process and waits for it to complete.
- *compensate:* Invokes compensation for the named processes.
- *delay:* Expresses the passage of time.
- *empty:* Does nothing.
- *fault:* Throws a fault in the current context.
- *raise:* Raises a signal.
- *spawn:* Instantiates a process without waiting for it to complete.
- *synch:* Synchronizes on a signal.

Complex BPML Activity Types

A *complex activity* is an activity that contains one or more child activities. It establishes a context for execution and directs that execution. Complex activities define hierarchical composition. This can be as simple as repetitive execution of a single activity or a means to establish a nested context for the execution of multiple activities. BPML supports other forms of composition, which include cyclic graphs and recursive composition. Complex activities are used when hierarchical composition is required, in particular to establish a new context for the execution of child activities. Examples include the following [11]:

- *all:* Executes activities in parallel.
- *choice:* Executes activities from one of multiple sets, selected in response to an event.
- *foreach:* Executes activities once for each item in an item list.
- *sequence:* Executes activities in sequential order.
- *switch:* Executes activities from one of multiple sets, selected based on the truth value of a condition.
- *until:* Executes activities once or more based on the truth value of a condition.
- *while:* Executes activities zero or more times based on the truth value of a condition.

A complex activity that contains multiple activity sets must, of course, select which one to use. Several typical logic constructs are used. The *choice* activity waits for an event to be triggered and then selects the activity set associated with that event handler. The *switch* activity evaluates conditions and selects the activity set associated with a condition that evaluates to true. All other complex activities defined in the BPML specification contain a single activity set and so do not have to make such decisions.

A complex activity also determines the number of times to execute activities from the total activity set. Typical logic constructs are as follows: the *until* activity, which repeats executing activities until a condition evaluates to true; the *while* activity, which executes activities repeatedly while the condition evaluates to *true*; and the *foreach* activity, which repeats executing activities, once for each item in the item list. All other complex activities listed execute activities from the activity set exactly once.

A complex activity determines the order in which activities are executed. The *sequence* activity executes all activities from the activity set's list in sequential order. The *all* activity executes all activities from the activity set's list in parallel. All other complex activities defined in BPML execute activities in sequential order.

A complex activity completes when it has finished executing all activities from the activity set. This includes all activities that are defined in the activity list and all processes instantiated from a definition made in the activity set's context. Nested processes and exception processes are considered activities of the activity set.

Simple activities *abort* and throw a *fault* if they cannot complete due to an unexpected error. Complex activities *abort* and throw a *fault* if one of their activities throws a fault from which they cannot recover.

With the addition of nested processes and other syntax and support, we can see that BPML is a superset of BPEL. When either WSCI or BPEL is used with BPML, an end-to-end view is provided that depicts the role of each individual business process in the overall choreography, and the business activities that are performed by each role.

We will now delve further into the BPML specification and extract examples that illustrate the definition of execution logic. This will help us appreciate its capability to define activity or process logic.

Based on BPML state transitions, the following example has been extracted from the BPML specification to illustrate the capability of the language. Figure 14.5 illustrates the synchronization of activities that execute in parallel, with the related BPML code in XML shown here:

```
<all>
    <context>
        <signal name="tns:completedA"/>
    </context>
    <sequence>
        <call process="activityA"/>
        <raise signal="completedA"/>
        <call process="activityB"/>
    </sequence>
    <sequence>
        <call process="activityC"/>
        <synch signal="completedA"/>
        <call process="activityD"/>
    </sequence>
</all>
```

Signals are used to synchronize between activities that execute concurrently. To enable synchronization, the *raise* activity signals activity completion of Activity A, whereas the *synch* activity is a synchronization barrier that waits for the completion of the relevant activity. The example in Figure 14.5 involves four dependent activities. Activity B is dependent on the completion of Activity A, but is not dependent on Activities C or D. Activity D is dependent on the completion of both Activity A and Activity C, but is not dependent on Activity B. Activities A and C are not dependent on any other activity. Several other signals can be used to model the example.

Activity A may be the source of a signal on which both Activities B and D synchronize. Activity C may be the source of a signal on which only Activity D synchronizes. Activities A, B, C, and D are started in parallel and use signals to ensure a proper order of execution. In this example there are two parallel sequences. One sequences Activity A followed by Activity B. The other sequences Activity C followed by Activity D. The signal is raised from one sequence and synchronized from the other.

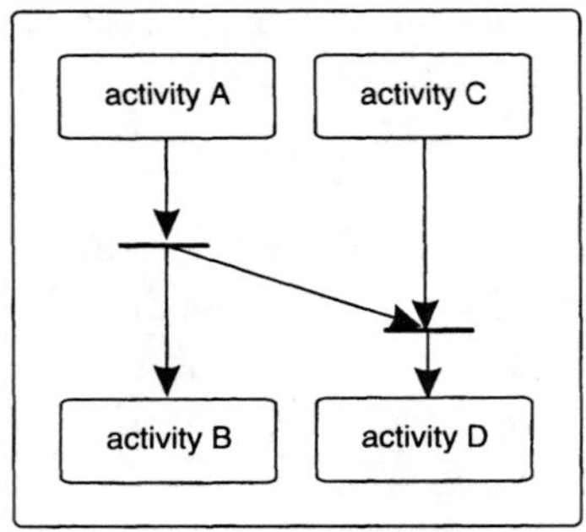

Figure 14.5 Example of BPML used to synchronize activities executing in parallel [11].

The BPML specification [11] includes several other examples that illustrate the use and the power of this BPM language. One example shows how BPML can use signals to detect the completion of an asynchronous process, based on concurrent quotations from different suppliers. Another example describes a more complex series of interactions in a two-step order process, illustrated in the BPML specification.

BPEL, WSCI, and BPML are all similar approaches to solve the same problem: the definition of process logic in XML so that it can be used as executable code by BPM-based software products. Each of these languages—WSCI, BPEL, and BPML—is evolving. A decision between them has not yet been resolved. All are solutions to the same problem, with specifications and languages that are conceptually similar; they may in time consolidate into one overall specification.

The cross-participation of organizations in two (and for some organizations all three) of these initiatives augurs well for possible convergence of the specifications. But until that time, most BPM tools will most likely need to support generation of all three BPM languages from workflow diagrams or process models.

14.2.4 ebXML Business Process Specification Schema (BPSS)

BPSS is the fourth BPM language that we will discuss. BPSS is part of ebXML, which has decades of experience in EDI behind its specification [10, 12]. BPSS differs from BPEL, WSCI, and BPML in that it defines a business process for physical business interchanges between parties so that collaboration and transactions can be carried out between commercial business partners [13]. It is designed to work in conjunction with the ebXML Collaboration Protocol Profile (CPP) and Collaboration Protocol Agreement (CPA), both defined in the ebXML specifications [13]. In contrast, the other BPM languages are generic to Web services: They do not provide explicit commercial semantics (or terms) as discussed next, nor do they have the intent of a trading partner agreement as with ebXML.

A Web service may have to be designed for internal and external uses. For this reason, internal-use Web services can be described in the three BPM languages, whereas external-use Web services may require further specification, which is described in commercial terms for business collaboration using ebXML BPSS. For example, if a supplier accepts a purchase order from a customer, this acceptance is a binding legal agreement: for the supplier to deliver the requested products or services to the customer at an agreed-on price and time; and for the customer to pay the supplier following delivery. The various messages and interactions sent between these external businesses constitute a binding contract between both parties. BPSS therefore includes the concepts of time periods for business response, plus *nonrepudiation*: Neither party can deny its legal obligations to the other party, once the purchase order has been issued and accepted.

A company may want to wrap its implementation of a given role in external-use BPSS collaboration, and additionally also as an internal-use Web service. To achieve this it can describe the Web service in any BPM language; nothing in the specifications prevents either of these two scenarios, but note that neither BPSS nor the other BPM specifications have been designed with the other approaches in mind.

BPSS 1.0 also specifies how models are used to generate XML-based BPSS definitions. It describes the XML-generation concepts using UML class diagrams and action diagrams. Because of its earlier start in 1999, the specification of ebXML BPSS is several years ahead of the other BPM specifications. BPSS focuses on BPMU [10].

In time it is expected that the three BPM languages—or a consolidated version of them—will evolve along lines similar to BPSS, but with broad applicability to all applications—not just for EDI and ebXML-based applications. In fact, BPSS is a clear pointer to a future when application development will be based on automatic generation of XML-based languages directly from workflow or other process models.

The architecture of the ebXML BPSS 1.0 specifications consist of the following functional components [13]:

- UML version of the BPSS;
- XML version of the BPSS;
- Production rules defining the mapping from the UML version of the BPSS to the XML version;
- Business signal definitions, which acknowledge receipt of messages.

Together these components allow complete specification of the run-time aspects of a business process model.

BPSS is the machine-interpretable run-time business process specification that is used by ebXML Business Service Interface software. The BPSS code is incorporated with or referenced by the ebXML trading partner CPP and CPA. Each CPP declares its support for one or more roles within the business process specification, documented by UML use case diagrams for BPSS 1.0. Within these CPP profiles and CPA agreements were added further technical parameters that resulted in a full specification of the run-time by ebXML Business Service Interface software at each trading partner.

The BPSS 1.0 Specification provided full documentation and guidance for automatic generation by UML modeling tools of XML-based BPSS code from class diagrams and action diagrams. The BPSS 2.0 specifications change from UML diagrams in BPSS 1.0 to process models defined as business process diagrams (BPDs) using BPMN. These BPDs are then used to generate BPSS XML-based code. (We will cover BPMN next.)

To define the commercial and legal nature of this transaction, the following BPSS "Create Order" *<BusinessTransaction>* requests: isNonRepudiation Required="true" with timeToAcknowledgeReceipt="P2D" (where "P2D" is a W3C Schema syntax standard that means Period=2 Days and timeTo AcknowledgeAcceptance="P3D"; (where P3D means Period=3 Days). These periods are all measured from the original sending of the request.

```
<BusinessTransaction name="Create Order">
    <RequestingBusinessActivity name=""
            isNonRepudiationRequired="true"
            timeToAcknowledgeReceipt="P2D"
            timeToAcknowledgeAcceptance="P3D">
    <DocumentEnvelope
```

```
                BusinessDocument="Purchase Order"/>
</RequestingBusinessActivity>
<RespondingBusinessActivityname=""
                isNonRepudiationRequired="true"
                timeToAcknowledgeReceipt="P5D">
        <DocumentEnvelope isPositiveResponse="true"
                BusinessDocument="PO Acknowledgement"/>
        </DocumentEnvelope>
    </RespondingBusinessActivity>
</BusinessTransaction>
```

14.2.5 Business Process Modeling Notation (BPMN)

Business Process Modeling Notation is emerging as a way to specify business process models and diagrams for any BPM language. As the following extract from the BPMN specifications [14] states:

> Business people are very comfortable with visualizing business processes in a flow-chart format. There are thousands of business analysts studying the way companies work and defining business processes with simple flow charts. This creates a technical gap between the format of the initial design of business processes and the format of the languages, such as BPEL4WS, that will execute these business processes. This gap needs to be bridged with a formal mechanism that maps the appropriate visualization of the business processes (a notation) to the appropriate execution format (a BPM execution language) for these business processes.
>
> Inter-operation of business processes at the human level, rather than the software engine level, can be solved with standardization of the Business Process Modeling Notation (BPMN). BPMN provides a Business Process Diagram (BPD), which is a Diagram designed for use by the people who design and manage business processes. BPMN also provides a formal mapping to an execution language of BPM Systems (BPEL4WS). Thus, BPMN would provide a standard visualization mechanism for business processes defined in an execution optimized business process language.

BPMN describes private processes, abstract processes, and collaboration processes, as discussed next.

Private processes are those that are internal to an organization. These are processes that have been generally called workflow or BPM processes. A single private process will map to a single BPEL XML inactivity. *Abstract processes* represent the interactions between a private process and another process or participant. Only those activities that are used to communicate outside the private business process are included in the abstract process. All other "internal" activities of the private process are not shown in the abstract process. Thus, the abstract process shows to the outside world the sequence of messages that is required to interact with that business process. A single abstract process may be mapped to a single BPEL abstract process.

Collaboration processes depict the interactions between two or more business entities. These are defined as a sequence of activities that represent the message exchange patterns between the entities involved. A single collaboration process may be mapped to various collaboration languages, such as ebXML BPSS, RosettaNet, or WSCI.

An example from the BPMN specifications is shown in Figure 14.6. This illustrates the message interactions between a patient and a doctor in establishing an appointment to see the doctor, who diagnoses the illness and prescribes medicine, with interactions to collect the medicine.

BPMN specifies standard diagrammatic notations or icons that can be used in process models to define a business process in a BPMN business process diagram (BPD). An example illustrating part of the process diagram in Figure 14.4 for the travel agent example is expressed as a BPMN BPD in Figure 14.7.

The BPMN specifications illustrate, using many examples, generation of XML-executable BPEL code from typical process models in BPMN. It describes, in detail, the mapping of BPMN diagrams to generated BPEL XML code.

A complete BPMN example of an e-mail voting process model is documented as Figure 92 of the BPMN specifications [14], with generated BPEL code from this BPMN process included as Appendix A of that document.

We have covered BPEL, WSCI, BPML, and BPSS as the four major BPM languages used today for the automatic generation of executable XML code from workflow diagrams. We have also discussed BPMN as an evolving standard for specification of process logic for all of these BPM languages. We are now ready to review some of the software products that support these languages.

14.3 SOA Business Process Management Products

We saw in Chapter 11 that many BPM development environments are available as commercial software products for EAI. Each of these has evolved based on proprietary approaches to define, generate, and execute business process execution logic.

As is evident from the previous section, XML-based BPM languages are evolving rapidly. During the next few years, a "standard" BPM language may emerge. But until that time, we will see different products released to support one or several

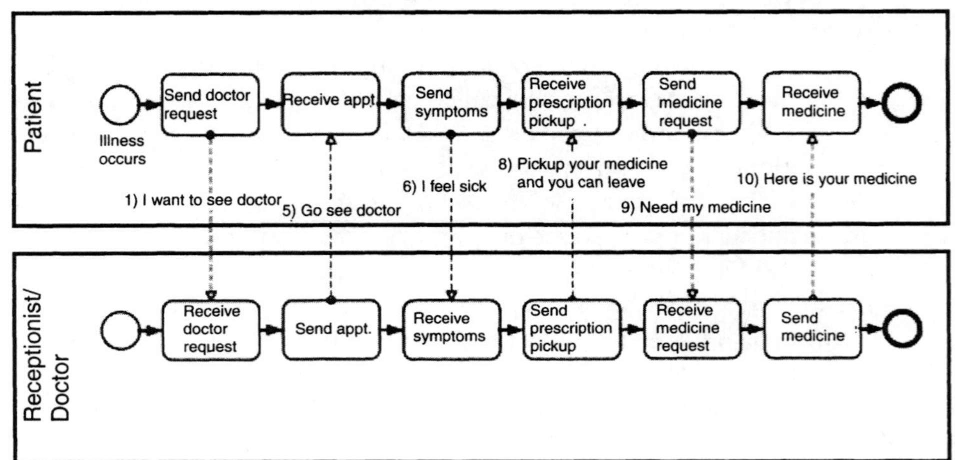

Figure 14.6 A process from different points of view using BPMN [14].

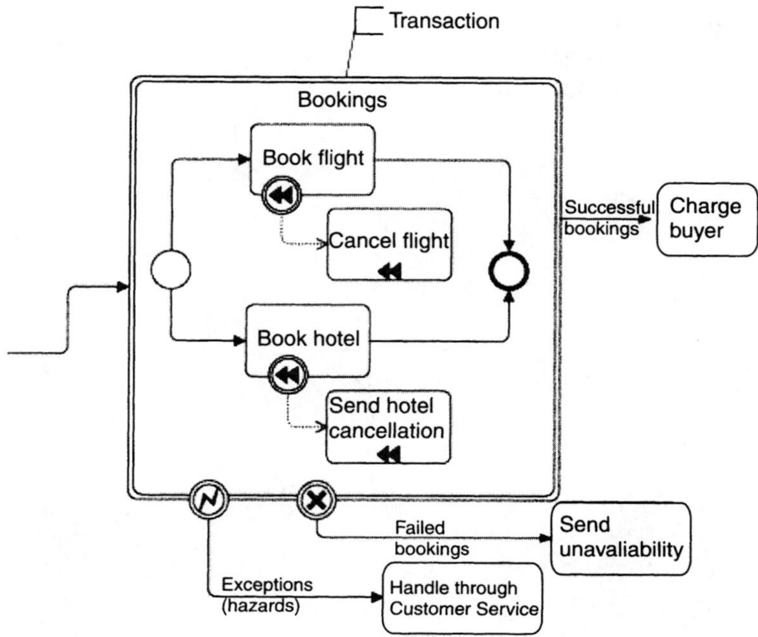

Figure 14.7 Part of travel agent example in Figure 14.4, shown as a BPMN BPD [14].

of the BPEL, WSCI, BPML, and BPSS specifications. Many of the EAI products introduced in Chapter 11 were the first to move in this direction. While migrating their customers toward these emerging languages, they will also likely continue to support their proprietary BPM approaches. Other BPM products will be released to support only these languages; they will not have to concern themselves with migrating customers from "legacy" proprietary BPM approaches.

This final section of the chapter will discuss many BPM software products for SOA. At the time of writing, some products are just starting to address their support of the BPM languages covered earlier. However, a new class of dedicated business process management system (BPMS) products and also a new category of managed enterprise service bus (ESB) products are starting to appear. These BPMS and ESB products are being developed specifically to support the BPM languages natively. They are discussed later in the Product Descriptions section of the chapter.

The chapter is therefore a "work-in-progress." Later editions of the book will update the concepts we have covered, to reflect the current status of BPM at that time.

The following SOA vendors and their BPM products are discussed in the Product Descriptions PDF file *Chap-14-Products.pdf* in the Book Materials folder on the accompanying CD-ROM:

Infrastructure Software Vendors

- Microsoft;
- IBM;
- Oracle.

Integration Vendors

- Software AG.

ERP Vendor

- SAP.

EAI Vendors

- webMethods;
- SeeBeyond;
- TIBCO.

Enterprise Portal Vendors

- Plumtree (now BEA);
- Vignette.

BPMS Vendor

- Intalio.

Management of SOA Development

- Infravio.

ESB Products

- Cape Clear 6.1;
- Cordys 4.2;
- FioranoESB Suite 3.7;
- FusionWare Integration Server 3.0;
- Iona Artix 3.0 Advanced;
- Polarlake Integration Suite 4.0;
- Sonic SOA Suite 6.1.

14.4 Summary

In this chapter we examined BPM languages for SOA:

- Business Process Execution Language for Web services combines IBM's WSFL and Microsoft's XLANG. BPEL is designed to support implementation of any complex business process, as well as being used to describe interfaces of business processes.

- Web Services Choreography Interface is an alternative specification to BPEL. It is used to define the flow of messages exchanged by Web services participating in coordinated activities with other services. WSCI is *not* a "workflow description language" as such, but describes the behavior of Web services that interact with a workflow, or a system that implements a workflow.
- Business Process Modeling Language defines a formal model for expressing executable business processes. It defines simple and complex activities, transactions and compensation, data management, concurrency, exception handling, and operational semantics. BPML provides a grammar as an XML schema to enable the persistence and interchange of definitions across heterogeneous systems and modeling tools.
- The ebXML Business Process Specification Schema (BPSS 1.0) defines a business process for physical business interchanges between parties so that collaborations and transactions can be carried out between commercial business partners. It works in conjunction with the ebXML CPP and CPA. It also defines the automatic generation of BPSS code from UML diagrams. BPSS 2.0 uses BPMN instead of UML for process models.
- BPSS defines commercial and legal terms and responsibilities between enterprises. This goes beyond the current intent of BPEL, WSCI, or BPML. These languages do not provide explicit commercial terms, nor do they have legal intent similar to a trading partner agreement.
- BPSS is also a pointer to a future where application development will be based on automatic generation of XML-based languages directly from process or workflow models. In time it is expected that the first three BPM languages—or a consolidated version of them—will evolve along lines similar to those of BPSS, but with broader applicability for all applications, not just for EDI and ebXML.
- Business Process Modeling Notation is emerging as a way to specify business process models and diagrams. This is as an evolving standard for the specification of process logic for all of the above BPM languages. The Business Process Management Initiative (BPMI) and the Open Management Group (OMG) have announced they are merging their BPM activities to advance the use of BPMN as an open standard.

On the CD-ROM we discussed a number of BPM vendors and their software products:

- Microsoft BizTalk Server automatically generates BPEL code directly from BizTalk Orchestration Designer diagrams.
- IBM WebSphere Business Server Integration Workbench automatically transforms between various UML diagrams. The IBM WebSphere Business Integration Server Foundation automatically generates BPEL code from process models.
- Oracle BPEL Process Manager automatically generates BPEL from process models. It runs on all of the major application servers, including Oracle Application Server, IBM WebSphere, BEA WebLogic, and JBoss.

- Software AG's Enterprise Legacy Integrator, Enterprise Information Integrator, Enterprise Service Integrator, and Enterprise Process Integrator are all tools for integration.
- SAP NetWeaver supports WSCI for BPM, with the stated intent of also supporting BPEL.
- webMethods Business Process Integrator offers proprietary automatic generation of executable code from process models.
- SeeBeyond e*Insight Business Process Manager supports process modeling, implementation, monitoring, and management, as does webMethods. Part of SeeBeyond ICAN, it provides automatic generation of BPEL from process models specified using BPMN. SeeBeyond has been purchased by Sun Microsystems.
- TIBCO BusinessWorks similarly uses graphical design tools to manage all aspects of a BPI project.
- Plumtree Enterprise Web is used to build composite applications. This is a development environment that offers a potential for future BPM language support. Plumtree has been purchased by BEA.
- Vignette Process Workflow Modeler uses Microsoft Visio. It supports XML Process Definition Language (XPDL), another BPM language for workflow modeling. It has the potential to support the other BPM languages discussed in this chapter.
- The final product that we discussed in this chapter was Intalio | n^3 Business Process Management System (BPMS). With its native support for BPML, BPEL, and use of WSCI, the Intalio | n^3 product family is clearly the direction of BPMS for the future.
- We discussed the need for metadata management of SOA development, using an SOA registry.
- We discussed the emergence of ESB products. This is a field that is expected to expand rapidly in the next few years.

As we have seen in this chapter, the SOA and BPM markets are consolidating, with some of the original innovators being purchased in 2005. Many BPM tools generate code in proprietary languages at present. It is expected that most will evolve in time to generate code in BPEL, WSCI, BPML, and/or ebXML BPSS based on BPMN. In Chapter 15 we will see how modeling tools and BPMS products can be used for rapid delivery of priority enterprise architecture areas into production.

Endnotes

[1] Search for *WS-Transaction* and *WS-Coordination* specifications on OASIS at http://www.xml.org.

[2] Event-driven architecture is defined for use in SOA at http://www.sys-con.com/story/?storyid=46560&de=1.

[3] The BPEL specifications are at http://www-106.ibm.com/developerworks/library/ws-bpel and also on the OASIS site at http://www.xml.org.

[4] The white paper "Business Process with BPEL4WS: Learning BPEL4WS, Part 2," by Rania Kalaf, August 1, 2002, at http://www-106.ibm.com/developerworks/webservices/library/ws-bpelcol2 is the loan processing example. The white paper at http://www-106.ibm.com/developerworks/library/ws-autopb/, "Automating Business Processes and Transactions in Web Services," by James Snell, August 1, 2002, is the travel itinerary example.

[5] White papers on BPEL are available from IBM at http://www.ibm.com, from Microsoft at http://www.microsoft.com, and from OASIS at http://www.xml.org. The examples in this section have been drawn from the IBM DeveloperWorks site at http://www-106.ibm.com/developerworks/library/ws-bpelwp and also at http://www-106.ibm.com/developerworks/library/ws-bpelcol1/?n-ws-8292.

[6] The BPEL4WS, WS-Coordination, and WS-Transaction specifications are all available from the OASIS Web site at http://www.xml.org.

[7] Details of ChoreoServer are available from http://www.choreoserver.com.

[8] Collaxa is now part of Oracle. The Collaxa BPEL Orchestration Server for Web services is now called the Oracle BPEL Process Manager. Details are available at http://www.oracle.com.

[9] The WSCI specifications are available from http://www.wsci.org/ and http://www.w3.org/TR/wsci, both of which have many white papers.

[10] As mentioned in earlier chapter endnotes, BPSS 2.0 uses BPMN for business processes, rather than UML. BPMN is discussed in this chapter and in Chapter 15 with modeling tools that support BPMN for generation at executable XML-based BPEL on BPML.

[11] Further details about the BPML specifications are available from the BPMI Web site at http://www.bpmi.org. Click on links also to OMG.

[12] The full ebXML specifications on http://www.ebxml.org and also htpp://www.xml.org should be read in conjunction with the discussion of the ebXML BPSS 1.0 specification in this section.

[13] The ebXML.org Web site at http://www.ebxml.org and also OASIS at htpp://www.xml.org both provide full documentation of the ebXML Business Process Specification Schema 1.0 (BPSS 1.0). See also specifications now published to ebxml.org.

[14] The BPMN specifications are on the XML cover pages at http://xml.coverpages.org/BPMNv10Draft.pdf. A white paper overview of BPMN is available from the Popkin Web site at http://www.popkin.com. (Popkin is now part of Telelogic at http://www.telelogic.com.) See also the latest on BPMN on OMG.org.

CHAPTER 15

Managing and Delivering Enterprise Architecture

This final chapter brings together the rapid delivery technologies we covered in Part III, with the rapid delivery methods discussed earlier in Parts I and II. I will start by examining the concepts of virtualization and "on-demand" computing. We will see how our existing IT infrastructure will evolve to this more flexible environment for better utilization of hardware, storage, networks, operating systems, and applications. I will next discuss modeling tools, which provide the modeling bridge from the methods in Parts I and II to the implementation technologies of Part III. The chapter concludes with a summary of key principles from the book on methods, technologies, and enterprise architecture directions for the future.

15.1 Virtualization and On-Demand Computing

In the 1990s we saw an increasing focus on *outsourcing*. Specific business functions—even entire departments—were transferred to external organizations that specialized in providing the relevant services. This was particularly true for many IT functions and departments. The IT resources that were previously used, such as equipment, facilities, and IT staff, were all transferred to the outsourcing supplier. These people and other resources moved from being part of the original enterprise to become part of a "virtual enterprise."

Today this move to outsourcing is an accepted fact of life. Enterprises now direct their efforts to their core business focus, for example, selling products through retail stores, delivering insurance services or banking services, manufacturing automobiles or planes, providing health care services, or delivering government services. The outsourcing suppliers also benefit from this delegation of noncore IT services to them. They can generate economies of scale that are passed back, in part, as savings to the original enterprise, while still enabling some of these savings to be retained as profit for the outsourcing supplier.

Now consider the infrastructure of a typical IT organization. It has hardware, memory, servers, storage, networks, and operating systems to satisfy the processing demands that are placed on it. We have traditionally had to configure this infrastructure to handle expected peak loads. Because of the need to ensure capacity for peak loads, not all equipment is fully utilized under normal loads; some may remain idle much of the time. This is inefficient and expensive. Yet it has been a fact of life that we have had to dedicate certain physical resources wholly to some critical applications just so we had the capacity to handle those peak loads needed to support the business. This problem will soon disappear. Instead of dedicating these IT resources, we can pool them all so they can be shared as needed. We can utilize only the specific resources that are needed; and we can do this dynamically. This is achieved through *virtualization.*

15.1.1 Virtualization Concepts

In the early days of computing, applications were written to utilize specific hardware. For example, in the 1960s programs were written to access data stored at precise disk sector addresses. With the advent of operating systems, we separated the program from reliance on specific hardware locations. We were able to access "virtual" disk locations to obtain the data that were needed.

Applications have traditionally been developed independently of each other. They were designed to access required data on their dedicated physical servers or set of physical servers. The servers used by these applications usually had low utilization rates, and the unused system resources sat idle and were wasted.

With this independent application development, the result has been progressive evolution to the redundant data problem that we discussed in Chapter 1 and have returned to often throughout the book. There was also little, if any, sharing of other physical resources such as memory, unless applications were deployed on mainframe-based machines or on machines that supported memory partitioning.

Technologies have since enabled some sharing of these resources. For example, servers can be partitioned to increase their utilization, or blade technology can be used to change server storage availability by dynamically adding or swapping out disk storage.

In the dynamic business environment of today, we discussed the fact that organizations must be able to change rapidly and often. They must be able to employ dynamic, *on-demand* strategies that drive implementations of end-to-end integrated business processes. The number of application systems that support those processes will continue to grow and will increasingly span multiple servers on different technologies. These heterogeneous cross-platform technologies will need to be managed, monitored, and measured.

Applications running on mainframes, servers, and desktops today now take advantage of technologies such as virtual memory, where each executing application thinks it has its own dedicated, real memory. Logical partitioning allows organizations to "slice up" a machine into virtual partitions; some operating systems offer the flexibility to dynamically change allocation of system resources for different environments. Today, virtual servers may run across many physical servers, so that disk resources can be shared. This makes it possible for the physical server to be run at very high utilization levels. As stated by IBM in its Virtualization Redbook [1]:

> The hardware-based virtualization capabilities of the IBM mainframe also allow virtualization and sharing of I/O paths, and allows for the definition of virtual TCP/IP networks connecting the virtual servers at memory speed.

Some operating systems support a virtualization technology called *physical partitioning,* in which each physical partition or virtual server owns a dedicated set of resources that is not used by others. This is also referred to as *hardware partitioning.*

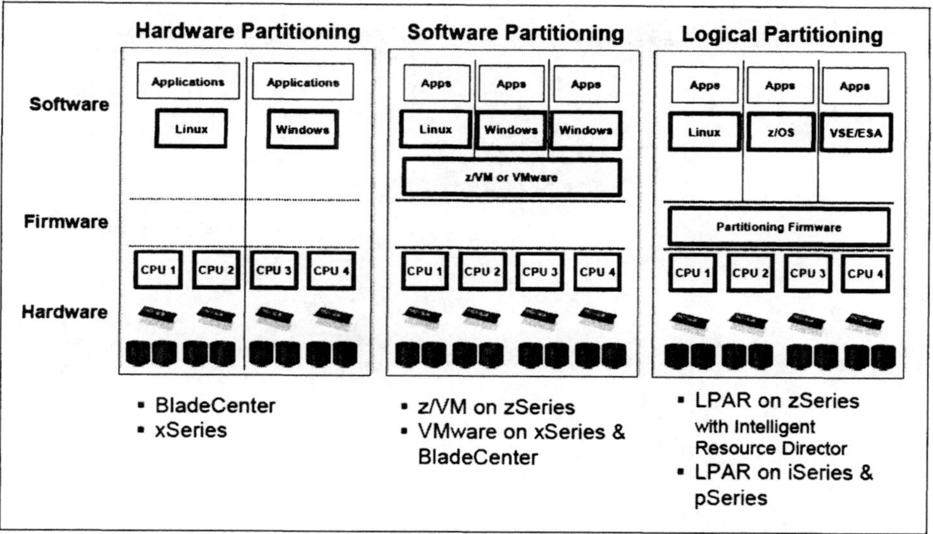

Figure 15.1 Different modes of partitioning. (*From:* [1]. © 2005 IBM Corporation. Reprinted with permission.)

There is also *software partitioning* and *logical partitioning,* as illustrated in Figure 15.1. This shows that hardware partitioning uses fixed resources, whereas software and logical partitioning have greater, more dynamic capabilities, depending on implementation and platform. In its Redbook, IBM makes the point that [1]:

> Virtualization is now expanded beyond the scope of one physical box and one architecture to deliver the classical benefits of virtualization on an end-to-end scale, across all architectures including servers, storage, and networks. This new level of virtualization is realized through technologies like provisioning and workload management ...
>
> IBM Enterprise Workload Manager (EWLM) . . . automatically monitors and manages heterogeneous workloads across an IT infrastructure. . . . It provides end-to-end resource optimization and load balancing of IT resources in heterogeneous, multi-tier application and server environments ...
>
> The goal of EWLM provides the ability to identify work requests based on service class definitions, track performance of those requests across server and subsystem boundaries, and manage the underlying physical and network resources to achieve specified performance goals for each service class.

An example of the IBM Enterprise Workload Manager is shown in Figure 15.2.

IBM is implementing its virtualization engine using industry standards that will enable the management of heterogeneous environments, described as follows [2]:

> IBM Director Multiplatform is the component of the Virtualization Engine that provides a simplified view of IBM eServer hardware from a centralized server. It delivers a comprehensive systems management solution for heterogeneous environments, such as support of IBM eServer BladeCenter, iSeries, pSeries, and xSeries servers. IBM plans to add similar functionality in future releases of IBM Director Multiplatform for supported platforms, including IBM eServer zSeries servers. IBM

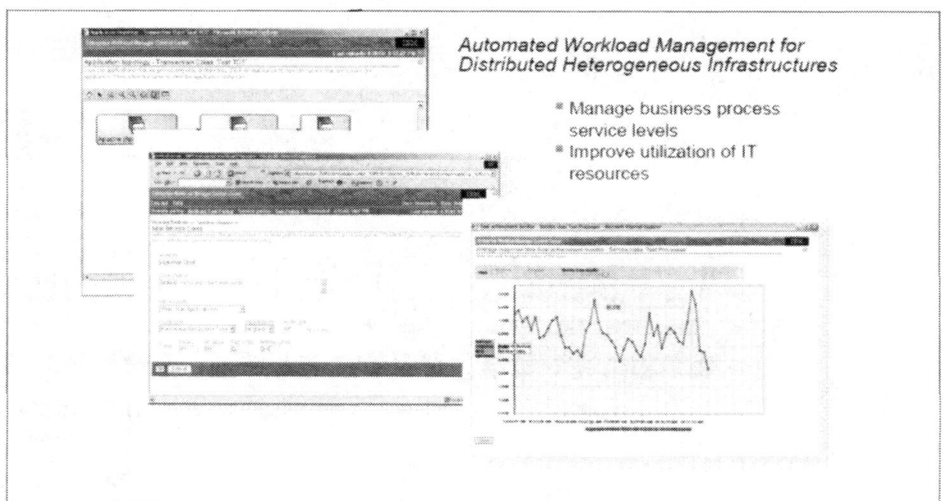

Figure 15.2 Enterprise Workload Manager. (*From:* [1]. © 2005 IBM Corporation. Reprinted with permission.)

Director Multiplatform's core infrastructure is designed to provide a single point of control for managing up to 5,000 systems.

By leveraging industry standards, the IBM Director Multiplatform provides an extensible architecture to enable solutions for easy integration with other systems management tools and applications, such as Tivoli Enterprise, Tivoli NetView, HP OpenView, Microsoft SMS, CA Unicenter, BMC Patrol, and NetIQ.

We have discussed some of the concepts of virtualization; further detail is available from the IBM Redbook [1]. We will now see how these capabilities are used in an on-demand environment.

15.1.2 On-Demand Concepts

IBM defines an *on-demand* operating environment as delivering "an open, industry-standard, accessible set of services interfaces for the creation and management ... of computing resources." To permit open architecture deployment, IBM states that [1, 3]:

> IBM Virtualization Engine, IBM Director Multiplatform [and other technologies] provide an abstraction of the interface and build workflows that can define, configure, build and deploy operating system images into containers. However, they provide these functions in a generic, industry standard way on which other hardware, software, and middleware developers are able to build on and incorporate into their products and offerings without making the IBM Virtualization Engine a prerequisite.

Figure 15.3 illustrates IBM's on-demand operating environment, showing all services. Those shown above the Enterprise Service Bus are related to business services and functions, whereas those below the bus are related to infrastructure man-

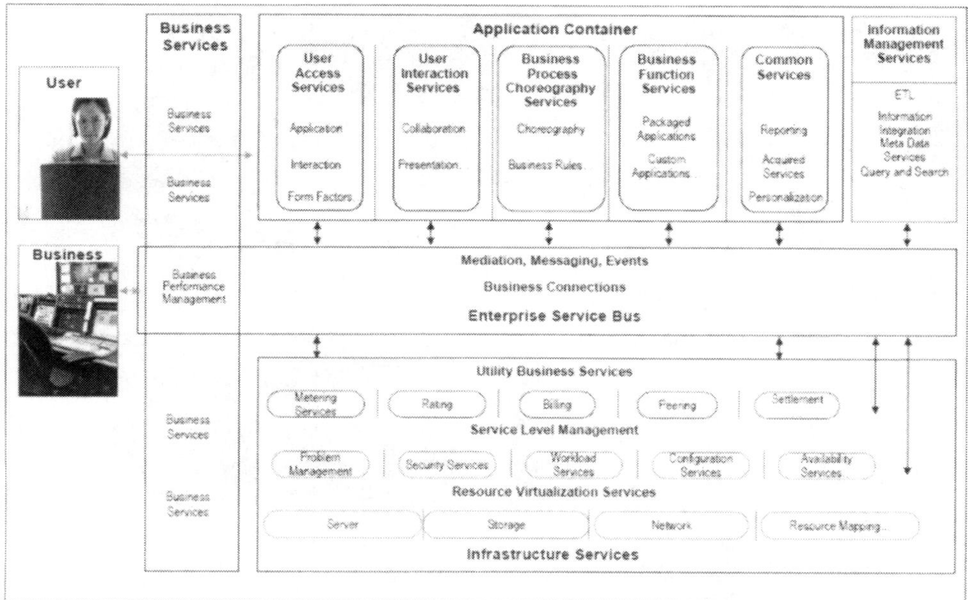

Figure 15.3 On-demand operating environment architecture. (*From:* [1]. © 2005 IBM Corporation. Reprinted with permission.)

agement. The bus and thus the services can be called using a variety of protocols such as SOAP, JMS (Java Message Services), and other forms of messaging. The bus can also be bridged using other messaging technology. Infrastructure services are run within the enterprise service bus, but they are not invoked directly by business logic.

Figure 15.4 provides a schematic summary of virtualization and on-demand concepts. It illustrates the key principles using five levels of abstraction. At the bottom (fifth level) of Figure 15.4, physical hardware (mainframes, servers), networks, storage, and other devices are pooled for shared use as required. Above this, at the fourth level, the virtualization engine allocates logical resources from this pool of physical resources. This allocation is based on the processing workloads that are determined by the on-demand operating environment above it (at the third level). The result is that each requesting system or application (at the second level) believes it has its own dedicated set of physical resources. At the highest (first) level, dynamic business services can be built as business applications using SOA and BPM languages as discussed in Chapter 14.

A characteristic of the systems of the future that will be built on SOA and BPM principles (as discussed in Chapter 14) will likely be unpredictable workloads. Previously, physical resources had to be dedicated to legacy systems, ERP and other packaged applications, and line-of-business systems. This need for physical resources inhibited the ability of these systems to accommodate increased workloads beyond their original design constraints. The virtualization and on-demand architecture illustrated in Figure 15.4 illustrates that required resources are now allocated dynamically as logical resources, on demand. The physical barriers to

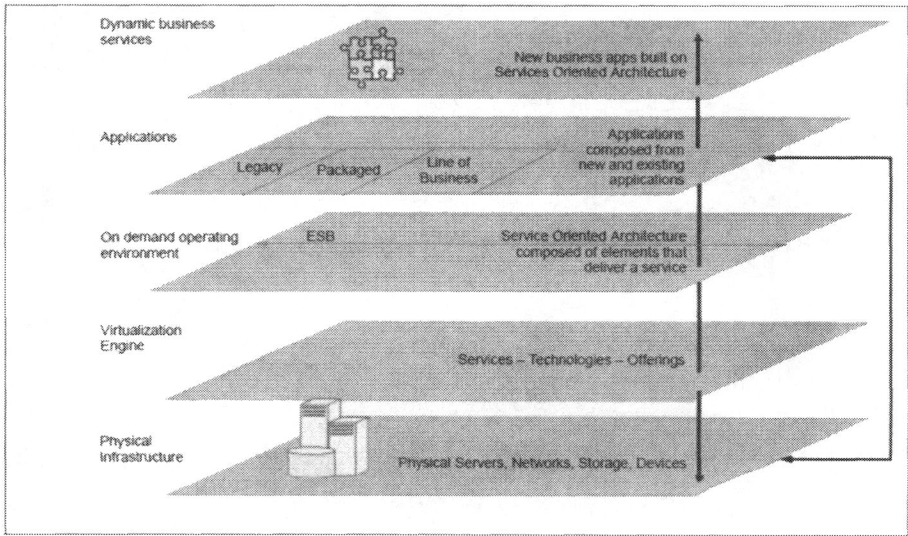

Figure 15.4 Summary of virtualization and on demand. (*From:* [1]. © 2005 IBM Corporation. Reprinted with permission.)

handle greater workloads, which previously inhibited growth, have now disappeared.

The improvement in development productivity that is offered by SOA and BPM languages can now be realized in full, without the hardware and resource constraints that previously would have inhibited this productivity improvement. We can see a potential for the future that is now unbounded.

15.2 Costs of Integration

In Part III we covered technology integration. We now need to consider the relative costs of these integration technologies: custom integration (through tailored programmatic solutions), traditional EAI or B2Bi (business-to-business integration), Web services, or SOA. Two papers by ZapThink will help us evaluate these costs. The first ZapThink paper helps us to determine the costs of technology integration [4], as shown in Figure 15.5. This examines the real cost of the above integration approaches across four stages: initial costs, customization, maintenance, and changes.

The low initial cost of *custom integration* in the first two stages of Figure 15.5—shown by the solid unbroken line—is offset by the high costs of maintenance and changes due to complex programmatic modifications that need to be made to custom integration code. These later maintenance and changes costs are reduced with the traditional EAI/B2Bi approaches—shown by the dashed line—but initial costs and customization are higher. This EAI/B2Bi approach works well with systems and business processes that change infrequently, but it suffers from cost "spikes" to accommodate later changes. In their paper, ZapThink comment that

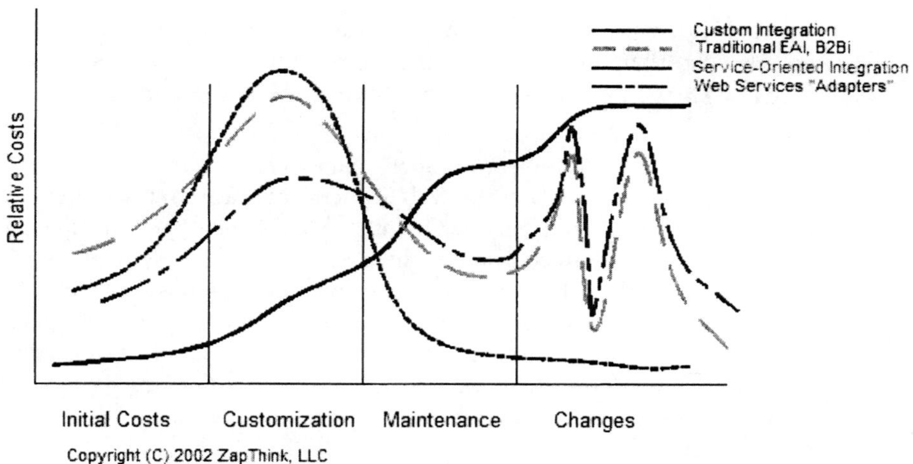

Figure 15.5 Relative costs of different integration approaches. (*From:* [4]. © 2002 ZapThink. Reprinted with permission.)

"EAI systems 'pour concrete on business processes' since they tend to solidify existing processes rather than enable an IT environment that allows companies to deal easily with change" [4].

The third approach—Web service adapters—shown by the dot-dash line in Figure 15.5 has lower initial costs and customization than traditional EAI or B2Bi. However, it suffers from similar cost spikes in the change stage. ZapThink comments that Web services now provide good standards for integration, but they observe that many developers write Web services interfaces as tightly coupled, static "SOAP wrappers"—so that "developers now pour standards-based concrete over existing business processes" [4].

The fourth approach—called *service-oriented integration (SOI)* by ZapThink—is based on SOA. This has the highest cost in the customization stage, as shown by the dotted line in Figure 15.5. Reviewing ZapThink's comments on this approach [4]:

> While tightly coupled SOAs have been around for a while—both CORBA and DCOM have elements of service-oriented architectures—Web Services technologies allow architects to build standards-based, loosely coupled SOAs that expose business functionality at varying levels of granularity. The real costs in building and integrating such SOAs are in the system re-architecting. In an SOI solution, it is not sufficient to simply wrap an existing API with a Web Services interface. It is too easy (and almost lazy) to create a one-to-one mapping between system APIs and Web Services interfaces. Rather, businesses must spend time analyzing their business processes and creating business Services at varying levels of granularity, perhaps even requiring the orchestration and choreography of multiple layers of Web Services to accomplish a single task. This support for multiple levels of granularity enables the SOA to support frequent changes in the underlying systems, as well as changes to business processes and underlying business assumptions, without the need to make interface changes that break the loose coupling of the Services. The real win with SOI, therefore, is in the reduction of cost at the maintenance and change phases of integration, as shown by the dotted line in the graph.

The second white paper by ZapThink addresses the question of *semantic integration* [5]. Another term for semantic integration is *business integration*, which is the focus of Parts I and II of this book. ZapThink comments that [5]:

> In today's early SOA implementations, companies often implement static service definitions, which mean that the Web Services' interface contracts are set at design time. While UDDI and Service-Oriented Management provide the means for dynamic discovery of such Services, those Services are still essentially static.
>
> In order to achieve the sort of semantic data integration we are seeking, we must implement **dynamic** service definitions. In essence, the definition of the Service interface must change based on the context of the Service requester. As a result, a Service can change its contract between invocations. For example, the fact that a Service provider requires first names to be no longer than 40 characters should not require the requester to know that fact.

They make the point [5] that this "just-in-time" integration style requires service requesters to decouple the data in an SOA from any technical assumptions (such as a specific data schema or format) so that the data can be accessed via discoverable, loosely coupled, dynamically bindable services.

Figure 15.6 shows the integration "zipper." This indicates that semantic integration is at the highest level, above business process integration, which is the focus of SOA and SOI. To achieve this level of integration, we need to bring together the business integration methods from Parts I and II with technology integration from Part III.

This leads us to consider the role of modeling tools. We need to discuss how the rapid delivery methods for semantic integration (i.e., business integration) that we covered in Parts I and II are used in conjunction with the rapid delivery technologies in Part III. The focus of modeling tools is this semantic integration of methods and technologies.

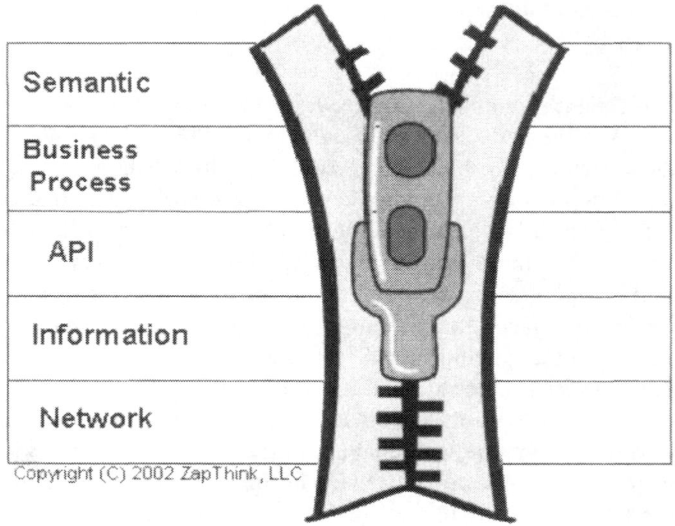

Figure 15.6 The integration "zipper." (*From:* [5]. © 2003 ZapThink. Reprinted with permission.)

15.3 Role of Modeling Tools

Computer-aided software engineering (CASE) tools first appeared in the early 1980s. (This term is not used today; instead they are referred to as *modeling tools.*) These tools were based on the premise that computer technologies could assist systems analysts and DBAs in their analysis and design efforts in much the same way that computer-aided design (CAD) tools provide design assistance to architects and product designers. Computer-aided manufacturing (CAM) tools further offer help by translating product designs to robotic commands, so that products can be manufactured using automated factory robots. These CAD tools are widely used today in building architecture and the automated robot-controlled manufacture of automobiles.

It was felt that modeling tools could be used to translate database designs developed by DBAs into the DDL required to implement and install those database designs using RDBMS products. Many data modeling notations existed in the 1980s; most are still widely used today. Some of these include entity/relationship (E/R) modeling [6], IDEF1X [7], information engineering [8], and modeling notations associated with specific RDBMS products, such as Oracle Designer. These different data modeling approaches were based on the relational theory and normalization principles defined by Edgar Codd [9, 10] and documented by Chris Date [11].

The rigor of the logical data modeling and physical database design methods used in the 1980s enabled this automatic DDL generation objective to be realized exceptionally well. Today it is standard practice for DDL code to be generated automatically by modeling tools from logical data models and physical database designs. In fact, it is now unusual to see anyone manually coding SQL *Create Table* and *Create Index* statements.

In the 1980s, it was also felt that the application designs developed by systems analysts could be translated automatically into executable program code. This task was much more difficult. These application designs were expressed diagrammatically as logic using software engineering [12]. In the 1990s, UML diagrams [13] supplanted software engineering and became widely used to document application designs and logic. UML diagrams were also perceived as a way to generate executable program code automatically.

There were some successes in automatic generation of executable program code from diagrams: one of the most notable was the Information Engineering Facility (IEF) in the late 1980s and 1990s [14]. Because of its initial complexity, this approach to automatic code generation was largely considered to be a failure by many. As a result, code generation—hyped by CASE tools in the 1980s and 1990s—eventually lead to "CASE" becoming a derogatory term. It was largely this market perception that saw the more successful of these tools launch themselves as "modeling tools." They wanted to distance themselves from the bad name that the other CASE tools had gained.

The software industry is now moving strongly into the twenty-first century. Today, modeling tools are seeing a renaissance in market interest. There is a resurgence in the innovation and application of technologies to automate software design, development, and automatic code generation. The following section discusses some of the major modeling tool vendors and the product capabilities that are available today.

15.4 Modeling Tool Products and Directions

We will discuss the product capabilities of some modeling tools in the Product Descriptions section of Chapter 15 on the accompanying CD-ROM, and the strategies used by their vendors. I will not attempt to cover all products in the market. I will only address specific products that, by their innovation, will enable you to see the technology trends that are developing.

Modeling tool products are discussed in the PDF file *Chap-15-Products.pdf* in the Book Materials folder on the accompanying CD-ROM. The following products are covered:

- Rational Software Architect (from IBM);
- System Architect (from Popkin Software, now part of Telelogic);
- Proforma Provision;
- IDS Scheer ARIS;
- Visible Advantage and Visible Analyst (from Visible Systems Corporation).

Please read this section on the accompanying CD-ROM now.

15.5 Summary of Key Enterprise Architecture Principles

This section summarizes key messages and principles from the book in terms of general concepts for each rapid delivery methodology discussed in Parts I and II and for each of the rapid delivery technologies in Part III. The chapter concludes with a discussion of the anticipated directions that Enterprise Architecture will take in the future.

15.5.1 Evolution to the Twenty-First-Century Enterprise

In the preface we discussed the changes that occurred following the publication in 1776 of Adam Smith's *Wealth of Nations*. We tracked the evolution of manual processes from the Industrial Age through to the Information Age. By the second half of the twentieth century, we recognized that our manual processes were operating in a state of manual chaos. But with the introduction of the computer we did not change those processes; we automated them with improvements—but essentially without much change. The result: *We moved from manual chaos to automated chaos*. Today we have twenty-first-century enterprises *functioning with eighteenth-century processes*. We have not effectively utilized the Internet technologies of today for the rapid-change environment in which most organizations find themselves.

15.5.2 Architects of the Enterprise

We also discussed in the preface that the real architects of an enterprise are not found in its IT departments, leading us to two important principles:

1. Enterprise architects are the senior managers who set the directions for the future, based on processes designed for that future and its technologies. The future cannot be based on eighteenth-century processes that no longer respond to the rapid-change environment of today and the even greater change environment of tomorrow.
2. The future will be based on business transformation through processes that use the technologies of today and tomorrow to complete in minutes and seconds what before took days and weeks, with strategic directions set by senior management and with business experts and IT experts working together in a design partnership.

15.5.3 Using the Zachman Framework for Reusability

In Chapter 1 we learned the basic concepts of the Zachman framework for enterprise architecture. Discussing the need for reusability, John Zachman commented in Chapter 1 that:

> Enterprise reusability is only achieved effectively by taking an enterprise-wide approach: not in detail across the enterprise, but broadly to encompass the whole enterprise.

We discussed the need for methods that defined a high-level "horizontal slice" across the width of each cell of the Zachman framework, representing an enterprise-wide subset. We also need methods to identify priority areas to be delivered first, defined as a "vertical sliver" down the complete depth of each cell as shown in Figure 1.7. We learned that reusability was particularly achieved from the Planner and Owner rows of the Zachman framework, with the key cells at the Owner row shown in Figure 1.8.

15.5.4 Systems Development Directions in the Twenty-First Century

In Chapter 1 we saw that traditional systems development methods that identify business needs from existing operational business processes are no longer responsive enough. The traditional systems development approach—interviewing users based on existing business processes and then identifying their future needs—do not work well in periods of rapid change, such as today. If we base our needs for the future on operational processes that we still use today, we are implicitly assuming that the future will be similar to the past. This is very dangerous; few industries and enterprises can say today that their future will be like their past. Most know that the future will be quite different. The only certainty we have is that the processes we will need then are quite different from the processes we use today.

We saw that the rapid delivery methods of enterprise architecture, when applied under the direction of senior management, result in business transformation, so the enterprise can compete in a future where *the only thing that is constant ... is change itself*. This brings us to a very important principle to accommodate change:

> We must design for tomorrow based on business plans for the future, not the existing business processes that we still have today.

Many of these existing processes reflect our needs for a pre-Internet past that will never return. Even if the same processes must remain for regulatory or legislative reasons, the rapid delivery methods and technologies that are available today enable these existing processes to be implemented so that they are more responsive.

15.5.5 Using Business Plans to Define the Future

In Chapter 2 we discussed the concepts of balanced scorecard and strategy maps. We saw how this approach communicated clearly key strategies and scorecard measures to achieve success in a business plan.

Chapter 3 introduced the business planning method of strategy analysis. We learned how to define business plans, if none presently exist, or to refine existing plans. This method can be used for business plans at any management level and for any project. It can be used to define personal scorecard measures for accountability, as part of each manager's job description.

Chapter 4 discussed implications of Sarbanes-Oxley compliance for financial reporting and other governance controls. Today, an inability to answer internal control audit questions has taken on a new personal meaning for senior managers. We saw the need for a governance analysis framework to obtain answers for relevant internal control reporting questions.

When enterprise architecture is used by senior managers, it enables precise governance analysis. We saw that governance analysis framework matrices are defined in a 25-day period, identifying key data, business activities and processes, locations, business units, and business events for business plans.

15.5.6 Enterprise Architecture in Government and Defense

Chapter 5 discussed the U.S. government's (FEAF) and the U.S. DoD enterprise architecture initiatives: DoDAF and the earlier C4ISR, which were originally based on Spewak's EAP. We also discussed TOGAF. These offer management guidance for complex projects, but we saw they provide *little methodology guidance* for the Planner and the Owner rows of the Zachman framework. We discussed the fact that the methods in this book are essential to identify integrated data and reusable processes to achieve business integration.

We discussed three implementation strategies in Chapter 5 for enterprise architecture in government, defense, and commercial enterprises:

1. The first strategy showed how enterprise architecture is used to build systems in *20% of the time* and *10% of the cost* of traditional systems development based on the use of AllFusion (previously called Coolgen or IEF). These savings are realized after multiple years, when business integration is achieved.

2. The second strategy discussed how to develop a business case for enterprise architecture. It can be used in conjunction with the first and third strategies.
3. The third strategy showed how the strategic methods of enterprise engineering deliver time and cost savings similar to the first strategy using any development tool, in 3-month increments. With this strategy, high-priority and high-ROI systems can be delivered rapidly for immediate benefit—with steady evolution by progressive business integration. It can be used for any enterprise architecture project, regardless of whether FEAF, DoDAF, C4ISR, TOGAF, Spewak's EAP, or some other enterprise architecture approach is being used.

15.5.7 Development of Integrated Data Models

Chapter 6 introduced the concepts of business data mapping. We saw that intersecting entities indicate the existence of business activities, processes, or systems that can be prioritized for rapid delivery as subprojects. These subprojects represent the priority "vertical slivers" discussed in Chapters 1 and 5.

In Chapter 7 we discussed the planning for and conduct of a facilitated modeling session with senior management and business experts. We progressively developed a strategic model on a white board, using business plans and business rules as catalysts.

We learned the entity dependency rules that are used to determine ownership of entities based on the strength of associations defined by business rules. We learned how to use these rules for entity dependency analysis of any data map. We used these concepts to derive reusable business activities. We learned how to develop project maps that defined the implementation sequence for separately deliverable subprojects in a larger project.

We reviewed four real-life strategic modeling projects that applied entity dependency analysis for different organizations. In each case the strategic modeling projects were completed in 20 days or less.

Chapter 9 covered the principles of business normalization. These principles were used to identify the data needed to support future business needs. We discussed the benefits of business normalization as follows:

- *Uncontrolled data redundancy is eliminated.* We saw that each nonkey attribute can reside in only one entity, where it is wholly dependent on "the key, the whole key, and nothing but the key." Homonyms or synonyms of attributes are clearly identified, appropriately named, and reside in their relevant entities.
- *Redundant data maintenance processes are minimized.* We saw that because data redundancy had been eliminated, redundant processes previously needed to keep redundant data versions up to date were also eliminated.
- *Data are more stable and able to accommodate business change.* We discussed that business processes change often, to reflect changed business conditions. In contrast, data are more stable and generally change only when the nature of the business changes.

- *Future business data needs are identified.* A normalization cross-check enables future business needs to be determined. The data model can thus be modified easily to incorporate these future business needs.
- *Expert knowledge is captured.* We saw that recursive associations or *many-to-many* associations between subtype entities of a supertype represent expert business knowledge or expert rules in a 5BNF structure entity.
- *Logic for processing 5BNF structure entities is generic.* Because every structure entity has a similar format, the logic that is developed for processing a structure entity is generic and reusable. This is an important principle: It means that this common logic can be used for processing expert knowledge.

15.5.8 Strategic Alignment Using the Zachman Framework

In Chapter 8 we discussed the principles of strategic alignment matrices. We aligned the columns of the Zachman framework across each row as matrices. These matrices are used for governance analysis as discussed in Chapter 4. Business plans in column 6 should be aligned with people in column 4, data in column 1, functions in column 2, time in column 5, and locations in column 3. These alignment matrices apply to each planning statement, organization unit, data entity, activity or process, business event, and location. These matrices answer the questions *why, who, what, how, when,* and *where.*

Activities in column 2 correspond to strategies in column 6. They both specify *what* has to be done. Processes in column 2 correspond to tactics in column 6. These specify *how* the tactics are implemented. We saw that functional areas in column 4 are used to manage functions in column 2 as organizational units. In turn, these functions group related activities; several functions can share common reusable activities.

15.5.9 Using Activity Modeling for Reusable Activities

In Chapter 8 we covered activity modeling and activity-based costing. Chapters 6, 7, and 9 identified reusable activities by the decomposition of *many-to-many* associations. Activities group related tasks; these tasks are then invoked by processes that execute required tasks in specific sequences based on business rules.

An activity model shows transformation of inputs into outputs, based on controls, such as business rules or constraints. Costs are associated with resources used as mechanisms for transformation. These resource costs can be used to calculate activity costs, using activity-based costing (ABC) to identify process improvements, for greater efficiency or reduced cost.

ABC forms the basis for economic analysis to evaluate the feasibility of alternatives to the current activities. These alternatives can utilize different technologies to achieve required process improvements or cost reductions.

15.5.10 Workflow Modeling and Business Rules

In Chapter 8 we also covered workflow modeling and business rules concepts. Project maps, developed from data maps by entity dependency analysis in Chapter 7, can be used to derive activity models and workflow models. We saw the progressive derivation from a project map of an activity model and a workflow model.

We discussed methods in column 6 that are used for business rules. In column 6, row 3, the BRS Proteus business rules methodology identifies business rules in a rule book. This is used also for rule design in row 4 and rule specification in row 5 [15].

15.5.11 Menu Structure Design and Screen Design

In Chapter 10 we learned that entity dependency analysis also offers guidance for menu structure design. We saw the design of simple hierarchical menus as well as tabbed menu structures. We discussed concepts for design of screen formats from a data model.

We analyzed a data model for physical database design and capacity planning. We learned that we could use the access paths taken through a data model by a transaction to calculate the transaction performance response time for performance analysis. We saw that we could optimize this response time by using different physical database design strategies for local access. We also saw how to optimize the response time for remote, distributed access.

15.5.12 Process Modeling to Define Reusable Processes

In Chapter 10 we also discussed a process modeling method for enterprise architecture that uses a business-driven, language-independent schematic and pseudo-code notation for business processes. Process models defined using this notation can be implemented in any object-oriented or procedural language.

A business process invokes data access processes (DAPs) to create, read, update, or delete occurrences of data model components. These are elemental methods used in object-oriented development, from which reusable processes can be implemented. We discussed the automatic derivation from a data model of parallel logic, shown in process maps for DAPs. We learned that these concepts are used today by code generators that generate executable code in various languages from the DDL scripts that define the database structure.

15.5.13 Technologies and Products for EAI

In Chapter 11 we learned that the typical cost for the manual entry and processing of a purchase order is $100 to $150, independent of the value of the items purchased. This cost typically drops to $8 to $10 when using EAI for transaction processing. We saw that this is a powerful business driver for EAI.

We discussed the role of trading communities in helping customers and suppliers to find each other, so they can do business together. We reviewed electronic message formats, drawing on examples from RosettaNet, Microsoft BizTalk, and ebXML. With BizTalk on the CD-ROM, we saw graphical process models used for BPM. This enables business logic to be defined by business users as orchestration diagrams, tested and then compiled for execution without further programming.

Industry markup vocabularies were discussed in Chapter 11 for some industries, including XBRL (for audit and financial reporting); IFX, OFX, and FpML (for banking and finance); and HL7 (for health care). Concepts for XML message interchange were discussed based on workflow processes and on data transformation between XML document formats. We saw how EAI can be used to keep redundant data versions up to date, using XML documents to synchronize data changes throughout the enterprise as replicated data in near real time.

On the CD-ROM we examined the EAI support provided by several EAI vendors. webMethods was used to introduce the technologies needed for EAI: business process modeling, with graphical workflow models for business process management; system integration, with adapters to access ERP packages, databases, legacy systems, messaging middleware, and other interfaces; business process monitoring, for real-time monitoring of business processes; and business process optimization, with real-time metrics for optimization of processes during normal EAI operation. Other EAI middleware products that we reviewed included IBM's WebSphere Business Integration Server Foundation, SeeBeyond's Business Integration Suite, Vitria's Businessware Business Process Integration; and Tibco's Businessworks.

15.5.14 Enterprise Portal Technologies and Products

Chapter 12 covered three portal categories: collaborative portals, business intelligence portals, and integration portals. Products were discussed on the CD-ROM in each category, covering their architecture and the technologies they use. We summarized the desired characteristics that should be exhibited by most portal products.

Enterprise portals can be implemented rapidly, with easy direct access to resources: to structured databases or warehouses; or to unstructured reports, documents, e-mail, audio, video, graphics, and images. But we saw that portals, of themselves, only provide integrated access. They do not provide business integration without other integration capabilities also being utilized.

If portals are used to access resources that exist redundantly and are not synchronized, the end result is only easy access to nonintegrated data. Portals should be used in conjunction with other technologies that can achieve integration and synchronization of redundant data resources and versions.

15.5.15 Technologies and Products for Web Services

Chapter 13 introduced the concepts of Web services for real-time program and code module integration that is language independent and platform independent. We learned that Web services specified in XML using SOAP, WSDL, and UDDI are interoperable.

Many software vendors and the products that they offer for Web services were covered in the Product Descriptions section on the accompanying CD-ROM:

- Microsoft is using .NET to transform the company based on Web services. All .NET languages are built on a common language specification to unify programming models for cross-language integration.
- IBM's Web services products are based on WebSphere and Java, with support and generation of SOAP, WSDL, and UDDI using J2EE.

- Software AG offers extensive integration tools for Web Services, Java/EJB, and RPC, with integration adapters for legacy applications, databases, CRM, and ERP.
- Oracle Application Server supports Java and Web services development with Oracle JDeveloper and Application Development Framework (ADF).

Web Services for Remote Portals (WSRP) was discussed on the CD-ROM. This offers a plug-and-play capability for easy inclusion of Web services in any environment.

15.5.16 Technologies and Products for SOA and BPM

Chapter 14 introduced the concept of SOA. Four BPM languages were covered:

- *Business Process Execution Language.* Microsoft's XLANG and IBM's WSFL were incorporated in BPEL to implement any complex business process, as well as describe interfaces of business processes.
- *Web Services Choreography Interface.* WSCI is used to define the flow of messages exchanged by Web services participating in coordinated activities with other services. WSCI is not a "workflow description language."
- *Business Process Modeling Language.* BPML defines simple and complex activities, with transactions and compensation, data management, concurrency, exception handling, and operational semantics. BPML is a robust BPM language comparable to BPEL.
- *ebXML Business Process Specification Schema.* BPSS defines a business process for physical business interchanges between ebXML parties. BPSS 1.0 defined the automatic generation of BPSS code from UML diagrams. BPSS 2.0 uses BPMN for process models. BPSS defines the commercial and legal terms and responsibilities between enterprises that go beyond the current intent of BPEL, WSCI, or BPML.
- *Business Process Modeling Notation.* BPMN is standard documentation to specify business process models and diagrams. It is an evolving standard for the specification of process logic for the BPM languages just described.

A number of BPM products were discussed on the CD-ROM: Microsoft BizTalk Server automatically generates BPEL code directly from Orchestration diagrams; IBM WebSphere Business Integration Server Foundation generates BPEL code from process models; BPEL code is generated from process models by Oracle BPEL Process Manager; while the SeeBeyond [16] e*Insight Business Process Manager automatically generates BPEL from process models specified by BPMN. Other products were discussed that offer the potential for future BPM language support.

The final product discussed in Chapter 14 was Intalio | n^3 Business Process Management System (BPMS). This provides native generation support for BPML, BPEL, and WSCI. The Intalio | n^3 product family is clearly the direction of BPMS for the future.

The critical need for metadata management of SOA development was discussed on the CD-ROM, with a white paper reference to a SOA metadata registry that included a discussion of the Infravio X-Registry for SOA metadata management.

15.5.17 Achieving Business and Technology Integration

Earlier in this chapter, we discussed how systems of the future will be built on SOA and BPM principles with unpredictable workloads. Virtualization architectures in an on-demand environment allow resources to be allocated dynamically as logical resources.

Productivity improvements from SOA and BPM languages can now be fully realized through virtualization, without the hardware and other resource constraints that previously would have inhibited this productivity improvement. The potential for the future is now unbounded in terms of the hardware resources that are needed to accommodate growing workloads.

We recognized the importance of *semantic integration* in achieving *business integration*, which was the focus of Parts I and II. We saw that modeling tools are used for business integration and technology integration, bringing together Parts I and II of the book with Part III. On the CD-ROM we discussed several modeling tools used to achieve this: IBM's Rational Software Architect, Telelogic's System Architect, Proforma's Provision, IDS Scheer's ARIS, and also Visible System Corporation's Visible Advantage, Visible Analyst, Visible Developer, and Visible Polaris.

- *IBM's Rational Software Architect* supports automatic transformation between business process models and UML 2 diagrams, with code generated in Java, C, and C++. It provides UML 2 support for software development in Zachman rows 3, 4, and 5 for the Designer, Builder, and Subcontractor.
- *Telelogic's System Architect* offers solid support for the Zachman framework as an interface. It also provides support for DoDAF and FEAF as well as for BPMN. This can use Intalio | n^3 for automatic generation of BPEL and BPML executable XML-based code for SOA.
- *Proforma's Provision* offers enterprise architecture support for DoDAF and FEAF, with support also for BPMN business process modeling.
- *ARIS from the European company IDS Scheer* offers extensive enterprise architecture support in a wide range of modeling tool products.
- *Visible Advantage* offers strategic planning and strategic modeling support, with automatic entity dependency analysis for rapid delivery of priority subprojects. It particularly addresses rows 1 and 2 of the Zachman framework for the Planner and Owner. Models are exported or imported to or from *Visible Analyst,* for software engineering and UML at rows 3, 4, and 5 for the Designer, Builder, and Subcontractor. *Visible Developer* imports DDL scripts from Visible Analyst for automatic generation of 80% to 90% of code in VB, ASP, VB .Net, ASP .Net, and C# .Net, leaving only application-specific code to be written. Both Visible Analyst and Visible Developer can be installed as add-ons and used within Microsoft Visual Studio .Net. These Visible products are included on the accompanying CD-ROM.

15.6 Future Directions in Enterprise Architecture

Enterprise architecture is a well-established discipline. Its use is mandatory for all U.S. governmental departments and agencies, including the U.S. Department of Defense. It is being adopted by governments and defense organizations in many other countries. It is also widely used in the private sector by large, medium, and even small enterprises.

15.6.1 Enterprise Architecture Skills Transfer

Considering the key role that enterprise architecture takes in managing change, to maintain control, EA should not be defined for you by an external consulting organization. Your organization should be directly involved in enterprise architecture so that you can use it to manage future enterprise change yourself. Business and IT experts in your organization must be self-supporting in your knowledge and application of enterprise architecture.

To become self-sufficient, the preface discussed enterprise architecture training through public or in-house courses with skills transfer. These course materials can be licensed by universities and other educational institutions for inclusion in educational curricula, or licensed for internal training use within government, defense, or commercial enterprises. The modeling, code generation, and change management tools provided on the accompanying CD-ROM will enable you to become proficient in these methods and technologies.

Many approaches and methods are used for enterprise architecture. In this book I have described an integrated set of methods and technologies that is used to achieve rapid delivery of enterprise architecture, with high-priority areas delivered into production in 3-month increments.

Many consulting firms have their own proprietary enterprise architecture methods. While rapid delivery is often their mantra, these companies derive consulting revenue from projects that extend over a long period of time. To complete enterprise architecture for any organization is a multiple-year project, but you should not have to wait years before any results are delivered.

In evaluating any methodology, the key characteristic is the ability of the methodology to accommodate your priorities. The benefit to your organization should be the capability to identify high-priority or high-ROI areas that can be delivered rapidly to address business needs.

We are now at the point where we can make reasoned judgments about the directions in which enterprise architecture methods and technologies will head during the next few years.

15.6.2 Methodology Directions

My observations of the key methodology directions for enterprise architecture follow:

- *Increased focus on the Planner and Owner rows:* In the book we saw that an enterprise-wide focus in rows 1 and 2 identifies integrated data with reusable business activities and processes.

- *Using business plans as a catalyst:* We must focus on the business plans for the future, rather than use existing business processes that reflect needs of the past.
- *Senior management must be actively involved:* Senior managers establish the business plans and are the true architects of the enterprise. They must remain actively involved to set priorities and provide direction when alternatives emerge.
- *Project teams comprise business experts and IT experts:* Methods based on interviewing business experts do not work effectively. Business and IT experts with enterprise-wide knowledge must work together in a design partnership, drawing on their respective business or IT expertise to achieve integrated data with reusable activities and processes.
- *Early delivery must be achievable:* Rapid delivery methods are needed so that priorities defined by senior managers can be used to address urgent business needs. Rapid delivery technologies enable these priorities to be delivered early.

15.6.3 Technology Directions

The technology directions during the next few years are now clearly apparent:

- *XML and Web services are the integrative technology:* Web services are now interoperable, and XML as an integrative data format is now ubiquitous.
- *SOA is the development paradigm:* Loosely coupled SOA logic enables Web services to be invoked dynamically and also replaced easily using alternative Web services for more effective solutions.
- *BPM languages will be used for development:* BPEL will subsume BPML and emerge as a de facto standard, along with BPSS for ebXML. These languages will increasingly be used with BPMN for design of business processes.
- *BPM code generation from process or workflow diagrams:* Executable code will be automatically generated directly from workflow or process diagrams as BPEL or BPSS XML-based code.
- *Modeling tools for business and technology integration:* The key to business integration and technology integration is based on utilization of BPMN by modeling tools.
- *BPMN uses business experts more effectively than UML:* BPMN used in the Owner row enables business experts to apply their business knowledge more effectively than does UML, which directs its focus more to the Designer row.

15.6.4 Standards for Enterprise Architecture

At the time of writing, several independent efforts were under way to define standards for enterprise architecture. These are all works in progress:

- The Enterprise Architecture Interest Group (EAIG) [17] is open to organizations that are interested in influencing "the practice and development of a common body of knowledge regarding Enterprise Architecture (EA)." It has several large organizations, including Sandia National Laboratories, Volkswagen of America, General Motors, Booz Allen Hamilton, Oakland University, FEAC Institute, and ATT Government Solutions. The EAIG is progressively establishing standards for each cell of the Zachman framework, with standards currently defined for rows 1 and 2 but still to be ratified at the time of writing.

- The Office of Management and Budget is defining standards for FEAF [18].
- The National Association of State CIOs is defining standards for enterprise architecture toolkits and frameworks [19].
- The Canadian government is establishing directions based on enterprise architecture for business transformation [20].
- The Object Management Group is defining open standards based on model-driven architecture and business process management through a merger of their BPM activities with those of the Business Process Management Initiative [21]. This merger augurs well for the possible future incorporation of BPMN as an additional diagramming notation within UML.
- John Zachman published his e-book in 2003 [22]. Recognizing the body of knowledge that has evolved from 1987 to the present, John Zachman and Stan Locke of Zachman Framework Associates are developing the definitive standards for enterprise architecture [23]. These are a significant extension of current standards, leading to EA certification for enterprises and individuals and also certification for vendors of methodologies, technologies, and tools.

The Zachman standards were released in late 2005, too late to make it into this first edition of the book. I will cover these new standards extensively in the second edition. I will visit you again in that edition, when I discuss further the evolution and developments of enterprise architecture methods and technologies.

Endnotes

[1] An excellent introduction to virtualization is available from the IBM Redbook (2004) titled *Virtualization and the On Demand Business* at http://www.ibm.com/redbooks.

[2] Many of these organizations and products offer management and virtualization capabilities similar to those of IBM.

[3] IBM defines the term *container* as the generic environment for installing, deploying, and running business services and operating systems; it is nonspecific or virtualized.

[4] Schmelzer, R., and J. Bloomberg, *Understanding the Real Costs of Integration,* ZapThink, October 2002; e-mail: rschmelzer@zapthink.com.

[5] Schmelzer, R., *Semantic Integration: Loosely Coupling the Meaning of Data,* ZapThink, August 2003; e-mail: rschmelzer@zapthink.com.

[6] E/R modeling is based largely on the principles established by Peter Chen in his paper "The Entity Relationship Model: Toward a Unified View of Data," *ACM Trans. Database Systems*, 1976, pp. 9–36.

[7] Bruce, T., *Designing Quality Databases with IDEF1X Information Models,* New York: Dorset House, 1991.

[8] The business-driven IE methods were first developed from 1976 to 1980 by Clive Finkelstein and popularized throughout the 1980s by James Martin (see the IE books referenced in Chapter 5). These business-driven IE methods have since evolved into the methods that are used today for the rapid delivery of enterprise architecture as discussed in this book.

[9] Codd, E., "A Relational Model for Large Shared Data Banks," *CACM,* Vol. 13, No. 6, 1970, pp. 377–387.

[10] Codd, E., "Extending the Database Relational Model to Capture More Meaning," *ACM Trans. Database Systems,* No. 4, 1979, pp. 397–434.

[11] Date, C., *Introduction to Database,* Vols. 1 and 2, Reading, MA: Addison-Wesley, 1982 (and later editions).

[12] See books by Michael Jackson, Ken Orr, Ed Yourdon, and Tom de Marco referenced in endnotes [1] through [4] in Chapter 5.

[13] See books by Grady Booch, Ivar Jacobson, and James Rumbaugh referenced in endnotes [14] through [18] in Chapter 5.

[14] The IEF was developed by Texas Instruments and was quite successful. But before code could be generated, a great deal of definition was needed to capture the detailed logic that was not expressed in diagrams. Once this initial definition had been completed, program code could be automatically generated from diagrams. Then, when the logic in these diagrams needed to be changed, the new program code could also be automatically regenerated. This is now known as AllFusion and is discussed in relation to strategy A in Chapter 5.

[15] See links for BRS Proteus from Business Resolutions in the endnotes of Chapter 8.

[16] SeeBeyond is now part of Sun (see http://www.sun.com).

[17] The evolving EAIG standards can be reviewed at the EAIG Web site (http://www.eaig.org).

[18] See the FEA Program Management Office reference models at http://www.egov.gov.

[19] Visit https://www.nascio.org/ for details about the National Association of State CIOs.

[20] Read a summary at http://www.tbs-sct.gc.ca/pubs_pol/ciopubs/egt-ftsg_e.asp.

[21] The merger announcement is at http://www.bpmi.org/downloads/BPMI-OMG_Merger.pdf. Visit OMG at http://www.omg.org. Visit BPMI at http://www.bpmi.org.

[22] Visit http://www.ZachmanInternational.com/ for the e-book by John Zachman, *The Zachman Framework for Enterprise Architecture: A Primer for Enterprise Engineering and Manufacturing,* Glendale, CA: Zachman International, 2003.

[23] Details of the new enterprise architecture standards will be published on the Zachman Framework Associates Web site, which is under construction at http://www.ZachmanFrameworkAssociates.com and also at http://www.zachmaninternational.com.

About the Author

Clive Finkelstein is acknowledged worldwide as the father of information engineering and is the managing director of Information Engineering Services Pty Ltd in Perth, Western Australia. He has more than 45 years of experience in the computer industry. He has published many books and papers and contributed chapters and forewords to several books. Mr. Finkelstein has coauthored or authored the following books: *Information Engineering* (Savant Institute, 1981); *An Introduction to Information Engineering* (Addison-Wesley, 1989); *Information Engineering: Strategic Systems Development* (Addison-Wesley, 1992); and *Building Corporate Portals with XML* (McGraw-Hill, 2000).

Mr. Finkelstein is an internationally renowned consultant and instructor and has completed projects for defense, government, and commercial organizations throughout the world and in most industries. The emphasis of these projects has been to bridge from strategic business plans to information systems, so aligning systems closely with corporate goals. Many projects have involved the Zachman Framework for Enterprise Architecture, using the latest methods and technologies for change management and rapid delivery of priority areas into production. These methods use enterprise engineering for rapid definition of enterprise architecture. Mr. Finkelstein's technology focus addresses enterprise integration technologies using XML, enterprise application integration (EAI), enterprise portals, Web services and service-oriented architecture (SOA) for business process management (BPM) using XML-based BPM languages. He provides training and consulting in all aspects of the Zachman Framework for Enterprise Architecture, with rapid delivery of priority areas using enterprise engineering.

Mr. Finkelstein writes a monthly column, "The Enterprise," for *DM Review* magazine in the United States. Past issues are available at http://www.dmreview.com/. He also publishes a free, quarterly technology newsletter via e-mail: *The Enterprise Newsletter (TEN)*. Past issues of *TEN* are available at http://www.ies.aust.com/. Click the *Papers* link on any page. Click on the *Courses* link on any page for his public and in-house skills-transfer courses. These are all summarized at http://www.ies.aust.com/cbfindex.htm. Mr. Finkelstein may be contacted at cfink@ies.aust.com.

Index

E

F

Recent Artech House Titles in Computing

Agile Software Development: Evalluating the Methods for Your Organization, Alan S. Koch

Agile Systems with Reusable Patterns of Business Knowledge: A Component-Based Approach, Amit Mitra and Amar Gupta

Discovering Real Business Requirements for Software Project Success, Robin F. Goldsmith

Engineering Wireless-Based Software Systems and Applications, Jerry Zeyu Gao, Simon Shim, Xiao Su, and Hsin Mei

Enterprise Architecture for Integration: Rapid Delivery Methods and Technologies, Clive Finkelstein

Open Systems and Standards for Software Product Development, P.A. Dargan

Practical Insight into CMMI®, Tim Kasse

Practical Software Process Improvement, Robert Fantina

A Practitioner's Guide to Software Test Design, Lee Copeland

The Requirements Engineering Handbook, Ralph R. Young

Software Configuration Management Handbook, Second Edition, Alexis Leon

Systematic Software Testing, Rick D. Craig and Stefan P. Jaskiel

Testing and Quality Assurance for Component-Based Software, Jerry Zeyu Gao, H.-S. Jacob Tsao, and Ye Wu

For further information on these and other Artech House titles, including previously considered out-of-print books now available through our In-Print-Forever® (IPF®) program, contact:

Artech House
685 Canton Street
Norwood, MA 02062
Phone: 781-769-9750
Fax: 781-769-6334
e-mail: artech@artechhouse.com

Artech House
46 Gillingham Street
London SW1V 1AH UK
Phone: +44 (0)20 7596-8750
Fax: +44 (0)20 7630-0166
e-mail: artech-uk@artechhouse.com

Find us on the World Wide Web at: www.artechhouse.com

CPSIA information can be obtained at www.ICGtesting.com
Printed in the USA
BVOW06*1952180114

342278BV00010B/104/P